# INTRODUCTION TO FORESTRY

## McGRAW-HILL SERIES IN FOREST RESOURCES

**Henry J. Vaux,** Consulting Editor

**Avery** / Natural Resources Measurements
**Baker** / Principles of Silviculture
**Boyce** / Forest Pathology
**Brockman and Merriam** / Recreational Use of Wild Lands
**Brown and Davis** / Forest Fire: Control and Use
**Chapman and Meyer** / Forest Mensuration
**Dana** / Forest and Range Policy
**Davis** / Forest Management: Regulation and Evaluation
**Davis** / Land Use
**Duerr** / Fundamentals of Forestry Economics
**Graham and Knight** / Principles of Forest Entomology
**Guise** / The Management of Farm Woodlands
**Harlow and Harrar** / Textbook of Dendrology
**Heady** / Rangeland Management
**Panshin and de Zeeuw** / Textbook of Wood Technology
    Volume I— Structure, Identification, Uses, and Properties of the
    Commericial Woods of the United States
**Panshin, Harrar, Bethel, and Baker** / Forest Products
**Rich** / Marketing of Forest Products: Text and Cases
**Sharpe, Hendee, and Allen** /Introduction to Forestry
**Shirley** / Forestry and Its Career Opportunities
**Stoddart, Smith, and Box** / Range Management
**Trippensee** / Wildlife Management
    Volume I—Upland Game and General Principles
    Volume II—Fur Bearers, Waterfowl, and Fish
**Wackerman, Hagenstein, and Michell** / Harvesting Timber Crops
**Worrell** / Principles of Forest Policy

*WALTER MULFORD WAS CONSULTING EDITOR OF THIS SERIES
FROM ITS INCEPTION IN 1931 UNTIL JANUARY 1, 1952.*

# INTRODUCTION TO FORESTRY

Fourth Edition

Grant W. Sharpe
Professor of Forest Resources and Outdoor Recreation
College of Forest Resources
University of Washington

Clare W. Hendee
Deputy Chief for Administration
Forest Service, U. S. Department of Agriculture
Forestry Lecturer
University of Maryland

Shirley W. Allen
Late Professor of Forestry
School of Natural Resources
University of Michigan

**McGRAW-HILL BOOK COMPANY**
New York  St. Louis  San Francisco  Auckland  Düsseldorf
Johannesburg  Kuala Lumpur  London  Mexico  Montreal  New Delhi
Panama  Paris  São Paulo  Singapore  Sydney  Tokyo  Toronto

Frontispiece

A 120-year-old second-growth redwood stand in Del Norte County, California. The trees average 200 ft in height. (*Courtesy of the U.S. Forest Service.*)

3 4 5 6 7 8 9 0 D O D O 7 8 3 2 1 0 9 8 7 6

This book was set in Times Roman by National ShareGraphics.
The editors were William J. Willey and Shelly Levine Langman;
the production supervisor was Judi Allen.
R. R. Donnelley & Sons Company was printer and binder.

**Library of Congress Cataloging in Publication Data**

Sharpe, Grant William.
    Introduction to forestry.

    (McGraw-Hill series in forest resources)
    First-2d ed. by S. W. Allen, 3d ed. by S. W. Allen and G. W. Sharpe
published under title: An introduction to American forestry.
    Includes index.
    1. Forests and forestry. 2. Forests and forestry—United States.
I. Hendee, Clare Worden, date joint author. II. Allen, Shirley
Walter, date An introduction to American forestry. III. Title.
SD373.S56    1976       634.9'0973      75-37680
ISBN 0-07-056480-9

# Contents

Preface     ix

Part   I / History, Influences, and Uses of the Forest

  1 / Human Use of the Forest    3
  2 / Building the Country with Forests    14
  3 / Forestry as a Federal Public Policy in the United States    26
  4 / Beneficial Influences and Services from the Forest    50
  5 / Outdoor Recreation    70
  6 / Management of the Forest Environment    93

Part  II / Forests and Forestry

  7 / How to Know Your Trees and Their Environments    115
  8 / Where Our Forests Are and What They Produce    145
  9 / The Tree, the Forest, and Forestry    173
  10 / Forestry Around the World    193
  11 / The Political Economy of Forestry    210

Part III / The Practice of Forestry

  12 / Silviculture: Reproduction Methods    227
  13 / Silviculture: Intermediate Operations    242
  14 / Measuring the Forest    251
  15 / Harvesting the Forest Crop    281
  16 / Making Forest Products Adaptable and Durable    299

Part IV / Forest Protection

  17 / Fire and the Forest    325
  18 / Insects and Mammals    356
  19 / Disease and the Elements    380

Part  V / Forestry and National Planning

  20 / How the Federal Government Practices Forestry    401
  21 / How the States and Communities Practice Forestry    427
  22 / The Practice of Forestry on Private Lands    442
  23 / Education in Forestry: Career Opportunities
in Forestry    463

24 / The Trends in Forestry and National Planning                    484

Appendix A / Legislation and Government Policy Influencing
                        the Development of Forestry in the
                        United States, by Time Periods                               493
          B / Metric Conversion Factors                                       499
          C / Common and Scientific Names of Trees Mentioned
                        in the Text                                                          501
          D / Professional Forestry Instruction in the
                        United States and Canada                                  505
          E / Forestry Employment and Income Tables                515

Index                                                                                        519

# Preface

Many changes have taken place in forestry since the publication of the third edition of this book in 1960. Uses and values of forest land have increased greatly. Forest technology and forest land management practices have changed. More people have become interested in the overall forest environment. More of the public are increasingly involved in policy decision-making, especially on the public lands.

In assessing the need for a fourth edition, the authors had the benefit of suggestions from numerous teachers in forestry and other schools who had used the book in their classes. Based on these suggestions and other evaluations, seven new chapters were added. The old text was completely revised to reflect the present-day situation. The entire book was rearranged and now is presented in five logical parts. Approximately 140 new illustrations have been added to this edition. English units of measure are followed by their metric equivalents where practical, making the book useful wherever the metric system (SI) is used or being considered. Sexist terminology has been eliminated making the book more acceptable to the growing number of women forestry students.

In accomplishing this revision, considerable help was received from several sources. We gratefully recognize the individuals, companies, and agencies who have helped with text and illustrations.

The several federal agencies that have helped include the Extension Service, Forest Service, Soil Conservation Service, and Cooperative State Research Service in the U.S. Department of Agriculture; the Bureau of Land Management, National Park Service, Bureau of Indian Affairs, and Bureau of Outdoor Recreation in the U.S. Department of the Interior; the Air Force, Navy, Army, and Army Engineers in the U.S. Department of Defense; the Tennessee Valley Authority and the Environmental Protection Agency.

The State Foresters of Georgia, Hawaii, Minnesota, Ohio, Oregon, Texas, and Washington furnished current program information and modern illustrations. Ken Pomeroy, Washington Representative of the National Association of State Foresters, furnished current data on state forestry programs and plans.

Frank Wadsworth, Director of the Institute of Tropical Forestry, furnished current information and pictures on the forests of Puerto Rico. The American Forest Institute and several of their company members furnished important data and photos. The American Forestry Association assisted in locating historical information and in helping with its use.

We are especially grateful to the authors of the several new chapters: Robert K. Winters for his review and suggestions for Chapters 1 and 2 and his new Chapter 10; Tom McLintock and J. B. Hilmon for Chapter 6; Robert Marty and Henry Webster for Chapter 11; and David R. M. Scott for his Chapters 12 and 13.

The authors would also like to thank the following: Dan Poole for his suggestions on wildlife in Chapter 4; Frank Brockman and John Hendee for their suggestions on outdoor recreation in Chapter 5; Frank Brockman again for his tree foliage photos in Chapter 7; David Scott for his suggestions on forest succession in Chapter 9; Reinhard Stettler for his suggestions on genetics in Chapter 12; Stanley Gessel for his comments on nutrition in Chapter 13; Bill Atkinson for his great assistance in updating Chapter 14; George Stenzel for his comments on Chapter 15; Robert E. Martin, Ed Loners, and Walter Schaeffer for their kind assistance with Chapter 17; Richard D. Taber, Robert Gara, and Robert Matthews for help on Chapter 18; Charles Driver for his input on Chapter 19; Richard Marks for his assistance on extension forestry in Chapters 20 and 21; and Donald Theoe for his help on Chapter 23. Thanks also go to G. F. Weetman for information on forestry instruction in Canada.

Acknowledgment is also made to those whose helpful criticism made earlier editions of this book possible. They include Dow V. Baxter, Dan Bonnell, L. W. Bryan, Ovid M. Butler, Henry E. Clepper, Glen R. Durrell, Samuel A. Graham, Guy Lemieux, John M. Molberg, W. J. O'Neil, Will F. Ramsdell, R. C. Smith, Henry H. Tryon, John Alan Wagar, and G. F. Weetman.

In conclusion, thanks go to Wenonah Sharpe for her many hours of editing the manuscript and her several illustrations.

*Grant W. Sharpe*
*Clare W. Hendee*

**With specially prepared chapters by:**

Chapter 6

Tom McLintock, Former Director
Environmental Research
Forest Service
U.S. Department of Agriculture
and
J. B. Hilmon, Director
Southeast Forest Experiment Station
Forest Service
U.S. Department of Agriculture
Asheville, North Carolina

Chapter 10

Robert K. Winters, Former Director
International Forestry
U.S. Department of Agriculture;
Consultant
International Forestry
Society of American Foresters

Chapter 11

Robert Marty
Professor of Forestry
Michigan State University
East Lansing, Michigan
and
Henry H. Webster, Chief
Forestry Division
Michigan Department of Natural Resources
Lansing, Michigan

Chapters 12 and 13

David R. M. Scott
Professor of Silviculture
College of Forest Resources
University of Washington
Seattle, Washington

# INTRODUCTION TO FORESTRY

# Part One

# History, Influences, and Uses
# of the Forest

# Chapter 1

# Human Use of the Forest

Most of the world is now faced with the problem of managing the forest environment in a complex social, economic, and political setting.

In the past, human triumph over the environment was dependent upon the ability to find food, fashion a means of protection from other animals, and find shelter from the elements.

Authorities now generally agree that our early ancestors were tree-dwelling primates living in regions having a warm, moist climate. Only there does nature provide vegetable foods that can be easily gathered throughout the year. Eventually our ancestors came down out of the trees. Perhaps a gradual weather change converted some tropical forest areas to open grassy savannas with scattered dry-land trees. The tree dwellers may have ventured out onto these open areas where cereals and other seeds could have provided their basic food needs.

As these early ancestors became more humanoid, they developed skills that enabled them to survive under a wide variety of conditions. Their clubs, fire-hardened wooden spears, and crude stone weapons enabled them to hunt for animal food and for skins to keep them warm as weather changes occurred and as they migrated to harsher climates. Although humans developed their civilizations fastest in areas having the open park-like forests characteristic of the Mediterranean region, eventually they learned to make the dense northern and tropical forests serve their needs.

Since the forest still furnishes many of our continuing needs, our past, present, and future dependence upon it makes worthwhile a consideration of those items provided by the forest.

**Food from the Forest**   As a breeding place and home of wild animals, the forest has been a rich hunting ground. It has thus contributed generously, if indirectly, to the food supply of primitive peoples and pioneer communities. Moreover, nuts, berries and larger fruits, buds, and roots from forests were quickly available, and it required little effort to harvest or to prepare them for use. They were direct products of the forest, less subject to failure than domestic crops, and for that reason they frequently stood between life and starvation for forest-dwelling people when fish and game were scarce. The forest also served as a "pharmacy" for primitive people. Early European explorers found the natives of the northern Andean countries using a decoction made from the bark of the *Cinchona* tree as a cure for malaria. Today, quinine, extracted from the bark of trees of the same genus, is used as an antimalarial agent.

Acorns that are thought to have been buried more than 1,500 years ago were found in the Ozark Mountains in 1923 by an expedition from the Museum of the American Indian (Cadzow, 1924). The storage pit was lined with grass, and the acorns were contained in a bag of twisted wild hemp. Acorns are, of course, a familiar article of food to some tribes of native Americans today.

In 1650 Jesuit missionaries exploring the Great Lakes region found that the native tribes there depended heavily upon the forest plant foods during years when the maize crop failed. Wild rice was an important vegetable staple, even preferred to acorns. Other foods were raspberries, blueberries, hazelnuts, wild apples, cherries, plums, cranberries, beechnuts, and chestnuts. Among the less common foods were lichens (rock tripe), boiled to make a "very black and disagreeable porridge." The bark of oaks and basswood, and other trees, was "cooked and pounded and then put into water in which fish had been boiled, or else mixed with fish oil, making an excellent stew."

As for game, even today settlers in the wilder parts of our country supplement their grocery list with venison and other meat from game animals taken in the forests. In Europe there are game markets where one may purchase the flesh of deer, wild boar, hare, and various birds. Although these animals do considerable damage to young trees, and expensive protective devices such as wire wrappings and fences must be used, game animals are considered a part of the crop of the managed European forest. It might be noted here that it is largely the foresters who have the privilege of hunting.

Although it is a far cry from hoarded acorns to the nutting parties of 75 years ago, or from venison taken with a primitive bow and arrow to the highly organized sport of deer hunting today, the American forest still yields these foods and can be managed so as to yield more of them.

**Clothing from the Forest**  Most of the important fur bearers inhabit wooded country, and so the forest has yielded another prime necessity of human life. Today the fur industry would shrink considerably without a forest habitat for wild fur-bearing animals. Rayon from wood pulp is still an important article of commerce. These examples represent direct products from the forest.

**Shelter from the Forest**  Even if there had been caves enough to go around people would probably have taken to living in trees to escape some of their enemies. After awhile, they learned to adapt the tree to their own use. Whether the primitive shelters called only for pole frames, as in Fig. 1-1, upon which a thatch of grasses or bark or the skins of animals might be stretched, or for logs and timbers in the heavier type of early dwelling and fortification, here was wood. Wood was a material at hand and one that yielded to harvesting and fashioning with the crude tools that had been developed. The hollow stumps of huge western redcedars provided shelter for early residents of the Pacific Northwest (Fig. 1-2).

In Gothic construction, as Lewis Mumford points out, it was not only that the great piers resembled tree trunks and the window tracery the branches through which light filtered as through leaves in a forest, but also that the structure would be impossible without its falsework of wood (Mumford, 1934).

Throughout the centuries wood has served the human need for shelter. Even today, with all the substitutes that have been developed, it is difficult to find a shelter structure that does not employ a material of the forest in considerable volume, and usually it is wood itself. Insulation, wood finishes, stains, and other building accessories also draw heavily on the forest for such products as paper pulp, rosin, tall oil, and sawdust.

**Fuel from the Forest**  Today more than 50 percent of the total consumption of wood is in the form of lumber; however, the use of wood for fuel outstripped every other use until about 1900 and was of first importance for centuries.

Over the entrance of the great railroad terminal in Washington, D. C., one may read:

Fire—Greatest of Discoveries—
Enabling man to live in various climates—

**Figure 1-1** A wigwam of poles and ash bark, built in 1899 by Chippewas, Lac Courte Oreille Reservation, Wisconsin. *(Courtesy of the Smithsonian Institution.)*

use many foods—and compel the forces of
nature to do his work.

Something had to feed the fire to get this work done, and wood has been that something for more than 500,000 years. Only in relatively recent times have other fuels become more important. Coal, for instance, has been produced in the United States since 1820, but the output remained small until the advent of the Civil War. The petroleum industry got its start about the same time (1859), with the bulk of production coming since 1910. Wood-burning locomotives were still in use in the early 1900s, and today some of the power for the sawmill industry still comes from wood waste.

**Figure 1-2** This western redcedar stump was used as a home in 1901, in western Washington State. A similar stump was once used as a logging camp post office. *(Photo by Darius Kinsey.)*

Some further decline, however, is expected in the use of sawdust, slabs, edgings, and other similar material used as fuel in industrial plants. A growing use of this wood waste is as raw material for the pulp and paper industry (*The Outlook for Timber in the United States,* 1973).

A curious comment quoted by Cameron (1928) illustrates the importance of wood as a fuel during colonial days in this country. Subsequent to the Revolutionary War, a surgeon who had been with the Hessian troops revisited the new nation and worried in his writings lest farmers and landowners should not "be taught how to manage their forests so as to leave for their grandchildren a bit of wood over which to hang the teakettle."

Fuelwood consumption in 1970 for the United States was estimated at 16 million cords, but consumption had dropped sharply in the first five decades of the present century because of the substitution of oil, gas, coal, and electricity in home cooking, heating, and industrial uses. In recent years, however, substantial markets have developed in metropolitan areas for fireplace wood. Expected increases in income, population, and residential construction indicate this market may continue to grow. The predicted energy crisis has also tended to increase fuelwood consumption. It is expected that rigid air pollution standards could reduce this use in some areas in the future (*The Outlook for Timber in the United States,* 1973).

As will be seen in Chap. 11, there are many places in the world where fuelwood for home heating and cooking is of major importance. In a few instances this demand is much greater than the supply.

The forest, however, has been historically indispensable as a source of fuel since human beings first learned to use fire for their greater comfort and readier adaptation to the environment.

**Products and Inventions from the Forest**   From the time of the primitive handle of the stone ax or the twig that served the earliest human beings for a pothook, through the period of wooden ships, to the innumerable forest products of the present day, people have coupled their inventive genius with the diverse materials from the forest to make life richer and easier.

It was probably the rolling section of a fallen tree that elicited the idea of the wheel. Through the discovery of fire and that wood will float, the notion of a burned-out log for a boat dawned on human consciousness.

It may have been that from the growth of a tree in the crevice of a great rock, watched until it split this hard and discouraging material, came the idea for shaping stones for building. Stone in a quarry can be broken by inserting dry wooden plugs into drilled holes along a desired line of cleavage and wetting the wood until its swelling splits the stone. There are indications that stone was thus prepared for some of the massive structures of antiquity.

When one of our early ancestors was first surprised by a twig in the forest snapping back in his face, the pain and noise and the thought of quick and easy availability might readily have produced in his inventive mind a whole line of ideas. He could make a bow; he could beat his family, or even some wild animal, producing enough pain to force his will upon another; he could produce a musical instrument; and so on, far into the prehistoric night.

**Tools and Conveniences from the Forest**   Should one attempt to catalogue the wooden and forest-grown articles in the households of primitive peoples, the greatest task would not be to list them but to name them. Should one advance to the time of Tutankhamen, the list would grow longer and to some extent it would be a measure of the advance of civilization. In a modern household this task would be tedious and discouraging, but it would be seasoned with surprises. In place of the paddles, baskets, twig brooms, oddly carved furniture, and ornaments that had been met before, there would be the problem of listing such things as cellophane on a lamp shade, the wooden handle of a coffee urn, the wood flour in the plastic telephone, the linoleum, the pigments in paintings, fabrics, and finishes, and the dozens of seen and hidden wooden parts in the comfortable furniture of this day. Most of these miscellaneous articles are merely taken for granted if, indeed, they are noticed at all.

The barrier, the column, and the lever, aside from its modification in the form of the wheel, seem unmistakably linked to the forest and to the human experience with it. The lathe, one of the first instruments of precision, had only wooden parts originally. The operator held the cutting tool against the revolving material that was to be shaped.

**Agriculture and the Forest**  It was Sulla who spoke of tillage and pasturage as "the two breasts of the state." These two uses of land constitute what we call *agriculture,* but the old Roman probably was not thinking of pasturage as the use of managed pastures, and there is reason to believe that the world he knew was not heavily covered with forest. On the other hand, domestic animals have roamed the forest throughout the ages, grazing on incidental meadows which occur in the woods, browsing on the foliage of trees and shrubs, and devouring the "mast" as the beechnuts, acorns, and other larger tree seeds are called. The use of various kinds of forest forage by cattle, sheep, horses, and swine on the public lands of the United States involves an annual total of approximately 9 million head and nourishes those animals that provide much of the meat, wool, and leather that help to keep our citizens well fed and comfortable. These animals belong, in large part, to the owners of ranches and farms that yield winter forage to feed them a part of the year. Almost invariably, the water used to irrigate the hay lands so tilled comes from a forest-covered and managed watershed. This widespread industry would be impossible without the water and forage of the forests.

Tillage has both gained and suffered from people's use and treatment of the forest. In the United States few farms east of the Mississippi River were open areas. Centuries of forest had matured, fallen, and grown again, building up a rich organic capital in the surface soil, and this was particularly true in river bottoms. The forest here was in the way. It had to be felled and destroyed to clear the ground for farming, and it generally surrendered virgin soil of great fertility. Tillage was its highest use. Unfortunately, agriculture was not successful on all cleared lands, and the false notion that removal of the forest assured the appearance of a farm eventually brought about abandonment of many unproductive farms, with erosion of soil following disastrously. Some of this very land is now the subject of considerable effort toward reclamation for other purposes by public agencies. Appropriately enough, a part of it will be reclaimed by reestablishing forests on it.

In European practice, removal of leaves and other organic matter from the forest for use on farmland has been common, with disastrous results to the productiveness of forest soil. With this practice now forbidden in the state forests of some European countries, peasants clean the gutters of forest roads in order to secure the leaves for use as animal bedding and later for the enrichment of their lands.

At one time, an American traveler in western Iran reported that lack of wood for fuel and ineffectiveness or expense of other fuels made necessary the drying of animal manure for "native fuel" when the soil itself was desperately in need of that fertilizer (Richards, 1922). Here the absence of a forest product caused a material that was needed in agriculture to be used instead as a fuel.

**National Defense and the Forest**  Forests were used as barriers against enemies in ancient times by Asiatic tribes and the Greeks and Romans. The early Germans also had their *Grenzmarken* set aside solely for use as frontier forests. These were frequently fortified by ditches and other artificial barriers and occasionally used as hiding places in case of need (Fernow, 1911).

For many centuries wooden ships made up the navies of the world. In fact, the earliest civilizations to attain dominance in their world and time were those having an abundant supply of ship timber. The Minoan civilization on Crete was perhaps the earliest. Until the advent of the iron man-of-war in the midnineteenth century, practically no nation achieved world dominance unless it had within its boundaries such a supply of naval timber or had conquered territories that did. The great concern over scarcity of quality naval timbers in the sixteenth and seventeenth centures in northern Europe gave rise to the science of forestry (Winters, 1974). Furthermore, the first real concern of the young American nation over a supply of timber came because a navy was needed to defend its merchant ships from the pirates of the Barbary Coast. The examples of military uses of the forest and its products can be multiplied indefinitely.

**Spiritual Needs and the Forest**  Trees and the forest have from very ancient times featured prominently in spiritual and religious life. Trees were larger, stronger, and lived longer than shrubs, weeds, and grasses and were accordingly more worthy of respect, and even worship. In the prehistory mythology of Egypt, the gods were identified with individual trees or with the forest generally. According to one version, the goddess Nut emerges from the branches of the sycamore fig tree and offers refreshing food and drink to the souls of the dead as they halt in the tree's shade on the journey to the abode of the dead. And in northern Europe and England the oak, particularly if heavily infested with mistletoe, was deemed sacred.

One of the early recorded acts of forest devastation, on the other hand, is the destruction of pagan groves that had been used by the sorely tempted Hebrews in Palestine after one of their periodic adventures in idolatry. But references to the Mount of Olives, the Cedars of Lebanon, and the Psalmist's exclamation, "All the trees of the field shall clap their hands," are only a few of the hundreds of Scriptural passages that indicate the extent to which the beauty and imagery of the forest appealed to the ancients. The spiritual yearnings of people throughout the ages have led them to seek the beauty and solitude of forests, and these sanctuaries still yield deep satisfaction.

The establishment and maintenance of the national parks in the United States, which are dedicated so completely to spiritual use and enjoyment that no commercial use is countenanced, stand out as a real recognition of the human need for recreation. It is the forests of the great majority of our national parks that make them attractive and frame the grandeur of canyons, plains, and mountains. All agencies managing forested lands have noted the tremendous increase in visitor use since World War II (Fig. 1-3).

**Figure 1-3** Many millions of visitors annually seek enjoyment in forested areas of the national forests and parks of the United States. George Washington National Forest, Virginia. *(Courtesy of the U.S. Forest Service, photo by Bluford Muir.)*

**Human Treatment of the Forest**   Because the forest yields certain things that humans need and can sell or barter, it has been vulnerable to quick exploitation, resulting in its destruction. And because it has been in the way of farms, cities, highways, and other space requirements, it has been drastically removed in many countries. Fire, insects, disease pests, and storms take their yearly toll, and yet defense of the forests seems expensive and unnecessary to many. Humans have used their scientific knowledge and their ability to organize to destroy the forest by overuse. Another human attribute, forethought, has not been properly employed.

A mass of scientific knowledge has gone into the tools, the financing, and the organizing of the forest exploitation that Americans have thought necessary for the building of this nation. What there is left of the forests of the United States—and that is still an amazing acreage— must be managed, extended, and built up to supply future needs and to render the services that are necessary for the safety and prosperity of the country's citizens. These services include the retarding of too rapid runoff, which carries away precious topsoil and increases the volume and destructiveness of floods; controlling to some extent the drying and soil-eroding power of high winds; and, finally, covering the scars of fire, erosion, soil exhaustion, and other similarly unsightly forms of poor land use.

An estimated one-half the commercial forests of the United States is under some degree of forest management. This includes the industrial ownerships, public lands, and a portion of small ownerships. The entire answer, however, is neither public effort nor private effort alone but the two together, and there is every reason to demand the sacrifices necessary on the part of owner and user to obtain from the forest a continuous harvest. The trends of the past two decades toward improved management and protection on industrial and public lands are encouraging but still leave a big job to be done on the 60 percent of commercial forest land in small ownerships.

The changing relationship in the United States between humans and the forest has been truly dynamic. The early settlers saw the forests as being in the way. At the turn of the twentieth century, forests were looked on as an aid in settlement and development. The nation proudly looked back on a century of progress. Since 1900 there has been competition for all the values of the forest. There has been a growing public concern in the 1970s, spoken of by some as the "decade of the environment," as to the adequacy of forests to meet the needs of the future.

The challenge to forest managers, public and private, is for demonstration of the renewability and potential of these forests. In a nation and a world with growing energy requirements—much of it from nonrenewable fuels—forests have an increasingly important role.

## BIBLIOGRAPHY

Allen, Shirley W., and Justin W. Leonard. 1966. *Conserving Natural Resources,* 3d ed., McGraw-Hill Book Company, New York.

*Annual Report of the Chief of the Forest Service for 1970–71.* Washington, DC.

Butler, O. M. 1935. *American Conservation,* American Forestry Association, Washington, DC.

Cadzow, Donald A. 1924. Ancient Dwellers of the Ozarks, *Amer. Forests and Forest Life,* **31:**70, Washington, DC.

Cameron, Jenks. 1928. *Development of Governmental Forest Control in the United States,* Johns Hopkins Press, Baltimore.

Chase, Stuart. 1958. *Some Things Worth Knowing,* Harper & Brothers, New York.

Fernow, B. E. 1911. *History of Forestry,* University Press, Toronto.

Mumford, Lewis. 1934. *Technics and Civilization,* Harcourt, Brace & Company, Inc., New York.

*The Nation's Range Resources: A Forest Range Environmental Study,* 1972. Forest Service, U. S. Department of Agriculture, Forest Resource Report no. 19.

*The Outlook for Timber in the United States.* 1973. Forest Service, U. S. Department of Agriculture, Forest Resource Report no. 20.

Pinchot, Gifford. 1900. *A Primer of Forestry,* Part I, Division of Forestry, U. S. Department of Agriculture, Bulletin no. 24, Washington, DC.

Richards, E. C. M. 1922. West Persia: The Wood Famine Country, *Amer. Forests and Forest Life,* **28:**579, Washington, DC.

Smith, Guy Harold (ed.). 1971. *Conservation of Natural Resources,* 4th ed., John Wiley & Sons, Inc., New York.

Winters,Robert K. 1974. *The Forest and Man,* Vantage Press Inc., New York.

Woods, John B. 1946. Report of the Forest Resource Appraisals, *Amer. Forests,* **52:**414, Washington, DC.

# Chapter 2

# Building the Country with Forests

In building the United States, forests were both in the way and in demand. It is no exaggeration to say that without forests there would have been no United States of America, as we know it.

In recent years some historians have interpreted the history of environmental practices as a positive part of the building of the country rather than as pure exploitation. An example is taken from Nash (1968) in which he writes:

> Most accounts of American conservation contain at some point an elegaic description of the "unspoiled" continent: once the country was beautiful and rich in resources, but then came the "greedy exploiters" who "raped" the "virgin" land. Such a representation unjustly uses the emotions of the present to describe the actions of the past. It fails to employ historical sympathy, to understand the past in its own terms. Neither the pioneers nor most subsequent resource developers considered themselves unthinking spoilers or were regarded as such by their contemporaries. Instead they acted in a manner consistent with their environmental circumstances and intellectual heritage when the forest seemed limitless, cut-out-and-get-out was an appropriate response. Certain-

ly early Americans made mistakes in using the land, but they became such only in the opinion of later generations. Rather than shaking moralistic fingers, conservation historians would do well to attempt to understand why men acted as they did toward their environment.

Any country is likely to experience changes in its development faster than they can be predicted. Steam, for example, was yet to be put to work when the exploring missionary, Father Hennepin, observed in 1678 that the forests of the Lake States "afford all manner of timber fit for building." These particular forests were not to be put to use in building the Middle West until a century and a half later. Meanwhile, the lumbermen of the early settlements in New England and New York had learned to make a living from their newfound forest resources. A strong young nation was showing its restlessness and realizing its need for a wooden navy to protect a growing commerce. All this must have seemed a fast-moving period of history to the American businessmen of that day, but it was not to compare with the speed of cutting during the nineteenth century.

**Wealth of Forests Substituted for Scarcity of Tools, People, and Money**    Let us consider what forests have contributed toward the building of the country. We shall find some justification for loss but greater reason for restoration. Where human strength and tools are scarce and natural resources are abundant, the easiest means to make these resources available are usually adopted. Thus incomplete use comes about, wilfully or otherwise, because, for example, tools and people are more important than trees. This was the case in colonial times as the use of wood for homes, fences, and fuel slowly expanded into crude extracting, manufacturing, and exporting industries. Ship masts, boards, staves for casks, and potash from wood ashes, tar, pitch, and turpentine were the principal items of trade. This expansion was inevitable. Something had to be bartered or converted into money with which to buy the commodities the colonists could not produce. Fish and tobacco could not take care of everything. Self-interest, too, prompted shrewd and provident individuals to make as good a living as possible, and the vagueness of the concept of land and timber as property at this time offered unusual freedom to logging and other forest businesses.

**Forest Industries in Colonial Times**    There is some argument as to whether the first sawmill in America and in the state of Maine started its shrill business at York in 1623 or at Berwick in 1631; but as time and as sawmills with their cuts of 500 board feet a day were considered then, the exact date is not so important. The circular saw was still to come, and the crude sash saws, driven by water power and slicing away vertically, could be tended by a crew of two or three hands. Possibly the boards that were exported in 1631 from New Hampshire to England were rived or hewed. At any rate, they found a ready market; and white pine, a soft, clean, fragrant, and reasonably strong wood, entered a market it was to dominate for 250 years.

Meanwhile, the rulers of England had counted on the forests of these new colonies to supply the mast timber for the Royal Navy. By about 1695 the surveyors general of William and Mary and their deputies went dutifully about picking out the best and straightest trees and reserving them with the King's broad-arrow mark (Fig. 2-1). This was in accordance with the new charter of 1691 issued to "The Province of Massachusetts Bay in New England," which set aside as property of the Crown and for the use of the Royal Navy all trees more than 24 in. (60 cm) in diameter 1 ft. (30 cm) from the ground. Penalties were provided for violation of this provision, and the decree was soon spread throughout New England, Nova Scotia, New York, and New Jersey.

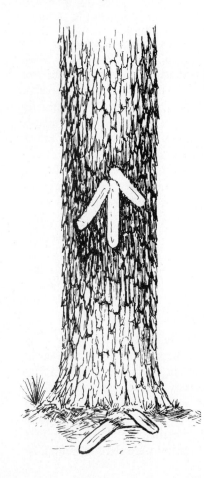

**Figure 2-1** The King's broad arrow. The trees so marked were to be reserved for masts for the English Navy during colonial days. Such a restriction was one of the irritations which led to the Revolutionary War.

The reaction of colonial lumbermen to such inconvenience was eloquent of what they thought of this prize timber and the part it played in their struggles for a livelihood. It also announced a New World attitude which declared in effect, "We're a long way from the old country, her needs may be important but the wilderness we live in is for us—let the job go on." And with that the axes continued to ring in the forest, the whips cracked over the oxen, and the surveyors general of the woods and their deputies had a season of stormy years. This was in spite of the fact that England's Navy was fighting to maintain its mastery over the French and to defend its commerce with the American Colonies, all of which constituted service to the latter!

The Colonies probably had no chambers of commerce, but the germ of this American institution was abroad in the land. The dependence of the new country, for prosperity, on a good international reputation for its forest products is reflected in various early regulations of exports imposed by the colonial legislatures. Masts must be without defect, staves of good sound wood, and those who would set fire to a forest that could produce these merchantable goods were to be punished. Trade was something to keep alive. Customers must be kept supplied whether they were Portuguese, Spanish, or British. Other laws had to do with abating thievery and keeping the wharves free of congestion with export forest products, which had acquired the name *lumber*.

There are few crumbs of conservation philosophy in these early laws and regulations, and yet even their flavor of self-interest indicates some respect for the forest.

**Building a Wooden Navy**   Following a period of growing resentment against the broad-arrow policy and of frayed nerves over other family quarrels with England, came the hard-fought war of the Revolution and out of it a young nation. One of the first surprising pieces of legislation then was reenactment in 1783 by the Massachusetts Assembly of a "broad-arrow" policy of its own, which later in modified form became the policy of the nation. The United States had a commerce to protect from Algerian pirates, and ships for the job must come from forests.

Following the establishment of the United States Navy in 1798 and up to 1833, several laws were enacted which provided for reserving lands on the Florida Gulf Coast as live-oak forests for the use of the Navy, purchasing actual ship timber and storing it for naval use, policing the federal live-oak reserves, and even authorizing the purchase of land for growing live oak. Although these purchases and experiments failed to achieve the objective of a continuous and satisfactory supply of naval construction material, they do reflect the conviction of our early statesmen that forests and sea power in those days were intimately related.

**Forests and the Early Villages**  It is of particular interest that more than the material products of forests were recognized as valuable forest dividends to this country at an early day. The power of forest cover to hold the soil in place was one of these. For example, there had been too severe grazing of domestic animals and some very heavy timber cutting near the town of Truro on Cape Cod peninsula, and the sand was beginning to drift. The Massachusetts Legislature thereupon, in 1709, attempted the regulation of these practices as a means of forestalling the encroachment of sand on the village. The productive character of soil enriched by the forest and the necessity of protecting it from injury by forest fires was emphasized by fire laws in Massachusetts in 1743 and in North Carolina in 1777.

Another significant matter in the literature of colonial days is mention of local shortages of wood. It was, of course, natural to use first the forest that was at hand, for distant and rapid transportation was unknown. Dr. Schoepf refers to the lack of wood for particular purposes in particular localities after the Revolution, and as early as 1720 the French in Canada had been forced by local shortages to enact severe timber trespass laws (Cameron, 1928). Even before this, certain communities in New Hampshire had limited the number of trees a citizen might have at any one time, and in one village a fine was imposed for every tree taken for other than home use (Ise, 1920).

**Industrial Revolution Finds the Lumber Business**  As in other instances where established trade relations are broken by war, the interruption of trade with England during the Revolution promoted in America what is now known as *economic nationalism*. The new nation "must make itself industrially as well as politically independent of the Old World." The factory system, which had made a weak start in Rhode Island after the Federal Tariff Act of July 4, 1789, finally became well established by 1815 (Ely, 1908). Although cotton mills were the first manifestation of the jump of the industrial revolution across the sea, there is little doubt that boom times, stimulation of invention, and the intervening War of 1812 had affected the forest industries. The local demand had not yet expanded tremendously, but population was moving westward, the first steam sawmill had started at New Orleans in 1803, and river-rafting of logs was a well-established technique. About this time also the wood-burning locomotive, traveling on wooden rails, had begun to prophesy widespread rapid transportation, although the first logging locomotive was not to come until 1852. In 1830 another steam sawmill made its appearance near Pontiac, Michigan. The center of lumber production was still in southeastern Pennsylvania, with the population center more than 100 miles southwest. The United States had entered upon that important period between 1820 and 1870, when population quadrupled. There was attendant demand for forest products, and a home market had become more important than foreign shipments of masts, boards, and staves.

**The Settler Pushes Westward** The agricultural expansion by this time had pushed beyond the central hardwood forest, and the prairie communities of Illinois, Iowa, and even Kansas were looking to the day when they would be states instead of territories. The sod-house farmer of the prairie had wood problems that had never occurred to the log-cabin dwellers of West Virginia or Ohio. To the latter, after the cabin, barn, fences, and woodpile were accounted for, the forest was literally in the way. To the prairie farmers the buildings for their needs, the towns where they must trade and market their crops, and the railroad ties on which these crops were to be shipped were still trees in the forests of the Lake States (Figs. 2-2 and 2-3).

**Subsidizing Farms and Transportation with Land and Forests** Two important groups of land laws enacted from 1841 to 1871 speeded up the exploitation of forests, the development of widespread rapid transportation, and the settlement of the country. During this period the United States had rounded out its boundaries with the annexation of Texas and by adding other cessions, purchases, and settlements. The first of these groups was made up on the Preemption Act of 1841, the Homestead Act of 1862, and others of less importance. The Preemption Act enabled heads of families with certain qualifications to establish prior claim to purchase cheaply 160 acres of public land for their own settlement, use, and benefit. The Homestead Act was similar but broader in scope. It provided for free patent for 5

**Figure 2-2** One of the thousands of logging crews in the Lake States supplying the needs of the settlers as they moved westward onto the treeless prairies. About 1875, near Newaygo, Michigan. *(Courtesy of the University of Michigan.)*

**Figure 2-3**  The largest load of logs ever hauled by one team. On its way to an exhibit at the World's Fair in Chicago, 1893. *(Courtesy of the St. Louis County Historical Society, Duluth, Minnesota.)*

years of residence and cultivation, and the claimant could elect to "commute" or pay up and secure patent at any time 6 months after time of filing. These two laws induced settlement but also made possible very wasteful forest exploitation.

The second group of laws has to do with grants of public land to subsidize internal improvement, such as post roads, canals, and railroads, and grants to states and territories in aid of education. The builder of a railroad, for example, was to have, besides an adequate right of way, a gift of land including each alternate square mile or "section" in a belt 6 mi (9.6 km) wide each side of the road. He was also to have the right to select elsewhere lands in lieu of those due him but already granted to other owners. The remaining government sections were to be sold at $2.50 per acre, and the railroad company was to sell its acquired lands at a low fixed price to actual settlers. The road was then to transport troops, mail, and supplies free of charge or at equitable rates fixed by Congress.

The first of these railroad land-grant acts was passed in 1850, subsidizing construction of the Illinois Central Railroad. The great Pacific Railway grants were made from 1862 on, and by the close of President Grant's administration in 1877, more than 155 million acres (62.7 million ha) of land had been allotted by the United States in place of money subsidies for internal improvement (Donaldson, 1884).

A vast proportion of this land was unfit for agriculture, and much of it was heavily timbered. No attempt was made at inventory of soil, cover, or minerals before the grants were made. As might be expected, therefore, title to vast areas of good timberland passed to private owners and from them to great natural-resource corporations. This was particularly true in the non-agricultural Lake States plains and in the West.

The development of transportation of course brought settlement on the better soils, started towns and cities, and generally invited the population to spread out over the Middle West (Fig. 2-4). Thus a new and great demand for building material was created, and by 1870 close to 27,000 lumber manufacturing plants were in operation, with more than $161 million of invested capital, turning out an annual product worth more than $250 million

**Figure 2-4** The land-grant railroad spread settlement to the treeless prairies and created a new demand for building material. By 1900 there were nearly 200,000 miles of railway lines, resting on wooden ties, and accompanied by wooden telegraph poles. *(Lithograph by Currier and Ives.)*

(Ise, 1920). The faster circular saws were standard equipment in the larger mills, and 13 billion board feet of lumber were chalked up as the yearly forest harvest in 1870—enough to build 650,000 houses (Reynolds and Pierson, 1925).

It must not be overlooked in passing that land and also forests, because they occupied so much of the land, were used in place of money, a thing the nation did not have (Fig. 2-5). And further, that by subsidizing internal improvement, a market for land and timber became available to a "land-poor" and "timber-poor" nation. The fact that these natural resources did

**Figure 2-5** Magnificient western redcedar "stood in the way" of farmland development in the states of Washington and Oregon. This historical photograph, 1898, shows two Northwest loggers posing with their falling saws, axes, and springboards before a large western redcedar in Whatcom County, Washington. *(Photo by John D. Cress; courtesy, Special Collections Library, University of Washington, Seattle.)*

not bring a good price and that fraud was practiced in many transactions is most unfortunate, but they did turn much-needed revenue into the Treasury. No less a statesman than John C. Calhoun (*Congressional Globe*) had announced his very simple grounds for supporting the land-grant bills as a course "highly advantageous to the treasury." The United States is not the only nation that has paid public bills with land and timber. Fernow (1911) mentions the sale of a part of the reforested lands in the sand dunes of Gascony by the French in 1865 to wipe out the expense of public reforestation.

**Changing Rates in Lumber Consumption**   Per capita consumption of lumber from the forests of the United States had reached 300 board feet by 1864 and in 1900 had risen to 539 board feet. However, 25 years later it was down again to 347, in 1955 it was 248 board feet (*Timber Resources for America's Future,* 1958). In 1970 it was 193 board feet and estimated to be 224 board feet by 1980 at 1970 relative price projections (*The Outlook for Timber in the United States,* 1973). This lumber has come from American forests. What has it been used for and why have Americans tightened their belts and restrained their appetites for forest products?

Lumber made up 51 percent of our wood consumption in 1970. Buildings, other construction, fences, crossties to cushion railroads, mine timbers, fuel, pulpwood for paper, and staves for cooperage were the leading kinds of use. Hundreds of other uses of wood, such as furniture, boats, picnic tables, shipping and tool handles, compete for mention.

**Contributions from the Forest Are Both Large and Varied**   One way of visualizing the contribution of forests to the building of the country is to consider that the equivalent of not less than 100 good tall trees, 18 in. (45 cm) in diameter at the stump, must be harvested to supply the complete buildings and equipment on the average farm. Remembering that farms were being established at the rate of 90,000 a year for the decades each side of the year 1900 and that a good large straight tree or two would be needed each year for repair material, the forests cut to build farms must have been dense, deep, and sound. Spread out 10 years' supply of the forest trees used for farm construction a few years ago, and they could form a heavy shelter belt entirely around continental United States.

Although some 90 percent of farm buildings and perhaps 80 percent of all dwellings, whether in country or city, come from the forest, the plank sidewalk has given way to a more permanent type of construction. Yet there are relatively few buildings of any character today in which the forest has not contributed something; if not wood, then it may be insulating material in great volume; and if not that, it may be oils, paints, or furnishings. Insulation alone has introduced a new way of using forests, and most insulating "wools," boards, and papers are made from wood fiber. Even those from other much publicized vegetable fibers need the admixture of wood to give them strength. Moreover, plywood, a product produced principally from trees of large diameter and finding its major use in construction, exhibits ever-increasing demand.

The United States uses considerable amounts of paper and paperpulp products. In fact, Americans in 1970 consumed about 567 lb (257 kg) of paper products per person. At 1970 relative prices and medium projections, estimated use by the year 2000 will be 1,114 lb (505 kg) per capita (*The Outlook for Timber in the United States,* 1973).

Since 1920, pulpwood consumption in United States mills increased 12 times, rising from 6 to 72.4 million cords in 1972. This is 5.6 billion cu ft (158,480,000 m³) which includes 3.7 billion cu ft (104,710,000 m³) of roundwood used directly in pulping and 1.9 billion cu ft (53,770,000 m³) of chips and sawdust obtained from slabs, edgings, veneer cores, and other residues of primary manufacturing plants. Export demand, including the pulpwood equivalent of pulp and paper, increased to 0.7 billion cu ft (19,810,000 m³) in 1972, a change from 0.5 million cords in 1920 to 9.5 million cords in 1972. As a result of such growth, nearly half of the cubic volume of timber harvested from domestic forests is now used as pulpwood.

Since 1920 the average use of pulpwood per ton of pulp produced has not changed materially, averaging about 1.6 cords per ton. Future technological improvements are estimated to decrease this to 1.5 cords of pulpwood per ton of pulp by the year 2000.

Importation of pulpwood from Canada continues at a considerable rate; pulp mills in the South contribute heavily to kraft-paper demands and produce paper containers and newsprint, but have to compete for wood with other industries; Rocky Mountain species suitable for pulping suggest establishment of more mills in that region if water, power, and pollution problems can be solved; the mills of the Northwest have to compete with other industries for suitable pulping species, although there is now greater use of poorer quality trees and sawmill waste. The vast forests of Alaska now support a pulpwood and paper mill industry.

Further development and widespread forest management of lands which produce pulpwood species throughout this country can supply much of our needs, assuming that the wood products come as now from the South, the Northeast, and Lake States, or the Northwest, *and* from the mature forests of the Rocky Mountains and Alaska. But such a happy picture will mean reforestation, further development in transportation, new mills and communities, and a more skilled harnessing of our boasted-of American ingenuity.

More than one great university, hundreds of banks, thousands of businesses, and millions of homes stand today because the forests of America furnished them and their owners with liquid funds, jobs, and articles of commerce or the actual materials of their construction.

Human brains, ingenuity, strength, and skill plus the tools that the citizens accumulated through saving the proceeds of their labor had to be combined with forests to build this nation. None of these factors could be dispensed with, and the great material contribution of forests may not be lightly considered.

## BIBLIOGRAPHY

Butler, O. M. 1935. *American Conservation,* American Forestry Association, Washington, DC.

Cameron, Jenks. 1928. *Development of Governmental Forest Control in the United States,* Johns Hopkins Press, Baltimore.

*Congressional Globe,* 29th Cong., 1st Sess., Washington.

Dana, Samuel Trask. 1956. *Forest and Range Policy,* McGraw-Hill Book Company, New York.

Defebaugh, J. E. 1906. History of the Lumber Industry in America, II., *Amer. Lumberman,* Chicago.

Donaldson, Thomas Corwin. 1884. *The Public Domain,* Washington, DC.

Ely, Richard T. 1908. *Outlines of Economics,* The Macmillan Company, New York.

Fernow, B. E. 1911. *History of Forestry,* University Press, Toronto.

Hotchkiss, George W. 1889. *History of the Lumber and Forest Industry of the Northwest,* George W. Hotchkiss and Co., Chicago.

Ise, John. 1920. *United States Forest Policy,* Yale University Press, New Haven.

Nash, Roderick (ed.). 1968. *The American Environment: Readings in the History of Conservation,* Addison-Wesley Publishing Company, Inc., Reading, Mass.

*A National Plan for American Forestry.* 1933. Sen. Doc. 12, 73d Cong., 1st Sess., Washington.

*The Outlook for Timber in the United States.* 1973. Forest Service, U. S. Department of Agriculture, Forest Resource Report no. 20.

*Report of the Chief of the Forest Service for 1970–71.* Forest Service, U. S. Department of Agriculture.

Reynolds, R. V., and A. H. Pierson. 1925. Tracking the Sawmill Westward, *Amer. Forests and Forest Life,* **31**:646, Washington, DC.

Ryan, J. C. 1973. *Early Loggers in Minnesota,* Minnesota Timber Producers Association, Duluth.

Sparhawk, N., and W. D. Brush. 1929. *Economic Aspects of Forest Destruction in Northern Michigan,* U. S. Department of Agriculture.

*Timber Resources for America's Future.* 1958. U. S. Department of Agriculture, Forest Service Report no. 14.

# Chapter 3

# Forestry as a Federal Public Policy in the United States

Forest policy can be defined as a settled or definite course or method adopted and followed by a government, institution, body, or individual. It generally has a body of laws, regulations, rules, and procedures. Changing times inevitably result in changing policies, so that policies are consequently in a constant state of flux (Dana, 1956).

To fully understand these policy changes one must have some background as to attitudes and public opinion toward the subject at the time. Most of the major changes evolved slowly from the impetus of a few people or a few organizations, generally both, who promoted and enlarged the general public support for a change. Policy changes on federal or state legislative acts frequently took several years for completion.

**The Development of Forest Policy**   Most people are amused when told the story of the boy who scorned the opportunity to earn a quarter because he had a quarter. And yet a similar disposition toward providential handling of natural resources, and forests in particular, has characterized the well-supplied American people. Progress leading away from such a viewpoint takes two paths. The first is *restriction* pure and simple, which was the principle of the greater part of all early American forestry legislation. The second is *use and renewal*, with restriction, of course, but with emphasis on the constructive phase of conservation rather than policing alone.

A nation that sprang from courageous people individualistic enough to leave restriction-ridden countries of Europe had little taste for restriction—too little at times for the public good. Shortages of timber in one locality have been overcome by the marvelous tools of transportation. Stark and desperate need for forest products is not even yet common in the United States. Let us see how these two things—rebellion against restrictions and overcoming real needs—have affected the development of forest policy in this country and whether forestry as a positive or as a negative policy is what we are settling on. Appendix A is a listing of major legislation and government policies and a brief summary of what they entail by time periods.

**Disposal of the Public Domain and Its Effect on Forest Policy** The period from 1841 to 1891 is most significant, but more as a time that demonstrated *need* for working out a forest policy than it is for any *accomplishment* in that direction. It was a period characterized by three rather universally accepted ideas: (1) the country must be settled at any cost; (2) it is appropriate for the government to subsidize internal improvements, education, and even agriculture with land in lieu of the money that it does not have; and (3) natural resources will gravitate into satisfactory ownership and management under a laissez faire policy. These three ideas brought about the disposal of more than two-thirds of an empire of 1,500 million acres (607 million ha), exclusive of Alaska, and four-fifths of all the timberland it contained to individuals, corporations, and new states. Brave provisions to assure bona fide development were recited in most of the laws under which land could be acquired, and these have been discussed briefly in Chap. 2. It will bear repeating here, however, that the preemptor under the act of 1841 was to improve the land, which was bought for $1.25 per acre ($3.09 per ha), and erect a dwelling; that the railroad, wagon road, or canal builders, from 1850 on, were to sell out at modest prices the bordering alternate sections of land that they had received as rich bonuses, and do some free hauling of troops and property for the government; that the homesteader under the acts of 1862 and later ones was to make of the claim a real home and a real farm and live on it; that the claimant under the Timber Culture Act of 1873 should plant 40 of the 160 acres (16 of the 64.7 ha) to trees; that the claimant and purchaser of 640 acres (259 ha) of land unfit for cultivation without water, under the Desert Land Act of 1877, should claim just that kind of land and irrigate it within 3 years; that miners should work their claims as well as purchase or hold them; and that most of these laws required that the persons who asserted a claim to land should swear that it was taken up for their own use and benefit.

Enforcement of trespass regulations, encouraged in 1850 by a Supreme Court decision confirming decision of the lower court in an action under the Timber Trespass Act of 1831, waxed and waned according to the views and the courage of the various Secretaries of the Interior.

"Speculation-and-fraud" came to be almost a single word, and "dummy entry men" were used by shrewd timberland grabbers to acquire land as if it were bona fide homesteads, preemptions, desert land, and other claims. The "rubber forty" came into the picture, which meant that a sawmill owner would buy 40 acres (16 ha) of timber and then cut everything within reach of it. The states had established agricultural colleges, partially financed from sale of land or scrip[1] granted them as special subsidy by act of 1862. They showed little interest in anything that approached management of other "school lands" reserved at the rate, first of one and then of two sections per township, or of the swamp and overflow lands granted to them by acts of 1849 and 1850. The best of federal timberland agents were in the position of one policeman in a disturbed town of 5,000. By 1891 the country was settled, and the government had done a generous turn of subsidizing internal improvements, education, and agriculture—however, natural resources *had not* gravitated into satisfactory ownership and management under the laissez faire policy. Instead, there were large tracts in the hands of comparatively few owners, a trend that persisted and increased; most of the choice and accessible timber had passed with little protest to those who firmly believed that "timber is a one-time crop"; and forest fires were seldom challenged. It is small wonder that a few thoughtful people were beginning to worry constructively. Others worried, but confined their efforts to crying, "For shame!" From 1870 on there was plenty of protest, and constructive suggestions were laying the foundation for profound changes in the care and use of the public forests that remained.

**Forestry Comes to Life Again**   In the period just reviewed, the new nation, feverishly busy on the work of settlement and internal improvement, had forgotten any forestry suggestions of the early days of the Confederation. The decades from 1871 to 1891 witnessed a resurrection of the forestry idea. This was evident in a resolution that followed the presentation of a paper by Franklin B. Hough before the American Association for the Advancement of Science at Portland, Maine, in 1873. This paper sketched the evils that have followed deforestation in other countries, urged the retention of forests on the public lands, and indicated their importance,

---

[1] Scrip was a form of negotiable certificate issued to the states that contained no public land. It was exchangeable for land and was purchased in considerable blocks from the Eastern states by companies which resold it or used it for selection of land in the public-land states.

when supplemented by reservoirs, for regulating the flow of streams. This was no dull speech, neither was the resolution in any sense a timid one, nor was the committee, with Dr. Hough as its chairman and the promotion of federal and state forestry commissions as its assignment, "just another committee." It had a report ready in 1874 that developed into a memorial to Congress, and brought about the establishment of a Division of Forestry in the Department of Agriculture by act of 1876. Dr. Hough was put in charge, and out of this division the present U. S. Forest Service developed (Fig. 3-1).

Still another service of the American Association for the Advancement of Science was a recommendation to the President of the United States in 1890 urging investigation of the preservation of forest areas on public land for maintenance of favorable water conditions. This recommendation also urged that, pending investigation and report, sales of public timberlands be suspended until they could be put under adequate administration and protection for the supplying of local wood and lumber needs. President Harrison referred the resolution to his Secretary of the Interior J. W. Noble, who was so impressed that he recommended action to the Congress (Van Hise, 1930). The next year, 1891, an act was passed authorizing the President to set apart and reserve from time to time any public lands that were wholly or in part covered with timber or undergrowth, and proclaim them as public reservations. The same law repealed the Preemption Act of 1841 and the Timber Culture Act of 1873, both of which had been abused, and halted

**Figure 3-1**  Dr. Franklin B. Hough, first head of the Division of Forestry established in 1876. *(Courtesy of the American Forestry Association.)*

sales of public land. President Harrison proclaimed the first "forest reserves," now known as national forests, within the same year, 1891. The American Forestry Association (organized in 1875) and assisted by others had urged the forest reserve clause in the 1891 act.

**Building Up the Federal Forests** Upon signing of the law of 1891, which gave him the power to reserve public forest lands, President Harrison promptly proclaimed some 2.5 million acres (1 million ha) in Wyoming and Colorado as forest reserves, and the combined total of his proclamations reached more than 13 million acres (5.3 million ha). These were impressive areas, and the new policy of public forests was well launched except for some authority to administer and protect them and to make their mature products available. Before such legislation was secured, vigorous criticism charged the federal government with hoarding and "locking up" the forests. Dr. Fernow (Fig. 3-2), still acting as head of the Division of Forestry, alert to the need of putting forests to use, was probably back of a request to the Secretary of the Interior Hoke Smith, early in 1896, to enlist the National Academy of Sciences in a study of the forestry situation, so that it might advise the government on how to provide for rational handling of the forest lands of the country. Mr. Smith complied, and this permanent "brain trust" had a commission, with Prof. C. S. Sargent of Harvard at its head, hard at work by July 1896. Out of this study came the recommendation for a measure very much like one previously urged in vain by the Secretary of the Interior. Also, the same commission had found time, along with its other

**Figure 3-2** Dr. Bernhard E. Fernow, who became chief of the Division of Forestry in 1886. *(Courtesy of the Department of Manuscripts and University Archives, Cornell University.)*

duties, to urge upon President Cleveland the proclamation of a new group of forest reserves involving more than 21 million acres (8.5 million ha). This the President did with a suddenness that created much Western opposition. The whole prospect appeared to the Western people as a drag on development of their part of the country and as unwarranted interference by the Eastern states. But the final outcome, following this opposition, was a law that cleared the way for real progress in public forestry. Known as the act of June 4, 1897, it provided, among other things, for the following:

Appropriation for surveying the existing and projected reserves
Modification of reserve boundaries by the President
Delay of effective date of the President's latest withdrawals
Creation of the reserves only for purposes of producing timber and protecting water supply
Protection of the reserves from fire and trespass
Making of rules and regulations by the secretary for the use and occupancy of the reserves, which should have the force of law
Sale of mature timber at market value
Free use of timber by miners and settlers under permit
Selection of other public lands in lieu of patented lands or valid claims within the reserves
Various other concessions to local users and to jurisdiction of local courts

This legislation, with little modification, constitutes the organic law under which the national forests are administered today by the Forest Service.

**Setting the Forest Reserves in Order**    Approval of the act of June 4, 1897, by no means marked the last of the withdrawals of public lands and proclaiming them forest reserves. That procedure was to continue for at least another 15 years, but the law did start the business of setting in order a goodly number of millions of acres. Dr. Fernow found himself with a Division of Forestry in one department, while the forests were in another. He retired in 1898, with the observation that the time had come for the division to have charge of the public forest reservations, which were in need of systematic management. This did not come about until 1905.

Meanwhile, Fernow had turned over the division to his successor, Gifford Pinchot, who, at the former's suggestion some years before, had studied forestry in France and had acquired varied experience upon his return (Fig. 3-3). He had managed the great forested Vanderbilt estate at Biltmore, N. C., had served with Professor Sargent and others on the special Commission of the National Academy of Sciences in 1896, and, for a year previous to assuming his position as Fernow's successor, had traveled over the forest reserves of the West as a special agent of the Department of the Interior. He

**Figure 3-3** Gifford Pinchot, who served as chief of the Division of Forestry, the Bureau of Forestry, and the Forest Service, successively, from 1898 to 1910.

continued the work of the division, which had become a bureau in 1901 and which had a public to inform but no forests to manage, until 1905. During this time, Pinchot and his organization made some excellent studies and plans for management of privately owned timberlands, and, although comparatively few of them were adopted by owners, the educational effect was far-reaching. His program differed from Fernow's, which had concentrated on the wood user.

By act of February 1, 1905, the forest reserves, which had been receiving improved management under a forestry division established in 1901 in the Department of the Interior and headed by Filibert Roth,[2] were transferred, after considerable opposition had been worn down, to the Department of Agriculture. In the same year, the name of the Bureau of Forestry was changed to the Forest Service, and, in 1907, the name *forest reserve* was changed to *national forest*.

Let us pause a moment to get our bearings in 1907, for there are stirring years just ahead. Gifford Pinchot, forester, was head of the Forest Service in the Department of Agriculture, which had been given charge of the national forests, heretofore called *forest reserves*. The act of February 1, 1905, which had made the transfer from the Department of the Interior to the Department of Agriculture, also provided that all receipts for 5 years

---

[2] There is a long story in the forestry relations of the two departments between 1898 and 1905. The Commissioner of the General Land Office soon ran into such difficulties in administering the reserves, that Secretary Hitchcock of the Department of the Interior called upon the Department of Agriculture for technical help, which was furnished for a time. Moreover, a division of its own having been established, as noted in the text above, and the Commissioner of the General Land Office meanwhile having looked with disfavor upon the cooperation between the two government departments, all negotiations ceased sometime in 1902, and Roth and his technical staff resigned in 1903. The next 2 years no doubt produced a kind of management that influenced the 1905 transfer to the Department of Agriculture.

from the forest reserves (national forests later) should be earmarked for expenditure by the Forest Service; that supervisors of national forests and forest rangers should be picked, where practicable, from the states in which the forests were situated; and that forest officers should have authority for arrest without warrant. Thus, the legal foundation for managing the federal forests was strengthened; there was unity of command. The setting in order of the national forests was progressing, and a crop of technically trained graduates was appearing each year from Biltmore, where Dr. C. A. Schenck, Pinchot's successor there, had organized a "master school" in 1898, patterned after the earlier German institutions. Other graduates were available from Cornell, where Dr. Fernow had organized the New York State College of Forestry the same year and kept it going until 1903. Still others were being graduated at Yale, where Henry S. Graves headed a school of forestry organized in 1900, and from the University of Michigan,[3] where Filibert Roth had become head of the department of forestry in 1903. More forest schools had been and were being established. The Society of American Foresters had been organized in 1900 and by 1905 had begun to publish its proceedings. The *Forestry Quarterly*, started by Fernow in 1902, published technical articles and news. Forestry graduates pooled their talents with those of a fine group of Western supervisors and rangers. Sawmill owners and workers, ranchers, cowmen, sheepmen, settlers, miners, and locators began slowly, if unwillingly, to adjust themselves to the increasing administrative activity on the national forests. President Theodore Roosevelt was keenly interested in the national forests and was giving the movement his aggressive support, having brought the total area of forest reserves to the figure of 100 million acres (40.5 million ha), with a disposition to make further withdrawals when examination had indicated their advisability.

Although the actual turning point between floundering attempts to set the public forests in order and really setting them in order is the moment of signing the Transfer Act of February 1, 1905, the 2 years from 1905 to 1907 were really occupied in making the turn. Certain finishing touches of policy were adopted in these 2 years, including the opening to settlement and entry, by act of June 11, 1906, of agricultural lands that were situated within the forest reserves; the granting of 10 percent of the receipts from the reserves for schools and roads, following an act of June 30, 1906, to the states in which they were located (later, in 1908, raised to 25 percent and made a permanent arrangement); the charging of a fee per head for grazing

[3] The first recognized course in forestry offered anywhere in the United States was given in 1881 at the University of Michigan although lectures on the subject had been given before at other schools. This course, taught by Professor Volney M. Spalding, continued for 4 years until the School of Political Science, in which it was then given, was discontinued in 1885 (Dana, 1953).

stock on the reserves; the limiting of the authority for Presidential withdrawals of land for reserves;[4] the changing of the names to *Forest Service* and *national forests* (as mentioned earlier); and the making of a generous appropriation for the work in the act of June 4, 1907.

Other significant events concerned repeal of the Forest Lieu Selection Act of 1897, beginning of an investigation of the Oregon and California Railroad land grant for violation of grant provisions, and appropriations for survey of lands in the Appalachians and White Mountains, which were later to figure in the creation of Eastern national forests.

**Decentralization of the U. S. Forest Service**   By 1907 the administration of the forest reserves had progressed to a point where decentralization appeared necessary; and six field districts were established in 1908, with headquarters at Denver, Albuquerque, Ogden, Missoula, Portland (Or.), and San Francisco. A *district forester,* with a technical and administrative staff, was given charge of each district, which comprised from 15 to 20 national forests, as the reserves had been renamed. Outbursts of Western dissatisfaction with the policies of the Forest Service had by no means ceased, and this decentralized organization found itself with a vast public-relations problem at its doors—one that a staff working wholly from Washington could never meet. In the same year the first forest experiment station was organized at Flagstaff, Arizona, cooperation was arranged between the Forest Service and the Department of the Interior for the management of timber on Indian lands, and the Attorney General was requested by Congress to institute proceedings to bring about forfeiture of the land grant of the Oregon and California Railroad. The latter was the most ambitious decision, thus far, to cancel a land-subsidy contract that had been violated by a favored company. The three events listed above are not closely related, but they serve to illustrate the vigor of the forestry movement during that period.

**The White House Conference of 1908**   The business of conserving natural resources is full of interlocking problems, and this truth had impressed itself so deeply upon the members of President Theodore Roosevelt's (Fig. 3-4) Inland Waterways Commission that they suggested to him the advisability of calling the governors of the states together to confer on the broad natural-resource problems of the country. The conference was called for May 13, 1908, and it is significant not only for what it accomplished but also because it was the first assembly of its particular character ever held. The invitation list had grown from the names of the governors to those of

---

[4] President Roosevelt had before him a report on some 16 million acres (6.5 million ha) of proposed reserves, which he neatly withdrew and proclaimed before signing the Agricultural Appropriation Bill, which carried a rider limiting his authority to do so.

**Figure 3-4**  President Theodore Roosevelt and Chief Forester Gifford Pinchot on the river steamer *Mississippi,* in 1907. *(Courtesy of the U.S. Forest Service.)*

the Supreme Court, the Cabinet officers, representatives of various national societies, and various groups of special guests. Politicians, scientists, and businessmen exchanged ideas under the leadership of the President and adopted a "Declaration of Principles," which had this to say about forestry:

> We urge the continuation and extension of forest policies adapted to secure the husbanding and renewal of our diminishing timber supply, the prevention of soil erosion, the protection of the headwaters, and the maintenance of the purity and navigability of our streams. We recognize that the private ownership of forest land entails responsibilities in the interests of all the people, and we favor the enactment of laws looking to the protection and replacement of privately owned forests.

The governors went home, and within a year and a half 41 of them had appointed conservation commissions for their own states. The President, shortly after the conference, appointed a National Conservation Commission of scientists, business people, and politicians in equal proportions, with Forester Gifford Pinchot as chairman. They met, undertook a natural-resource inventory with the help of the federal bureaus, reported to the President and the second meeting of governors in less than a year, and in spite of a very unfriendly attitude upon the part of Congress, had given the conservation movement, including forestry, a tremendous start toward an adequate program.

One specific and important result of the White House Conference and the work of its National Conservation Commission was the wholesale withdrawal of public lands by President Theodore Roosevelt for examination, study, and the subsequent proclamation of various natural-resource reserves, including generous additions to the national forests.

Forest policy gained, therefore, both nationally and in the states from this busy but short-lived series of conferences and investigations, which were discontinued abruptly because of congressional opposition.

**Formal Recognition of Research**    The establishment of the first forest experiment station on the Coconino National Forest in Arizona in 1908 (already mentioned) and of the Forest Products Laboratory at Madison, Wisconsin, in 1910 had put the Forest Service emphatically into the business of forest research. Even these were not completely new ventures, for timber preservation, forest nursery, and other problems had been investigated both inside and outside the Forest Service for several years. But in 1915, the Branch of Research was set up as one of the major divisions of the work of the Forest Service. Under this branch some eight stations now operate in as many localities, in addition to the great Forest Products Laboratory in Madison. The work of these institutions is discussed in Chap. 20.

**The Establishment of the National Park Service**    Up to 1917, the Army had been charged with patrolling the national parks, 10 of which had been created in the United States, beginning with Yellowstone in 1872. The real task of supervising and protecting them, however, was a part-time responsibility of the Department of the Interior. Any road building that was undertaken fell to the lot of the Army engineers. The only definition of the purposes of the parks was contained in the language of the act of March 1, 1872, which set aside Yellowstone National Park "as a public pleasuring ground" and ordered "the preservation from injury or spoliation of all timber, mineral deposits, natural curiosities, or wonders within said park, and their retention in their natural condition." This was no task to be handled on a part-time basis, and the National Park Service was therefore established in April 1917, as a bureau of the Department of the Interior, under the act of August 25, 1916. Stephen T. Mather became the first director

**Figure 3-5** Stephen T. Mather, first director of the National Park Service (NPS), 1917 to 1929. Much of the present-day policy in the NPS was established by Mather. *(Courtesy of the National Park Service.)*

(Fig. 3-5). Upon his death, in 1929, after a highly successful and tireless term of service, he was followed by Horace M. Albright, and upon resignation of the latter in 1933, Arno B. Cammerer was appointed director. He served for 7 years and upon his retirement because of ill health was succeeded by Newton B. Drury in 1940, who held the office until early in 1951. Arthur E. Demaray served until December of that year. Conrad L. Wirth was director from December 1951 until 1964. George Hartzog was director from 1965 until December 1972. Ronald Walker became director in January 1973 followed by Gary Everhardt, January 1975. The work of the National Park Service is discussed further in Chaps. 5 and 20. For an inside look at that agency the reader is referred to Everhart (1972).

**The Clarke-McNary Act of 1924**   Out of the agitation for control of forest devastation on private timberlands came a report on forest conditions and needs by the Forest Service, in response to a resolution introduced by Senator Capper of Kansas; a nontechnical digest of this report; a long series of hearings on the Snell and Capper bills; the appointment of a Senate Select Committee on Reforestation, which held hearings in Washington and throughout the country; and the introduction of practically identical bills in the Senate by Senator Charles L. McNary of Oregon and in the House by Congressman John D. Clarke of New York. The final whittling down produced the Clarke-McNary Act of June 7, 1924, which is much more significant in its provisions affecting forestry on public lands than on any control of destructive practices on private lands. Two of its provisions affect the conditions under which forestry practice might be inaugurated by large owners of private timberlands. These are (1) amendment of the Weeks Law of 1911 to extend federal cooperation in fire control to *any* timber or forest-producing lands, regardless of their effect on flow of navigable streams; and (2) authorization of a study of the effect of taxation laws and methods upon forest perpetuation. A third provision, which is also in the nature of an amendment to the Weeks Law, authorizes acquisition by the federal government of cutover lands "for the production of timber." This gave an "outlet for a price," heretofore not available to lumber companies, for certain of their cutover lands. Other provisions of importance include setting up a financial program for the recommendation of appropriate forestry practices to various regions by the Forest Service; for cooperating with states and through them with private owners[5] in fire control; and for making the taxation study. State cooperation was also authorized for procuring, producing, and distributing tree seeds and plants for use in farm forestry and for advice and assistance to farm owners in reforestation and management of existing forests. The remaining provisions had to do with addition of certain public lands to the national forest system and with the acceptance of donations of privately owned lands.

**Establishment of the Civilian Conservation Corps (CCC)**   One of the first important recommendations of President Franklin D. Roosevelt, upon assuming office in March 1933, was an attack on the problem of unemployment, which had developed since the 1929 financial crash. It called for the establishment of a Civilian Conservation Corps to be made up of unemployed young men who were to be organized for conserving natural resources. It is clear from earlier campaign utterances of the President, from the language of the act of March 31, 1933, and from eventual assignment of the work camps that forestry was the activity which offered the greatest opportunity to the proposed enterprise. An act giving broad powers to the President was passed in record time and signed by him on March 31, 1933. Immediate funds were made available from unexpended and unobligated balances of public-works appropriations and from the $300 million relief appropriation which had been made available under an act of the previous year. Six classes of forestry work are mentioned in the act of March 31,

---

[5] There was something of a gentlemen's agreement in the original hearings, but not incorporated in the bill, that the forests of the country could be protected adequately for $10 million a year, that it would be equitable for private owners to assume one-half the burden, the state one-quarter, and federal government the other quarter. The amount authorized annually in the bill was, therefore, not more than $2,500,000. Since then the authorization has been raised. In 1971 the authorization was raised to $40 million and $25 million was appropriated for Fiscal Year 1973. In F. Y. 1971 the federal expenditures were $15,119,942, state and county $106,687,874, private $1,383,033, for a total of $123,191,849.

1933, including forestation, fire control, and forest research. Others, such as erosion and flood control, construction of paths, trails, and fire lanes in national forests and national parks, also were mentioned. Authority was granted the President to extend the work to state, county, and private lands so long as it was of a nature in which the federal government was legally authorized to cooperate.

The organization and work of the CCC is a story in itself, which is the more remarkable because dual "command" involving Army officers and project supervisors managed somehow to iron out minor differences in viewpoint and policy and to accomplish a vast amount of valuable work. From the strict standpoint of public policy, it should be added in passing, however, that the legislation, the operation of the corps itself, and the stimulus given by both of these to the expansion of public forestry and the conservation of human resources were far-reaching.

In the period following World War II, there was some public agitation for a revival of the CCC. Many bills were introduced in Congress. This interest resulted in the establishment of a peak of 87 Job Corps Conservation Centers on the public lands from 1965 to 1968. Of these centers, 26 were still active in 1974. Program emphasis was on training and educating disadvantaged enrollees to 21 years of age, with conservation work being secondary.

In 1970 a Youth Conservation Corps program was started on an experimental basis with a small summer enrollment. In 1974 the enrollment was 5,500 in 178 camps. This involved youths 14 to 18 years of age and the emphasis was on training and education. In September 1974 the YCC was made a permanent organization.

The legislative history of the Job Corps Conservation Centers and the Youth Conservation Corps contains many testimonials to the value of the CCC program of the 1930s. Much public opinion is favorable for a continuation of some aspects of this program, for example, the Job Corps and YCC.

In addition to the favorable public opinion that persists, it is possible now to evaluate the past results more fully. Thousands of CCC enrollees learned a trade and how to become useful citizens. Many enrollees went on to colleges or universities for further education; some entered the military and were better for their CCC service. Professionals in the supervision of CCC activities gained experience. Tree planting, timber-stand improvement, recreation improvements, roads and other improvements, and all other authorized land-management activities were accelerated. Policies governing all conservation work were currently reviewed and revised to meet the growing program needs. Most policies were restated and viewed in a different light. The CCC made a real impact on most of the enrollees, the communities, the land resources of the United States, and on the subsequent forest land development policies of the supervisory federal and state agencies.

**Forests and Soil Conservation**   The Soil Conservation Service, now in the Department of Agriculture and formerly in the Department of the Interior, where it was established by executive order in 1933, includes a staff specialist whose efforts are devoted to supervision of the work of a force of Woodland Conservationists in the field. This is in accordance with a policy of using vegetative as well as mechanical methods and amounts to recognition of the importance of forests in conserving soil. The work of this section is discussed in Chap. 20.

**Extending Federal Help in Farm Forestry**   The Norris-Doxey Act, approved May 18, 1937, provided for federal aid to the extent of 50 percent of the cost of reforestation of farmlands in the Plains regions and for extending further encouragement to the management of farm forests. Both these functions were cooperative through state agencies. Cooperation was established either with the State Forester's office or the extension division of the land-grant college. In 1950 the Norris-Doxey Act was repealed through the enactment of the Cooperative Forest Management Act of August 25, 1950. This new act enlarged the authority and increased authorizations of appropriations contained in the earlier act and specified that the use of private agencies and individuals offering service to timberland owners should be encouraged. Federal expenditures were not to exceed those of the state for like purposes.

In 1970 the authorization for cooperative forest management was increased to $20 million. In F. Y. 1972, the federal expenditures were $4,284,000 and the 50 states expended $10,321,000. A total of 867 service foresters were employed full or part time by the states under this cooperative forest management program. Services were rendered to more than 272,000 owners, involving an estimated 11,150,000 acres (4.5 million ha) of private woodlands during F. Y. 1972.

**Status of State Forestry Departments**   Beginning with their management of vast CCC and other relief projects and continuing with new responsibilities under the Norris-Doxey Act, the Cooperative Forest Management Act and state forest tax laws, the administrative forestry organizations in the states have assumed increasing importance in the national picture. Meanwhile, they have kept up their regular work in educating the public, acquiring and organizing state forests without federal help, assuming responsibility for controlling wildfires on state and private lands, reforesting state lands, cooperating with private owners in forest management, and making no small contribution to forest research. New York has the oldest of the state departments, one having been created as a Forest Commission in 1885. How the states practice forestry is discussed further in Chap. 21.

**American Forest Congresses**  Forest congresses have been called by the American Forestry Association on six important occasions. Each congress had a significant effect upon subsequent decisions and thus became a milepost in the evolution of forest conservation. These historic dates, the situation at the time, and major developments thereafter are as follows:

*1882*  Fears of timber famine resulting from the combined effects of wanton exploitation and unchecked forest fires caused farsighted civic leaders to convene the first forest congress.

*1905*  The national economy continued to favor exploitation. Federal and state forestry organizations found themselves woefully inadequate to cope with the monumental task confronting them. A second forest congress helped arouse the public to the meaning of "conservation through wise use."

The American Forestry Association did not call a forest congress during the 1920s or 1930s but continued to hold its regular annual meetings in various sections of the nation. Its objectives had been defined so clearly in the 1905 congress that another special session was considered unnecessary.

*1946*  During the preceding four decades two world wars and a 70 percent increase in population made severe demands upon the nation's forests. The American Forestry Association called for review of the situation and convened a third forest congress.

*1953*  Attempts to implement the program soon revealed some gaps in the framework. Accordingly, the Association invited three dozen conservation leaders to draft a new program. This instrument became the basis of intense debate at the fourth American forest congress. Immediate results included passage of legislation leading to curtailment of fraudulent mining claims on the public domain. Then the Association aimed another broadside at "woods burners" in a Southern forest fire prevention congress. It conducted landownership studies in three major regions of the United States. And it continued to maintain an alert watch on exploiters, to keep the public informed about all phases of conservation, and to press for more effective management of the nation's forests.

*1963*  Pyramiding requirements for water by a rapidly expanding population and an explosive increase in outdoor recreation cast new demands upon the forests during the 1950s. These important uses had only been touched upon lightly in earlier programs for American forestry. They needed to be evaluated and accorded adequate roles in the management of forest and rangelands. There was also an increased interest in world forestry, forest protection, intensified management, and research and education. Hence the fifth forest congress was called.

*1975*  Early in that year, 75 national conservation leaders appointed by AFA met and proposed planks for AFA's future policy. These planks were grouped under World Forestry, Interrelationships of all Natural Resources, and Domestic Forest Programs.

The planks were discussed at the 1975 "Centennial" Forest Congress held in Washington, D.C. During this sixth congress, more than 100 recommendations evolved, which were voted on by members in 1976. The adopted recommendations now guide American Forestry Association policy.

**Forest Pest Control Act of 1947**   More effective forest pest control programs have been developed during the more than 25 years of operation under this act. Federal, state, and local agencies and private owners have all contributed to this cooperative program. In any one year most of the forested acreage is examined from the air or from the ground. Federal expenditures under the act have run in excess of $10 million annually in recent years.

**Mining Claims on National Forests**   Long-established abuses of mining laws by claimants interested in resources other than minerals were dealt a telling blow by the enactment in 1955 of an amendment to the Mineral Disposal Act of 1947. Locators on fraudulent mining claims had for years been able to interfere with timber management and general land administration by asserting that valuable timber on the claims was needed for development and sometimes by obtaining fraudulent patent to the land. The purposes for which such patented land was used might vary from resort or residence to shop or store. Many of the claims were filed for sand, gravel, stone, pumice, pumicite, or cinders. Others were for gold, silver, or uranium. The law removed the former group of minerals from the operation of the mining laws and made them no longer the basis of mineral discovery. Furthermore, it gave the agency in charge of the area the right to dispose of the vegetative surface resources and to manage the other surface resources, provided such management did not interfere with legitimate mining. Claims filed previous to July 23, 1955, the date the law became effective, would retain their status unless defaulted or the claimant had waived surface rights or the claim had been adjudged invalid. A generous appropriation was made to the Department of Agriculture to be used in clearing up ownership claims to the existing locations. This law is important in putting a halt to unwarranted patenting of invalid claims and to freeing the Forest Service from interference with timber management. Much credit is due the American Forestry Association for bringing about a meeting of minds among federal bureaus concerned and the mining industry, so that legislation could be agreed upon.

As a result of the 1955 amendment and other efforts, ownership claims to existing mining locations have been largely resolved. However, increased prices for minerals in recent years have increased mining. This resulted in issuance of new regulations in 1974 on National Forest lands subject to location and entry under United States mining laws of 1872. These regulations would require miners and prospectors to spell out in advance how they planned to search for or develop deposits. Beginning in 1974 they were required to post a bond to ensure restoration work where necessary.

**"Conservation Reserve" Feature of the Soil Bank Legislation**   There are two kinds of limitations on crop reduction contained in the 1956 Soil Bank Legislation. One is known as "acreage reserve" and the other as "conservation reserve." Benefits are paid to farmers for both, the former being concerned with limiting crops now in surplus, but the conservation reserve contracts, in order to qualify, must run from 3 to 10 years as against the annual acreage reserve agreements. Moreover, the land thus withdrawn from the production of critical crops must be used for purposes of erosion control, wildlife habitat, or timber production; and no crops may be marketed during the life of the contract. (Christmas trees, for example, may not be sold.) One effect of this legislation has been an increase in demand for forest planting stock, and a number of states have expanded their nursery capacity. About 2.2 million acres (890,000 ha) of cropland were planted to trees under the soil bank legislation (Cliff, 1973).

In the Agriculture and Consumer Protection Act of August 10, 1973, Title X allows for long-term contracts with landowners for installing conservation practices. These contracts also can be used for (1) improving fish, wildlife, and recreation resources; (2) enhancing the level of management of nonindustrial private forest lands (see Chap. 22); and (3) developing long-term cover for wildlife.

This act gives authority for setting aside croplands now in wheat, feed grains, and cotton under multiyear contracts for the years 1974 through 1978. Prior to 1973 as much as 60 million acres (24.3 million ha) had been set aside on an annual basis with no requirement for protective cover. Land retired under a multiyear contract under this act would be required to have a protective cover crop and grazing would be prohibited.

The Secretary of Agriculture proclaimed there would be no set-aside program for 1974. All cropland was to be in production. What the future holds in terms of cropland conversion is speculative at this point.

From a forestry standpoint the forestry incentives section above is significant. It directs the Secretary of Agriculture to encourage development of nonindustrial private land for timber production. Each owner must have a plan of management approved by the State Forester. The plan becomes the basis for a signed contract of 1 to 25 years' duration; it limits contracts to ownerships of 500 acres (202 ha) or less; and 50 to 75 percent of the cost of reforestation, timber-stand improvement, and related activities are authorized.

**Interstate Compacts for Forest-Fire Control**   The 1947 fires in the state of Maine demonstrated that fire situations could develop which exceed the normal capabilities of any fire-control agency. As a result the concept of an interstate compact was developed in the northeastern United States. An interstate compact allows the tapping of reserve equipment and manpower in states which are not having serious fire problems.

In 1949, congressional approval was given for the Northeastern Interstate Forest Fire Protection Compact to go into action as soon as any two of the states of Maine, New Hampshire, Vermont, Rhode Island, Connecticut, New York, and the Commonwealth of Massachusetts gave their consent. This compact also permitted any contiguous state to join the compact, and any contiguous province of Canada to join with congressional approval. All seven of the states and the provinces of Quebec and New Brunswick were members in 1973.

Congressional approval was given in 1954 for South Central Interstate Forest Fire Protection Compact, permitting Arkansas, Louisiana, Mississippi, Oklahoma, and Texas to become members. The additional approval of Congress for the Southeastern States and Middle Atlantic Compacts has resulted in the entire East Coast entering into compact agreement.

In 1972, the Middle Atlantic and Southeastern States Compacts entered into an intercompact agreement, permitting interchange of personnel and equipment among all members of either compact.

Activation of the several compacts for fire use has been light, although training meetings and technical exchange of information has been extensive. The use of Eastern fire crews on fires in the West in 1967, 1970, and 1973 has proved the value of the compact concept.

Some discussion has been developed toward a compact on a nationwide scope, which would provide state fire organizations a highly mobile, well-trained, equipped back-up force for emergency fire fighting.

**Termination of Federal Supervision over Indian Lands**   In 1954 two acts were passed by Congress providing for the "orderly termination" of federal supervision of Indian lands, the Menominee Reservation in Wisconsin and the Klamath Reservation in Oregon. Each of these reservations had important stands of timber and considerable controversy arose as to the continuation of sound forest management on the Klamath lands by the Forest Service or by private enterprise, either of which might be allowed to purchase the timberlands in order to pay off the Indians. Late in the Eighty-fifth Congress in 1958, an amendment was passed to the act providing for termination of federal control over the Klamath Indian Reservation. This amendment authorized the offering of 700,000 acres (283,000 ha) of timber- and marshland for sale to private companies on bid, if they would agree to manage the timber for sustained yield as it has been managed for years by the Bureau of Indian Affairs. Should there be no takers at appraised value by the spring of 1961, the amendment provided for purchase of the lands from the Indians by the Forest Service, to be added to national forest, and by the Fish and Wildlife Service for inclusion in the national wildlife refuge system.

The forest area was divided into 11 large units to be managed under sustained yield. One of these units, 91,541 acres (37,000 ha), was purchased by a pulp and paper corporation, but there were no other bids. The remaining 10 units, totaling 525,680 acres (212,736 ha), were acquired as national forest. The marshlands, consisting of 14,641 acres (5,925 ha), were purchased by the federal government through the Department of the Interior's Fish and Wildlife Service.

One-fifth of the Indians exercised an option, in an election in 1958, to hold their tribal interests. Approximately 144,000 acres (58,275 ha), consisting of 135,000 acres (54,632 ha) of forest and 9,000 acres (3,642 ha) of other lands (farm, grazing, and marsh), were set up in a management trust. After 10 years, in an election in 1969, the majority of the Indians involved voted to terminate the management trust. This remaining 135,000 acres (54,632 ha) of forest land was approved for purchase by the federal government in 1973 to be added to the Winema National Forest by P. L. 93-102.

After several years of negotiations and legislative considerations, P. L. 93-197 was signed by the President on December 22, 1973. This act repeals the act of June 12, 1954, as it relates to the Menominee Indian Tribe of Wisconsin; recognizes them as a sovereign Indian Tribe; and restores to them those federal services furnished American Indians. Their forest lands will continue to be managed under sustained yield.

**Use of Pesticides**   The President's Executive Orders establishing the Environmental Quality Council placed increased emphasis and restrictions on the use of pesticides. Only those that have minimal environmental impact were to be used. Land-managing agencies were committed to not using persistent pesticides in action programs where research and field tests demonstrated that nonpersistent chemicals or nonchemical methods will accomplish control objectives. The focal point in the control of forest pests in the years ahead was for integrated control, using natural enemies, forest cultural practices, and effective but safe pesticides.

**Studies of Land Ownership by the American Forestry Association**   By its vote, the members of the American Forestry Association had approved, in 1954, a study "state by state . . . of the desirable relationships between Federal, state and private ownerships with a view to mutual understanding and agreement among all classes of forest owners as to further Federal and state acquisitions." Under this plan and with a foundation grant, such a study was completed for California in 1957–1958 (Dana and Krueger, 1958), and a second one completed for Minnesota in 1960, by Dana, John W. Allison and Russell N. Cunningham.

North Carolina was selected as the third state since four-fifths of its commercial forest land is held in relatively small private tracts. Pomeroy and Yoho (1964) conducted the study. In the foreword to this report, Edward P. Stamm, President, The American Forestry Association, stated:

North Carolina Lands completes the Association's program of pilot studies in the ownership, use and management of forest and related lands. These studies provide the essential background for projects of this type. Having pointed the way, we now urge each state to undertake a similar review for its own future economic welfare.

**American Forest Policy a Part of Cooperative Agreement**    Dana (1956) concludes that:

> . . . forest and range policies of the timber states are not single entities but are made up of the policies of governments, associations, companies and individuals. Each of these policies in its turn has its own characteristic components. All have evolved gradually in response to stimuli exerted by ever-changing conditions.
>
> That evolution has now reached the stage where the activities of public and private agencies form a pattern that gives promise of relative stability. The task of managing the country's forest and range lands so as to assure an adequate and permanent supply of products and services has become largely a cooperative enterprise. . . . The main problem today is not to invent new methods of attaining the goals which all agree to be desirable, but rather to sharpen the tools already in existence.

**Multiple Use**    The Multiple-Use, Sustained-Yield Act of June 12, 1960, had a profound effect on not only management of the national forests but other public and private lands. Legally it applied only to the national forests, but foresters and segments of the public embraced the concept as a part of the answer in stretching forest resources. The law stated it to be the policy of the Congress that the national forests shall be administered for outdoor recreation, range, timber, watershed, and wildlife and fish purposes. The purposes of the act were supplemental to, but not in derogation of, the original intent for which the national forests were established as set forth in the act of June 4, 1897, commonly called the Organic Act.

The law also defined multiple use and sustained yield and these definitions are quoted from the act (*The Principal Laws Relating to Forest Service Activities*, 1974):

> Multiple use means the management of all the various renewable surface resources of the National Forests so that they are utilized in the combination that will best meet the needs of the American people; making the most judicious use of the land for some or all of these resources or related services over areas large enough to provide sufficient latitude for periodic adjustments in use to conform to changing needs and conditions; that some land will be used for less than all of the resources; and harmonious and coordinated management of the various resources, each with the other, without impairment of the productivity of the land, with consideration being given to the relative values of the various resources and not necessarily the combination of uses that will give the greatest dollar return or the greatest unit output. Sustained yield of the several products and services means the achievement and maintenance in perpetuity of a high-level annual or regular periodic output of the various renewable

resources of the National Forests without impairment of the productivity of the land.

**Policy Trends**   The advice by Dana (1956) to "sharpen the tools already in existence" was prophetic. The ensuing decades since 1956 have seen dynamic changes in the attitudes of the general public. Population increases and high economies have made increased pressures on forest land. While markets were calling for more products, certain segments of the public were calling for more attention to management of recreation, aesthetics, wildlife, and watersheds. Concern for all phases of the environment was expressed in many ways. There was renewed interest in preserving wilderness and in the intangible values of the forest land. Clearcutting of timber became suspect largely because of its appearance. Many federal land management decisions were challenged in the courts. Many organized groups and interested individuals called for more opportunity for public involvement in public land management decisions.

In addition to the long list of legislation during the 1960s and 1970s cited earlier in this chapter, there were congressional hearings on clearcutting and other environmental issues. There were several studies and reports with policy implications for the times. Some of these reports are listed in the Bibliography at the end of this chapter and will be discussed in Chap. 24.

The increased public interest and concern have resulted in changed policy direction for the public lands. There is more emphasis on forest amenities use. Some increases in wilderness designations appear desirable. More care will be needed in laying out and supervising clearcutting. Multiple-use management will need to be more carefully done, including more attention to all land uses. There is a trend towards more intensive forestry on the better sites on all forest lands, including federal-state cost-sharing incentives for small owners. It appears there will be more public involvement on public land management decisions. Environmental impact assessments will be increasingly important. Forestry professionals and managers will be increasingly involved in public hearings, special studies, and public opinion.

## BIBLIOGRAPHY

Allen, Shirley W. 1929. *Conservation Aspects of the History of the Oregon and California Railroad Land Grant,* Iowa State College, Ames.
American Forestry Association. 1975. A "Centennial" Program for AFA. Washington, DC.
American State Papers, 1832. (1861 ed.). *Naval Affairs* IV, Washington, pp. 191–202.
*Annual Report. U.S. Environmental Protection Agency.* 1971, 1972, 1973.
Butler, O. M. 1935. *American Conservation,* American Forestry Association, Washington, DC, p. 147.

Cameron, Jenks. 1928. *Development of Governmental Forest Control in the United States,* Johns Hopkins Press, Baltimore.

Clepper, Henry. 1975. Crusade for Conservation. The Centennial History of the American Forestry Association. *Amer. Forests,* **81**:17–113.

Cliff, Edward P. 1973. *Timber: The Renewable Material; Perspective for Decision.* Prepared for the National Commission on Materials Policy, Washington, DC.

Collingwood, G. H. 1935–1937. Forestry in Congress, *Amer. Forests,* vols. 41, 42, and 43, nos. 2–6.

Coyle, David C. 1957. *Conservation,* Rutgers University Press, New Brunswick, NJ.

Dana, Samuel T. (ed.). 1953. *History of Activities in the Field of Natural Resources,* University of Michigan Press, Ann Arbor.

————. 1956. *Forest and Range Policy,* McGraw-Hill Book Company, New York.

————, and Myron Krueger. 1958. *California Lands, Ownership, Use and Management,* American Forestry Association, Washington, DC.

————, John H. Allison, and Russell N. Cunningham. 1960. *Minnesota Lands: Ownership, Use, and Management of Forests and Related Lands,* American Forestry Association, Washington, DC.

Donaldson, T. C., 1884. *The Public Domain,* 3d ed., Washington, DC.

Everhart, William C. 1972. *The National Park Service,* Frederick A. Praeger, Inc., New York.

Fairchild, Fred R., and Associates. 1935. *Forest Taxation in the United States,* Washington, DC, pp. 635–640.

Fernow, B. E. 1911. *History of Forestry,* University of Toronto Press, Toronto.

*Fifty Years of Forestry in the U. S. A.* 1950. Society of American Foresters, Washington, DC.

*Forestry and Irrigation* (now called *American Forests*). 1906. vol. IX, no. 1.

Ise, John. 1920. *The United States Forest Policy,* Yale University Press, New Haven, p. 20.

Kaufmann, Herbert. 1967. *The Forest Ranger,* Johns Hopkins Press, Baltimore.

Kinney, J. P. 1917. *The Development of Forest Law in America,* John Wiley & Sons, Inc., New York.

*One-Third of the Nation's Land: A Report to the President and to the Congress by the Public Land Law Review Commission,* 1970. Washington.

*Outdoor Recreation Action.* Winter 1972–1973. Bureau of Outdoor Recreation, Report 26, U.S. Department of the Interior.

*Outdoor Recreation: A Legacy for America.* 1973. Bureau of Outdoor Recreation, U.S. Department of the Interior.

*The Outlook for Timber in the U.S.* 1973. Forest Service, U.S. Department of Agriculture, Forest Resource Report no. 20.

Pomeroy, Kenneth B., and James G. Yoho. 1964. *North Carolina Lands, Ownership, Use, and Management of Forest and Related Lands.* American Forestry Association, Washington, DC.

*The Principal Laws Relating to Forest Service Activities.* 1974. U. S. Department of Agriculture, Forest Service Agriculture Handbook no. 453.

Redington, Paul G. 1926. Fifty Years of Forestry, *Amer. Forests,* **32**:719–724, 750.

*Report of the Chief Forest Service.* 1970–1971. U. S. Department of Agriculture.

*Report of President's Advisory Panel on Timber and the Environment.* 1973. Washington, DC.

*Timber Trends in the United States Forest Resource Report no. 17.* 1965. Forest Service, U. S. Department of Agriculture.

U. S. Department of Agriculture. *Timber Management,* Forest Service Manual, Title 2400, and *Cooperative Fire Control,* Forest Service Manual, Title 3100.

―――. 1973. Press Release Announcing Proposed Mining Regulations on National Forests.

Van Hise, Charles R., and Loomis Havemeyer (and Associates). 1930. *Conservation of Our Natural Resources.* The Macmillan Company, New York.

*What's Ahead for Our Public Lands? A Summary Review of the Activities and Final Report of the Public Land Law Review Commission.* 1970. Compiled for the Natural Resources Council of America by Hamilton K. Pyles Project Coordinator, Washington, DC.

# Chapter 4

# Beneficial Influences and
# Services from the Forest

Concepts and attitudes towards forests have changed greatly since World War II. Many more people accept multiple-use management of forest lands. A philosophy of preservation rather than use, however, is a growing trend.

Forests, in addition to their aesthetic effect on the landscape, are able to modify local climate, regulate the flow of water, reduce soil erosion, support a grazing industry, and provide recreational opportunities for millions of people. Although it is not customary to group shelterbelts, wildlife areas, forested grazing lands, watershed protection forests, and forest influences, they will be discussed together in this chapter as a matter of convenience. Because of its growing importance and appeal, outdoor recreation will be considered separately in Chap. 5.

## FOREST INFLUENCES ON THE ATMOSPHERE

**Weather** This is the short-term condition or state of the air or atmosphere. We think of the weather in such terms as hot or cold, wet or dry, clear or cloudy, and calm or stormy. Generally speaking, the forest has little effect on the weather but it does have some effect on climate, which is the weather in a given area over a longer period of time. Local climate at least is one feature of environment that humans modify in their manipulation of forest cover. Such effects differ, of course, with combinations of the kind and size of trees, the density of the forest, the area it covers, its degree of slope, and its aspect (the direction it faces), but certain generalizations concerning local climate can be made.

**Wind**   The air flow that cools the territory adjacent to a forest might be thought of as a small wind, but wind is usually considered as air moving horizontally over considerable territory and with noticeable velocity. It may be cold or warm and it may remove moisture from the soil, damage property or crops mechanically, and reinforce fire or other damaging agencies. Climate includes wind, and the forest accomplishes one of its greatest local modifications of climate by dissipating the velocity of wind and by producing vertical detours in the path of wind. Normally, wind velocities within a forest are but a few miles per hour. The most interesting demonstrations of these influences occur in the use of belts of trees called windbreaks or shelterbelts, which if properly designed can show an effect for a distance of over 40 times the height of the trees on the leeward side, and somewhat less to the windward (Fig. 4-1). Evaporation from the soil is reduced, transpiration from vegetation is lessened, drifting snow is checked, and the movement of soil halted. The effect is that of a barrier, and the more impervious to air it is, the more effective it will be. Usually the trees that grow tallest where windbreaks are in demand are cottonwoods or other hardwoods that retain fewer lower branches. Therefore, other species are used, planted in rows in the shape of a low-pitched roof, with taller trees forming the top of the roof and shrubs forming the low edges. A planted L-shaped windbreak on a farm in southwest Minnesota is seen in Fig. 4-2. The farmstead planting is more common today than the type of widespread shelterbelt planting conceived in the midthirties.

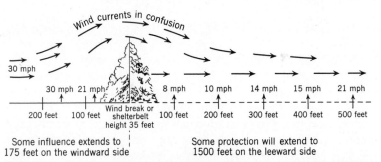

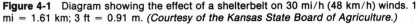

**Figure 4-1**   Diagram showing the effect of a shelterbelt on 30 mi/h (48 km/h) winds. 1 mi = 1.61 km; 3 ft = 0.91 m. *(Courtesy of the Kansas State Board of Agriculture.)*

**Figure 4-2** An L-shaped windbreak planted to protect a farm in southwest Minnesota. *(Courtesy of the University of Minnesota.)*

**Air Temperature**   The forest which intercepts the sun's rays should be cooler inside than an area in the open. The extent of influence is dependent on the density of the stand. The effect of lowering temperatures is most apparent during the summer months when it may be 6 to 8 degrees cooler under the forest canopy. The average winter high temperatures are lowered only 2 or 3 degrees. The overall moderating influence is to lower maximum temperatures and raise minimum temperatures. In the summer months the forest has a slight influence on the temperature of the adjacent locality. Because the cooled air can move around, it flows by drafts or currents to the surrounding territory and has a limited cooling effect.

**Humidity**   Loss of water by evaporation from the soil surface is considerably less in a forest than in an open field, but relative humidity is generally slightly higher. Transpiration from the herbaceous material and from reproduction, along with that from the lower part of the crowns of older trees, no doubt contributes to the humidity. Total moisture lost by transpiration is often much greater from forest than from open-field vegetation. These considerations have led to much speculation as to whether forests influence rainfall, but, although there are some interesting records in Europe showing apparent increases following reforestation, there is not sufficient proof to conclude that this influence really exists or is of importance.

**Precipitation**    The discussion above concerning transpiration is the basis for the belief that forests may increase precipitation, especially rainfall. There are tremendous amounts of water lost to the atmosphere through forest transpiration. It is believed by some researchers that forests transpire more water than is evaporated from an equivalent area of open water. From this we know that forests contribute heavily to atmospheric moisture. The factors which cause the release of this moisture as precipitation over wide areas are little affected by the presence or absence of forests, however.

On the other hand, most scientists feel that the cooling effect above forests may increase rainfall by 2 or 3 percent over that of nonforested areas. The role of the forest and water will be considered at greater length farther along in this chapter.

**Evaporation**    We have seen that forests influence wind movement, temperature, and humidity. The rate of evaporation from the ground, also affected by these three factors, is therefore influenced by a forest cover. Not only is water evaporated at a decreased rate within the forest but the forest's influence is felt for some distance to the leeward. One of the reasons for planting shelterbelts is to lower the rate of evaporation on the lee side and thus increase crop production. Many a crop of grain or potatoes has been gathered close in the lee of a prairie shelterbelt, when there was none to gather a few dozen feet further away.

## FOREST INFLUENCES ON THE SOIL

**Soil Temperature**    As in the instance of air temperature, the temperature of the soil is affected by the forest canopy, but to a greater extent. If, for example, the temperature of the soil just below the ground level in an open area during the summer is 90°F (32°C), the soil temperature at the same depth but within the forest may be only 70°F (21°C). This change naturally varies with the depth of the soil and also with the season. It takes longer for forest soils to freeze in the winter than soils in the open and certainly the depth of freezing is much less in the forest soil. On the other hand, the protection the canopy affords the soil from the sun may keep the ground frozen longer in the spring.

The general influence of the forest on temperature of the soil is a cooling one, partly because of shade and partly because of the insulating effect of the litter on the ground.

Although the soil of a forest on the whole remains cooler than open-field soil, the variation in extremes of temperature is not great. In the open the high temperatures of the summer and low temperatures of the winter would kill many plants which are able to survive under the protection offered them by the forest.

Both these influences—cooling and moderation—vary with the kind of forest, whether broad-leaved or evergreen. The influences on winter soil temperature, for instance, are less if the forest is deciduous.

**Soil Composition**    The manner in which the individual soil particles are arranged is called soil structure. A forest cover will have a considerable influence on this structure. Leaves, twigs, and branches create a large annual accumulation of litter on the forest floor. This litter furnishes food for rodents, insects, earthworms, and numerous microorganisms which create favorable soil structure and soil fertility. The burrows and holes left by these animals and the channels left by decaying roots all aid in making the soil porous, permit free air movement, and favor infiltration and storage of water in the soil. Much litter becomes mixed with mineral soil to form the humus layer. Solutes of decomposing litter are carried downward into the soil by water to add to the nutritional value of the soil. The influence of a forest on soil composition varies with the kind of forest and the region it is in, but the general effect is similar. An open bare soil quickly becomes compact and impermeable whereas a forest floor remains loose and porous.

**Soil Moisture**    In Fig. 4-3 the cycle through which water moves from the ocean to the atmosphere, to land, and back to the ocean is portrayed.

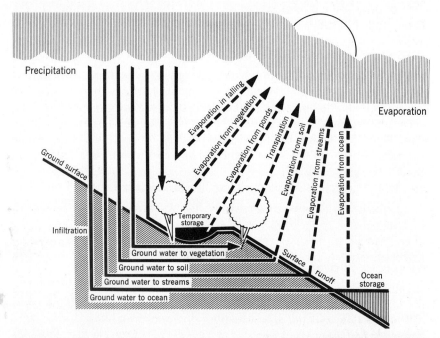

**Figure 4-3**   The hydrologic cycle, showing the movement of water from the atmosphere to the land and ocean, and back to the atmosphere. *(Courtesy of the Soil Conservation Service.)*

This is called the *hydrologic cycle*. Air masses lying over the ocean collect large amounts of water through evaporation. As these air masses or clouds containing water vapor move over land, they are often forced to rise, and on cooling they precipitate moisture in the form of rain, snow, hail, or dew.

As the water falls, some is lost by evaporation. Much of the water is intercepted by the leaves of trees and other vegetation and it, too, is lost by evaporation. The water that runs off the leaves to the ground wets the surface and infiltrates the soil. Approximately 50 percent of most soils are made up of air spaces of different sizes and water entering the smalller pores is held there against the pull of gravity. A considerable amount of this water is taken up by tree roots; some is used for growth but most is transpired by the tree and goes into the air as water vapor. A large amount of water may be held in storage in a forest soil. The thicker and more decomposed the litter and humus layers are, the more water the soil will hold. In this way forest soils act as a reservoir. Excess water percolates deeper and deeper and joins the *ground water*. The ground water may move laterally to feed into streams and lakes, or it may lie under the surface of the ground to be used as water pumped from wells. The upper level of ground water is known as the *water table*, which fluctuates with precipitation and surface use.

A forest soil will absorb water up to 50 percent of its own dry weight. If rain falls faster than the soil can absorb it, the water runs off as *surface water*. An unprotected exposed soil has poor infiltration, and most rain water flows off the surface, resulting in erosion and floods. Not all surface runoff is serious, since its contribution to stream flow is not usually in the nature of a flood. It finds its way into streams and lakes where some is lost to evaporation, or used by stream-side vegetation, or may be used for domestic water systems or irrigation. The remainder may serve the purposes of hydroelectric power, recreation, and many other uses before eventually reaching the ocean where it completes the hydrologic cycle.

## EROSION, FLOODS, AND WATERSHED MANAGEMENT

**Erosion**  Crowns of trees reduce the mechanical beating power of rainfall on the soil, while roots reinforce the soil and, along with forest litter, keep it absorptive and make it less vulnerable to erosion. When water strikes bare soil, it becomes muddy, the amount of muddiness depending on the character and condition of the soil. Muddy water tends to clog soil openings and the absorptive rate rapidly decreases. Rather than infiltrate the soil, the water moves over the surface. The steeper the slope the faster will be the flow and the greater will be the water's carrying and grinding power. At first, only small particles of soil are moved. The particles become larger and larger and eventually large boulders will be moved. Topsoil is carried away and huge canyon-like gullies may appear. Rivers, lakes, and reservoirs are silted in. An example of silting is the case of the Santa Ynez River in California. Since 1920 three dams have been built only to have their reservoirs silt in (two of these within 2 years after completion of the dams). A fourth dam has now been built to obtain the much needed water for the city of Santa Barbara.

Soil is always being moved from higher to lower elevations by the forces of nature—by water in particular—without disturbing the vegetative cover. This slow process, measured in centuries, is known as *geologic erosion*. The faster more destructive process, which rips open gullies and causes great economic loss, is called *accelerated erosion*. The farmer in preparing soil through tillage, strip-cropping, and terracing can effectively reduce erosion.

**Floods**  Stories of flood damage are among the oldest recorded, and even in America a 40-day flood of the Mississippi was one of the hardships that pursued De Soto's men more than 400 years ago. More recent floods on the Ohio, Mississippi, Columbia, and other rivers have caused damage running into the hundreds of millions of dollars, and floods have invaded the homes of more than a million people. Each catastrophe stimulates public action to attempt control of the particular stream.

The influence of forests upon floods has been both championed and discounted for years, but few have denied that volume and velocity of surface runoff are reduced greatly, and that silting of reservoirs and channels is lessened in completely forested watersheds. A few inches in height of flood stage may cause millions of dollars in additional damage, and the effect of the forest on these inches, added to other economic values and products from the forest, justifies forest maintenance in extensive areas. In fact, the soil-holding power of a forest by keeping mud and silt out of the flood water may alone justify a forest cover.

Forests cannot prevent abnormally high precipitation from running off when it falls on frozen soils. Similarly, if the soil reservoir is already full, there is nothing for additional water to do but runoff.

A relatively small canyon in southern California gave an exhibition a few years ago of the efficiency of forest cover (principally chaparral) as a means of retarding runoff in comparison with other burned-out canyons. Thirty-four persons were killed and 200 homes were destroyed by a sudden flood following a heavy storm over Pickens Canyon in Los Angeles County. Fire had removed the cover from 5,000 acres in this comparatively small watershed. San Dimas Canyon, a few miles to the east of Pickens Canyon, experienced the same storm but no flood resulted. Here the forest cover was intact. Similar contrasts have been noted in other watershed areas. Dana (1956) reports evidence *is* conclusive that in most regions surface runoff is very small or negligible from areas of undisturbed vegetation, while it may amount to half of the precipitation where vegetation has been destroyed or seriously disturbed.

**Watershed Management**   As stated in an earlier chapter, forests cover approximately one-third of the total land area of the United States. From this forested area comes more than half the nation's stream flow (Fig. 4-4). Thus it becomes the forester's job to manage these lands not only for timber, wildlife, range forage, and recreation, but also for maximum water yields and for flood control.

A watershed is the area contributing to a stream or river. The size may extend from a single creek draining a few acres to a huge river flowing from many states. Like other natural resources of the forest, this water is subject to good and bad management. Water, however, is the least understood of the natural resources. The watershed manager does not attempt to increase precipitation but seeks more efficient management of the water that does fall.

In mountainous Western evergreen forests, 80 percent of the precipitation falls in the form of snow. If more of this snow can reach the ground, rather than stay in the treetops, it will be protected from the evaporating

**Figure 4-4**  The forest provides clean water for a great variety of uses to humans. Newhalem Creek, Ross Lake National Recreation Area, Washington State. *(Photo by Grant W. Sharpe.)*

winds. By making scattered openings in the forest small enough to avoid erosion but large enough to catch snow, more water can be stored and conserved than in an uncut forest. Accordingly, by manipulating the forest cover with partial cuttings, transpiration by a dense forest may be reduced and stream flow increased.

From this brief discussion, we can see that the forest exhibits considerable influence on the soil as a water reservoir. The best forest soil for water storage is the porous soil and this can be maintained through proper forest management. By controlling fires, heavy grazing, and improper cuttings—all of which result in depletion or destruction of the soil structure—the resultant erosion, sedimentation, and floods are curtailed.

In general, the objective of watershed management is to obtain the maximum quality and quantity of usable water for domestic and industrial uses, for maintaining conditions favorable for fish and wildlife, and for recreation. Since the job of the water resource manager is comparatively new to forestry, it might be well to list the ways in which these objectives are carried out:

**A**    In holding down floods and other high water flows, the water resource manager tries to:
     **1**    Maintain high infiltration rates and increase the capacity of the soil to store water at the start of a storm.
     **2**    Encourage deep percolation of water to recharge the water table.
     **3**    Reduce snow-melting rates.
     **4**    Reduce surges of flow by using mechanical barriers.

**B**    To control water quality, the water resource manager tries to:
     **1**    Maintain or increase the protective cover, thus anchoring the soil against erosion.
     **2**    Obtain better infiltration so that water filters through the soil rather than flows over it.
     **3**    Protect stream banks and beds against erosion.
     **4**    For fish habitat, maintain or increase shade over streams to hold down water temperatures.

**C**    To increase water yield the manager tries to:
     **1**    Reduce evaporation-transpiration losses.
     **2**    Reduce losses to interception.
     **3**    Increase snow accumulation.
     **4**    Decrease evaporation from streams and reservoirs.

**D**    To alter the timing of water yield, which usually means reducing yield during the high-flow season and increasing it during the low-flow season, the manager tries to:
     **1**    Reduce snow melting in winter and prolong it in spring.
     **2**    Spread water into subsurface storage areas such as meadow fills for later return to streams.

  3  Raise lake outlets or create reservoirs for increased temporary storage.
E  To control and prevent erosion, the watershed manager attempts to:
  1  Reduce the exposure of bare soils by:
     a  Preventing wildfires.
     b  Regulating grazing.
     c  Discouraging cultivation of easily eroded slopes.
     d  Encouraging favorable methods of logging.
     e  Planting vegetation.
  2  Slow down runoff by:
     a  Constructing small check dams, and contour trenches and ditches.
     b  Introducing beaver.
     c  Covering eroded areas with brush, litter, or other debris.

## RANGE MANAGEMENT

In a recent study it was stated that range is intimately related to other environments (U.S. Department of Agriculture, 1972). It questioned that a clear definition could exist between range and pasture and between range and forest and some other kinds of land with respect to grazing use. Hence, all natural ecosystems that produce or can produce forage were called forest-range.

This study was designed to explore the current (as of 1970) and prospective production of resources and role of grazing on all forest and range ecosystems—of the 48 conterminous United States. Other federal agencies participated in the study. See Table 4-1.

For the nation, 52 percent of the forest-range lands are in the West, 18

**Table 4-1  Acres of Forest Range, Improved Private Pasture, and Other Land by Geographic Region, in the 48 Conterminous States, 1970.**

| Geographic region | Forest-range environment | Improved private pasture | Other land | Total land area |
|---|---|---|---|---|
| Western | 621.7 | 8.9 | 122.4 | 753.0 |
| Plains | 213.9 | 24.0 | 169.3 | 407.2 |
| Northeast | 182.0 | 39.9 | 219.4 | 441.3 |
| Southeast | 184.1 | 28.3 | 88.0 | 300.4 |
| Total | 1,201.7 | 101.1 | 599.1 | 1,901.9 |

Note: 1 acre = 0.40 hectare.

percent are in the Plains, and the Southeast and Northeast regions contain 15 percent each.

Much of the Western grazing land is in an area of low rainfall and, because most of it has never been plowed, is termed *natural vegetation*. This land is at low elevation where it is in use year round, although mountainous areas are used, especially as summer range.

The history of grazing in the West has been a matter of too many animals for too long a period (or at the wrong time) on insufficient land. Erosion and an invasion of noxious plants characteristic of overgrazed lands resulted in serious depletion of the range. Through more than a century of trial and error in determining the suitable species of cattle or sheep to use and the carrying capacity of the area to be grazed, much has been learned. Practices of range management, such as systematic salting away from water holes, eradication of poisonous plants, careful observance of grazing seasons, repairing of erosion damage, seeding when appropriate, development of water, and use of fences for confining stock, have come into being.

In spite of the low rainfall, the grasses found in the park-like openings of pine forests in the 11 Western states are rich in protein. In addition to beef and mutton, wool and leather are products of the Western range. Many of the larger tree farms are finding it profitable to run their own cattle and sheep on company-owned forest lands. Other owners, strictly in the timber- and forest-products business, lease their lands to stock raisers for grazing purposes.

The rise of the livestock industry has created a colorful phase in American history. Although trail herds were known before the Civil War, the soldiers returning from the war in 1865 saw an opportunity to make money marketing cattle. Expanding Eastern markets, extension of the railroads to the West, settling of native claims money invested from abroad, and millions of acres of free forage on public land caused a phenomenal rise in the cattle industry over a 20-year period. In the winter of 1885, one of the severest blizzards ever recorded hit the already overstocked range and this, coupled with a drought in 1886, all but wiped out the industry. During the next few years, the cattle business became somewhat stabilized but now had to compete with a fast-growing sheep industry. Cattle were not easily moved from one range to another. The people who raised sheep, on the other hand, whose headquarters were their wagons, could move from one grass range to another and, if grass became scarce, move to the proverbial "greener pastures." The cattle raisers, forced to remain with nonmigrating herds and permanent ranch facilities, took a dim view of sheep and sheepherders, and the result was the bitter range wars known to all who read westerns or watch television.

With the coming of the homesteader and homestead laws and the fencing of open range, the stock raisers were forced westward into the desert and mountains. Just as in the timber industry, the cattle industry passed from a period of exploitation to one of sound management practices.

Since World War II there has been a great change in the range industry. The numbers of sheep grazed have decreased, mainly due to high production costs; cattle numbers have been more stable; and high labor costs and other expenses have resulted in more mechanization in all phases of range management.

In 1970 the federal government maintained jurisdiction over 373 million acres (151.7 million ha), or 31 percent of the 1,201.6 million acres (486 million ha), while the nonfederal owners controlled 829 million acres (335.5 million ha) or 69 percent of the total forest range. Ownership by ecosystem, however, varied widely (U.S. Department of Agriculture, 1972).

In December 1973, the Bureau of Land Management, Department of the Interior, and the Forest Service, Department of Agriculture, jointly announced increases in grazing fees for 1974. This was a grazing fee program initiated in 1969 and designed to raise fees on a graduated basis to fair-market value by 1980. The average 1974 fee per animal unit month (equivalent of grazing for a mature cow for one month) on Bureau of Land Management (BLM) lands was to be increased from 78 cents to $1.00. The average 1974 fee per animal unit month on Forest Service lands was to be increased from 91 cents to $1.11.

About 25,000 operators now hold permits for grazing approximately 9 million head of cattle and sheep on lands administered by the two agencies, for a total of about 19 million animal unit months (Fig. 4-5). The permits specify the location, duration, and quantity of use for individual permit holders. Range areas under permit are in most cases being currently improved by the cooperative efforts of permittees and the federal agencies (Press Release, 1973).

The job of range regulation on both public and private lands frequently involves a forester who specializes in range management. For that reason the subject has been introduced here. The interested reader will find the bibliography very helpful in gaining better understanding of this phase of land management.

## WILDLIFE MANAGEMENT

Wildlife once fed and clothed the native people and early settlers of this country, but there were not too many residents, weapons were primitive, and the habitat was extensive. It is interesting to note that the diaries of early American missionaries and explorers indicate that they saw relatively few game animals in the dense forests. Records show, too, that in the early 1800s in the Lake States, the fur trappers who lived off the land were

**Figure 4-5**  *Upper,* a sheep drive in the Bighorn Mountains of Wyoming; *lower,* cattle grazing on the range in Colorado. *(Courtesy of the Bureau of Land Management.)*

compelled to exist almost exclusively on a diet of fish. The magnificent virgin forest was a biological desert, as far as wildlife was concerned, for the dense shade crowded out browse plants. Natural wildfires, as well as those set by the native people, opened up extensive areas which, before closing over, supported an abundance of wildlife.

With the arrival of settlers, subsistance hunting persisted, at least for a while. As the forests were logged or cleared and burned for croplands and pasture, the habitat, instead of being opened up enough to promote browse, was opened up so much it was destroyed. Livestock competed with wildlife, and the resident settlers shot the wildlife that ventured too near. Game grew more scarce and some disappeared. By the time of the Civil War most elk and white-tailed deer had been eliminated in the eastern United States, and the range of the wild turkey had been greatly reduced.

Not all the land that was cleared was suited to agriculture, and these submarginal farmlands soon began growing trees again. As scientific forest management began to be practiced, it was found that, within the managed forest, wildlife flourished. The largest populations of deer were being supported on second-growth forests, not necessarily because of wildlife management practices, but because there was abundance of deer browse on these lands.

Forestry and wildlife management have many factors in common. Both fields are concerned with the utilization of a natural resource, one with trees, the other with game animals. The educational background of the two professions is very similar, at least in the first few years. Both are concerned with forest ecology, fire management, excessive numbers of livestock and wildlife, and pressures from environmentally concerned citizens. Their common denominator is a sustained yield of harvestable crops for public benefit.

Forestry had its beginning in this country around the turn of the century, while wildlife management got its start as an offshoot of forestry in the early 1930s. Aldo Leopold, a forester, saw wildlife management as habitat manipulation to increase wildlife and to convert hunting from exploitation to cropping. Sensible wildlife practices, he and others felt, could keep history from repeating itself. The number of animals an area will support is limited by the amount of food available during the winter season. Those animals in excess of the carrying capacity of the area are considered surplus and should be harvested through controlled hunting rather than allowed to starve.

Early wildlife practices in the United States developed by trial and error. Excessive hunting was allowed in some areas, while in others populations built up beyond desirable numbers, and the habitat was destroyed. The use of bounties and paid hunters to control predators had serious consequences in many sections of the country. Taking an animal census or maintaining proper sex ratios was not understood, or at least was not in common usage, until the midthirties.

Due to the influence of Leopold and others with an understanding of wildlife management, the forester and wildlifer began to understand better each other's needs. For example, each type of forest in the United States is, biologically speaking, a different ecosystem. Each forest type supports its own community of plants and animals, with each member of that community mutually dependent and mutually interactive on all members of the community. It must be recognized that forests of each major type support or have the potential of supporting a variety of wildlife populations and densities during their various stages of plant succession (Jahn and Trefethen, 1974).

Foresters, for several reasons, have overlooked the tangible and intangible values that wildlife offer. As brought out in the last part of Chap. 18, some mammals, such as porcupine, black bear, and deer, are sometimes in conflict with forest management. As more is known about the management of wildlife, these mammals will be kept in balance with their environment, particularly where wildlife specialists are allowed a free hand.

A thriving animal population in a forest is an asset to both the local and the national economy. Such fur-bearing mammals as beaver, fox, otter, fisher, mink, raccoon, martin, muskrat, and rabbit, which spend much of their lives in the forest, support a large fur industry. Migratory waterfowl, dependent on forested watersheds for lakes and marshes, attract a large number of duck and goose hunters. Streams and lakes which sustain a large population of trout, bass, salmon, and other fish contribute to an immense tackle industry. Small game such as quail, pheasant, grouse, turkey, rabbit, and squirrel exist principally in open fields and wooded areas and these also lure large numbers of hunters. Deer, elk, moose, bear, and mountain lion are forest-dwelling big-game animals pursued by the hunter in North America (Fig. 4-6). National and state forests permit hunting and fishing under state regulation, and considerable private forest land is open to hunting. The income from licenses and from the manufacture and sale of guns, ammunition, fishing tackle, clothing, camping gear, gasoline, and related items, as well as the amount spent for accommodations and the services of guides and packers, represents a multibillion-dollar annual industry.

There is now a growing interest in nonconsumptive use of wildlife resources, mostly observation of wildlife or "hunting" them with a camera. This nonconsumptive use, which frequently coincides with hiking or traveling, has increased faster than hunting or fishing.

Since early in the century, professionals have recognized that the aesthetic "nonconsumptive enjoyment of wildlife in the out-of-doors is by far the greatest value of this resource."

In addition recent evaluations indicate "our most neglected and crucial research needs are those concerning human social behavior. . . ." "There are many long-term decisions of quantity versus quality. The biologist alone, the social scientist alone, the economist alone cannot deal with these questions. Their combined effort is required and it must do great things" (Allen, 1973).

Wildlife refuges and other public lands are reporting a phenomenal increase in visits from bird watchers and nature photographers. On national forests alone, there are over 20 million visitor days annually attributed to wildlife viewing, and another 20 million are reported from federal wildlife refuges for the same reason.

**Figure 4-6** Elk grazing in the mountains of western Wyoming. *(Courtesy of the Bureau of Land Management.)*

The forester, in his or her position as a land manager, has an opportunity to provide the wildlife benefits the public is demanding, while at the same time satisfying the need for recreation, water, and forest products. To accomplish this, however, the forester must work more closely with the wildlifer than has been the case in the past.

Intensive forest management must be blended with the needs of the wildlife specialist. Each species of wildlife has a habitat need which differs from all other species. The forest type, plant species composition, successional stages, length of cutting rotation, and other management practices will govern the population of wildlife species the forest ecosystem will support. Where there is a diversity of habitats, dozens of different animal species may use the same general area (Jahn and Trefethen, 1974).

Some animals, including several endangered species, have very specialized needs. Two examples directly under the forester's control are the availability of snags, which make good den trees, and wolf trees, which offer excellent nesting sites and places of refuge from storms. Several public and private forests have set aside undisturbed tracts of forest, including substantial acreages of mature timber, because of the protection they afford an animal species. In this instance the production of wildlife takes precedence over timber production.

Managing the stand for both wildlife and timber production is an important research activity.

Research on cutting practices and their effect on deer populations is already bearing fruit. A mature stand of Douglas-fir in western Washington State supports a maximum population of 10 black-tailed deer per sq. mi. (2.58 km²). After 20 years of harvesting, the same acreage peaks at 60 deer per sq. mi. (2.58 km²), and this drops back to 10 as the stand closes in (Dasmann, 1971). In Minnesota, aspen is managed to produce wood fiber and simultaneously produces a series of successional stages needed to provide breeding and nesting habitat, food, and shelter for ruffed grouse. Here the aspen is (1) clearcut on a 40-year rotation to assure aspen regeneration and (2) cut in blocks of 10 acres (4 ha) or less to provide seasonal food and cover within the usual travel distance of adult grouse. Individual trees are left to supply winter buds as food for grouse.

In central Michigan, stands of jack pine are being periodically subjected to prescribed burning to perpetuate open stands as nesting sites for the endangered jack pine (Kirtland's) warbler (Fig. 4-7). The nesting requirements of this warbler which were once maintained by natural fires, are trees in the 5- to 20-ft. height range.

These case histories illustrate how the forester and wildlifer work together in providing both timber for people and habitat for wildlife.

Jahn and Trefethen (1974) offer these five factors as essential to maintaining critical wildlife habitats on commercial forest lands.

**1** *Retain buffer strips of trees along streams and highways.* Such buffers serve in many ways. Along streams the natural cover checks erosion, enhances water quality, improves forest aesthetics, and fish and wildlife values are assured. Leaving standing timber along highways can screen clearcuts. As the adjacent clearcut grows to an aesthetically pleasing cover, the strips can be selectively harvested. In the meantime both wildlife and the environmentally aware public have benefitted.

**2** *Keep clearcuts to 50 acres or less wherever possible.* Clearcutting in recent years has come under intense and bitter public criticism, in spite of the fact that with certain tree and wildlife species it appears a sound management practice. It is the large-scale clearcutting operations, particularly those which do not blend in with topographic features, which are both aesthetically upsetting and of limited value to wildlife during much of the period of regeneration.

When fitted into the landscape, and applied in comparatively small irregularly shaped blocks of 50 acres or less and separated by tracts of uncut timber, their value to many forms of wildlife is undisputed. This practice is also more acceptable to the general public—perhaps because it is less noticeable.

**3** *Lay out forest management units so prescribed burning can be used, where applicable, to benefit both vegetation and wildlife.* Prescribed burning is valuable, particularly in the South, for managing both forests and wildlife. Here pine stands are burned periodically to control brown spot disease, reduce hardwood competition, minimize the buildup of organic matter, and reduce

**Figure 4-7** A prescribed burn in a jack pine stand in central Michigan to provide nesting sites for the Kirtland's warbler. *(Photo by Robert E. Martin.)*

the chances for destructive wildfire. The understory plants, following a prescribed burn, are favorable to seed-eating wildlife, such as bobwhite quail and songbirds.

4 *Retain and maintain openings in forest compartments and stands.* Most wildlife does best near openings where forest *edge* is provided. Where a forest abuts along a clearing, larger numbers and a greater variety of animals will be found where the two types of cover meet, than will be found in the interior of the forest stand or in the center of the clearing. Any forest practice that increases edge should inevitably increase the local wildlife population.

5 *Maintain some overmature and even diseased, dying, and dead trees.* Here there is some chance for minor differences between foresters and wildlifers. To the forester, snags create both a fire hazard and a safety hazard. To the wildlifer on the other hand, snags provide nesting cavities essential for the survival of hole-nesting species such as chickadees, nuthatches, screech owls, and woodpeckers. Snags are the favored perching spots and nesting sites for eagles, hawks, and owls that in turn prey on rabbits, mice, and other rodents, which, if uncontrolled, can be a serious pest in a newly seeded or planted area.

Foresters are beginning to recognize wildlife as an important value of forested lands, not only for the ecological balance and the aesthetic considerations involved, but one that can produce crops that can be harvested annually.

Revenue from sportsmen can be derived in a number of ways. Hunting clubs often lease animal hunting privileges on privately owned forests for one to several dollars per acre. Other forest owners sell hunting rights on a daily fee basis, realizing from $5 to $25 per day for each hunter using the land. Here the returns are considerable.

The private landowner must have something to sell, however, for the experienced hunter will not spend money to hunt where there is no game. Technical assistance is available from both state and federal forestry, soil, and game and fish departments and from extension departments of universities.

## BIBLIOGRAPHY

Allen, Durwood L. 1962. *Our Wildlife Legacy*, rev. ed., Funk & Wagnalls, New York.

———. 1973. Chairman Report of the Committee on North American Wildlife Policy, *Transactions of the Thirty-eighth North American Wildlife and Natural Resources Conference*, Wildlife Management Institute. Washington, DC.

Allen, Shirley W., and Justin W. Leonard. 1966. *Conserving Our Natural Resources*, 3d ed., McGraw-Hill Book Company, New York.

Buckman, Harry O., and Nyle C. Brady. 1971. *The Nature and Properties of Soils*, Macmillan & Co., Ltd., London.

Callison, Charles H. 1967. *America's Natural Resources*, The Ronald Press Company, New York.

Dana, Samuel T. 1956. Forest Influences. *A World Geography of Forest Resources*. Edited by Stephen Haden-Guest, John K. Wright, and Eileen M. Tefclaff for The American Geographical Society. The Ronald Press Company, New York.

Dasmann, R. F. 1968. *Environmental Conservation*, 2d ed., John Wiley & Sons, Inc., New York.

———. 1971. *If Deer Are to Survive*. Stackpole Books. Harrisburg, Pennsylvania.

Daubenmire, R. F. 1974. *Plants and Environment*, 3d ed., John Wiley & Sons, Inc., New York.

Forbes, R. D. (ed.). 1956. *Forestry Handbook*, The Ronald Press Company, New York.

George, E. J. 1961. *Shelterbelts for the Northern Great Plains*, Farmers Bulletin no. 2109, U.S. Department of Agriculture.

Guggisberg, Charles A. W. 1970. *Man and Wildlife*, Evans Brothers, London.

Heady, Harold F. 1975. *Rangeland Management*, McGraw-Hill Book Company, New York.

Jahn, Laurence R., and James B. Trefethen. 1974. *The Resource Situation Regarding Wildlife (Game) Species*. Wildlife Management Institute. Washington, DC.

Leopold, Aldo. 1933. *Game Management*. Charles Scribner's Sons, New York.

Mason, George F. 1966. *The Wildlife of North America*, Hastings House, Publishers, Inc., New York.

Press Release. 1973. Public Lands Grazing Fees, announced for 1974, issued jointly by the U.S. Departments of Agriculture and the Interior.

Satterlund, Donald R. 1972. *Watershed Management*. The Ronald Press Company, New York.

Scheffer, Victor B. 1974. *A Voice for Wildlife*, Charles Scribners Sons, New York.

Shirley, H. L. 1972. *Forestry and Its Career Opportunities*, McGraw-Hill Book Company, New York.

Smith, Guy-Harold (ed.). 1971. *Conservation of Natural Resources*, John Wiley & Sons, Inc., New York.

Stoddard, Charles H. 1968. *Essentials of Forestry Practices*, The Ronald Press Company, New York.

Stoddard, Laurence A., Arthur D. Smith, and Thadis W. Box. 1975. *Range Management*, McGraw-Hill Book Company, New York.

Street, Philip. 1970. *Wildlife Preservation*, McGikken & Kee, London.

U.S. Department of Agriculture. 1972. Forest Service, *The Nation's Range Resources, A Forest Range Environmental Study*, Forest Resources Report no. 19. Washington, DC.

Wildlife Management Institute. 1974. Placing American Wildlife Management in Perspective, Washington, DC.

# Chapter 5

# Outdoor Recreation

The general area of resource-oriented recreation will be categorized here simply as outdoor recreation, and does not include such nonforestry (activity-oriented) forms of recreation as those dependent on playfields, tennis courts, and swimming pools. Outdoor recreation depends upon some particular element or a combination of elements of natural resources. The resource, such as a forest, often dictates the location and type of activity people participate in and shapes the kind of experience they receive. Each year millions obtain inspiration and relaxation through access to a variety of natural environments, and this suggests a very simple definition:

**Outdoor recreation** Leisure activities characterized by a relationship between people and the resources of nature.

Natural resources provide a variety of recreation offerings: hunting and fishing, picnicking and camping, walking, hiking and mountain climbing, driving vehicles in forest settings, boating and other water sports, winter sports, photography, painting, and nature study. As millions of citizens

**Figure 5-1** The forest provides outdoor recreation opportunities for millions of people in North America. *(Courtesy of the U.S. Forest Service.)*

in North America annually participate in these resource activities, they become personally involved in a very important aspect of forestry: the recreational use of the forest (Fig. 5-1).

## THE FACTORS AFFECTING THE DEMAND FOR RECREATION

Before entering into further discussion of outdoor recreation, it would be of interest to look at the reasons why the demand for recreational land is increasing:

**1** The population of the United States has increased dramatically. In 1800 the population was only 4 million; in 1960 it reached 179 million; in 1975 it exceeded 200 million, and by the year 2000 it is expected to be over 300 million. Since the early 1900s there has been a shift from a rural to an urban society. Many of these people have chosen to reestablish contact with nature through outdoor recreation experiences.

**2** Leisure time has increased. The standard work week slowly but inevitably continues to shorten; vacations become longer; and 3-day weekends are now common. Modern conveniences add free time to each day, and earlier retirements and an extended life expectancy add years to our free time.

**3** Incomes have increased; for many at least, incomes are in excess of that needed for the bare essentials of life, making more money available for a great variety of recreation equipment and travel.

**4** Travel facilities have improved. Today we have better highways and autos to use in reaching distant recreational areas. Accommodations have improved. Packaged tours, involving everything from bicycles to aircraft, provide planned trips for almost any taste and income, and to all corners of the earth.

**5** The awakening of environmental concern has broadened people's interest. Increased exposure to wildlife and wilderness concepts through television and other informational media has made people more aware of opportunities available to them.

**6** Miscellaneous demand factors include perceiving certain forms of outdoor recreation as one of the things to do to "keep up socially." The purchase of expensive equipment, and the desire to show it off, contributes also for another group. The relatively low cost of some forms of outdoor recreation is appealing to still others.

These demand factors are affected or tempered by people's knowledge of the opportunity, their financial and physical ability, and the competition for their time from other forms of leisure activity. Education has increased, and with it an appreciation of nature. Numerous studies document the relationship between higher education and participation in outdoor recreational activities.

## THE FACTORS OF OUTDOOR RECREATION SUPPLY

We have looked at the demand factors, now let us turn our attention to the supply factors, where these demands presumably are being met. Furnishing land for outdoor recreation is commonly held to be a government function, although government cannot and is not doing it alone.

The management of large tracts of land just for outdoor recreation is seldom a profitable venture and is thus impractical for most private concerns to undertake. Some exceptions to this include ski resorts and hunting clubs, and those parks on industrial lands maintained in the interests of public relations, as mentioned on pages 82, 83. Because many government agencies, municipal to federal, control large areas of wild land set aside for various purposes, the task of administering parts of them for recreation becomes theirs. The policy of dedicating land solely for public recreation is well established, getting its start with the setting aside of such well-known areas as New York City's Central Park in 1853, or the country's first state park, The Yosemite Grant, in 1864 (now incorporated into Yosemite National Park), or the world's first national park, Yellowstone National Park, in 1872. This principle, public recreation on large public ownerships, has now been adopted by public agencies in all parts of the world.

The suppliers of land for outdoor recreational purposes may be grouped into the categories discussed below.

## Local Government

This would include both municipal and county governments which provide some resource-based outdoor recreation. Their concern traditionally has been to provide user-oriented recreation areas such as playgrounds, tennis courts, swimming pools, beaches, zoos, and botanical gardens. Because of their proximity to large numbers of people, these parks receive more recreational use than all state and federal areas combined. County parks are usually larger than municipal parks and, being located in more rural settings, are able to preserve the natural environment more easily.

Another example of local government participation is the Metropolitan Park Authority, a level of government which may include several counties. This type of organization is usually near a large city and functions to provide recreational opportunities in rural areas for all residents of those counties. Because open space for parkland expansion is in the surrounding county, while the population and source of income for funding such parks are largely in the city, it becomes a mutually beneficial program. Such systems are found around several major cities in the eastern United States (Fig. 5-2).

## State Agencies in Outdoor Recreation

State lands have a variety of designations: parks, parkways, forests, wildlife areas, memorials, recreational areas, and historical sites. These names have different connotations in different states and may be administered by one of a number of state agencies.

States make their major contribution to outdoor recreation through their state park system. The visitor use of the state parks is greater than the combined total use of the national parks and forests, reaching well over 400 million annual visits. Approximately 95 percent, however, is day use. The reasons for this heavy use is that the more elaborate state park systems are (1) located in states with large populations, (2) purposely located to be easily accessible to large numbers of people, and (3) designed for use by large numbers of people. (This is in direct contrast to the reasons for locating national parks.)

Attendance in most state parks tends to be concentrated on weekends, particularly on Sunday afternoons. The result is serious overcrowding for a few hours each week. On the other hand, some state parks are filled to capacity all summer long (Fig. 5-3).

**Figure 5-2** Patrons using one of several bathing beaches at Stony Creek Metropark, near Detroit, Michigan. The Metropolitan Park Authority is an example of local government participation in outdoor recreation. *(Courtesy of the Huron Clinton Metropolitan Authority.)*

Funds for operating and maintaining state parks come mainly from state legislative appropriations, although some income may be derived from fees, permits, and miscellaneous revenues. Land acquisition today comes mostly from Federal Land and Water Conservation Fund Act monies, matched by funds from voter-approved state bond issues, referendums, or tax levies. To qualify for federal funds each state must submit an approved statewide outdoor recreation plan, including a recreation demand survey, to the Bureau of Outdoor Recreation.

There are nearly 8 million acres (3.2 million ha) in state parks, but about half of the parks are 100 acres (40 ha) or less. Of the nearly 4,000 state parks, 8 are huge, containing over 60 percent of the total state park acreage in the United States.

State parks may be logically classified into three groups: (1) *utilitarian areas*, which generally support such physical activities as camping, boating, and swimming; (2) *significant areas*, which preserve features of historical, geological, biological, or archeological interest at the state level; and (3) *scenic or dual purpose areas* offering extensive outdoor recreation opportunities and often combining features of the two types mentioned above. The dual purpose area is usually large, the setting is scenically attractive, and

**Figure 5-3**   An overcrowded state park in Alaska, a scene typical of many state parks today. *(Photo by Neil C. Johannsen, Alaska Division of Parks.)*

these areas are of sufficient scope to allow for hiking and horseback riding (Brockman and Merriam, 1973).

Many state recreation agencies now maintain interpretive programs similar to those long in use by the National Park Service (see page 86).

The value of state parks in the nation's overall recreation picture cannot be overemphasized. They provide recreation opportunities reasonably close to home, and they relieve much of the pressure which otherwise might be directed to overcrowded federal areas.

### Recreational Use of Federal Lands

About a dozen federal agencies are directly concerned with some phase of outdoor recreation. Some serve only in an advisory capacity, but most conduct recreation programs on the lands which they administer. Only one, the National Park Service, is maintained for the sole purpose of administering lands for outdoor recreation. The others, including the Forest Service of the U.S. Department of Agriculture which manages the national forests, provide recreation as one phase of their program. Other important agencies involved in outdoor recreation are the Bureau of Outdoor Recreation, Bureau of Land Management, the Fish and Wildlife Service, and the Bureau of Reclamation, all in the Department of the Interior. The Army Corps of Engineers and the Tennessee Valley Authority also provide outdoor recreation in areas under their Jurisdiction.

**The National Park Service**   The National Park Service, a bureau of the Department of the Interior, was created by Congress in 1916.

The national park concept was well established by this time; however, the various parks and monuments were administered by other governmental agencies such as the Forest Service and U.S. Army.

The NPS administers approximately 286 different areas, each of which has national significance in one or more of the following classifications: scenery, geology, archeology, biology, history, or outdoor recreation. All of these areas, however, are managed under one of three categories:

*Natural Areas*   Use must be consistent with the preservation of the natural environment.

*Historic Areas*   They must maintain the historical integrity of the site, eliminating any uses which are not compatible with historic preservation.

*Recreational Areas*   The dominant or primary resource is outdoor recreation. Natural resources may be utilized as long as the activity is compatible with the recreation mission.

Most national monuments and all national parks but one (Mesa Verde) fit the natural area category (Fig. 5-4). Most military parks, battlefields, historic sites, memorials, and some monuments are managed under the historic area objectives. In the third category are the national recreation areas, seashores, lakeshores, and parkways. Each of the three categories has its own set of resource management and use objectives, which dictate the kinds of physical development allowed in each. Of the three, those guidelines established for the recreation area category, have the greatest flexibility.

The 286 National Park Service areas include the following:

|  | Number of<br>areas | Approximate<br>acreage |
|---|---|---|
| National parks | 38 | 15,100,000 (6 million ha) |
| National monuments | 83 | 9,900,000 (4 million ha) |
| National recreation areas | 16 | 3,800,000 (1.5 million ha) |
| National seashores and lakeshores | 12 | 670,000 (271,000 ha) |
| National preserves | 2 | 655,000 (265,000 ha) |
| National parkways | 6 | 150,000 (60,700 ha) |
| National memorial parks | 1 | 70,400 (28,500 ha) |
| National scenic riverways | 4 | 50,000 (20,000 ha) |
| National historical parks | 14 | 65,000 (26,300 ha) |
| National historic sites | 45 | 10,300 (4,170 ha) |
| Miscellaneous areas | 65 | 62,000 (25,090 ha) |
| Total | 286 | 30,532,700 (12,901,520 ha) |

**Figure 5-4** The National Park Service has the task of preserving areas of outstanding beauty while at the same time making them accessible to large numbers of people. Providing special transportation systems is a method of doing both. Yosemite National Park, California. *(Photo by Grant W. Sharpe.)*

The 65 miscellaneous areas are mostly military parks, battlefields, and other memorials, and include the National Capital Parks in and around Washington, D.C. New areas are continuously being added to the system by Congress; therefore, the above list, current in 1975, must not be considered final.

The NPS has the difficult, if not impossible, task of catering to an increasing number of visitors while at the same time maintaining these areas "in such manner and by such means as will leave them unimpaired for the enjoyment of future generations." This basic rule, from the 1916 act creating the NPS, requires that there be (1) careful planning of all roads and facilities; (2) resistance to pressure from those who would exploit timber, forage, minerals, or construct water storage in the parks; (3) a firm stand against attempts to legislate inferior areas into the national park system; (4) protection of wild animal life; (5) acquisition of private inholdings (which now allow the owners of these lands to ignore some park policies); (6) control of acts of vandalism and other acts of depreciative behavior which destroy and deface park values; and (7) careful weighing of the problems of protection of park resources from insects, disease, and fire, which in themselves are usually natural phenomena.

One of the ways the NPS is able to carry out its mission is to present its story to its millions of visitors through its elaborate interpretive programs, discussed on page 86. The NPS also serves ably in the international scene as an international consultant to countries throughout the world on matters related to national park management, interpretation, and planning.

The National Park Service is now under pressure to designate roadless areas in the national parks for study as to which of them are suitable for classification as wilderness under the Wilderness Act (1964).

The NPS is criticized by preservationist groups for being too recreation-oriented and for departing from park standards in its management policies. On the other hand, other recreationists (mostly sportsmen's organizations) and mining, timber, and grazing interests have objected to national park establishment because of the preservation orientation. Given the dual directive of *preserving* and *using* the parks, these criticisms appear inevitable and very likely will continue. The director of the NPS has a challenging task.

**Forest Service**    National forests were established primarily for the protection of timber and watersheds. The original laws, formulated around the turn of the century, did not consider recreational uses of the forests. As people discovered the recreational opportunities  on the new national forests, the agency began to recognize the recreation values of its lands and cater to the visitor's needs. By 1925 outdoor recreation was considered a valid use of its lands.

Since passage of the multiple-use act in 1960, recreation has had legal standing as one of the five major national forest uses along with timber, water, wildlife, and forage. Policy today emphasizes the integration of recreation with these other uses. As a result the Forest Service today is very much in the business of providing recreation, as is shown by its over 200 million annual visitors.

Forest Service lands possessing recreation values are classified under several designations. The largest are the wilderness areas, most of which are in the West, where travel is by foot or horseback and where visitors must rely largely on their own skills to survive (Fig. 5-5). Though timber harvesting is not permitted, grazing is, where it was established prior to the Wilderness Act of 1964. Wilderness areas total well over 10 million acres, and more roadless areas are being set aside each year under this act.

The Forest Service also has a large system of campgrounds, some of them highly developed but most having minimal facilities. Other recreational assets include organization camps and winter-sports areas. Special-interest areas include geological, archeological, historical, and botanical areas, and observation sites. Interpretation is an important activity for visitor education on these latter areas (Fig. 5-6). The Forest Service also manages several national recreation areas. Approximately 50 percent of the big-game animals of the United States are found on Forest Service lands.

Hunting, fishing, hiking, camping, picnicking, and winter sports are the major recreational uses of the national forests. Facilities are provided on

**Figure 5-5** The Mt. Dana–Minarets Wilderness Area of California is one of 61 areas to be kept in its natural state for wilderness-related recreation. The Forest Service administers approximately 10 million acres in wilderness. *(Courtesy of the U.S. Forest Service.)*

the intensively used sites for the convenience of the visitors and to protect the environmental integrity of the areas. Among the previously overlooked assets of the national forests are the 200,000 miles of logging roads, which are added to each year. With the advent of recreational vehicles, motorbikes and snowmobiles, these roads attract increasing dispersed recreation use.

One very important recreation function of the Forest Service is its research division. It has become the leader in the field of recreation research, providing material of significant value to recreation agencies at all levels of government (see the Bibliography for a sample of Forest Service recreation research publications).

**Bureau of Land Management** The Bureau of Land Management (BLM), established in 1946, manages the public domain, the federal lands of Western states not already in some other category. Approximately 460 million acres (186 million ha), 63 percent of which is in Alaska, are under BLM jurisdiction. Grazing, timber production, and mining are important activities on these lands. As hunting, fishing, camping, and picnicking use

**Figure 5-6**  A Forest Service naturalist and young visitors examine fossil-bearing shales in the George Washington National Forest, Virginia. *(Courtesy of the U.S. Forest Service.)*

increases, BLM is expanding its interest and expertise in matters related to outdoor recreation. A current concern of conservationists is the need for legislation giving BLM authority and responsibility for managing and protecting recreation values and other multiple uses of the public domain.

**U.S. Fish and Wildlife Service**    This newly reorganized bureau (July 1, 1974) maintains a system of fish hatcheries and wildlife refuges, which have substantial visitor interest. Approximately 30 million acres (12 million ha) are managed by the FWS in 356 national wildlife refuges and 93 national fish hatcheries. Hunting, fishing, and nonconsumptive activities, such as wildlife viewing and interpretive programs, are important FWS outdoor recreation activities. The Bureau also works in habitat preservation, water pollution control, protection of endangered species, and predator control and coordinates its activities with other land and wildlife managing agencies.

**Bureau of Reclamation**    The Bureau of Reclamation is in the water-storage business, and its reservoirs, used for irrigation, hydroelectric power, municipal and industrial water, and flood control, also attract people for recreation. If the area has national significance the recreation administration is turned over to the National Park Service (or the Forest Service if the project area is within a national forest). On areas of less than national significance, the recreation opportunities are turned over to a local or state agency to administer.

**Army Corps of Engineers**  Known as the Corps of Engineers, this agency is involved in flood control, navigation, beach erosion control, shore protection, flood-plain planning, boat harbor development, and navigable water protection. The Corps of Engineer project reservoirs have seen a phenomenal increase in boating use. Efforts to meet recreational needs include providing access, boat launching, swimming areas, camping and picnicking sites, and limited interpretive programs. Public interest, in the form of visits to project areas, exceeds that of any other federal agency. The responsibility for recreation on Corps projects is usually transferred to other federal, state, or local agencies.

**Tennessee Valley Authority (TVA)**  TVA, created in 1933, concerns itself with the overall development and control of the Tennessee River. Projects include hydroelectric power generation and flood control. Fishing, boating, vacation cabins, marinas, and other water-related recreation on TVA projects is usually transferred to other agencies for administration.

A noteworthy exception, administered by TVA itself, is the Land Between the Lakes, a multiple-use area which places a strong emphasis on outdoor recreation and environmental education, and is located between two reservoirs on the Tennessee and Cumberland Rivers, in Kentucky and Tennessee (Fig. 5-7).

**Bureau of Outdoor Recreation**  The Bureau of Outdoor Recreation (BOR) has a service role to play in the recreation field. The Bureau, established in 1962, coordinates all federal outdoor recreation programs. Established through a recommendation of the Outdoor Recreation Resources Review Commission, the BOR concerns itself with policy, planning, assistance, and coordination. Among other things, it prepares the nationwide outdoor-recreation plan, approves state outdoor-recreation plans, handles federal-state assistance programs, administers the Land and Water Conservation Fund Act of 1964, and activates various studies, research projects, and other educational programs.

### Outdoor Recreation on Private Lands

The private sector can be broadly grouped by motive into two categories: profit and nonprofit. The profit category includes those enterprises which charge for providing facilities and services, as well as equipment manufac-

**Figure 5-7** An aerial view of a forested campground located on Kentucky Lake. This is in the 170,000-acre (68,800-ha) outdoor recreation area known as the Land Between the Lakes. *(Courtesy of the Tennessee Valley Authority.)*

turers. The nonprofit category includes lands owned by clubs and conservation societies and industrial and agricultural owners.

The private sector's role in outdoor recreation is not as well defined as is the role of the public sector, largely because there are so many different enterprises, with widely divergent recreational opportunities.

The private contribution comes from a vast array of individuals, groups, and organizations which involves more people and just as much land as the public sector. At least 50 percent of all recreation opportunity is directly attributable to the private sector (Bureau of Outdoor Recreation, 1973).

**Profit Recreation Offerings** Profit-oriented recreation enterprises include a wide spectrum of activities. There are approximately 46,000 commercial enterprises in the United States providing amusement and spectator sports activities, which receive 400 million visits annually and occupy about 18 million acres (7.3 million ha) of land. There are an additional 37,000 full-time enterprises attracting 600 million visitors on 4 million acres (1.6

million ha) of land and water. These include dude ranches, vacation farms, hunting and fishing camps, campgrounds, resorts, beaches, winter-sports areas, and marinas. There are an additional 2,000 other enterprises of a similar nature offered on a part-time basis. These cater to 150 million visitors on 1 million acres (405,000 ha).

If they are to show a profit, these enterprises must be carefully planned and located. They do best if located in close proximity to mountains, seashores, winter-sports areas, hunting areas, or on the routes to major attractions, such as state or national parks, and where climate is favorable for an extended season of use. Sizes range from a few acres to very extensive areas offering a wide variety of activities. Income is usually derived by offering overnight accommodations, food services, rentals, and entertainment. Such areas may be run by individuals, families, or corporations, and success depends on such factors as supply and demand, location, access, and the quality of the enterprise. The temperament of the manager is of importance here, as these enterprises thrive on repeated visits, and word-of-mouth advertising by satisfied customers.

**Nonprofit Recreation Opportunities**   According to the Bureau of Outdoor Recreation there are more than 1 million nongovernmental enterprises offering outdoor recreation without a profit motive in the United States. They control about 467 million acres (189 million ha) of land and receive about 800 million visits annually.

In this group are an estimated 32,000 membership clubs which operate their facilities for members and their guests. These groups include such interests as hiking, hunting, fishing, swimming, boating, skiing, horseback riding, and recreation vehicle clubs.

Other quasi-public lands include those controlled by conservation societies; garden clubs; fraternal, union, and religious organizations; and youth groups (Scouts, 4-H), which alone have over 20 million members.

Finally, industrial organizations control or own over 100 million acres (40.5 million ha) of land, much of which is available for outdoor recreation. These include the lands belonging to utilities, industrial timber companies, agriculture enterprises, and similar areas where something other than recreation is the primary use of the land (Fig. 5-8). The basic reason for permitting recreation on these lands is the enhancement of public relations. Many companies offer a variety of free facilities and services, including campgrounds, covered kitchens, picnic tables, boat-launching sites, hiking trails, and roadside rest areas. A few of the more progressive companies offer the visitor self-guided auto tours or walking trails through company areas, and detailed maps of company lands where visitors are welcome to fish, hunt, camp, or drive vehicles. Some companies print animal and tree identification charts, and others establish "natural areas" on company lands for the protection of unusual plant or animal species. Today most

**Figure 5-8**  A public campground provided on privately owned industrial forest lands in Washington State. St. Helens Tree Farm. *(Courtesy of the Weyerhaeuser Company.)*

companies work closely with public agencies in matters related to wildlife management, watershed protection, and public recreation. The multiple use of the forest is stressed in most promotional material, pointing out that these lands provide jobs, pay taxes, and benefit recreationists. Such efforts contribute greatly to the public's understanding of the private timberland owner's viewpoint.

The offering of recreational opportunities has attendant difficulties. Catering to urban people unfamiliar with the forest environment requires great patience. Often the foresters in charge of these recreational areas have difficulty justifying expenses, especially when the facilities and resources are misused or destroyed by vandalism. Most visitors, such as hunters, fishermen, snowmobilers, campers, trailbikers, rock hounds, hikers, and berry pickers, appreciate these efforts. Unfortunately, despite the approval and enjoyment of the majority of users, signs are shot up, picnic tables are defaced, self-guided walking trails are "chewed up" by motorcyclists, and toilets are damaged and burned. Some companies decide that providing recreation is too costly. However, the presence of family groups on the site may prove a deterrent to vandalism. A high-quality offering also may serve as a deterrent to destruction. For this reason the development must be carefully planned and the method of promoting the facility carried out with finesse. An oversell of company "propaganda" receives a negative response, whereas a more subtle approach usually wins public support. A small entrance charge for the privilege of using the land may also serve as a deterrent to damage and brings in money to help defray costs.

Personnel should have some understanding of visitor behavior and their wants and needs. They should be instructed in the objectives of an interpretive program which helps gain public support. For example, Conner Forest Industries, of northeastern Wisconsin, offer an unusual summer educational experience. Visitors can ride a steam locomotive train (Fig. 5-9), visit a logging museum and country store, see a blacksmith at work, and view a film about the century-old logging company's past and present operations. Presenting Wisconsin's logging heritage is their objective, and their actions have won them awards as well as public support.

The private sector has some peculiar problems. Outdoor advertising laws may not permit them to use signs to promote their campgrounds. The improvement of their lands for recreation may result in increased taxes, even if no fees are charged. Sanitation laws may be more rigid for the private than the public sector. By granting permission for others to use their

**Figure 5-9** A steam locomotive train called the *Lumberjack Special* provides paying visitors with an educational and entertaining experience. This is one of several methods the company uses to interpret Wisconsin's lumber history. *(Courtesy of the Connor Forest Industries, Laona, Wisconsin.)*

land, owners may be liable for injuries to recreationists, unless the state where the land is located has adopted a law which relieves the landowner of liability. Also, liability may be increased if entrance fees are charged. Liability insurance is available at reasonable cost, however. Working directly with the public requires managerial skills different from those needed for growing trees. Foresters with a speciality in outdoor recreation should be considered. Assistance, of course, is available through a variety of government and university sources.

Though many of the above activities are not forest related, they do show the great diversity of opportunities in which the private sector is involved. In addition to providing an extremely important element in the overall recreation economy, these private recreation opportunities serve to relieve the pressure on the overcrowded public recreation areas. Private enterprise, therefore, plays a major role in supplying needed outdoor recreation resources and facilities.

## PUBLIC OPINION AS A FACTOR IN RECREATION

Outdoor recreation deals with people and the resources of nature. These resources are no longer taken for granted, and their management is now under close public scrutiny. With the diverse user-groups and type of lands involved, policy decisions related to outdoor recreation have become the subject of acrimonious debate, and at times, legal action.

The organized conservation clubs, such as the Friends of the Earth, the Mountaineers, the National Audubon Society, the Sierra Club, and the Wilderness Society, have been active in influencing public opinion. These groups are national in scope and are active in matters related to open space, wildlife conservation, wildland preservation, and environmental quality.

These powerful manifestations of organized public opinion are important factors in the setting aside of land for outdoor recreation and in the consequent use of this land.

## INTERPRETIVE PROGRAMS

Parks and equivalent areas are more than places in which to play, picnic, and camp. Though visitors come to these places for relaxation, some may wish to learn about an area's natural and cultural resources. Interpretive programs make this possible.

Interpretation is a service offered to visitors to parks, forests, and similar outdoor recreation areas. It seeks to achieve three objectives: (1) to assist the visitor in developing a keener awareness, appreciation, and understanding of the area visited; (2) to accomplish management goals by reinforcing the idea that parks are special places requiring special behavior, and also to minimize human impact on the resource by guiding people away

**Figure 5-10** An interpretive specialist discusses the natural history of the park during a guided tour. Jasper National Park, Alberta. *(Photo by Grant W. Sharpe.)*

from fragile or overused areas; and (3) to promote public understanding of an agency and its programs (Sharpe, 1976).

The objectives of interpretation are carried out through the use of carefully chosen media. The examples of personal activities include information duty, talks, guided tours, and living or cultural interpretation (Fig. 5-10). The nonpersonal or unattended media include exhibits, signs and labels, self-guided trails, self-guided auto tours, audio devices, and publications on specific topics such as flora, fauna, and geology. These are the basic tools which the interpreter uses to communicate with the recreation visitor. Selection is based on such visitor characteristics as age, education, and place of origin, as well as other considerations such as cost, climatic conditions, and potential for vandalism.

The interpretive program is an educational program, but not in the formal sense. Visitors participate voluntarily and are usually receptive to learning, as long as it is *easily absorbed.*

## PLANNING THE SMALL OUTDOOR RECREATION SITE

Whether it be on private or public lands, the forest manager may very easily become involved in looking for and planning a small recreation camp or picnic area. Items to consider in the potential site are its environmental attractions, terrain (some facilities require level ground, others may be well adapted to irregular ground), soil (its drainage and ability to retain or permit establishment of vegetation and its susceptibility to damage through compaction and erosion), condition of cover for shade, availability of a suitable water supply, the wind velocity, snow depth, temperatures, flood and avalanche potential, and other possible hazards.

### Facilities Needed in Recreation Areas

The enjoyment of a public recreation area, once it is selected, is greatly increased if it contains adequate facilities. These facilities should include picnic tables, fireplaces, toilets, water and garbage receptacles, roads, parking areas, and directional and interpretive signs. If overnight camping is permitted, level camper and trailer space must be provided. The facilities must be sturdy, economical, and easily maintained. These will be discussed briefly.

*Picnic Tables*   The table should be heavy enough to discourage rearrangement by visitors. Most tables are made of wood or a combination of wood planks for seats and tops and concrete or pipe bases. A surface treatment protects the wood and serves to inhibit the "pocketknife artist."

*Fireplaces*   These may consist of simple grates set in rocks or may be waist-high charcoal stoves mounted on pipes. This type, as well as the iron swivel models that rest on the ground, may be rotated to take advantage of the wind direction. Rock and mortar units, because of exposure to extremes of heat and cold, require frequent repair but are still the most common type. There is a trend toward the use of smaller fireplaces that require less wood and are less expensive to construct. If the trend toward visitors' bringing their own portable gasoline stoves continues, perhaps a stove holder, consisting of a post and flat steel plate, should be considered instead of fireplaces (Fig. 5-11).

*Toilets*   Adequate sanitation is frequently the limiting factor in determining the carrying capacity of a recreation site. Toilets may be of either the pit or flush type, but should be sufficient in number, easily accessible, screened, conspicuously labeled, and placed at a safe distance from water supplies and swimming areas. An innovation in pit toilets is a type which is set over a large buried tank. It is periodically emptied by a tank truck equipped with a suction device.

*Water Supply*   Although a lake or stream greatly enhances the popularity of a recreation area, an adequate, uncontaminated, domestic water system must be an important consideration in the location of a campground or picnic site. Subsurface water is frequently used, and since any water source is susceptible to contamination, periodic checks must be made on its purity.

Once the water is piped to the area where it is to be used, combination drinking fountains and hydrants are the most efficient means of dispensing it. These facilities can be worked into the natural surroundings by encasing them in stone or wood. There should be numerous signs pointing out the

**Figure 5-11**  The enjoyment of outdoor recreation is increased if adequate facilities are provided. Note the use of the charcoal grill. A portable gasoline stove has been placed on it. Land Between the Lakes, Tennessee and Kentucky. *(Courtesy of the Tennessee Valley Authority.)*

water by routes which do not cross other campers' areas. Visitors must be instructed not to wash utensils at the spigot, since a coating of grease in the soil will eventually prevent drainage. Where a hand pump is in use and the supply of water is limited, the temptation to waste water may be lessened by shortening the handle on the pump.

**Garbage Disposal**  Cleanliness in a camp or picnic site is best maintained by numerous covered garbage cans and frequent garbage pickups. The cans should be situated so that they serve several units, thus reducing the tendency to litter. In an area where there are bear and other mammals there should be provision for keeping the cans covered and erect.

**Roads, Trails, Parking Areas, and Barricades**  The width, grade, surface material, drainage, and similar features of entrances and connecting roads will differ with the area's topography and other characteristics, but should conform to the agency's minimum standards. Features to consider are good visibility, adequate turning radius, and, where possible, a loop design. Parking areas should be planned with different types of use in mind. A campsite spur will have individual parking for a car or recreation vehicle.

If travel trailers are permitted, then greater maneuverability is essential. The ideal design is a pullthrough, which eliminates the necessity of backing the trailer. Individual parking units are not necessary in picnic areas. To protect vegetation, the boundaries of parking areas are usually defined with barriers of logs, concrete or wooden posts, or partly buried rocks. Trails are needed for access to water, toilets, and points of interest.

**Signs** Well-placed signs give the visitor a feeling of welcome and encourage proper use of the site. It is frustrating at the end of a long drive to have to search an area for water or toilet facilities. In addition to directing visitors to facilities, signs should point out hazards and scenic areas, rules and regulations, and can be used in the area's interpretive program. Sign location has a definite bearing on effectiveness, as does the brevity of the message. Signs must be sturdily constructed to withstand the elements, animals, and human vandalism.

**Miscellaneous Facilities** Depending on the sort of recreation site being planned, the type of visitor it is intended to serve, and many other factors, facilities in addition to those indicated above may be necessary. These might include artificial plantings, maintenance and administration areas, play areas, a shower house, shelters, garbage pits, reservoirs, steps and bridges, ramps and other modifications for handicapped visitors, boat-launching sites, and guard devices to protect visitors from areas of danger. The visitor's interest in natural or human history is encouraged if well-laid-out loop, self-guided trails, and other interpretive devices are used.

In addition to developed sites, dispersed recreation on forest roads is an increasingly popular activity. Many recreation vehicles are self-contained and these give people the opportunity to camp virtually anywhere on forest roads. While the impact of such use bears careful watching to safeguard against environmental impacts, in many places it is an appropriate activity and exemplifies recreation in multiple-use forestry.

A large number of areas of recreational interest are on forested lands and their management is part of the general field of forestry. Training in forestry, combined with electives in social science, outdoor recreation, natural history, wildlife management, park structures and facilities, landscape design, law and procedure, and public administration, can effectively prepare a student for employment in this rapidly developing field. The reader desiring additional information on outdoor recreation will find the Bibliography helpful.

## BIBLIOGRAPHY

Bannon, Joseph J. 1972. *Problem Solving in Recreation and Parks,* Prentice-Hall, Inc., Englewood Cliffs, NJ.

Brockman, C. Frank, and Lawrence C. Merriam, Jr. 1973. *Recreational Use of Wild Lands*, McGraw-Hill Book Company, New York.

Brown, William E. 1971. *Islands of Hope*, National Recreation and Park Association, Washington, DC.

Burch, William R., Jr. 1966. Wilderness: The Life Cycle and Forest Recreational Choice, *Jour. Forestry*, **64**:606–610. Washington, DC.

Cordell, Harold K., and George A. James. 1972. *Visitors Preferences for Certain Physical Characteristics of Developed Campsites*, U.S. Department of Agriculture, Forest Service Research Paper SE-100, Asheville, NC.

Driver, B. L. (ed.). 1974. *Elements of Outdoor Recreation Planning*, The University of Michigan Press, Ann Arbor; and Longman Canada, Ltd., Don Mills, Canada.

Everhart, William C. 1972. *The National Park Service*, Frederick A. Praeger, Inc., New York.

Gray, David E., and Donald A. Pelegrina. 1973. *Reflections on the Recreation and Park Movement: A Book of Readings*, Wm. C. Brown Company, Publishers, Dubuque, IA.

Hendee, John C. 1969. Appreciative versus Consumptive Uses of Wildlife Refuges: Studies of Who Gets What and Trends in Use, *Transactions of the Thirty-Fourth American Wildlife and Natural Resources Conference*, Wildlife Management Institute, Washington, DC.

———, and Richard L. Bury. 1971. Does Recreational Development Pay Off? *West. Conservation Jour.*, **28**:28–30.

———, and Frederick L. Campbell. 1969. Social Aspects of Outdoor Recreation: The Developed Campground, *Trends in Parks and Recreation*, **6(4)**:13–16, National Recreation and Park Association. Washington, DC.

———, and William R. Catton, Jr. 1968. Wilderness Users: What Do They Think? *Amer. Forests*. **74(9)**:28–31, 60, 61.

———, ———, Larry D. Marlow, and C. Frank Brockman. 1968. *Wilderness Users in the Pacific Northwest: Their Characteristics, Values, and Management Preferences*, U.S. Department of Agriculture, Forest Service Research Paper PNW-61, Portland, OR.

Jensen, Clayne R. 1970. *Outdoor Recreation in America*, Burgess Publishing Company, Minneapolis, MN.

Kraus, Richard G. 1971. *Recreation and Leisure in Modern Society*, Appleton Century Crofts, Inc., New York.

———, and Joseph E. Curtis. 1973. *Creative Administration in Recreation and Parks*, The C. V. Mosby Company, St. Louis.

Malbon, Sidney A. 1976. Buildings, Structures, and Other Facilities. *Interpreting the Environment*, Grant W. Sharpe (ed.). John Wiley & Sons, Inc., New York.

McIntosh, Paul A. 1976. Signs and Labels. *Interpreting the Environment*, Grant W. Sharpe (ed.). John Wiley & Sons, Inc., New York.

Outdoor Recreation Resources Review Commission. 1962. *Outdoor Recreation for America: A Report to the President and to the Congress*, Washington, DC.

Romeny, G. O. 1972. *Off the Job Living: A Modern Concept of Recreation and Its Place in the Postwar World*, McGrath Publishing Co., Washington, DC.

Sharpe, Grant W. 1976. An Overview of Interpretation. *Interpreting the Environment*, Grant W. Sharpe (ed.). John Wiley & Sons, Inc., New York.

———, 1976. Self-Guided Trails. *Interpreting the Environment*, Grant W. Sharpe (ed.). John Wiley & Sons, Inc., New York.

Stankey, George H., and David W. Lime. 1973. *Recreational Carrying Capacity: An*

*Annotated Bibliography*, U.S. Department of Agriculture, Forest Service General Technical Report INT-3, Ogden, Utah.

Stein, Thomas A., and H. D. Sessoms. 1973. *Recreation and Special Populations*, Holbrook Press, Boston.

Tildon, Freeman. 1967. *Interpreting Our Heritage*, The University of North Carolina Press. Chapel Hill.

————, 1954. *The National Parks: What They Mean to You and Me*, Alfred A. Knopf, Inc., New York.

U.S. Department of the Interior, Bureau of Outdoor Recreation. 1970. *Islands of America*, Washington, DC.

U.S. Department of the Interior, Bureau of Outdoor Recreation, 1973. *Outdoor Recreation: A Legacy for America*, Washington, DC.

U.S. Department of the Interior, National Park Service. 1972. National Parks and Landmarks, *Areas Administered by the National Park Service and Related Properties as of January 1, 1972*, Washington, DC.

U.S. Department of the Interior, National Park Service. 1968. *Administrative Policies for Historical Areas of the National Park System*, Washington, DC.

U.S. Department of the Interior, National Park Service. 1968. *Administrative Policies for Natural Areas of the National Park System*, Washington, DC.

U.S. Department of the Interior, National Park Service. 1968. *Administrative Policies for Recreation Areas of the National Park System*, Washington, DC.

U.S. Department of the Interior, National Park Service. 1973. *Outdoor Recreation— A Legacy for America*, Washington, DC.

U.S. Environmental Protection Agency. 1974. *Studies in Environment:* Vol. V *Outdoor Recreation and the Environment*, Washington, DC.

Washburn, Randel F., and J. Alan Wagar. 1972. Evaluating Visitor Response to Exhibit Content, *Curator*, 15:248–254.

Wetterberg, Gary B. 1976. Self-Guided Auto Tours. *Interpreting the Environment*, Grant W. Sharpe (ed.). John Wiley & Sons, Inc., New York.

Chapter 6

# Management of the Forest Environment

Management of the forest environment in the sense of protecting it against damage and destruction has always been an important part of forestry. Recent concern about overall decline in the quality of life has tended to bring environmental values of the forest into sharper focus and to assign them higher priority in setting policies and defining objectives. Environmental aspects of forest management have also included control or modification of practices which contribute to broader problems, such as the far-reaching effects of persistent pesticides. A third and more positive aspect which has been too often overlooked is the opportunity to manage the forest specifically for the enhancement and greater use of its environmental values.

**Historical Perspective** In the second half of the nineteenth century, disposal of the public domain had accelerated, unchecked by enactment of

This chapter was prepared by T. F. McLintock, Retired Director of Environmental Research, Forest Service, U.S. Department of Agriculture, and J. B. Hilmon, Director, Southeast Forest Experiment Station, Forest Service, U.S. Department of Agriculture, Asheville, N C.

many well-intentioned but poorly written and administered land laws. A laissez faire attitude in Congress toward land speculation, timber trespass, fraudulent practices, and corrupt officials was rationalized by the generally accepted notion of resource inexhaustibility and by the need to open up and settle the country. The government had shown little concern over the excessively wasteful practices common to resource extraction and use.

Change in established attitudes and abuses could come only through pressure from an enlightened and aroused citizenry or through the initiative of far-sighted political leaders. The reform movement, small and fragmented at first, gradually attracted a number of articulate and dedicated advocates—respected men with varied backgrounds like Marsh, Muir, Sargent, Powell, McGee, Hough, Schurz, Fernow, and, of course, Pinchot.

Rampant deforestation, often followed by catastrophic uncontrolled fires, had evoked warnings as early as the 1850s about a possible timber famine. Beyond such pragmatic considerations, however, uneasiness was increasingly expressed about damage to other, less tangible values. The overall implications of reckless resource exploitation were not fully understood, but the more readily observable consequences were being sharply condemned. The importance of forests in regulating streamflow had long been recognized, and the effects of bad cutting practices, fire and overgrazing on erosion, stream siltation, and local flooding were there for all to see. The too common failure of natural regeneration following forest removal and the lack of any conscious effort to accomplish it were viewed as being improvident in principle as well as being a short-sighted timber policy. John Muir was particularly vocal about the need to preserve and protect large, representative areas of unspoiled forest, mountains, lakes, and streams before they all vanished under relentless human assaults. By the 1870s the efforts of the crusaders had begun to have some effect. The next 40 years saw the establishment of the statutory, institutional, and philosophical framework necessary for the development and acceptance of effective resource protection and—ultimately—management.

Although the most conspicuous issues in this early conservation movement were those of wasteful practices, political chicanery, and potential timber shortages, strong environmental elements were deeply embedded in it from the very beginning. In 1864 Congress granted to the state of California the Yosemite Valley and the Mariposa Big Tree Grove "for public use, resort and recreation." The first federal reserve was set aside in 1872, not for timber production but "as a public park or pleasuring ground for the benefit and enjoyment of the people." It was Yellowstone National Park. The first large state area withdrawn from development and commercial use was the huge Adirondack Preserve, set aside in 1885 to be held "forever wild." The American Antiquities Act was passed in 1906, and in the next 5 years, 23 national monuments were proclaimed by the President, including what later became Grand Canyon and Olympic national parks.

This period was notable for the organization of a number of societies and organizations representing a broad spectrum of conservation interests: the American Ornithologists Union (1873), American Forestry Association (1875), American Fisheries Society (1884), Audubon Society (1886), and the Sierra Club (1892), to name a few. This was also a fruitful era for the passage of legislation and the organization of commissions to protect vanishing bird, mammal, and fisheries resources. Massachusetts had created the first state fish and wildlife agency in 1865 and within the next decade most other states followed. The federal Biological Survey, forerunner of the Fish and Wildlife Service, was set up in 1896. The first federal wildlife refuge was established in Florida in 1902, and others, notably the National Bison Range in Montana, came soon after.

The waning of the Roosevelt-Pinchot influence and gathering clouds of World War I ended the era that solidly established conservation, including an appreciation of what we now call a *land ethic,* as one of America's enduring social and political philosophies. In the next half century, progress was sporadic. The National Park Service was formed in 1916, and under Stephen Mather's dynamic leadership, the park system flourished. The Forest Service, as part of its emerging multiple-use philosophy, gave official birth to the wilderness movement in 1924 and set aside some 13 million acres (5 million ha) of wilderness and primitive areas within national forests over the next 20 years.

During the 1930s economic depression, dust storms and catastrophic floods brought a temporary revival of the mood and tempo of turn-of-the-century conservationism. Establishment of the Tennessee Valley Authority and the Soil Conservation Service, enactment of such laws as the Pittman-Robertson, Omnibus Flood Control, and Taylor Grazing Acts, formation of the Civilian Conservation Corps, and initiation of the shelterbelt program provided mechanisms for putting husbandry and use of land, water, forests, and wildlife on at least a partially scientific basis. The country had moved gradually from a purely custodial toward a managerial forest policy—an undramatic but highly significant step.

**The Environmental Movement**   Shortly after the end of World War II the United States entered its third conservation era. This would have much wider social and ecological implications than the first two and would become part of a worldwide reaction to progressive decline of the quality of life. Although the "conservationism" of the two Roosevelts and the "environmentalism" of the 1960s and 1970s had some common elements, they had such different origins, objectives, scope, and strategies that it is almost meaningless to describe one in terms of the other. The early conservationists were impelled primarily by wholesale dissipation of natural resources as raw materials and sought to reduce waste and establish wise use. In contrast, the new crusade was motivated by the threats to people's personal health and welfare presented by disruption of essential life-support systems on a global scale.

Initially attention focused on pollution of air and water by virtually unrestricted release of industrial wastes. The immediate effects of this long accepted practice could be seen, felt, tasted, and smelled, and the sources could usually by traced. The hidden or delayed public health implications became the object of much research. Similarly, there was growing anxiety about widespread use of new chemicals, particularly synthetic organic materials, without knowledge of their biological consequences. Publication of Rachel Carson's *Silent Spring* in 1962, which vividly dramatized potential dangers of pesticides, keynoted the popular reaction against injury to wildlife from introduction of toxic chemicals into their food chains. Finally, there were growing and insistent demands that massive physical assaults on air, water, and land be halted until the full nature and extent of their effects could be determined. Thus the development of the supersonic transport, off-shore oil drilling, strip mining, construction of the Alaska pipeline, and clearcutting of timber were stopped, delayed, or subjected to restrictive regulations.

Much of the impetus and effectiveness of the environmental movement came from a proliferation of concerned citizens' organizations, some of long standing, some more recent, and some almost spontaneously created on an ad hoc basis to deal with a specific issue. Greatly expanded funding for environmental research became available from federal agencies, universities, foundations, and other sources. Much was learned in a short time, both about the true nature of problems and of the best strategies for halting or changing objectionable practices. The crucial nature of people's role in, and their impacts on, the operation of the total biosphere was elucidated and proclaimed, as was the close interrelationship and interdependence of all living organisms. The opening sentence of Commoner's *The Closing Circle* puts it very well: "The environment has just been rediscovered by the people who live in it."

Let us now see how the foresters and their work have been affected by the environmental movement. In the time-honored tradition of Pinchot, foresters had become accustomed to a self-image which embodied all that was good in resource protection and management. They were the people who put out fires, planted trees, practiced selective cutting, and took care of wildlife. In the decades since the first Roosevelt they had progressed from custodians to managers. They had accepted as natural and proper the roles of pioneers, leaders, and molders of public attitudes in conservation matters. They knew that silvics was the very essence of ecology and that silviculture was the skillful application of a pure science as an advanced art form. If any group understood cause-and-effect relationships in nature, foresters surely did. They had been taught that conservation questions require technical answers. Their competence and versatility had been tested and proved in the control of regeneration, growth, deer herds, insects, campers, fire, streamflow, livestock, and logging contractors. Through dedication and professionalism foresters were largely responsible for keeping conservation alive through long periods of public apathy.

But as the environmental movement gathered momentum and gradually encompassed all potential threats to the quality of life, many conventional forestry practices came under fire. Foresters suddenly found themselves accused of indiscriminate use of pesticides, destructive cutting practices, disregard of aesthetics, neglect of wildlife, and opposition to wilderness. The forestry profession stood indicted of default of principles, insensitivity to national needs and public attitudes, and defiance of the will of the people.

Foresters generally had a conservative background, their contacts too often were with people of like views; they were professional in outlook, better trained in timber than in full multiple use; too often their responsibilities had given them a self-sufficiency and even a feeling of self-righteousness. Their influence, which had been considerable and predominantly favorable, had too long been confined to a rather isolated body of technical problems and technical solutions. Foresters recognized shifting patterns of forest use, but failed to sense or understand the profound changes in society's goals and value standards. Nor did they comprehend the degree to which "their" dominion of forest, land, wildlife, and water had become part of a much larger and more complex dominion, for which they could claim only limited proprietary rights or paternalistic responsibility. Their traditional role was not just being challenged, it was being ignored by the new generation of self-proclaimed ecologists who had forgotten, never knew, or did not care about past history and who had suddenly and dramatically captured the imagination and support of large segments of the public. Technical competence without a sensitive and responsive social conscience was not enough.

On the other hand, the environmental movement had become a vast and enormously fragmented crusade. The organized or institutionalized effort, which was the dominant force, included many special interest groups who tended to define environmental problems and solutions in the narrow terms of their own particular concerns. They were strongly polarized and showed little sympathy for compromise, which they regarded as a sellout. This created extreme demands and often irreconcilable conflicts between equally dedicated groups. They were impatient and wanted instant solutions, not understanding how long it takes to develop safe and workable alternatives. They repeatedly invoked the unanswerable argument that if a practice could not be conclusively shown to be free from all environmental hazards then it was unacceptable and should be discontinued.

Foresters were subjected to the same kinds of constraints on their freedom of decision and action as had been imposed on other offenders: investigations, appeals, injunctions, petitions, protest meetings, restrictive legislation. The implications were clear—change or shut down. It was equally plain that grudging compliance with court orders was not sufficient. What was required was a new approach to the theory and practice of forestry which would reflect contemporary values and priorities.

Meaningful reform had to start with reestablishment of mutual trust and respect with the public. Through local hearings, open meetings, listening sessions, and other forms of public involvement, programs must be explained and objectives justified on a broader base, and while still in the planning stage. Possible environmental impacts must be identified and assessed, safeguards proposed, and total costs and benefits analyzed. Safe, effective alternatives to unacceptable practices must be developed and tested. Performance standards and controls must be strengthened on all operations to assure proper protection of soil, water, wildlife, scenic beauty, and other nonmarket values. Intangible resource values should also figure more prominently in setting management objectives, especially on public lands, and opportunities for adequately funding such activities should be exploited. The prevailing concept of multiple use should be examined for its validity under more strongly environmental policies and goals.

There are dangers in this kind of responsiveness, of course; to try to satisfy everybody usually is to satisfy nobody, and unfortunately, the gentle virtue of compromise is not characteristic of reformers. The extreme preservationist factions were unlikely to accept anything less than complete surrender on the question of timber harvest and use. Those interested in maximum timber harvest would view any abridgement of traditional cutting practices as unreasonable and any proposed withdrawals of commercial timberlands as confiscatory. However, history seems to suggest that, when the American public is given a meaningful role in policy formulation and decision making, it generally favors moderation. Furthermore, a landmark act of Congress which became law in 1970 would go a long way toward public reassurance by providing a mechanism for detailed disclosure of potentially hazardous programs and for a broader-based control. This was NEPA, the National Environmental Policy Act of 1969.

**The National Environmental Policy Act**   The act requires that before a major federal program is undertaken the responsible agency must identify and evaluate all possible environmental effects. If they are likely to be significant, an environmental impact statement must be developed and used as an integral part of the planning and decision-making process. During its preparation the public is informed of the proposed action and of its possible consequences and is given an opportunity to express its views. Other concerned agencies are also consulted and provide formal review of the draft statement. Feedback from all individuals and groups is considered and is incorporated in the revised final statement to the extent possible or desirable. The statement is filed with the President's Council on Environmental Quality and made available to the public.

Criteria for judging "significant" effects and for determining whether a proposed action justifies an impact statement were not spelled out in the act, but it has been generally conceded that congressional intent was for coverage to be broad. Consideration is given not only to visible, immediate, and local impacts, but also to what is known about obscure, long-range, and off-site effects. Thus, statements are prepared for projects which will cause extensive ecosystem disturbance; may have delayed chain reactions in birds, fish, or other animals (including humans), or could impair unique values of parks, wilderness tracts, archeological sites, and other special-use areas. A key element of the statement is the description of alternative practices or substitute projects which would avoid or minimize environmental damage. Agencies were expected to use imagination and vigor in devising such options. Also, the likelihood of unavoidable environmental impacts was to weigh heavily in the cost-benefit balancing which would influence final "go" or "no-go" decisions.

NEPA has had important effects on the conduct of federal forestry operations and, to a lesser degree, on other public and private activities. For one thing, the environmental consequences of all kinds of development and management practices are becoming better understood. Preparation of impact analyses has obliged planners and managers to dig deeply into available knowledge about ecosystems and how they are altered by various types of stresses induced by forest uses. Second, it has engendered greater sensitivity and responsiveness to public attitudes and needs. It has led to new and mutually rewarding modes of public involvement and communication and should eventually reduce the unfortunate polarization which often beclouds environmental issues. Third, it has increased workloads of public forest officers and delayed progress on many programs. The necessity not only to explore fully hazard potentials but to find alternatives to unacceptable practices has made heavy demands on available personnel. And finally, compliance with NEPA has helped bring foresters face-to-face with contemporary realities of social climate and culture, reducing their isolation, broadening their environmental consciences and responsibilities, and perhaps instilling in them a measure of humility.

**Environmental Law** In the past decade conservation organizations, and the concerned citizen as well, have found a sympathetic and powerful ally in the courts, and environmental law has become an important field of jurisprudence. Much of the legal action has focused on lowering barriers to litigation against federal agencies, and two of the most troublesome have been substantially reduced. Definition of "standing to sue," the right to take the federal government to court, has been liberalized by a series of decisions, beginning with the Storm King case.[1] In effect, these rulings permit the "personal injury" required as a basis for legal action to include environmental damage. Previously, true economic loss had to be shown. Second, immunity of federal agencies to judicial review of their decisions has been virtually overthrown. Traditionally, resource management had been regarded as a technical matter for which the responsible agency had discretionary authority, but the concept of leaving public forest management to the professionals, without citizen access to judicial review, has been repeatedly challenged in the courts, for the most part successfully.

The roster of important cases affecting federal forestry practices is much too long to enumerate. Three examples will illustrate the kinds of projects involved.

*Mineral King*   In 1969 the Forest Service and National Park Service were sued to prevent construction of a highway to provide access through a national park to a huge recreational development in a national forest. Violation of several laws that protect park and wilderness values from commercial encroachment was cited. The court ruled plaintiff had no standing to sue. Ruling was upheld by the Supreme Court in 1972, 3 years after the project was halted.

*East Meadow Creek*   Plaintiffs obtained an injunction against Forest Service timber sale under the Wilderness Act of 1964. The sale area, adjacent to a designated primitive area, had potential for wilderness classification. This ruling, which has been sustained, has given rise to the concept of de facto wilderness, and has severely limited discretionary authority of the Forest Service to manage all undeveloped areas of 5,000 acres (2,023 ha) or more.

*Monongahela*   A restraining order halted all clearcutting on the Monongahela National Forest in West Virginia because timber sale contracts do not limit cutting to dead, mature, and large growth trees which had been marked, and because purchaser is not required to remove all cut trees. The court ruled this to be in violation of the Forest Reserve Organic Act. By implication and extension this ruling could, if sustained, have a profound influence on more than half of all national forest timber sales.

The entire field of environmental law is in a state of flux. Legislation is still evolving, judicial attitudes are still being formed and precedents set. NEPA will need further interpretation in the courts. But one thing is fairly certain: federal foresters will have to learn to live with judicial review and

[1] Scenic Hudson Preservation Conference sued Federal Power Commission (354 F 2d 608; 2d Cir., 1965) to revoke license to a utility company to build a power generating plant. Precedents set: (1) citizen groups given standing to sue; (2) federal agency responsibility to develop environmental information on impacts of projects under its jurisdiction was established.

court-imposed restraints for some years, as environmentalists demand, and the public supports, limitations on administrative discretion.

**Forest Use Impacts on the Environment**   The principal environmental impacts from forest uses arise from road construction, timber harvesting, controlled burning, type conversion, and use of chemicals. These activities can be managed so as to minimize or eliminate harmful or undesirable effects. Failure to do so can usually be traced to faulty administration or heavy management costs, although sometimes the full extent and significance of the damage was unforeseen, or the leverage or strong public pressure to improve performance had not developed.

Whenever the ground is broken and vegetation is uprooted, there will be some soil movement from gravity, wind, or washing. Where disturbance is severe, as in road construction, substantial erosion and sedimentation may occur (Figs. 6-1, 6-2, 6-3). Engineering knowledge and skills can assure proper road location and grade, provide for drainage, and stabilize fills and backslopes. Transport of logs from stump to landing, even on gentle slopes,

**Figure 6-1**   A broad-based dip, built into a logging road, prevents roadbed destruction and erosion. The surface water is intercepted and diverted, and thus is not allowed to develop sufficient volume and velocity to do serious damage. *(Courtesy of the U.S. Forest Service.)*

**Figure 6-2**  A well-constructed culvert at an intermittent stream crossing. The road slopes into the crossing from both directions so that water from surface runoff goes into the stream. *(Courtesy of the U.S. Forest Service.)*

can create compacted or deeply disturbed soil conditions which will concentrate water and permit erosion and siltation. Skillful location of skid trails, use of suitable equipment, and postlogging stabilization of disturbed areas can virtually eliminate these hazards. Excessive soil movement and water pollution, often charged to timber cutting, are in fact usually caused by poor design or careless construction of the log transport system. Normally tree removal per se, even clearcutting, will produce little soil movement. On very steep and unstable terrain, decay of root systems following cutting often results in localized land slippage, particularly in sections of the Pacific Northwest and Alaska. But such areas can usually be recognized prior to logging and should be avoided.

Timber harvesting may, however, degrade the environment in other ways. Logging along roads and shorelines of lakes presents an objectionable sight to travelers and recreationists unless cuts are light and debris is removed. When cutting extends to stream margins, debris can clog the stream channel, logs dragged across it may stimulate stream bed erosion, and exposure to sunlight raises water temperature. These disturbances create condi-

**Figure 6-3** This temporary truck road, built on contour, was closed immediately after logging was completed, and the roadbed seeded to grass. *(Courtesy of the U.S. Forest Service.)*

tions unsuitable for fish and unattractive to people who fish. Adverse impacts can be greatly reduced, if not prevented entirely, by leaving undisturbed, or very lightly cut, buffer zones.

Although the evidence is not yet conclusive, it appears that some wildlife species inhabiting remote and secluded areas can tolerate only limited human presence during certain phases of their life cycles. The breeding season is often critical. The California condor and the southern bald eagle, for example, have been known to abandon nest sites as a result of relatively minor disturbance by humans. Some large mammals, such as elk and bighorn sheep, can also be adversely affected by human encroachment. Where such situations are known or suspected, wise resource management would dictate delineation of critical areas as off limits to logging, restricting operations to nonsensitive periods, or perhaps establishment of formal sanctuaries.

Clearcutting is a special and highly controversial case. Silviculturally, it is a subsystem of even-aged management whereby a timber stand is regenerated by removal of all the overstory at one time. But in practice it "has purposes which are easily misunderstood and effects that are prone to intuitive misinterpretation" (Smith, 1973). The reaction against clearcutting derives primarily from the appearance of devastation which is often left behind, from which other environmental damage has been inferred and ascribed to it. Research has failed to support most such allegations, *provided clearcutting is wisely planned and properly executed.* Clearcutting generally favors wildlife, so long as habitat needs are not overlooked. Stone (1973) states that it does not cause significant soil nutrient losses, nor does it deserve blame for erosion resulting from road construction or poor logging practices.

Clearcutting as a silvicultural system is, however, uniquely vulnerable to abuses. Effects of carelessness or unwise practices that may not be evident under other harvesting systems become highly visible with clearcutting. Slash is more of a problem and can be a fire hazard and an eyesore for many years if not disposed of. Clearcut areas are often too large, accentuating the impression of ecological desolation. The system has been misapplied to forest types and stand conditions which called for some other method, resulting in poor utilization, destruction of growing stock, and regeneration failure. Where artificial regeneration was required, site preparation to ensure planting success has often been crudely done, leaving ugly and persistent scars. If care is not taken, clearcutting operations tend to steamroller indiscriminately through patches of young growth, small streams, good wildlife cover, or other natural enclaves which should be left intact.

Burning of logging slash has always been a cheap, effective, and fairly uncomplicated disposal method, especially in the Northwest where residues commonly exceed 150 tons per acre (366 t/ha). In the South prescribed burning has long been an important pine management tool for fuel hazard reduction, enhancement of wildlife cover and browse, improvement of herbage for livestock grazing, control of forest disease, and for other purposes. Fuel volumes are usually small but areas are large, with close to 2.5 million acres (1 million ha) treated annually. Until fairly recently smoke from slash fires and prescribed burns was of little public concern. It was associated with naturally occurring wildfires; burns were of short duration; and, in the West at least, burning operations were generally carried out in remote areas. But as air pollution became a critical national problem, all sources came under critical scrutiny and many local ordinances and some state laws were enacted to prohibit or curtail open burning.

Proper burning techniques can, however, materially reduce the smoke problem. One precaution is to burn only when atmospheric conditions are such that smoke will move strongly upward several thousand feet before spreading out laterally. Burning may be restricted to times when fuel condition favors complete combustion, minimizing release of unburned gases and particulates. Firing patterns and techniques can also be adjusted to produce desirable combustion.

During the past decade many environmental organizations have become increasingly critical of various large-scale type conversion programs. Some of these have arisen as a result of dramatically accelerating demands for all products and services of the forest and have as their objective more complete and efficient use of the available land. Projects have been undertaken to reclaim extensive areas from "useless brush" in order to favor timber production, water yield, or livestock grazing. In other cases wide swaths of vegetation have been cleared for ski slopes, firebreaks, and transmission lines. All these activities usually employ heavy machinery, chemical herbicides, or fire, singly or in tandem.

Both the means and the ends of many of these projects have been condemned as socially unsound, scientifically unproved, and economically unjustified. Replacement of natural ecosystem diversity by artificial uniformity is considered unwise and objectionable. Injury to aesthetics, wildlife, air and water quality, and in some instances to human health has been cited. Supporting cost-benefit analyses have been discredited because intangible benefits and environmental values have been ignored. As a result, public pressure has forced careful review of objectives and thorough study of total environmental impacts, as required by NEPA. Resource managers have backed away from some of these ventures and have redesigned others, giving proper recognition to environmental considerations. Still others, such as the establishment of fire-stop zones in southern California, are under litigation and their future is uncertain.

The vast array of synthetic chemicals produced during the technological revolution included many new herbicides and insecticides which, supplemented by increased availability and versatility of small aircraft, gave foresters powerful weapons against plant and insect pests. Though most of them seemed "safe" to handle at first, evidence of subtle, long-range environmental damage soon began to accumulate. Persistent, broad-spectrum compounds like DDT killed beneficial organisms as well as the target insect. Carried by air or water, these compounds remained active to injure biota far from the application site. Some chemicals were found to contain minute quantities of toxic impurities; others formed dangerous decomposition products. Some, caught up in food chains of fish, birds, and mammals, had obscure and complex cumulative effects.

If all the deleterious environmental consequences attributed to them could not be substantiated, enough could be to inspire a profound suspicion of pesticides and their users in the minds of a public already in revolt against chemical effluents from industrial plants. A series of restrictions of pesticide use was gradually imposed, and for a time it appeared that large-scale application of any chemical might be prohibited. It now seems probable that some tentative middle ground will be cautiously agreed upon, pending more complete understanding of the biological effects of each chemical. In any event, whether motivated by a real concern for environmental quality, or whether merely responding to society's imperatives, the forester will have to apply more knowledge, skill, and common sense in the future regarding the use of pesticides.

**Managing Environmental Values of Forests**   It is axiomatic that the first goal of environmental management is to prevent unnecessary or unacceptable damage. However, the forester should not be satisfied with just reacting to pressures to change bad habits. Intangible resources so important to public well-being should not be merely protected, but should be constructively managed. There are numerous opportunities for exercise of initiative and imagination, and for the deployment of multidisciplinary teams, to expand or enhance specific environmental benefits.

Although silviculture is usually defined in terms of timber production, it is based on ecological principles and can be applied to gain other objectives as well. Its use in forest landscaping is a good example. More people derive pleasure and relaxation from driving through forested areas than from any other forest-related recreational activity. Yet much wooded landscape which should be a delight to the beholder presents instead an impenetrable wall of vegetation or an endless expanse of fully stocked monotony. Silvical knowledge and silvicultural skill, supported by the special expertise of the landscape architect, can impart to such stands a natural beauty that will greatly enrich the outdoor experience. Judicious thinning will allow deeper visual penetration into the forest and create pleasing patterns of light and shadow. Flowering species or picturesque specimen trees can be released or highlighted. Diversity of vegetational composition, texture, and spatial arrangement can be developed. Mountains, lakes, meadows, and rock formations can be given visibility by opening the stand at strategic points. Native wildlife can be made a perceptible component of the forest scene by creating favorable habitats for birds and other small animals at roadside parks, turnouts, rest areas, and picnic sites and for larger species in glades, marshes, or forest openings visible from the road.

Timber harvesting, type conversion, wildlife clearings, watershed improvements, ski slopes, and other types of resource development and use can create discordant anomalies in otherwise undisturbed forest landscapes. To an already highly mobile society, expanded networks of forest highways and access roads have exposed such operations to view even in the most remote locations. The unfavorable effects of scars left by logging or herbicide treatment may be heightened by geometrical shapes or spatial regularity completely out of phase with natural land forms or vegetational patterns. When spread across a valley or mountain slope, they may so dominate the entire landscape that scenic values are cancelled out, and the viewer is left with a sense of frustration and disappointment.

Multiple-use management should include the visual resources, as well

**Figure 6-4** Logging cuts can be designed to blend with natural patterns, textures, and contours of the landscape. *(Courtesy of the U.S. Forest Service.)*

as timber, water, and wildlife, and landscape design should have as much weight as logging engineering, silviculture, or ecology. Job planning and execution should not only avoid impairment of scenic values but should attempt to enhance visual acceptability whenever possible. The openings can be designed to blend with natural patterns, textures, and contours of the landscape. Size, shape, and spatial arrangement can be varied and sculptured to minimize the impression of unnatural disturbance. Excessive contrast, or destruction of existing contrasts, would be avoided. Visual diversity should be maintained, if present, or tastefully introduced if it is not (Fig. 6-4).

Some 130 species of wildlife in the U.S. are classified as scarce, endangered, or unique. For many of these, their precarious status is at least partially due to habitat failures that can be repaired, once specific requirements are known. Thus, the use of prescribed fire to reestablish essential jack pine cover in Michigan has probably saved the Kirtland's warbler from extinction. In the West it is known that scarcity of nesting snags near lakes and reservoirs has contributed, along with DDT, to declining populations of the osprey. Breeding areas can be restored or enlarged by providing for preservation of suitable dead trees or for the killing of live trees when necessary. Limited populations of other species such as the Kaibab squirrel which are unique to small ecological niches can be maintained, if not augmented, by habitat management that will ensure continuance of their special food or cover requirements.

Almost any kind of timber cutting will favor wildlife to some extent by increasing the diversity and availability of low-growing vegetation. But much more can be accomplished by planned and skillful integration of timber and wildlife management prescriptions, with objectives of both clearly spelled out. Imaginative collaboration between silviculturist and wildlife ecologist can create suitable openings, margins, escape routes, den trees, mast sources, nest areas, and other habitat needs for many of the species valuable for both hunting and for increasingly popular noncon-sumptive use (Fig. 6-5).

The relatively recent concept and practice of urban forestry has been a natural outgrowth of efforts by city and regional planners, zoning boards, real estate developers, and civic groups to improve the quality of life in densely populated areas. The many benefits of woodlands, parks, and greenbelts within the urban community are being realized. Resource inventories are being made, and ways of taking better care and making better use of existing trees and wooded areas are being studied. Opportunities for making trees an integral and harmonious component of housing developments, industrial complexes, transportation systems, and urban renewal projects are being explored.

**Figure 6-5** Imaginative collaboration between silviculturist and wildlife ecologist can create or maintain habitat needs for many animal species valuable both for hunting and for increasingly popular nonconsumptive use. *(Courtesy of the U.S. Forest Service.)*

Trees—in groups, strips, small woodlands, or large forest—can serve an even wider spectrum of functions in an urban-suburban setting than in the conventional context of commercial forests. Of great significance is the physical and psychological therapy provided by even the small wooded park as a temporary haven from the confusions and frustrations of the daily struggle for existence in the city. The natural and intrinsic beauty of trees can confer a special grace and charm on human structures. Enjoyment of recreational activities is enhanced by wooded surroundings, and miniature forests can support a surprising variety of birds and small mammals even in the heart of the city. Forested watersheds have historically protected the quality of municipal water supplies. The ameliorating effects of trees against wind and sun are taken for granted, but less appreciated is the capacity of belts of trees and understory vegetation for absorption and attenuation of sound.

The full potential for application of forest-management knowledge and techniques to urban forestry opportunities and problems has not yet been realized. But even when needs and possibilities have been obvious, there has seemed to be a lack of awareness, both by city planners and by foresters themselves, of the key role the latter can play. By training, experience, and outlook, the forester is equipped with a unique set of qualifications that can contribute in an important way to the early design and planning of urban projects so that optimum benefits from the use of trees will be assured and costly mistakes avoided.

Because social and environmental rather than biological and physical considerations dominate, and because an entirely different set of economic forces are operative, much more imagination and flexibility will be required than is customarily needed in wildland management. Existing urban-suburban woodlands, whether publicly or privately owned, are likely to have single rather than multiple-use objectives as watersheds, parks, wildlife sanctuaries, or cemeteries; or for beautification, barriers against dust or noise, nature trails, or just "open space." Vegetation must be protected from hazards of air pollution, trampling, and vandalism, as well as from the usual pests, and much higher investments in protection will be justified. Decisions about tree planting—what species, where, when, and how—will be more complicated. Management for timber production will nearly always be a strictly minor objective.

Purists are generally inclined to vigorously resist proposals for "managing" wilderness areas. Nevertheless, where greatly expanding use may endanger wilderness integrity or prevent full enjoyment of the wilderness experience, imposition of some managerial controls will probably be required. Wilderness carrying capacity is limited in two ways. First, too much use can cause ecological retrogression; particularly in high mountain country, delicate balances are readily upset; fragile soils once disturbed can quickly erode; rare alpine flowers once trampled may not return; crystal-clear springs and sparkling brooks may be defiled; and the essential solitude of such animals as the bighorn sheep and the mountain lion is easily broken. Second, most wilderness users have a low threshold of tolerance for encounters with other people or for evidence of human presence; "over-crowding" may occur when more than two or three other parties are seen; and latent antagonisms may emerge between backpackers and horseback riders. Litter and wornout camping sites can spoil an otherwise satisfying wilderness visit.

For both of these problems, "people management" is the primary solution. More even dispersal of visitors throughout an area will reduce use impacts and minimize encounters. This can be accomplished by more and better trails, additional camping sites, improved signing and maps, and opening new access points. More drastic measures include the rationing of use under a permit system, closure of heavily used trails and sites to allow rehabilitation, and limitations on group size. Since wilderness purists are suspicious of any tampering with freedom of use or the introduction of inappropriate improvements, management strategies should be subtle, carefully justified, clearly explained, and discreetly applied.

**Strategies for Realistic Goals**   The ultimate overall goal of renewable resource management will be the effective integration of products and uses for the maximization of net social welfare. This means that in the future environmental values will be treated much more explicitly in policies and plans of all forest ownerships. Even anticipating some reversal of the recent pendulum swing toward environmental conservatism, society will never allow return to complete freedom of managerial discretion and action. However, definition of management objectives in terms of optimum balance between production and environmental protection and enhancement will continue to be difficult until a satisfactory information base for measuring both tangible and intangible values is available.

Although much has been learned of the specific ecological consequences of some forest practices, too many decisions are still made on the basis of speculation and unproved premises. Large-scale application of insecticides, herbicides, and fertilizers, for example, is still suspect because important questions about effects on living organisms remain unanswered. Habitat requirements of wildlife, particularly nongame species, must be better understood before management prescriptions can be designed for their benefit. Fundamental to virtually all practices is a greatly amplified knowledge of the structure and functioning of critical forest ecosystems, and of their assimilative and regenerative capacities under various humanly induced stresses.

The oft-repeated economic maxim, "there is no free lunch," has special relevance for environmental management. The public no longer tolerates unrestricted use of land, air, and water as free disposal sinks, either for deliberately discarded wastes or for inadvert by-products of careless operations. Both the avoidance of environmental damage and the enhancement of benefits will entail additional costs. Rational decisions as to what expenditures can be justified and how charges will be levied will be governed by the value of environmental elements that may be affected and by the extent to which the public will agree to bear part of the cost. The concept of an effluent charge, which would be essentially payment for permission to pollute, has been proposed as one possible approach to the problem of industrial wastes. A reasonably sound and workable basis for calculating and incorporating externalities into pricing systems and for determining trade-offs would facilitate the design of resource development strategies acceptable both to the public and to land managers.

A corollary problem was pointed up in the National Environmental Policy Act. Section 102 directs federal agencies to develop procedures to "insure that presently unquantified environmental amenities and values may be given appropriate consideration in decision making along with economic and technical considerations." How to measure nonmarket products or uses of managed forests (such as aesthetics, songbirds, or noise abatement, for example), or to develop value indicators that have some basis for comparison with genuine market values, has puzzled economists for years. This remains a relatively unexplored area.

A vital requirement for effective management of environmental values in the forest is their recognition and inclusion in multiple-use planning and decision making. At that stage critical questions must be answered relative to use compatibility and balance, probable environmental impacts, public needs and attitudes, cost-benefit ratios, production goals, and ultimately the allocation of funds and personnel for program execution. It is here that the most experienced judgment, the greatest sensitivity to public interest, and the broadest base of ecological understanding are demanded. Political and social awareness are as important as technical knowledge and managerial excellence.

## BIBLIOGRAPHY

Carter, Luther J. 1973. Environmental Law (I): Maturing Field for Lawyers and Scientists, *Science,* **179:**1205–1209.

————. 1973.Environmental Law (II): A Strategic Weapon Against Degradation?, *Science,* **179:**1310–1312, 1350.

Commoner, Barry. 1971. *The Closing Circle,* Alfred A. Knopf, Inc., New York.

Cook, D. I., and D. F. Van Haverbeke. 1971. *Trees and Shrubs for Noise Abatement,* Research Bulletin 246, Agriculture Experimental Station, University of Nebraska, Lincoln.

Dana, Samuel Trask. 1956. *Forest and Range Policy: Its Development in the United States,* McGraw-Hill Book Company, New York.

Davis, Kenneth P. 1970. Land: The Common Denominator in Forest Resource Management: Emphasis on Urban Relationships, *Jour. Forestry,* **68:**628–631.

Duncan, Donald P. 1971. Managing the Forested Environment: Role of the Professional, *Jour. Forestry,* **69:**8–11.

Graham, Frank, Jr. 1971. *Man's Dominion: The Story of Conservation in America*, M. Evans and Company, Philadelphia.

Hagenstein, Perry R. 1971. Multiple Use and Environmental Decisions on the Public Lands, *Jour. Forestry,* **69:**21–24.

Krygier, James T., and James D. Hall (eds.). 1971. *Forest Land Uses and Stream Environment: A Symposium,* Oregon State University, Corvallis.

Litton, R. Burton, Jr. 1968. *Forest Landscape Description and Inventories: A Basis for Land Planning and Design,* U.S. Department of Agriculture Forest Service Research Paper PSW-49, Berkeley, CA.

McDonald, Philip M., and Raymond V. Whitely. 1972. Logging a Roadside Stand to Protect Scenic Values, *Jour. Forestry,* **70:**80–83.

McGee, Charles E. 1970. Clearcutting and Aesthetics in the Southern Appalachians, *Jour. Forestry,* **68:**540–547.

McLintock, Thomas F. 1972. Criteria for a Managed Environment, *Jour. Forestry,* **70:**556–558.

Marsh, George P. 1974. *The Earth as Modified By Human Action: A New Edition of Man and Nature,* Scribner, Armstrong & Co., New York.

Mock, H. Byron. 1971. Forest Management and Litigation, *Jour. Forestry,* **69:**200–205.

Murphy, James L., Leo J. Fritschen, and Owen P. Cramer. 1970. Research Looks at Air Quality and Forest Burning, *Jour. Forestry,* **68:**530–535.

National Research Council. 1970. *Land Use and Wildlife Resources,* National Academy of Sciences, Washington.

Norris, Logan A. 1971. Chemical Brush Control: Assessing the Hazard, *Jour. Forestry,* **69:**715–720.

Reidel, Carl H. 1971. Environment: New Imperatives for Forest Policy, *Jour. Forestry,* **69:**266–270.

Smith, David M. 1973. Maintaining Timber Supply in a Sound Environment, in *Report of the President's Advisory Panel on Timber and the Environment,* Washington, pp. 369–426.

Stankey, George H. 1973. *Visitor Perception of Wilderness Recreation Carrying Capacity,* U.S. Department of Agriculture, Forest Service Research Paper INT-142, Ogden, UT.

Stone, Earl. 1973. The Impact of Timber Harvest on Soils and Water, in *Report of the President's Advisory Panel on Timber and the Environment,* Washington, pp. 427–467.

Udall, Stewart L. 1963. *The Quiet Crisis,* Holt, Rinehart and Winston, Inc., New York.

U.S. Congress, Subcommittee on Science, Research and Development. 1968. Managing the Environment, ser. S, Washington.

U.S. Department of Agriculture. 1973. *National Forest Landscape Management,* vol. 1, Agriculture Handbook 434, Forest Service, U.S. Department of Agriculture, Washington.

University of Massachusetts. 1970. *A Symposium on Trees and Forests in an Urbanizing Environment,* University of Massachusetts Cooperative Extension Service, Amherst.

Webb, William L. 1973. Timber and Wildlife, in *Report of the President's Advisory Panel on Timber and the Environment,* Washington, pp. 468–489.

# Part Two

# Forests and Forestry

# Chapter 7

# How to Know Your Trees and Their Environments

The forested one-third of the earth's surface includes several thousand species of trees. Within North America there are about 845 forest tree species of which more than 165 are commercially used. The Society of American Foresters lists 147 forest *types*, 97 in eastern United States and 50 in Western states. Forest types are further consolidated into 17 major groups reflecting the prevalence of key species.

**Scientific Names**   Because of great confusion in the use of common names, it is necessary to have some universal system which can be used not only in a single country but throughout the world. Such a system was developed through the use of Latin names, many of which were first applied when Latin was used by scientists of all countries. Scientific names have been in common use since the middle of the eighteenth century when Linnaeus published his monumental *Plantarum* (1753). In this book Linnaeus gave the generic or group name, then the species designation, which usually consists of a short descriptive phrase. This practice gives a generic name followed by a species name for each plant, the combination constituting binomial nomenclature.

**Identification**   Trees may be divided into two main groups called *angiosperms* and *gymnosperms*. The angiosperms are mainly hardwoods and the gymnosperms mainly softwoods. The angiosperms have broad leaves, and the gymnosperms have needle-like or scale-like leaves. The angiosperms are generally deciduous and the gymnosperms generally evergreen. The angiosperms bear hard seeds, and the gymnosperms bear cones with seeds.

Having decided that your tree is a gymnosperm or an angiosperm, there are many ways to identify the genus and then the species. One way is to become familiar with the variations in form and size of leaves, fruits, flowers, twigs, and bark. Pictures can also be used and there are many illustrated field guides that are very helpful.

### Trees and Their Environments

Trees are a vital part of the natural scene; they are affected by their environment and in turn affect their surroundings.

This total environment is a complex integration of numerous interrelated physical and biological factors. These involve physical factors such as climate, including the varying temperatures, rainfall, and various measures of radiation. Movement and composition of the air is also significant. Factors of the soil such as texture, structure, depth, moisture capacity, drainage, nutrient content, and topographic position are important.

Biological factors include the plant associates: the larger mammals that use the forest as a source of food and shelter; the many small mammals, insects, and insect-like animals; the fungi to which the trees are host; and the myriads of microorganisms in the soil, especially those whose functions are beneficial to the tree.

Because of the complexity of the total environment and the difficulty with which some factors are measured, complete and exact quantification of the environment is difficult (U.S. Department of Agriculture, 1965).

Ten species of hardwoods and ten species of softwoods have been selected to give the reader a view of their characteristics, their ranges, their site requirements, and their uses.[1] This should allow for study in more depth of a few species.

**Eastern White Pine** *(Pinus strobus)*   Eastern white pine is an important eastern conifer. For about 250 years eastern white pine was the leading commercial species. Because of its former abundance and the cheapness and varied usefulness of its lumber, it was important in the development of the states in which it grew, as well as of regions far outside its natural range.

Eastern white pine grows naturally from Newfoundland to Lake Win-

---

[1] The detailed information on these 20 species of trees was taken from the individual species writeups, Useful Trees of the United States, FS-71, Forest Service, U.S. Department of Agriculture.

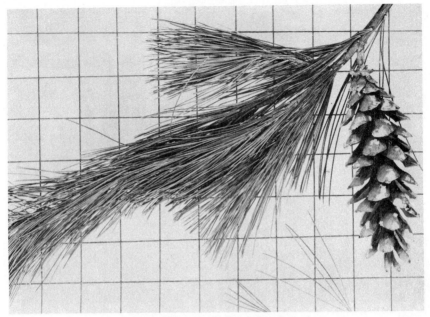

**Figure 7-1**  Eastern white pine. *(Photo by C. Frank Brockman.)*

nipeg in Canada, southward through the Lake States and New England. It also grows in the southern Appalachians, as far south as northern Georgia. The species grows best, however, in the humid and cool situations in northern latitudes, making a slower growth in the Lake States than in the Northeast, where 80-year-old trees in favorable situations may have a diameter of 16 in. (40 cm) and a height of 100 ft. (30 m). Under some conditions white pine may reach diameters of 3 to 6 ft. (0.9 to 1.8 m), and trees more than 200 ft. (60 m) high have been reported. Extensive stands containing from 20,000 to 50,000 board feet per acre were formerly not at all uncommon.

Eastern white pine is distinguished from all other eastern pines because its leaves, or needles, occur in bundles of five. They are 3 to 5 in. (7.6 to 12.7 cm) long, bluish green on the upper surface and whitish beneath.

The wood of eastern white pine is light, soft, durable, and very easily worked. It is straight-grained and takes paint well. Practically all of the eastern white pine taken from the forest today is converted into lumber. The lumber is probably put to a greater variety of uses than any other wood, with the possible exception of oak. Eastern white pine can be used for practically every part of a house, and houses built of it in New England 300 years ago are still in excellent condition.

**Western White Pine *(Pinus monticola)***   Like its eastern relative, western white pine is a very important timber tree. The wood of few trees among

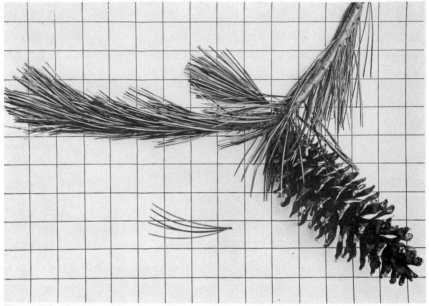

**Figure 7-2**   Western white pine. *(Photo by C. Frank Brockman.)*

its associates in the Western forests can command a higher price on the lumber market.

Western white pine develops its greatest size and highest economic values in deep porous soils on gentle north slopes and flats in northern Idaho and Montana. It seldom grows in pure stands and is most frequently associated with western hemlock, Douglas-fir, several Western firs, and lodgepole pine.

Western white pine grows from the lower part of British Columbia southward into western Montana and along the Cascade and Sierra Nevada Ranges through Washington and Oregon to central California. As is usual in white pines, the needles are borne in bundles of five. They are pale bluish green with a white frosty appearance, 2 to 4 in. (5 to 10 cm) long, and thicker and more rigid than those of the eastern white pine. Young cones are green or dark purple, first standing erect, then drooping by the end of the first season. The cones usually attain a length of 6 to 10 in. (15 to 25 cm), and upon maturing at the end of the second season, become yellow-brown in color. The cones are slightly curved and longer than those of eastern white pine. The winged seeds are a pale red-brown and are shed in September soon after the cones ripen.

Practically all of the western white pine taken from the forest is sawed into lumber, which is used principally in building construction, match planks, boxes, and millwork such as sash, frames, and doors.

**Sugar Pine** *(Pinus lambertiana)*   Sugar pine is the largest of all the pines. A tree of the Western mountains, it grows at an altitude of from 1,000 to 7,000 ft. (300 to 2,100 m) above sea level from the Coast and Cascade Ranges of southern Oregon, along the Coast Range and Sierra Nevada of California, and through the southern part of that state in scattered stands into Lower California. It attains its largest size and heaviest stands in California from Tulare to Eldorado Counties, where it is found on cool moist sites on the west slope of the Sierra at elevations ranging from 4,500 to 6,000 ft. (1,400 to 1,800 m).

The name *sugar pine* comes from the white, sugary substance that forms from sap exuded in drops on the bark or wood when the tree is wounded. This substance is sweet, pleasantly flavored with resins, and reportedly has laxative properties.

Botanically, sugar pine belongs to the white pine group, along with eastern white pine and western white pine. Its members can usually be readily identified by their five needles per bundle. The leaves have the deep blue-green and whitish tinge that is typical of true white pines. They are 2 ½ to 4 in. (6 to 10 cm) long, stout, stiff, and twisted, remaining on the twig through the third year.

With a life-span of about 500 years, this tree is remarkable because of the fact that it keeps on growing to a very advanced age. It grows to a larger

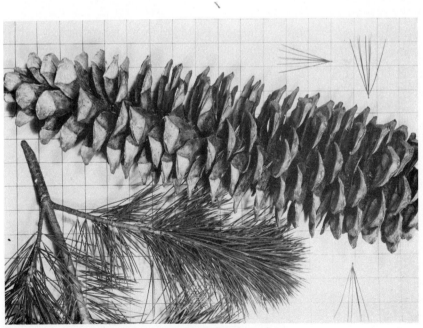

**Figure 7-3**   Sugar pine. *(Photo by C. Frank Brockman.)*

size than any of its associates, except the giant sequoias with which it is occasionally found. Trees 160 to 180 ft. (48 to 55 m) high with diameters from 2 to 3 ft. (0.6 to 0.9 m) are common, but heights of 250 ft. (76 m) and diameters of 10 ft. (3 m) or more have been reported.

It is practically always associated with other species, chiefly ponderosa pine, California incense-cedar, white fir, and Douglas-fir.

Moisture in both soil and air is necessary for the rapid development of sugar pine throughout all stages of its life, but especially during the seedling and sapling periods. Except in early youth the tree demands a large amount of light.

The wood of sugar pine is very much like eastern white pine in both appearance and properties and has practically the same wide range of uses. It is light in weight, moderately weak, not stiff, and fairly soft. It takes paint well and does not split in nailing. Almost the entire cut of sugar pine goes into lumber and its products. The uses which consume the largest amounts are building construction; boxes and crates; sash, doors, frames, and general millwork; and foundry patterns. It is a favored wood for raisin trays and boxes.

**Ponderosa Pine** *(Pinus ponderosa)*  Ponderosa pine, formerly known as western yellow pine, is one of the most widely distributed and important

**Figure 7-4**  Ponderosa pine. *(Photo by C. Frank Brockman.)*

of Western timber trees. It is found in every state west of the Great Plains, as well as in southern British Columbia and northern Mexico. It is the most valuable species of the Southwest, where it forms great open forests at 3,500 to 8,500 ft. (1,000 to 2,500 m) above sea level and is to that region what eastern white pine has been to the Northeast or longleaf pine to the Southeast.

The total stand of ponderosa pine is greater than that of any other pine in North America, and the total supply or volume is second only to that of Douglas-fir.

Ponderosa pine grows in pure stands and in mixture with other species on a wide variety of soils, sites, and elevations. Although it shows a preference for sunny climates and warm situations, it is able to endure severe winters. Having a deep taproot and long, strong side roots, the tree can resist drought better than its associates. Excellent stands of ponderosa pine are therefore found where the annual rainfall is only 18 in. (45 cm). Ponderosa pine forests are nearly always rather open, because the tree cannot tolerate dense shade and also because, in the drier locations especially, of the competition of the far-reaching roots for soil moisture.

Growth characteristics of the tree are apt to vary with the region, there being a noticeable difference in tree measurements, in length and thickness of needles, size of the cones, and color of the bark in various parts of its range. Average measurements show diameters of full-grown trees to be from 5 to 8 ft. (1.5 to 2.4 m) and heights from 150 to 230 ft. (46 to 70 m), but they are larger in California and Oregon than in Arizona and New Mexico. The needles are usually dark yellowish green and may be from 8 to 11 in. (20 to 30 cm) long, occurring in clusters of three (occasionally two or, in the *P. ponderosa* var. *arizonica*, mostly five) at the ends of naked branches. Cones are 3 to 6 in. (7.6 to 15 cm) long, often clustered, bright green or purple when fully grown, becoming light reddish brown as the seeds ripen. They fall from the tree soon after opening and discharging their seed. The winged seeds are 1 to 1 ½ in. (2.5 to 3.8 cm) long and about 1 in. (2.5 cm) wide, and are produced rather abundantly after the trees reach middle age.

This pine has a wide range of uses from highly finished products to the roughest construction. The soft, high-grade lumber, resembling white pine, is extensively used for planing-mill products, and large quantities go into sashes and doors. This wood is also used to some extent by pattern makers, but is not equal to white pine for that purpose. Ponderosa pine is also used for caskets, furniture, fixtures, toys, and various other manufactured products.

**Shortleaf Pine** *(Pinus echinata)*    Shortleaf pine, one of the four important pines in the Southern states, has a wide botanical range. It grows more or less abundantly in 24 states from Staten Island and Long Island, New York, and parts of Pennsylvania southward to northern Florida, and west-

**Figure 7-5**  Shortleaf pine. *(Photo by C. Frank Brockman.)*

ward to eastern Texas and eastern Oklahoma. In a considerable part of its range, shortleaf excels all other conifers as a timber tree.

Shortleaf pine, in common with longleaf, slash, and loblolly, is called "yellow pine" or "southern yellow pine" by the lumber trade.

Shortleaf pine usually grows in the uplands and foothills, but it also spreads into the lower levels. Although often associated with loblolly pine, red oaks, hickories, and sweetgum, shortleaf grows best in pure stands. It forms densely crowded stands of many small-sized trees per acre. Under average conditions, this species reaches a height of 34 ft. (10 m) and a diameter of 4.5 in. (11 cm) in 20 years, and attains a height of 82 ft. (25 m) and a diameter of 12 in. (30 cm) in 70 years.

The trunk of shortleaf pine is remarkably straight and clear, slightly tapering at the top with numerous short branches which form a narrow pyramidal top, or crown. The bark is pale reddish brown and coarsely fissured. The needles, or "straw," are mostly in clusters of two or three, since the shortleaf pine belongs to the group of two-leaved pines. Dark bluish green in color, these needles are soft and flexible and from 2 to 5 in. (5 to 13 cm) long.

The cones of this species, which are very abundant, are among the smallest of pine cones, measuring from 1 ½ to 2 in. (3.8 to 5 cm) in length, in size resembling a small pullet egg. The cone scales are tipped with very fine needle-pointed prickles. The seed likewise is very small and, when the cones open, may be carried several hundred feet. The seeds germinate quickly and evenly. Because shortleaf pine seedlings frequently take over abandoned open fields, this species, as well as loblolly pine, has been called "oldfield pine."

The wood of shortleaf pine is moderately hard, strong, straight-grained, and dark yellow or light brown in color. By reason of its comparative freedom from resinous matter, its stiffness, and its ease of working, it is especially fitted for house construction. The wood is used principally for building material such as interior finish, flooring, ceiling, frames, sashes, wainscoting, weatherboarding, sheathing, joists, lath, and shingles. It also goes into boxes and crates, railroad-car construction, barrels, agricultural machinery, excelsior, wood pulp, mine props, low-grade furniture, wood-enware, and toys.

**Douglas-fir** *(Pseudotsuga menziesii)* Douglas-fir is an outstanding American forest tree. A native of the Western part of North America, it grows from the Rocky Mountains to the Pacific Coast, and from Mexico to central British Columbia.

Douglas-fir thrives under a wide range of soil and climatic conditions. It nevertheless grows most rapidly in fairly deep, moist but well-drained

**Figure 7-6**  Douglas-fir. *(Photo by C. Frank Brockman.)*

soils in locations having at least 40 in. (100 cm) of rainfall a year and a long growing season. It attains its fastest rate of growth and largest size in Washington and Oregon, in the region between the coast and Cascade Mountains. Here trees having diameters of 3 to 6 ft. (0.9 to 1.8 m), and heights of 200 ft. (60 m) or more are not uncommon. Under favorable conditions individual trees sometimes grow to be over 300 ft. (90 m) tall and 10 to 15 ft. (3 to 4.6 m) in diameter and live for 1,000 years or more.

Douglas-fir trees have thick, furrowed bark, which is smoky brown in color. Their needles are usually deep yellow-green and are ¾ to 1 ¼ in. (1.9 to 3.1 cm) long. The cones are 2 to 4 ½ in. (5 to 11.4 cm) long, with small winged seeds ¼ in. (0.6 cm) long and about ⅛ in. (0.3 cm) wide.

Although Douglas-fir is suitable for many purposes, it is used principally for building and construction in the form of lumber, timber, piling, and plywood. Its value as a structural timber is due to its strength and stiffness combined with its moderate weight, as well as the fact that timbers of Douglas-fir can be cut as large as 2 ft. square (0.6 m²) and 60 ft. (18 m) long. Douglas-fir plywood is used for sheathing and for concrete forms, interior paneling, prefabricated house panels, other structural forms, and boats. Considerable quantities of Douglas-fir also go into railroad ties, cooperage stock (largely staves for casks, half barrels, and kegs), and mine timbers.

**Western Hemlock** *(Tsuga heterophylla)* Western hemlock, like its eastern cousin, has often been considered an inferior wood. In recent years it has nevertheless become important for building construction and products such as furniture, as well as for wood pulp.

Growing along the Pacific Coast from Alaska to Sonoma County, California, western hemlock is an associate of Douglas-fir, western redcedar, and Sitka spruce.

Western hemlock grows best in cool, moist situations, where it sometimes reaches an age of 500 years and grows to heights of 175 to 225 ft. (55 to 70 m) with diameters from 3 to 5 ft. (0.9 to 1.5 m). At 100 years of age, however, trees average from 17 to 21 in. (43 to 53 cm) in diameter and 130 to 150 ft. (40 to 45 m) in height.

The bark on fully grown trees is from 1 to 1 ½ in. (2.5 to 3.8 cm) thick, of a dark russet-brown color, and deeply furrowed with narrow cross ridges. On young trunks the bark is thin, dark orange brown, with shallow fissures. The foliage is a glossy yellow green with small leaves not over an inch (2.54 cm) long, which remain on the tree from 4 to 7 years. The small, drooping dark-purple cones are ¾ to 1 ¼ in. (1.9 to 3 cm) long. The narrow winged seeds are small [ 1/16 in. (0.15 cm) long].

Western hemlock is used principally for pulpwood and lumber. Substantial quantities of rough-sawn lumber are now used for exterior house siding. The lumber goes largely into building material such as sheathing,

**Figure 7-7**   Western hemlock. *(Photo by C. Frank Brockman.)*

subflooring, joists, studding, planking, rafters, siding, and flooring. Other products include millwork, boxes and crates, ladders, grain doors, car construction and repair, prefabricated house panels, refrigerators, woodenware, and novelties.

**Eastern Hemlock *(Tsuga canadensis)***   Although botanically known as *canadensis*, eastern hemlock is abundant in the United States as well as in Canada. It is a native of the Northeastern and Lake States and is frequently an important member of the forest in New England, New York, and Pennsylvania. Pennsylvania has chosen eastern hemlock as its state tree. In the Appalachian Mountains this species extends as far south as northern Georgia and northern Alabama.

A tree mostly of medium size, eastern hemlock usually grows to be 60 to 80 ft. (18 to 24 m) tall and 2 to 3 ft. (0.6 to 0.9 m) in diameter. Occasional trees are 100 ft. (30 m) in height and 4 ft. (1.2 m) in diameter. The species usually reaches its largest size in the southern Appalachians, principally near streams on the slopes of high mountains in North Carolina and Tennessee. There, trees 200 years old average about 20 in. (50 cm) in diameter and 87 ft. (26 m) in height. In the Lake States where conditions are not so favorable to this species, the diameter and height growth are somewhat slower. Eastern hemlock grows rather slowly, maturing at 250 or 300 years and sometimes living for 600 years. The record age is 988 years.

**Figure 7-8**  Eastern hemlock. *(Photo by C. Frank Brockman.)*

Though occasionally occurring in pure stands, eastern hemlock commonly is mixed with other tree species, such as white pine, red spruce, sugar maple, beech, and yellow birch. The tree grows best in cool, moist places. Hemlock is very tolerant of shade and will survive many years in the undergrowth of dense forests. The trees are handsome when planted for ornament or shade.

The foliage of eastern hemlock is particularly graceful and especially lovely in early summer when each branchlet is tipped with the delicate light green of new growth. The needles ordinarily are dark green and shiny on the upper surface, and pale green and dull beneath with two bands of white dots. They are flat, ⅜ to ⅝ in. (0.95 to 1.6 cm) long and ¹⁄₁₆ in. (0.15 cm) wide, rounded or notched at the tip, minutely stalked at the base, and attached to the branchlets by short stalks, which persist after the leaves fall. Although spirally arranged around the twig, the leaves appear to be in two rows, like a flat spray.

Eastern hemlock cones are among the smallest of the pine family, being about ⅝ to ¾ in. (1.6 to 1.9 cm) long. At maturity in autumn, they are reddish brown and hang down singly from short stalks, usually remaining on the tree during the first winter. The tiny seeds are ¹⁄₁₆ in. (0.15 cm) long, each with a wing twice the length of the seed.

Eastern hemlock is valued principally for lumber and paper pulp. The lumber is used largely in building construction for farming, sheathing, subflooring, and roof boards, construction and repair, and general millwork. Besides lumber, eastern hemlock now furnishes large quantities of pulpwood, used principally in making newsprint and wrapping papers and some book and high-grade printing papers.

**Sitka Spruce** *(Picea sitchensis)*  Sometimes called the "glorious Sitka spruce" because it is a tree of splendid form, this species also produces wood of high commercial value. Larger than any other spruce in North America or perhaps in the world, its size is comparable to that of the huge Douglas-fir. The great size of the trees makes it possible to obtain clear lumber of almost any desired width and length of grain.

During World War I its exceptional fitness for aircraft construction was discovered and it became well known both in this country and abroad. Sitka spruce grows in a strip along the Pacific Coast from northern California to a little beyond Cook Inlet in Alaska. It is rarely found more than 40 miles from the coast.

Although Sitka spruce occasionally forms pure stands, it generally grows in mixture with other species. In Oregon and Washington it is associated with Douglas-fir, grand fir, western hemlock, and western redcedar. Forest-grown trees are tall and straight, with open conical crowns. Those approaching maturity have long cylindrical trunks, frequently free of branches for 40 to 80 ft. (12 to 24 m), and often with spreading bases.

**Figure 7-9**  Sitka spruce. *(Photo by C. Frank Brockman.)*

Mature trees in Washington and Oregon commonly measure from 4 to 6 ft. (1.2 to 1.8 m) in diameter and more than 200 ft. (60 m) in height [300 ft. (90 m) under ideal conditions] and attain an age of 400 to 450 years. In Alaska, average dimensions of mature trees are somewhat less.

Bark on trees of this species is thin. The sharp-tipped leaves are slightly flattened, lustrous green, and almost covered with white bands of numerous rows of stomata on the upper surface. They stand out from all sides of the branches and are often nearly at right angles to them, frequently bringing their white upper surface to view by a twist at the base. For the most part they remain on the tree from 8 to 11 years.

The cone grows on a short stalk. It is oblong and cylindrical, pale yellow, and often tinged with dark red when fully grown, becoming lustrous and pale yellow or reddish brown. The cones fall mostly during their first autumn and winter. The tiny, rounded seeds are pale reddish brown with narrow, slightly oblique wings.

The principal uses for Sitka spruce are lumber and paper pulp. Material sawed for lumber is used for construction purposes, but most of it goes into remanufactured products, including boxes and crates, planing-mill products, sash, doors, blinds, and general millwork, refrigerators and kitchen cabinets, woodenware, novelties, furniture, fixtures, and boat building.

**Redwood (*Sequoia sempervirens*)**   Redwood, also known as *coast redwood*, grows in a very narrow strip along the coast of California from the extreme southwestern corner of Oregon to 150 miles (240 km) below San Francisco. This area is about 500 miles (800 km) long and rarely more than 20 or 30 miles (32 to 48 km) wide, in a region of frequent fogs and considerable soil moisture.

The original redwood forests covered 1,454 million acres (588,000 ha), and in 1909 the total stand of this species was estimated to be over 100 billion board feet. By 1925 more than one-third of the redwood area had been logged. The amount of timber remaining in 1963 was placed at 31,257 million board feet on commercial forest land. With the help of public-spirited citizens, a number of mature groves have been purchased and placed under state or federal supervision so that future generations may know and enjoy the beauty and worth of these trees. The Redwood National Park was established in 1968 in Del Norte and Humboldt Counties in northern California.

Redwood is a rapid grower and reaches a greater height than any other American tree. In favorable situations, trees 20 years old may average 51 ft. (15.5 m) in height and 8 in. (20 cm) in diameter. Average mature trees are 200 to 240 ft. (60 to 75 m) high with diameters of 10 to 15 ft. (3 to 4.6 m). Exceptional individuals sometimes reach a height of 350 ft. (107 m), a diameter of nearly 20 ft. (6 m), and an age of approximately 2,000 years.

This large tree has small leaves and cones, for neither one is more than

**Figure 7-10**   Redwood. *(Photo by C. Frank Brockman.)*

an inch in length. The needles are olive green, flat and sharp-pointed. The purplish-brown cones are egg-shaped and only ½ in. (1.27 cm) wide. Under each cone scale are four or five brown seeds with winged margins. They are shed slowly and carried only relatively short distances by the wind.

A large proportion of the redwood lumber produced by the sawmills is used without further manufacture in the form of planks, dimension boards, joists, beams, stringers, and posts. Much of this material goes into framing for houses and industrial buildings, bridges and trestles, and other heavy construction.

The lumber is also remanufactured into planing-mill products, such as siding, flooring, ceiling, sash, doors, blinds, and general millwork. Among other major uses for redwood lumber are tanks, silos, caskets, outdoor furniture, boxes for cigars and tobacco, and musical instruments. A comparatively small amount of redwood is used for shingles and split products, including shakes (hand-split shingles), grape stakes, pickets, fence posts, and ties. Richly colored redwood paneling makes a very pleasing interior finish.

**Sugar Maple** *(Acer saccharum)*   Sugar maple, the official state tree of New York, Vermont, West Virginia, and Wisconsin, is one of the most valuable hardwoods in the United States. It is by far the most important, as well as the most abundant, of all the maples.

**Figure 7-11**   Sugar maple. *(Photo by W. D. Brush.)*

Sugar maple is widely distributed in the eastern United States and southeastern Canada, from eastern Minnesota to Maine, New Brunswick, and Nova Scotia and southward to northern Georgia, Alabama, Mississippi, and northeastern Texas.

Although sugar maple is a comparatively slow-growing species, it is vigorous, aggressive, and persistent. On suitable soil it is able to hold its own with any trees. It is one of the surest and most prolific seeders in the forest. Sugar maples planted in farm woodlots and along farm roads and boundaries will increase the value of farms and provide a source of revenue in maple products. It is also a popular shade tree.

Leaves of sugar maple are paired 3 to 5 in. (7.6 to 12.7 cm) across and lengthwise. They have three to five long pointed lobes. The divisions between the lobes are rounded. Leaves are dark green on the upper surface and lighter green underneath. In autumn the leaves turn clear yellow, orange, scarlet, and dark red. In spring yellowish-green flowers on long threadlike stalks appear with the leaves. Male and female flowers may be in the same cluster of flowers or in separate clusters. The fruit consists of a two-winged samara, or key. The wings are spreading and about 1 in. (2.5 cm) long. Each wing contains a seed. The seeds ripen in the fall and are scattered by the wind.

Sugar maple reaches a maximum height of 100 to 120 ft. (30 to 37 m), with a trunk diameter of 3 to 4 ft. (0.9 to 1.2 m) at breast height. In the forest the trunk may be clear for 50 to 60 ft. (15 to 18 m), but in the open the branches grow lower on the trunk and form an oval-shaped crown.

Sugar maple wood is heavy, hard, strong, tough, and compact. It takes an excellent polish. Its heartwood is light reddish brown, and its sapwood is generally white, sometimes tinged with reddish brown. It is not durable in contact with the soil.

Sugar maple is one of the best and most durable floor woods, and large amounts are used for this purpose. It is the best wood for shoe lasts because it is hard, finishes smooth, checks very little when carefully seasoned, and does not warp out of shape. Sugar maple is the only wood used for bowling pins. This species is used extensively in making furniture. Although it is usually straight-grained, sugar maple provides most of the figured maple, such as bird's-eye, wavy, and curly maple, used in the manufacture of furniture. It is also used for planing-mill products, boxes and crates, agricultural implements, vehicles, musical instruments, sporting and athletic goods, and woodenware. It makes excellent fuelwood. As its name implies, sugar maple is the source of maple sugar and syrup.

**White Ash** *(Fraxinus americana)* White ash is a valuable hardwood as well as the most important of the sixteen native species of ash in the United States. Five others also of commercial value are green ash, black ash, pumpkin ash, Oregon ash, and blue ash. Three eastern species—white ash (including Biltmore ash), green ash (including red ash), and black ash—produce probably 90 percent of the total cut, with white ash alone making up 40 percent.

Not forming pure stands, the species occurs singly or in small groups with other hardwoods, such as basswood, yellow-poplar, beech, maples, oaks, and hickories, sometimes with such conifers as eastern hemlock and eastern white pine. Thriving on a variety of soils, it is most frequently found in comparatively well-drained locations, along streams, and on north and east slopes. White ash is widespread in eastern United States, New Brunswick, and Nova Scotia. It extends southward to northern Florida and Louisiana and northeastern Texas.

The paired or opposite, pinnately compound leaves are 8 to 12 in. (20 to 30 cm) long, with eight to nine, usually seven, short-stalked elliptic leaf-

**Figure 7-12** White ash. *(Photo by C. Frank Brockman.)*

lets. These are 2 ½ to 5 in. (6.3 to 12.7 cm) long, mostly short-pointed, inconspicuously toothed or without teeth on edges, dark green on upper surface, and paler beneath. Flowers appear in spring before the leaves, male and female on separate trees. The staminate flowers form dense reddish-purple masses, but the inconspicuous greenish pistillate flowers grow in more open clusters.

Ash is used principally for handles, furniture, boxes, baskets, crating, and sporting and athletic goods. Baseball bats are made almost exclusively from ash. Other sporting goods for which ash is widely used are oars, paddles, tennis rackets, snowshoes, skis, polo sticks, hockey sticks, and bows.

**White Oak** *(Quercus alba)* The oaks are among the most important hardwood species in America. They are important because of the large quantity of oak timber available as compared with other hardwoods and because of the strength and beauty of the wood. Nearly 60 species of oaks grow in the United States; they are scattered over practically all parts of the country, especially toward the South and West. In addition there are numerous varieties, hybrids, and shrubby species.

White oak is probably the most outstanding native timber species of the oak group. Forest-grown white oaks have long, clean trunks that taper very little until they branch into comparatively narrow tops. When white

**Figure 7-13** White oak. *(Photo by C. Frank Brockman.)*

oak grows in the open, the trunk is short and often of large size, the top forming an impressive dome with many great branches gnarled and twisted, and the entire tree giving an impression of sturdiness and strength.

White oak formerly occupied extensive areas of rich land in the group of states centering about Kentucky, and trees 400 years old, 6 ft. (1.8 m) in diameter and 130 ft. (40 m) high were not uncommon. Forest trees 3 ft. (0.9 m) in diameter are now rare. In this country the reputation of oak as a high-grade, all-purpose wood was built largely on white oak. It is doubtful that any other native oak possesses the combination of strength, hardness, toughness, ability to stay in place, durability, and beauty of grain to the same degree as this species.

White oak grows from southeastern Minnesota to Maine and into southeastern New Brunswick, and south to northern Florida and Louisiana and southeastern Texas.

White oak is a valuable tree for ornamental planting, provided it has plenty of space and good soil for its development. Although it grows slowly, in a comparatively few years it will begin to show the characteristic impressive form.

Our native oaks are often divided into two groups: white oaks and red (or black) oaks. The fruit of the white oak ripens in 1 year. The lobes of the leaves are rounded and free from bristles, and the bark and wood are ligh ₍

colored. The fruit of the red oaks, except the California live oak, matures in 2 years. The leaves or their lobes are tipped with bristles, and the bark and wood are darker than in the white oaks. The fruit of all oaks is the acorn, which distinguishes the oaks and the tanoaks from all other trees. Few oaks bear acorns before they are 20 years old.

Oak is one of the oldest furniture woods. A third to a half of the oak lumber manufactured is used for furniture and other products such as flooring, railroad cars, boxes and crates, and millwork. Smaller amounts of lumber are consumed in making pallets; radio, phonograph, television, and sewing machine cabinets; agricultural implements; and building ships and boats. Oak is also used extensively for railroad ties, fuelwood, cooperage, and mine timbers. The bark of some oaks is an important source of tanning materials.

**American Basswood (*Tilia americana*)**   American basswood is a compact symmetrical tree valued for its shade and beauty, as well as for the quality of its wood. It is widely distributed over much of the northern half of the states east of the Mississippi.

American basswood grows rapidly and under a wide variety of soil and climatic conditions, making its best growth in moist, fertile soil and under

**Figure 7-14**   American basswood. *(Photo by C. Frank Brockman.)*

the climatic conditions of the northern part of its range. It is recognized as an important soil-improving tree. It grows in mixture with other species and only rarely forms pure stands. This species reaches a height of 75 to 130 ft. (23 to 40 m), with a diameter of 3 to 4 ft. (0.9 to 1.2 m). Under favorable conditions, trees sometimes attain a height of 140 ft. (43 m) and a diameter of 4 ½ ft. (1.37 m). The life-span may reach to 100 or 140 years.

The bark of American basswood is dark brown and deeply furrowed on trunks, gray on the branches, and reddish on twigs. The leaves are heart shaped, 3 to 6 in. (7.6 to 15.2 cm) long, and saw-toothed. The flowers develop into clusters of woody, pealike balls, covered with a short thick brownish wool and containing two or three seeds. These fruit clusters remain attached to the leafy bract, which later acts as a wing to bear them away on the wind. They ripen in September or October.

The heartwood of basswood is creamy brown with occasional darker streaks. The sapwood is wide and creamy white or pale brown, merging more or less gradually into the heartwood. Basswood is light in weight, soft, uniform in texture, straight-grained, holds nails well, and has low strength values. It is slightly softer and lighter in the air-dry condition than yellow-poplar, cottonwood, and white pine, which are often put to the same uses. The wood is without taste or odor. In damp situations basswood discolors and is subject to mold and decay.

Basswood is used mainly in the manufacture of products made from lumber, although veneer, cooperage stock, and excelsior are also made from it. Limited and decreasing quantities are used for pulpwood. Among the products manufactured from basswood lumber are boxes, apiarists' supplies, woodenware, trunks and suitcases, venetian blinds, shade rollers, picture frames, molding, and furniture.

**American Beech** *(Fagus grandifolia)*    American beech has long been a favorite tree because of its unusual beauty and dense shade. With its smooth bluish-gray bark, its delicate tracery of graceful branches and twigs, and its shiny pointed buds, beech is as lovely in winter as in summer when clothed in a mantle of dark green foliage.

Beech usually occurs in mixture with other hardwoods and, with sugar maple and yellow birch, forms the typical northern hardwood forest. This species is found on a variety of soils where the surface layers remain moist and thrives on rich alluvial bottom lands. A slow-growing species, beech withstands shade better than most of its faster growing but shorter lived associates and often displaces them. Trees may reach a height of 100 ft. (30 m) and a diameter of 3 ft. (0.9 m), or occasionally larger. Beech may attain an age of 300 years or more. Small trees sprout readily, but trees of all sizes may develop large numbers of root suckers, usually, but not necessarily, after injury to the stem or the roots. Distribution of American beech is mostly east of the Mississippi River and southward to northern Florida.

**Figure 7-15**   American beech. *(Photo by C. Frank Brockman.)*

The elliptic, short-stalked leaves grow in two rows, 2 ½ to 5 in. (6.3 to 12.7 cm) long, usually hairless, and coarsely toothed, each of the parallel lateral veins ending in a tooth. The dull upper surface is dark bluish green and the underside light green. The inconspicuous flowers appear after the leaves unfold, male and female being borne on the same tree. The seeds mature in 1 year. The fruit is a prickly burr usually containing two triangular, pale brown, thin-shelled beechnuts about ½ in. (1.27 cm) long, which are sweet and edible. They are also excellent wildlife food.

Beech is used principally for lumber, railroad ties, veneer, pulpwood, cooperage, and fuel. The lumber goes into the manufacture of boxes, crates, baskets, and fruit packages; planing-mill products such as flooring; furniture, particularly chairs; handles; woodenware and novelties; toys and spools. Beech has no characteristic taste or odor; consequently, it is especially suitable for food containers. Because it can be satisfactorily bent after steaming, the wood is also well suited for the curved parts of chairs. This species is not decay resistant in contact with the soil, but though difficult to treat with preservatives, it is used in large quantities for ties.

**Yellow Birch *(Betula alleghaniensis)***   Yellow birch, the most important native birch, is a common and valuable forest tree of the Northeastern and Lake States.

**Figure 7-16**   Yellow birch. *(Photo by C. Frank Brockman.)*

The best stands are near the Canadian border, where mature trees are 60 to 80 ft. (18 to 24 m) tall and 1 to 3 ft. (0.3 to 0.9 m) or larger in trunk diameter. Relatively slow growing and long lived, the trees often take 150 years to reach sawtimber size. Generally yellow birch is found on moist, cool uplands, such as north-facing slopes of mountains. It is characteristic of the northeastern hardwoods, associated with sugar maple, beech, eastern hemlock, red spruce, balsam fir, and eastern white pine. Moderately tolerant of shade, forest-grown trees develop long clean trunks, which make good lumber. Seedlings are numerous in the forests, especially on moss-covered logs, stumps, and boulders or where the forest floor has been disturbed.

The elliptic or egg-shaped leaves 3 to 4 in. (7.6 to 10 cm) long are often in pairs. They are dull dark green above and yellow green beneath becoming yellow in autumn. Long- or short-pointed, the leaves are sharply and doubly toothed.

The upright fruit is 1 to 1½ in. (2.5 to 3.8 cm) long, conelike and elliptic in shape and ripens in late July and August. The small winged nutlets ⅛ in. (0.31 cm) long, produced in abundance, are wind-disseminated.

The lumber production is gradually declining, probably because this birch has been heavily logged and does not reproduce well on many cutover lands. The principal uses of birch are lumber, veneer, distillation products, and crossties. Lumber and veneer go into such products as furniture, boxes, and millwork, including interior finish, doors, plywood, and fixtures. The largest and best logs are used for veneer, and much of the low-grade lumber serves for boxes and crates. Birches are among the leading furniture woods, ranking fifth in quantity. Because of its handsome color, the heartwood is taken for the visible parts of furniture, and the sapwood goes into inside sections. Among the other uses for birch wood are woodenware and novelties, shuttles, spools, bobbins, handles, and dowels. A small quantity is made into barrels.

**American Elm** *(Ulmus americana)*    Six species of elm grow naturally in the United States—American elm (including its variety Florida elm), slippery elm, rock elm, winged elm, cedar elm, and September elm. Although all of these are native only to the territory east of the Rocky Mountains, they can be successfully planted in the Western states. American elm perhaps has the widest range, but slippery elm is a close second. Both are generally distributed east of the Rockies. The distribution of the other species is limited.

American elm is the largest of the elms in this country. Perhaps best known as one of the most beautiful trees shading our city streets, its lovely

**Figure 7-17**   American elm. *(Photo by C. Frank Brockman.)*

vaselike form naturally graces many northern landscapes. Unfortunately millions of American elms have died in recent years from the Dutch elm disease (see Chap. 19).

This elm grows on moist, rich lands along the borders of streams or on low fertile hills. In such favorable situations, trees may attain a height of 100 ft. (30 m) and a diameter of 6 ft. (1.8 m), although average trees are 60 to 70 ft. (18 to 21 m) high and 4 to 5 ft. (1.2 to 1.5 m) in diameter.

The lopsided leaves are 4 to 6 in. (10 to 15 cm) long, rather thick, double-toothed on the margin, and generally slightly rough on the upper surface and softly hairy on the lower with very pronounced veins running in parallel lines from midrib to leaf edge. The flowers are small and greenish, and are on slender stalks, sometimes an inch long. They appear in early spring before the leaves. The fruit is a green oval-shaped samara, in which the center seed portion is entirely surrounded by the wing. A deep notch in the end of the wing is distinctive of the species. The seed ripens in the spring and is scattered by the wind.

As a source of lumber, American elm (known to the trade as *white elm*) is by far the most important. Considerable amounts are also cut from slippery elm and rock elm, but the other species are of slight commercial importance.

Lumber from the different species of elm is used for many products. It is used principally in the manufacture of furniture, plywood, boxes and crates, containers, and pallets. Other important uses are millwork and fixtures; handles, chiefly of the bent-wood type; caskets and burial boxes; musical instruments; sporting goods; woodenware; novelties; and toys. In the past the principal use of elm has been for slack cooperage staves sliced directly from the log, and elm is still considered better than any other wood commonly used for slack staves.

**Yellow-Poplar** (*Liriodendron tulipifera*)  Yellow-poplar or tuliptree is one of the most valuable broadleaved trees or hardwoods in the United States. Common in forests and woodlots, this tree is also widely planted around homes and in parks for both shade and ornament.

Yellow-poplar is native in all states east of the Mississippi River, except Maine, New Hampshire, and Wisconsin, and extends westward into Missouri, Arkansas and Louisiana. It is the state tree of Indiana, Kentucky, and Tennessee.

In size, yellow-poplar ranks among the tallest native broad-leaved trees; its maximum recorded height of 200 ft. (61 m) exceeds all except black cottonwood of the Far West. The usual height at maturity is 80 to 120 ft. (24 to 36 m) and the trunk diameter 2 to 6 ft. (0.6 to 1.8 m) but giants with trunks 8 to 12 ft. (2.4 to 3.6 m) in diameter have been reported. The straight columnar trunk develops without branches for much of its length. Yellow-poplar grows rapidly and attains an age of 200 to 250 years or more.

**Figure 7-18**   Yellow-poplar. *(Photo by C. Frank Brockman.)*

This species develops best in moist, deep, rich, neutral soils, such as mountain coves and bottom lands. Yellow-poplar must have plenty of light for growth, and the young plants will not survive in dense shade. The trees usually occur in mixed stands with other species such as hickories, black walnut, butternut, white oak, and basswood. Pure stands also occur, often on the most productive land. Yellow-poplar propagates from stump sprouts as well as from seed.

The name tuliptree refers to the large handsome tulip-shaped flowers 1 ½ to 2 in. (3.8 to 5 cm) in width and length. Borne in large numbers in spring, the perfect flowers are greenish yellow with darker yellow and deep orange at the base of the six petals.

The leaves, flowers, and fruits are all distinctive and easy to identify. Of unusual squarish shape with four to six points, the leaves measure 3 to 6 in. (7.6 to 15 cm) in length and width and have a wide-notched or nearly straight apex. They are shiny dark green, paler beneath, and turn clear yellow in fall. The upright conelike fruit 2 ½ to 3 in. (6.3 to 7.6 cm) long matures in autumn. It is composed of about 80 light brown, narrow, scale-like samaras, each usually containing one good and one aborted seed near the base and shedding from the axis. Although produced in abundance, the seeds germinate poorly, apparently due to inadequate or incompatible pollination.

Yellow-poplar is valuable for many purposes, but principally for lumber, veneer, particle board, and pulpwood. The wood is widely used for furniture (especially corestock) and fixtures and for millwork and siding. It is also manufactured into boxes and crates; radio, television, and sewing machine cabinets; caskets; musical instruments; and excelsior as well as numerous other products. Large quantities of veneer are used, especially as inner plies and crossboards in hardwood plywood manufacture. The large size of the trunks and comparative freedom from defects make it possible to saw unusually broad clear planks.

**Sweetgum** *(Liquidambar styraciflua)*   Sweetgum (also widely known as *redgum*) is one of the most beautiful and important of our hardwood trees. Although growing as far north as southwestern Connecticut, it is primarily a tree of the Southern and Southeastern states, where it attains its best development.

Sweetgum trees may reach large size, especially in the South. Diameters range from 1 ½ to 3 ft. (0.45 to 0.9 m), and heights vary from 60 to 120 ft. (18 to 36 m) at maturity. In exceptional cases sweetgum may attain a diameter of 5 ft. (1.5 m) and a height of about 150 ft. (45 m). The biggest trees are usually found in rich southern bottom lands subject to flooding. Straight, clear trunks are common in forest-grown trees.

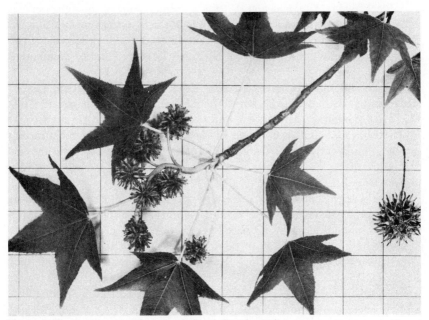

**Figure 7-19**   Sweetgum. *(Photo by C. Frank Brockman.)*

The leaves of sweetgum are perhaps its most distinguishing characteristic. They are star-shaped, having five to seven points, up to 7 in. (18 cm) broad, and are responsible for the name "star-leaved gum" by which the tree is sometimes known. The leaves are aromatic. They are conspicuous in the fall by their brillant color, typically deep red but varying to pale yellow, orange, and bronze. The flowers unfold with the leaves, male and female occurring on the same tree. The compound fruit is a spherical head, 1 to 1 ½ in. (2.5 to 3.8 cm) in diameter, made up of many capsules ending in projecting spines. The fruit frequently clings to the tree on its long swinging stem until late in the winter.

Because of the handsome grain and coloring of the wood and the ease with which it can be finished, sweetgum is used extensively for inside trim and furniture. In fact, for this use it exceeds all other American species except yellow-poplar. Much of the sweetgum lumber shipped from this country previous to World War II returned in furniture under the pseudonyms "satin walnut" and "Circassian walnut." A large amount of sweetgum veneer and lumber is used for containers; considerable quantities go into slack barrels. Large amounts of sweetgum lumber are also used for sewing machine and kitchen cabinets, moldings, and musical instruments. The use in decorative wall panels has increased because of the grain variations and coloring natural to the wood.

**Black Walnut** *(Juglans nigra)*    Black walnut is one of the most beloved of American trees, as well as a most valuable commercial species. Besides producing a wood having a rare combination of desirable qualities, it is the source of nutritious nuts that have become a food product of commercial value.

Black walnut at its best is a tree of majestic size and surpassing beauty. Trees having diameters from 4 to 6 ft. (1.2 to 1.8 m) and a height of 150 ft. (45 m) were common at one time, but today a tree 2 ½ ft. (0.75 m) through and 100 ft. (30 m) tall is unusual. Black walnut is one of the most rapidly growing hardwoods and is decidedly intolerant of shade except in the first few years of its life. It grows in a mixture with other hardwoods and is seldom found in pure stands.

The species is native to the Eastern part of the United States, growing from western Massachusetts to eastern Nebraska and southward to northwestern Florida and eastern Texas.

The bark of black walnut is thick, dark brown and is divided by rather deep fissures into rounded ridges. The alternate leaves are compound, consisting of 15 to 23 yellowish-green leaflets in a featherlike arrangement along both sides of a leafstalk, which is 1 to 2 ft. (0.3 to 0.6 m) long. The leaflets are about 3 in. (7.6 cm) long, extremely tapering at the end and toothed along the margin. The nuts are borne singly or in pairs, and enclosed in a solid green husk which does not split even after the fruit is ripe.

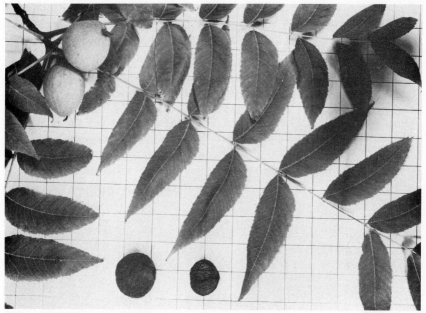

**Figure 7-20**   Black walnut. *(Photo by C. Frank Brockman.)*

The nut is black with a very hard, thick, finely ridged shell, enclosing a rich, oily, edible, and highly nutritious kernel.

Black walnut is used principally for lumber and veneer in such products as furniture, gunstocks, fixtures, radio and television cabinets, musical instruments, caskets, interior finish, and sewing machines. To a limited extent it is also used for railroad ties, fence posts, and fuelwood, although defective material generally goes into these products. The nuts have long been an article of food, and in recent years shelled black walnuts have become a commercial product. *502*

In Appendix C (page 429) are the common and scientific names of trees mentioned throughout the text.

## BIBLIOGRAPHY

Brockman, C. Frank. 1968. *Trees of North America: A Field Guide*, Western Publishing Company, Inc., New York.

Harlow, William M., and Ellwood S. Harrar. 1969. *Textbook of Dendrology*, 5th ed., McGraw-Hill Book Company, New York.

Ketchum, Richard M. 1970. *The Secret Life of the Forest*, conceived and produced in cooperation with the St. Regis Paper Company, American Heritage Publishing Co., Inc., New York.

Little, E. L. 1953. *Check List of Native and Naturalized Trees of the United States*, Agricultural Handbook no. 41, U.S. Forest Service.

Shirley, Hardy L. 1973. *Forestry and Its Career Opportunities*, 3d ed., McGraw-Hill Book Company, New York.

Smith, Guy-Harold (ed.). 1971. *Conservation of Natural Resources*, 4th ed., John Wiley & Sons, Inc., New York.

Society of American Foresters. 1971. *Terminology of Forest Science, Technology, Practice and Products,* edited by F.C. Ford-Robertson, Washington DC.

U.S. Department of Agriculture, Forest Service. 1965. *Silvics of Forest Trees of the United States*, Agriculture Handbook no. 271.

Vereck, Leslie A., and Elbert L. Little, Jr. 1972. *Alaska Trees and Shrubs*, Agriculture Handbook no. 410. Forest Service, U.S. Department of Agriculture.

# Chapter 8

# Where Our Forests Are and What They Produce

In previous chapters we have learned why forests occur where they do. We have reviewed many of the values, services, and benefits modern human beings receive from the forests. But we are looking at this subject with considerable hindsight and knowledge compared to the first explorers and settlers. Hence, it is hard for us to imagine the feelings with which the explorers of the seventeenth and eighteenth centuries viewed the virgin forests of the American continent. Europe was already crowded and partitioned into estates; wood was scarce and expensive. As explorers, with no need to prepare the soil for tillage, they could afford to marvel when confronted with unending miles of luxuriant trees. Charlevoix wrote of the forests of the Lake States, explored by him in 1721, as "the greatest forests of the world," and felt that "there is nothing perhaps in nature comparable

to them." The colonists of the Atlantic seaboard 100 years earlier saw the
forest in a different light—to them this was a barrier to be cut through for
roads and to be cleared for farms. Considering the multiplicity of their
problems, we can forgive these colonists if the vast potential of such forests
did not seem important to them.

These courageous settlers were not so much given to description as
some who came even earlier. For it is recorded that Thorfinn Karlsefni, the
Viking, in A.D. 1012, somewhere on the eastern shore of North America
"caused the trees to be felled, and hewed into timbers, wherewith to load
his ship, and the wood was placed on a cliff to dry." These probably were
timbers from a land "level and covered with woods," which another passing
Viking, Bjarni Heriulfsson, reported 26 years later as he skirted the shores
seeking his way back to Greenland after being driven off his course in a
storm.

More than 500 years later, in 1539, Don Ferdinando de Soto found
traveling in Florida "cumbersome with woods" and trees "as big and as
rancke as though they grew in gardens digged and watered." Four years
later his men were building small ships—"brigandines"—from "wilde pine-
trees," on the banks of the Mississippi.

Captain John Smith, in 1614, also issued certain publicity on a country
farther north and back on the Atlantic Coast. He found the land "over-
grown with all sorts of excellent goode woodes for building houses, boats,
barks or shippes." Still farther north and a little earlier, Hudson and Champlain had written of "goodly oakes" and "fine trees." And so the new
continent was explored and reported until in 1805 Lewis and Clark were
finding in the northern Rockies "the top of a mountain covered with pine"
and, going down a western slope, "arbor vitae . . . from two to six feet in
diameter." Finally, the observing Captain Lewis records that the "whole
neighbourhood of the Coast is supplied with great quantities of excellent
timber" (Butler, 1935).

The vast expanse of original forest over which these men might travel
covered almost one-half the total area of the country and is estimated at
822 million acres (332.7 million ha). The trees varied in size; the wood, in
hardness and workability. Soft and easily seasoned woods were usually
available to the early settlers. The situation was therefore unlike some of the
more recently penetrated tropical forests where few specimens of any given
tree, such as teak in Burma, are harvested or in West Africa where only one
tree on several acres may be economically available.

This diversity of species no doubt impressed Europeans whose home
countries yielded comparatively few species.

With the building of the country the forests have shrunk for better or
for worse to about one-half the original area. More than 400 million acres
(161.9 million ha) have passed into private ownership, some of them to be

abused and abandoned, some to be cleared and farmed or settled or held for speculation. A growing acreage, particularly in the South and West, and to a less but increasing extent in other parts of the country, is held for permanent and productive forest management.

## FOREST TYPES AND REGIONS

In such great areas as the United States and its possessions, there are hundreds of groupings of species known as forest types and subtypes. There are also broad characteristics which mark great geographical regions. Within these regions the species have determined to a large extent the character of forest industries.

The forests of Eastern United States differ widely from those of the West and are completely separated by the Great Plains, which are practically treeless. The Eastern forests have both hardwoods and softwoods of commercial importance and, probably because of favorable rainfall conditions, are widely distributed. The Western forests, although rich in variety and commercial value of softwoods, have few important hardwoods and cover considerable less area than those in the East. These two groups of forests meet in northern Canada.

There are six major "natural forest regions" or "forests" in the United States. Three are east of the Great Plains: the Northern Forest, the Central Hardwood Forest, and the Southern Forest. The Rocky Mountain, Pacific Coast, and Alaskan Forests are west of the prairie states. These forests are indicated on the map of Fig. 8-1 and will now be discussed individually. All tree names are in accord with *Check List of Native and Naturalized Trees of the United States* (Little, 1953). The scientific names for all common names used appear in Appendix C.

**The Northern Forest** This region covers almost all New England, New York, and the Lake States—Michigan, Wisconsin, and Minnesota. Also, it extends in a strip from northern and central Pennsylvania southwest through the Appalachian Mountains to northern Georgia. This forest is found in 19 states. Most of the soils of this region or forest can be classified as poor agriculturally, although the forest has given way to many farms. Some of the poorer ones are surrounded with rock fences thrown up through years of clearing, but for more than two centuries they have yielded a living only through application of intense human effort. The Northern Forest presents a vast problem in planning and in reconciling its use for mining, agriculture, recreation, manufacturing, and for regulation and utilization of rainfall runoff.

Of the five trees whose ranges are most characteristic of the Northern Forest, four are conifers. These are balsam fir, northern white-cedar, east-

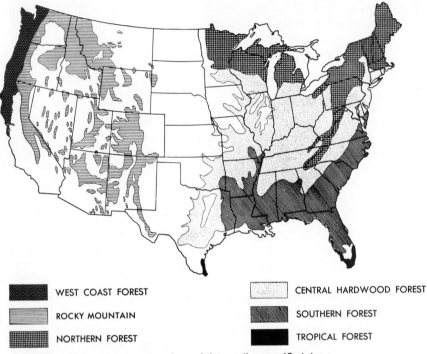

| | | | |
|---|---|---|---|
| WEST COAST FOREST | | CENTRAL HARDWOOD FOREST | |
| ROCKY MOUNTAIN | | SOUTHERN FOREST | |
| NORTHERN FOREST | | TROPICAL FOREST | |

**Figure 8-1**  The natural forest regions of the contiguous 48 states.

ern white pine, and eastern hemlock. The characteristic hardwood is the yellow birch. Sugar maple is a common tree also, but it is even more typical of the forest region to the south.

Within the Northern Forest (Fig. 8-2) are several local forest types of importance. In the northern portion of Minnesota, Wisconsin, and Michigan are eastern white pine and red pine. Jack pine, the principal pine marketed in the Lake States today, now occupies great areas in these three states where white and red pines were once abundant. It was only after logging and repeated uncontrolled fires in the late 1800s and early 1900s destroyed the humus layer of the soil and the seed source of red and white pines that jack pine flourished. In moist or swampy areas northern white-cedar, black spruce, and tamarack are common associates. Balsam fir requires moderate moisture, and in wet places in the northern part of the region it may occur in pure stands. On drier sites of the north it occurs with white spruce; in the northeast with white and red spruce; and in the Appalachians with red spruce.

A common hardwood type throughout the Northern Forest is a mixture of American beech with yellow birch and sugar maple. Eastern hemlock is commonly associated with these three hardwoods. Aspen (quaking and bigtooth), a producer of root suckers, and paper birch, a prolific seeder, are both common over large burned areas of the Lake States where moist mineral soil has been exposed. A dozen more hardwoods are found to some extent, and these include walnuts, hickories, elms, ashes, and American basswood.

In the southern part of the Northern Forest (Appalachian Mountains), in addition to the red spruce and balsam fir mentioned above, are the shortleaf, eastern white, pitch, and Virginia pines; eastern hemlock; white, northern red, and scarlet oaks; yellow-poplar; magnolia; black tupelo; and other hardwoods common in the northern part. American chestnut was at one time the most abundant tree in the Appalachians. The chestnut blight, a virulent foreign disease which was accidentally introduced into the United States in 1903, has nearly obliterated this once fine tree.

There are small areas in the eastern part of this forest where one might imagine oneself in the rugged and timbered iron or copper ranges of the Lake Superior country. Along the New York shores of Lake Ontario a person might readily feel that this was northern Wisconsin. It is difficult to think, however, of the entire forest as having much in common socially, industrially or in the matter of population. The eastern section saw the

**Figure 8-2** The Northern Forest. Eastern white pine about 100 ft (30 m) tall. Superior National Forest, Minnesota. *(Courtesy of the U.S. Forest Service.)*

earliest establishment in this country of sawmills, pulp mills, wood-distillation plants, and shipyards. It witnessed a westward march of forest industries to the Lake States as the virgin forests of the Atlantic seaboard were consumed, but it is now coming back into the forest production picture. About the middle of the last century, New York, Pennsylvania, and Maine were the leaders in lumber production. By 1870 Michigan, which had for 10 years been a runner-up, nosed into first place and stayed out in front until 1890. Minnesota and Wisconsin also produced heavily from 1860 to 1890. Shortly after 1899 the Northern Forest lost its lumber production lead to the Southern Forest.

It was the Northern Forest that furnished a large share of the lumber used in this country for the first 250 years of settlement. The bulk of this lumber came from eastern white pine. Today it is still considered the most desirable northern lumber species, followed closely by red pine and white and red spruce. A lower-quality softwood lumber is manufactured from jack pine, eastern hemlock, tamarack, and balsam fir. Until recently the Northern Forest was the leader in the production of pulpwood. The three species of spruce and balsam fir are the most desirable pulp species, although all northern conifers except tamarack and northern white-cedar are used successfully today in one pulp process or another. Aspen, a "Cinderella tree" once considered a forest weed, accounts for nearly half of the pulpwood harvest in the Lake States. The main use for the very durable northern white-cedar is for poles, posts, and shingles.

The region's hardwoods have kept thousands of woodenware plants supplied. Handles, flooring, furniture, ladder rungs, novelties, and athletic equipment such as bats and bowling pins are made from the more dense woods such as sugar maple, yellow birch, black cherry, white ash, and American beech. A highly prized veneer for kitchen cabinets is made from yellow birch. Visit any north woods curio shop and you will see a variety of novelties made from the bark of paper birch. Tons of charcoal today are produced from the lower-grade dense hardwoods and some from wood residue. Basswood lumber is used for cooperage and woodenware; as veneer it is made into cabinet linings, mirror backings, drawing boards, and utilized in other places where a fine-grained, soft wood is desirable. Basswood flowers are favored by some bee keepers for the tart honey they yield. Millions of Christmas trees are cut annually in this region from both native and nonnative evergreens grown on hundreds of plantations.

**The Central Hardwood Forest**   This vast area of broad-leaved trees stretches from Cape Cod almost to the Rio Grande in Texas and northwest to the southern half of Minnesota. Its western boundary is very irregular where it meets the Prairie Plains. This forest is invaded by the Northern Forest along the Appalachian Mountains and by the Southern Forest up the Mississippi Valley to southeastern Missouri. The Central Hardwood

Forest is scattered over a greater area than any other of the great forests of the United States, except the Rocky Mountain Forest, and touches about 30 states.

In numbers and usefulness of species the region measures up well with the others, but because much of the forest originally occupied deep rich soils, thousands of productive farms have appeared. Traveling in summer from Washington, D.C., approximately straight west to St. Louis, Missouri, one is impressed not only by forest of almost tropical luxuriance but also by prosperous and stable agricultural development. Most of the time one will be within the limits of the Central Hardwood Forest (Fig. 8-3).

More than 20 genera and twice as many species of trees are represented here. Because of the great diversity of climate and soils, however, few species grow throughout the entire region. White oak, the region's most important and widely distributed tree, is one exception. Other oaks include the northern red; southern red; black, bur, and chestnut oaks; and, to a lesser extent, the post, overcup, swamp white, and chinkapin oaks. Most of these trees lose their identity and become either "white" or "red" oaks when

**Figure 8-3**   The Central Hardwood Forest. White ash over 100 ft (30 m) tall, with sugar maple associates. Hoosier National Forest, Indiana. *(Courtesy of U.S. Forest Service.)*

manufactured into forest products. American beech, sugar maple, American and slippery elms, black willow, eastern cottonwood, black walnut, shagbark and bitternut hickories, hackberry, yellow-poplar, American sycamore, black cherry, honeylocust, and white and green ashes, although enjoying differing degrees of importance and abundance, are all found throughout the Central Hardwood Region. Other less widespread species of hardwoods include butternut; several more oaks and hickories; sweet and river birch; cucumbertree; sassafras; sweetgum; black locust; black, red, and silver maples; Ohio and yellow buckeye; American basswood; black tupelo; black and blue ashes; osage-orange; and northern catalpa. American chestnut is nearly a forgotten tree, for the same reason mentioned in the discussion of the Northern Forest.

The conifers are confined to shortleaf, pitch, and Virginia pine; eastern redcedar; and occasionally eastern hemlock.

With such a variety of tree species, it is understandable that the Central Hardwood Forest produces a large assortment of forest products. Among the more important are the products from the white oaks—railroad ties, tight cooperage, flooring, furniture, cabinets, and ship and boat timbers. From the harder maples come flooring, fancy veneer, furniture, and a wealth of sporting equipment such as bowling pins and croquet mallets.

Handles of various shapes and sizes come from the hickories, oaks, and ashes. Fine quality furniture, cabinets, veneer, and gun stocks are produced from black walnut. Other cabinet woods are black cherry and yellow-poplar. Hardwood lumber is cut from sweetgum, elm, and sycamore. Other products such as mine timbers, posts, poles, piling, light millwork, and a host of other lesser items, come from the hardwoods of this forest.

The fruit of such trees as American beech and the walnuts, oaks, and hickories is called mast, and serves wildlife as a food.

From eastern redcedar, a highly aromatic and colorful wood with moth-repelling properties, comes material for chests and closets. Wood pulp for paper products comes not only from the region's limited conifers but also from an ever-increasing tonnage of hardwood species, such as cottonwood, oak, beech, and maple, to name a few.

Over the past 30 to 40 years several national forests have been established in this forest region. There are two national parks and several small but important state forests. Generally, the majority of the private forest land is in small ownerships.

The vast extent of this forest, originally covering no less than 150 million acres (60.7 million ha) and now scattered over about 132 million acres (53.4 million ha), makes it less a unit, socially or economically, than any of the great forest regions.

**The Southern Forest**   This forest extends along the Atlantic Coastal Plains from southern Virginia south to all but the lower end of Florida, and west along the Gulf Plains to east Texas, northward to Oklahoma, and up the Mississippi Valley into Missouri. Four important pines characterize the Southern Forest—shortleaf, longleaf, slash, and loblolly (Fig. 8-4). Two less significant pines are pitch and pond pines. In traveling, one may suddenly find oneself out of the pine forest and into swamps supporting baldcypress and water tupelo. In moist bottom lands will be found sweetgum, black tupelo (blackgum), and numerous oaks, such as Nuttall, willow, cherry-bark, water and swamp chestnut oak, and in other moist areas, American elm, red maple, and eastern cottonwood. Less common bottom-land species are sugarberry, swamp poplar, water hickory, planertree (waterelm), and common persimmon. The southern magnolia and live oak, the latter fes-tooned with "Spanish moss," are the picturesque southern trees of drier sites. Other upland trees include cucumbertree, yellow-poplar, pecan, mockernut hickory, American beech, and several more species of oak.

**Figure 8-4**  The Southern Forest. Loblolly and shortleaf pine. *(Courtesy of the Interna-tional Paper Company.)*

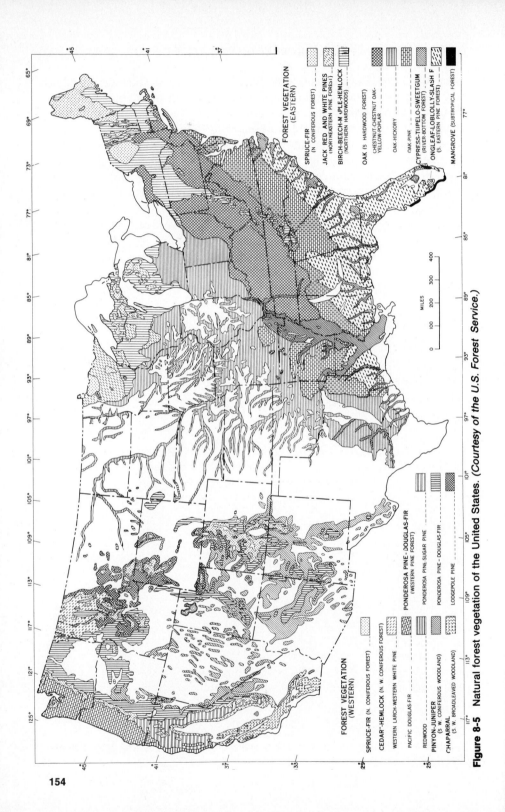

**Figure 8-5** Natural forest vegetation of the United States. *(Courtesy of the U.S. Forest Service.)*

FOREST VEGETATION (EASTERN)

SPRUCE-FIR (N CONIFEROUS FOREST)

JACK RED AND WHITE PINES (NORTHEASTERN PINE FOREST)

BIRCH-BEECH-M\PLE-HEMLOCK (NORTHERN HARDWOODS)

OAK (S HARDWOOD FOREST)

CHESTNUT-CHESTNUT OAK-YELLOW-POPLAR

OAK-HICKORY

OAK-PINE

CYPRESS-TUPELO-SWEETGUM (RIVER-BOTTOM FOREST)

ONGLEAF-LOBLOLLY-SLASH F (S. EASTERN PINE FOREST)

MANGROVE (SUBTROPICAL FOREST)

FOREST VEGETATION (WESTERN)

SPRUCE-FIR (N. CONIFEROUS FOREST)

CEDAR¨-HEMLOCK (N. W CONIFEROUS FOREST)

WESTERN LARCH-WESTERN WHITE PINE

PACIFIC DOUGLAS-FIR

REDWOOD

PINYON-JUNIPER (S. W CONIFEROUS WOODLAND)

CHAPARRAL (S. W BROADLEAVED WOODLAND)

PONDEROSA PINE-DOUGLAS-FIR (WESTERN PINE FOREST)

PONDEROSA PINE-SUGAR PINE

PONDEROSA PINE-DOUGLAS-FIR

LODGEPOLE PINE

MILES

0    100    200    300    400

This wide southeastern border of the United States was once the source of large timber production. It had captured the lumber lead from the Lake States group in about 1900 and held it until 1920, when the production lead shifted to the West Coast. The once great cotton industry of the South moved westward also; thus thousands of acres of plantations on sandy soil ill adapted to agriculture reverted to southern pine. Because of an abundant rainfall and a long growing season, these second-growth forests in comparatively few years produced huge volumes of wood more suited to high-grade wood pulp than lumber. The northern pulp industry, looking for places in which to expand, moved South. By 1972 approximately 146 pulp mills were operating within the 12 Southern states. Southern mills are favorably located with respect to markets and generally have an ample supply of raw materials due to a large land area and rapid tree growth. Excellent transportation facilities are available and also an abundant supply of relatively cheap labor, water, chemicals, and power. Once again southern pine has assumed a position of great importance.

With a market for thinning and salvage timber in the pulpwood mill, there is an incentive today to practice good forestry, thus assuring the pulpwood industry a place of permanence. No species or group of species in the United States equals the four southern pines in their annual pulpwood cut. In 1970 the South accounted for 45 percent of the nation's output of roundwood products and net growth of timber. (*The Outlook for Timber in the United States,* 1973).

Lumber from the southern pines is still a major industry in many Southern Forest communities. Timbers for heavy construction, such as bridges and large buildings, come mostly from longleaf pine. Slash pine produces some heavy construction timbers also. From loblolly and shortleaf come material for lighter construction.

Longleaf and slash also produce gum or crude resin, the raw material of a small naval-stores industry. This region once supplied more than 60 percent of the world's natural production of turpentine and rosin. Much of it today, however, is produced as a by-product of the southern kraft pulping process.

The extremely durable baldcypress is manufactured into a variety of products such as beams, bridge timbers, cooperage, stadium seats, poles, and piling. The hardwoods of the Southern Forest are used essentially for the same purposes as are the hardwoods of the Central Forest region.

Although not so far-flung as the Central Hardwood region, the Southern Forest has the largest tree-covered area of all the natural forest regions. It embraces approximately 195 million acres (78.9 million ha) or almost 30 percent of the forest area of the United States, including coastal Alaska.

**The Rocky Mountain Forest**   A glance at Figs. 8-1 and 8-5 reveals the spattered pattern of the Rocky Mountain Forest. It extends from Canada on the north to Mexico on the south, from the vast prairies on the east to the Cascades and Sierra Nevadas of the Far West. Moreover, the treeless areas between these 50 or more patches of forest are not rich agricultural lands. Natural prairie and other grasslands account for some of them, and it is said that the early Spanish ranchers and their descendants, wishing pasture for sheep and goats, burned the mountains regularly to extend the open stretches. Prospectors, too, in search of gold, silver, and copper ore outcroppings, found the forests in the way and fired them so that the surface of this highly mineralized country would be easier to explore. Most of this prospecting came after 1850 and the annual burnings were no doubt helped along by later travelers, whose thoughtfulness has not made them famous.

If a family were to set out on a trip to see the "Rocky Mountain Forest," their wanderings would not only be over great distances horizontally, but in order to see all the types they would have to climb to higher elevations than those common in the East. Starting at 5,000 ft (1,500 m) above sea level in the drier sites of the central Rockies of New Mexico or Colorado, they could see two or three species of juniper, several pinyons or nut pines, and some shrubby species of oak. Willows would appear if water were nearby. At about 6,000 ft (1,800 m) they would notice the beginning of the ponderosa pine forest, so characteristic of all Western states. Should their day's journey carry them upward even further they would see more and more quaking aspen, Douglas-fir, and white fir mixing with the now disappearing ponderosa pine, until at their camping place at night there would be almost a pure forest of these two coniferous species. The next morning on their upward climb, they would travel through almost pure forests of blue and then Engelmann spruce (Fig. 8-6) for another 1,000 ft (300 m). At 9,000 ft (2,700 m) they would run into a forest of Engelmann spruce, subalpine fir, and limber pine which would continue until they reached timberline at 11,000 or 12,000 ft (3,300 or 3,600 m). Above the upper fringes of the ponderosa pine they may have seen patches of lodgepole pine in old burns.

Tired of climbing, our family might drive from Denver northwest to Missoula, Montana, and the "Inland Empire."[1] Much of what they would see would be ponderosa pine and heavy patches of lodgepole pine, a species that grows in thick stands soon after a fire. Reaching Missoula, they could travel northwest to Idaho, through fine stands of ponderosa pine, into the heart of the Inland Empire where they would also find magnificent forests of western white pine, western larch, and occasional mixtures of western hemlock, grand fir, Douglas-fir, and western redcedar. At higher elevations this far north would be Engelmann spruce and subalpine fir, again the

---

[1] Eastern Washington and Oregon, northern Idaho, and the west slope of the Rocky Mountains in Montana.

**Figure 8-6**  The Rocky Mountain Forest. A stand of Engelmann spruce in the mountains of Colorado. *(Courtesy of the U.S. Forest Service.)*

timberline species. This close to the Canadian boundary, timberline is around 7,000 ft (2,100 m) above sea level. Travelers to the Black Hills of South Dakota will find forests largely of ponderosa pine, with white spruce in the valleys and some scattered bur oak and hophornbeam. In eastern California they will find ponderosa mixed with Jeffrey, lodgepole, western white, and sugar pines, white and California red fir and Douglas-fir.

The principal commercial timbers of the Rocky Mountain Forest as a whole are ponderosa pine, western white pine, Douglas-fir, lodgepole pine, and Engelmann spruce. The rather spotty distribution of the forest really brings it close to local demand and so helps the smaller forest industries, while major operations are confined largely to the heavily timbered northwestern portion and, to a lesser extent, to the southeastern territory.

The southern Rocky Mountain Forest region, in the states of Arizona, Colorado, Nevada, New Mexico, Utah, and eastern California, has a total of approximately 100 million acres (40.4 million ha) of forest land. Most of the commercial forest is in national forests. Industry is limited mostly to sawmills which prepare lumber for local use.

The northern Rocky Mountain Forest region includes eastern Washington and Oregon, Idaho, Montana, Wyoming, and western South Dakota, for a total of 80 million acres (32.3 million ha) of forest land. Sawmills are the chief forest products industry.

The Rocky Mountain section contained 14.2 percent of the nation's timber inventory in 1970 and accounted for 7.1 percent of the total national output of roundwood products. Some 4 percent of the nation's lumber and wood products establishments were located in this area in 1967; these produced 6 percent of the value added in United States production of lumber and wood products.[2]

Forest areas in the Rocky Mountains that were classed as suitable and available for timber production in 1970 amounted to 61.6 million acres (25 million ha) or 3 million acres (1.2 million ha) less than in 1962.[3]

Taking the Rocky Mountain Forest as a whole, high mountain recreation, forage for sheep and cattle, and water production for domestic and municipal use and for irrigation are the most important uses of the forest. Here lie eight of the country's best-known national parks and over 50 national forests. Most of the larger reservoirs are in this region also. The lumber industry, on the other hand, centered mostly around ponderosa pine, although never in violent competition with the Pacific Coast, the Lake States, or the South, has had a tremendous local importance and also furnishes lumber, poles, and ties in considerable quantity to the Great Plains region.

**The Pacific Coast Forest**   The forests of this region extend southward from British Columbia through western Washington and Oregon, and into California to the San Francisco Bay area. The entire forest lies west of the Cascade and Sierra Nevada ranges. Although it is the smallest of the natural forests in the United States, this forest produces over one-third of this country's total timber products.

Douglas-fir is the nation's most important commercial species, accounting for one-fourth of the total standing sawtimber volume, even after 80 years of large-scale harvesting. Two-thirds of this volume is concentrated in the forests of western Washington and Oregon.

The entire Pacific Coast Forest produces trees of such remarkable size that it is no wonder this forest is one of the most famous in the world (Fig.

---

[2] *The Outlook for Timber in the United States,* 1973.
[3] Ibid.

8-7). Trees of such enormity are found nowhere else. In the rain forests of Olympic National Park, for example, on the Olympic Peninsula in the state of Washington where the annual rainfall is over 150 in. (381 cm) four of the Northwest's most important trees reach their maximum sizes. Further south, along the fog belt of coastal California, are the magnificent redwoods with average diameters of 8 to 12 ft (2.4 to 3.6 m). Even more impressive are their heights which average 200 to 300 ft (60 to 90 m), the loftiest of which is 368 ft (110 m). Further inland, in groves at middle elevations in the Sierra Nevada, stand the most famous of all trees, giant sequoias. What these 270-ft (80-m) trees lack in height they make up in diameter. The General Sherman tree in Sequoia National Park is nearly 30 ft (9 m) in diameter at breast height. Diameters of 12 to 14 ft (3.6 to 4.2 m) are relatively common in the giant sequoia groves. Most of the giant sequoias, however, as well as the record-sized trees of the other species are under some form of protection. They contribute to the economy of the region mainly through their aesthetic value rather than through their use as lumber. Hundreds of thousands of tourists annually spend thousands of dollars just to look upon or camp beneath these dignified western giants which stand in state and national parks and national forests.

   In the northern part of the range, as already mentioned, Douglas-fir is

**Figure 8-7** The Pacific Coast Forest. Western redcedar in the Chilliwack River Valley, North Cascades National Park, Washington. *(Photo by Grant W. Sharpe.)*

the most characteristic tree. Along the coast its principal associates are Sitka spruce, western hemlock, western redcedar, and Pacific silver and grand firs. At higher elevations these species give way to subalpine fir and whitebark pine. Further inland but still west of the Cascades, Douglas-fir is found with western white pine and noble fir. The most important hardwoods of the Northwest are red alder, bigleaf maple, black cottonwood, Pacific madrone, and Oregon ash. The drier eastern slope of the Cascades supports a forest which is more characteristic of the Rocky Mountain Forest.

In the coastal California section of the Pacific Coast Forest, redwood is an important tree. Its common coniferous associates include Douglas-fir, Sitka spruce, western hemlock, and grand fir. Port-Orford-cedar is limited to a small coastal area of Oregon and California. The hardwood associates of redwood are red alder, Pacific madrone, bigleaf maple, tanoak, and California-laurel. As one moves inland, away from the 50-mi-wide (80-km) fog belt, most coastal species disappear, although Douglas-fir and bigleaf maple are still encountered. Incense-cedar, western white and sugar pines, Pacific madrone, Oregon white oak, California black oak, and golden chinkapin become more common. At somewhat higher elevations, Jeffery and ponderosa pine and giant sequoia appear with sugar pine and incense-cedar. At about 6,000 ft (1,800 m), white, California red, and Shasta red firs appear. Further up the mountain slopes grow mountain hemlock and lodgepole pine.

The lead in lumber production shifted from the South to the Pacific Coast Forest in 1920. Washington was the nation's number one producer of lumber from 1909 until 1938, the national lead shifting then to Oregon which has held it since. From the three Pacific Coast states with their reserves of uncut Douglas-fir comes a high grade of softwood lumber, timbers, and veneer for plywood, which is exported throughout the world. Substantial quantities also go into pulp, poles, and piling and a variety of other items. Douglas-fir is considered to be the most widely used commercial species in the world. Western hemlock, Sitka spruce, and the several species of western true firs are the region's important pulp species. Western redcedar, because of its durability, has many uses but is best known as the nation's leading wood for shingles. Redwood, because of its durability and strength, is used for many items ranging from cigar boxes and coffins to siding and building construction. Incense-cedar is the principal wood used in making pencils. Port-Orford-cedar is known to the archer as the leading wood for arrows. The region's hardwoods are limited. Red alder, long considered an inferior species and for years cleverly disguised as other woods by the local furniture industry, has come into its rightful place as the Northwest's leading furniture wood. Bigleaf maple is cut for flooring and furniture, and black cottonwood is used for pulp, excelsior, and veneer for boxes and crates.

The forests of the region's vast high country are important for recreational use as indicated by the eight mountainous national parks and several wilderness areas in its twenty-four national forests. The growing population of the West Coast is also dependent on these forests for water production. The very size of the timber, its location in rugged sites, and its distance from the greatest consuming centers of the country have brought about unusual and, to a certain extent, unavoidable destructiveness in exploiting the forests of the Pacific slope. In no other region are logging and milling of the product more costly.

The Pacific Coast Forest is more compact, and perhaps its communities have more in common socially and industrially than do those of some of the other natural forest regions. On the other hand, its ruggedness; vulnerability to wildfires; importance in conserving water for irrigation, power, and municipal use; and the demand for it as scenic playground country present unusual problems of planning, which require the best of skill and knowledge if its forests are to reach their highest degree of usefulness.

**The Alaskan Forest**   The forests of this huge state are divided into two natural forest regions, the coastal and the interior (Fig. 8-8). The coastal forest extends 800 mi (1,287 km) from the "panhandle" of southeastern Alaska, along the south coast through the Kenai Peninsula to Kodiak Island, from sea level to approximately 2,500 ft (750 m) in the south to 1,500 ft (450 m) in the north. The greater part of this region lies adjacent to northwestern British Columbia and mostly in the 16-million-acre (6.46-million-ha) Tongass National Forest (Fig. 8-9). The tree species in this area are chiefly western hemlock and Sitka spruce, and in some areas western redcedar, Alaska-cedar, and mountain hemlock. In the muskegs, lodgepole pine is a component of the vegetation. Among the hardwoods are red alder and black cottonwood.

Most of the commercial timber lies within a few miles of tidewater. Western hemlock makes up about 74 percent of the timber volume and Sitka spruce about 20 percent. These two trees, considered as pulpwood species, cover nearly 4.3 million acres (1.7 million ha) of commercial forest, the vastness of which gives some indication of the pulp potential of Alaska's coastal forest. The pulp industry has become established in southeastern Alaska and centered at Ketchikan and Sitka, and mills elsewhere are contemplated, further enhancing the state's economic outlook.

The interior of Alaska contains an estimated 106 million acres (42.8 million ha) of forest land on about 32 percent of Alaska's 365 million acres (147 million ha) of land area. Its commercial forests cover about 22.5 million acres (9.1 million ha) capable of growing 20 cu ft/acre (1.4 m³/ha) per year.[4] Although yields for the most part are inferior to the coastal forest, some of the local stands are highly valuable because of the excessive cost of

----

[4] *The Outlook for Timber in the United States.*

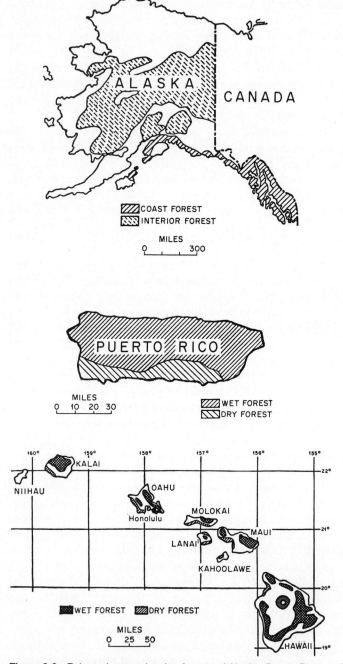

**Figure 8-8** Enlarged maps showing forests of Alaska, Puerto Rico, and Hawaii. *(Courtesy of the U.S. Forest Service.)*

**Figure 8-9** The Alaskan Forest. An aerial view of the tree-covered islands on the Seymour Canal. Tongass National Forest, Alaska. *(Courtesy of the U.S. Forest Service.)*

transporting wood products either in or out. The U.S. Bureau of Land Management, which controls the larger part of the state's interior forest, is plagued with wildfires which burn a million or more acres (405,000 ha) each year. Nearly all the interior forest has been burned at one time or another. Insects and disease also take a large annual toll.

Limited rainfall, low humidity, high winds, high temperatures, and long hours of summer sunshine combine to create one of the most dangerous fire conditions in any North American forest. An expanding road system, increasing population, and a greater invasion of tourists are not going to improve the fire situation when one considers that 75 percent of all interior fires are caused by people.

In spite of this there are fine commercial forests of white spruce, quaking aspen, balsam poplar, black cottonwood, and paper birch in the Alaskan interior, especially along stream courses, lake shores, flood plains, and other well-drained lowlands. Black spruce is a common muskeg type and depending on the locality, may be associated with tamarack. These muskeg forests are not unlike those found throughout other parts of northern North America. Several species of willows and alders occur in the interior but seldom grow to commercial sizes.

Alaska's interior forest is going through the same phase of use and misuse that the forests of other states were witnessing a half to two and a half centuries earlier. The state and the nation must face the huge problem of educating the indifferent forest user to the need for caution in the use of fire. Greater utilization of the interior forest and an expansion of markets in the state are possible since all but logs and rough materials for house construction are brought in from the "outside."

Commercial fishing is Alaska's top industry, but her coastal pulpwood and other forest industries and income from recreationists are becoming more significant. The 49th state, with an area one-fifth the size of the contiguous 48 states, has 119 million acres (48 million ha) of forest, 28 million (11.3 million ha) of which are classified as commercial (Viereck and Little, 1972). Three of the National Park Service's four largest showpieces are in Alaska.

The Alaska Native Claims Settlement Act of 1971 called for recommendations to Congress by the Secretary of the Interior concerning disposition of some 80 million acres (32 million ha) of federal land. In December 1973 the Secretary recommended to Congress the doubling of the National Park and National Wildlife Refuges from 30 to 60 million acres (12 to 24 million ha), the adding of 20 new units to the National Wild and Scenic River System, 18.8 million acres (7.6 million ha) to the National Forest System, and the remainder for various uses by the Bureau of Land Management. Final disposition is up to Congress and it may take several years for completion. It is obvious that these several federal agencies will contribute to the forestry and recreation picture and the future of Alaska (U.S. Department of the Interior, 1973).

**Forests of Hawaii**    Almost 2 million acres (808,000 ha) of assorted wet and dry forest cover about one-half of the total area of the seven main islands in the Hawaiian group (Fig. 8-8). Slightly more than half the commercial forest land is privately owned and under such management as will best build up and maintain the depleted stands. People and grazing animals have been the principal causes of the destruction of the native forest.

Vegetative conditions range from rain forest jungle to desert in just a few miles. Weather is extremely variable. Despite the heavy rainfall and lush vegetation, several thousand acres burn over annually; hence, fire is a serious problem. There is also occasional loss on the island of Hawaii from lava flows.

Water is the principal product derived from Hawaiian forests and the original act of the old Territorial Legislature, which created the present Division of Forestry, stressed this activity and directed that ways and means be devised for "protecting, extending, increasing and utilizing the forest and forest reserves, more particularly for protecting and developing the springs, streams and sources of water supply so as to increase and make such water available for use."

There are fewer forest types in Hawaii than are found in most main land areas. One native tree, ohia lehua, not only grows in pure stands, but it is the predominant species (Fig. 8-10). Surprisingly, very little of it is used as sawn timber. In fact, the 50th state had only three sawmills in operation in 1974. Koa is a valuable cabinet wood which can be manufactured into fine plyboard, and most of this species, in accessible areas, has already been

**Figure 8-10**   The Hawaiian Forests. Ohia lehua growing at 3,000 ft (900 m) elevation where the annual rainfall is 100 in (254 cm). Island of Hawaii. *(Courtesy of the Division of Forestry, State of Hawaii.)*

harvested. Mamani, which occurs as a short tree at high elevations [5,000 to 10,000 ft (1,500 to 3,000 m)] furnishes a very durable wood, which is used locally as fence posts. Kukui, the candlenut tree, is the state tree, and oil from the nuts is burned for light. These trees grow in moist draws in mixed stands, cover only a small area, and have no timber value. Kiawe (mesquite, algaroba) grows well in the dry lowlands and is valuable for fuel, fence posts, forage, and honey.

Many foreign trees have been introduced to Hawaii, particularly a species of eucalyptus from Australia. A recent survey indicates that there are presently in excess of 170 million board feet of lumber ready to harvest from these exotic stands, 75 percent of this being eucalyptus. Other outstanding species are Mexican ash, Australian redcedar, redwood, and silk-oak. The growth rate of some of these planted trees is rapid. Flooded gum has been known to reach an average height of 133 ft (40 m) in 16 years with a diameter at breast height (dbh) of 18 in. (45.7 cm), and from a single 40-year-old tree of this same species, 2,800 board feet of lumber has been obtained.

From the above you will see that the Hawaiian environment is a limited land mass with many rare species. Rapid population growth is occurring on limited land resources.

Examples of native ecosystems are being preserved. Habitat for rare plant species are being maximized. The multiple-use land management concept is being followed on state lands and promoted for the private lands. Recreation use on the state lands is increasing. Watershed management annually becomes more important. Pressures for increased land use are mounting. Conflicts in most land use, especially timber harvesting, are increasing, but with some compromise on both positions, they can be resolved.

The Division of Forestry operates under the state government through the Department of Land and Natural Resources. This Division is headed by the State Forester with four district foresters for each of the four land districts of the state. The work is carried on by a ranger force, district fire wardens, general laborers, and others as needed. Trees are raised or held in one of the five nurseries close to area of use. Nursery trees for forest, windbreak, and erosion projects are distributed for a nominal charge. The average annual tree distribution is about one-half million.

The Forest Service maintains a small research staff at the Institute of Pacific Islands Forestry in Hawaii to assist the state and others in some of the research problems.

Hawaii Volcanoes National Park is located on the island of Hawaii. It includes a tropical forest wilderness area. The Haleakala National Park is on the island of Maui. Both are receiving increased recreation use. The area of these two National Parks is 299,423 acres (121,000 ha) (Tagawa, 1974).

**The Tropical Forest**   Covering a total of not more than 400,000 acres (162,000 ha) at the southern tips of Florida and Texas is the commercially unimportant Tropical Forest within the United States. More subtropical than tropical, the forest is composed largely of palms and mangroves.

The mangroves, composed chiefly of four salt-tolerant species of trees, form a protective buffer in estuaries and along the coasts of south Florida.

Mixed forests more representative of the tropics are found in the Commonwealth of Puerto Rico, a 100-mile /160-km/ long rectangular American island in latitude 18°N in the eastern Caribbean. Formerly all forested, the island still bears a variety of coastal and mountain vegetation ranging from dry to rain forest. The more than 500 native tree species include Spanish cedar and lignumvitae, but no mahogany or pines. The moist forests, on the north side of the east-west mountain chain, called the Cordillera Central, are evergreen and grow to 100 feet /30 m/ or more in height. They contain as many as 40 tree species per acre, none of which are widely distributed in the continental United States (Fig. 8-11).

**Figure 8-11**   The Tropical Forest. A plantation of a veneer wood *Anthocephalus chinesis* in Puerto Rico. Trees are 5 years old and have 11-in. (28 cm) diameters. *(Courtesy of the U.S. Forest Service.)*

Only about 15,000 acres *[6,000 ha]* still bear virgin forest but the recent decline of agriculture in the interior has led to rapid extension of secondary forests, now covering more than 700,000 acres *[283,000 ha]*, or about 30 percent of the island. These new forests contain many valuable and fast-growing hardwoods with a potential for management and use. About 15,000 acres *[6,000 ha]* of mangrove forests cover estuaries and other protected coastal lands. The island is self-sufficient only in fence posts and imports almost all of its lumber, plywood, and other forest products. One paper mill uses waste cartons and sugar cane bagasse.

The Forest Service of the U.S. Department of Agriculture has administered the 28,000-acre *[11,300-ha]* Caribbean National Forest in the eastern mountains since its proclamation in 1903. Operated also as the Luquillo Experimental Forest, and managed by the Institute of Tropical Forestry, silvicultural research is an important activity in this forest. Included within it are a 2,000-acre *[808-ha]* natural area containing four types of forest in virgin condition, many forestry experiments and demonstrations, and recreation areas visited by more than a million persons per year.

The Forest Service of the Puerto Rico Department of Natural Resources, in existence since 1918, administers a system of 13 Commonwealth Forests totalling about 60,000 acres *[24,000 ha]*. Within these forests are more than 8,000 acres *[3,230 ha]* of forest plantations, most of them dating from the CCC period (1935–1943). They also contain heavily-used public recreational areas.

The Federal and Commonwealth Forest Services cooperate in encouraging production and utilization of forests by private interests. Trees and incentive payments are provided for farm plantings, and technical assistance is offered to landowners, wood processors, and consumers of forest products.

The Department of Agriculture of the United States Virgin Islands has since 1950 undertaken a farm forestry program with technical and financial cooperation from the Institute of Tropical Forestry in Puerto Rico. Some 200 small forest plantings have been established, mostly with mahogany, and the Institute utilized the 134-acre *[54-ha]* Estate Thomas Experimental Forest on St. Croix for research and demonstration purposes (Wadsworth, 1974).

**Ownership of United States Forests**    The total forest area in the United States at present is about 754 million acres (305 million ha) out of a total land area of 2.27 billion acres (918.6 million ha).

Of that total, about a third—254 million acres (103 million ha)—is set aside in parks, wilderness areas, and watersheds or is not suitable for growing commercial timber.

The remaining 500 million acres (202 million ha) of the total forest base is the commercial forest. The biggest single owner of the commercial forest is government; local, state, and federal. About 136 million acres (55 million ha) of the commercial forest land is publicly held—27 percent of the total.

Private individuals, about 4 million persons, own almost 60 percent of the commercial forest, about 296 million acres (119.8 million ha).

The forest products industry comes in a distant third, with about 13 percent of the commercial forest, something like 67 million acres (27 million ha).

## CANADA'S FORESTS

Canada is the world's leading exporter of forest products, with three-fourths of its exports going to the United States.[5] Of Canada's nearly 2.3 billion acres (931 million ha) of land, 25 percent or 588 million acres (237 million ha) are classified as productive forest land. Another 191 million acres (77 million ha) are not suitable for regular harvest. 17 million acres (6.8 million ha) are reserved.

Because of the size of the trees, most of Canada's vast forest land is best suited to pulp and paper production rather than lumber. Of pulp paper and paperboard, 10.4 million tons (9.36 million t) were imported by the United States in 1971. Close to 75 percent of all newsprint used in the United States comes from Canada, and nearly 9 billion board feet of lumber were also shipped to American markets in 1971.

Approximately 93 percent of the forest land is publicly owned, being administered either by the Dominion or Provincial government, and is referred to as Crown land. Compare this with the United States where nearly three-fourths of the forest land is privately owned. Table 8-1 gives some indication of the ownership and location of Canada's forests.

[5] *The Outlook for Timber in the United States,* 1973.

**Table 8-1  Forest Land Areas in Canada by Province, 1967 [in million acres or hectares (ha)]**

| Province | Total | | Suitable for regular harvest | | Not suitable for regular harvest | | Reserved | |
|---|---|---|---|---|---|---|---|---|
| | acres | ha | acres | ha | acres | ha | acres | ha |
| Atlantic* | 56.7 | 22.7 | 47.7 | 19.1 | 8.3 | 3.3 | .65 | .26 |
| Quebec | 171.8 | 68.7 | 121.8 | 48.7 | 49.9 | 19.9 | .062 | .025 |
| Ontario | 120.5 | 48.2 | 115.5 | 46.2 | .105 | .042 | 4.9 | 1.98 |
| Prairie† | 132.7 | 53.1 | 119.6 | 47.8 | 4.98 | 1.99 | 8.1 | 3.24 |
| British Columbia | 138 | 55.2 | 134.8 | 53.9 | . . . . . . . | . . . . . . . | 3.2 | 1.28 |
| Northwest Territories & Yukon | 176.5 | 70.6 | 48.8 | 19.5 | 127.7 | 51.1 | | |
| Total | 796.2 | 318.5 | 588.2 | 235.2 | 191.0 | 76.4 | 17.0 | 6.8 |

*Includes Newfoundland, Prince Edward Island, Nova Scotia, and New Brunswick.
†Includes Manitoba, Saskatchewan, and Alberta.
*Source:* From *The Outlook For Timber in the United States, 1973,* Table 107, p. 134; Glenn H. Manning and H. Rae Grinnell, *Forest Resources and Utilization in Canada to the Year 2000,* Canadian Forestry Service Publication 1304, Ottawa, 1971.

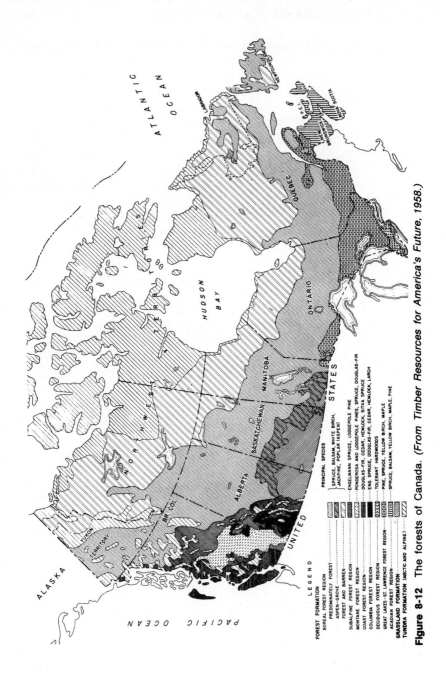

**Figure 8-12** The forests of Canada. *(From Timber Resources for America's Future, 1958.)*

LEGEND

FOREST FORMATION — — — — — PRINCIPAL SPECIES

BOREAL FOREST REGION
PREDOMINATELY FOREST— — — — — — SPRUCE, BALSAM, WHITE BIRCH,
ASPEN-GROVE— — — — — — — — — — (JACKPINE, POPLAR (ASPEN)
FOREST AND BARREN—

SUBALPINE FOREST REGION— — — — — ENGELMANN SPRUCE, LODGEPOLE PINE
MONTANE FOREST REGION— — — — — — PONDEROSA AND LODGEPOLE PINES, SPRUCE, DOUGLAS-FIR
COAST FOREST REGION— — — — — — — DOUGLAS-FIR, CEDAR, HEMLOCK, SITKA SPRUCE
COLUMBIA FOREST REGION— — — — — — ENG. SPRUCE, DOUGLAS-FIR, CEDAR, HEMLOCK, LARCH

DECIDUOUS FOREST REGION— — — — — — TOLERANT HARDWOODS
GREAT LAKES-ST. LAWRENCE FOREST REGION— PINE, SPRUCE, YELLOW BIRCH, MAPLE.
ACADIAN FOREST REGION— — — — — — — SPRUCE, BALSAM, YELLOW BIRCH, MAPLE, PINE
GRASSLAND FORMATION—
TUNDRA FORMATION (ARCTIC AND ALPINE)—

The forest of the southern tip of Ontario is a continuation of the Central Hardwood Region of the United States (Fig. 8-12). Just north of this in both Ontario and Quebec and in the Maritime Provinces is an extension of the Northern Forest of the United States. The numerous streams throughout southern Quebec are used for log driving and make logging operations economical despite the small size of the trees and the large areas that have to be cut annually. North of this area is a wide belt of white and black spruce, tamarack, jack pine, balsam fir, quaking aspen, balsam poplar, and paper birch which extends across Canada and is known as the *boreal forest*. All but balsam fir and jack pine are transcontinental, that is, they grow from Labrador and Newfoundland into Alaska. The grasslands in the southern parts of the Prairie Provinces—Manitoba, Saskatchewan, and Alberta—are similar to the treeless areas of eastern Montana and the Dakotas. In the mountainous region of southwestern Alberta and southeastern British Columbia are Engelmann spruce, subalpine fir, western larch, Douglas-fir, western redcedar, and western hemlock. Ponderosa, lodgepole, and western white pines occur at lower elevations in the interior of the province. Along coastal British Columbia are concentrated the massive Douglas-fir, Sitka spruce, western hemlock, and western redcedar. There are no significant differences in the uses of these species from those uses listed earlier in this chapter.

In recent years Canada's national economy has witnessed a phenomenal growth due to the expansion of industry such as development of water power, oil, and uranium and iron ores. This industrial expansion, coupled with an increasing population, will place a greater demand on Canada's forest products.

> Output of both the lumber and pulp and paper industries in Canada has climbed steadily in recent decades. Between 1950 and 1971 annual production more than doubled. Timber utilization practices have improved. Fuelwood use had declined. . . . The 1970 timber cut of about 4.3 billion cubic feet [121.7 million m³] in Canada is well below calculated sustainable allowable cut of 10.7 billion cubic feet [302.8 million m³]. Economics might lower the attained cut to 8 billion cubic feet [226.4 million m³]. The Outlook report and Canadian studies indicate that future exports to the United States may be substantially increased (Manning and Grinnell, 1971).

## BIBLIOGRAPHY

*Annual Report of the Land and Natural Resources Department to the Governor of Hawaii,* 1971-1972.

Brown, H. P., A. J. Panshin, and C. C. Forsaith. 1949. *Textbook of Wood Technology,* McGraw-Hill Book Company, New York.

Butler, O. M. 1935. *American Conservation,* American Forestry Association, Washington, DC.

# Chapter 9

# The Tree, The Forest, and Forestry

Earlier chapters have dealt with trees and forests from the standpoint of history, beneficial influences, recreation, and their economic importance. It is time to look at trees as individuals. How does a tree grow, how does it survive with other living things, how does it react to environmental influences? How do trees, forests, and forestry fit together? This chapter will attempt to answer these questions.

Trees exert a fascination on the human race. They were probably our prehuman home, and they remain deep in our affections and occupy a central place in folklore. Perhaps it is the longevity of the tree, lasting beyond human generations; perhaps it is the yearly renewal of the seemingly dead branches of the deciduous species; perhaps the whispering leaves and bountiful fruits and nuts. Although we no longer worship the spirits of trees, most of us still experience a feeling of awe when in a forest of big trees.

The oldest as well as the longest-living things, trees express bountiful diversity in form and utility. Even in old age they have great beauty (Fig. 9-1).

**Figure 9-1**  A 3,200-year-old Rocky Mountain juniper *(Juniperus scopulorum)* in Logan Canyon, Utah. Although it is in a relatively isolated area, this ancient tree has considerable visitor interest. *(Photo by S. Ross Tocher.)*

**The Soil**  A few plants locate themselves in water, some take up residence on other plants, but most trees must obtain water and certain mineral substances directly from the soil. Six major and six minor elements are needed for tree growth. The major elements are nitrogen, phosphorus, sulfur, calcium, potassium, and magnesium. The minor elements, needed in less concentration, are iron, manganese. copper, zinc, boron, and molybdenum (Bonner and Galston, 1952). Each of these minerals, taken up from the soil through the roots, is necessary for proper functioning of the tree. For example, phosphorus and sulfur are protein builders, iron and magnesium become part of the chlorophyll molecule, and potassium is an aid to cell division. These materials are, of course, in addition to the vast quantity of carbon which comes from the air.

The many shrubs and other plants of the forest utilize the same 12 essential elements that the trees use. Because animals eat these green plants, their bodies also contain these essential elements. It would seem that eventually all the essential elements of the soil could be tied up in other organisms. Without some means of being returned to the soil, the dead bodies of animals, leaves, twigs, and trunks of trees would soon accumulate into great continuous heaps of nightmarish undecomposed matter so that eventually life in the forest, and everywhere for that matter, would cease. Because of the decaying action of bacteria and fungi, organic matter with its valuable minerals is returned to the soil. This orderly decomposition of the organic materials of the forest builds what is called a *humus* layer, a kind of storehouse upon which future generations of forest organisms can depend for the nutrients necessary for growth.

**The Tree**    Trees are woody plants that usually grow upright with single stems and have thier roots well anchored in the soil.

The stems or boles of the trees that extend above the soil surface support the crowns and supply them with water and mineral substances from the soil. Above and in the sunshine are crowns, forming a cover of branches, buds, and leaves in which the materials brought up from the soil and taken in from the atmosphere, during periods of favorable temperature, are elaborated and distributed over each tree of the forest. This process, which results in growth, will be considered in greater detail.

There are almost as many habits or forms of trees as there are species, and the great visible differences occur in the crowns and in the minor characters of the stems. In this country it is the trunks or stems that are harvested from the forest. The branches of the roots and the crown are of small cross section, usually crooked, and although useful as fuel are very expensive to handle. The crowns of felled trees are called *slash* in logging operations and often become a fire hazard. For this reason, they are usually burned by controlled fire or chipped on site and returned to the forest floor. With this brief introduction to a tree, we go on to see how it becomes one.

### How a Tree Grows

Trees usually start from seeds (Fig. 9-2). These may be tiny and windborne, such as the ones attached to the drifting "cotton" of the cottonwood or other poplars, soft-shelled nuts such as acorns, hard-shelled ones like walnuts or hickory nuts, fleshy, winged seeds such as those of maple, beans such as the ones from the locusts, or even the pits of fruit like those from cherries. The pines and spruces have their naked, nutlike, winged seeds falling from the bracts or scales of cones. These may ride far with the wind

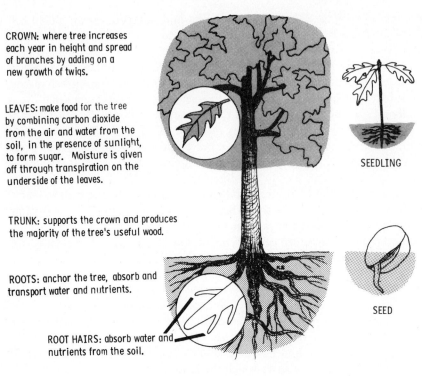

CROWN: where tree increases each year in height and spread of branches by adding on a new growth of twigs.

LEAVES: make food for the tree by combining carbon dioxide from the air and water from the soil, in the presence of sunlight, to form sugar.  Moisture is given off through transpiration on the underside of the leaves.

TRUNK: supports the crown and produces the majority of the tree's useful wood.

ROOTS: anchor the tree, absorb and transport water and nutrients.

ROOT HAIRS: absorb water and nutrients from the soil.

SEEDLING

SEED

# HOW A TREE GROWS

HEARTWOOD: inactive sapwood, which gives the trunk strength and stiffness.

SAPWOOD: (xylem) carries the sap (water plus nitrogen and mineral nutrients) from roots to leaves.

CAMBIUM: microscopic layer of cells where diameter growth occurs with the formation of an annual ring.

INNER BARK: (phloem) carries sugar made in the leaves down to the branches, trunk and roots, where it is converted to substances vital to growth.

OUTER BARK: protects the tree from insects and disease, excessive heat and cold, and mechanical injuries.

TRUNK CROSS-SECTION

**Figure 9-2**   How a tree grows. *(Modified from USDA Forest Service.)*

**Figure 9-3** The forest floor covered with mosses, herbaceous plants, and conifer seed-lings. Note the seedlings are beginning to evidence treelike form. *(Photo by Grant W. Sharpe.)*

or drop close to the parent tree, depending on their size. Seeds may also float, roll, or be carried by birds or mammals for great distances. Some trees, like the willows, may reproduce themselves by cuttings or twigs that float or fall to muddy or sandy places and take root. Others may regenerate by sprouts from the stump of their seed-sown parent. These methods of propagation will be discussed later in the book. Here we will start with the germinating seed.

A tree seedling that has just pushed through the ground has little to distinguish it from the seedling of any other plant. It is usually tiny and frail and often must compete with plants its own size that are themselves full grown. But by 3 or 4 weeks in the instance of hardwoods, and the end of the second year in the instance of softwood conifers, the seedling begins to show plainly its single-stem character and other evidences of treelike form (Fig. 9-3). Growth is taking place, and wood, the material of so many uses, is being formed. Growth in a tree, as in other living organisms, is the forma-tion of tissue from raw materials. These materials are water, mineral matter, and carbon dioxide. For growth to take place, there must be an interaction between several parts of the tree.

**Roots** One part of the tree whose function is little known by the average person is the roots. Briefly, they are responsible for absorption and conduction of water and mineral salts; anchorage of the tree to the soil; and in some species, reproduction by sprouting. In Fig. 9-4 we can see the four kinds of roots and their relative locations.

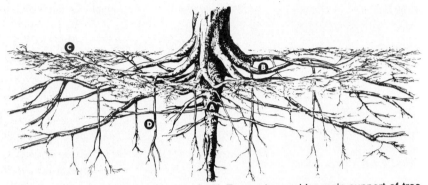

**Figure 9-4** The tree and its root system: (A) *Tap root*—provides main support of tree and anchors it firmly in the ground. (Not all trees have one.) (B) *Lateral roots*—help support and anchor trunk, may extend far out, beyond crown spread. (C) *Fibrous roots*—masses of fine feeding roots close to ground surface. (D) *Deeply descending roots* ("Sinkers")—grow downward from lateral roots. *(From Conservation Teaching Aid. Forest Service and Soil Conservation Service. U.S. Department of Agriculture.)*

The roots of herbaceous plants, shrubs, and trees, constitute the forest underground—the part that is *in* the soil discussed earlier. This part of the tree is seldom harvested although tree and shrub roots are used to some extent in medicine and the arts. Occasionally they are salvaged for some purpose when land is cleared. Storage of food is a function of the roots of many vegetables and other small plants but is of little importance with trees.

Water and dissolved mineral salts enter the tree by absorption. This occurs in tiny, thin-walled root hairs, only 0.01 mm in diameter which live but a few days and occur only near the tip of the growing root. Therefore, it is necessary for even the oldest trees to be continuously growing new roots. Some tree species depend on a fungus growth called *mycorrhiza* to serve in the same capacity as root hairs. The mycorrhiza produces a sheath around the roots from which grow fingerlike mycelia that extend into the soil, assisting the tree to absorb mineral food and moisture. Once the solution of water and minerals enters the roots, it is carried up the trunk of the tree to the leaves.

**Leaves**   The leaves might be called the "chemical laboratories" of the tree. They contain small green bodies called *chloroplasts*. These bodies contain chlorophyll, a substance that gives the green color to the leaves. In the presence of sunlight, these chloroplasts are able to start a chemical reaction in which the raw materials of carbon dioxide (taken from the air and entering the leaves through millions of tiny openings called *stomata*) and water (which comes up from the roots) are involved. This reaction breaks down the molecules of carbon dioxide and the molecules of water. The reaction, called *photosynthesis,* produces a new combination of atoms of carbon, oxygen, and hydrogen, and may be expressed in the following equation:

$$6CO_2 + 6H_2O + \text{radiant energy} \rightarrow C_6H_{12}O_6 + 6O_2$$

carbon      water        (expended)      glucose      oxygen
dioxide

This equation indicates that six molecules of carbon dioxide are combined with six molecules of water to form one molecule of glucose (a carbohydrate) and six of oxygen. The oxygen, a by-product, is released to the atmosphere and the carbohydrate, which may be converted into cellulose, is transported to all parts of the tree which are less than a year old. Cellulose is the main constituent of wood, making up approximately 60 percent of the tree. Lignin, also composed of carbon, oxygen, and hydrogen, but of a different chemical structure than cellulose, makes up most of the remainder of the tree.

Another life process, called *respiration* or breathing, takes place in the leaves. The chemical reaction of respiration is the opposite of the reaction of photosynthesis, and it may be presented as follows:

$$C_6H_{12}O_6 + 6O_2 \rightarrow 6CO_2 + 6H_2O + \text{energy}$$

glucose      oxygen      carbon      water      (released)
                              dioxide

In this instance, some of the energy is retained by the tree and is used to do much of the internal work needed for its growth. Photosynthesis will stop during the night, because of the absence of light, whereas respiration goes on in the tree 24 hours a day. Excessive respiration could be fatal to the tree. Note above that in one process oxygen is released and in the other carbon dioxide is released. All the carbon dioxide released in respiration is used in photosynthesis and only some of the oxygen released in photosynthesis is needed in respiration (Wilson and Loomis, 1957). (As pointed out earlier, additional carbon dioxide for photosynthesis comes from the air.) Because respiration, which uses up food (the glucose), goes on night and day, and photosynthesis, which manufactures food, takes place during the day only, it would seem the tree could respire itself to death. Fortunately, photosynthesis normally proceeds during the day at a rate 10 times that of respiration, and from this comes the food necessary for growth.

**Trunk** The trunk of the tree has many internal parts. Let us look at a cross section of a tree trunk, such as the top of a stump or the end of a log. Starting with the innermost part, one finds the *pith,* a small area of dead cells around which the first woody growth takes place. Next comes the *heartwood,* the inactive area whose main function is support and rigidity for the tree. The heartwood is usually dark in color. the 1- to 3-in. (2.5- to 7.5-cm) layer of wood surrounding the heartwood is the *sapwood,* or *xylem.*

The water and dissolved minerals pass upwards through the xylem on their way from the roots to the leaves. As new xylem is added to the tree, the old becomes heartwood (Fig. 9-2).

Growth in the tree takes place in the *cambium,* a microscopic layer of cells just outside the xylem. As the cells of this cambium layer divide and subdivide, the inner cells form the xylem; the outer cells form the *phloem* or *inner bark.* The inner bark is a layer of soft moist tissue whose function it is to carry the carbohydrates prepared in the leaves down to the branches, trunk, and roots. Gradually the inner bark changes to *outer bark.* The outer bark serves the tree in two ways: (1) It protects it from mechanical injury such as from a hard blow or from fire, and (2) because the bark is impervious to water, it prevents water loss from within and keeps outside water, which could be contaminated with decay-bearing organisms, from entering.

The trunk increases in diameter each year as a layer of wood is added, and an *annual ring* is formed. Early in the growing season of each year a layer of large, thin-walled, light-colored cells is formed, called the *springwood.* A darker layer of smaller thick-walled cells called *summerwood* forms later when there is plenty of building material available but a shortage of water. Side by side, the springwood and summerwood appear as a single annual ring in both the heartwood and the xylem, and in cold and temperate regions, where growth is interrupted during the winter, these rings serve to indicate the age of the tree. When growth conditions are favorable and food and water are abundant, the rings are wide. When drought occurs, the growth slows down and the rings are narrow. In the tropics, where the growing season is 12 months long, there usually are no annual rings.

The growth at the ends of branches and at the top of the main stem (and at the ends of the roots for that matter) is due to an increase in the number of cells, through cell division. From this it is hoped that the reader will realize that the wood at the "top" of the tree or even at a given spot on the trunk, once established, will never grow further from the ground, but rather the tree will add new wood each year to give the tree its height and diameter growth.

### The Tree and Water

We have seen that water is needed to carry dissolved minerals from the soil to the leaves. Water is also necessary in the chemical processes of photosynthesis where its hydrogen molecules combine with those of oxygen and carbon dioxide to make a sugar called glucose. We have seen how water moves this food to all those parts of the tree less than a year old. Water has other functions too. Various pressures, which require the presence of water, are built up in the growing cells of the tree to "inflate" those cells and give them rigidity. Soft fruits of trees, such as apples and peaches, are 85 percent water. It is the major constituent (75 to 90 percent) of *protoplasm,* the living material of cells themselves.

As vital as water is to trees and their growth, most of it entering the tree escapes through the stomata of the leaves as water vapor. This process is called *transpiration.* Only a very small amount of water is needed to carry on the processes of metabolism (the chemical changes associated with protoplasm outlined above). The water loss, due to transpiration, might then be thought of as a necessary evil. The leaves must open their stomata to admit carbon dioxide if photosynthesis is to take place. When the stomata are open, the tree loses its water by evaporation. The more the tree evaporates, or transpires, the more demand there is on the water in the soil.

The mechanics of transpiration are interesting, but not well understood. A phenomenon by which water can be drawn 368 ft (110 m) high, as in the instance of the tallest redwood, certainly deserves more study. Each of the several current theories have weaknesses. The most logical one is the *cohesion theory,* in which there are columns of water molecules between the leaves and the roots. The water molecules, which are in stress, are like links in a moving chain, each link pulling up the one behind it. As water is evaporated from the leaf surface, water molecules in the leaf stomata pull up those in the xylem, which pull up water molecules from the roots and soil.

The amount of transpiration varies with the time of day, and is greatest on hot dry summer days. The drying action of the wind tends to increase transpiration.

Transpiration is also influenced by the available amount of moisture in the soil. If soil moisture is low, the water molecules are more tightly held to soil particles, putting greater stress on the water columns in the tree. If the amount of water being transpired begins to exceed the amount available in the soil, considerable stress is established, and the cells around the leaf stomata, called *guard cells,* lose turgor pressure, closing the stomata. Though this conserves water, the closed stomata stops the intake of carbon dioxide, and photosynthesis is stopped, resulting in a growth loss to the tree.

The reader might wonder just how much water a tree transpires. One acre of pulpwood-sized southern pine transpires 750,000 gal (2.85 million l) of water per year. One sawlog-size tree in the South can transpire 80 gal (304 l) of water per day during a hot summer.

## THE FOREST

The forest offers us an excellent opportunity to observe interrelationships. Here a change brought about by either humans, animals, or natural elements has an effect on the overall forest association.

This association, or *ecosystem,* is a complex community of organisms composed of trees, shrubs and small plants, animals of many kinds, and soil and water. The forest is located both *on* and *in* the soil. It might include mountains, canyons, streams, and even open spaces (Fig. 9-5). The forest is

**Figure 9-5** The forest is a complex community of organisms. This one has been altered many times by insects and other animals, the natural elements, and in the last 200 years, by human beings. Yet the forest persists, creeping back to cover all scars. Pisgah National Forest, North Carolina. *(Courtesy of the U.S. Forest Service.)*

renewable. It is the great responsive and flexible natural resource that is dealt with in the practice of forestry.

According to the lexicographers, our word "forest" comes from the Latin *foris* or *foras,* which meant outdoors, and there was a Low Latin expression *forestis,* which is said to have described open ground reserved for the chase. This, with the addition of trees for cover, is the meaning that persisted to a greater or lesser degree throughout Europe until the Middle Ages and gave rise to the definition of a forest in English law as a tract of woodland used for hunting, usually belonging to the sovereign. It had its own laws and policing organization.

The popular definition of a forest today is a large tract covered with trees. It is thought by some to be natural growth. There are of course many privately and publicly owned forests that have grown up from seedlings which were hand planted many years ago. All this makes a short, comprehensive definition difficult. To understand how a forest grows the reader should have a brief exposure to forest ecology, competition, and succession.

**Forest Ecology**    Organisms, both plant and animal, in a forest community affect and are in turn affected by their respective environments. The study of the interaction between an organism and the elements of its surroundings, including both other organisms and physical factors such as soil, water, and temperature, is called *forest ecology*. When study is focused on the environmental relationships of a single individual or species it is termed *autecology*. When the study includes the dynamics of an entire forest community it is termed *synecology*.

**Forest Competition**    One of the things foresters are particularly interested in is *why* different tree species grow where they do.

For example, we sometimes find a north-facing slope covered by one species and a south-facing slope covered by another. The reasons for this include competition between species, as well as differing environmental conditions on the two slopes. South slopes receive more sunlight and hence are warmer and dryer than north slopes. The tree species on the south slope are better adapted to the warmer, dryer conditions than the tree species on the north slope.

In reality, however, it is seldom so simple. The ability of a particular plant to grow successfully on a site is influenced by many environmental factors including light, temperature, moisture, soil conditions, *and* the presence of the same and different species. What frequently happens in nature is that the limited supply of essentials (amounts of water, space, light, and soil nutrients) is unable to satisfy the full growth potential of all plants that are present. That is, there is a density-induced deficiency of the essentials. When such a deficiency occurs the organisms are said to be in competition.

In general, competition may result in a reduction in size of some or all of the individual competing organisms. Competition may also result in reduced numbers of organisms. The end result of competition is usually that while many "stragglers" die, other plants thrive, and in the instance of trees, the stand is left with fewer, bigger individuals.

Taking the example of the north and south slopes, it is probable that the tree species on the south slope were best adapted to conditions there and thus "defeated" the species now found on the north slope. It is likely that both species started on south slopes, but because there was a deficiency of something, competition resulted. Species A grew faster than B on the south slope and B faster than A on the north slope. The result was that A was successful and took over the south slope and vice versa on the north.

Why is this important? Because we are dealing not only with tree-environment interactions, but also in interactions between trees of the same and different species. Understanding both how a tree responds to the environment and to other species helps us know why trees of different species occur where they do.

**Figure 9-6**  *Upper*, a clear cut area photographed just after logging; *lower*, the same area 10 years later, showing the natural invasion of pioneer species. St. Joe National Forest, Idaho. *(Courtesy of the U.S. Forest Service.)*

**Forest Succession**  Not only are plants in a forest community affected by their environment, but they in turn exert modifying influences on their environment. The forest environment may thus be changed to the extent that the original species may no longer successfully compete. Therefore, the competition and nature of the forest community is modified as new species invade and others decline in importance. This internally controlled process of community change is called *succession.*

In order for the basic stage of succession (the pioneer stage) to begin there usually is some kind of a disturbance, such as the removal of the forest by fire, wind, erosion, or harvesting (Fig. 9-6).  The first plants to invade an area of relatively open conditions are called *pioneers.* Once the pioneers are established, their presence alters the site and a new series of plants begin to appear, plants with somewhat different tolerances for shade than the pioneers. These intermediate or subclimax plants may occupy the site for many years, until they too are gradually replaced. The changes in the species population continue until equilibrium is reached. The resulting "stable" community is referred to as the climax stage.

These successional stages are strictly theoretical. There are no well-defined or specific stages in succession, because there are too many environmental factors which influence plants. Harvesting, wildfire, disease, animals, and wind are all factors which cause change by altering seed sources and seed bed conditions. With so many variables in soil moisture, temperature, light, and nutrients, the stages of succession are difficult to distinguish.

The forest is a dynamic system, one constantly changing. With a changing overstory there is a changing understory, which even means a changing habitat for wildlife. Though it changes daily, the changes in the forest of interest to the forester are measured in years. As we saw above the changes come from various forces, i.e., competition for water, soil nutrients, shade or sunlight, and forces over which the forester has some control. Many of the species of trees having commercial value are in the intermediate or subclimax community, which means the forester must know how to control succession so the most favorable regeneration conditions of the desired tree species are reached. These methods will be taken up in greater detail in Chap. 13.

**Forest Classification**  To facilitate forest management, foresters have arbitrarily classified the forest trees into several groups. One classification is based on the size of the individual tree, for example.

Seedling—up to 3 ft (9 m) tall
Sapling—a young tree less than 4 in. (7.6 cm) dbh[1] and from 3 to 10 ft (0.9 to 3 m) tall

[1] dbh (diameter at breast height) = 4 ½ ft (1.35 cm) above the ground.

Pole—from 4 to 12 in. (10 to 25 cm) dbh
Standard—from 1 to 2 ft (0.3 to 0.6 m) dbh
Veteran—over 2 ft (0.6 m) dbh

Other classifications treat age and species. Trees in a forest that are essentially the same age, such as those coming in after a devastating fire, are said to be *even-aged*. A forest with trees ranging from small seedlings to poles to large veterans, for example, is said to be *all-aged*. Foresters talk of a *pure forest* if it is composed mainly of one species, and a *mixed forest* if it contains several species. Botanists and foresters refer to *tolerant* trees as those which can grow in the shade of other trees. Species which cannot survive in shade are said to be *intolerant*. From this it can be seen that a mixed forest of all-ages could have intolerant trees standing over those which are tolerant.

Foresters may want to know the *stand density* of a tract of timber, which tells whether it is well stocked, medium stocked, or understocked. A medium-stocked stand has 40 to 70 percent of its canopy closed over; the other two classifications are more or less than this.

Another common classification of trees is based on the relative position of their crowns (Fig. 9-7).

**Dominant** Pertaining to trees with large crowns which extend above the general level of the forest canopy and receive full light from above and partial light from the sides.

**Codominant** Pertaining to trees with crowns which form the gener-

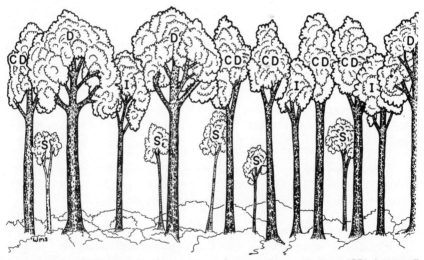

**Figure 9-7** A crown classification showing dominant (D), codominant (CD), intermediate (I), and suppressed (S).

al level of the forest canopy and receive full light from above but relatively little from the sides; crowns smaller than dominants.

**Intermediate**  Pertaining to trees with small crowns crowded into the general level of the forest canopy, receiving some light from above but none from the sides.

**Suppressed**  Pertaining to trees with small crowns that are entirely below the level of the canopy receiving no direct light from above or from the sides. Also called *overtopped.*

A knowledge of these basic classifications will aid the reader in understanding Chap. 13.

**What a Forest Is**  From the above we may conclude that, *a forest is a community of trees and associated organisms covering a considerable area; utilizing oxygen, water, and soil nutrients to attain maturity, and reproduce itself; and capable of furnishing people with useful products and services.*

## WHAT FORESTRY IS

The first part of this chapter has dealt with what a forest is. This section will concern itself briefly with what forestry is.

The Society of American Foresters has adopted the following definition of forestry:

> The science, the art and practice of managing and using for human benefit the natural resources that occur on and in association with forest lands (Ford-Robertson, 1971).

The subject matter of forestry as a science is further divided and includes many aspects by their own special names. Most of these subjects are either elaborations of natural sciences or have a close relationship to the social sciences.

### The Science of Forestry

The science of forestry is young. Even the Germans based their management practices on accumulated observations and trial-and-error experiences until about 1863, when experiment stations were established and research methods were used to develop a scientific foundation for the art. There had been some experimenting among the ancients in the growing and care of individual trees, and things that nowadays seem obvious had been discovered and recorded. Pruning, pollarding to produce small fuelwood, winter storage of tree seeds in sand, and transplanting to increase the vigor of nursery stock were known to the Romans and probably taught by the counterpart of our modern extension forester. Fernow suggests that some of the agricultural and silvicultural knowledge of the Romans was picked up by the German tribes in the fourth century (Fernow, 1911).

To Germany and France particularly, the United States is deeply indebted, for all the early foresters in this country were educated in or had visited these countries and had learned from their studious and skillful foresters.

**Fundamental Aspects of Science in Forestry**   Forestry has to take account of air, water, earth, fire, plants, animals, property, human relationships, and the needs of people. All these things have profound effect upon efforts to learn how to produce, manage, and utilize forests, and upon actual work in laboratory, forest, field, and mill. Geology contributes its established knowledge of the earth's crust, the formation of soil, and the action of wind, water, and ice. Biology classifies, identifies, and describes the living things whose growth and harvest forestry would manipulate. Ecology deals with adaptation by living things to their environments. Mathematics enters into surveys of property, measurement of forest products, calculations of growth and yield, analysis of investments, and forecasting of needs. Physics and chemistry help in subtle problems of growth, injury, fire control, and the engineering phases of harvesting the forest crop. Economics investigates supply and demand, factors of production, and analyzes investments. Sociology adds knowledge of the human element which is necessary to successful forest development and use. All these are contributors, but they are outside the immediate field of the science of forestry.

### Specific Divisions of Forestry as a Science

*Forest Soils*   A highly developed branch of the science of forestry is the study of soils. Early foresters were concerned with it, and one of the first true forest experiment stations was established in 1865 in Prussia to study problems arising from the removal of litter from the forests. The *site* of which the forester speaks and which is a combination of numerous locality factors, cannot be rated or understood without knowledge of the composition, physical and chemical character, and behavior of the soil upon which the forest is to be established, managed, and utilized. The recognition of forest cover as a means of holding soil in place has stimulated the interest of foresters in the study of soils. Their endless search to understand the part that soil elements play in causing growth or stagnation in the forest has resulted in forest-research centers building up a body of scientific knowledge of forest soils under North American conditions.

*Dendrology*   In North America the number of useful species of trees emphasizes the need for thorough description, classification, and recognition of them. Furthermore, the distribution of trees, the how and why of their grouping themselves into types, and the way they grow individually must be understood by the forester. The body of knowledge built up on these principles and particulars is called *dendrology,* and it owes much to investigators in systematic botany, plant anatomy, and physiology.

**Silvics** The term *site* as used in forestry integrates such environmental factors as climate, slope, soil, fire, and biological considerations. They all affect the forest ecosystem and go far in dictating the occurrence of forest types. The study of these basic ecological processes (silvics) develops insight into the practices of silviculture.

**Silviculture** Introducing forest growth on bare land, whether it has formerly supported forests or not, is one of the difficult tasks that must follow well-established general principles to succeed. These principles, and the established body of knowledge that accompanies them, also guide the manipulation of existing forests to assure their natural reproduction and perpetuation. Thinnings and cuttings to improve tree form and hasten growth in both natural and artificial forests proceed successfully through knowledge of requirements for soil, light, moisture, space, and defense against wind and mechanical injury. Principles and organized knowledge of these matters of forest cultivation constitute the basic subject of *silviculture.*

**Forest Management** This subject is more a family of subjects than a single one and is variously interpreted to include mensuration, regulation, valuation, and preparation of working plans or is interpreted to cover all financial aspects of forestry. It is the business arm of the science but is mentioned here along with the subjects that it may include.

**Mensuration** One of the characteristics of science is its earnestness to appraise and to measure. The scientific approach is a quantitative one. Forestry has its branch called *mensuration,* which is an adaptation of mathematics to the measurement of timbered areas or whole forests, of single trees and of logs, and other pieces and units of forest products. But the forest is dynamic, and its size, volume, and yield vary. What it contains today must be projected into the future, if control of the resource is to be achieved and if future wants are to be met. Forest mensuration, furthermore, is not a problem that one may solve at a desk or in a library or wholly in a forest. Above all, it will remain unsolved without precise methods for peculiar forms and arrangements of trees, their distribution on forest land and their products.

**Protection** Humans conquer their enemies by skillful maneuvering, strength, and artifice, all of which must be exerted at the right place and the right time and with the fullest possible knowledge of the enemy and its position. The forest likewise combats many enemies through its own devices, but people must help in this defense or else sacrifice to the enemy the benefits and products that they seek. Fire, insects, disease, wind, and animals may steal the forest. Knowledge of the behavior of these enemies and development of strategy in outwitting them constitute *forest protection.*

Without this accumulated knowledge, practices in defending forests frequently turn into boomerangs. Thus, so-called backfires for defense may develop into conflagrations, or introduction of certain insect-control measures may cause some other useful form to move out. This particular subject is so baffling and concerns so many destructive agencies that it is usually further divided into forest-fire control, forest entomology, and forest pathology.

**Regulation**   As noted heretofore, there is a general group of inventory and planning activities known in the forest as the art of forest regulation. A considerable literature covers the principles and observations that guide this work. In the somewhat narrow sense of fixing in advance what and when certain cuttings of the forest shall be made for definite cultural and economic ends, this kind of planning is governed by the subject called *forest regulation* or *regulation of the cut.*

**Valuation**   In considering forestry as a business, whether public or private, it is essential to know whether it will pay. Because "guessed at" values introduce disorder into any business, there must be principles and an accumulation of knowledge to guide the putting of a value on forest properties, and this accumulation is known as *forest valuation.* The term *forest statics* is sometimes used almost synonymously, but it has to do with weighing one viewpoint of value, or treatment at a given value, against some other viewpoint or possible financial result of treatment. Assumptions of the soundness or unsoundness of forest investments are made and used as business guides through the application of this valuation division of forestry.

**Administration**   Getting things done on a forest or the carrying out of plans has been referred to as *forest administration.* Such an understanding is at variance with the technical definitions of administration in the broadest sense. Nevertheless, as it concerns forestry in the United States, administration has principally to do with personnel and its direction and use in accomplishing desired ends. How forest workers and forest executives are selected, trained, assigned, compensated, and used in carrying out forest policies and procedures forms an array of knowledge known as *forest administration.*

**Policy**   In the sense that a course of conduct must be decided upon in broad terms, a business, a government, or an individual usually sets up a sort of code. This may, of course, be subject to change, as in examples of amendments to laws and ordinances, reconsidering broad decisions of boards of directors, or of an individual. For any given time, however, there is a policy that serves as a guide to action. Forestry is a policy; but, depending upon its promoters, it also has a body of laws, regulations, rules, and procedures that make up forest policy. Most of these are the results of "battles of opinion," and many of them are subject to more than one interpretation. Knowledge, record, and interpretation of these various "codes" constitute a subject known as *forest policy.*

*Utilization* Trees standing in a forest may some day make up houses, packaging containers, or newspapers, and between the trees and their final utility is the art and the business of forest utilization. It is full of engineering, manufacturing methods, adaptation of product to particular use, transportation, and even fabrication. It is so vast in its organization and has so many "business" aspects that these characteristics overshadow the established set of principles and compiled knowledge that amounts to the subject, *forest utilization.* This is a division of forestry as a science, closely allied to engineering, economics, and the natural sciences: chemistry, physics, and biology.

*Wood Technology* By far the greatest direct product of the forest by volume is wood. There are numerous variations of structure, physical and mechanical properties, and behaviors of wood under varying conditions. Knowledge of these characteristics is labeled *wood technology,* and in forestry it is closely allied to forest utilization.

*Other Subjects* Of the subjects that have been discussed, dendrology, silvics, silviculture, forest mensuration, forest protection, forest management (usually including regulation and valuation), forest administration, forest policy, forest utilization, and wood technology are familiar divisions of the *science of forestry.* Other subject names, such as forest economics, forest pathology, forest zoology, forest organization, forest finance, and forest engineering, are subdivisions, variations in name or groupings. Still other related subjects or specialties are outdoor recreation, wildlife management, watershed management, and range management. There is also the so-called municipal and utility forestry, which is largely tree preservation and landscape work. The latter, of course, seldom involves a forest.

**Professional Courses of Study** The Society of American Foresters has established educational standards for the profession of forestry. An account of the Society's procedure in accrediting forestry schools is contained in Chap. 23.

**BIBLIOGRAPHY**

Ahlgren, Clifford E. 1973. The Changing Forest, pts. 1 [79(1):40–43] and 2 [79(2):16–18], *Amer. Forests.*

Bonner, J., and A. W. Galston. 1952. *Principles of Plant Physiology,* W. H. Freeman and Company, San Francisco.

Clepper, Henry, and Arthur B. Meyer. 1965. *The World of the Forest,* prepared in cooperation with the Society of American Foresters, D. C. Heath and Company, Boston.

# Chapter 10

# Forestry Around the World

## The World's Forests

A few points regarding the forests of the world are basic to a proper understanding of their importance to humans through the ages. As was indicated in Chap. 1, early people made the forest serve some of their basic needs and gradually made inroads upon it with fire, stone ax, and eventually the goat. After the last glacial period, some 10 to 12 thousand years ago, we may presume that the land area of the earth was forested except for deserts, natural prairies, and areas of marshes, tundra, and treeless mountain tops. According to recent estimates only 29 percent of the land area of the earth is now forested. The reduction has been caused by actions of the human race, except for some relatively minor and mostly localized changes in climate.

The forests of the world are, broadly speaking, of two kinds, the coniferous forest composed of "needle" trees and the usually deciduous broad-

This chapter was prepared by Robert K. Winters, formerly Director of International Forestry, Forest Service, U.S. Department of Agriculture, and currently Consultant in International Forestry of the Society of American Foresters.

leaf trees. In general, the conifers are to be found on the cooler, drier situations, and the broadleaf species are predominant in the warmer, usually moister areas of the world. Because the Northern Hemisphere contains the bulk of the world's land area having a temperate climate, the coniferous forest is largely found there. Tropical forests consist almost exclusively of broadleaf species. Mixed broadleaf and coniferous forests are found near the boundaries between these two climatic zones. From this it is apparent that trees, like *Homo sapiens* and other animals, are in constant competition for living space. Thus trees of a given species generally occupy those areas where their natural characteristics best equip them to compete with other species.

What then are some of these characteristics, and how do they affect the composition of a forest? The influence of moisture has already been mentioned. Some species can exist under relatively dry and even semidesert conditions. They usually have a long and deeply penetrating taproot that can obtain water from considerable depths. Their leaves are usually small, compact, and covered with a cutaneous layer that minimizes water evaporation. In this category are many of the needle trees and the tiny-leaved and thorny acacias of the semideserts.

On the other extreme, some species can compete successfully on wet, even periodically inundated tidal and river-margin areas. Their roots must have access to oxygen, and most trees will die if their roots are denied it for any considerable period of time. Under such circumstances, some species send up "knees" that, in some way not clearly understood, enable the roots to survive the submersion period.

Character of seed also has much to do with the distribution of a given tree species. The seed of light-seeded species like cottonwood can be widely distributed by the wind or can be carried miles downstream by water. They thus regularly establish themselves on river banks and on newly made sandbars. The fruits of certain tree species have food value and are eaten by birds and other animals; the seeds are then distributed with the feces. Throughout the range of eastern juniper in the United States, for example, this species is frequently found along fence rows and beneath telephone wires on which birds perch.

A third characteristic that importantly affects the forest composition of any area is the ability of the component species to endure shade. Some cannot long endure any shade. Others are able to persist for years in deep shade and, when the overtopping trees are cut or die, accelerate their growth rate and eventually take over the area. Thus, light-demanders, especially those having lightweight seeds, often establish themselves on clearcut areas, on abandoned agricultural land, and on new-made river margins. Subsequently the seed of some shade-endurer becomes established under the initial cover and ultimately replaces that cover.

Because of these varying characteristics of individual tree species, the kind and distribution of the forests of the world are largely determined by local conditions. Each combination of temperature, rainfall, and soil has its peculiar association of tree and other vegetation that can hold the site in competition with all other combinations of vegetation. Occasionally hurricanes, fires, or other catastrophies destroy this natural state of equilibrium. Subsequently the affected area is ordinarily restocked by one or more of the light-demanding species. Gradually shade-endurers establish themselves beneath this forest cover and ultimately replace it, thus ending the competitive cycle by reaching another temporary state of equilibrium.

The distribution of the principal forest associations of the world is shown in Fig. 10-1. Each is characterized by the natural tree association that is predominant in the area. Within any of these forest regions a variety of localized forest associations or types may occur. They would ordinarily be the result of variations in climate, soil, and the influence of the human race. Figure 10-1 reveals that over wide areas of relatively uniform climate similar forest associations have developed. In the frost-free equatorial region, tropical broadleaf forests abound. Adjacent to the tundra in the north, coniferous forests occur. Between these extremes of climate are found, often in mixture, coniferous and broadleaf species. Of course, a parallel zonation of tree associations is found in the altitudinal ranges of a mountain system. Not all land area within the geographic distribution of these associations is forested, far from it; the map merely indicates the general kinds of forest that are found where forest still exists. In densely settled areas much land is in agricultural crops.

Table 10-1 shows the approximate distribution of the forest area of the world by the principal geographic regions. Overall, some 29 percent of the earth's land surface is forested. The Americas show a relatively high concentration of forest land. Within North America the land area is almost equally divided between the United States and Canada, but Canada is 45 percent forested as against 32 percent for the United States. The U.S.S.R. also shows a relatively high proportion of forest area.

As to species composition, about one-third of the world's forest area bears a coniferous forest, mainly located in the temperate zone of the Northern Hemisphere. The U.S.S.R. possesses 45 percent of this total, and North America 36 percent. Of the area of broadleaf forest, somewhat more than three-quarters is found in South America and Africa, especially West and Central Africa. This results, of course, from the fact that the broadest portion of these continents lies in the equatorial belt where warm moist conditions favor the tropical rain forest. Overall, three-fourths of the area of broadleaf forest is found in the less industrialized regions and, in the main, constitute a relatively untapped resource.

According to the best available data (FAO-1963), nearly 85 percent of

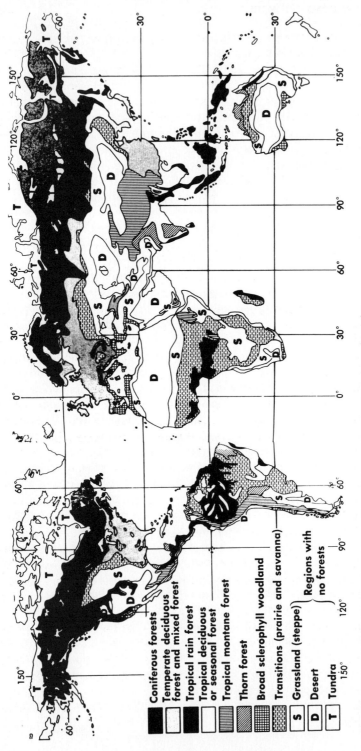

**Figure 10-1** Generalized distribution of the principal forest associations throughout the world. *(From A World Geography of Forest Resources, edited for the American Geographical Society by Stephen Haden-Guest, John K. Wright, and Eileen M. Tchlaff. Copyright © 1956, The Ronald Press Company, New York.)*

Coniferous forests

Temperate deciduous forest and mixed forest

Tropical rain forest

Tropical deciduous or seasonal forest

Tropical montane forest

Thorn forest

Broad sclerophyll woodland

Transitions (prairie and savanna)

S Grassland (steppe)

D Desert

T Tundra

Regions with no forests

**Table 10-1  World Forest Area as a Percentage of Land Area,\* by Regions**

| Region | Land area (millions) acres | Land area (millions) hectares | Percentage forested |
|---|---|---|---|
| North America | 4,633 | 1,853 | 38 |
| Latin America | 5,019 | 2,007 | 44 |
| Africa | 7,339 | 2,935 | 24 |
| Europe | 1,129 | 452 | 29 |
| U.S.S.R. | 5,297 | 2,119 | 34 |
| Asia | 6,727 | 2,691 | 19 |
| Pacific Area | 2,081 | 832 | 11 |
| Total | 32,225 | 12,890 | |

\*Food and Agriculture Organization of the United Nations, *World Forest Inventory*, 1963, Table 1.

the total timber volume in the forests of the world is found in North America, the U.S.S.R., and South America. Data for the latter are largely based on estimates of experts, but for the other two regions the data are based largely on field inventories. Accordingly, the supply situation of the world's coniferous timber, the most important industrial wood, is known with relative accuracy.

Although reliable forest ownership data are not available for a considerable part of the world, it is estimated that 77 percent of the forest area is publicly owned, and in North America nearly three-fourths is similarly owned. This high proportion is primarily caused by the large area of Canadian forest that is owned by the various provinces.

Although data on the worldwide timber cut are none too reliable, the best estimates indicate that 83,860 million cu ft (2,373 million m³)were removed in 1970. Of this total approximately 54 percent was for industrial use and the remainder was for fuel and other domestic uses. About four-fifths of the domestic-use wood was consumed in the less industrialized parts of the world, this mostly of broadleaf species. This wood contributed substantially to the local economies of the producing countries. Particularly in the less industrialized nations, the forest has been a resource ready for conversion into lumber, paper, plywood, and other processed items that provide employment and add materially to the gross national product (GNP).

Forest products are also important items in international trade. Available trade statistics are considerably more reliable than production statistics. Table 10-2 presents export and import data for logs and sawn wood, two items for which volume summaries can readily be made. However, they account for only about half the dollar value of all forest-product international trade. The other half is chiefly accounted for by trade in wood pulp and the various grades of paper and paperboard.

**Table 10-2   1970 Trade in Logs and Sawn Wood**

| | Exports (in 1,000 m³) | | | |
| | Logs | | Sawn wood | |
| | Conifer | Nonconifer | Conifer | Nonconifer |
|---|---|---|---|---|
| North America | 13,391 | 368 | 20,057 | 674 |
| Latin America | 10 | 365 | 1,677 | 557 |
| Africa | · · · · · · | 6,505 | 109 | 760 |
| Europe | 1,676 | 1,544 | 19,202 | 2,435 |
| U.S.S.R. | 7,351 | 98 | 7,980 | · · · · · · |
| Asia | 486 | 28,227 | 165 | 2,623 |
| Pacific area | 1,829 | 394 | 274 | 44 |
| Total world trade* | 24,743 | 37,501 | 49,464 | 7,093 |

*Because of reporting errors the world totals of exports only approximate the world total of imports.

The regional breakdown of exports and imports of logs and sawn wood reveals a number of significant points. The developing countries in Asia and Africa are heavy exporters of logs, principally nonconiferous. This export of logs is characteristic of nations with a substantial forest resource that have not yet developed an advanced forest-product manufacturing industry. However, North America and the U.S.S.R. are large exporters of conifer logs. North America, Europe, and the U.S.S.R. are large exporters of sawn wood, mainly coniferous. With respect to imports, Japan is seen to be a very large importer of logs, both coniferous and nonconiferous. Europe is a significant importer of logs, and a very heavy importer of sawn wood. A considerable proportion of the North American exports and imports of both logs and sawn wood is the result of the movement across the Canadian–United States border.

### The Beginnings of the Science of Forestry

The beginnings of the science of forestry had their roots in the shortage of ship timbers in northern Europe during the seventeenth century, in France and Britain, especially. During the 1660s and 1670s, Jean Baptiste Colbert, Prime Minister of France, attempted to strengthen France's sea power. During his tenure he increased the annual expenditures for this purpose 44-fold, but the existing readily available French forests were then in no position to supply the high-quality naval timbers in the required quantities. Although his ultimate aim was to make France self-sufficient in naval timber and other forest products, much timber had initially to be purchased abroad.

To accomplish this goal of self-sufficiency, Colbert issued the celebrat-

| Imports (in 1,000 m³) | | | |
| --- | --- | --- | --- |
| Logs | | Sawn wood | |
| Conifer | Nonconifer | Conifer | Nonconifer |
| 1,786 | 477 | 13,859 | 1,008 |
| 20 | 266 | 1,560 | 154 |
| 52 | 279 | 1,600 | 490 |
| 3,592 | 8,152 | 27,297 | 3,701 |
| 400 | 68 | · · · · · · | 287 |
| 18,762 | 26,771 | 3,768 | 972 |
| 5 | 205 | 710 | 276 |
| 24,617 | 36,218 | 48,794 | 6,888 |

ed Ordinance of Waters and Forests of 1669. It attempted to bring all French forests under systems of cutting that would provide a continuous yield of timber. At that time only the simplest and most rudimentary of forestry principles were known and employed. A given forest ownership was merely divided into as many equal areas as the age in years of the trees at the anticipated harvest date. One such area was cut over each year. To obtain reproduction a definite number of seed trees was left, and some species sprouted from the stump. Because of variations in the productivity and species composition of the annual cutting areas, there was no way in which the owner could forecast the quantity and character of the yield in any year. In fact, the science of forestry was not yet developed. The research needed to supply rates of growth of individual species and other scientific data was not undertaken until more than a century had passed.

About this time, the modern age of science was being born. In 1609 Galileo invented the telescope and taught that the earth revolved around the sun. Anton van Leeuwenhoek invented the microscope; Robert Hooke identified living cells; and later Sir Isaac Newton established the laws of physical motion. German forest masters apparently were in tune with the new scientific spirit. Soon they were applying mathematical formulas to calculate forest growth, were developing cutting budgets to spread equally the volume of forest yield over the number of years required to produce a new crop of timber, and were preparing systematic forest operational plans. They then began to establish experimental plots to measure the effect of various practices on timber production, i.e., thinning frequency and intensity and yields at various ages. Thus, through research they were pioneering in the science of forestry.

Gradually these early pioneers attracted pupils and eventually some of them established schools of forest practice. One of the earliest of these was established in 1768 at Ilsenburg, Germany, by Hans Dietrich von Zanthier. Others followed, headed by Johann Jacob Trunk at the University of Freiburg in Bresgau in 1791; by G. L. Hartig in Huningen in 1791; by Henrich Cotta in Zillbach in 1795; and by still others. Most of them depended entirely on the reputation of their founders and passed out of existence at their death. Two, however, were exceptions; the ones established by Trunk in Freiburg, which has continued to this day, and the one established by Cotta. The latter was later moved to Tharandt where it was officially designated as a Forest Academy and in the 1930s was made a unit in the University of Dresden.

Although the French foresters had for some time held leadership in the practice of what might be called rule-of-thumb forestry, the Germans eventually changed all that. At first the French viewed the German theoretical forestry as impractical and clung to their old ways. After a time, however, the French leaders began to accept the new science and established a forestry school in Nancy in 1825. J. B. Lorentz, the first director, had been educated in the German school at Tharandt under the progressive leader, Cotta. Lorentz faced opposition at first, but gradually the conservative elements in French forestry accepted the German concepts. As the nineteenth century advanced, the Germans and the French emerged as the undisputed leaders in developing the science of forestry.

From these two countries this science has moved out, modified wherever necessary to fit local conditions in other parts of the world. German foresters were involved in the launching of forestry in Russia, Sweden, Spain, and other European countries. One of the more significant extensions of the science was to India, where the European principles had to be adapted to subtropical forests.

By the early nineteenth century British officials were becoming alarmed concerning the supply of teak ship timbers in India and Burma. In 1855 Lord Dalhousie, then Governor General of India, laid down the basic principles of what was to become a permanent forest policy for India. To implement this policy he brought a German forester, Dr. Dietrich Bradis, to Burma as Superintendent of the forests of the Province of Pegu (Burma). After adapting the European principles to Burmese forest conditions with considerable success, he was asked to extend his operations to the whole of India. To assist him he brought two young German foresters, William Schlich and B. Ribbentrop. Arrangements were also made to send five young French-speaking Englishmen to Nancy for scientific training in forestry. Simultaneously two young German-speaking Englishmen were sent to Germany for similar training. Thus was instituted the Indian Forest Service, which ultimately grew to more than 600 foresters plus more than 10,000 subprofessionals and forest guards.

From India and Burma the British carried the science of forestry to practically all their colonies. The usual procedure was as follows: An officer of the Indian Forest Service would be temporarily detailed to study the forest situation in a British colony that was contemplating the creation of an indigenous forest service. When his report had been studied and approved, he would usually be transferred to become the first head of the newly created service. In this manner the science of forestry was introduced into practically all the British colonies. The other important European colonial powers were generally following a similar practice. Noncolonial powers, such as China and Japan, brought in German or French foresters to assist in establishing a forestry science.

The first extension of the science to the United States came when a young German forester, Bernhard Eduard Fernow, came to this country in 1876. He was first employed by mining companies to handle their forests that were involved in charcoal operations. Gradually he extended his influence to the then young forestry organizations and still later was appointed Chief of the Division of Forestry in the Department of Agriculture. In 1887 young Gifford Pinchot sailed for Europe and for a period of study at the Forest School at Nancy, France. He also was greatly influenced by the then retired Dr. Dietrich Brandis and by a period of practical forestry experiences in Switzerland. Fernow and Pinchot were, therefore, the primary pioneers in the introduction of the science of forestry to the United States.

### Worldwide Forestry Organizations

International forestry cooperation began in the field of forestry research. In 1892 the International Union of Forestry Research Organizations, often referred to as IUFRO, was organized in Vienna, Austria. Its primary objective was to stimulate effective research in forestry. To this end it first attempted to standardize basic research procedures and to institute international studies of important tree species and international timber-testing programs. During World Wars I and II its activities were interrupted, but currently Union Congresses are held at 5-year intervals, and 22 specialized committees coordinate a program of international research in all fields of forestry.

In 1921 Anders Fjelstad, permanent Norwegian delegate to the International Institute of Agriculture (IIA) in Rome, Italy, initiated within the Institute a program for gathering international forestry statistics. Later he persuaded the Institute's governing board to organize the First World Forestry Congress. This Congress, held in Rome in 1926, was attended by some 1,200 delegates from 58 countries.

In the early 1930s when the worldwide depression threatened the forest-products industries of the Northern Hemisphere, the inadequacy of the existing statistics on forest resources, timber production, and timber trade in Europe became obvious. Rumors circulated, concerning accumulated stocks and forthcoming supplies, and this, in turn, aggravated the crisis. As a result, the Economic Committee of the League of Nations convened, in the spring of 1932 in Geneva, an international conference of timber experts. One month later a second conference decided on the creation of the Comité International du Bois (CIB) with headquarters in Vienna. Its principal functions were to assemble, coordinate, and publish statistical data on the production, trade, stocks, and prices of forest products and to promote timber trade. Ultimately 15 European nations, as well as Canada and the United States, affiliated with CIB. Germany was never a member. At first merely an outsider, it eventually became a bitter foe.

As the Nazis attained power in Germany they perceived in wood a raw material that could help them in their bid for world power. Science had developed methods for converting wood into textiles, motor fuel, cattle feed, and other materials that were in short supply in parts of Europe. They apparently reasoned that the prestige of German forestry and the worldwide connections of German foresters could be used in the economic and political penetration of other countries.

Their moves in this direction became apparent during the Second World Forestry Congress, held in Budapest in 1936. Having become disenchanted with the CIB they set about to establish a competing organization they could control. Accordingly, they introduced a resolution creating in Berlin a Centre International de Silviculture (CIS) as an autonomous unit within the International Institute of Agriculture. Its primary functions were (1) to prepare, convene, and organize, regularly, World Forestry Congresses; (2) to carry out the recommendations of those Congresses; (3) to coordinate matters in the field of international silviculture; (4) to study problems of silviculture in the international field, referring those in forestry-related areas to other units in the Institute; and (5) to publish the results of such studies.

From its inception in 1938 the CIS had organizational difficulties. Its members were chiefly German satellites. Norway and Sweden, both important European timber producers, refused to join. But early Nazi war successes changed all that. Inevitably the conquered governments became members of CIS. During the war years CIS assembled a quantity of information on international forestry, which was published in bulletins and in a quarterly journal, *Intersylva*, which was issued in French and German with Finnish, Italian, and Spanish resumés.

When the Nazis overran Austria, the CIB office was moved to Brussels, and a branch office was established in Geneva. Eventually these were also closed, and the Secretary-General, Egon Glesinger, escaped to the United States, where he hoped to keep alive an interest in the CIB organization. The wartime plans to create the Food and Agriculture Organization (FAO), which later became one of the United Nations family of organizations gave him that opportunity.

The scope of the activities of the FAO was initially established during a conference convened at the request of President Franklin D. Roosevelt at Hot Springs, Virginia, in April 1943. At that conference the agriculture and nutrition leaders of 43 nations considered ways and means of improving the food and agricultural conditions around the world. In spite of the urging of Anders Fjelstad, forestry was not included as a discipline within the FAO organization. Soon thereafter Glesinger contacted Clarence Forsling of the Forest Service, U.S. Department of Agriculture, to report that some of the European delegates to the Hot Springs Conference were disappointed that a forestry unit had not been included in the proposed organizational structure of the FAO. As a result, the support of President Roosevelt was obtained, and forestry became one of the important disciplines of that organization.[1] Subsequently FAO officially took over from the Permanent Committee of the IIA its functions (including those of the CIS), its library, archives, and property. The FAO intended to do the same for the CIB, but there is no available evidence that its Permanent Committee took the necessary action.

The initial responsibilities of the Forestry Division of the FAO were primarily (1) the promotion and coordination of forestry research among its member nations; (2) the dissemination of statistics on forest area, timber volume and growth, and international trade in forest products; (3) advisory functions to member nations, especially where one nation had developed techniques of value to others; and (4) cooperation with other public international organizations. The very rapid increase in the number of member nations during the 1950s and 1960s resulted in some shift in emphasis, although there was no fundamental alteration in the four primary responsibilities. The urgent need for assistance to the new developing nations in formulating and carrying out an adequate forestry program forced expanded funding to care for their previously unforeseen needs.

The regular FAO program is financed by a biennial assessment on member countries according to an agreed-upon formula. Initially the United States provided nearly one-third of the biennial budget; other nations contributed lesser sums. In 1972 Congress limited the United States contribution to 25 percent of the total, effective January 1, 1974. Many of the developing nations are assessed only token amounts, and some of them are continually in arrears. As the FAO membership grew (it was 103 in the summer of 1973), additional funding became an absolute necessity. As a result the United Nations Development Fund, later renamed the United Nations Development Program (UNDP), was established in 1958. With headquarters in New York, and with substantial funding contributed biennially by voluntary offerings of donor nations, it is in a position to help finance 2- to 5-year projects in developing countries designed to strengthen

---

[1] For further details on this development refer to Winters (1971), and Winters (1974).

their forestry, agricultural, and nutritional programs. Recipient nations are required to contribute half or more of the project costs. For the 11-year period from 1959 to 1969, 65 forestry and forestry-related projects had been approved by the UNDP, involving approximately $60 million of its funds. Roughly 40 percent of this sum was allotted to finance preinvestment surveys designed to indicate the feasibility of establishing or expanding forest industrial plants. Invariably the developing nations are eager to manufacture and use any of their resources. To do so provides employment and the commodities needed for domestic growth and foreign trade. In many of these countries the forest constitutes an important natural resource. National planners, therefore, want to know the extent and nature of their forest resource in order to decide what kinds of plants (sawmills, pulp mills, veneer or plywood plants) to build and what a reasonable capacity might be, depending upon the quantity and character of the forest resource.

Approximately 30 percent of the UNDP fund allocations were used to establish or expand forestry educational and training facilities. This activity has been very important because, as many of the new nations emerged from colonial status, their colonial administrators and scientists returned to their home countries. This left the new nations with a great need for the facilities to educate and to train their own national leaders. The remaining 30 percent of allotted funds provided for the financing of projects in the fields of forestry research, forest management, and a variety of miscellaneous projects. Since the beginning of the UNDP, approximately 25 percent of the funds allotted to all projects in the broad field of agriculture have financed forest projects. This is a firm indication of the relative importance of the forest resource to the developing countries as they prepare their national plans.

In 1973 the approximate number of professional forestry specialists assigned to projects operated by the Forestry Department of FAO is shown in the following tabulation:

| Professional forestry specialists | Approximate number |
| --- | --- |
| Rome headquarters | 61 |
| Regional offices | 19 |
| Field projects | |
|     UNDP | 284 |
|     Trust and other funds | 80 |
|     Total | 444 |

Of this number 41 are citizens of the United States. A few of these are permanent specialists with the FAO, but most are on leave from their career

United States positions for a few months to a few years. In addition to the above, forestry specialists are also assigned to projects operated by other departments in the FAO, such as those in range and watershed management. Furthermore, a number of countries assign to FAO for one to several years young graduate foresters who assist regularly employed forestry specialists as associate experts. The number of these is subject to such long- and short-term fluctuations that meaningful data are not available.

In addition to the multilateral forestry aid of the FAO a number of nations have operated bilateral assistance programs in forestry. Although the United States'[2] program has probably been the greatest in absolute amount, a number of other nations have made greater contributions in proportion to their gross national product. These include Canada, Great Britain, France, the Netherlands, Belgium, and others.

The United States program came as an outgrowth of the Marshall Plan (1948), which assisted in the recovery of European nations following World War II. In his inaugural address of 1949, President Truman made the following statement:

> The United States is preeminent among nations in the development of industrial and scientific techniques. The material resources which we can afford to use for the assistance of other peoples are limited. But our imponderable resources in technical knowledge are constantly growing and are inexhaustible.
>
> I believe that we should make available to peace-loving peoples the benefits of our store of technical knowledge in order to help them realize their aspirations for a better life.

The plan that these words suggested became widely known as the Point Four Program.[3] Subsequently it was administered by the Foreign Operations Administration (FOA), International Cooperation Administration (ICA), and the Agency for International Development (AID). Under AID the program has continued, although in recent years on a greatly diminished scale.

Precise figures indicating the monetary size of the program cannot be given. Some projects that were classified as "forestry" in published statistics were strongly oriented toward water conservation and erosion control and vice versa. Some grants for sawmill construction were classified in the "industrial" category along with steel mills and chemical plants. Furthermore, summarized statistical data prior to 1955 are nonexistent. Nevertheless, the grants classified under the heading "forestry" during the fiscal years 1955 to 1970 aggregated approximately $24 million.

---

[2] Authorized by Public Law 535, 81st Congress.
[3] Ibid.

The sums allotted to individual developing countries from these funds also included the salaries and expenses of experts from the United States who were assigned to advise in the planning and operation of specific projects. For the most part these specialists were recruited by AID or its predecessors from other government agencies or from private organizations. In a few instances the responsibility for advice in planning and operation of certain projects was contracted by AID to private institutions. For example, the Syracuse University New York College of Environmental Science and Forestry operated under a contract designed to assist in strengthening of the Philippine College of Forestry.

Normally the recipient country was required to contribute at least half the project cost. Thus these projects represent a total investment of approximately $50 million. The sums allotted to forestry assistance were greatest in the 1950s—some $2.5 million annually. Subsequently they decreased gradually until in the late 1960s they were less than one-tenth of that sum. A possible explanation is that the Food and Agriculture Organization has a relatively large number of professional foresters in the field and on its supervisory staff and was in a good position to handle this forestry assistance.

The United States Agency for International Development also makes available development loans, and a number of countries have obtained such loans for forest-product industrial construction and other forestry purposes. Still another way in which United States funds have helped to spread forestry in the developing lands has been through local currency funds that accrued from the sale of its grain gifts during past years. Public Law 480, which provided for such gifts, stipulated that local-currency funds resulting from the sale of such grains could be used within the country for certain types of development projects, including forestry. Considerable amounts of such funds have been approved for forestry and related projects in such countries as India, Morocco, and Israel.

The Peace Corps has also made a considerable contribution to forestry in some of the countries in which it has operated. In 1971 it had forestry programs in more than 25 nations of Asia, Africa, and Latin America. About 75 volunteers were requested to service these programs for a 2-year period beginning in June 1971. Some were graduate foresters and others had only practical experience in forestry (Fig. 10-2). The volunteers have been especially active in reforestation projects. Also in demand are foresters with skills in the field of outdoor recreation to help plan, establish, and maintain forest-park recreation facilities. Some of the young forestry graduates in the Peace Corps work under the informal guidance of highly skilled professionals from FAO and AID. These more senior officers make the initial surveys of the needs and resources of the developing nations and the Peace Corps volunteers participate in the work program that implements the recommendations.

**Figure 10-2**   A Peace Corps volunteer in a forest in Chile, one of hundreds who worked overseas in forestry. *(Photo by Grant W. Sharpe.)*

Not all international forestry activities have been government sponsored. In developing countries, especially, foreign companies have often held logging concessions and have extracted the more valuable and readily accessible portions of the timber resource. In only a few instances, however, has any attempt been made to apply appropriate forestry principles and to leave the forest area in a condition such as to perpetuate effectively the valuable elements of the timber crop. For many years a paper company has operated a pulpmill in the state of São Paulo, Brazil, that has consumed eucalyptus and slash pine from company-owned local plantations. In Chile, European-trained foresters pioneered in the establishment and management of plantations of Monterey pine and eucalyptus that are now supplying raw material for a number of pulpmills and board mills.

At the Sixth World Forestry Congress, held in 1966 in Madrid, leaders in the Society of American Foresters proposed the formation of an international organization of professional forestry societies. An organizing meeting was held in Washington, D.C., in August 1969, and the International Union of Societies of Foresters officially came into being. Its purpose is "to promote international cooperation for the advancement of the practice and profession of forestry and of professional foresters throughout the world." At the time of organization 11 national societies became members. At the

end of 1973, the organization was composed of the professional forestry
societies in 19 nations.

## World Forestry Literature

As has been mentioned, the International Union of Forest Research Organizations stimulated a coordinated international forestry research program.
In general, the results of research projects in a given country were published
in its own professional journals, usually however, comparing results obtained elsewhere under the coordinated research program. The published
proceedings of the First World Forestry Congress, held in Rome in 1926,
probably constitute the first truly international forestry literature. The statistical and other publications of the CIB and CIS have already been mentioned; the proceedings of successive World Forestry Congresses have
provided a considerable body of world forestry information. Since 1939 the
journal, *Forestry Abstracts,* has been published quarterly by the Commonwealth Forestry Bureau in Oxford, England. It contains brief English-language abstracts of the world's literature in forestry and related fields.

With the establishment of FAO the production of international forestry literature was materially stimulated. *Unasylva,* a quarterly forestry journal, was published from 1947 to 1971 and publication was resumed in 1974.
In addition, the *Yearbook of Forest Products* contains annual worldwide
statistics on the production and trade in important forest products. At approximately 5-year intervals FAO has compiled and published the *World
Forest Inventory*, containing for the countries of the world data on forest
area, timber volume, growth, and removals. The FAO has also published a
variety of handbooks and manuals dealing with forestry practices in various
parts of the world. In addition, a series of mimeographed reports has provided detailed forestry information for many individual countries.

As worldwide travel and communication improve, foresters around the
world are becoming more knowledgeable regarding world forest conditions
and diverse practices. Consequently the better-known professional forestry
journals are being more widely read. As English increasingly becomes an
important second language of world foresters, the importance of forestry
publications in English has increased. To still further increase the usefulness of international forestry literature, the Joint FAO/IUFRO Committee
on Forestry Bibliography and Terminology in 1954 published the basic
English version of the *Oxford System of Decimal Classification for Forestry*.
This has provided an extremely useful tool for the retrieval of important
forestry publications in all important subject areas. In 1949 the Joint Committee also began the preparation of a multilingual forestry terminology.
French, German, and English foresters initiated the compilation of a standard glossary of technical forestry terms. In 1971 the English-language version was published by the Society of American Foresters under the title,

*Terminology of Forest Science, Technology, Practice, and Products.* The others will contain direct translations of the English definitions plus those of other terms that are important in their national literature. Each English term has been given a permanent number by means of which the definition of that term in any of the other languages can quickly be found in the appropriate language terminology. Subsequently the revisions of the various language versions will be so coordinated that each contains numbered definitions that are exact translations of the identical term in the other language versions. By these means the very large body of technical forestry literature will continously be made available to foresters having diverse language backgrounds.

The shared findings of research and practice have been effective in improving forestry around the world. It is hoped that this cooperation will continue and increase.

## BIBLIOGRAPHY

Fox, Gordon D. 1972. *Forestry in Developing Countries* (preliminary survey), Office of Science and Technology, Agency for International Development, Washington, DC.

Kelts, Lora I. 1973. International Directory of Professional Forestry Associations and Their Principal Publications, *Jour. Forestry,* **8:**506–511.

Shirley, Hardy L. 1973. *Forestry and Its Career Opportunities,* 3d ed., McGraw-Hill Book Company, New York.

Winters, Robert K. 1974. *The Forest and Man,* Vantage Press, Inc., New York.

———. 1971. How Forestry Became a Part of FAO, *Jour. Forestry,* **69:**574–578, 711.

# Chapter 11

# The Political Economy of
# Forestry

## FOREST ECOLOGY AND ECONOMY

### People and the Natural World

The human race impacts the natural world in three principal ways: (1) by extracting raw materials, (2) by modifying the land surface for food production and other purposes, and (3) by discarding wastes and residues of various sorts. It has been estimated (Knesse et al., 1970) that in 1965 Americans extracted and used 2.5 billion tons (2.25 billion t) of ore, fuel, wood, crops, and animal products from the world's fields, forests, mines and waters. This amounts to 15 tons (13.5 t) per person per year—15 tons of materials extracted from nature for each American.

The human race also intrudes on the natural world by substantially altering the land. One-half of the United States is so altered, as is shown in

This chapter was prepared by Robert Marty, Professor of Forestry, Michigan State University, and Henry H. Webster, Chief, Forestry Division, Michigan Department of Natural Resources.

this listing:

| Land use | Percentage |
|---|---|
| Urban areas, roads, etc. | 2 |
| Strip and open-pit mines | 3 |
| Cropland | 20 |
| Improved pasture | 25 |
| Substantially unaltered | 50 |
| Total | 100 |

Finally, the natural world is impacted through discards. Virtually everything taken from this natural world eventually is discarded. If each of us requires 15 tons of nature's materials to sustain our standard of living then you can be sure that something like 15 tons of waste also will be discarded in one form or another—as mine tailings, manufacturing residues, trash, smoke, water pollution, or any of a large number of other forms of residue.

Wood constitutes about 10 percent of total raw material extractions. The following listing shows the annual materials balance for wood and wood products as an example of how materials cycle through our economy.

| Production | cu ft | Millions m$^3$ |
|---|---|---|
| Trees harvested | 15.0 | 424.5 |
| Discarded logging residues | 2.0 | 56.6 |
| Logs, poles, bolts, etc. | 13.0 | 368.0 |
| Used as fuelwood | 1.3 | 36.8 |
| Roundwood for industrial use | 11.7 | 331.0 |
| Discarded as primary manufacturing residues | 1.7 | 48.0 |
| Primary wood and paper products | 10.0 | 283.0 |
| Discarded secondary manufacturing residues | 0.7 | 19.8 |
| Final wood and paper products | 9.3 | 263.0 |
| **Consumption** | | |
| Additions to the inventory of wood and paper products | 0.6 | 17.0 |
| Recycled paper waste | 1.1 | 31.0 |
| Used and discarded as wood and paper waste | 7.6 | 215.0 |

Human ecology is the study of how people interact with their environment—how they go about making their living and what the results of these efforts are, both for the individual and for the world. A full understanding of these processes must include consideration of how individuals and societies decide how they will live from and with nature. Economics is the study of how people make these choices, and the economics of forestry is the study of how we utilize our forests to satisfy human wants and needs.

## The Economic Importance of Forests

The forested lands of the United States contribute to our well-being in many ways. About one-third of America is forested, and because of their pervasiveness no complete inventory exists of all the goods, services, and satisfactions stemming from these lands. Forest lands provide timber and minerals important in many industries, they provide recreation of many sorts; they are the habitat of many fish and wildlife species; they constitute the watersheds that provide much of this nation's water for residential, industrial, and farm use; and they encompass substantial areas of wilderness.

The national forest system is made up of about 187 million acres (75.6 million ha) of land, predominately forested and mainly located in the western United States. The system is made up of 154 national forests and is administered by the U.S. Forest Service. In the year ending June 30, 1971, the system produced these outputs (U.S. Department of Agriculture, 1973a):

| Output | Volume of production | Receipts (millions of dollars) |
|---|---|---|
| Timber | 10.5 billion board feet | 317.8 |
| Minerals, gas, and oil | . . . . . . . . . . . . . . . . . . . . | 29.4 |
| Forage for domestic livestock | 7.36 million animal unit-months | 4.8 |
| Recreation use | 184 million user-days | 8.1 |
| Big game harvest | 576 thousand animals | |
| Wilderness primitive areas | 14.3 million acres (5.8 million ha) | |
| Water production | 50% of the water supply of the West | |

Except for timber and minerals, receipts represent only a small portion of the economic value of the outputs provided. Nonetheless, the listing makes apparent the kinds of output available from forests and something about their relative economic importance. Timber, recreation, and water are the three most important outputs that forested lands provide in most circumstances.

Long-continued research in the economics of timber production and use gives us a much better picture of the economic importance of this traditionally most important forest output. A study of the timber economy (Hair, 1963) indicated that about 6 percent of the nation's gross national product and about 5 percent of its civilian employment originates in timber-based economic activity. These activities include forest management; harvesting of forest products; primary manufacturing to produce lumber, plywood, and paper; secondary manufacturing to produce final goods such as furniture; construction of housing and other structures; and transportation of wood products between the forest, the manufacturer, and the ultimate consumer. In the principal timber production and manufacturing areas, timber and wood products often are among the most important industries. Hair's study indicates that, for every dollar of timber harvested, the final products created are worth about $25.

### The Economic Structure of the Wood Products Sector

The structure of economic activity is complex and there are many interactions among firms in the wood products industries. Economists have developed transaction tables to display these relationships with more clarity. Table 11-1 is a transaction table for wood products industries in the South Atlantic census region (Kaiser, 1972).

Each column in the table shows how much the indicated industry sector purchased from other sectors. For example, firms manufacturing wood household furniture (sector 9) purchased $127 million worth of material from sawmills and planing mills, $75 million worth of materials from veneer and plywood plants, $15 million worth of other wood products, $2 million worth of inputs from the other wood furniture sector, $261 million worth of labor, and $446 million worth of other inputs like power, services, glues, fabrics, and others. Similarly, each row in the table shows how much the output of each sector was sold to other manufacturing sectors and to consumers. These transaction tables allow the calculation of technical coefficients which indicate how each sector will be influenced by an increase or decrease in the volume of output wanted by consumers. Table 11-2 shows some of these relationships, again for the South Atlantic region. For example, every $1,000 increase in the amount of wood household furniture produced requires $34 worth of stumpage and an additional $44 of activity in the harvesting sector.

## THE CONTRIBUTION OF THE FOREST ECONOMIST

### Decision Processes

A forest may be managed in many ways and for a variety of purposes. What is the best alternative? Should this forest be developed for recreation, or timber, or both or left as wilderness? On the one hand there are the

**Table 11-1  Transactions Matrix for Wood Products Industries, South Atlantic Region (in Millions of Dollars)**

| Selling sector | Purchasing sector — South Atlantic | | | | | | | | | | | | | | Final demand | | | | |
|---|---|---|---|---|---|---|---|---|---|---|---|---|---|---|---|---|---|---|---|
| | 1. Logging contractors | 2. Sawmills and planing | 3. Veneer and plywood | 4. Millwork plants | 5. Prefabricated wood products | 6. Wooden containers | 7. Wood preserving | 8. Other wood products | 9. Wood household furniture | 10. Upholstered wood furniture | 11. Other wood furniture | 12. Wood partitions and fixtures | 13. Paper mills | 14. Paperboard mills | Manufacturing and transportation | Construction and maintenance | Final consumer | Exports | Total |
| **Hardwood stumpage** | 27 | 33 | 2 | | | | | | | | | | | | | | | | 122 |
| **Softwood stumpage** | 168 | 20 | 1 | | | | | | | | | | | | | | | | 388 |
| *South Atlantic:* | | | | | | | | | | | | | | | | | | | |
| 1. Logging contractors | | 177 | 34 | | | | | | | | | | 67 | 215 | | 193 | | 33 | 533 |
| 2. Sawmills and planing | | 83 | 4 | 32 | | 8 | 22 | 6 | 127 | 27 | 6 | 2 | 11 | 53 | 23 | 12 | | 18 | 635 |
| 3. Veneer and plywood | | | 61 | 22 | 10 | 17 | 16 | 17 | 75 | | 4 | 3 | | | | 124 | | 48 | 225 |
| 4. Millwork plants | | | | | 1 | 6 | | 5 | | | | | | | | | | | 173 |
| 5. Prefabricated wood products | | | | 13 | | | | | | | | | | | | 54 | | 10 | 64 |
| 6. Wooden containers | | | | | | | | | | | | | | | 66 | | | 19 | 86 |
| 7. Wood preserving | | | | | | | | | | | | | | | | 65 | | 25 | 90 |
| 8. Other wood products | | 2 | 2 | | | | | | 15 | | | | | | 36 | 7 | 19 | 33 | 117 |
| 9. Wood household furniture | | | | | | | | | | 19 | 1 | 3 | | | | 11 | 242 | 670 | 926 |
| 10. Upholstered wood furniture | | | | | | | | | | | | | | | | 91 | 91 | 301 | 417 |
| 11. Other wood furniture | | | | | | | | | 2 | 19 | | | | | | 16 | 16 | 42 | 58 |
| 12. Wood partitions and fixtures | | | | | | | | | | 2 | | 3 | | | | | 14 | 35 | 49 |
| 13. Paper mills | | | | | | | | | | | | | | | 3 | | | 352 | 534 |
| 14. Paperboard mills | | | | | | | | | | | | | | | | | | 713 | 1.114 |
| **Employment** | 192 | 150 | 55 | 42 | 64 | 25 | 16 | 30 | 261 | 120 | 18 | 17 | 109 | 190 | | | | | 2.932 |
| **Other inputs** | 146 | 172 | 66 | 72 | | 30 | 36 | 53 | 446 | 251 | 29 | 24 | 347 | 657 | | | | | 5.602 |
| **Total** | 533 | 635 | 225 | 172 | 64 | 86 | 90 | 117 | 926 | 417 | 58 | 49 | 534 | 1.115 | 2.285 | 1.221 | 1.038 | 4.499 | 21.530 |

Source: Kaiser, 1972

**Table 11-2   Direct and Indirect Effects of a $1 Increase in Final Demand for Southern Forest Economy (in Dollars)**

| | Sector | Stumpage input | Harvesting sector | All forest product industries |
|---|---|---|---|---|
| 1. | Logging contractors | 0.451 | 0.000 | 1.352 |
| 2. | Sawmill and planing | 0.211 | 0.142 | 1.496 |
| 3. | Veneer and plywood | 0.099 | 0.225 | 1.681 |
| 4. | Millwork plants | 0.056 | 0.060 | 1.511 |
| 5. | Prefabricated wood products | 0.045 | 0.042 | 1.341 |
| 6. | Wooden containers | 0.065 | 0.091 | 1.521 |
| 7. | Wood preserving | 0.116 | 0.274 | 1.571 |
| 8. | Other wood products | 0.035 | 0.069 | 1.298 |
| 9. | Wood household furniture | 0.034 | 0.044 | 1.404 |
| 10. | Upholstered wood furniture | 0.011 | 0.010 | 1.158 |
| 11. | Other wood furniture | 0.020 | 0.028 | 1.272 |
| 12. | Wood partitions and fixtures | 0.019 | 0.032 | 1.286 |
| 13. | Pulp mills | 0.034 | 0.159 | 1.249 |
| 14. | Paper mills, except building | 0.035 | 0.162 | 1.256 |
| 15. | Paperboard mills | 0.041 | 0.196 | 1.287 |
| 16. | Building paper and board mills | 0.010 | 0.049 | 1.074 |
| 17. | Paper coating and glazing | 0.010 | 0.046 | 1.337 |
| 18. | Bags, except textile | 0.018 | 0.085 | 1.674 |
| 19. | Other converted paper | 0.011 | 0.052 | 1.409 |
| 20. | Paperboard boxes | 0.017 | 0.084 | 1.542 |
| 21. | Corrugated shipping containers | 0.024 | 0.117 | 1.768 |
| 22. | Other paperboard products | 0.012 | 0.061 | 1.423 |

Source: Kaiser, 1972.

technological or biological possibilities—the physical condition and capability of the land. On the other hand, there are the persons who are interested in this land, those who want products or services from it. Economics builds a bridge between the technology of forestry and the human interests and concerns about forests. Forest economists are interested in how people go about deciding forestry questions and how well they do it.

Decisions about forestry are made every day by those who control forest lands. They make these decisions on the basis of experience, markets, and politics. These are the three great processes that guide decision making in forestry and most other human activities as well. One of the great questions that has intrigued economists is how producers and suppliers of commodities manage to know what and how much to produce. How does it happen that the lumberyard has available the kinds and sizes of wood needed by builders and other users? How is it that the state park has developed a set of recreation facilities that are approximately what most users would prefer? Part of the answer is simply experience. People in any business gradually become aware of the needs and desires of their patrons, what they are willing to pay for, and the regular ups and downs of their demands or requirements. Indeed, experience would be all that was ever needed if society's wants and needs never changed. But change they do, and there have evolved two parallel and complex institutions to help us adjust to these changes: markets and government.

A good deal of forested land in the United States is held for commercial purposes, i.e., to supply timber or minerals to industry and increasingly to provide commercial outdoor recreation opportunities such as camping or skiing. The managers of these properties receive their major signals about what and how much to produce through the market for their products or services. Markets establish prices for commodities, and as these prices change, both sellers and buyers may change their minds about what to do. For example, the price of timber may increase because processors are anxious to have more and bid against one another for the available supply. Timberland owners supplying this market may try to increase their offerings to the market in response to this price increase and they may decide to try to grow more wood than heretofore, as well. They do these things because the higher price makes a change in sales and production desirable; they can make more profit in this way. These forest owners and managers respond to the price signals provided by the market, and in this way the amount of output made available is adjusted to the buyers' demands.

But a good proportion of our forests is held in public ownership, principally by the federal government and by the states. Some outputs from these public lands are sold and some consideration is given to price signals in deciding how these lands are to be used. But for the most part, production decisions on public lands are arrived at through a political process. Put very simply, legislators make the decisions about the use of public forest lands. Legislatures act very much like a committee of purchasing agents for the public at large. First they collect money from all of us, mostly through various types of taxes; then they decide how much of it should be spent for various public goods and services—how much for defense, education, welfare, roads, forestry, agriculture, and so on. Then within each major area they decide in detail what activities will be authorized and what funds appropriated for the various products and outputs.

Legislators get a great deal of advice and counsel in doing their job. They receive recommendations each year from the bureaus that manage public forest lands, and they hear from interest groups each year when they hold hearings on the budget. The legislators' job is to decide what is in the public's best interest after weighing all the facts and opinions provided by others and considering their own experience and convictions. This is the governmental decision process.

The decisions about how to use forest lands are always influenced by all three decision processes: experience, markets, and politics. Forest management adapts to new private and public needs through signals received from markets and from government. An increased private need results in an increase in the market price for the output in question, and this encourages price-responsive forest managers to increase their production of this output. An increased public need results in expanded authorization of activities and additional appropriations of funds for the output required. In the first case, it is individuals demanding more output in a market which generates the response, and in the second case, it is individuals and groups demanding more output from legislators which causes the change.

## The Rules of Efficiency

Economists study how decisions actually are reached, but they have an equal concern for how decisions *should* be reached. Over the years they have developed the concept of economic efficiency and some procedures for decision making which help to improve economic performance.

Forested properties ordinarily are subdivided into areas, compartments, allotments, and other production units, each devoted to a primary output like timber, forage, recreation services, and so forth. Production is the physical or tangible process of translating certain necessary elements or inputs into a desired output on a particular production unit. For example, corn (the output) is grown by combining seed, fertilizer, labor, and machinery (the inputs) in a given sequence of plowing, planting, cultivating, and harvesting (the operations) on a particular field (the production unit) having certain environmental conditions. A production plan is a recipe which identifies the inputs and operations required to produce a given quantity of output for a particular production unit. A production function is a sequence of production plans and shows how output increases as additional quantities of inputs are employed. For example, the forester's variable density yield tables show how timber output changes with soil quality, rotation length (i.e., time), and the number of trees established per acre. Production functions are summaries of technical information and indicate how managers can control the production process.

These functions are all alike in one regard. They all obey the law of diminishing returns. It seems to be an invariable rule that for a given production unit, after some level of output is reached, each additional unit of output requires the application of a larger amount of input than the one before.

It is apparent that additional quantities of output are not desirable regardless of their cost. For example, a private forest producing timber for sale would increase output as long as the cost of extra input was less than the revenue to be derived from the added output. This idea of looking at successive increments in output, determining their cost, and finding the last increment where the value of the output exceeds its cost is termed *marginal analysis* and is a fundamental concept in defining economic efficiency.

Public forests produce such outputs as scenic attractiveness or the opportunity for viewing wildlife which are not sold and so have no established market or monetary value. There is a production function for these outputs, too, and the cost of additional scenic attractiveness or added wildlife-viewing opportunities will increase as higher levels of these outputs are wanted. Evidently it would be desirable (i.e., economically efficient) to augment these nonmarket outputs as long as the value of the added output exceeded its cost, just as with any other output. The only difference in these cases is that output value cannot be precisely known since there is no market process to establish it. Instead the decision maker substitutes a personal estimate of value. Thus, the logic is identical but the estimate of value is arrived at differently—objectively in one case, subjectively in the other.

The principles of marginal analysis, then, allow the forest manager to find the most efficient level of production for each production unit. These decision rules are logical and often helpful, even when some of the information on production functions and on the value of inputs or outputs is not completely accurate.

### Economics in the Practice of Forestry

The administration of forested properties is a complex business made up of many different kinds of activities. One aspect of forest management is planning to achieve greater economic effectiveness, and here the forester is most likely to make use of economic concepts and methods. Most forest properties are organized and operated according to an annual plan or program of work. Most of this work is routine—maintaining boundaries; examining resource conditions; maintaining fire and pest surveillance and protection; maintaining and building roads, buildings, and other facilities; undertaking resource treatment projects of various sorts; arranging for the harvest; extraction or use of timber, minerals, forage, and other outputs; and controlling public use of the property for recreation and other purposes. A very important part of the job of administration is to consider changes in the ongoing program which may improve the management of the property.

Contemplated changes in management programs are the creative part of forestry. They result from an examination and prescription process carried out by trained and experienced professionals as they work with particular production areas on the property. The professional can often quickly identify whether or not the unit is in a satisfactory condition, and if not, what action or steps can be taken to improve productivity and condition. Usually the general course of action to be recommended is straightforward. The overstocked timber stand needs thinning; the chronically overused campground needs expansion, replication at another site, or a fallow period with remedial management; an eroding watershed needs revegetation; a declining big-game herd needs more winter range; and so forth.

After the opportunity for improving the condition and productivity of a production unit is recognized, the task becomes one of deciding whether or not the improvement is worthwhile. This task involves, first, designing the action in detail, that is, deciding exactly what is to be done and making an estimate of the effects of this action on resource condition and productivity. Second, it is necessary to subject this action to the economic test of efficiency by contrasting its cost and benefits. How much will the action cost? What are the benefits worth and when will they occur? Do benefits outweigh costs? If benefits do exceed costs, then this action can be viewed as a desirable one. If not, then perhaps it would be best to forgo it.

Forest economists work in three different ways to help forest managers in evaluating new management actions. First, foresters and other resource professionals are trained by forest economists in economic principles so that they have a general understanding and appreciation of economic analysis and can carry out their own evaluations in many instances. Second, most large forestry organizations have forest economists who are available to managers to help them in evaluating large and complex management changes. Third, there is a long-continued effort in forest economics research to provide increasing economic evaluation of common forestry practices over a wide range of conditions. Therefore, a precalculation of economic efficiency frequently is available to the manager in the research literature. These constitute the contribution of economics to the practice of forestry.

## FORESTS AND SOCIETY

### The Balance of Forest Land Uses

The various uses made of forest land reflect the relative importance society attaches to alternative purposes for which forests can be protected and managed. There are roughly 500 million acres (202 million ha) of commercial forest land, and 254 million acres (102.8 million ha) of noncommercial forest land in the United States. Thus, two-thirds of the total is at least potentially available for production of commodity products (i.e., timber), while one-third is not so available (U.S. Department of Agriculture, 1973a). The noncommercial forest land includes areas specifically reserved for noncommodity uses and areas too low in timber growth productivity to be seriously considered for forest commodity use.

There are several important trends in the use of forest land. Reservation of forest land for noncommodity purposes such as parks and wilderness areas is gradually increasing. Some of these actions involve well-publicized events and a considerable level of controversy at the time decisions are being made. Examples of such actions during the last decade include the creation of Redwood National Park in northern California and enlargement of the "no-cut zone" in the Boundary Waters Canoe Area in northern Minnesota. This latter area has also been the scene of a major use conflict concerning mineral exploration, with the result that this use has been proscribed by court action. One current important issue involves proposals for creation of Wilderness East, a system of naturalistic areas in national forests east of the Great Plains. Despite this activity, only 3½ percent of the forest land capable of producing commercial stands of timber are in designated noncommodity-use areas.

One associated shift in uses of forest land is occurring in areas being converted to urban uses. This shift in forest use is obviously most frequent in the suburban-rural fringe adjacent to major cities, but is also occurring well beyond that zone in many regions. Not only is urban development increasingly dispersed, but vacation- and second-home sites are found scattered or forming small communities within the forested environs of the major cities. Another associated shift in land use is occurring in forest areas marginally useful for agriculture. One example is the lower Mississippi Valley, where soybeans and hardwoods are competitive crops. This is only one of many such regions where this problem exists. Net losses of approximately 6 percent of commercial forest land over the next 30 years (primarily to urban development) have been foreseen by knowledgeable observers (Vaux, 1973).

There have been proposals and legislative actions for administratively stabilizing uses of forest land. These include land-use incentives, especially various forms of special tax treatment to reduce pressure for premature conversion of forest and agricultural land to urban uses (California Extension Service, 1972). No less strikingly, these also include proposals for directly increasing stability of uses within forest land. For example, the Public Land Law Review Commission (1970) called for designation of "dominant use zones" in national forests for intensive management of timber production and prompt designation of additional areas to be reserved for noncommodity uses. More recently (1973), the President's Advisory Panel on Timber and the Environment has recommended prompt completion of the National Wilderness System and intensification of timber management elsewhere. Both proposals provided important ideas for more systematic land resource management—ideas that have not, unfortunately, entered public discussion in any really productive form to date.

When and if they are considered, forest-use patterns will likely be more well defined and will involve zones where naturalistic, noncommodity values are designated as primary, with all other uses secondary. Other zones where commodity values are achieved by intensive management will be defined as primary, with all other uses similarly defined as secondary; still other zones will be defined as mixed-use areas. These latter areas will resemble current multiple-use practice. The likely net effect on the balance of forest uses will be sharper delineation and appreciably less forest land in mixed-use zones (James, 1973).

### The Path of Forest Development

The current balance of forest land use is one stage in a continuing process. A simplified view of other, preceding stages will give perspective.

Development of forests in a particular nation or region characteristically begins with an exploitative stage. During this stage, forests serve primarily as a source of development capital for other sectors of the economy. Large quantities of old-growth timber are frequently the area's most readily converted source of value. Some of the timber products go directly into structures in the area, but the greater part frequently is exported to other, more developed regions in return for investment capital. The primary management problem is to accomplish this with minimal damage to long-term productivity of forests. Unfortunately, this goal frequently is not accomplished due to wildfires and related catastrophes.

A protective custodial form of management commonly follows the exploitative stage. This is a constructive response to the destructiveness of exploitation. Protection against fire, theft, and related catastrophes is gradually extended to essentially all forests in the area. Relatively simple management involving primarily regeneration practices and more orderly harvesting is gradually undertaken, beginning in areas with particularly favorable conditions for growth. The focus is frequently still entirely on timber, but with a markedly more constructive emphasis.

When this more constructive stage is well developed, it is often followed by a mulitple-use stage. The importance of recreation, water, wildlife, and amenity-related values of forests increases, based on widespread public preferences, and is recognized in official policy documents and in management plans for individual forest units. This stage develops first on publicly owned forests, where lack of markets for these values do not create difficulties experienced on privately owned forests. Nevertheless, effects of the multiple-use stage are finally felt on both in varying degree, frequently as an accommodation to intense public pressure. The multiple-use stage is often a time of intense controversy among groups pursuing conflicting resource management goals.

These three stages have all occurred to varying degrees in major portions of North America over the last 100 to 150 years. A new stage, which might be termed a "fully planned stage," now seems to be taking hold. Its full dimensions remain partially obscure, but a pattern of primary and secondary uses (some giving priority to commodities and others to amenities) with decreased forest land in mixed-use areas, is developing. A particularly high level of managerial skill will be required to identify and execute these patterns.

## Economics in the Political Process

What is the contribution of economics to management and policy decisions concerning forests and related natural resources? This vital question depends upon two relationships: that of economics to other sciences, and that of science to public decisions.

Biological and social sciences are equally important in analysis of nat-

ural resource questions and are especially vital in estimating the consequences of policy and management actions. Some of these actions have a
direct impact on the natural world, others have direct effects on humans,
relating closely to their preferences and to successful resource programs.
Nearly all important policy and management actions have effects of both
kinds, making both sciences equally important and the links between them
vital.

Economics applied to forestry and related natural resources has a key
role in combining the biological and social consequences of policy and
management actions. Until recently, this role has been considered the full
evaluation of such consequences from a human viewpoint (Duerr and
Vaux, 1953; Webster, Marty, and Skok, 1963). But the role of other social
sciences (especially sociology, political science, and public administration)
has become more developed in relation to forestry and other natural resources. The result is more complete understanding of changing human
goals and preferences and their implications for resource management. This
trend has somewhat altered the role but increased the importance of economics and related quantitative analysis in incorporating biological and
social consequences of management. These quantitative sciences provide a
framework for effective evaluation of both the relative difficulty of various
courses of action and the relative value of their results, in both cases utilizing biological and social sciences for these comparisons.

The overall role of all sciences in relation to public decisions is to
clarify alternative courses of action and to identify their major consequences. What are the alternative ways in which forests of particular type
and location could be managed? What would be the consequences of each
course of action in terms of scenic attractiveness, regional development,
availability and cost of timber products, abundance of wildlife, and related
values? Are there alternatives that involve notably less conflict among these
values than do others being considered? These are questions that the sciences can answer, particularly if biological and social sciences are effectively linked. Final choice among feasible and relatively desirable alternatives
is then a political question, in that the political process (involving legislative
bodies, public media, and many different forums for discussion) is a method for expressing and ultimately unifying public preferences on important
resource issues.

This process, where science identifies alternatives and major consequences and political processes choose among them, depends on a distinction between facts and values. This is an important distinction but one that
can be constructively changed to some degree, given sufficient time and
effort. Science can enlarge the area of fact in terms of both knowledge of
biological consequences and exploration of settled public preferences on
matters related to natural resources. Where such preferences exist, careful

understanding of them can help to bring order to decision processes, some of which have become very turbulent in the recent past (Sax, 1970). Such order can help resource managers, analysts, and citizens to focus more effectively on relevant and generally acceptable alternative courses of action, and economics and related sciences can effectively provide this order.

## BIBLIOGRAPHY

California Extension Service. 1972. An Environmental Controversy: The Williamson Act and State Land-Use Policy, Suppl. 7 in a series on California's environment, Cooperative Extension Service, University of California.

Duerr, William A., and Henry J. Vaux. 1953. *Research in the Economics of Forestry,* Charles Lathrop Pack Forestry Foundation, Washington, DC.

Hair, Dwight. 1963. *The Economic Importance of Timber in the United States.* U. S. Department of Agriculture, Forest Service Miscellaneous, Publication 941.

James, Lee M. 1973. Land-Use Planning: Why Forestry Professionals Should Be Involved, *Proceedings of Society of American Foresters National Convention.*

Kaiser, H. F., Jr. 1972. Multiregional Input-Output Model for Forest Resource Analysis, *Forest Science,* **18(1):**46–53.

Knesse, Allen V., Robert U. Ayres, and Ralph D'Arge. 1970. Economics and the Environment, RFF (Resources for the Future), Washington, DC.

President's Advisory Panel on Timber and the Environment. 1973. *Report of the President's Advisory Panel on Timber and the Environment,* Washington, DC.

Public Land Law Review Commission. 1970. One-Third of the Nation's Land, *A Report to the President and to the Congress by the Public Land Law Review Commission,* Washington, DC.

Sax, Joseph L. 1970. *Defending the Environment: A Strategy for Citizen Action,* Alfred A. Knopf, Inc., New York.

U.S. Department of Agriculture. 1973a. *The Outlook for Timber in the United States,* Forest Resources Report no. 20.

———1973b. Report of the Chief, 1972.

Vaux, Henry J. 1973. Timber Resource Prospects, in William A. Duerr (ed.), *Timber: Problems, Prospects, Policies,* Iowa State University Press, Ames.

Webster, Henry H., Robert J. Marty, and Richard A. Skok. 1963. Biological Research, Economic Analysis, and Forest Management, *Jour. Forestry,* **63:**754 –759.

# Part Three

# The Practice of Forestry

Chapter 12

# Silviculture: Reproduction Methods

There are a number of ways to define silviculture, but in the broad sense, this aspect of forestry includes all the manipulating operations that go into the development and maintenance of a socially determined form of forest stand. Stopping a wildfire or insect epidemic in a park or a wilderness is just as much a silvicultural practice as is planting tree seedlings on an area devoted to wood products. In these terms, silviculture includes not only the subject matter covered in this and the following chapter, but is related to many other chapters of this book as well.

Forest ecology deals with how the forest (or forest ecosystem) operates, while silviculture is the applied science of reproducing and manipulating a forest.

This chapter deals with reproduction methods used in replacing one forest stand with another. Chapter 13 covers the tending of an existing forest community so that it will develop in a desired manner.

This chapter was prepared by David R. M. Scott, Professor of Silviculture, College of Forest Resources, University of Washington.

Replacing one forest community with another or starting a forest in an area dominated by a nonforest plant community calls for three broad categories of activities: (1) altering the existing forest community to provide space for the tree reproduction desired, (2) manipulating the surface of the soil to provide the conditions necessary for the desired reproduction, and (3) providing a source for the new population of trees.

## Manipulating the Existing Stand

A wide range of manipulative possibilities may be employed. At one extreme, the existing forest community is entirely removed. This is called *clearcutting* and produces for the subsequent reproduction an environment that is not influenced by the presence of any members of the previous community. At the other extreme, a single tree of the existing stand is removed to provide space for reproduction. This is called the *selection* method and creates a seedling environment that is strongly influenced by the proximity of individuals of the existing stand.

Clearcutting makes the entire area available for reproduction and therefore results in an even-aged stand (Fig. 12-1).. The selection system makes only part of the stand area available for reproduction, and an uneven-aged stand structure is produced (Fig. 12-2). The clearcutting method is appropriate only to tree species that can reproduce on the site in question without any modification of the environment by other vegetation, namely, those species that normally reproduce following severe natural disturbances. Such species usually are termed *intolerant.*

The selection system is appropriate for obtaining reproduction of tree species that naturally reproduce in small openings of the canopy. Such openings develop as trees of the preceding stand are reduced in numbers and space occupancy by competition and old age. These species are termed *tolerant* and are naturally dominant in the late successional stages.

Intermediate between clearcutting and selection is the *shelterwood* method of providing space for reproduction. In this method, a partial removal of the existing stand is carried out, sufficient to make the entire area available for reproduction (Fig. 12-3). The rest of the stand remains to modify the environment of the new generation for the first few years, after which it also is removed. Selection and shelterwood environments also exist on an area where all the trees are cut, adjacent to an uncut stand (Fig. 12-4).

The shelterwood system probably produces a wider range of seedling environment than either the clearcutting or selection system. The seedling environment of a heavy residual shelterwood is very similar to that of selection and a very light residual shelterwood gives seedling conditions that closely resemble clearcutting. Therefore, variations of the shelterwood method are applicable to a wide spectrum of ecological requirements in tree reproduction.

**Figure 12-1**  A clearcutting reproduction method. Seeding came from the uncut trees above. *(Courtesy of the U.S. Forest Service.)*

Quite possibly, much successful natural reproduction in forests occurs in what is essentially a shelterwood environment. Natural disturbances which open up the stand occur so frequently that selection-type environments are not sustained for long periods of time, a fact attested to by the relative scarcity of climax forest stands. At the same time, most natural disturbances rarely result in as complete a removal of the existing stand as

**Figure 12-2**  A selection method of reproduction in a mixed hardwood stand in northern Michigan. Note the seedlings and younger trees in the background. *(Courtesy of the U.S. Forest Service.)*

**Figure 12-3**  A shelterwood cutting of ponderosa pine in eastern Oregon. The old forest is serving as a shelter for the new one. Once reproduction becomes established, the remaining stand will be removed. *(Courtesy of the U.S. Forest Service.)*

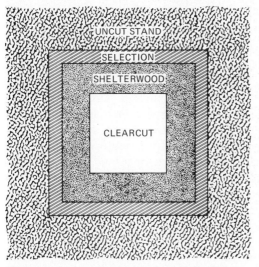

**Figure 12-4** A schematic of a hypothetical 20-acre (8-ha) square cut showing the various types of environments for reproduction.

does clearcutting. Even a forest of dead trees, following a catastrophic fire or insect epidemic, has some sheltering effect for ensuing reproduction.

This is not to imply any particular social virtue in naturalness, but simply to point out the factual relationships between natural reproduction conditions and the several methods used by foresters.

It is also possible to consider the environment for reproduction in a cut area as shown in Fig. 12-4. By retaining the same absolute size but simply changing the shape of the cut, the result is predominantly a strip shelterwood (Fig. 12-5).

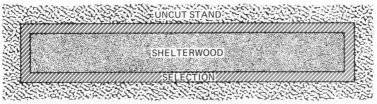

**Figure 12-5** A schematic of how altering the shape of the same-size cutting (see Fig. 12-4) changes the proportion of environments for reproduction.

## Site Preparation

Site preparation, as commonly practiced, may include (1) the control of nontree plant species that offer both competition and environmental modification for the future forest reproduction; (2) the reduction of debris left from the previous stand, after the harvesting operation has removed the material with economic value; and (3) soil preparation. Sometimes all these objectives are accomplished in a single operation, such as by using prescribed fire or a heavy machine that breaks down living and dead organic material and tills the surface soil. In many ways, number one, above, is more similar ecologically to manipulating the existing stand (as described in the previous section) than it is to number two and three above. Nonetheless, all are frequently essential to successful establishment of tree reproduction.

Many forests, particularly those older ones that have not been manipulated, have well-established vegetation beneath the main canopy. Changing the tree canopy alone may not provide the growing space needed for reproduction, particularly where the understory is already established. With release from the overstory this understory may develop vigorously and provide serious competition for the desired forest reproduction. Of course, such vegetation may be beneficial in modifying microclimate on certain sites and at appropriate densities.

Logging debris or slash may offer a physical impediment to tree reproduction or to the operations necessary in tending a new stand. It may also be a fire hazard. On the other hand, this same material may be a valuable source of environmental modification, especially in reducing high air and soil surface temperatures on some sites.

Soils in forested ecosystems are frequently typified by surface layers of organic material in various stages of decomposition, because of the annual deposit of foliage, dead tree parts, and individual trees that have died in the normal course of community dynamics. These organic layers are inclined to have extreme variations in water and temperature and therefore are generally not good rooting media for tree seedlings, especially when the tree canopy, with its climatic modification, is removed. A mineral soil or mixture of mineral and organic materials is usually much more favorable. However, on some sites a significant portion of the nutrient supply may be in the humus layers of the soil, and these same layers may also have a function in the stability and physical property of the underlying mineral soil.

The point to be made is that site preparation methods are dictated by a given ecological situation. A treatment that is too severe may be a deterrent to reproduction, while measures that are too conservative may result in poor growth rates.

The use of prescribed fire in site preparation is common in many forest areas. Historically, natural fires have been the single most common disturbance that created conditions for the regeneration of new forests; thus, this method imitates nature. Under some conditions fire is easy to work with and therefore economical to use. However, in other forest systems fire does not result in the site preparation required; it is too dangerous or has deleterious side effects, such as loss of soil fertility and high soil surface temperature. Under these conditions mechanical site preparation is an alternative. The logging operation itself may result in a satisfactory site preparation on some areas, since the skidding equipment and the moving logs eliminate vegetation, break down slash, and scarify the soil. Because this does not always occur, equipment has been developed specifically for site preparation. This includes disks, drums, and blades mounted on or dragged by various types of power sources (Fig. 12-6). Mechanical site preparation frequently demands substantial effort and has limitations in that some terrain is too steep or certain soils are too subject to compaction or erosion to allow it. Again, site preparation methods must be governed by the ecological and physical site characteristics.

**Sources of Reproduction**

Once suitable space has been made available for reproduction and the site has been prepared, the final step in establishing a stand involves making certain that there is an appropriate source for a new generation of the desired tree species. This source may already exist on the area itself or on a nearby area, or it may be necessary to transport it from some distance.

**Figure 12-6** A duplex brush cutter being used in site preparation prior to planting in Florida. *(Courtesy of the U.S. Forest Service.)*

Tree reproduction can originate vegetatively in many hardwoods and a very few conifers and by seed in nearly all tree species.

**Vegetative Reproduction**    The cutting of mature individuals frequently results in vegetative sprouting from dormant buds in the stumps (Fig. 12-7). In some tree species, vegetative reproduction after cutting also arises from root suckers whose origin is from adventitious buds which develop on roots near the soil surface. Either of these events can produce a successful stand, although stump sprouts are frequently poorly spaced (because of the wide spacing of the old stumps) and may be subject to early rot if originating too high on the stump.

Vegetative sprouts may also arise from adventitious buds developing in the callous tissue formed by the cambium in cut stumps. These usually are short-lived and cannot be considered a reliable means of obtaining reproduction.

Vegetative reproduction usually develops very rapidly in size at first, probably due to food reserves stored in the root system. As a result, initial yield may be higher than in stands originating from seed. However, these advantages are usually offset by an early decrease in vigor, reduced longevity, and occasionally inferior form and shape. Vegetative sprouting is usually

**Figure 12-7**    Vegetative sprouting of dormant buds in hardwood stumps in a Michigan forest. *(Courtesy of Morbark Industries, Inc.)*

most vigorous following cutting done in the dormant season, when food reserves in the roots are presumably high.

Vegetative reproduction can also be carried out in some tree species by means of cuttings. In this technique, portions of the parent tree are cut off and planted, sometimes after a treatment with some artificial hormone to encourage root development. These cuttings range in size from that of a common lead pencil upward.

One of the interesting features of vegetative reproduction is its apparent desirability as browse for herbivores. Rabbits and deer, for example, will frequently eat sprout vegetation while adjacent seed-originated reproduction of the same tree species is not utilized. This may be due to the food reserves available to the sprout reproduction.

**Seed Reproduction** Seed is the origin of most natural stands. After passing through a juvenile period, trees produce seeds. However, age of seedbearing, periodicity of seed crops, amount of seed, and exact characteristics of the seed in terms of longevity, resistance to environmental extremes, dispersal mechanisms, and germination requirements vary tremendously with species and environment. Some tree species produce frequent and abundant crops of highly germinable and thoroughly dispersed seeds at an early age. Others produce infrequent, light crops of poorly germinable seed that are not well dispersed. Others are intermediate between these extremes. These characteristics greatly affect natural regeneration.

Seed can already have fallen to the forest floor from trees that were harvested or can be still attached to branches that remain in the area after cutting. More frequently, however, seed comes from trees that are left in the area for this purpose, as in the seed tree or shelterwood methods, or from adjacent uncut stands in the clearcutting method. If seed of the desired genetic constitution is not available as required, it may be collected elsewhere and directly seeded (usually aerially) on the site.

Because of the substantial loss of seed from predation, infection, inhospitable environments, and additional losses during germination and juvenile seedling stages, large amounts of seed are frequently required to establish a relatively small population of young trees. As a result of these uncertainties in securing reproduction by natural or artificial seedings, foresters frequently rely on planting young trees or seedlings that have been grown either in outdoor nurseries or in greenhouses. This technique, while perhaps requiring more effort and expense initially, has advantages in control of the timing and population characteristics of the new generation of trees.

Seed is collected during years of abundant production. This can be done in a variety of ways, but usually there is an attempt to identify the

**Figure 12-8**  Collecting loblolly pine seed by net in a seed production area. *(Courtesy of the Georgia Forestry Commission.)*

source as accurately as possible. Parent trees, in stands of high quality reserved for seed production, are usually harvested of their cones by skilled employees using special techniques (Fig. 12-8). Seed is also bought on the open market. Frequently the pickers utilize tops from trees that have been cut at seed-maturing time or try to locate squirrel caches of cones.

The seed is then extracted from the cones, cleaned, sorted, and stored in a very cold, oxygen-free environment. The seed of some species will maintain much of its germinability for many years if properly stored, but in other species, seed storage for even a few months leads to a substantial loss in viability.

When the seed is needed for sowing, it is removed from storage, moistened, and kept at temperatures just a little above freezing for several weeks. This is called *stratification*. It simulates the moist, cool environment of a forest floor and readies the seed for immediate germination when exposed to warmer temperatures.

The seed is then sown in carefully prepared beds, at a spacing that is intended to produce a given density of seedlings. An intensive regimen of weed and disease control, together with equally rigid control of soil fertility and water, is undertaken to produce seedlings of uniform, desired quality (Fig. 12-9). Nursery sites are carefully selected for correct soil and climate. Depending on species, location, and type of seedlings, time in the nursery may vary from 1 to 6 years. Roots are often pruned to promote a compact root system. If a larger size is desired, the seedlings may be transplanted to a wider spacing after a year or two, and then allowed to develop for a given period of time.

After the seedlings have reached the prescribed stage of development, they are lifted from the nursery beds in a dormant season, sorted and graded for quality, and packaged in manageable numbers. It is important that these steps be carried out quickly to prevent dehydration. If possible, seedlings are shipped immediately to the field and planted. Frequently there is some delay in planting crew availability, or planting site conditions may prevent ideal timing. In these circumstances, the packaged seedlings are refrigerated and can be safely held for several weeks or months, depending on their physiological condition when lifted.

A comparatively recent development in seedling production is the use of container techniques. These involve growing the seedlings in individual

**Figure 12-9** A forest nursery in Oregon. Seedlings will later be lifted, graded, root-pruned, bundled, and shipped to the planting site. *(Courtesy of the Weyerhaeuser Company.)*

**Figure 12-10**  A greenhouse holding 150 thousand seedlings being grown in individual containers of special rooting media. Forestry Science Laboratory, Corvallis, Oregon. *(Courtesy of the U.S. Forest Service.)*

**Figure 12-11**  Six-week-old red pine seedlings being grown in tubes. Note the growth of the roots at right. Superior National Forest, Minnesota. *(Courtesy of the U.S. Forest Service.)*

containers of special rooting medium in a greenhouse with a closely controlled environment (Fig. 12-10). After a relatively short time, often about 4 months, the seedlings are planted at the site with the root medium intact (Fig. 12-11). This technique was originally established by foresters in cold, northern climates, where the difficulties of successfully producing and planting conventional bare-root seedlings were substantial. It is now being used much more widely. Under some conditions it offers a number of advantages: flexibility of production, improved success in seedling survival on some sites, and extension of the planting season. For some species which are difficult to propagate in bare-root nurseries, this method is often more successful.

Planting of seedlings in the field is done both by hand (Fig. 12-12) and by machine (Fig. 12-13), depending on the availability of labor, the characteristics of the soil, terrain, site preparation, and the seedlings. Generally, modern planting is done at lower densities (400 to 600 trees per acre or 988 to 1,482 trees per ha) than was common several decades ago (1,200 or more per acre or 2,964 trees per ha).

**Figure 12-12** Hand-planting tree seedlings in a burn in Montana. Bitterroot National Forest. *(Courtesy of the U.S. Forest Service.)*

**Figure 12-13** Machine-planting in the Chippewa National Forest, Minnesota. The tractor is equipped with a hydraulic plow which prepares the site for planting. The rear wheels close the furrow and compact the soil around the seedling. *(Courtesy of the U.S. Forest Service.)*

### Genetic Considerations and Manipulation

Of economically important plant species, forest trees are among the least genetically altered by humans. In many locations in the world their gene pools remain essentially intact. However, silvicultural reproduction practice frequently includes various levels of genetic manipulation to more nearly meet social objectives, whether these include better individual tree characteristics, higher yields by populations, or resistance to some parasite or predator.

In silvicultural systems involving natural reproduction, efforts are made to select trees with desirable qualities as seed sources. It is also important that a large enough population is left and that it be properly spaced;

otherwise, negative inbreeding may result. In fact, an adequate population of seed producers may be more important than rigid selection for superior qualities, particularly in pioneer species, i.e., those characteristic of early successional stages. This type of seed-producer selection is aimed at little more than maintaining the existing gene pool in the succeeding generation.

When reliance is placed on reproduction by nursery-raised seedlings, a number of genetic controls are possible. Quite common in operational silviculture is the use of local seed sources (provenances) to produce seedlings for a particular geographical location, usually based on climatic characteristics. There appears, however, to be evidence that soil variations within climatic zones may also be important. Careful seed-selection procedure is designed to assure reproduction that is safely adapted to a particular environment.

Another technique involves the use of selected tree stands to serve as seed production areas. These are of unusual quality for a particular environment and are further cultivated by removal of the less desirable individuals, by proper spacing, and possibly by fertilizing. Seed production is relatively abundant due to this cultivation, and the process of selection may provide certain genetic gains.

Serious attempts at improvement of genetic pools revolve around selection based on rigorous criteria. The resultant superior individuals in tree populations are called *plus trees*. These individuals are then transferred to seed orchards by grafting a cutting to a root stock or by rooting the cutting. When a number of such individuals are allowed to interbreed freely, they produce seedlings which show some genetic gain. Controlled breeding between individuals is also carried out and the ensuing progeny is tested for desirable qualities. Matings that produce populations with abnormal concentrations of the desirable properties are then repeated on a production basis. However, it is important to continue the selection process in the progeny to further the genetic gain. There is danger, of course, in narrowing the genetic base, particularly in relation to disease susceptibility.

Vegetative propagation of superior individuals is also possible. Exact genetic construction of stands can be repeated in this manner.

## BIBLIOGRAPHY

Barrett, John W. 1962. *Regional Silviculture of the United States,* The Ronald Press Company, New York.

Libby, W. J., R. F. Stettler, and F. W. Seitz. 1969. Forest Genetics and Forest-Tree Breeding, *Ann. Rev. of Genetics,* 3:469–494.

Smith, David M. 1962. *The Practice of Silviculture,* 7th ed., John Wiley & Sons, Inc., New York.

U.S. Department of Agriculture, Forest Service. 1973. *Silvicultural Systems for the Major Forest Types of the United States,* Agriculture Handbook no. 445.

# Chapter 13

# Silviculture: Intermediate Operations

When a forest plant population consisting of both tree and nontree species is first established, the individuals are small. However, as they develop rapidly in size and occupy all the growing space, interactions such as competition and mutualism come into play, and changes in the characteristics of both individual plants and of plant populations take place. These features of the natural community dynamics may or may not be socially desired either in detail or timing, and so cultural practices may be required to obtain wanted characteristics. The following cultural practices are some of the methods directed toward controlling the plant population or changing the physical environment.

*Release cuttings* have several forms. As the young forest community develops in the seedling and sapling stage, the desirable individuals may be at a competitive disadvantage relative to other members of the population. This usually is caused by lack of control of seed sources or sprouting by undesired elements of the previous plant community. In any instance, a

This chapter was prepared by David R. M. Scott, Professor of Silviculture, College of Forest Resources, University of Washington.

*cleaning* operation is required. This operation usually removes undesired species, but occasionally is directed at poorly formed individuals of a desirable species.

If a similar type of operation is required when the stand is older, it is referred to as a *stand improvement cutting* (Fig. 13-1). When undesirable older individuals have been left from the preceding stand and must be removed because of their effect on the reproduction, the operation is referred to as a *liberation cutting* (Fig. 13-2).

Each of these operations may be implemented by cutting if the undesirable individuals are small, or by girdling if they are large. The latter operation consists of cutting through bark and phloem thoroughly enough to interrupt the flow of food to the roots (Fig. 13-2). This eventually causes the tree to die. However, cutting and girdling may result in sprouting from dormant buds below the cut in many angiosperms and occasionally in a few gymnosperms, particularly if the cut individuals are young. Such sprouts may develop in height so rapidly that competition to the desired young trees is equal to or greater than the precutting condition.

The use of chemicals, whether with a hormonal or poisonous effect, may reduce both the effort required in release operations and the probability of sprouting. Such chemicals may be applied to individual stems or may be sufficiently specific to be applied on an area basis, usually by spraying from aircraft.

Another intermediate operation is *pruning*. This is somewhat different from other manipulations in that it is aimed at altering the form of individual rather than population characteristics. Cutting of entire lower branches, close to the stem, is a method for improving stem wood quality by the premature removal of knots caused by branches.

The ends of branches are cut to give trees a desired shape and to cause new terminal growth to be initiated by buds at lower positions on the trees. This type of pruning is commonly practiced on trees that are to be used for ornamental purposes.

Still another intermediate operation is the *sanitation cut*. In any plant community, certain individuals, either because of genetic variation or competitive position in the community, are more susceptible to disease or predator attack than are the remainder. Hence, they may serve as the initiators of an epidemic outbreak that will severely affect the entire population. If these susceptible individuals are eliminated, the chances of an epidemic will be greatly reduced. This entails the same techniques used in release operations, but subsequently the treated individuals may also be burned or chipped (see Fig. 13-1).

*Salvage* operations remove valuable material from the stand. Since this material is usually dead or dying, its removal has little ecological impact on the community (Fig. 13-3).

**Figure 13-1** *Upper:* a natural stand of mixed hardwoods in northern Michigan, prior to an improvement cut; *Lower:* the same stand after removal of unwanted, diseased, and deformed trees. A chipping machine was used to alter the unwanted trees. *(Courtesy of Morbark Industries, Inc.)*

**Figure 13-2** A forest worker in the Lake States girdling scrub oaks with an ax. The oaks will eventually die, liberating the red pine reproduction. *(Courtesy of the U.S. Forest Service.)*

**Figure 13-3** A salvage operation where dead western redcedar shake bolts are being removed from the stand. Mt. Baker–Snoqualmie National Forest, Washington. *(Courtesy of the U.S. Forest Service.)*

*Thinning* (or forest stand density control), though perhaps the most well-established method of intermediate silviculture operations, is probably the least understood. In spite of a great deal of professional attention, the control and results of thinning are imperfect.

After a developing forest stand has been satisfactorily structured in terms of species composition, susceptibility to disease, and other features, there is still a great deal of variation or flexibility both in the manner in which the individual trees may develop or in the way the entire community may grow. This is brought about by the tremendous difference in size of trees, and therefore in growing space needed, with increasing age. An area of land that will support literally thousands of seedlings or saplings may be fully utilized by only a few score of the same population 30 or 40 years later. This means that there is tremendous loss of numbers due to competition. However, as the forest ages, its genetic constitution and spatial arrangement, as well as the nature of the physical environment, can cause great differences in this population reduction. After a group of young trees develops in size sufficiently to occupy all the growing space, the continued growth and competition changes individual tree morphology and physiological processes, compared with these same features in noncompetitive circumstances. At a comparable height, competitively grown or forest-grown trees tend to have shorter crowns (because basal branches die) and straighter and less tapered stems than do noncompetitively grown or open-grown trees. In addition, when trees are at too great a competitive disadvantage, their physiological processes may be so affected that they do not grow efficiently in proportion to the growing space occupied. As a population of trees fills the available growing space and continues to develop, it is differentiated into social positions, or crown classes. Some trees fall behind others in height and size, lose growing efficiency, and eventually may die, leaving their spaces vacant until refilled by the continued development of the adjacent individuals. Thus at a particular stage in the life of a forest stand, it consists of both efficient and inefficient individuals, and there are gaps in space occupancy. The proportions in each of these categories depend on the characteristics of the tree population (numbers, genetic make-up, spacing, age) and the physical environment. When there is a very large number of very similar trees and therefore little or no competitive advantage, almost the entire stand may be growing very slowly and inefficiently. This is called *stagnation*.

Thinning is the cultural adjustment of numbers and arrangements so that the stand and the individual tree in the stand will grow in a more socially valuable manner than would otherwise be the case. At the same time, thinning provides a harvest of some of the population that otherwise might be lost, and at an earlier time than if no procedure were undertaken until the final crop was ready for removal. Generally, thinning reduces immediate total yield because it results in loss of space occupancy, although this may be offset by subsequent reduction of stagnation. However, total yield may not be the objective of management and thinning, although reducing the total, will increase the yield of the desirable form of growth.

There are several methods of thinning, based on the structure of the stand. A thinning that removes the smaller individuals and leaves the larger is classified as a *low thinning* and most nearly simulates the reduction of stand numbers through natural competition (Fig. 13-4). This technique also is most likely to result in greatest total growth, since inefficient trees are generally removed, leaving the space they occupied available for utilization by efficiently growing trees. However, the stems cut are small and may not have any value. In *selection thinning* the bigger trees are cut and the smaller trees are left. This is usually done because the smaller trees have some desired qualities, such as stem straightness or lack of taper, or because the big trees have undesired qualities, such as being too branchy. On the other hand, the larger trees may have more value on the current market. This technique is more likely to reduce total growth or lengthen the time required for the final crop to reach a certain size.

*Crown thinning* removes some of the large trees, leaving other large trees as well as the smaller trees. Obviously this type of operation is a compromise between the advantages and disadvantages of the first two.

In some circumstances a *mechanical thinning* is used. This method spaces the stand with little regard for any crown differentiation and is most frequently used in stands where the latter is relatively unimportant. This is usually because of youth or lack of genetic variation (for example, in clonal populations). Mechanical thinning may also be employed because of operational feasibility or simplicity.

When the trees removed in thinning young stands are not useful and therefore have no value, the operation is termed *precommercial thinning*. Thinnings of this nature are then investments to provide future values, as are most other intermediate operations. In older stands, the trees removed usually have value as wood. However, wood values may not necessarily be the management objective.

*Fertilizing*, much like genetic modification, has only recently become an important aspect of silviculture. In spite of the fact that fertilizer was applied to forest communities in India and Western Europe as early as the middle of the nineteenth century, the practice was never widespread. Unfortunately, these early attempts were made with little knowledge of the required nutrient elements. The measurement techniques used to assess response were also imperfect. As a result, it was commonly believed that forests were relatively insensitive to fertility levels in the soil.

In the 1930s symptoms of nutrient deficiencies developed in the otherwise extraordinarily successful exotic pine plantations in Australia. This,

**Figure 13-4** *Upper:* A 50-year-old red pine plantation in Michigan, before thinning; *Lower:* The same stand after a heavy, low thinning. *(Courtesy of the U.S. Forest Service.)*

**Figure 13-5** The effect of nutrient deficiencies on seedling growth. Each of the three Douglas-fir seedlings at left was deprived of one nutrient: number 1 was deprived of nitrogen; number 2, of phosphorus; and number 3, of potassium. Seedling number 4 received all nutrients. *(Courtesy of the University of Washington, College of Forest Resources.)*

together with a renewed interest in increasing wood yields of forests in Europe and North America, brought about an expanded fertilization research and development program.

Reasons for fertilizing forests include the remedying of nutrient deficiencies, the increase of wood yield, the improvement of tree or forest appearance, the stimulation of seed production, and the increased production of subordinate plant species that are valuable as forage for domestic or game animals. Deficiencies are frequently associated with scarcity of the so-called micronutrients (those required in very small amounts, such as copper, zinc, and boron), while increases in productivity often require additional available quantities of macronutrients (needed in relatively larger amounts, such as nitrogen, calcium, phosphorus, and potassium) (Fig. 13-5). Obviously, the effort required for addition of macronutrients is much greater than for micronutrients. In northwestern United States, 200 lb (90 kg) of nitrogen per acre is a common operational fertilizer application, while 1 lb (0.45 kg) per acre will cure some zinc deficiencies in Australia. However, substantial gains in productivity, perhaps 25 percent or more, have resulted from macronutrient additions, and relieving deficiencies can mean even greater gains. As a result, fertilizing has become an economically attractive and fast-growing silvicultural practice, particularly in Australia, Scandinavia, and southeastern and northwestern United States.

Recently there has been some concern about the effects of timber harvesting on soil fertility, particularly as a result of such practices as clearcutting and prescribed burning. Except for a few specific examples, it appears that removing crops of forest trees at the intervals presently proposed (by many public and private agencies) has little impact either on the nutrient element supplies or on nutrient cycling. However, each ecological situation has to be judged on its own merits. The cycle of each nutrient element should be assessed and the importance of that portion removed in a timber harvest should be considered, as well as the role that the vegetation plays in nutrient cycling. Frequently it appears that nutrient problems in forest ecosystems arise not from the total amount of a particular element that is present, but from its chemical or physical availability for plant use.

## BIBLIOGRAPHY

Bengtson, G. W. (ed.), 1968. *Forest Fertilization: Theory and Practice*, TVA National Fertilizer Development Center, Muscle Shoals, AL.

Smith, David M. 1962. *The Practice of Silviculture*, 7th ed., John Wiley & Sons, Inc., New York.

Chapter 14

# Measuring the Forest

In Chap. 3 and elsewhere in this book, trends towards more intensive protection and management of forest lands are discussed. Public concern in North America is directed toward the adequacy of our forest land, with people questioning whether their forests can produce all the products and services that are required. This concern has resulted in increased attention being paid to the estimation of forest growth and potential yield. Values of timber products have increased dramatically in recent years so that accurate measurements are essential. Sorting for higher value products has become extremely selective in pulp, plywood, and sawtimber operations. Weighing of logs is also common practice. Forest measurement is thus an area of great importance in forestry.

That phase of forestry which seeks to measure the present and future volume, growth, and development of individual trees and stands, and their timber products, is known as *forest mensuration.* It measures ages, diameters, heights, basal areas, and volumes of standing timber. It also measures the volume of logs, piles of pulpwood, and cords of fuelwood and considers single pieces such as posts, poles, piling, mine props, and railroad ties.

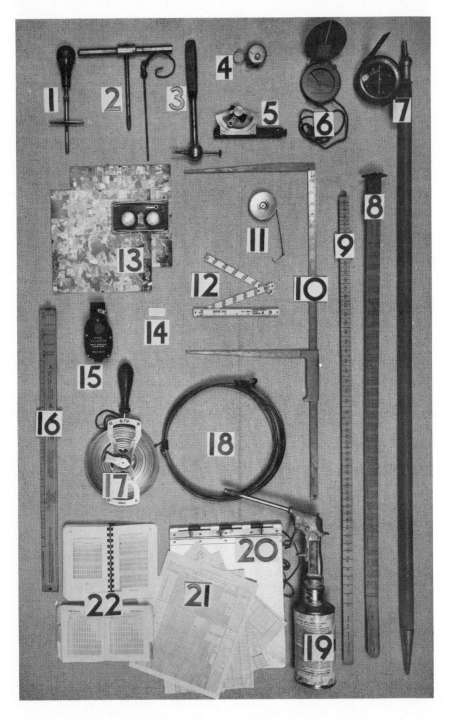

Forest measurement also includes surveying or measuring the land on which the forest grows. The science of mensuration recognizes the forest as a dynamic community that loses by damage, is reduced by harvesting, and gains by growth.

The forester's equipment for forest mensuration includes a Biltmore stick, hypsometer, log-scale stick, Abney level, clinometer, diameter tape, wedge prism, tree calipers, compass, surveyor's tape, aerial photographs, pocket stereoscope, volume table, maps, tally sheets, and a tatum board (Fig. 14-1). In this chapter we shall see how this equipment is used. We will discuss the measurement of logs, trees, land area, and finally, forest sampling.

## MEASURING LOGS

### Board-Foot Log Rules

A log rule is a formula or table which gives the volume of a log, based on its diameter and length. Board-foot log rules are designed to predict the lumber which may be sawn from the log. The board foot represents a piece of wood 1 in. thick by 12 in. wide by 1 ft long (2.54 cm by 30.48 cm by 30.48 cm).[1] It is a common unit of log measurement throughout the United States, although it is gradually being replaced by the cubic foot unit in many areas.

The buyer of a saw log knows that not all of the log can be used for lumber. The log is not square; worse yet, it is tapered. The first cuts which square the log remove *slab;* each pass of the saw through the log produces sawdust (the width of this cut is the *saw kerf*); side trimming of each board or plank removes *edging*. Still, log buyers cannot wait until the log is sawn into boards to find out its board-foot volume; therefore, they use a board-foot *log rule* to tell them what can be cut from the log.

Log rules must take into account the volume of wood lost to saw kerf, slabs, and trimmings. As we shall see, there is considerable variation in the design of log rules, although each has several common features. Most

---

[1] Board feet in a plank $= whl/12$ where $w$ and $h$ are nominal width and height in inches and $l$ is the length in feet.

---

**Figure 14-1** Some equipment used for forest, tree, and log measurements: (1) bark-thickness gauge, (2) increment borer and extractor, (3)increment hammer, (4) tally register, (5) Abney level, (6) hand compass, (7) staff compass and Jacob staff, (8) scale stick, (9) Biltmore stick, (10) tree calipers, (11) diameter tape, (12) folding cruiser stick, (13) aerial photographs and pocket stereoscope, (14) wedge prism, (15) Relaskop, (16) tree volume stick with angle gauge at upper end, (17) 100-ft tape, (18) 1-chain tape, (19) tree marking paint and gun, (20) tatum board, (21) plot sheets and blank maps, (22) volume tables. *(Photo by Grant W. Sharpe.)*

board-foot rules assume that the log is a perfect cylinder and that it will be cut into inch-thick boards only. A few of the more common board-foot rules are described here.

**The Scribner Log Rule**  This is an example of a diagram rule devised by J. M. Scribner over 135 years ago. In circles representing the small ends of logs of many diameters, Scribner drew in all the 1-in. boards the circles would hold—allowing room for slab, edgings, and a ¼-in. saw kerf (Fig. 14-2). The volume represented by these boards was then computed for various lengths and put into table form. The Scribner rule underestimates the amount of lumber which can be recovered from logs, particularly small-diameter logs sawn with modern sawmill techniques. Since this rule does

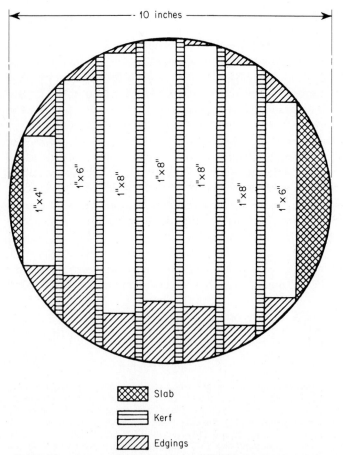

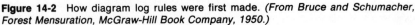

**Figure 14-2**  How diagram log rules were first made. *(From Bruce and Schumacher, Forest Mensuration, McGraw-Hill Book Company, 1950.)*

not take taper into account, it also underestimates the lumber contained in long logs. This is the oldest rule in general use and is the official rule in many parts of the United States. A modification in which values are rounded off to the nearest 10 board feet and the final digit dropped is called *Scribner decimal C.* A log containing 486 board feet would be recorded as 49, thus facilitating the work of the tallyman.[2] The Scribner decimal *C* rule is an official rule of the United States Forest Service in western national forests.

**International Log Rule**   This rule is based on a series of formulas and was first published in 1906. It allows ½-in. taper for each 4 ft of length and ⅛-in. shrinkage for each 1-in. board. In one form the International rule assumes a ⅛-in. saw kerf. In modified form, in which it assumes a ¼-in. kerf, it is an official rule of the United States Forest Service generally in eastern national forests.

**Doyle Log Rule**   This rule is from the formula

$$V = \left(\frac{D - 4}{4}\right)^2 L$$

where $V$ = number of board feet in the log, $D$ = diameter in inches inside bark at the small end, and $L$ = log length in feet.

The Doyle rule is also very old; it was developed prior to 1837. It is a poor log rule and serves to dispel the idea that a mathematical rule is always the most accurate. Its values for small logs are absurd, giving an error of as much as 300 percent. Yet the rule is used extensively in the eastern and southern United States. It underestimates the volume of small-diameter logs, is most accurate at 28 in. (71 cm), and overestimates volumes of larger logs.

**Variation in Board-Foot Log Rule Values**   For various reasons, including prevalence of particular defects in many localities, character of timber, peculiarities of rule construction, and size of logs, wide differences occur in measuring the same log by different rules. For example, a 16-ft log 12 in. dib (diameter inside bark) at small end contains the following amounts of lumber in board feet by the following rules: International ¼ in., 95; Scribner, 80; Doyle, 64. Actually such a log, if perfect, would turn out a squared timber 8 by 8 in. by 16 ft, which would contain approximately 85 board feet. In addition, several 6-in. boards 16 ft long could also be secured by a good sawyer. Even if sawn into 1-in. boards with a reasonably thin saw, this log should produce more than 100 board feet.

[2] No metric equivalent of the board foot exists; therefore, no simple conversion is possible. Because these rules were designed for English units, no attempt has been made to convert them to metric equivalents.

## Cubic-Foot Log Rules

Cubic-foot log rules are used in a manner similar to board-foot rules, except that they are designed to estimate cubic-foot volume of logs. Because of its greater accuracy and usefulness for conversion to a variety of forest products the cubic foot is being used increasingly to measure logs and trees. Frequently cubic-foot volumes are expressed in *cunits* or hundreds of cubic feet (e.g., 600 cu ft = 6 cunits).

Cubic-foot log rules generally assume the log to be a truncated paraboloid, and its volume is the average basal area in square feet multiplied by the length of the log in feet. The rules differ mainly in which part of the log is used in arriving at the average basal area.

By assuming log ends are circles we can calculate their basal area in square inches or square feet. The area of a circle in square inches is:

$$
\begin{aligned}
A &= \pi r^2 \\
&= 3.1416 r^2 \\
&= 3.1416 \left(\frac{D}{2}\right)^2 \\
&= 3.1416 \frac{D^2}{4} \\
&= \frac{3.1416 D^2}{4} \\
&= 0.7854 D^2 = \text{area in sq in.}
\end{aligned}
$$

where

$A = $ basal area (in.$^2$)
$r = $ radius (in.)
$D = $ diameter (in.)

Thus area in square feet is $(0.7854D^2)/144 = 0.00545D^2$ because 144 is the number of square inches in a square foot. Area in square meters is $0.00007854D^2$ when $D$ is measured in centimeters.

**Smalian's Formula**  In this formula both end diameters (inside bark) are considered. To obtain $V$ (log volume in cubic units) by the Smalian method:

$$
V = \frac{B + b}{2} L
$$

where $B = $ basal area at large end of log and $b = $ basal area at small end of log.

By substituting values of a 16-ft log in which the large diameter is 20 in. and the small diameter is 18 in., we find:[3]

$$V(\text{ft}^3) = \left[ \frac{0.00545(20)^2 + 0.00545(18)^2}{2} \right] 16$$
$$= [0.00545(400) + 0.00545(324)]8$$
$$= (2.18 + 1.77)8$$
$$= 3.95(8)$$
$$= 31.60 \text{ cu ft}$$

Using metric measurements, a log that is 5 m in length, 51 cm in diameter at the large end, and 46 cm in diameter at the small end will have a volume of

$$V(\text{m}^3) = \left[ \frac{0.00007854(51)^2 + 0.00007854(46)^2}{2} \right] 5$$
$$= 0.926 \text{ m}^3$$

It is also possible to calculate cubic-foot volume of a log using Smalian's formula, small-end diameter, and an estimate of log taper: [4]

$$V(\text{ft}^3) = \left[ \frac{0.00545(D)^2 + 0.00545\left(D + \dfrac{L}{A}\right)^2}{2} \right] L$$

where

$D$ = small-end diameter of log (in.)
$L$ = log length (ft)
$L$ = log length in feet required for 1 in. of taper

This approach is useful if it is only possible to measure diameter at one end of the log. For example, if a 16-ft log is 18 in. in diameter at the small end,

---

[3] If it is desired to maintain a complete accounting for log volume, an allowance for trim must be added to log length. This is necessary because wood in the trim frequently ends up as chips or other products. Assuming an 8-in. trim in this example, actual log length is 16.67 ft and cubic-foot volume becomes

$$V = \frac{(3.95)(16.67)}{2} = 32.92 \text{ cu ft}$$

[4] Average log taper can be estimated from accurate measurements of both end diameters for a representative sample of logs to be scaled. Since butt logs exhibit considerably more taper than other logs in a tree, a separate sample for butt logs is good practice.

and a 1-in. taper per 10 ft of log length is assumed, cubic-foot volume (not including trim) is

$$V(\text{ft}^3) = \left[ \frac{0.00545(18)^2 + 0.00545\left(18 + \frac{16}{10}\right)^2}{2} \right] 16 = 30.9 \text{ cu ft}$$

The metric equivalent of this formula is:

$$V(\text{m}^3) = \left[ \frac{0.00007854(D)^2 + 0.00007854\left(D + \frac{L}{A}\right)^2}{2} \right] L$$

where

$D$ = small-end diameter of log (cm)
$L$ = log length (m)
$A$ = log length in meters required for 1 cm of taper

**Huber's Formula**   This rule requires only one diameter measurement, the center of the log. Huber's formula is stated: $V = CL$, where $C$ = area at the center of the log. In a 16-ft log with a center dib of 19 in. we find

$$V(\text{ft}^3) = 0.00545(19)^2(16)$$
$$= (.00545)(361)(16) = 31.48 \text{ cu ft}$$

In a 5-m log with a center dib of 48 cm,

$$V(\text{m}^3) = 0.00007854(48)^2(5)$$
$$= 0.905 \text{ m}^3$$

The disadvantage of Huber's rule is that obtaining dib at the middle of decked or loaded logs is seldom practicable.

### Scaling

**Scale Sticks**   A person who determines the volume of logs is called a *scaler.* Log-rule values are stamped or printed on *scale sticks,* which are strong, flat, wooden measuring sticks that the scaler places against the small end of the log, and the contents, barring defect, are read directly from the stick (Fig. 14-3).   There are several log length values for each diameter division. The stick usually has an iron hook fastened at right angles to the zero end to facilitate the measurement of diameter inside bark (dib). There are different kinds of scale sticks in use to fit the log rule being used.

**Figure 14-3**  A log scaler reading the log volume directly from numbers on a scale stick. The scaler must recognize log species and how to deduct for defect. *(Courtesy of the U.S. Forest Service.)*

**Where Logs Are Scaled**  Depending on the terms of the sale, method of paying timber fallers, and type of log transportation in use, logs may be measured at various locations. They may be scaled in the woods before being skidded to a landing; or be scaled on trucks, in mill yards, or sorting ponds; or as they are entering the mill on a conveyor or jack ladder. The scaler usually numbers each log and frequently stamps it with a marking hammer. The number is also placed in a scale book with the volume opposite it. Two diameter measurements are taken and averaged when the cross section is irregular in shape. Length of logs must be checked frequently, and this can often be done by comparing log lengths with the known length of cars, trucks, or decks, or by pacing or measuring with a tape.

There is considerably more to log scaling than reading numbers off a scale stick. A scaler must be able to recognize the log species from the wood or bark. Scalers must know all the rules and regulations concerning log specifications and how to recognize certain defects and must know how to apply this knowledge to the log itself. Even a scaler with experience will make periodic visits to a mill to observe the interior of the logs as they are cut open.

**Deducting for Defect**  Defects which reduce the usable portion of the log must be considered in log scaling. Gross volume is determined from log dimensions, using a log rule. Net volume is calculated by deducting an estimated volume of defect (called "cull") from gross volume. Decay is the most common form of cull, but several other factors cause defect such as splits, cracks, and breaks, fire scars, and log sweep (crookedness).

A number of methods of deducting for cull are in use. A hollow, showing as a hole in both ends of the log, may be scaled as a log of somewhat larger diameter than the hole, and the result deducted from the gross scale of the log. Or the actual diameter of the hole may be increased slightly, squared, and figured as a useless squared timber of so many board feet to be substracted from the sound scale. Thus, if a 16-ft log 20 in. dib were to exhibit the opening of a hollow 7 in. in diameter, the scaler might add 2 in. to this diameter and scale the cull area as a 9-in. diameter log-inside-a-log. The result by the Scribner rule is 40 board feet of cull to be subtracted from 280 board feet gross scale, leaving a net scale of 240 board feet.

Where decayed sapwood or other log surface defect, such as fire or insect injury, is severe, the scale is simply taken as if the diameter were inside the injured zone. If serious defects are concentrated at one end of the log, scaling length may be reduced. Hidden defects may sometimes be identified by the fruiting body of a fungus or the spot where it has been broken off, and these logs should be carefully studied and treated on principles similar to those used with visible defects. Observing logs with cull indicators being sawed in the mill is an instructive experience, a great deal of which is needed to assure sound judgment on the amount to allow for cull.

Standard practice on sales of national forest timber is based on deduction of the number of board feet in a squared block of timber that would include the deductible defect in question. Thus, if a catface or fire scar on the surface of the first log of a tree were deeper than the thickness of the first slab, that additional depth in inches times the greatest width of the deductible defect in inches times its length in feet, with the product divided by 12, would equal the number of board feet to be deducted. An arbitrary reduction of 20 percent, however, is already made for saw kerf of the sound log and should not be deducted again when allowance is made for defect. This "standard rule" is expressed algebraically as follows: Let $w$ and $h$ be width and height, respectively, in inches of the end cross section of a deductible defect. Let $l$ be length of the defect in feet. Let $D$ be the number of board feet to deduct. Then

$$D = \left(\frac{whl}{12}\right)\frac{80}{100} = \frac{whl}{15}$$

Solving for a defect enclosed by a space 10 in. wide, 6 in. high, and 5 ft long,

$$D = \frac{10 \times 6 \times 5}{15} = 20 \text{ board feet}$$

If the gross scale of the log is 200 board feet, net scale would be 180 board feet.

Cubic volume deductions can be made in an analogous manner, using one of the basic cubic log rules to calculate defect volume in the case of circular defects, or by using the following formulas to determine volume of rectangular defects:

$$\text{Cubic foot } V(\text{ft}^3) = \begin{bmatrix} \text{end area} \\ (\text{sq ft}) \end{bmatrix} \begin{bmatrix} \text{defect length} \\ (\text{ft}) \end{bmatrix}$$

$$\text{Cubic meter } V(\text{m}^3) = \begin{bmatrix} \text{end area} \\ (\text{m}^3) \end{bmatrix} \begin{bmatrix} \text{defect length} \\ (\text{m}) \end{bmatrix}$$

### Cordwood Measurement

A measure of stacked round or split wood for fuel or pulpwood is a *cord,* which somewhat loosely occupies 128 cu ft of space.

**The Standard Cord**   Such a cord is a stacked pile 4 ft by 8 ft by 4 ft (1.22 m by 2.44 m by 1.22 m) high. Of the 128 cu ft (3.62 m³) in a cord, solid wood or wood and bark occupy only 75 to 100 cu ft (2.1 to 2.8 m³), depending on the size of the sticks, their straightness, smoothness, and how well they are limbed and piled.

**The Short Cord**   The short cord is often called a *rick* or a face cord, which is used for short-length fuelwood. Since a rick is 8 ft long and 4 ft high, and the depth is the length of the pieces, it would take several ricks to make a standard cord. It should be pointed out that the term *rick* has various connotations in different parts of the country.

**The Long Cord**   This is a cord in which the length of the stick exceeds 4 ft. The length varies with region and purpose. A cord for destructive distillation to obtain wood tar and charcoal may be 8 × 4 × 4 1/16 ft or 50 in. A shingle bolt cord on the West Coast is often 8 × 4 × 4 1/3 ft. In the Lake States, the sticks are often 8 ft long (actually 100 in.) and stacked 4 × 4 to make a theoretical 133 cu ft. A long cord in the South, often called a *unit,* may be 4 × 8 × 5 ft (actually 63 in.) to make 168 cu ft of stacked volume.

**Measuring the Cord**   The number of cords in a stack of cordwood is determined by measuring its length and height (an average of several heights taken at points along the pile) and calculating the face area. This area divided by the face area of a standard cord gives the volume of the pile.

## Log Weight

Log purchases on the basis of their weight are used now by many pulp mills. Loaded trucks are driven onto scales and weighed as they enter the mill yard. After the load is dumped, trucks are weighed again, and the difference is the weight of the wood. This method has several advantages. For one thing it is easy and accurate. Pulp mills have found that logs left in the woods too long become infested with blue stain fungi and insects, and with this method of measure they are more assured of getting the logs soon after they are cut. The log owner who is paid by the pound for logs makes considerable effort to get them to the mill before they dry out.

## Product Recovery

Wood harvested from forests is channeled into numerous products such as lumber, plywood, pulp and paper, composition board, shingles, and fuel. Because of the variety of end uses possible, it is frequently inaccurate to measure tree and log volumes in traditional board-foot units. Not only are board-foot log rules based on long-outdated sawmill capabilities, but a large volume of wood is not being sawn at all, rather it is peeled, chipped, split, or diverted to other nonlumber uses. A more useful approach to predicting product recovery from a log or tree is to measure wood volume in cubic feet and then to apply recovery factors pertinent to the ensuing product (Table 14-1).

A product recovery factor, when multiplied by the volume of raw material input, will provide an estimate of the amount of that product expected

## Table 14-1   Estimated Product Recovery From a Log Under Three Manufacturing Processes*

(Log size: 14-in. Diameter Small End, 16-in. Diameter Large End, 16 ft Plus Trim in Length, 20 cu ft, 110 bd ft Scribner)

| Product | Process no. 1† | Process no. 2‡ | Process no. 3§ |
|---|---|---|---|
| Lumber (bd ft) | 146 | 21 | |
| Compacted chips (cu ft) | 13 | 22 | 50 |
| Plywood (sq ft ³/₈ in. basis) | · · · | 280 | |
| Sawdust (cu ft) | 7 | trace | |
| Glue-contaminated chips (cu ft) | · · · | 4 | |

*Source:* Adapted from Hartman, Atkinson, Bryant, and Woodfin, 1976.

*Actual recovery will depend on specific manufacturing techniques and equipment. This is meant to be an example only.

†Saw for lumber with bandsaw headrig, chip solid residue.

‡Peel for plywood to 4¹/₂-in. core; saw core for lumber; chip usable residue.

§Chip entire log.

to be manufactured from the input. For example, a lumber recovery factor of 7.3 indicates that 7.3 board feet of lumber will be produced from each cubic foot of log-scale input. Hence, a 20-cu ft log will be expected to provide 20 (7.3) = 146 board feet of lumber. Recovery factors are most accurate when based on the particular equipment, product mix, and log characteristics of a specific production facility. By using cubic foot units to measure input volume and appropriate product recovery factors, accurate estimates of output quantities can be made.

### Metric Volume Measurement

The use of metric units of measurement is fast approaching in American forestry. First will come metric sizes for lumber, plywood, and other manufactured products. Eventually foresters will be measuring log and tree volumes in metric units. The conversion from cubic feet to cubic meters is straightforward—merely multiply the number of cubic feet by 0.02832 (for example, 225.0 cu ft = 6.4 m³). The eventual conversion to metric units for log and tree volumes will be facilitated if foresters are already using cubic feet rather than board feet to measure log volumes. See Appendix B for a useful metric conversion table.

## MEASURING TREES

### Tree Diameter

The diameter of a tree is most commonly measured at breast height, which is understood to be 4 ½ ft. (137 cm) above ground. Adjustment is made for leaning trees, abnormal growth, and trees on a steep slope. The *diameter breast height,* or dbh, of a tree is taken to the nearest 0.1 in., 1 in., or 2 in. (or 1 cm), depending on the accuracy desired.

One instrument used to obtain dbh is the *tree caliper,* made of either wood or metal. It is a simple device, consisting of an arm and two prongs, one of which is free to slide along a graduated scale on the arm. The prongs are placed against opposite sides of the tree and the diameter is read on the scale. The *diameter tape* is a steel pocket tape with a scale on each surface and a bark hook at the zero end. The outside surface is graduated in inches and tenths of inches, and although the tape is placed around the tree, the scale is calibrated to give the tree's diameter. The reverse side is a regular surveying tape, 20 ft long and divided into feet and tenths of feet. A third instrument for obtaining dbh is the *Biltmore stick,* a solid stick or folding pocket rule, which is held against the trunk (Fig. 14-4) at the customary height above ground. Most Biltmore sticks are designed for use by the average arm length of 25 in. (63.5 cm). Experienced estimators can "eyeball" a tree's dbh within half an inch or so, but will check their accuracy frequently with one of the above instruments.

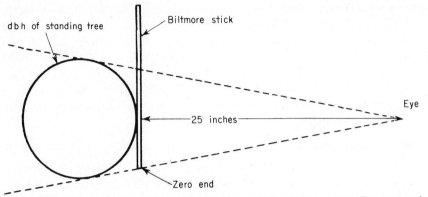

**Figure 14-4**  Measuring the dbh of a standing tree with the Biltmore stick. The zero end is held to the left, the tree's diameter is read at the point where the line of sight, from the observer's eyes to the right of the tree, intersects the stick.

## Tree Height

Suppose the total height of a standing tree or perhaps only its merchantable height [for example, up to a 5-in. (12.7-cm) top diameter] is needed. An accurate hand instrument used to obtain this measurement is the *Abney level*. Simply by sighting at the top of the tree and at the base of the tree and adding the readings or subtracting them, depending on the position of the observer, the tree height is obtained. The distance that the Abney is used from the tree is important. Abneys have two scales. The topographic scale is used with the 1-chain or 2-chain tape (1 chain = 66 ft). The percent scale is used with a 100-ft tape. Since the percent Abney and 100-ft tape combination is commonly used in forestry work, we will use it as the example cited in Fig. 14-5.

In situation 1, on level ground, assume the Abney reading of OT = 86; and the reading of OB is 5. Since horizontal distance is 100 ft, tree height is 91 ft. In the instance of a very tall tree, or one with the top hidden in a dense canopy, it may be necessary to move out farther than 100 ft horizontal distance. If, for example, horizontal distance is 135 ft, multiply the sum (or differences, as the case may be) by 1.35 (91 × 1.35 = 122.8 ft). If horizontal distance is 75 ft, tree height is 0.75(91) = 68.2 ft.

The *clinometer* is another instrument that may be used to measure angles (Fig. 14-6). When the percent scale is used, the procedure for measuring tree heights is identical to that for the Abney level.

Another method of obtaining tree heights is with the *Merritt hypsometer*. By placing the hypsometer scales or graduations on one surface of the Biltmore stick a convenient tool called a *cruiser's stick* is made. The hyp-

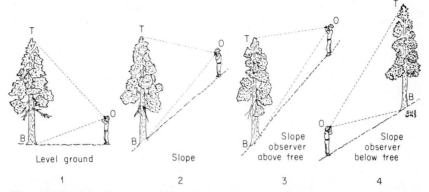

Level ground | Slope | Slope observer above tree | Slope observer below tree

1            2            3            4

**Figure 14-5** Using the percent Abney in four situations. The observer is 100 horizontal feet from the tree. In situation 1 the Abney reading of OT + OB = BT, the distance from the base to the top. Similarly in 2 where observer is on a slope but not above the top T, then readings of OT + OB = BT. In 3, observer is above T; therefore, OB − OT = BT. Likewise in 4, OT − OB = BT. Remember this rule: When the observer is between the base and the top, add the readings; if the observer is above the top or below the base, the readings are subtracted. This may be stated simply: Between—add; above or below—subtract.

**Figure 14-6** The forester at right is using a clinometer to determine the height of a tree. At left the forester is demonstrating the use of the hand held "ranger" compass. *(Photo by Grant W. Sharpe.)*

someter permits one to determine tree heights expressed in 16-ft (4.88-m) logs. There are two sets of scales, one for readings from a distance of 1 chain from the tree, the other for 1 ½-chain distances. The use of a 1-chain hypsometer is illustrated in Fig. 14-7. If the tree is too tall for either scale, the distance from the tree is doubled and the resultant reading doubled. Measurements on a slope are possible so long as the appropriate distance from the tree is the horizontal distance. Since the Biltmore stick and Merritt hypsometer must be read at exact distances from the eye and the hypsometer held exactly vertical for height measurements, these instruments are principally valuable for making rough estimates. Both are inaccurate unless designed for the exact arm reach of the individual who is to use them. The average-sized man has an arm length of 25 in. (64 cm); the average-sized woman has an arm length of 23 in. (58 cm).

## Tree Age

In Chap. 9 we learned that in temperate climates a tree forms a *growth ring* by adding new wood each year. When a tree has been felled, its age can be determined by counting these rings. The rings also tell an experienced observer about the tree's environmental history: did the tree receive adequate

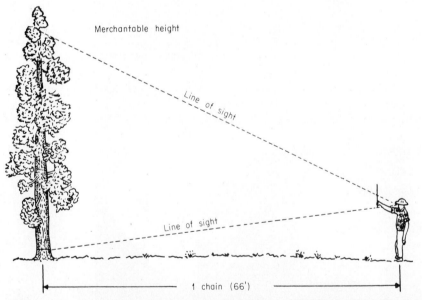

**Figure 14-7** Using the Merritt hypsometer. The observer holds the zero or bottom end of the hypsometer so that it intercepts the line of sight between the eye and the stump height of the tree. Without moving the head or the stick a second sighting is made on the merchantable top of the tree; the point at which the line of sight intercepts the hypsometer scale will indicate the tree's length, either in feet, meters, or the number of 16-ft logs.

**Figure 14-8** Using the increment borer to determine the age of a tree. Here the borer has been twisted into the tree, and the core is being removed with the extractor. *(Courtesy of the U.S. Forest Service.)*

moisture; were soil nutrients available; did its neighbors crowd it or shut off its light; was it ever defoliated by insects or burned in a fire? Often a forester wishes to learn the history or age of a standing tree. A hollow augerlike tool called an *increment borer* is twisted gradually into the trunk. As the leading edge is forced toward the center, it cuts a core of wood which may be removed with an extractor (Fig. 14-8). The rings appear as dark and light bands. If the growth characteristics of the outside inch of wood are all that is needed, the *increment hammer* in Fig. 14-1 (item 3) may be used.

### Tree Volumes

Tree volumes, like log volumes, are measured in board feet and cubic feet, and are based on log rules. Foresters have long made use of tree volume tables which provide an estimate of volume contained in the standing tree (Table 14-2). Three types of volume tables are in general use:

    **1  Form class volume tables**  Volume estimates are based on species, dbh, merchantable or total height, and form (taper) of the butt log.
    **2  Standard volume tables**  Volume estimates are based on species, dbh, and merchantable or total height.
    **3  Local volume tables**  Volume estimates are based on species and

dbh only. Local volume tables are usually developed for local conditions from form class or standard volume tables.

### Tree Growth

Wood production is frequently a major goal of forest management and for that reason foresters devote a great deal of attention to measuring and controlling tree growth. Growth can be measured for an individual tree, such as height growth, diameter growth, basal area growth, or volume growth, but most often foresters are interested in growth of a forest stand or a collection of trees. Stand growth is expressed on a unit area basis, for example, volume growth per acre or basal area growth per acre.

Forest growth can be visualized as consisting of three components: (1) increment of the stand during a period of time (growth period), (2) ingrowth into the smallest measurable diameter class from trees that were too small

**Table 14-2   Portion of a Cubic-Foot Volume Table for Douglas-fir**
(Volumes in Cubic Feet. Four Merchantability Standards)

| dbh | Merchantable top | Total height (ft) | | | | | | |
|---|---|---|---|---|---|---|---|---|
| | | 40 | 50 | 60 | 70 | 80 | 90 | 100 |
| 8 in. | TS* | 5.7 | 7.3 | 9.0 | 10.6 | 12.3 | 13.9 | 15.5 |
| | 4 in. | 4.9 | 6.4 | 7.8 | 9.2 | 10.6 | 12.1 | 13.4 |
| | 6 in. | 3.0 | 3.9⁻ | 4.8 | 5.6 | 6.5 | 7.4 | 8.2 |
| | 8 in. | . . . | . . . | . . . | . . . | . . . | . . . | . . . |
| 9 in. | TS* | 7.0 | 9.1 | 11.1 | 13.2 | 15.2 | 17.2 | 19.2 |
| | 4 in. | 6.3 | 8.2 | 10.0 | 11.9 | 13.7 | 15.5 | 17.3 |
| | 6 in. | 4.8 | 6.2 | 7.6 | 9.0 | 10.4 | 11.8 | 13.1 |
| | 8 in. | 1.0 | 1.3 | 1.6 | 1.9 | 2.1 | 2.4 | 2.7 |
| 10 in. | TS* | 8.5 | 11.0 | 13.4 | 15.9 | 18.4 | 20.8 | 23.2 |
| | 4 in. | 7.8 | 10.1 | 12.4 | 14.7 | 17.0 | 19.3 | 21.5 |
| | 6 in. | 6.6 | 8.6 | 10.5 | 12.5 | 14.4 | 16.3 | 18.2 |
| | 8 in. | 3.5 | 4.5 | 5.5 | 6.6 | 7.6 | 8.6 | 9.6 |
| 11 in. | TS* | 10.0 | 13.0 | 15.9 | 18.9 | 21.8 | 24.7 | 27.6 |
| | 4 in. | 9.4 | 12.2 | 15.0 | 17.7 | 20.5 | 23.2 | 25.9 |
| | 6 in. | 8.5 | 11.0 | 13.5 | 16.0 | 18.5 | 20.9 | 23.4 |
| | 8 in. | 6.0 | 7.7 | 9.5 | 11.2 | 13.0 | 14.7 | 16.4 |
| 12 in. | TS* | 11.7 | 15.2 | 18.6 | 22.1 | 25.5 | 28.9 | 32.2 |
| | 4 in. | 11.1 | 14.4 | 17.6 | 20.9 | 24.1 | 27.3 | 30.5 |
| | 6 in. | 10.4 | 13.4 | 16.5 | 19.6 | 22.6 | 25.6 | 28.6 |
| | 8 in. | 8.4 | 10.9 | 13.3 | 15.8 | 18.2 | 20.7 | 23.1 |

*TS: Total stem, including top and stump. Volumes to top diameters inside bark exclude 1.5 ft (45.7 cm) stump.
*Source:* Adapted from Hartman, Atkinson, Bryant, and Woodfin, 1976.

to measure at the beginning of the growth period, and (3) mortality or loss of trees to death. Increment and ingrowth increase measured stand volume while mortality decreases volume. Terms used to express forest growth are

Gross growth = increment + ingrowth
Net growth = gross growth − mortality

For example, trees on an acre of forest land grow 150 cu ft (10.5 m³/ha) in a year (increment = 150), trees totaling 2 cu ft (0.1 m³/ha) in volume enter the stand by growing into the smallest measurable diameter class (ingrowth = 2) and trees totaling 14 cu ft (1.0 m³/ha) in volume die during the year (mortality = 14). Then

Gross growth = 150 + 2 = 152 cu ft/acre (10.5 + 0.1 = 10.6 m³/ha)
Net growth = 152 − 14 = 138 cu ft/acre (10.6 − 1.0 = 9.6 m³/ha)

It is also important to define the time period to which forest growth estimates apply. Current annual increment (cai) refers to growth in a specific year, periodic annual increment (pai) is the average growth per year over a short period of time, and mean annual increment (mai) refers to average annual growth over the life of the stand. For example, suppose net growth for a stand is 138 cu ft/acre at age 20 and 130 cu ft/acre at age 21. Total volume present in the stand at age 21 is 3,675 cu ft/acre. Then

$$\text{cai (age 20)} = 138 \text{ cu ft/acre}$$
$$\text{cai (age 21)} = 130 \text{ cu ft/acre}$$
$$\text{pai (2-year period)} = \frac{138 + 130}{2} = 134 \text{ cu ft/acre}$$
$$\text{mai (at age 21)} = \frac{3{,}675}{21} = 175 \text{ cu ft/acre}$$

### Forest Yield

The concept of forest yield differs from that of forest growth in that yield refers to the total amount of volume, basal area, or number of trees expected to be present in the stand at a given age, while growth refers to an *increment* in volume or basal area. In the previous example, yield at age 21 is 3,675 cu ft/acre while growth at age 21 is 130 cu ft.

Yield estimates are generally presented in yield tables, several types of which are in use.

**Normal yield tables**   Tables based on measurements made in natural unmanaged forest stands that exhibit complete crown closure. In terms of modern forest management, "normal" stands are considerably overstocked, especially at young ages.

Normal yield tables have been developed for pure-species stands of the major forest species in the United States. Yield estimates are tabulated by stand age and site index. Since most forests today are managed, normal yield tables are declining in usefulness.

**Empirical yield tables**  Tables similar to normal yield tables but which are based on stocking as found in average natural stands rather than on dense "normal" stands.

**Variable density yield tables**  Tables of yield estimates which are based on stand density as well as on age and site index, and are useful for predicting yields under a forest management regime that includes stocking control.

**Managed stand yield tables**  Tables which include as variables not only age, site index, and stocking but also other forest management practices, such as fertilization and genetic improvement, and which are regarded as the ultimate objective of research in forest yield estimation.

## MEASURING LAND AREA

### Systems of Land Survey

In the New England and Atlantic Coastal states (excluding Florida) and in Pennsylvania, West Virginia, Kentucky, Tennessee, and Texas, the method of subdividing land is called *metes and bounds*. Where this confusing system prevails, property lines may begin at physical features such as streams, lake shores, or ridge tops, or at artificial features such as fences and roads. Although the corners were once marked with monuments, their descriptions are vague and many corners themselves have long been lost. Locating the legal forest boundary here is indeed a problem, and often a forester or surveyor must spend days seeking information which might lead to "who owns what." Although not a complete solution, the more practical *rectangular system of surveys* applies to most of the rest of the United States. It is from this system, established in 1784, that such familiar terms as *township* and *the lower forty* were derived.

**The Rectangular System of Surveys**  This system uses established *meridians* and *base lines* as references from which land surveys are made and is employed by all states not on the metes and bounds system. Each state or a small group of states will have a common east and west base line which parallels (but does not necessarily coincide with) the major parallels of latitude. Similarly, one or more states will have a north and south principal meridian. The point where the base line intersects the principal meridian is called the *initial point*, which was the starting point of the survey (located by latitude and longitude). It is here that the systematic numbering of the square *townships* north and south of the base line begins. Township distances east and west of the principal meridian are measured by *ranges*.

By referring to the grid of Fig. 14-9a this numbering system will be easier to understand. Township 1 North, Range 3 West, is usually stated T 1 N, R 3 W, and others have been located on this grid.

Each township is theoretically 6 mi sq (9.66 km), contains 23,040 acres (9,324 ha), and is divided into 36 sections, as illustrated in Fig. 14-9b. Section number 1 is in the northeast corner of the township. A section, 80 chains (1 mi or 1.61 km) square, containing 640 acres (259 ha), is further divided into quarter sections of 160 acres (64.75 ha) each, which in turn are divided into four 40-acre squares. This last subdivision of 40-acre (16.19-ha) squares is termed ¼-¼ (quarter-quarter) section. The legal descriptions of the single forties are designated in Fig. 14-9c. Irregular areas within a section caused by lakes and surveying errors become lots. The numbering of lots is left to the judgment of the surveyor, although by convention they are usually numbered from east to west and north to south.

Because of the convergence of the meridians, the northern boundary of a township is supposed to be somewhat shorter than the southern boundary, and both may be less than 6 mi across. The nearer the North Pole the township lies, the greater this convergence is. Occasionally early surveyors were not particularly careful, and the discrepancies found now may not follow this theoretical pattern.

The actual laying out of section corners started in the southeast corner of the township so that human survey errors and discrepancies due to convergence fall in the northern tier of forties of sections 1, 2, 3, 4, 5, and 6, and the western tier of forties of sections 6, 7, 18, 19, 30, and 31, which often makes "forties" lying along these boundaries more or less than 40 acres. For each 24 mi east or west of the principal meridian, a guide meridian is established; similarly, a standard parallel is established each 24 mi north and south of the base line, as shown in Fig. 14-9a. These lines are termed *correction lines* and are established to prevent further extension of error.

**Marking Corners**    In the early days, section corners were indicated by *monuments* of marked stones, piles of rock, or more often by wooden posts and blazed trees, many of which have since disintegrated. Many survey notes of early surveyors in Western and Prairie states make colorful reading. Often surveyors were "paid by the monument" and would leave town to mark corners only when they ran out of money. One account tells of "rolling rocks off the wagon every mile while counting wheel rotations and being fired on by natives."

The Bureau of Land Management, charged with locating corners on public lands, suggests using iron or concrete posts with an appropriately stamped brass cap at the top. Whatever material is used, the field notes should include such information about the corner and its monument as the kind of post, its diameter, depth set in ground, and any markings on the

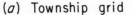

### (a) Township grid

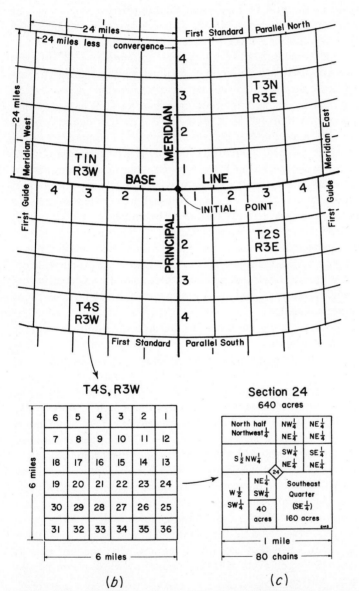

**Figure 14-9** Generalized diagram of the rectangular system of surveys, *(a)* Township grid showing initial point, base line, principal meridian, standard parallels and guide meridians, and examples of township and range designations. *(b)* Subdivision of township into 1-mi sections and the systems of numbering sections from 1 to 36. *(c)* Subdivision of section into half sections, quarter sections, and forties. *(Adopted from the Bureau of Land Management, U.S. Department of the Interior.)*

**Table 14-3  Units of Land Measurement**

| Units of linear measure |
| --- |

1 link = 0.66 ft = 7.92 in. = 20.12 centimeters (cm)
1 rod = 16.5 ft = $^1/_4$ chain = 5.03 meters (m)
1 chain = 100 links = 66 ft = 20.12 meters (m)
1 mile = 80 chains = 5,280 ft = 1.6093 kilometers (km)

| Units of area |
| --- |

1 township = 36 sq mi = 36 sections = 23,040 acres = 9,324.3 hectares (ha)
1 section = 1 sq mi = 640 acres = 259.0 hectares (ha)
$^1/_4$ section = 160 acres = 64.75 hectares (ha)
$^1/_4$ of $^1/_4$ section = 40 acres = 16.19 hectares (ha)
1 acre = 43,560 sq ft = 10 sq chains = 0.4047 hectare (ha)

monument. If a tree or stone is used, the appropriate information is included, as well as the nature of the surrounding objects. Distances and bearings to witness trees are also recorded in the field notes. Frequently these trees provide good clues for locating the original corner. It might be mentioned that corners are located every 40 chains (804.8 m) (quarter section corners) and 80 chains (1,609.6 m) (section corners). Interior lines of the sections were not run by the original surveyor. (See Table 14-3 for units of linear measurement and units of area).

## MEASURING FORESTS BY SAMPLING

### Timber Cruising

Timber areas in the United States are often very large. The cost of determining the volume of even a segment of a forest understandably prohibits the measurement of every tree. The total volume, therefore, is estimated by obtaining the volume on part of the stand and multiplying this sample by the appropriate "blow up" factor. The sampling can be done in several ways.

**The Random Sample**  A system which gives each part of a forest an equal and independent chance to be sampled is called a *random sample*. The following is an example of this method. A forest tract is divided evenly into 100 plots, and numbers from 1 to 100 are placed in a hat. By drawing 10 numbers, a tenth of the tract has been selected at random. If the timber volume of these 10 plots is measured, the sampling will be 10 percent of the total. Naturally a uniform coverage of the forest tract is left up to chance. In Fig. 14-10a, it can be seen that certain swampy, grassland, or brush areas can be missed. Obviously the point has been exaggerated to show its disadvantages since some provision can be made to select a certain number of

40 ACRES                                    40 ACRES

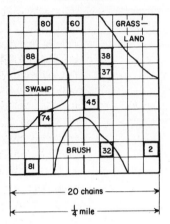
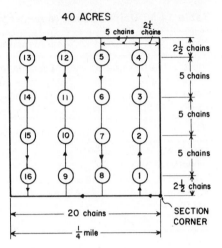

(a) Random sampling                    (b) Mechanical sampling

**Figure 14-10** *(a)* Random sampling method where plots are selected by drawing numbers from a hat. As indicated in this example the plots are seldom evenly distributed. Though the cruise covers 10 percent of the total, it is not representative of the true cover because no plots fall in the swamp or grassland. *(b)* Mechanical sampling method showing sixteen 1/4-acre plots, each with a radius of 58.9 ft. The cruise is 10 percent of the forty or 4 acres. The arrows indicate the direction of the cruise. The plot centers are 5 chains apart. The cruiser has offset 2 1/2 chains west of the section corner and then 2 1/2 chains north before location of the first plot.

plots from each of the four subdivisions. Usually, in order to determine the area of timber types, the timber cruiser will want to map the area traversed while locating the plots. The location of lakes, streams, roads, changes of timber type, and topography are some of the features needed for planning future forest management and logging operations. Such a map requires passing through the area systematically. Random sampling does not lend itself well to map making or to locating the plots easily.

**Mechanical Sampling**   A method of cruising which *does* lend itself to map making and assures an even distribution of plots is *mechanical sampling,* in which plots are located along predetermined lines. The estimator or timber cruiser following these lines (usually located with a compass) will establish plots at given intervals. Because this method is the one foresters ordinarily use, it will be used to illustrate both timber cruising and map-making techniques.

In Fig. 14-10b, a quarter section or "forty" illustrates cruise lines and plot locations which give the estimator a 10 percent cruise. The plot size chosen here is a circular 1/4 acre. Although the area covers 40 acres, only 4 acres need be sampled to obtain the desired 10 percent cruise. This would

**Table 14-4   Sample Plot Dimensions (acres)**

| Plot size (acres) | Circular plot radius (ft) | Square plot size (ft) |
|---|---|---|
| 1 | 117.8 | 208.8 |
| $1/_2$ | 83.3 | 147.6 |
| $1/_4$ | 58.9 | 104.4 |
| $1/_5$ | 52.7 | 93.3 |
| $1/_{10}$ | 37.2 | 66.0 |
| $1/_{250}$ | 7.45 | 13.2 |
| $1/_{1,000}$ | 3.7 | 6.6 |

mean sixteen ¼-acre plots are needed in the forty. Plot radius in this case is 58.9 ft. The plot boundary may be located by pacing or measuring several radii from the plot center. An advantage to a circular plot over a square plot is that it is easy to determine if borderline trees are in or out of the plot. Circular or square plots of other sizes are also used. The larger and more scattered the trees, the bigger the plot should be. Tables 14-4 and 14-5 gives the dimension of most sample plots in use.

Strip cruising is another means of mechanical sampling in which the cruiser measures all trees for a given distance on each side of the compass line. Since the strip is usually 1 chain wide, the cruiser finds it rather easy to estimate a distance of 33 ft to left and right. The strips are run parallel through the forty, and if a 1-chain width is used each pass through covers 5 percent of the area.

A simple rule for determining the acreage and percentage cruised is

$$\text{Acres} = \frac{\text{chains} \times \text{chains}}{10}$$

**Table 14-5   Sample Plot Dimensions (hectares)**

| Plot size (hectares) | circular plot radius (m) | Square plot size (m) |
|---|---|---|
| 0.20 | 25.2 | 44.7 |
| 0.10 | 17.8 | 31.6 |
| 0.08 | 15.9 | 28.2 |
| 0.05 | 12.6 | 22.3 |
| 0.02 | 7.9 | 14.1 |
| 0.01 | 5.6 | 10.0 |
| 0.005 | 3.9 | 7.1 |

If a single strip 1 chain wide and 20 chains long is run through a forty, we find that

$$\frac{1 \times 20}{10} = 2 \text{ acres} \quad \text{and} \quad \frac{2}{40} = 0.05 \text{ or } 5\%$$

Therefore, a 10 percent cruise would require two strips through the forty. This simple acreage rule has other uses. If one wished to determine the acreage of a section and knew that it was $80 \times 80$ chains, then:

$$\frac{80 \times 80}{10} = \frac{6,400}{10} = 640 \text{ acres}$$

**The Survey Crew**   The normal cruise party consists of two persons—a person with a compass and the estimator or timber cruiser (Fig. 14-11). If additional data are required, such as information on reproduction, ground cover, rate of growth (or a topographic map to be made), a third person may be added to the crew, although two can usually perform all these duties. The least experienced of the two-person party is the one with the compass, who keeps the party on line with either a hand compass or a staff compass. One of the two takes the head end of the chain, the other the rear, and they follow the compass course marking off distances until the location of the plot center is reached. The timber cruiser makes a map as they go, recording location of streams, topographic changes (read from the Abney level or clinometer), and forest type changes. When the plot is reached and its boundaries defined, a tally begins of all trees in the plot on the tally sheets. Each tree's diameter is recorded, using the dot-bar system (illustrated below)  opposite the diameter and below the appropriate species according to tree height. The cruiser also records defect and anything else

of a pertinent nature. The other person may assist in tallying, taking tree heights, or boring a representative dominant or codominant tree to determine its age. When a new plot is reached, a new tally sheet is used, and the process starts all over again. When the last plot in a given line is measured, the party continues in the same direction until the section or ¼ section line is reached. Here they "tie in" on their map and move to the next cruise line.

Office work includes determining the volume on each tally sheet from *volume tables*. Such a table, discussed earlier, simplifies the cruiser's field-work. The number of square feet per acre or *basal area* of the standing timber may also be obtained from the dbh's of the cruise plot data. Basal

**Figure 14-11** A crew of two persons running a cruise. A staff compass is being used here to locate the lines run at intervals through the forest. The person with the compass is recording the tree dbh's which are being determined with a Biltmore stick by the cruiser in the background. *(Courtesy of the U.S. Forest Service.)*

area information tells the forester the stocking density of the forest. They may indicate that a young stand may be too dense for optimum vigor and growth and require thinning to reduce the basal area.

### OTHER METHODS OF CRUISING AND MAPPING

**Variable Plot Cruising**   As indicated above, foresters may wish to know the basal area of the growing forest. A new technique in timber cruising was introduced into the United States from Germany by Dr. L. R. Grosenbaugh, of the Forest Service in 1952, and is called the "Bitterlich method of direct basal area determination." *Variable plot cruising,*[5] as it is also called, is a timesaver, since plot boundaries are not laid out. It requires that the cruiser stand on a spot in the forest and, while rotating, count all the trees whose diameters appear greater than the width of a small vertical object, called an angle gauge, held outstretched at eye level (Fig. 14-12a).

[5] Variable plot cruising is also known by several other names, including *prism cruising, angle count, point sampling, plotless cruising,* and *variable radius plot sampling.*

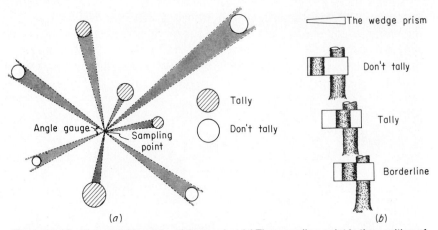

**Figure 14-12** How variable plot cruising works. *(a)* The sampling point is the position of the observer's eye. The circles represent the dbh of trees. The shaded area shows the angle of projection defined by the edges of the angle-gauge. Only those trees which intercept a greater angle are tallied. *(b)* The wedge prism and how it tells which trees to count. If the displacement of the tree, as seen through the prism, is beyond that part of the tree not seen through the prism, the tree is not counted. If the displacement is less, the tree is tallied. If the displacement coincides with the tree's edge, it is borderline and is counted as half a tree.

The object used will vary in complexity from the cruiser's own thumb, a coin, or a piece of metal mounted on a sighting stick to an optical device such as the wedge prism or more elaborate Spiegel Relaskop held next to the eye (see Fig. 14-1, items 14, 15, and 16). The wedge prism is a piece of glass that bends light rays. It may be held at any convenient distance from the eye, provided the prism is held over the fixed sampling point as the cruiser rotates to check all the trees. Trees to be included in the count will not be completely displaced from the line of sight over or under the prism, as seen in Fig. 14-12*b*. When the number of trees has been determined by a prism, or other form of angle gauge, the basal area in square feet per acre may be computed by multiplying the tree count by the basal area factor (BAF) of the prism. If the dbh's of counted trees are known it is possible to estimate volume per acre using volume/basal area ratios ($V$/BAR).

**Aerial Photographs in Forestry**   To a passenger in an airplane flying at 12,000 ft (3,658 m), the trees on the ground appear quite small. An estimate of a tree's height from that altitude, would be only a wild guess. Yet by viewing aerial photographs taken at that same altitude, it is possible to measure tree heights to within 1 or 2 ft (30 to 60 cm) of accuracy. Stand density, stand area, and crown diameter are a few of the other measurements that foresters can determine by reading aerial photographs. With the aid of a stereoscope placed over two photos of the same object (Fig. 14-1, item 13) photographed from different positions in the air, a third dimension is shown which makes such measurements possible. Aerial photos have other applications, also. A photo interpreter with experience can delineate insect-damaged stands, determine the width of a river and the direction of its flow, decide where logging roads should be located, and perhaps most useful of all, can make maps of and inventory the volumes of vast forest areas. The map-making disadvantages of laying out random sample plots can be overcome when maps are made from aerial photos.

**Continuous Forest Inventory**   Basically foresters are concerned with timber volume, both present and future. A means of obtaining long-range information on growth (and mortality) of a forest is by *continuous forest inventory*. This method, commonly referred to as CFI, employs permanent sample plots which are located mechanically either on the ground or on aerial photographs. Mensuration data from these plots, such as species, dbh, height, and form class, are collected periodically (Fig. 14-13) and are computed on data processing equipment. CFI is also used to tabulate changes in species and quality of a given forest.

**Trends in Measurement**   The application of intensive forest management, high values for timber, increased wood recovery in logging, and the use of specialized mill equipment all point toward changes in forest measurement practices. The board foot is being replaced by the cubic foot,

**Figure 14-13**   Punch card data being collected for Continuous Forest Inventory work in Louisiana. *(Courtesy of the Crown Zellerbach Corp.)*

volume tables and yield tables need revision, and there may be a change-over to the metric system within a few years. Forest measurement continues to be an actively expanding area in American forestry.

## BIBLIOGRAPHY

Allan, Arthur L. 1968. *Practical Field Surveying and Computations,* American Elsevier Publishing Company, Inc., New York.

Avery, T. E. 1966. *Forester's Guide to Aerial Photo Interpretation,* U.S. Department of Agriculture Handbook no. 308.

——— 1968. *Interpretation of Aerial Photographs,* Burgess Publishing Company, Minneapolis, MN.

——— 1975. *Natural Resources Measurements,* 2d ed., McGraw-Hill Book Company, New York.

Binek, A. 1973. *Forest Products in Terms of Metric Units,* P. O. Box 7, Westmount, (Published by the author) Quebec, Canada.

Bruce, D. 1968. Literature on Timber Measurement Problems in the Douglas-fir Region, U.S. Forest Service Resource Paper no. PNW 67-1968, Pacific Northwest Forest Range Experiment Station, Portland, OR.

Dilworth, John R. 1965. *Variable Plot Cruising,* Oregon State University Bookstores, Inc., Corvallis.

———. 1974. *Log Scaling and Timber Cruising,* Oregon State University Bookstores, Inc., Corvallis.

Freese, Frank. 1967. *Elementary Forest Sampling,* U.S. Department of Agriculture, Forest Service Handbook no. 232.

Hartman, David A., William A. Atkinson, Ben S. Bryant, and Richard O. Woodfin, Jr. 1976. *Conversion Factors for the Pacific Northwest Forest Industry.* Institute of Forest Products, University of Washington, Seattle.

Husch, Bertram, and Charles I. Miller, and T. W. Beers. 1972. *Forest Mensuration,* 2d ed., The Ronald Press Company, New York.

Mark, Gordon G., and Robert S. Dimmick. 1971. Managing the Family Forest, *Farmers' Bulletin,* vol. 2187, Forest Service, U.S. Department of Agriculture.

Spurr, S. H. 1952. *Forest Inventory,* The Ronald Press Company, New York.

———. 1960. *Photogrammetry and Photo Interpretation: With a Section on Application to Forestry,* The Ronald Press Company, New York.

*Surveying Our Public Lands.* 1960. U.S. Bureau of Land Management.

U.S. Department of Agriculture, Forest Service. 1969. *National Forest Log Scaling Handbook.*

Wilson, Robert L. 1972. *Elementary Forest Surveying and Mapping,* Oregon State University Bookstores, Inc., Corvallis.

Chapter 15

# Harvesting the Forest Crop

A managed forest is a scene of constant activity. Silvicultural cuttings may be going on in several areas. Perhaps salvage of fallen, diseased, or insect-infested trees will support a fuel business in one area. In another area trees are being removed for a pulp mill or sawmill. Perhaps improvement cuttings are occupying the labor force in another. These are all scenes of harvest. Part of the forest crop is being removed. In this chapter we shall review the methods by which trees are felled and transported.

### The Logging Plan

Before timber harvesting actually occurs a *logging plan* should be prepared. Such a plan might vary with regions, but basically it should include the location of the area to be harvested; the road system (which may have to be built); the most economical and environmentally sound harvesting methods; the intended market for the logs; estimation of labor needs for felling, bucking, loading, and transporting the logs; and the assignment of personnel to these jobs. The plan should also be concerned with inventory of equipment needed, maintenance of equipment, alternatives in case of equipment failure, and safety precautions for personnel.

Other considerations include the effect of harvesting on other forest features, such as the possibility of silting a fish spawning stream, the appearance of the logging area from nearby public recreation sites, or how it will look from the surface of a lake or well-traveled road or highway (Fig. 15-1). Accurate maps must be prepared, environmental impact statements written, and in some instances, public hearings held. The importance of these considerations was cited in Chap. 6. Before the plan is approved many revisions may be needed.

The logging plan should also determine what the total cost of removing the timber will be to a prospective buyer.

### Characteristics of Lumber and Its Handling as a Crop

North American forests in general produce trees of great size and weight. The resulting logs are seldom milled into lumber in centers close to the forest. Rail transport for distances of 200 to 300 mi (320 to 480 km) is not uncommon, and water transportation varies from 100 to 1,000 mi (160 to 1,600 km). Truck hauling is the system most commonly used, and distances

**Figure 15-1**   The illustrations at left show three examples of discordant cutting layouts. In each the sharp-edged patterns contrast conspicuously with the landscape characteristics. At right the same three cuttings examples show shape variations which have greater visual harmony with the landscape. *(Courtesy Branch of Landscape Architecture, Forest Service, U.S. Department of Agriculture Northern Region.)*

may run as much as 250 mi (400 km) or more. Skidding or dragging the logs from stump to landings involves comparatively short distances, generally with tractors or with rubber-tired skidders. Skidding covers distances up to a mile (1.6 km), but the average is much less. In the West some experimental logging by helicopter and balloon involves distances of ¾ to 1 mi (1.2 to 1.6 km).

Felled trees are "bucked" or sawed to log lengths or merchantable tree lengths, trimmed of branches, and assembled by means of powerful high-speed machinery. Some may now be bundled by steel strapping for unit loading onto trucks, barges, and railcars. Most products are moved promptly from the forest to the mill.

### The Logging Camp and Woods Labor

An institution truly North American in character was the lumber or logging camp of yesterday. Typical lumber camps varied from a group of crude log buildings with almost primitive conveniences, established by the poorer type of "gyppo" or contractor in the Lake States, to groups of portable houses in the Northwest, still used to some extent. These portable camps are of a size and design adapted to transportation on flatcars, trucks, and trailers and accommodate four to eight men. The dining quarters in these camps are larger and built in sections. Between these two extremes are the rude log or frame camps, found in all regions, made up of a bunkhouse for sleeping quarters, cookhouse or dining room, garages, shops, small store, and an office. In large camps there may be more than one large bunkhouse or a number of smaller living quarters.

These camps are still necessary for the accommodation of employees in out-of-the-way locations in the woods in both the United States and Canada, but are not used if commuting labor is available.

In recent years there has been a greater trend toward contracting for all phases of logging. Wages for labor are good. Generally they exceed the minimum wage set by the United States Fair Labor Standards Act. Piecework payment for felling and pulpwood and chemical woodcutting is the general rule. Contracts on the basis of either M (thousand) board feet or cord are used, and a good worker makes good wages. Woods work requires strength, skill, alertness, and endurance and certainly much more resourcefulness than assembly-line work in the average factory.

### Felling and Cutting into Logs

To fell a tree so that it will not lodge against another, will not break because of uneven ground, and will lie so that it can be trimmed of branches, cut or bucked into logs, and skidded or dragged to the landing with least obstruction is the task of the sawyer. The way in which the tree leans and the side that has the heaviest part of the crown will determine to some extent which way it must fall. A skillfully placed undercut, which produces a sort of hinge, will often assure a very accurate dropping of the tree (Fig. 15-2). When a properly managed forest is being cut, there are other considerations such as cutting the stump close to the ground, avoiding injury to reproduction by selecting the best place to drop the tree, and felling certain undesirable specimens which slow down a crew operating on a piecework basis. As in other operations, these extra precautions must be compensated by higher straight pay, a bonus for complete compliance with contract terms, or some other incentive device.

**Figure 15-2** Felling a ponderosa pine with a power saw. The undercut is made by removing a wedge-shaped section of the trunk in the direction of fall. The back cut (seen here) is made on the reverse side. *(Courtesy of the Boise Cascade Corporation and American Forest Institute.)*

**Figure 15-3** Felling a tree with tractor-mounted, hydraulically operated shears. The wedge action of the scissorlike blade controls the direction of fall of the tree. *(Courtesy of the Boise Cascade Corporation and American Forest Institute.)*

The seller or forest manager has also had the expense of spotting or marking the particular trees for felling. Since the advent of the chain saw, many fallers prefer to work alone. After felling the tree, fallers have the task of sawing the tree trunk into logs, bolts, poles, or other rough products. Generally a faller owns the chain saw, or in some instances, it will be owned by the contractor if the work is on a contract basis. In larger timber, especially in the West, fallers usually work in pairs.

One of the trends is towards felling timber by use of hydraulic power shears. There are various kinds of shears similar to the one illustrated in Fig. 15-3. In addition there are harvesting machines that shear and limb the entire tree.

### Measuring the Product

This step has been discussed in Chap. 14. Scaling in the woods is feasible even though it is done under difficulties because of limited access to the small end of the log. It is necessary, however, to scale in the woods in order to keep records of piecework. Care must be used to assure sufficient length on logs to allow for trim when the lumber is manufactured. Softwood logs are usually cut to even lengths such as 10, 12, 16, 20, and 32 ft (3, 3.6, 4.8, 6, and 9.6 m). Hardwood logs may be cut to odd lengths. There is a growing tendency to handle long logs or entire trees and to cut later to desired lengths at the mill. Another trend is the use of cubic feet in expressing measurements.

## Log Handling

**Skidding or Transporting Logs from Stump to Landing**    The first kind of power used for skidding logs from stump to landing in the United States was a team of oxen. They were used at the start in almost every logging region, even in the redwoods of California. Timbers 80 to 100 ft (24 to 30 m) long and straight as an arrow are reported as having slid along behind twenty-five yoke of oxen on the St. Clair River in Michigan, more than 140 years ago. Skidding tongs, which resemble gigantic ice tongs, were attached to the log, and two hooks joined by chain were sometimes used to attach other logs to the first one in tandem. Teams of oxen would then be hitched to the log or crude sleigh, known as a *go-devil,* and cries, goads, curses, and bellows accompanied the slow but steady parade. Horses gradually took the place of oxen, only the larger and hardier animals being used. Tractors and other motorized equipment have gradually replaced horses on most operations.

The tractor, in various sizes, has been an integral part of timber harvesting since World War I, and particularly since the early 1930s. It is well adapted to skidding single logs and "bunched" lots of logs. This is accomplished by raising the logs with a winch so that only the rear ends drag (Fig. 15-4). Tractors are also used for cold-decking logs. This amounts to assembling the logs for future haul to the mill. On some logging areas rubber-tired skidders similar to the one in Fig. 15-5 are used. They are more mobile and can travel at faster speeds than tractors.

One of the methods used in large timber is direct cable skidding or yarding to a portable steel spar. The general idea of this method is as follows: A cable is attached to one or more logs, and yarding is accomplished by pulling and jerking the logs in, as the cable is rewound on a drum or a winch. The logs may slide flat along the ground, drag one end while the other swings from an overhead cable, or swing free as when crossing intervening canyons or low spots (Fig. 15-6).

Helicopter logging is presently being tried on an experimental basis in a few areas. Its major advantage is that timber can be removed from steep hillsides or inaccessible pockets without having to build a road. It is customary to use two helicopters; while one is flying logs the other is on standby. Gas tanks are only partly filled to give maximum lifting power; thus, there is a need for frequent refueling.

**Figure 15-4**  A track-type tractor with integral arch and winch that elevates the front end of the logs for the haul to the landing. *(Courtesy of the Caterpillar Tractor Company.)*

The logging crew and their equipment are flown in to the logging site by helicopter. A service area and a separate large landing area (for logs) is necessary. These of course must be adjacent to a road.

Cost becomes a major factor. Hauls over 1 ½ mi (2.4 km) are not practical. The timber must have premium value and be out of reach by conventional logging methods. Costs vary from $15 to $25 per minute, depending on the type of helicopter being used.

**Figure 15-5**  Rubber-tired skidders are mobile and adaptable to varying soils and topography. *(Courtesy of the Caterpillar Tractor Company.)*

**Figure 15-6** A portable steel spar used in the highlead system of cable yarding in western North America. The yarder or power unit is at right. The heel-boom loader at left is loading the truck. *(Courtesy of the Weyerhaeuser Company.)*

Balloon logging is another method of aerial logging. It was first tried out in Sweden in 1956 (Pearce and Stenzel, 1972). It is now in use in western Canada and the United States and has numerous advantages over conventional log transportation methods. These are best realized in steep areas with unstable soils unsuitable for road building. Balloons can also be used in tropical swamps and in areas with pockets of timber where the volume generally is too low to justify the construction of roads.

Balloons of various shapes have been tried, including the British barrage type of World War II. Because of the elliptical shape of this type of balloon, it is at the mercy of winds which can blow it off course.

A more popular design is the spherical balloon illustrated in Fig. 15-7,

**Figure 15-7**  Balloon logging in Washington State. The balloon provides the lift for the turn of logs. A drum on the yarder at lower left pulls the logs down by means of the main-line cable attached to the balloon tether line. The balloon is returned for new logs by means of a second drum pulling on the haulback line attached to corner blocks and the tether line. *(Courtesy of the Department of Natural Resources, Washington State.)*

whose shape makes it less subject to wind deflection. The line extending from the balloon to the logs is called the tether line, which in turn is fastened to two places on the ground, one to the main line to the balloon yarder (Fig. 15-8) and the other end to the haulback line. Contact between the yarder operator and the choker setter is by two-way radio. Helium is the gas used in the balloon.

Though quite efficient, the balloon method of transporting logs is not intended to replace conventional log-hauling methods, but is intended for use where these methods are not practicable.

**Loading Logs**   Loading in the past was backbreaking work since much of it, with smaller logs at least, was done by lifting or by use of a peavey. The crosshaul was commonly used with larger logs. Crosshauling consists of rolling logs up inclined skids from the ground to a truck or railroad flatbed by means of a cable passing under the log and doubled back over the vehicle to a power source; either animals, a winch, or tractor. It is still in use in smaller operations.

**Stationary Loading**   Most log loading today is done mechanically, and the methods are numerous. A relatively inexpensive stationary loader is the gin pole, a small tree held in a leaning position by guy wires so that the loading block is centered over the vehicle to be loaded. The A-frame is

**Figure 15-8**  The balloon yarder showing the massive size of equipment necessary to operate the balloon system. The upper cable is the main line and is attached directly to the tether line of the balloon. The lower cable is the haulback line, which is attached to several corner blocks on the ground to form a loop, and is then attached to the tether line. *(Courtesy of the Department of Natural Resources, Washington State.)*

**Figure 15-9** The single tong and heel boom loading a logging truck in Idaho. *(Courtesy of the Boise Cascade Corporation and American Forest Institute.)*

similar but uses two poles separated at the bottom to give greater stability to the operation.

Another stationary loading method is the spar tree boom loader, which utilizes a standing spar, boom poles, several blocks, and two tongs. The boom is swung out over the vehicle being loaded. Power comes from a diesel or gasoline engine equipped with drums to hold the wire rope used in lifting the logs and swinging the boom. A variation of this is the heel boom which uses only one tong. Here, one end of the log is heeled against the boom as it is lifted into position over the vehicle being loaded.

**Mobile Loading** Modern logging methods include a great variety of mobile loading devices. Some are spar-tree and A-frame devices (or slight modifications) mounted on trucks or tractors. A modified crane loader, utilizing a heel boom, is seen in Fig. 15-9.

In recent years there has been an increased use of huge forklift-mounted loaders. Long in use in warehouses, they are now a common sight in both the loading and unloading of logs of all sizes. As noted in Fig. 15-10, the forklift operates at right angles to the vehicle being loaded.

**Figure 15-10**  Loading a truck by forklift. This equipment is available in massive sizes for bigger logs. *(Courtesy of the Caterpillar Tractor Company.)*

Several manufacturers today offer a hydraulic loader mounted permanently either on the log-hauling truck or on a tractor. The boom arm has two segments of similar lengths and operates much like a person's arm, with a hydraulic grapple at the end operating like a wrist with fingers. This device is known as a "knuckle-boom."

**Unloading Logs**  The unloading operation utilizes most of the above loading devices. Because the unloading area is a terminus for many loads of logs, the equipment may be considerably larger. One device found in the unloading area is a huge crane mounted on steel rails. The entire load is lifted by means of hydraulic grapples or tongs.

### Log Transportation

Several methods of transporting logs, both by land and by water, have been tried in the United States with almost every conceivable variation. Today most logs are promptly hauled by truck to the mill or processing plant.

**Water Transportation**  In the past the number of important woods that would float, the frequent occurrence of streams in log-producing territory, and the small investment needed to improve the streams as ways for logs influenced the custom of floating logs. Only pulpwood is still floated on rivers, mostly in the Northeast and in eastern Canada. Rafting of logs, once a common practice, is limited today mostly to tidewater areas of Oregon, Washington, Alaska, British Columbia, and the Maritime Provinces. Some rafts are oceangoing and are designed to withstand heavy seas by lacing several layers of logs together with wire rope. In the more protected waters of the West Coast, the rafts are flat, long, and narrow and are made up in sections approximately 75 ft (22.5 m) square, with the logs lying parallel to each other. As many as a dozen sections are held end to end and towed by tug boats for distances of 50 to several hundred miles (80 to several hundred kilometers).

Barges are used to transport logs in some parts of the country, particularly hardwood logs that will not float.

As in the early days of logging, ships are still in use for transporting logs to world markets. Several West Coast ports load logs daily for export to Japan and other countries.

**Rail Transportation of Logs**  Railroad logging in the United States dates back to the early 1850s. During its development, specially geared locomotives were designed to pull heavy loads up steep grades. They were also equipped with special joints allowing the shaft to change length when negotiating sharp curves (Pearce and Stenzel, 1972). Railroad logging peaked in the 1930s, but was soon all but replaced by the truck. A few logging railroad spurs have persisted in some parts of the country. Since these railroads are standard gauge, cars loaded in the woods can be picked up by common-carrier railroads and transported to the mill.

**Hauling Logs by Truck**  Trucks are now the most common means of hauling logs from forest to the mill. The efficiency of the truck or tractor-trailer type of log transportation comes largely from its ability to penetrate the forest more easily than could the locomotive. Trucks are also better suited for use in scattered stands of timber or where logs are picked up here and there, as in certain cutting systems.

Truck sizes vary from the 1-ton pickup of the woodlot operation to the 22-or-more-ton trucks, which because of weight, height, width, and length limitations on public roads are permitted only on private company roads where state laws do not apply. The size of truck to be used will depend on the products to be hauled, the type of roads and bridges over which the haul is made, the distance of the haul, and the economic means of the logger.

In most Western logging operations and elsewhere, if logs of 32 ft (9.6 m) or longer are being hauled, a truck-trailer combination is required. The bed of the truck supports one end of the load and the trailer the other end (Fig. 15-11). On the return trip from the mill or log dump to the landing, the empty trailer rides the truck "piggy-back."

**Pulpwood Transportation**

In the discussion above we were generally concerned with methods of transporting long logs for use both in sawmills and pulp mills. In this section we shall deal with those short roundwood logs used specifically for pulpwood, which ultimately become paper or a paperboard product.

**Figure 15-11**   A loaded truck-trailer combination for logs over 32 ft (9.6 m). *(Courtesy of the Kenworth Truck Company.)*

Pulpwood is the leading forest product in many sections of the country. Pulpwood lengths are usually standardized within regions, with the lengths varying from one region to another. Most are between 48 and 96 in. (122 and 244 cm), the length depending on custom and the requirements of the pulp mill equipment. Because of the small sizes of logs, it is economically and physically possible for many small landowners to become pulpwood producers.

**Felling and Loading Pulpwood**   With the many thousands of pulpwood operations in North America today, there are no standardized methods of carrying out the task of felling and loading. Operators use the method best suited to the terrain, type of species, and their economic means. The tree is felled with power saws, bucked to the appropriate length, and loaded. The trend is away from hand loading to mechanized methods. In some areas full-length trees are skidded to the landing for cutting into pulpwood lengths, rather than cutting the short lengths at the stump. As labor costs continue to rise, and fewer people are willing to work without machines, new equipment is continually appearing in the woods. One- and two-person machines today can fell the tree by shearing, delimbing it, crosscutting it, and stacking the sticks onto a pallet or truck, at the rate of a tree per minute or three to five cords per hour.

Shearing trees at ground level is advantageous in that the stumps are now utilized, and tree planting machines can maneuver more readily in the woods.

Other loading methods include the knuckle-boom with log grapple and the forklift mentioned earlier. The truck-mounted self-loader is also popular today.

**Transporting Pulpwood**   A variety of skidding methods are used to transport the pulp logs to a central crosscutting and loading point. These include the use of horses, mules, and small tractors by the small producer, and tractors of many kinds for larger operations. Pallets are in common use with truck hauling. The pallet has a sledlike bottom and may be hauled about the woods empty with a tractor. Loading is made easier because the pallet sits on the ground. The truck, which unloads its empty pallets in the woods, reloads with power loaders (Fig. 15-12). While the truck is on its way to the mill with a loaded set, empties are being loaded in the woods. Pulpwood is also hauled by railroad or barge.

Pulp mills are using increasing amounts of chips produced from sawmill waste and logging residues. Chipping machines, which operate in the forest, are now being used to harvest diseased, dying, and other formerly unmerchantable material for wood fiber. Total tree harvesting appears to have great promise (Fig. 15-13).

**Figure 15-12**  A loaded pallet being pulled aboard a truck in Maine. *(Courtesy Scott Paper Company and American Forest Institute.)*

**Figure 15-13** This total tree harvesting method produces wood chips from material once considered unmerchantable. *(Courtesy Morbark Industries, Inc.)*

### Miscellaneous Forest Products

**Chemical Wood and Fuelwood**  The use of wood for destructive distillation also furnishes a way to utilize the waste products of logging and milling and to manage hardwoods on short rotations. Cull logs are now accepted at some plants and paid for by weight. This salvages a considerable amount of material.

In the past charcoal was a by-product of destructive distillation of wood. Today much charcoal is produced as a primary product.

Compared with coal, wood has the advantage of cleanliness and low ash content. About 80 cu ft (2.3 m³) of air-dried hickory or oak will yield more heat than a ton of coal. Eastern white pine and aspen compare least favorably with coal at 60 percent and 57 percent, respectively. Wood for use in fireplaces finds a ready market in towns and cities throughout the country and this use is increasing.

**Other Log Products**  Cooperage stock, railroad ties, fence posts, handle bolts, shake and shingle bolts, utility poles, and piling come from specially graded logs and species. In many instances they emerge from regular logging and are as well adapted to production through forest management as are other products. They represent uses for wood that demonstrate its practical indispensability.

**Naval Stores Production**   The gum that flows from longleaf and slash pine is used in naval stores production to make rosin, turpentine, wood tar, and rosin oils.

Formerly, the raw gum or pitch and the tar were used in shipbuilding. Today the principal products are turpentine, which comes from the distillation of the crude gum, and rosin, which is the finer part of the residue. Turpentine serves principally as a thinner in paints and varnishes, while rosin finds its way into the manufacture of paper, paints, varnishes, lacquers, soaps, greases, printer's ink, synthetic camphor, synthetic pine oil, insecticides, perfumes, odorants, pharmaceuticals, shoe materials, and polishes. Rosin oils are used for selective flotation in metallurgy and in paints and varnishes. Tar and pitch go into rubber goods and waterproofing or serve as binders in numerous materials and processes. The region comprising southern Georgia and northern Florida accounts for most of the production at present (Rolston, 1974).

At the end of the naval stores cycle the entire tree can be used for pulpwood, poles, or sawtimber.

Increased yields by genetically superior high-gum-yielding slash pine trees hold promise for the future. They yield up to twice as much gum and grow 10 to 15 percent more merchantable wood (Cox, 1973). The limiting factor in naval stores production appears to be the dwindling supply of skilled labor (Rolston, 1974).

**Miscellaneous Small Forest Products**   Maple syrup and sugar, cascara bark, huckleberry branches, and fern fronds for floral pieces, branches of evergreen trees for grave lining, Christmas trees, nuts of the pinyon and of certain hardwoods, mistletoe, conifer cones, holly leaves and berries, spruce gum, Canada balsam, and various drug plants and substances are also classified as forest products. Maple sugar, cascara bark, walnuts, and ginseng are the principal revenue producers on the list.

Sugar and syrup making from maple sap is an incidental industry, well adapted to management of farm forests. The product is one of our oldest agricultural commodities, one of the few solely North American crops, and the only crop that must be processed on the farm before it is in suitable form for sale.

Maple syrup production has declined since the turn of the century. Production dropped off because of labor shortages, rising production costs, changing rural customs, plus competition from less expensive cane and beet sugars. In the face of declining United States production, Canada has continued increasing maple syrup exports to the United States to supply the stable annual consumption of 3 million gallons (11.4 million l).

The bark of cascara is sold for medicinal purposes from the forests of the Northwest. No trees of diameters less than 4 in. (10 cm) [measured 12 in. (30 cm) from the ground] are to be peeled; all peeled trees are to be felled, the bark to be left on stumps to assure sprouting; all brush is to be piled to reduce fire hazard; and bark is to be removed from all wood down to 1 ½ in. (3.8 cm) diameter, including branches. This is unique forest management for an incidental but valuable product.

**Forest Management and Forest Harvesting**   Someone has said that a ship cannot be steered unless it is moving. A forest and its environment cannot be manipulated if it simply grows and is allowed to stagnate or to die of old age, insects, disease, or lightning fires. To manage a forest, the crop must be harvested when it is economically or biologically ripe, using methods that will assure regeneration and continuous growth. When order and regularity are achieved in these steps, sustained yield has usually been achieved; that is, the growth in the sense of economic increment over any given period will be equivalent to the volume removed in the harvest for that period. Whether or not sustained yield is to be achieved and maintained depends largely upon harvesting practices as well as protective and cultural work. Prompt and modern harvesting methods will promote and increase sustained yield.

## BIBLIOGRAPHY

American Forest Institute, Correspondence and Literature 1973–1974. Washington, DC.

Boise Cascade Correspondence and Literature 1973–1974. Boise, Idaho.

Cox, R. G. 1973. *Naval Stores Report for 1972 Crop Year,* Forest Service, U.S. Department of Agriculture, Olustee, FL.

Lysons, Hilton H., and Roger H. Twito. 1973. Skyline Logging: An Economical Means of Reducing Environmental Impact of Logging, *Jour. Forestry,* **71**:580 –583.

Pearce, J. Kenneth, and George Stenzel. 1972. *Logging and Pulpwood Production,* The Ronald Press Company, New York.

Peters, Penn A. 1973. Balloon Logging: A Look at Current Operating System, *Jour. Forestry,* **71**:577–579.

Rolston, K. S. 1974. Executive Secretary, American Pulpwood Association. Personal Correspondence.

U.S. Department of Agriculture, Forest Service. 1973. *Sugar Maple Sap Production Research,* Burlington, VT.

Wackerman, A. E., W. D. Hagenstein, and A. S. Mitchell. 1966. *Harvesting Timber Crops,* 2d ed., McGraw-Hill Book Company, New York.

# Chapter 16

# Making Forest Products Adaptable and Durable

In previous chapters it was emphasized that forests are renewable and that forest products are indispensable to human welfare. Wood products are harvested and manufactured with the least overall damage to the total environment, and compared to other competitive materials, less energy is used in their manufacture. Wood is biodegradable; it has many uses; and its future use looks promising (Seaman, 1970). Some of the uses and trends will be reviewed in this chapter.

The forest is a natural resource, a part of the wealth of nature, but wealth *in place*. Logs are raw material, not yet processed, but one step nearer to availability for human use. Lumber is an advanced material; it is easier to handle and easier to use than logs. A wooden chair is a manufactured product ready for use.

In Chap. 1 the forest was introduced as a natural resource "ready to use," but this term assumed the viewpoint of primitive human beings who were painfully aware that clubs, firewood, wheels, and boats must at least be reached for and rudely fashioned for use. That day and viewpoint are a long way from the modern tendency to assume that water originates in a faucet and chairs in a furniture store.

**Figure 16-1** Wooden beams, paneling, and furniture adds warmth and beauty to this home. *(Courtesy of the National Forest Products Association, Washington, DC.)*

Wood has been used for many centuries, yet technology makes it a modern substance. In the home, for example, it becomes a material superior to competitive products in strength, economy, versatility, and beauty (Fig. 16-1). Although wood is a wonderful material, to provide greatest service it must be properly processed and used. The following discussion starts with the log at the mill and considers the processing of wood for utilitarian demands.

### Making Lumber

Crudely fashioned construction timbers, such as railroad ties, telephone poles, fence posts, and piling, are frequently used in the form in which they leave the forest, receiving at most a treatment that includes peeling, drying, hewing, and coating or impregnation with some material to increase durability. Pulpwood, veneer, plywood, particle and fiberboard must be mechanically or chemically processed. Lumber,[1] on the other hand, is sawed

---

[1] The term *lumber*, first used to designate miscellaneous stored household furniture and like articles of the Lombard pawnbrokers in Europe, and later applied to staves and boards on the Boston wharves in colonial days, is strictly a North American term for sawed products. The English use the term *timber* to refer to sawed products.

into almost innumerable sizes; dried; trimmed to length and width; planed and surfaced to accurate dimensions; worked into special patterns; and even treated with chemicals to make it resistant to fire, decay, and insects. Today it is found on the market in packages, ready-cut to length for the customer.

Logs are sawed into lumber in the mill, with a heavy circular saw which has great chisel-like teeth, or a thinner band saw which runs like a belt on two enormous pulleys and may have teeth on one or both edges. Logs also may be cut with gang saws, which consist of many single saws secured in a frame that works up and down through slabbed logs (called *cants*), and can saw many boards or timbers simultaneously. The carriage that advances the log against the band or circular saw is fitted with devices to hold the log in the desired position and to set it for the desired thickness of lumber. The carriage is driven by steam, gasoline, diesel, or electric power directly or by cable and pulley arrangement. The sawyer drives the carriage by means of levers and push buttons. The thickness of the cut desired is signaled to the person who rides the carriage, or on riderless carriages, the sawyer sets the thickness from the control panel (Fig. 16-2). The sawyer also turns the log and puts it in desired position by means of a steam mechanism. The latter is a device for lifting-pulling-turning-pushing work, which it does with weirdly human efficiency under the influence of steam and the sawyer's lever. As boards or timbers are sawed, they fall onto live rollers, move a short distance, and are "kicked" off to a conveyor and thence to the edger, if they need to be edged or ripped, and are kicked from the edger to another conveyor, where they rejoin the boards that needed no

**Figure 16-2** The log at left is being sawn into lumber on a riderless carriage. The sawyer (at right) sets the thickness of the cut from a control panel. The thin band saw blade is barely visible in front of the sawyer. *(Courtesy of the Boise Payette Lumber Co.)*

edging. Trimming for length is accomplished by numerous circular saws, which rise or fall through a kind of table at the trimmer's control. Bad defects are also cut out in trimming. From the trimmer, the lumber is slowly conveyed over a sorting table where a grader indicates grade by a cryptic mark on each piece. The lumber then arrives at a "buggy" station where it is picked up by straddle trucks or forklift trucks and carted to a yard or kiln for drying or is conveyed by crane or other devices.

Coincident with the journey of the boards and timbers manufactured above, cants, which are really thick interior slabs from logs, are being kicked off the live rollers to gang saws. Thick slabs or outside slabs take a fast ride to resaws, which cut out their lumber, or to the other saws which cut them to fuel lengths. Uses for mill waste will be discussed later in the chapter.

Skillful manufacture of lumber involves not only fine and well-aligned machinery, but the judgment, dexterity, and coordination of many workers. The amount of waste material is also determined by these factors. The sawyer at the head rig, the edgers, and the trimmers are key people, who can "make or break" a lumber mill. The mills operated by stationary steam, gasoline, electric, or diesel engines or tractor, truck, or old car engines and housed informally, to say the least, operate in every part of the country where sawtimber is available. They vary from the portable farm-to-farm mills of New York and New England to the smaller shingle or tie mills of the West. There are also many medium- and small-sized mills manufacturing lumber of every quality for both local and wholesale consumption. Efficient forest management can keep a stable number of large and small mills going if they have a good logging crew, an efficient and true cutting rig, and an experienced sawyer. The mills and the demand for their products can give the forester an opportunity to manage the forest. In this sort of relationship, the public as a whole gains in employment, in materials that add to comfort and well-being, in sustained beauty of the general landscape, and in assured continuation of these benefits if all phases of the operation are well carried out.

### Integration of Wood-using Industries

Many companies today, or groups of companies, will own a sawmill, pulp mill, plywood mill, a housing component fabrication plant, a post and pole yard, perhaps a fuel yard, and have some means to utilize waste. High-valued peeler logs go to the plywood mill, and cull logs and other logging wastes might economically find their way to the pulp mill or charcoal plant. The biggest improvement in utilizing previously wasted material is in the establishment of wallboard, insulation board, and particle board plants. A smaller percentage of waste goes into box material, lath, fence stock, soil conditioners and mulches, wood flour, linoleum filler, and other similar uses. Waste may be used as fuel for boilers which provide the energy to operate manufacturing plants. Many products are manufactured from waste by an explosive separation process, using steam to separate the wood fibers. The fibers can then be reconstituted into a variety of low, medium, and high density boards used for paneling and cabinetry.

Chips and sawdust are extensively used in making paper pulp. Some mills get all of their wood requirements from chipped waste and sawdust.

### Trends in Use of Residues

Wood residues from primary processing at sawmills and other wood processing plants provide an important part of the fiber supply for the pulp industry and a significant potential for further expansion of wood-based industries.

In recent years the wood-using industries have made much progress in utilization of the roundwood delivered to sawmills, veneer mills, and other primary wood processing plants. In 1970, an estimated 2.8 billion cu ft (800 million m³) of slabs, sawdust, veneer cores, and other similar material resulting from the manufacture of lumber and other wood products was used for pulp, particle board, fuel, or other products. This represented about 74 percent of all such by-product material produced.

Use of these plant by-products by the pulp industry was of chief importance, almost 1.8 billion cu ft (54 million m³) or about 22 million cords being used for pulp in 1970, including nearly 2 million cords of chip exports to Japan. Use of such material for pulping increased nearly 18-fold between 1952 and 1970.

Volumes of plant by-products used for other products such as particle board, although small, also have increased substantially. Use of sawdust, slabs, etc., for industrial and domestic fuel, on the other hand, has declined sharply (U. S. Department of Agriculture, 1973).

Production can be greatly enlarged by more complete utilization of the wood grown. Some 2 billion cu ft (60 million m³) of wood are annually discarded in harvesting operations in the form of limbs, tree tops, defective or broken logs, not to mention stumps and even roots (Lassen and Hair, 1970). Processing losses remain substantial despite great gains in recent years. Improved sawmilling could raise the proportion of the log turned into lumber, which at present is only 45 percent. Similarly, chemical pulping processes can be improved to yield more fiber than the 45 to 50 percent now generally obtained. Lassen and Hair estimate that residues of primary and secondary manufacturing can be more thoroughly utilized, yielding as much as 1.7 billion cu ft (50 million m³) annually.

Coupled with some 1.4 billion cu ft (40 million m³) of harvesting residues believed utilizable, processing losses that might be captured each year total 3.1 billion cu ft (90 million m³). Even that is not the entire picture.

Through more efficient manufacturing and construction techniques, the equivalent of up to 300 million cu ft (8.5 million m³) can be saved. For example, more efficient engineering designs can achieve fully satisfactory and safe structures with less lumber and plywood.

Lassen and Hair estimate that potential annual savings through recycling of paper, fiberboard, and wood debris would amount to an additional 1.3 billion cu ft (3.9 million m³) of useful wood substance. Altogether, they estimate annual gains from residues and more efficient use at 4.7 billion cu ft (135 million m³). This is equal to more than one-third of all the wood used in the United States in 1971.

From the standpoint of meeting human needs in the coming decades, then, wood has tremendous potential (Cliff, 1973).

Unused plant residues in 1970 were largely at some distance from markets or in areas where supply currently exceeded demand. Use of residues is increasing rapidly, however, and it seems likely that within the next decade or so most of the coarse softwood residues and a substantial part of the fine residues will be utilized for pulp and particle board (U. S. Department of Agriculture, 1973).

### The Structure of Wood as a Material

How wood is formed from the raw materials—water, mineral matter, and carbon dioxide—was discussed earlier, and some information on structure was included. This was from the viewpoint of growth. But when a tree becomes a load of logs or a pile of pulpwood, growth has ceased. The way the wood behaves from then on and its adaptability for use and demand are matters of structure and properties. One seeks to know, therefore, how a piece of wood is put together and what the minute parts look like. The knowledge gained aids in understanding shrinkage, swelling, strength, and elasticity of wood; its reaction to paints and stains; and other properties of wood that satisfy or disappoint users of forest products.

Wood is a structure comprising a multitude of minute cellular units, which differ from each other in shape, size, opening, thickness of walls, contents, and arrangement. They are more or less firmly grown together, and most of them are slender and drawn out to points on the ends. If this type of cell is isolated and examined, it may be as long as ⅓ in. (0.84 cm) in spruce or only ¹⁄₂₅ in. (0.1 cm) in some of the hardwoods. Cells of this sort are called *tracheids* or, more commonly, fibers, and in the softwoods they conduct water longitudinally in the tree. Other cells of greater diameter and called *vessels*, occur in the hardwoods for this kind of waterway service. Water or sap is conducted in a radial direction in both softwoods and hardwoods by cells that comprise the so-called medullary rays or wood rays. They show in a stump cross section of oak trees as tiny spokelike marks from center to bark and give to oak its well-known "silver grain" when the cut parallels the rays or intersects them at a sharp angle.

No two woods have identical structure. The firs, pines, cedars, spruces, and other needle-bearing softwoods have relatively few kinds of cells, while the hardwoods, such as the oaks, hickories, beeches, and maples, have many kinds. These cells have varying functions, such as conducting water, storing building materials, and reinforcing the structure. The ranks of thin-walled open cells are formed in spring, the thick-walled ones later in summer, and the parallel positions of these two rankings give the *annual* or *growth* ring pattern characteristic of cross sections of logs.

### The Properties of Wood as a Material

It is not enough to explore the structure of a wood; its properties must be learned. A few examples of properties follow, with certain of their advantages:

**Workability**    Sharp tools skillfully used can do wonders with almost any wood, but something that is easily shaped and fitted and that is still reasonably strong and serviceable is said to be "easily worked." White pine has long been a favorite among carpenters for this reason, and yellow-poplar took its place in the hardwood regions for the same reason.

**Bending Strength**    Hickory and ash find their way into sporting equipment, wheels, implements, and tool handles because of their toughness and the ease with which they may be bent without breaking or weakening.

**Resistance to Decay**    Certain natural oils and other materials in cedars and the redwoods enable them to resist the attack of organisms causing decay. Both these woods are rather soft, but they are used in contact with soil and moisture as posts and telephone poles and as outside covering for buildings because of their decay-resisting properties. Osage-orange, white oak, mulberry, and catalpa are decay-resistant hardwoods used for fence posts.

**Hardness**    Where abrasion from the walking of people or animals or the moving of heavy objects is likely to wear away floors, pillars, docks, or steps, hardness is an advantage. Sugar maple and red and white oak possess this property.

**Combined Strength and Light Weight**    Boats and certain sporting goods demand a wood that is both durable and light weight. Port-Orford-cedar and several of the spruces exhibit the happy combination of these needed characteristics.

**Permeability**    Woods possessing the type of structure and communication between cellular units that permits chemicals to enter under reasonable pressure are adapted to treatment for fire, insect, and decay resistance. Red oak is a good example of such a wood.

**Heat and Sound Insulation**   We have come to expect protection from heat, cold, and disagreeable sound, and it is usually wood in some reconstructed form that serves this purpose. Insulation board helps keep our houses at a constant temperature. The wooden coffee-pot handle also serves as an insulator. Acoustical tile absorbs sound.

**Response to Sound Vibrations**   Resonance sought in musical instruments is achieved by the use of wood in sounding boards, woodwinds, and the bodies of large and small stringed instruments.

**Odor**   This property works both ways. Eastern redcedar, for instance, adds a delightful fragrance along with its moth-deterrent services. If the white fir of the West, on the other hand, is built into a new but unfinished house and gets rained on, the odor is temporarily intolerable.

**Color and Grain**   The greatest proof of the beauty of color in wood, aside from the testimony of our own eyes, is the universal attempts at imitation of it on metal and other materials. An example is the photographing of wood grains and laying the paper photo under a transparent top in products like Formica. The mellowness and richness of oak, cherry, walnut, and redcedar, are particularly evident in aged pieces of furniture. Grain, in the sense of figure revealed by various ways of cutting through or across the annual rings, also imparts special beauty to various woods and is accentuated by stains, oils, and polishes. Texture, which is a term indicating size and proportional amounts of woody elements, is also a way of describing the beauty of wood.

**Strength Under Weight and Shock**   The ability of wood to withstand bending, shock, and splitting makes it adaptable for many uses, from mallets to bridge timbers.

**Plasticity**   In bending wood to permanent forms such as one sees in chairs and sporting equipment, a considerable volume of wood must be "upset" or compressed to stay compressed. Beech is a good example of a wood that has this valuable property, which is known as *plasticity*. This differs from *resiliency,* for the latter means the ability to spring back to original shape.

**Chemical Characteristics**   Slow combustibility, resistance to damage by acids and alkalies, and the character of volatile and water-soluble contents and of other extractives are interesting and useful properties of certain woods. Because of these properties we have wooden tanks and vats at chemical works, wood-extracted dyes and tannins for textile and leather industries, and separation plates in some electric batteries. Food additives, drugs, and adhesives are also obtained from wood.

### Fiber Products from Wood

Physical characteristics of wood which are needed in papermaking are tear resistance, shear strength, bending and shock resistance, and ability of the fibers to accept color.

Paper, insulating material of various kinds, rayon, synthetic wool, wallboard, and cellophane all result from separating, treating, and reassembling wood cells or the materials in their walls and the materials between the individual cells. The two major constituents are cellulose, which comprises about 72 percent of the substance of wood, and lignin, which makes up 28 percent. These proportions are consistent in all species, but the remaining materials do vary and thus give to different species some of their peculiar characteristics. Cellulose makes up the framework of the cell wall. It is colorless and insoluble in ordinary solvents. Lignin is somewhat soluble in dilute alkalies, and because it is the binding material that holds the cells together, as well as a part of the cell walls, it is possible to separate the cells by dissolving the lignin. This is what occurs in chemical pulp and papermaking.

**Pulp and Paper**  Pulpwood comes by sluiceway or conveyor from the yard to the mill. If it is to be manufactured by one of the three common chemical processes,[2] it is washed, debarked, and chipped into small pieces by forcing the log or bolt against powerful rotating disks equipped with knives. The chips, a considerable amount of which may come from wood processing residues, are elevated by conveyor to the top of great cylindrical digesters. The chips, depending on the process employed and the species of wood being used, are cooked in a liquor for a certain number of hours at different pressures and temperatures. After the lignin and other binding materials have been separated or dissolved, the pulpy cottony mass of fibers goes to large tanks for washing in large quantities of water. After the pulp, now nearly pure cellulose, is washed and bleached, it goes to the beaters where clay, dyes, rosin, and other additives are mixed in to give the finished product its color, reduce its absorbing qualities, and give it other surface features. Next the pulp flows evenly onto a woolen carrier or screen where the wet sheet loses much of its water before passing over fast-moving rolls. Here it is pressed, dried, and comes out in rolls of paper at the other end (Figs. 16-3 and 16-4). Some mills process the wood only through the pulp stage, leaving the papermaking and other manufacturing to other plants.

Other processes besides chemical ones are employed to reduce the wood to fibers. One is the *mechanical* or *groundwood* process in which the wood is forced against a huge grindstone. The rough surface of the rotating

---

[2] The *sulfate* (*kraft*) and *soda* processes use alkaline cooking liquors; the *sulfite* process uses an acid cooking liquor.

**Figure 16-3**   The Fourdrinier paper machine. The wet pulp on the large screen is flowing to the left and into the presses and driers at the far left. *(Courtesy of the Gaylord Container Corporation, Bogalusa, Louisiana.)*

wheel tears the fibers from the wood. Water is used to cool the wheel and wash off the pulp. Next the pulp is screened to remove any larger pieces of wood, and proceeds to the mill to be made into paper.

**Figure 16-4**   The other end of the paper machine in Fig. 16-3. This machine is capable of producing 600 to 650 tons (540 to 585 t) of heavy paper each day. The paper speeds onto the roll at the rate of 800 to 1,500 ft (240 to 450 m) per minute, depending on the paper grade. *(Courtesy of the Gaylord Container Corporation, Bogalusa, Louisiana.)*

A fifth method of making pulp involves a combination of chemical cooking and mechanical action. Here the chips are softened with steam or chemical cooking and later "beaten apart" in an attrition mill. This method is known as the *semichemical* process.

The investment in a paper mill will be anywhere from $100 million to $300 million. A larger paper mill today can produce up to 2,000 tons (1,800 t) of paper per day.[3] In the chemical process it takes about 2 tons (1.8 t) of wood to make a ton (0.9 t) of paper. The yield is somewhat higher in the semichemical process.

Consumption of paper and paperboard reached 58.7 million tons (52.8 million t) in 1972 which was equivalent to 615 lb (277 kg) per capita. In 1972, printing and writing paper, which includes groundwood, coated printing, uncoated book paper, writing and related bleached Bristols, was the greatest requirement [12.3 million tons (11 million t)], followed by newsprint [10.4 million tons (9.4 million t)], packaging and industrial [5.6 million tons (5 million t)], tissue [4 million tons (3.5 million t)]. Paperboard, new and recycled, used 26.4 million tons (23.7 million t). This makes a total of 58.7 million tons (52.8 million t) (Slatin, 1973).

**Insulating Products**   Most of the insulating boards are pressed paper pulp or sawmill waste that has been macerated or broken up by a heat-and-pressure process, which accomplishes a kind of explosive reduction. One product, which resembles a rough brownish wool, is blown into attics as a loose layer. Formerly it was sold as insulating board, which also functions as a sheathing, and is widely used in the walls of dwellings.

**Rayon**   Previously known as *artificial silk*, rayon is now produced throughout the world from cotton linters (a short-staple cotton, which is salvaged from the seed after ginning) and from wood pulp. In the viscose process, either wood pulp or cotton is digested with strong alkali and becomes alkali cellulose. This product, treated with carbon disulfide, becomes cellulose xanthate and is dissolved in caustic soda to make viscose. This is the clear gumlike product that is spun into raw cellulose or viscose silk. There are several processes; all are highly technical and require vast investment in plant facilities. Most rayon manufacturing companies ordinarily are not in the forest- or cotton-production business, but with world production of nearly 7,787,000 lb (3.5 million kg) in 1972 and the United States producing 1.4 million lb (627,000 kg) or 18 percent of the total, wood pulp is in considerable demand (Rolston, 1973).

Other materials aside from cloth and yarn, obtained from the viscose cellulose solution are films, cellophane, sausage casings, core layer of shat-

---

[3] One example is the Union Camp Mill at Savannah, Georgia.

terproof glass, waterproofing, wallpaper surfacing, paints and lacquers, and viscose rubbers and leathers. From the filament forms come rayon waste and artificial wool, horeshair, and straw.

**Plastics**  The term *plastic* includes a variety of compounds or their mixtures which may or may not involve wood. A plastic product may include coloring, solvents, lubricants, fillers, plasticizers, and binders, the latter being the principal constituent. Cellulose binders are made either from cotton linters or sulfite-processed wood pulp. Fillers for use in plastics are made principally from wood flour, which is obtained by disintegrating the wood in an attrition mill. The lighter-colored, low-density woods such as cottonwood, basswood, spruce, balsam fir, and white pine are preferred. Flour from walnut shells is also used as a filler in some plastics. The other constituents of cellulose plastics are nonwood in origin. A variety of plastics, although of less importance, are now manufactured from lignin from both hardwoods and softwoods.

The interested reader may learn more about wood in the plastics industry by referring to Panshin and de Zeeuw (1970) in the Bibliography at the end of this chapter.

### Products of Wood Distillation

In burning wood to produce charcoal in earlier days, shallow pits were used, and the stacked wood that had been placed in them was covered with soil and fired with as little air as possible. The heat for carbonizing the wood was produced by burning a part of the charge itself. Tar and liquid products were lost in the smoke. Charcoal was the product sought. It was used in the manufacture of pig iron and gunpowder.

Charcoal is still an important commodity, although plants which manufacture it are fewer in number than in earlier years. The larger plants take the production of an unknown number of small independent producers and combine it with their own.

Hardwoods of the North, such as beech, birch, and maple, because they contain little gum, tannin, or resin are excellent woods for distillation. The stumps or pitchy remnants in Southern pine forests are also distilled for "stump turpentine," wood oils, tar, and charcoal.

The wood-distillation industry at the present time uses a variety of oven sizes. The larger ovens will accommodate several steel buggies or cars (Fig. 16-5). The loaded cars run on narrow-gauge tracks into the ovens; the oven doors are closed, sealed, and heat is applied. After about 24 hours of heating with only a limited amount of air present, the cars of partially glowing charcoal are pulled into another oven. This oven can be closed to let the charcoal cool without a supply of oxygen, which would allow it to burn up. Here it stays for a period; then it may go to a second oven for

**Figure 16-5** A wood-distillation plant which makes charcoal and chemical products from low-grade wood. *(Courtesy of the Michigan Department of Natural Resources, Lansing, Michigan.)*

cooling, or to an open-air waiting yard before it travels to bins for sacking, or to cars for shipping. The principal products of wood distillation are acetic acid, methyl alcohol, derivatives of wood tar, and of course, the most important item today, the charcoal itself. Charcoal is used for domestic cooking in some parts of the country, and its use in restaurants and for outdoor cooking at home and in recreation areas provides a rapidly growing market. Another demand for charcoal is in the fast-growing light-metals industries. Most of the other products of wood distillation are made more cheaply by the petroleum industry.

The charcoal industry affords opportunity for close utilization and intensive management of hardwoods on short rotations. Cull material in northern Michigan, West Virginia, and Missouri, for example, is purchased by weight and used by wood-distillation plants.

## WOOD PRESERVATION

### Drying Wood to Proper Moisture Content

Returning to the sawmill, which after all is the destination of a large part of all the wood harvested in the United States, one finds a heavy investment in drying kilns or tremendous acreage for piling lumber to be air-dried. Often both methods of drying are in operation. Undried or green lumber may contain from 30 to 250 percent water, based on oven-dry weight. Green lumber has little chance in the market, first, because it is heavy and, second, because it shrinks and warps and seldom does it gracefully in public. Checks or cracks may also appear. Again, it may seem to be dry and well seasoned and prove to be hardened only on the surface. Upon ripping or resawing, such a board will frequently assume a fantastic curved shape which makes it useless.

Free water, which is that held in cell cavities of the wood, is driven off first in drying. When the free water is gone, the *fiber saturation point* is reached. In other words, wood that holds only the water in its cell walls is at the fiber saturation point. This is a good reference point, for below it shrinkage occurs and above it there is no change in size with loss of water. Woods vary in their tendency to shrink, both in size and amount per direction. For example, few woods shrink appreciably in length or "endwise," and any wood that does this causes trouble when the ends of pieces must be fitted together. Flooring and siding in residence construction could easily demonstrate this. Figure 16-6 indicates that shrinkage varies with respect to the arrangement, in the piece, of the annual ring pattern.

Wood must have some moisture left in it when it is to be used for any purpose. It can then maintain a sort of equilibrium and be less affected by changes in atmospheric moisture. The Forest Products Laboratory recommends various average moisture contents for interior-finishing woodwork in different regions of the United States. For the lower coastal plains of the states starting with North Carolina and ending with Texas, and for a narrow strip of coastal territory in the southern half of California, 11 percent is the figure. For Nevada and adjacent belts in the states that bound it, 6

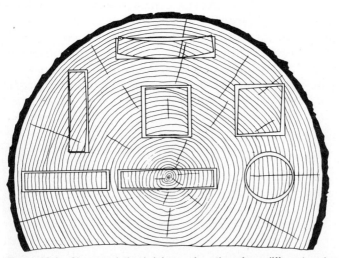

**Figure 16-6** Characteristic shrinkage of sections from different parts of a log. *(Courtesy of the Forest Products Laboratory, Madison, Wisconsin.)*

percent is the average. For the balance of the country, 8 percent is recommended.

**Air Drying and Kiln Drying**   Air drying takes a long time and may not get wood dry enough for its intended use. Kiln drying can cut drying time with safety and can also control the moisture content to levels appropriate for the use of the wood. Shipping and handling costs are reduced in both cases, but kiln drying has the advantage. Both methods tend to reduce the prospect of shrinking, warping, and checking in use, but kiln drying strikes a fatal blow at fungi and insects, while air drying helps in hindering insects and fungi but cannot be depended upon. Careful drying by either method increases the strength of the timber and prepares it for paint and other protective coatings and impregnating materials. Kilns are costly to install and operate and, if not skillfully handled, can ruin lumber in a number of ways. On the other hand, they are timesavers, and they make it possible to dry wood to specific moisture contents for specific purposes. They vary in design from the complicated brick and metal ovenlike affairs, which take whole trainloads of lumber at a charge and have the most delicate temperature and control instruments, to very simple ones. Some of the latter are practically tents, so arranged with draft and moisture controls that rate of drying may be regulated. The old "hotbox" type, which emphasized heat only and often caused wood to case harden on the surface while retaining moisture in the interior, has been replaced by designs that use controllable moisture spray or steam to avoid this particular trouble.

**Treatment to Prevent Decay, Insect Attack, and Shipworm Damage**   Of the factors of decay—heat, moisture, oxygen, and the presence of a living organism—there is only one that can be successfully outwitted under most of the ordinary conditions of use. That factor is the decay organism itself, and its most vulnerable weakness is its dependence on "food" supply.[4] If this food can be successfully poisoned, the organism, if present, dies, or, if about to attack, finds life impossible. The same is true of attack by termites, carpenter ants, and shipworms or marine borers. With the problem of decay and attack by insects and marine organisms met, wood finds myriad uses in contact with the soil, water, and weather.

The most common method of treating timber to make it decay resistant is to impregnate the outer portions with coal-tar creosote or solutions of chemical salts. A great industry has been built up for wood preservation, and many firms purchase or produce wood products for treatment and later sale as treated stock.

----

[4] A good example of excluding another decay factor is shown in the long and uninjured life of wood that has been completely submerged in water. Here there has been too little oxygen for fungi to thrive. Another is oiling and painting, which tends to exclude moisture.

The simplest and least effective of these treatments is brushing the wood with the particular preservative. Another crude method is the thermal treatment or hot and cold process, where wood is wholly or partially immersed in a hot bath of creosote or other preservative and left until it absorbs a part of the preservatives and the heat has expanded the air in the cell walls. The wood is then changed to a bath of cold preservative, where the air in the cells contracts, forming a partial vacuum. Atmospheric pressure then forces more liquid into the cells.

Pressure treatment involves heavy and expensive plant equipment consisting of the necessary cylinders, metal cars, tanks, pumps, and hoisting and transportation devices. The bulk of the business in which the entire stick is pressure-treated involves railroad ties, piles, telephone, telegraph, and power-line poles, fence posts, and. heavy structural timbers such as those used in bridges.

Timbers are loaded on cradlelike cars and run into long cylinders 50 to 180 ft (15 to 56 m) long and 6 to 9 ft (1.8 to 2.7 m) in diameter, which are sealed (Fig. 16-7). A vacuum may then be created, and after that the preservative introduced and pressure applied. Impregnation is quicker and easier in a lengthwise direction. To aid penetration of side surfaces some timbers are incised on the surface. The creosote or other preservative then enters at the numerous shallow cross sections.

A large number of processes are used in treating timber, some of them employing new materials and others using either the standard coal-tar creosote or a mixture of coal tar and creosote, or zinc chloride. Pentachlorophenol has high toxicity and is now established as an effective wood preservative. The amount of any preservative varies with the intended use of the timber. In so-called full-cell treatment, the preservative is forced to the point of refusal. This is necessary in treating marine timbers against the attack of borers, which are mollusks of many forms and wormlike in appearance. The most important are species of *Teredo* and *Limnoria*.

Factors upon which the relative value of preservatives may be judged, include cost, tendency to leach out in service, toxicity to typical wood-destroying fungi, toxicity to insects, and effect on steel or other materials that must be used with the wood in service. Toxicity to marine borers and prospect of continued availability are also important. Impregnation of lumber and structural timber with ammonium and other salt solutions produces fire resistance through release of nonflammable gases when heated.

One of the impressive uses of treated timber is in shelters and other types of buildings. These are known as pole-type structures and use creosote-pressure-treated poles set in the ground, serving both as support and wall members. The floors may simply be dirt or concrete; treated poles do away with the need for masonry foundations.

**Figure 16-7**  A load of wood about to be run into a long pressure cylinder for chemical treatment. Such treatment inhibits attack from fungi, insects, and marine borers. *(Courtesy of the Forest Products Laboratory, Madison, Wisconsin.)*

**Preservatives and Forestry**  A tendency toward quick decay is a problem in some wood species, and indeed, certain species that are plentiful in given localities are severely discriminated against for this reason. Preservative treatment may give such woods odors or a soiled appearance, but it does make them marketable. The forest manager thus has a market for otherwise unwanted species and small-dimension material from improvement cuttings and thinnings. Furthermore, preservation makes it possible for wood to compete with substitute metals and concrete. Metal and concrete are handicapped by weight, cost, and lack of easy workability, but have the advantage of relatively long service without replacement. Preservative treatment of wood produces and increases the market for wood through giving it greater serviceability. Market demand for such wood promotes good forestry practices by requiring only infrequent replacement, thus extending our wood supply.

## MAKING WOOD MORE VERSATILE BY FABRICATION

Wood in separate pieces may be much less useful than in partially assembled form. Laminated construction timbers, layers of veneer glued together to make plywood, and particle board are all examples of transforming the properties of wood and reassembling it. In the latter two, the grain is reoriented.

**Laminated Beams, Arches, and Trusses**  A laminated beam, arch, or truss is made by gluing and clamping many small boards together. If the boards, often 1 or 2 in. (2.5 or 5 cm) in thickness, are not long enough, they may be trimmed on the end at the angle or shaped to form a finger-type profile. Two boards so trimmed may be joined together to form a scarfed or a finger joint. Only carefully selected, specially dried lumber is used. After the boards have been stacked, glued, and pressed to form the desired shape, the beam is removed from the clamping device and is planed, trimmed, and finished according to customer specifications. These specifications usually include a curve and shape impossible to attain with solid wood. The finished article is used in such structures as churches, schools, auditoriums, and other large buildings (Fig. 16-8).

**Figure 16-8**  Laminated beams gave a new dimension to wood utilization. The curved laminated arch provides graceful lines and brings out the natural beauty of wood. *(Courtesy of the Forest Products Laboratory, Madison, Wisconsin.)*

**Figure 16-9** Veneer being peeled from a Douglas-fir peeler block. The lathe operator stands at the left. *(Courtesy of the American Plywood Association, Tacoma, Washington.)*

The use of laminated wood offers flexibility in design, greater structural strength, and brings out the decorative beauty of wood. In laminations of this type, the grain of all component parts is parallel.

**Plywood**   This is a wood product in which the grain of each component layer of veneer is placed at right angles to its neighbor. A simple piece of plywood is a three-ply panel. The outer pieces are called *face* plies or *skin* and their grain is parallel. The piece of veneer in the center is called *core* and its grain is at right angles to the grain of the face pieces. Plywood may be made of any odd number of layers of veneer, depending on its use. Three, five, and seven layers are most common; however, plywood is usually sold by the thickness (i.e., ¼, ⅜, ½, ⅝, ¾ in.).

Veneer is a thin sheet of wood of uniform thickness, usually peeled on a large rotary lathe (Fig. 16-9) or sliced from a large board called a *flitch*. Freshly cut veneer is dried either in the open, in well-ventilated rooms, or in conveyor kilns (driers) over 150 ft (45 m) long. Some veneer is used in making crates, containers, and other packaging materials, thus never gets to the plywood stage. If it is to be used as plywood, it must go through many more steps after the drying stage.

Much of the plywood in the United States is made from Douglas-fir. Once the *peeler blocks*, as the logs are called, are cut to length and debarked, they are brought to the rotary lathe. Here the block is rotated against a keen cutting edge, which literally unwinds the log in a continuous strip of veneer. At the end of a tier of storage trays, the veneer strip is clipped into various widths up to the maximum size of 4 ft (1.2 m). The next step is the steam-heated conveyor kiln. Once dried, it is sorted and graded, and each pile is sent to different departments of the mill for further treatment. One pile may go to a machine that replaces each knot with a tight-fitting patch; another pile goes to storage for later use; another cartload, mostly of sapwood, may be run through the drier again to reduce the moisture content to the desired level. The dried material eventually gets to the glue spreader (Fig. 16-10) where it loses its identity as veneer. The core sheets are spread evenly with glue on both sides and placed at right angles to the face sheets to give the plywood its strength. From here the stack of "sandwiched" panels is taken to an accordion-like press, where each panel is subjected to intense pressure and heat. The resulting bond of glue is stronger than the wood itself. The panels go next to end- and edge-trim saws and then onto sanding machines where both surfaces are sanded to satin smoothness. Each panel is inspected and if it passes goes to a brander, where the grade is burned into the end of the panel. The panel is now ready for shipment.

The plywood industry has had a fantastic growth since just before World War II, especially in the South and West. Its importance in construction is indicated by the fact that 60 percent of the plywood produced is used for that purpose. Panels, forms, entire walls, boats, and packages all employ this product. Production of plywood rose from 480 million sq ft (43.2 million m²) on the basis of ⅜-in. three-ply in 1935 to 23.5 billion sq ft (2.1 billion m²) in 1972. This now includes southern pine and some other species. New markets include highway signs and pallets for forklift trucks.

The manufacture of sandwich-board panels for light construction has been notable . The skin may be paper, wood, fabric, plastic, or metal. The interior may be mill residue, or wood from trees formerly considered inferior. A sandwich panel now used in roof, ceiling, wall, and floor sections has a plywood skin and a honeycomb core, and exhibits great structural strength. A major stride forward in heavier construction, where load is an important factor, is the use of fabricated hollow box plywood beams and trusses. Since they are built to specifications they have the advantage of being ready for installation when they reach the job, are corrosion resistant and light in weight, yet have great strength.

**Wood Particle Board**   A newer product known as wood particle board is made of actual wood particles or flakes which have not been pulped.

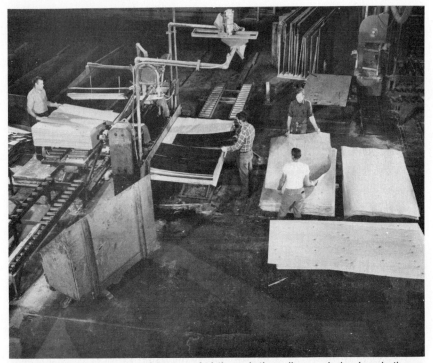

**Figure 16-10**  Veneer core sheets are fed through the rollers and glued on both surfaces. Two full sheets of the face veneer are then placed on top, one sheet for the panel below and one for the next panel to be assembled. *(Courtesy of the American Plywood Association, Tacoma, Washington.)*

These are put under pressure with an adhesive and made into thick boards used in place of plywood and may one day replace lumber.

There are three types of wood particle board. *Chipboard* is composed of random-sized wood chips ranging from sawdust to chunks the size of hazelnuts. Mixtures of softwood and hardwood can be used dry and, because the final product is usually veneered, strength is not too important. *Shaving board* is frequently made from planing-mill waste. Shavings are hammered into suitable sizes and the long fiber obtained produces boards of higher strength properties. *Flakeboard* or *splinter board* requires green waste and this is cut into flakes of carefully controlled length, width, and thickness. Each flake is like a miniature piece of veneer. When pressed together, a better distribution of properties is achieved because the veneers are oriented in all directions rather than at 90° as in plywood.

**Building Board Consumption and Demand**  Building board consumption including insulation board, hardboard, and particle board reached 14.1

billion sq ft (1.27 billion m²) (⅜ in. basis) in 1972—over four times the volume consumed in 1950.

In the 1950s and 1960s particle board consumption showed the largest increase, rising from less than 50 million sq ft (4.5 million m²) in 1950 to 6.3 billion sq ft (567 million m²) in 1972—an average annual rate of about 25 percent. Hardboard use also rose rapidly, with an average annual increase of 9.5 percent. Although use of insulation board has been relatively stable, this product still accounted for 40 percent of all building board consumed in 1972.

The fast growth in use of particle board largely reflects the substitution of this product for lumber and plywood used as core stock in the manufacture of furniture, doors, and cabinets. Much of the growth in use since the late 1950s reflects similar substitution for floor underlayment. Present work on the development of structural grades of particle board also suggests the likelihood of further substitution for softwood plywood used as subflooring and roof sheathing in construction.

Much of the recent increase in the use of hardboard also reflects substitution for lumber and plywood, especially in the furniture industry. Use of insulation board on the one hand, has been closely related to the construction industry (U. S. Department of Agriculture, 1973).

**Timber Connectors and Framing Anchors in Wood Construction** A wooden pin or dowel or a nail or bolt is the usual fastener for wood construction. The amount of load each can carry in timber construction, such as in trusses where load is important, is somewhat limited. Timber connectors can assume considerably more load than can any of these devices. Of the many kinds of connectors now used, most are modifications of steel rings which are inserted in grooves cut with power equipment or toothed plates embedded in the wood by pressure.

A bolt to complete the assembly is passed through the wood at the center of cach connector (Fig. 16-11). The load on the ring or plate is exerted parallel or vertical to the grain or at an angle. The purpose of the connector is (1) to distribute the weight of the structure over a greater area of the end of the truss or member and (2) to increase the sheer resistance of the members which are held together. Connectors have done much to improve construction with wood by increasing joint efficiency.

Framing anchors are devices made from sheet steel formed in such a way as to permit the fastening in place of joists and trusses. They are used in combination with nails but eliminate the need for toenailing. Framing anchors are placed outside the joint as seen in the lower half of Fig. 16-11.

**The Forester and the Processing of the Forest Harvest** It is natural to

**Figure 16-11** *Left,* a split ring timber connector, placed in the precut grooves, will serve to transmit the loads between the pieces of wood. *Right,* framing anchors are devices formed from sheet metal and used in combination with nails to hold framing members in place. *(Courtesy of the Timber Engineering Co., Inc.)*

ask, "What has all this manufacturing business to do with the forester's work?" The answer may be summed up by saying that anything which makes it possible to use wood effectively creates demand for wood and gives the forester a chance to harvest the forest regularly. Because more residue, inferior species, and poorer grades of wood can be utilized today, the forester's job is getting easier. This greater utilization is good conservation. In a broader sense, foresters have a profound responsibility to the conservation movement as a whole. Their product, which is *replaceable,* must supplement and be substituted for those resources which are *irreplaceable.* These products, then, must be efficient, economical, and attractive. Foresters play an important role in providing this sort of quality in wood products.

## BIBLIOGRAPHY

Cliff, Edward P. 1973. *Timber: The Renewable Material,* prepared for the National Commission on Materials Policy, Washington, DC.

Lassen, L. E., and D. Hair. 1970. Potential Gains in Wood Supplies through Improved Technology, *Jour. Forestry,* **68**:404–407.

Panshin, John A., and Carl de Zeeuw. 1970. *Textbook of Wood Technology*: Vol. 1, *Structure, Identification, Uses, and Properties of the Commercial Woods of the United States,* 3d ed., McGraw-Hill Book Company, New York.

*Report of the President's Advisory Panel on Timber and the Environment.* 1973. Superintendent of Documents, Washington, DC.

Rolston, K. S. 1973. Executive Secretary, American Pulpwood Association. Personal correspondence with American Forest Institute.

Seaman, Jerome F. 1970. *The Wood Resource and the Environment: Some Options*

# Part Four

## Forest Protection

Chapter 17

# Fire and the Forest

Fire, which is said to be the greatest of all human discoveries, becomes an agent of merciless destruction when it is out of control. It changes from the Doctor Jekyll, symbolized by the cheerful flame of the campfire, to the Mr. Hyde of a free-spreading conflagration. Wildfire is one of the three greatest enemies of the forest and when out of control it defeats the objectives of forest management.[1] On the other hand, a carefully controlled fire can be a useful tool in forestry under specific circumstances. The controlled or herded fire, frequently called a *prescribed burn*, can be used to prepare a favorable seedbed for certain species, eliminate disease and insects, and remove undesirable hardwoods or brush. The controlled fire is one of the least expensive and most practical means of ridding a clearcut area of logging slash, or reducing accumulated forest debris, both of which could add fuel to a fire at a less desirable time. Fire, it seems, can be both a friend and an enemy to the land manager, which brings up the subject of *fire management.*

---

[1] The term wildfire is now preferred to "forest fire" in order to differentiate between an uncontrolled fire, and a prescribed fire.

# Table 17-1 Some Large Wildfires of North America since 1825

| Name of fire | Location | Date | Acres burned | Hectares burned | No. of lives lost |
|---|---|---|---|---|---|
| Miramichi | Maine and New Brunswick | 1825–Oct. | 3 million | 1.2 million | 160 |
| Pontiac | Quebec | 1853–May | 1.6 million | 0.65 million | |
| Peshtigo | Wisconsin and Michigan | 1871–Oct. | 1.280 million (Wis.) 2.5 million (Mich.) | 0.52 million | 1,500 |
| Michigan | Michigan | 1881–Sept. | 1 million | 0.4 million | 282 |
| Hinckley | Minnesota | 1894–Sept. | 160,000 | 64,000 | 418 |
| Yacolt | Washington | 1902–Sept. | 239,000 | 96,700 | |
| Adirondack | New York | 1903–May, June | 637,000 | 257,800 | |
| Great Idaho | Idaho and Montana | 1910–Aug. | 2 million | 0.81 million | 85 |
| Cloquet | Minnesota | 1918–Oct. | 250,000 | 101,000 | 432 |
| Tillamook | Oregon | 1933–Aug. | 300,000 | 121,000 | 1 |
| Maine | Maine | 1947–Oct. | 240,000 | 97,000 | 16 |
| Malvern Hill | Florida | 1956–March | 100,000 | 40,000 | |
| Wenatchee | Washington | 1970–Aug. | 131,000 | 53,000 | |
| Laguna | California | 1970–Aug. | 185,000 | 75,000 | 10 |

Fire management is based on the concept that *fires in the forest may be either good or bad*. The same fire may be good for some aspects of the forest ecosystem and at the same time be bad for forest industry or public safety.

Fire management is designed to resolve these conflicts. It applies management policies and technology for both wildfires and prescribed fires. It recognizes that factors of time, location, fuel flammability, ecology, and economics make forest fires either wanted or unwanted.

Fire management provides systematic application of the alternatives for fire use, fire prevention and fire suppression. (Barrows, 1973)

### Historic Significance of Wildfires

". . . for a fire hath devoured the pastures of the wilderness and a flame hath burned all the trees of the field . . ." This and like expressions of the poets and prophets of Biblical times indicate that the destructiveness of range and forest fires was not unknown to the ancients. Ordinances against fires were being enacted in Germany as far back as the end of the sixteenth century. One of the oldest forest fires for which there is real evidence in the United States occurred, according to scars on California's giant sequoias, in A.D. 245. Others burned in 1441 and 1580 in the same locality, and Colorado fires have left their traces from the year 1676 on. More than 200 sq mi (516 km²) is believed to have burned south of Mount Katahdin in Maine about 1794.

The Great Idaho fire produced "dark days," requiring the use of artificial light in daytime, over an extensive area.

The Cloquet fire was swift and terrible in its toll of life and property. The federal government, having waived its immunity in the courts upon taking over operation of the railroads during World War I, was charged with starting the fire in the operation of its trains, and was sued. Most of the claims were for buildings and equipment, rather than for standing timber. The latter was destroyed over large areas of Minnesota, and loss of young growth was particularly severe. Total property damage has been generally estimated at $30 million.

In 1933 more than $20 million worth of choice timber was sacrificed in the Tillamook fire in Oregon. Translated into wages and value of manufactured products, the figure is ten times this amount. The fire is thought to have started from friction in the power skidding of a log through a tangle of dry cedar, just as the operation was about to shut down because of fire weather. About 200,000 acres (81,000 ha) burned a second time in 1939, and more than 180,000 acres (72,800 ha) burned again in 1945.

Terrible chaparral fires occur in southern California every few years over large areas (Fig. 17-1). These destroy brush cover necessary for retarding rapid runoff of rainfall, and the domestic and municipal water supplies of many communities are affected. In 1947 one of this country's most seri-

**Figure 17-1** A brush fire in southern California. Note the fire fighters and bulldozer at lower left. *(Courtesy of the U.S. Forest Service.)*

ous wildfires occurred in Maine. In October, because of a prolonged summer and fall drought, a number of uncontrollable fires literally exploded into one large fire. Over 200,000 acres (81,000 ha), most of them forested, were burned. In addition to the great loss of timber, property loss was high. Over 1,000 houses burned to the ground. About 400 homes, including 60 large estates, were destroyed in the summer resort center in Bar Harbor alone. In Acadia National Park 8,000 acres (3,200 ha) of forest burned. In all 16 lives were lost.

The South has also seen large wildfires in recent years. In 1955, a fire burned 50,000 acres (20,000 ha) in Clinch County, Georgia. Near Lake City, Florida, in 1956, the 100,000-acre (40,000-ha) Malvern Hill fire was "so intense that it created a wind storm of almost cyclonic proportions at its center" (Daniels, 1957).

In 1967, in north Idaho, the combination of low humidity, high temperature, and three summer months without rain, produced one of that area's longest periods of severe fire conditions (Fig. 17-2). The Sundance fire, which started September 1, during one 8-hour period, burned at an average rate of 100 acres per minute. The total area burned was 56,000 acres (23,000 ha). In July and August of 1970, during one of the worst possible fire weather combinations, a series of intense electrical storms accompanied by strong winds and little or no rain, struck the Wenatchee National Forest of Washington State. The 431 separate fires soon lost their identity when they formed 4 large fires, burning over 131,000 acres (53,000 ha) before being stopped by 12,000 men and women (Fig. 17-10).

## The Wildfire Situation in the United States

Fire is potentially the forest's greatest enemy because of its power to destroy so much timber and other forest values in such a short time. However, because of the protection afforded most of the forests in this country, fire loss is actually lower than the loss from either insects or disease. Of the millions of acres of land vulnerable to wildfires in the continental United

**Figure 17-2** A crown fire in an Idaho forest. *(Courtesy of the U.S. Forest Service.)*

States and coastal Alaska, 92 percent are under some form of organized protection.

Several factors have contributed to the improvement in this country's forest-fire situation in the past few decades. First of all, much reduction of loss has been on lands which are under protection for the first time. Secondly, there are two national fire prevention programs. One is the National Cooperative Forest Fire Prevention Program (better known as the Smokey Bear Program). The other is the Keep Green Program sponsored by forest industries through the various state Keep Green Associations. These will be discussed later in this chapter.

Other forces are at work in the United States to improve the wildfire problem. Forestry, civic and youth organizations, conservation and environmental societies, sportmen's and garden clubs are among those supporting fire prevention.

### Protection from Wildfire in the United States

As indicated earlier, 92 percent of our forests, excluding interior Alaska, are protected from wildfire. The degree of protection, of course, varies greatly with areas and ownerships. Also, because of variable fire weather, fuel buildups, and a fluctuation in the activities of the fire-causing agencies, the adequacy of fire protection organizations will vary.

The protected areas of the United States consist of national forests, national parks and monuments, Indian lands, Bureau of Land Management areas, and other federal areas; state forests, parks, school lands, and miscellaneous public areas; and tracts of private holdings. Most public lands have their own fire-control organization. The private owners may have their own elaborate fire organization, or by paying a given fee per acre may "contract" the fire-control job to public agencies, or they may be a contributing member in a fire-control cooperative. Two legislative acts, the Weeks Law of 1911 and the Clarke-McNary Act of 1924, provide for the appropriation of federal funds to states cooperating with the government in a fire-control program. In this arrangement the state accepts the responsibility for supervising and handling the job; the federal government provides technical help and leadership, if needed, and funds for specified expenses.

### The Causes of Wildfires

There are nine standard causes of wildfires in the United States. Keeping track of the frequency of these causes is the job of the Forest Service.[2] The major causes today are listed by these categories: lightning, campfire, smoking, debris burning, incendiary, equipment use, railroad, children, and miscellaneous. Though there may be occasional regional variations in caus-

---

[2] Data on these causes are compiled by the Division of Cooperative Forest Fire Control, Forest Service, and are presented annually in *Wildfire Statistics*.

es, the pattern remains relatively stable over the years. For example, incendiary fires have led all causes in this country for over 30 years, and they are still the number one cause today.

**Lightning**   Wildfires in this category cannot be prevented to any appreciable extent. Approximately 11 percent of the wildfires throughout the United States start from lightning. This nationwide percentage will naturally increase in the future if the number of fires of human origin can be reduced. Though 11 percent may seem like a small number of fires, the picture is altered when viewed by regions, as some areas are much more susceptible to lightning fires than are others. Between 1970 and 1973, lightning caused 48 percent of the fires in the Rocky Mountain states and 32 percent in the Pacific Coast states. Because of weather satellites and radar-tracking stations, meteorologists now have the ability to predict the occurrence and path of lightning storms. Such information makes early detection and attack  more effective.

**Camper**   This category includes fires started by campfires for cooking or for  providing light or warmth. For 30 years this group has been responsible for 4 to 5 percent of all wildfires.

**Smoker**   These are wildfires caused by smokers who are careless with matches, lighters, tobacco, or other smoking material. During the 1930s it was the number one cause. In the 1940s it moved to second place, in the 1950s to third place, where it remains today. Between 1970 and 1973, 10 to 12 percent of the wildfires were from this cause.

**Debris Burning**   This is defined as a wildfire spreading from clearing land; burning trash, range, stubble, meadow, rights-of-way, logging slash; or other prescribed burning. Debris burning is the number two cause of fires today. Between 1970 and 1973 it varied from 19 to 24 percent.

**Incendiary**   An incendiary fire is one willfully set by anyone to burn, or spread to, vegetation or property not owned or controlled by that person, or a fire set without the owners consent. It is the number one cause of wildfires, a distinction it has held most of the years since the 1940s. Between 1970 and 1973 incendiary fires were 24 to 26 percent of the total.

**Equipment Use**   These are wildfires caused by any mechanical equipment other than railroad operations. Between 1970 and 1973 such fires accounted for 2 to 5 percent of the total in the United States.

**Railroad**   These are wildfires caused by all railroad operations, including burning rights-of-way and ties. Approximately 6 to 7 percent of wildfires were in this category between the period 1970 to 1973.

**Children**   This category includes all wildfires set by children less than 12 years old. It accounts for 6 to 9 percent of the total wildfires from 1970 to 1973.

**Miscellaneous**   These are wildfires that cannot be properly classified under other general causes. In the years 1970 to 1973 the group accounted for 7 to 9 percent of the total number of wildfires.

### The Prevention of Wildfires

Reducing *fire risk* is a fascinating and challenging field. Of the wildfires in the United States, 89 percent are caused by people. Theoretically, we should be able to stop wildfires before they get started, or at least reduce their numbers. In spite of the fire prevention campaigns mentioned earlier, we find the percentage of people-caused versus lightning-caused fires has not changed much in the last 30 years. One wonders what these figures would have been if there had been no fire prevention efforts.

**Incendiary Fire**   Let us look again at the number one cause of wild-fires, the incendiary fire, of which 38 percent are in the Southern states. As noted, an incendiary fire is one set on someone else's property without the owner's permission. Motives are numerous. One of the more common is related to personal economic gain. This includes obtaining employment; improving grazing and hunting conditions or a berry crop; forcing the land-owner to cut trees earlier than desired; a personal grudge against a neigh-bor; or just "stirring up a little action." Some fires are set to divert attention from an illegal whiskey still or to destroy evidence of a theft or other tres-pass. An element of vandalism and revenge against the establishment is also at the root of some incendiary fires. Beyond these are the pyromaniacs—the "firebugs"—who set fires for reasons that are more apparent to the psychol-ogist than to the forester.

Because incendiary fires are deliberate their numbers are the most dif-ficult of any group to control. Prejudice toward the large landowner may be slowly overcome through public relations. It should eventually become evi-dent to the most recalcitrant incendiarist that a thriving forest industry offers better jobs than does a thriving wildfire. In this vein, demonstrations of how forest products improve the local economy have helped to reduce the number of incendiary fires in some communities. It is largely a matter of law enforcement and education, although further research into the moti-vation of incendiarists seems necessary if the percentage of incendiary fires is to be reduced appreciably.

**Debris Burning**   The number two cause, debris burning, is another group which bears discussion. This group has moved from third to second place nationwide, and in the Lake States area is the number one cause.

Debris burning, as a land management practice, is a way of life. It is traditional to burn dead leaves in the fall or dead grass in the spring. Carelessness and the reluctance to incur the expense and labor of providing necessary controls, coupled with an obstinate desire to burn during hazardous weather, account for the majority of these fires. Most states require burning permits, usually in particular seasons, which must be obtained from forest officers or other officials. In applying for the permit, the applicants are usually requested to use caution, often told how to burn safely, and are required to sign an agreement that they will take the necessary precautions (Fig. 17-3). In cases of extreme hazard the permit may be refused. Offenders, those who do not obtain permits or who violate conditions of the permit, must be prosecuted for their violations. The penalty in the form of a fine or payment of costs of suppression hopefully serves to deter the offender and also those who hear of the punishment. New air-pollution laws, which regulate against debris burning, should help reduce the number of fires in this category.

**Smokers** The third cause of wildfires, smokers, has gone from number one cause in the 1930s to number three cause in the 1970s. Whether or not this reflects real improvement, however, is debatable. The number of smoker-related fires has not been reduced, rather the percentage of other causes has increased. Since no smoker fire need ever happen, one wonders what kind of people are included in the term *smokers*. The Forest Service many years ago classified smokers under *campers* and grouped them with "children, tramps, drunks, and lunatics." This is a harsh classification; however, public opinion is now becoming hardened against the habit of smoking, and it may not be an outdated description. Hopefully the percentage of smokers will be reduced in the future, but the numbers will probably remain high because of increasing population.

The problem lies with the smoker's unconscious motion of lighting a cigarette, cigar, or pipe. Most summer users of the forest live the rest of the year where the streets are paved and develop the habit of carelessly tossing aside burning material. In a city, in most instances, this does little harm. Once the habit is formed, it is hard to break and is unconsciously repeated while in the forest. Most prevention material is aimed at breaking this habit of careless disposal. Examples of this type of risk-reduction are signs and posters, reading "Don't be a Flipper" or "Break Your Match," which are placed along trails and highways in areas having a history of smoker fires.

"Smokers" is a general term which includes all users of tobacco who frequent forest areas. It may be a berry picker, a hunter, a bulldozer operator, a picnicker, a highway traveler, or any one of more than a hundred types of forest users. For this reason, the "No Smoking While Traveling" rule may have to be enforced on forest or park trails.

Rev. 6-1-73

FORM 629-1-1-2-400

# State of Oregon -- Department of Forestry

## BURNING PERMIT

NO. 77-111

In accordance with ORS 477.515, OAR 43-040, 43-041, 43-045

RFD Farm No. _Y-82_

Name _JOHN P. JONES_

Address _3290 WEST HILLS ROAD_

City _PHILOMATH, OR_    State    _97370_ Zip Code

Telephone: _929-1234_

is hereby granted a permit to burn on: Forest Land Class. _1_ 1 2 3

Type: **Check one or more:** ☐ Agricultural ☐ Land Clearing ☐ Silvicultural ☐ Debris Disposal ☐ Non-Forest Land ☑ Hazard Reduction

Material: **Check one or more:** ☐ Grass, Grain, Stubble ☐ Debris ☐ Slash ☐ Rubbish ☑ Woody Materials

☐ Other

Acres _3 STACKED PILES_    Sec. _10_    Tons _____    Twp _16S_    Rge _8W_    County _BENTON_

Location: _SE¼ NE¼ 14_

_2 MILES N OF PHILOMATH CITY LIMITS ON WEST HILLS ROAD_

The permittee must provide the following men, equipment, and precautions on the fire until it is out: _1 COMPETENT MAN WITH FIRE TOOLS AND 5 GALLON WATER CONTAINER_

_BURN 1 PILE AT A TIME IN THE LATE EVENING_

☑ Burning will be confined to the hours of _6:00 PM_ to _10:00 PM_ on days when open burning is permitted by Air Quality Regulatory Authorities. This permit, with its terms and conditions, is effective from

_MAY 20, 1976_ through _MAY 29, 1976_, inclusive

Date Issued: _MAY 20, 1976_    Received By: _____

Issued By: _____

_____
(Forest Officer)

CAUTION: This permit does not relieve permittee from responsibility of fire damage as a result of fire escaping from above permit area

_____ DISTRICT

**Figure 17-3** A burning permit is required by many states before debris may be burned. Note the permit has certain precautions spelled out for individual permittees. *(Courtesy of the Oregon Department of Forestry.)*

**Miscellaneous** Prevention of some wildfires is virtually impossible, particularly those in the miscellaneous group. A live wire may break and fall into flammable cover; an automobile may leave the road and catch fire; sparks from the chimney of a summer cottage may be carried into dry leaves; or an oil stove in a resort may explode. From these incidents fire may spread to the forest.

On the other hand, public education, regulating public use of the forest, and enforcing fire laws, are proven means of preventing wildfires.

### Educating the Forest User

The camper and the smoker are often the same person and fire prevention material aimed at one is applicable to the other. All kinds of advertising media are employed today to bring to the public an awareness of the fire danger and the need for their cooperation. Warnings are seen on everything from matchfolders and posters to highway billboards; spot announcements are made repeatedly on radio and television; comic books, magazines, and newspapers carry the fire prevention theme; private and public foresters, or their representatives, make appeals to groups ranging from children's gatherings to service clubs. Interpretive messages in the forests and parks in the form of exhibits and talks carry the wildfire prevention theme also. The timing of such campaigns is important. An appeal to "put out your campfire" in the dead of winter does not make much impact. The same annoucement, heard by a family heading for their favorite campsite, is more likely to produce the desired effect—an attitude of caution and responsibility while in the forest.

Let us look at an example of regulating public use. In most developed recreation areas the camper is encouraged or required to use designated sites, which are equipped with fireplaces. The interests of the camper, smoker, or forest employee may often take them beyond developed areas. For this reason, various methods of prevention are justified, including "Closed to Entry" periods during hazardous conditions.

Examples of fire law enforcement would include closure of logging operations during periods of hazardous conditions, discriminate disposal of logging slash, regulating debris burning, installing spark arresters on locomotives and internal combustion engines used in the forest, and requiring a watchperson on duty after the day's activities cease. Law enforcement is an important tool in preventing wildfires.

### The Wildfire Prevention Programs

**The Smokey Bear Program** During World War II, State and Federal Foresters appealed to the War Advertising Council, now known as The Advertising Council, Inc., for help in curbing the smoke and wildfires threatening airfields, military installations, watersheds, rangelands, and standing forest needed in the war effort. For the first time a nationwide forest-fire prevention campaign was launched utilizing the talents of a professional advertising firm, Foote, Cone, and Belding, of Los Angeles, which volunteered its services. After experimenting with various slogans and symbols during the war, the campaign settled on a friendly, peacetime symbol, a bear in a ranger's hat and fire fighter's dungarees. Smokey appeared first in 1945 with the slogan "Care Will Prevent 9 out of 10 Forest Fires." Two years later the familiar "Remember—Only You Can Prevent Forest Fires" was initiated, and this slogan has persisted into the 1970s. A live bear, found badly burned in a forest fire in New Mexico, added appeal to the campaign. The bear was named Smokey and served as a living symbol and a popular live exhibit at the National Zoo in Washington, D.C. A new Smokey now carries on the tradition. As a trademark, Smokey is one of the best-known symbols in the United States. Through the Advertising Council, Inc., millions of dollars of free space and time with radio and television, transit companies, outdoor advertisers, and magazines and newspapers, is provided. Another advertising firm, Liller, Neal, Battle, and Lindsey, Inc., of Atlanta, Georgia, has voluntarily taken on the responsibility of working on specific Southern forest-fire problems. Movie and TV personalities have also donated much time to the Smokey Bear campaign. It is estimated that the program thus far has saved America more than $17 billion in losses that did *not occur* during its first 30 years.

**The Keep Green Program**   The Keep Green movement began in Washington State in 1940, followed by Oregon a few months later, and has now spread throughout the country. Some Keep Green support comes from state forestry departments but mostly from private forest owners. The timber industry, with an investment in the billions of dollars, saw an early need to promote a wildfire prevention program aimed at their employees and the visiting public.

Many states with a Keep Green organization are well organized. Consider the structure of "Keep Washington Green." A slate of officers serves as its staff with the executive secretary serving as the director. There is an executive committee made up of prominent forestry-oriented people. vice-presidents representing the 10 congressional districts of the state, a board of trustees, local county committee chairpersons, an advisory committee representing 18 forestry and other organizations within the state, and a group of honorary lifetime trustees. All major forest industries have input, and the association is financed largely by private contributions. Individual memberships are encouraged.

The public is reached through newspaper, radio and television, stamps and decals, leaflets, and novelties. School children throughout the state in grades 1 to 12 participate in the annual poster contest.

The Keep Green organizations depend heavily on local support, and they thrive best in states with a strong forest industry. In recent years they have become more closely tied to the Smokey Bear program and serve effectively in distributing its materials, in turn better solidifying the human-caused wildfire prevention program. In all there have been 39 states with a Keep Green Association.

## ANOTHER WAY TO THINK OF WILDFIRE PREVENTION: FIRE HAZARD REDUCTION

In the earlier treatment of causes of wildfires and their prevention, we have been discussing fire risk reduction. This is the logical time to compare fire risk with fire hazard.

*Fire risk* is the chance of fire starting from some causative agent, such as a match, lightning bolt, spark from a campfire, or cigarette; in other words, the means by which fuels catch fire. *Fire hazard* is the fuel that, by its kind, arrangement, volume, condition, and location, forms a special threat of ignition or suppression difficulty. Dry leaves along a frequented trail, tall snags in an area vulnerable to lightning, logging slash, and dry roadside shrubbery are examples of fire hazard. Fire hazard reduction is as vital a part of fire prevention as is fire risk reduction. It receives less publicity, however, and depends less on those outside the forestry profession; thus it could be considered more a part of the forester's general land management practices. Fire hazard reduction is essentially the removal of fuels in areas of high fire risk exposure.

Examples of fire hazard reduction are:

The removal of fuels along a railroad right-of-way

The removal of fuel in a plowed strip around an area of high hazard such as logging slash

The removal of dead snags capable of throwing sparks if the snags should become ignited

The removal of light ground fuels through a periodic prescribed burn

The expense of hazard reduction is often high. The *extent* and *location* of hazards to be reduced depend on local conditions. It therefore becomes necessary to weigh factors of risk against factors of hazard. When both risk and hazard in an area are high, it follows that this area should receive attention rather than one of low risk and low hazard, or even one of limited risk and high hazard. If the overall value of an area for any purpose does not justify the expense of reducing the hazard, or if the hazardous situation will change within a short period of time, there is an understandable reluctance to incur this expense. Hazard reduction is, however, an accepted means of wildfire prevention, and its expense is included in the budgets of many forest owners. Some states have enacted laws governing the amount of logging slash they will permit to accumulate, making a reduction of the hazard legally necessary.

## PREPARATION FOR ATTACKING WILDFIRES, OR "PRESUPPRESSION"

With the best of fire prevention service, wildfires are bound to occur, and carefully planned campaigns against these fires have all the problems of preparation that characterize relief undertakings in great disasters. Accumulated knowledge is needed of the terrain, character of cover, occurrence of risk and hazard, weather records, labor supplies, transportation routes, communication facilities, possible cooperative help, special times when and places where people will be concentrated, a history of past wildfires which includes their behavior, and other items of similar character. This material is kept up to date for areas that require protection and provides a source of information from which a *fire-control plan* is made. Into this plan go instructions for each person or group of persons in the organization in the event of fire. Such a plan would be used on a national forest, comprising a mountain range with all or parts of great watersheds, or a vast stretch of wooded plain, mesa, or swamp, or a combination of all of these. In a private corporation's holdings, the fire-control plan may cover territory similar to that of a national forest, but more likely it will be in several noncontiguous areas, and it may even be a part of one great area protected by an association formed for the express purpose of fire control. In the latter case, the fire plan will cover the entire holdings of the association.

### Activities Dictated by the Plan Before Wildfires Break Out

All details of a fire-control plan cannot be treated in a chapter of this length, but at least the more important items will be discussed.

**Financing Fire-Control Objectives**   Every fire-control organization is faced with the problem of acquiring sufficient funds for its wildfire prevention and suppression work. Budgets for fire control compete with budgets for protection from insects and diseases, as well as with financial demands from other departments in the corporation or government agency administering forest lands. Fire control has one factor in its favor. Without it, timber production, watershed management, recreation, grazing, and all the other resource management activities will suffer.

The question becomes *how much* money must be available to accomplish the desired fire control. Certainly such a figure is never appropriated or allotted by guesswork. Needs, of course, are estimated but only after careful study of the value of the land which is to be protected. It is a simple matter to determine the value of commercial timber and weigh this with the cost of protecting it. The picture becomes complicated when an attempt is made to determine other resource values. How does one evaluate long-range damages to soil fertility or damage to young trees, wildlife, recreational values, or loss to the remaining timber due to insects and disease which come in after a fire? How does one weigh the cost of these intangible values especially in this day of acute environmental concern? Some land managers today are thinking of the advantages of letting natural wildfires burn, particularly in national parks and national forest wilderness areas. There are after all some ecological as well as economic benefits from wildfires. These seem to be problems for the resource economist to answer rather than the fire-control specialist. No one can come up with an actual cost for fire control because this will change with fire weather and other unpredictable factors. The best of calculations can fall to pieces in an unusually bad fire year and few control organizations can expect to be financed to meet the worst that can happen. The best that can be done is to arrive at some kind of compromise between adequate fire control for that to be protected and the funds available. Many studies have been made to determine what constitutes a reasonably adequate level of fire control. Brown and Davis (1973) reveal that most such studies follow a common pattern of (1) a statistical analysis of control costs, fire occurrence, and area burned, (2) estimates of damage, and (3) an attempt to define some justifiable level of control.

The economic objective of fire control is to obtain adequate protection for the least cost. One method of arriving at the total cost of fire control proposed years ago by the Forest Service for any protection agency is the sum of the costs of control plus the damage losses. This is referred to usually as the *least-cost plus-damage* concept. It is based on the assumption that the sum of the costs of prevention, presuppression, suppression, and damage, or $P + P + S + D$ = total fire costs. As the costs of P, P, and S increase it is assumed D will decrease. This least-cost approach also has some problems in that measuring fire damage is difficult. The commercial value of a stand of timber is relatively easy to determine. Evaluations of losses to soil, water, wildlife, and recreation, as mentioned above, are more difficult to make. However, by finding reasonable combinations of P, P, and S, a fire-control agency is provided with a guide for determining expenditures needed to keep D to a minimum.

**Recruiting, Assigning, and Training Personnel** Fire control cannot, of course, be entirely separated from other duties of the administrative and labor forces of any forest enterprise; but, because it is seasonal so far as peak load is concerned, untrained temporary help must often be employed, and new equipment and methods must be mastered yearly by the regular force. First, second, and third lines of defense are provided for. These may consist of the following for most of the public forests at the present time:

**First Line**    "Smokechasers" stationed at lookouts or other points such as ranger stations and logging camp crew houses, and ready to go immediately to nearby fires afoot, by horse, or pickup truck. Special small crews kept at central points with fast vehicles, ready to go, but often temporarily engaged in other work. Smokejumper and helitack crews of variable size, highly trained, well equipped, and strategically located at airfields, are also on standby.

**Second Line**    Road construction crews, logging operation crews, railroad section hands close to the fire, and special labor crews on various types of work for the agency in charge of the forest. May or may not have their own foreman, tools, and supplies. Within a few hours of the fire, and will be supervised by skilled foremen from the forest itself. When labor not available, nearby labor of any kind from farms and towns will be used.

**Third Line**    Unskilled labor, such as employment agencies are able to recruit, or skilled crews from inmate camps, ranches, and neighboring forests. (The trend today is to avoid untrained and unconditioned people when possible.)

As the third line of defense is called in, more and more skilled personnel are required, not only on the fire itself, but to attend to equipping, feeding, and keeping time records of the crews and equipment. Even blacksmith shops, first-aid stations, temporary landing fields, pack-train corrals, and elaborate telephone and radio setups may be required with the attendant overhead force. These things require the work of trained personnel.

Training of everyone who takes part in fire control is customary and essential. Special fire schools are held on or within various units, such as whole national forests or groups of them; ranger districts that are subdivisions of national forests; individual labor camps, logging camps, and construction crews; and even among temporary or recently recruited forest or park rangers, or special patrol personnel for railroads, lumber companies, or recreation enterprises.

Typical programs at these fire schools are filled with coaching, in groups and individually, in the use of particular hand tools, weather instruments, radio and telephone equipment, in map interpretation, compass reading, law-enforcement procedure, general fire-control tactics, dramatization of arrests and court trials, and review of the action on recent and important fires. The stance taken and the way the hands grip the handle in using a shovel are not considered unimportant, nor are the exact precautions to take in preserving evidence of the cause of a fire under stress of first attack. More technical items are also covered. Examples include estimating the perimeter of a going fire and rate at which it will increase, mapping the seen and unseen areas from a given observation point to be used in securing greater detection coverage, reconnoitering terrain or an active fire by means of observation from aircraft, sinking a temporary well, or using special hose and portable pumping equipment from a backpack, pickup truck, or heli-

**Figure 17-4** A Forest Service smokejumper descending toward a forest fire in Montana. Air escaping through the steering slots and three tail lobes gives the jumper maneuverability. *(Courtesy of the U.S. Forest Service.)*

copter. Highly organized schools for "smokejumpers," where fire fighters are trained to parachute onto isolated fires, are maintained and operated by the Forest Service (Fig. 17-4). Special helitack crews are also being trained in western Canada and the United States. These crews are transported by helicopter to near the fire and are rappelled to the ground on 250-ft (75-m) ropes (Fig. 17-5) or jump directly to the ground from low hovering craft.

**Figure 17-5**  Rappelling from a helicopter to the vicinity of a wildfire in British Columbia. *(Courtesy of the International Forest Fire Systems, Ltd., Vancouver, BC.)*

Programs are also underway in the western United States for the training of interagency personnel from land management agencies from Canada, Mexico, and the United States. Sessions are conducted in fire management, fire prevention, fire behavior, fire generalship, and the training of air control officers. The Departments of the Interior and of Agriculture also conduct sessions for "fire overhead teams" which train as a group to supervise project fires.

### The Detection System

To be attacked properly, fires must be discovered promptly. Four means of detecting fires are employed—the fixed-point detectors, moving ground detectors, aerial detectors, and the combined air-ground detector. Each will be treated individually.

**The Fixed-Point Detector** Such a detector is the lookout house or tower, and in some parts of the country remains an important means of discovering fires. Steel towers as high as 100 ft (30 m) from the ground are used in flat or rolling forest country such as the South and the Lake States. Dwelling quarters adapted for observation purposes and elevated or built directly on the surface of prominent points are more frequent in the rugged country of the West (Fig. 17-6).

The location of fires from lookout houses and towers requires accurate maps, oriented and leveled so that a sighting instrument may be used to determine the exact direction of the fire in question. This is done by pivoting a straightedge, with accurately mounted sights, on a pin inserted in the center of the map at the point which corresponds to the actual location of the lookout building. This device, called a fire finder (Fig. 17-7) is rotated until the sights are in line with the fire seen through the lookout windows. The azimuth (arc of the horizon measured clockwise) is then read from a graduated 360° scale, located on the rim of the fire finder. The reading is reported to a dispatcher who plots it on his or her map. If the fire can be seen by other lookouts, it can be more accurately located on the

**Figure 17-6** The lookout house, still an important element in fire detection, is often used in combination with aerial detection. Near Mount Shasta, California. *(Courtesy of the U.S. Forest Service.)*

**Figure 17-7**  A fire lookout locates the position of a fire with a fire-finder alidade in Washington State. *(Courtesy of the U.S. Forest Service.)*

dispatcher's map. The point of intersection of the projected lines of sight from two or more lookouts gives the location of the fire. This method is often referred to as *crosscut*. If only one lookout can see the fire, vertical readings on the fire finder must be taken which give a reasonable estimate of the distance to the fire. The theoretical location is then checked by any means possible, or a smokechaser is dispatched with the best information available. The detector or observer is generally on duty throughout daylight hours. He or she may be a forestry student or a teacher whose vacation comes during the fire season, or a local man or woman if the fire season occurs during school months. Some agencies employ husband and wife teams for their two-person lookouts. When the man goes to a fire or is on his days off, the woman takes over the lookout duties. Such duties, in addition to detecting fires, are to report other information of value to the dispatcher: the size of the fire, the type of fuel in which it is burning, the best way to get there—anything that will aid the dispatcher in knowing how many people to send to the fire and how long it will take them to get there. Lookouts also record observation on weather and lightning storms, and must do what they can to keep their communication facilities in repair.

Lookout duty requires concentration, patience, alertness, good eyesight, accuracy, and devotion to duty under lonely conditions. As soon as possible, the lookout must become familiar with the landmarks around the station, the location of areas of high risk and hazard, and the position of permanent smokes such as sawmills and campgrounds. Additional equipment to help in detection would be binoculars, a haze cutter, goggles, and accurate maps of areas adjacent to the lookout's territory.

**The Moving Ground Detector** The second means of detection is the moving ground detector—a person in a car or truck or on foot, who patrols areas of high risk or hazard, or areas not visible from the fixed lookout. Such patrols take place mostly during periods when the danger of wildfire is high. Before the days of two-way radio, the moving detector method had several weaknesses. Reporting fires quickly was a problem and, being out of touch with the dispatcher, the person on patrol could not be sent on fires discovered by others. The two-way radio has made the roving fire patrol more efficient.

**Aerial Detectors** Aerial discovery of wildfires, the third means of detection, is almost as old as airplanes, and its overall use in detecting, reconnaissance of fires, and in directing ground attacks continues to grow in importance. (Uses other than the detection of fires will be discussed later in this chapter.) The area to be covered by most lookout systems usually contains several blind spots. During the fire season there often are periods when the fire danger is low and the lookout person is not really needed. By using aircraft, nearly all the area can be observed and the observations need be made only during periods of high fire danger. A smoke detected by aircraft can be scouted from close range. Fuel types, natural barriers, access routes, and information concerning the fire itself can be determined quite easily from aircraft. Aerial detection is gradually replacing fixed-point detectors. For example, in the Northern Region of the Forest Service (Montana, Idaho, and eastern Washington) in the 1930s, nearly 2,000 lookout towers were in operation. In 1973 only 132 were still being used, the detection being taken over by spotter planes.

The exclusive use of aerial detection has some disadvantages. Poor flying conditions may render the aerial detection system inoperative. There can be little coverage at night since night flying is not safe. Also, because it is not economical to maintain a staff of pilots, much of the flying is contracted, and an experienced pilot is not always available on short notice. For these reasons it is highly improbable that aerial detection will ever completely replace the ground detector.

**The Air-Ground Detection System** The Forest Service and various states have developed a combination air-ground detection system for areas under their jurisdiction. A few lookouts are located over a broad area, often near places having a high incidence of fires. One of the functions of the lookout in the air-ground combination is to make the weather observation used in forecasting fire danger which determines when aircraft are needed. Tracking paths of lightning storms which will establish fire search routes for air patrols is another important function for the lookout. Also, when a distant fire is reported by a ground detector, a plane can be sent to make a more detailed inspection. Since each part of this system overcomes inadequacies of the other, and because it gives a less expensive coverage over a greater area, the combination air-ground detection system will probably see wider use in the future.

### Other Presuppression Activities

**Communication**  It does little good for an observer to spot a fire if it cannot be reported to those concerned with putting it out. This calls for some dependable means of rapid communication, which as a rule is an independent telephone system or radio.

Telephones are an oddity today in fire lookouts, as most of them have been replaced with the two-way AM or FM radio. In fact, the radio has proved to be so effective that almost all federal, state, and private fire-control organizations use it not only for detection but in general administrative communication as well. Both aerial and ground detectors are dependent on the two-way radio. Needless to say, their radio equipment must be on the same frequency as that used by the local fire-control system.

Commercial telephone facilities are of course heavily relied upon for outside communication, especially when additional forces are required. The sign "Report Fires Here" so often seen along remote forested highways is an invitation to the traveler who has recently seen a fire to report it immediately to the local warden.

**Reporting the Fire**  The period between the time when the fire was ignited and when it was first seen is called the *discovery time*. The period between its discovery and report is known as the *report time*. The less time taken for each, the sooner the dispatcher can take steps to get a suppression crew or inspection plane to the fire.

**The Dispatcher**  This important individual in the fire organization may be an experienced clerk in the main office of a logging company, or a ranger in a state or national forest or national park, or a specially trained person at a logging camp or supply depot. When a fire is reported there is plenty of systematic hustling. The dispatcher tries to get an estimate of the perimeter of the fire, its "rate of spread," the type of fuel in which the fire is burning so that he or she will know its "resistance to control" (see page 351), the presence or absence of water for fire-fighting purposes, and all other factors which will aid in determining the strength necessary for the initial attack force.

**Transportation to the Fire**  The dispatcher, of course, does not go to the fire, but sends someone else. Once again quick action is necessary. The people going to the fire have two periods of time against which they are working. From the time the crew is notified until it starts, there is a period called *getaway time*. Many things can delay the crew unless it is ready, correctly directed, efficiently outfitted with equipment, and provided with adequate transportation. The period from the time the crew leaves until it reaches the fire is known as *travel time*. To avoid delays enroute to the fire, a systematic study of the road and trail system would be an essential presuppression activity. Maps should be prepared which indicate the travel time, based on safe speeds for vehicles, to various points. It may be necessary to provide more travel routes if the present system is not reasonably adequate. In some inaccessible areas of western United States, the initial attack comes from smoke jumpers or helitack crews.

**Service of Supply**   Tools, provisions, bedding, gasoline, and radio equipment are needed in quantity during busy fire seasons. The equipment plan, another presuppression task, would show the kinds and numbers of tools and equipment available at both large and small depots, as well as caches located at strategic points. Advanced plans must be made for services such as air drops which might be needed for big fires.

**Tools and Equipment**   The type of tools and power equipment needed on a fire depends mainly on such things as the character of fuel, topography, soils, availability of water, and accessibility of the fire. Even with bulldozers, power saws, water pumps, and aircraft, few wildfires are fought without some hand tools (Fig. 17-8). In fact, many wildfires can be con-

**Figure 17-8**   Fighting a wildfire with Pulaskis and shovels in California. *(Courtesy of the U.S. Forest Service.)*

trolled by a few people with simple tools if they arrive when the fire is reasonably small. Hand tools differ with regions because that which is an effective tool in one area may be useless in another. They all must have essentially the same qualities, however. For example hand tools must be easy to carry, simple to operate, efficient, versatile, and easily repaired or replaced. Some of the more widely used hand tools include the ax, shovel, Pulaski (a combined cutting and digging tool), grub hoe, council tool (a four-toothed rake), brush cutter, swatter, fire rake, and saw (crosscut or chain saw). Because the uses and needs of tools differ so greatly, even on a single fire, a few of each appropriate type are issued to a fire crew who usually work the tools in small groups. For example, a dozen people might work along a fireline in this order: two brush cutters, two people with axes, one with a saw, four with shovels, and two with grub hoes, and possibly a back pump can operator. The order would of course depend on the conditions of soil, fuel type, number of people, size of fire, and type of attack.

Because fighting fire by hand is expensive as well as unpopular, fire-control agencies are continuously looking for ways to fight fire with power equipment. The versatility of the bulldozer makes it the most effective piece of ground equipment in use in the forests today (Fig. 17-9). Other power tools, used mostly in construction of fireline, include tractor-drawn plows

**Figure 17-9** Building a fireline with a bulldozer, one of the most versatile pieces of heavy ground equipment used in fire-fighting. *(Courtesy of the Caterpillar Tractor Company.)*

and rotary trenchers. Pumping units, usually on pickup trucks, are used mostly in extinguishing fires, although they have been used to wet down fuel in order to make a temporary fireline. The use of aircraft will be discussed later in the chapter.

**Interpreting Weather and Other Factors of Fire Danger**   Another presuppression activity is the measurement of conditions which affect *fire danger*.[3] Temperature, relative humidity, the direction and velocity of wind, the moisture content of the fuel, the number of days since the last precipitation, the amount of precipitation, the condition of the vegetation, and the clearness or cloudiness of the day must be recorded and interpreted. This work continues throughout the fire season and serves to forecast severe fire conditions, to warn travelers and woods workers, to expand the first line of defense, intensify patrols, restrict burning permits, and to indicate the necessity of closing some areas to entry. These are all prevention or presuppression activities, which may be expanded when fire breaks out.

An outgrowth in the study of those environmental factors which control the moisture content of fuels, now in use in the United States, is the National Fire-Danger Rating System (Deeming et al., 1974). An abstract on this new approach to a nationwide method of rating fire danger follows:

The National Fire-Danger Rating (NFDR) System produces three indexes—OCCURRENCE, BURNING, and FIRE LOAD—that measure relative fire potentials. These indexes are derived from the fire behavior components—SPREAD, ENERGY RELEASE, and IGNITION—plus a consideration of RISK.

Three innovations in fire-danger rating are introduced in the NFDR System. First, it is solidly based on the physics of fire behavior—it is not empirical or statistical. Second, it makes use of the fuel model, an open-ended means of treating the myriad of naturally occurring fuel situations. Third, the system is designed so that improvements can be incorporated with a minimum of impact on the users.

FUEL MOISTURE, WIND and RISK are the principal variables accounting for the day-to-day fluctuations of fire danger. In the NFDR System, three classes of dead fuels and two of live fuels are recognized. Rainfall duration is the best predictor of the effect of rainfall on the moisture content of dead fuels. Very important, also, is the time fuels are exposed to solar radiation (sunshine).

Nine fuel models are introduced; each represents a broad grouping of fuel types with common characteristics. These characteristics, when evaluated, are the numerical fuel inputs required to solve the mathematical equations

---

[3] Fire danger is defined as "the resultant of both constant and variable fire danger factors, which affect the inception, spread, and difficulty of control of fires and damage they cause" (*Fireman's Handbook*, Forest Service, 1966).

which yield the SPREAD and ENERGY RELEASE components. The number of fuel models can be increased to provide the resolution necessary to meet the future needs of fire management organizations.

RISK is evaluated for lightning and man-caused fires. Both evaluations are subjective, but the schemes presented are considered adequate until more objective approaches can be developed.

**Obtaining Cooperation**   Various neighbors of the agency in control of any forest needing protection will have staff, supplies, transportation equipment, or money. Also, their interest in fire control will resemble and sometimes overlap that of the area concerned. A water utility in a valley, which depends on the steady flow of a stream which gets its start in the forest, will frequently contribute personnel, supplies, or money in case of need. A resort whose guests travel through the forest may be willing to assist in maintaining a telephone line. A mining company that purchases timber from the forest will transport fire fighters on its railroad. The county whose citizens enjoy a recreation area in the forest will be willing to maintain a section of a forest highway important in fire control. A logging company with several large bulldozers will place them at the disposal of the fire-control agency. Such cooperation is effective only if definitely agreed upon and coordinated. Obtaining this agreement and working it into the fire-control plan is a part of presuppression.

## SUPPRESSION OF WILDFIRES

**Fighting the Fire**   Let us assume a wildfire has been detected, reported, and a crew dispatched to suppress it. The character, volume, arrangement, and condition of the vegetative cover and other fuels such as dry dead wood, plus the slope, the wind or local draft, and the volume of heat, will determine what kind of fire there is to fight. It may be a *surface fire* which is consuming the loose debris and smaller vegetation on top of the ground. Possibly it has eaten its way along a pitchy root or through an animal burrow onto the organic materials below the surface of the forest floor. This may occur easily and quickly in a dried-out swamp, and the result is a *ground fire*, which is more difficult to extinguish. If the wind is high and the crowns of the trees are low or the trunks are covered with dead vines or moss, the fire is likely to rise to the branches and foliage of the forest, and then a *crown fire* occurs.

Most wildfires start as surface fires and these are the most common of the three kinds. A fire in the crowns of trees is not necessarily a true crown fire until its forward spread is outrunning and is independent of the surface fire. Embers from the crown fire may fall and start new surface fires, which in turn might develop into an obstinate ground fire. Ground fires have been known to spring into surface fires which soon rise to become crown fires.

From this it is seen that the three are closely related and all may be occurring at the same time.

These three classes are based on the vertical location and the behavior of a fire. Unfortunately, there is usually horizontal advance in two or more directions, or spread along a slope on which the fire creates its own draft. In a relatively flat area, a fire is likely to spread fanwise ahead of the wind from the point of origin; and it may burn into radiating fingers or strips, or develop, through embers blown ahead, into several separate fires, called *spot fires*. Fires will travel faster in some fuels than in other fuels. Light flashy fuels such as grasses, leaves, and fine brush will ignite easily, permitting fire to travel through them rapidly. The heavier fuels such as large limbs and logs burn more intensely, but the transfer of heat is slower; thus the fire spread is slower. The speed with which a fire moves through fuel is called the *rate of spread*. Similarly, fuels may affect the ease or difficulty of building a fireline or other means of fighting the fire, and this degree of difficulty is known as the *resistance to control*.

Methods of extinguishing fires are all based on the theory of removing any one of the sides of the so-called fire triangle: fuel, temperature, and oxygen. The fire is robbed of its fuel by raking or digging a cleared line which breaks the fuel continuity, or by making the fuels nonflammable by applying chemicals, dirt, or water. Temperature is reduced through the cooling effect of water, dirt, or chemicals being thrown on the fire. Oxygen is eliminated by smothering the fire with these same three materials.

Four methods of fighting wildfires without water are quite generally recognized. When the actual burning or smoldering edge of the fire can be worked safely, it is scraped, pushed, dug out and shoveled in, or "spanked" out. A real "spanker" or wide, flat piece of belting on a sturdy handle is needed for the latter trick, which works fairly well in light grass or thin litter of needles. Extinguishing the actual fire at its advancing edge is called the *direct method* and is used whenever it is possible to do so safely. Raking a line clear of all fuel, a foot or two ahead of the flaming edge of the fire, and allowing it to burn up to the line is known as the *two-foot method*. Should it be impossible to work so near the fire, a cleared line is constructed from 10 to 50 ft (3 to 15 m) ahead of, and roughly parallel to, the edge of the advancing fire, and the intervening strip is burned out. This is called the *parallel method*. It is occasionally used with weak crown fires that are not too unruly and quiet down at night. On fires that are crowning badly or advancing through slash, down timber, or other fuel where a great volume of heat is generated, there is no choice but to fall back for a safe distance to a ridge, or stream, rockslide, or plowed area and construct a line, if necessary, joining two or more of the previously mentioned natural barriers, and then backfire the area between the line and the advancing fire. This is the *indirect method*. It must frequently be used where a dense forest of pole size is afire, and crowning is to be expected, even at night.

Line construction (with appropriate environmental considerations being taken) is done by any means available, by hand, plows, or bulldozer. Water is used for mopping up and for cooling down fires. In organizing for handling a large fire, one person is given authority, the line is divided into sectors, and a sector boss for each is given a small crew and made responsible for that sector. Definite shifts with their own foremen are arranged. Of course reconnoitering has preceded this division, and constant vigilance on the progress or change of the fire is obtained by periodic reconnoitering by the chief or the assistants, or by aircraft equipped with two-way radios or loudspeakers.

Attack at the front is invariably made on small fires. However, in handling those which are not likely to crown or to endanger workers assigned to the uphill side, the attack is made on each flank of the rear, and an attempt is made to pinch them out at the head when advantage can be taken of some natural feature or change of wind. It is good business on small fires to use large crews for extinguishing them promptly. Delay may result in real damage. Extra-period fires are those which continue to burn after the temperature rise of the second day, referred to as the 10 A.M. policy. (Control the fire by then, or make new provisions for controlling the fire by the next 10 A.M.) *Control time* is the duration of the fight up to the point where assurance of victory is reached. After the fire is contained, the duties of patrol, falling of burning snags, extinguishing other burning material within the boundaries of the fire, and making breakovers impossible are the tedious duties called *mopping up*.

On all large fires, patrol is maintained for several days after the fire is apparently completely out. This practice is dictated by the many fires which "got away" in former years when personnel, money, and equipment were insufficient to afford even a single patrolman, or when faith in sketchy fire-fighting was too great.

**Trends in Fire Control**  Because of a greater area under protection and the continuing research in the various phases of fire prevention, detection, and suppression, the trend in the number of forest fires in the United States and Canada is downward. A larger application of power equipment, use of aerial photographs for fuel analysis, the development of more efficient detecting and dispatching procedures, a more elaborate network of fire roads and trails, the more rigorous training of all fire-control personnel, and greater use of water and chemicals have contributed to a reduction in both numbers and size of fires. Studies correlating abnormal atmospheric conditions with the behavior of large fires of the past have told us much about the blowup conditions existing at the time of these fires. Such studies help in predicting when these conditions will again prevail. It is conceivable that television, radar, or heat-sensitive alarms may be employed as means of detecting fires of the future.

One of the greatest developments in fire control since World War II is the extensive use of aircraft. Their use in detection, reconnaissance, and ferrying personnel to fires has already been mentioned. Air drops of food and supplies have been standard procedure for many years. Drops of larger pieces of equipment such as lightweight bulldozers, jeeps, and fire plows are reaching some degree of perfection. The dropping of water bombs and chemical retardants has proved so effective that the use of fixed-wing air tankers or helicopters has become standard procedure in some forest regions (Fig. 17-10). There are several ammonium phosphates which make effective air-dropped chemical retardants. The solution is dyed for visibility, thickened to improve coating, and treated with a wetting agent to permit greater penetration into fuels, and serves to cool or smother a fire, or fireproofs the fuel before it is reached by the fire.

Helicopters have many advantages over fixed-wing aircraft. By virtue of their ability to land and take off vertically, thus eliminating landing strips, helicopters can ferry equipment and personnel directly to the fire's perimeter. Picking up smokejumpers or injured fire fighters is another effective use.

The use of thermal infrared imagery, where heat shows up on a pho-

**Figure 17-10** Aerial suppression of a forest fire on the Wenatchee National Forest in Washington State. *(Courtesy of the U.S. Forest Service.)*

tograph, is a useful tool in fire detection. It is particularly helpful in pin-pointing fire in mop-up operations, once control lines have been established. One advantage of flying and photographing a contained fire with infrared imagery is that the photo reveals the extent of the hot spots and aids in determining how large a crew should be retained for mopping up. Signals from orbiting satellites are being used to give very early indications of fire outbreaks. This technique is particularly useful in locating fires started from dry lightning storms.

For a thorough coverage of wildfire protection the reader is referred to the Bibliography, especially the text by Brown and Davis, 1973.

## BIBLIOGRAPHY

Barrows, Jack S. 1973. Forest Fire Management: For Ecology and People, *Fire Management*, vol 39, no. 3, U. S. Department of Agriculture.

Brackebusch, Arthur P. 1973. Fuel Management: A Prerequisite, Not an Alternative to Fire Control, *Jour. Forestry*, **71**:637–639.

Brown, Arthur A., and Kenneth P. Davis. 1973. *Forest Fire: Control and Use*, 2d ed., McGraw-Hill Book Company, New York.

Craig, James B. 1975. Herding Fires, *Amer. Forests*, **81**:39, 50–51.

Crocker, C. S. 1949. Fighting Fires from the Air, *Trees*, Yearbook of Agriculture, U. S. Department of Agriculture.

Crow, A. B. 1973. Use of Fire in Southern Forests, *Jour. Forestry*, **71**:629–632.

Daniels, Jonathan. 1957. *The Forest Is the Future*, International Paper Company, New York.

Davis, M. H. 1954. Maintaining an Effective Organization to Control the Occasional Large Fire, *Jour. Forestry*, **52**:750–755.

Deeming, John E., J. W. Lancaster, M. A. Fosberg, R. M. Furman, and M. J. Schroeder. 1974. The National Fire-Danger Rating System, U. S. Department of Agriculture Forest Service Research Paper RM-84, Fort Collins, CO.

Harris, H. K. 1955. Helicopter Use: Fire Suppression, *Fire Control Notes*, **15**(2):7–12.

Hartman, A. W. 1949. Fire as a Tool in Southern Pine, *Trees*, Yearbook of Agriculture, U. S. Department of Agriculture.

——— 1949. Machines and Fires in the South, *Trees*, Yearbook of Agriculture, U. S. Department of Agriculture.

Hays, G. L. 1949. Forest Fire Danger, *Trees*, Yearbook of Agriculture, U. S. Department of Agriculture.

Jayaweera, K. O. L. F., and Kristina Ahlnas. 1974. Detection of Thunderstorms from Satellite Imagery for Forest Fire Control, *Jour. Forestry*, **72**:767–770.

Kimmey, J. W. 1955. Rate of Deterioration of Fire-killed Timber in California, U. S. Department of Agriculture Circular 962.

McGuire, John R. 1975. Fire as a Force in Land Use Planning, *Amer. Forests*, **81**:36–38.

Mobley, Hugh E. 1974. Fire: Its Impact on the Environment, *Jour. Forestry*, **72**:414–417.

Neuns, A. G. 1950. Water vs. Fire: Fighting Forest Fires with Water, U. S. Forest Service, California Forest and Range Experiment Station, Berkeley, CA.

NFPA. 1966. *Air Operations for Forest Bush and Grass Fires*, National Fire Protection Association, Boston, MA.

Peirce,  E. S., and C. A. Gustafson. 1949. Building a Fire Organization, *Trees*, Yearbook of Agriculture, U. S. Department of Agriculture.

Rothermel, Richard C., and Charles W. Philpot. 1973. Predicting Changes in Chaparral Flammability, *Jour. Forestry*, **71**:640–643.

Schaefer, V. J. 1957. The Relationship of Jet Streams to Forest Wildfire, *Jour. Forestry*, **55**:419–425.

Sutherland, Charles F., Jr. 1973. Cost of Forest Closure in Two Oregon Counties, *Jour. Forestry*, **71**:644–647.

Tyler, J., and C. H. Lewis. 1953. Air Patrol for Better Detection and Protection in the South, *Jour. Forestry*, **51**:444–446.

U. S. Department of Agriculture, Forest Service. 1956. *Glossary of Terms Used in Forest Fire Control*, U. S. Department of Agriculture Handbook 104.

———. 1970. *Smokey's Record.*

———. 1970, 1971, 1972, 1973. *Wildfire Statistics.*

Chapter 18

# Insects and Mammals

Chapter 17 was concerned with wildfire and its managament. In Chaps. 18 and 19 we shall find that there are other factors capable of destroying entire forests. This chapter deals with the zoological phase of forest destroyers: the insects and mammals.

## INSECTS

More than one scientist has speculated on the eventual chances for the human race to maintain itself on the earth against the insects. Food supplies, shelter materials (including even buildings themselves), clothing materials before and after fabrication, and even the bodies of beasts of burden, meat animals, and of humans are considered to be legitimate and fruitful fields of conquest by these small but numerous animals. One shudders, after an experience with blackflies or mosquitoes, to think what would happen if all natural and artificial controls were abandoned.

We should not forget that some insects are beneficial, even to the forests. Many prey on other insects, some are scavengers that feed on organic remains, and still others are pollinators of flowering trees and smaller plants. Unfortunately many insects feed on healthy trees, although even this may not be destructive to the tree. Under normal conditions the leaf-eating insects, for example, can find ample food yet render the tree little harm. Foresters are not concerned with such minor damages. They must act when the insects increase to the point where their depredations are killing trees and affecting the health of the forest as a whole.

### Timber Losses from Insect Damage

Although fire is potentially the greatest enemy of our forests, insects destroy more timber each year in the United States than any other single factor. The assistant chief of the Forest Service once said:

> Any way you look at it, the forest insect is a serious threat to be reckoned with. It can cripple trees, it can kill trees, it can stunt growth. Sometimes in a few months it can snuff the life out of a forest that has taken perhaps three hundred years to grow; and with its aftermath of fire, it can destroy soil that was a thousand years in the making. It can help trigger floods, it can help destroy wildlife and make the habitat untenable to certain wildlife for years. It can help pollute the streams and lakes with silt and ash, much to the detriment of the fish life therein. (Swingler, 1959)

Actual losses of timber from insect depredations run into billions of board feet each year. Some reports of insect epidemics for various areas and years might help to illustrate this: Annual losses due to insects from 1925 to 1936 in national forests of California reached 895 million board feet (Salman, 1937). Spruce budworm in Quebec between 1910 and 1920 destroyed 200 million cords of balsam fir. Larch sawfly in Minnesota between 1910 and 1926 destroyed 1 billion board feet of tamarack. Damage by larch sawfly to Eastern forests each year is approximately 400 million board feet (Graham and Knight, 1965). Between 1942 and 1948 the Engelmann spruce beetle destroyed 4 billion board feet of standing timber in the Colorado Rockies (Wygant and Nelson, 1949). A beetle epidemic occurred in 3 million acres (1.26 million ha) of timber in western Oregon and southern Washington in 1951. Insects destroyed 5 billion board feet of timber in the United States in 1952 (Crafts, 1958). In the 5 years following 1954, the balsam wooly aphid spread to 600,000 acres (0.24 million ha) of federal, private, and state forest lands in the Pacific Northwest. Montana's Christmas tree industry suffered economic loss of $450,000 in 1957 because of spruce budworm. *Ips* engraver killed 1 million board feet per month of southern yellow pine in east Texas during part of 1958 (Swingler, 1959), and in 1962, in the same region, the southern pine beetle killed over 93 million board feet of pine (Coulson et al. 1972). Insects kill enough timber each year in the United States to build 600,000 five-room houses (Baker, 1959).

These statements could have been headlines in a city newspaper, but few of them were. Insect populations build up quietly, without the spectacular smoke and blaze and loss of human life that accompany major fires. An insect epidemic can reach its peak unnoticed, and then it may be too late. Insects use clever strategy in their warfare on forests. This taxes the knowledge and ingenuity of forest managers to such an extent that they lean heavily on the forest entomologist, who may be a graduate forester but often has advanced training in the study and control of forest insects. The entomologist's task and the forester's, for they work together, is not merely one of spraying, dusting, shielding—methods such as are employed in one's garden—but of seeking out and plotting the strategic use of the particular insect's natural enemies and environmental problems, starving it out, or trapping and destroying it outright.

### Insect Populations

The forest has always been the natural home of thousands of species of insects. Fortunately, not all of them are destructive insects, and those that are tree damagers or destroyers are usually held in check by their natural enemies or an unfavorable environment. The population of a destructive insect is said to be in an *endemic* stage if it is present in normal numbers and is doing little or no damage to trees. According to Graham and Knight (1965), when the insect population reaches the point where annual losses of the forest exceed annual growth, the insect reaches *epidemic* proportions. This ability of an insect to multiply in the absence of any control is termed the *reproductive potential*. The potential of insect progeny is fantastic. Take, for example, an insect species which has a very high ratio of females to the total population of that species. If each female lays 100 female eggs, then the progeny of just two females could hypothetically reach 2 trillion individuals in only six generations. The force which works against the insects' reaching such proportions is called the *environmental resistance*. Food, competition, parasites, predators, unfavorable temperatures, light, moisture, tree vigor, and climate and weather are all factors of environmental resistance. If nature failed to maintain insects in some sort of balance through these factors, the forests would never reach maturity. Should the resistance factors for a particular insect become appreciably lowered, this balance is temporarily upset. Relieved of whatever was holding its numbers down, the population literally explodes and an *outbreak* is said to occur. If the outbreak increases in destructiveness, then the forest manager is faced with the epidemic mentioned above.

**Classes of Forest Insects**  The forest manager does not have time nor is it necessary to learn the names of all the insects in the forest. In the care of the forest the manager must, however, become familiar with the general groups of insects and should be able to recognize the characteristic damage of the various kinds. The forester must recognize the comparatively few species that are potentially destructive.

The insects most important to forestry are included in the following seven groups:

| Name | Order | Wing characteristics |
|------|-------|----------------------|
| Beetles | Coleoptera | Hard first pair of wings |
| Butterflies/moths | Lepidoptera | Scales on the wings |
| Wasps | Hymenoptera | Four membranous wings |
| Flies | Diptera | Only one pair of wings |
| Scales/aphids | Homoptera | Wings held "tentlike" over back |
| Bugs | Hemiptera | Half of front wings hard |
| Termites | Isoptera | All wings are same length |

Adult insects can be distinguished from other small animals by their jointed bodies consisting of three parts—the head, the thorax, and the abdomen; by the fact that adults generally are winged, and have a single pair of antennae and three pairs of legs. Forest managers have no trouble recognizing the adult, but unfortunately they most frequently encounter the insect in some phase of its life cycle other than the adult. The beetles, butterflies and moths, wasps, and flies pass through four stages of development, therefore undergoing *complete metamorphosis*. These four stages are egg, larva (the growing stage), pupa (resting stage), and adult. The larvae of some beetles are called grubs; those of butterflies and moths are caterpillars; those of flies are called maggots; and the larvae of the wasps are grubs, or caterpillar-like. Scale insects, aphids, bugs, and termites undergo only three stages—the egg, nymph, and the adult, and have a life cycle that is called *gradual metamorphosis*. Here growth takes place in the nymph stage, during which time the juvenile is similar to but smaller than the adult.

The forest is the home of many potentially destructive insects which differ widely in the kind and amount of damage they inflict and in the period of their life cycle in which they do the damage. Some attack trees only when in their larval stage; others do their destructive work as adults. Some insects attack only flowers; others, cones, buds, or leaves; still others damage only the trunk of the tree. Insects may be classified in several ways; but the most practical grouping, at least from the forest manager's standpoint, is the following method based on the manner in which insects do their damage:

**1　Sucking Insects**　Attack foliage and stems; equipped with sucking mouth parts which pierce tissues and suck fluid from the tree; mostly aphids and scales. Seldom kill the tree but may weaken it and slow its growth. The balsam wooly aphid, deadly to true firs, is an exception.

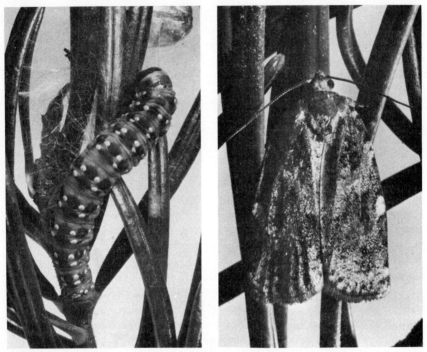

**Figure 18-1** The spruce budworm, a serious insect pest. *Left,* the nearly full grown larvae. It is this stage of the insect's life cycle against which aerial spraying is directed. *Right,* the newly emerged adult. *(Courtesy of the U.S. Forest Service.)*

    **2**  *Defoliators*  These are the needle and leaf eaters (Fig. 18-1); most damage is caused by larvae of certain moths and sawflies (Hymenoptera), some by adults and larvae of beetles; all are chewing insects. They strip the tree of its leaves and food manufacture stops; the tree becomes weakened and may die if defoliation continues.

    **3**  *Bark Beetles*  Insects with chewing mouth parts which attack the trunk and larger branches; larvae and adults, belonging to the Scolytidae, burrow into the phloem "engraving" (mining and eating) the soft tissue. Tree killed by girdling effect of engraving, and by introduced blue stain fungi.

    **4**  *Wood Borers*  Insects with chewing mouth parts which burrow in the sapwood and heartwood; mostly larvae of beetles (flat-headed and round-headed borers). Seldom kill the tree but ruin it for lumber or other manufactured wood products; bark openings permit entrance of fungi. Some insects attack dry wood (termites and powder-post beetles).

    **5**  *Terminal Feeders*  A group which feeds in the terminal growth of twigs, buds, and shoots; usually the larvae of moths and beetles. Causes tree deformity such as forking which affects the value of timber. Kills the tree only when tip damage is repeated.

**6  Root Feeders**  Insects which attack roots of small trees; some eat the roots, others only the bark; mostly beetle larvae called "white grubs," some weevils, also wireworms (click beetle larvae). Most serious to seedlings.

**7  Gall Makers**  Insects which produce conspicuous galls on leaves, twigs, limbs, and trunk; mostly wasps, mites, aphids, gnats, midges, and others. Rarely kill the tree but cause deformity, however the balsam wooly aphid also fits this group.

**8  Seed Insects**  Insects which deposit eggs within developing cones, where the larva feed unnoticed, destroying the seeds or nuts; mostly wasp-like insects (chalcids), larvae of small moths, and beetles (scolytids).

### Methods of Controlling Forest Insects

There are several methods for reducing the damage that insects may inflict on a forest. For example, in Chap. 13 we discussed sanitation and other types of silvicultural cuttings. These harvests remove the overmature, diseased, wind-thrown, lightning- or fire-killed trees and other defective timber. Though this removal may serve other purposes, it also destroys the insect's host material and breeding grounds. Such trees have little or no defense against insects and are a factor in building up insect populations, which spread to healthy timber. Generally, the healthier the forest, the more resistant it is to insect attack. A forest with mixed-age classes and species is considered more resistant to insect attack, especially the disastrous outbreaks, than is an even-aged or pure forest. Selective cuttings of susceptible trees, thinnings that accelerate growth, and other similar long-range forest management practices that help to make a "bug-proof" forest are termed methods of *indirect control*.

**Direct Control**  Another approach to reducing insect numbers is that of *direct control*. Dying trees often contain millions of insect larvae which, if allowed to emerge as adults, will spread to living trees. Effective direct controls include (1) trapping the insects by various methods, (2) piling and burning slash after logging, (3) felling and removing infested trees, (4) dunking them in a millpond, if one is available, (5) debarking the logs and exposing the larvae to the sun, (6) burning the peeled bark, (7) piling the logs and burning or spraying them with insecticides, (8) spraying the standing trees from the ground with toxic chemicals, (9) spraying from above with low-flying aircraft. These methods differ in their effectiveness and each has certain advantages and disadvantages, but all methods of direct control are expensive. Costs vary from $1 to $5 per tree, depending on the character of the infestation, species of insects (and tree) involved, and the

**Figure 18-2** Aerial spraying by helicopter to the Douglas-fir tussock moth in north-eastern Oregon. *(Courtesy of the U.S. Forest Service.)*

method used. The cost of treating large individual trees, such as sugar pine, can go as high as $20 per tree.

Many new insecticides have been developed in recent years. Power and hand spraying of the bark of infested trees with a toxic chemical such as BHC (benzene hexachloride) which acts both as a contact insecticide as well as a stomach poison, proved effective. Forest entomologists estimate that for each infested tree treated, attacks on two or more other trees will be prevented (Benedict, 1959).

DDT and other newer synthetic insecticides such as Zectran have been used in many of the large-scale aerial spraying projects undertaken since World War II. Aircraft flying from treetop level to several hundred feet above the trees (Fig. 18-2) can be credited with saving millions of acres of both private and public forests in the United States and Canada. One such project in 1974 serves to illustrate the effectiveness of aerial spraying.[1] Federal, state, and industrial forestry groups cooperated to combat a severe tussock moth outbreak on ½ million acres (202,000 ha) of public and private timber holdings in eastern Oregon and Washington. Walla Walla,

[1] DDT is permitted under special circumstances for large-scale aerial spraying only when permission is granted by the Federal Environmental Protection Agency.

Washington, was designated as the central mixing station (batch plant) where the insecticide DDT and its diluent were prepared in huge quantities. The prepared formulations then were trucked to holding tanks established at tussock moth control units. Tank trucks carried the spray material from the control units to nearby heliports and loaded it into the spray helicopters.

The spray consisted of ¾ lb (0.089 kg/l) of DDT mixed with a gallon of diesel oil at a cost of $1.00 per gal ($0.26/l). A total of 434,154 gal (1,649,000 l) of insecticide was sprayed over 433,000 acres (175,000 ha) at a cost of $6.00 to $7.00 per acre ($15 to $17/ha). This cost included chase planes which continually monitored the operation. In all, 630 helicopter-hours and 2,104 monitor-plane-hours were involved in the tussock moth operation. A system of checking the amount of spray and kill (100 percent effective in the treated area) was established, using oil-sensitive cards for the insecticide and larval counts/1,000 sq in. (6,540 cm²) of foliage to determine the percentage of control.

The above example is but one of many aerial operations, some of which were much larger, that have been used effectively against such defoliators as the Douglas-fir tussock moth, spruce budworm, and hemlock looper. Aerial spraying is not intended to be a cure-all for the control of foliage-feeding insects but certainly its application has reduced the annual loss due to defoliators by millions of dollars.

Care must be taken in the use of insecticides, both in the strength of the preparation and in their use near water in order to prevent injury to fish and other wildlife.

**Biological Control**   Another means of reducing insect populations is the rearing of a natural predator, or parasite, of the harmful insect. Fungi, bacteria, viruses, and even other insects are used in *biological control* as it is called. Parasitic and predatory insects proved to be very efficient and have been transported from one part of North America to another with success. Carabid beetles, for example, have been released for the purpose of reducing gypsy moth populations. Several foreign insects have been accidentally introduced into North America and have become our most serious pests. With no natural enemies to control them, they have spread rapidly. Their natural enemies from home have been brought over for control purposes with some success. The idea is sound but difficulties of rearing suitable numbers, providing sufficient food in the laboratory, and keeping them in supply are problems which need further exploration. There are many harmful insects that fortunately have not yet gained access to the forests of North America; but the chances of their eventual entry are depressingly good, and biological control probably will be used to control these unwanted visitors.

## The Application of Direct Control Methods

Earlier in the chapter, the general categories of tree-destroying insects were mentioned briefly. Controls of each category will now be discussed.

**Sucking Insects** The sap sucking insects of importance include certain aphids (Fig. 18-3), scales, true bugs, and cicadas. Control with stomach poisons is difficult because their sucking parts extend into the plant tissues, beyond the reach of the poison. The contact or systemic poisons are the most effective. Damage to forests from sucking insects generally is not serious and controls are seldom needed, the balsam wooly aphid being an exception. Moreover, due to the immense biotic potential of this insect, no direct control method is applicable. Control of the less serious sucking insects sometimes is needed on ornamentals and shade trees. Many of the newer organic phosphate and carbamate insecticides are effective, but extreme care in their use is mandatory. Other sprays in use are lime sulfur and miscible oils: application is recommended during the tree's dormant season.

**Defoliators** Thousands of forest insect species feed on the needles and leaves of trees. The most injurious ones are the caterpillars of moths and butterflies, some sawfly larvae, and a few beetles. Equipped with chewing mouth parts, they can mine down the center of the needles, skeletonize

**Figure 18-3** The aphid is one of several sucking insects found in North America. Control of the aphid is difficult because of its enormous reproductive potential, due to its ability to reproduce asexually. *(Photo by Ed Holsten.)*

the leaves by eating the chlorophyll-containing tissue and leaving the veins, or consume the entire leaf. They can defoliate not only one or two trees but an entire forest. This and the next classification, the bark beetles constitute the two most damaging insect groups. Deciduous trees can usually stand as many as three successive years of complete defoliation without serious harm; evergreens on the other hand will often die after one complete defoliation. The more vigorous trees, of course, have a better chance for recovery than the weakened ones.

The most harmful members of the group, those capable of defoliating many hundred thousand acres of timberland a year, are:

**1** The spruce budworm; attacks all true firs of North America as well as Douglas-fir, but will defoliate any conifer in its path.
**2** The Douglas-fir tussock moth; Douglas-fir and the true firs are its favorite hosts.
**3** The pine butterfly; ponderosa, western white, and lodgepole pine appear to be most susceptible.
**4** The hemlock looper; destructive to hemlock, spruce, and balsam fir in the Northeast; western hemlock first, then any coniferous associates will be attacked.
**5** The gypsy moth; attacks eastern hardwoods. The larch sawfly; attacks eastern larch (tamarack). Both insects were accidentally introduced from Europe.
**6** The tent caterpillar; this ubiquitous pest defoliates many different species of trees across North America (Fig. 18-4).
**7** The pine sawfly; perhaps a dozen species, native and European, which attack most eastern and southern pines.

Direct control of these insects today is usually a large-scale operation involving the aerial application of insecticides already described. Timing is important if the spraying is to be effective. It should come just after the eggs are hatched and the army of caterpillars is on the move. Biological control also has been effective in reducing defoliater populations (Balch, 1960). For example, a small chalcid wasp was introduced to control the larch sawfly. This effective parasite is now distributed through the eastern United States and Canada and is reducing outbreaks of the sawfly wherever they occur.

**Bark Beetles** Considered to be more destructive than the preceding group, the bark beetles are potentially more damaging because they are not controllable in the mass by means of aerial spraying. The greater part of their life is spent in the bark of living or dead trees, depending on the beetle species. There are too many kinds of bark beetles to cover their various life histories, but most of them follow this pattern. The emerging adults are in the open only long enough to find their particular host material, either standing trees or downed material such as logs or branches (Fig. 18-5). The

**Figure 18-4**   The western tent caterpillar. *Left,* the egg mass on a twig. *Right,* the larvae just emerging from their protective tent. *(Photo by Ed Holsten.)*

first-attacking females enter the tree and sever the resin ducts. If the tree cannot repel the attack, the successful females send out a powerful chemical message—an attractant (pheromone)—which informs the dispersed population that new breeding grounds have been located. Thousands of males and females within range of the message are guided to the source and congregate on the host material. The tree may try to "pitch out" the intruders but the mass attack usually overwhelms the host and it succumbs. As the tree dies, the females mate and bore egg galleries into the fresh phloem, or inner bark tissues (Gara, Holsten, and Manewal, 1972).

Eggs are deposited along the margins of the egg galleries singly or in groups, or at the ends of the gallery, each species following its typical pattern. Soon the eggs hatch and minute larvae bore larval mines at right angles to the main egg galleries. As hundreds of larvae eat their way into the phloem layer of a single tree, the tree is girdled and killed from within (Fig. 18-6). Generally, insects overwinter within the tree and emerge the

**Figure 18-5** The adult Douglas-fir beetle. *Upper,* just after emergence, with the thick forewings raised, exposing the hindwings, ready for flight. *Lower,* on a tree trunk ready to bore through the bark to the phloem. *(Upper photo by Ernest Manewal; lower photo by Ed Holsten.)*

following spring as adults to seek a new host and start the process over again. Some of the more destructive bark beetles are:

**1** The southern pine beetle; inflicts periodic damage on most of the southern pines.
**2** The turpentine beetle; attacks all species of pine and spruce in North America.
**3** The western pine beetle; an important insect enemy of ponderosa pine.

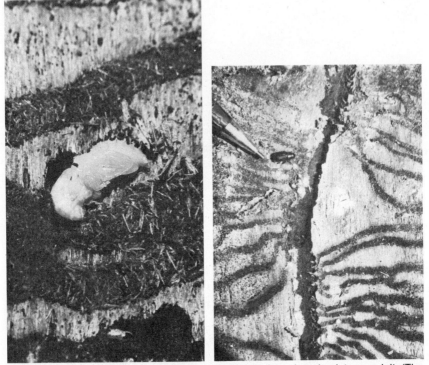

**Figure 18-6** *Left,* the Douglas-fir beetle pupae just before changing into an adult. (The larval mines in the phloem were made by a wood borer.) *Right,* the vertical egg gallery is shown at center, with larval mines at right angles on either side, all made by the Douglas-fir beetle. An adult Douglas-fir beetle (about natural size) appears at upper left. *(Photo by Ed Holsten.)*

    **4**  The mountain pine beetle; attacks all species of western pine, has wiped out thousands of acres of lodgepole and western white pine. The beetle is also very destructive to ponderosa pine in the Black Hills and Rocky Mountain regions.

    **5**  The Douglas-fir beetle; the most important insect enemy of Douglas-fir (Figs. 18-5 and 18-6).

    **6**  The Engelmann spruce beetle; causes periodic destruction to Engelmann and other western spruces in the Rocky Mountain Region and Alaska.

    These six are species of *Dendroctonus,* which when translated means *tree-killer.* Next, most important in the bark beetle group are the pine engraver beetles, belonging mostly to the genus *Ips,* and the fir engraver (*Scolytus ventralis*) (Fig. 18-7). These and other Coleoptera are largely secondary enemies which attack severely weakened trees, or healthy trees when the insect population is high—during outbreaks initiated by massive amounts of weakened host material.

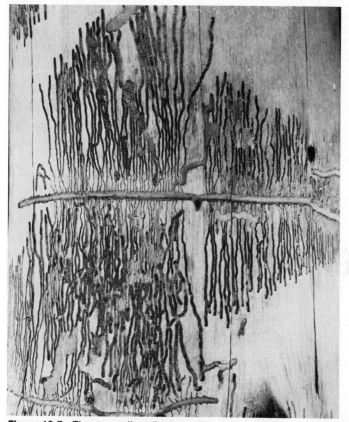

**Figure 18-7** The egg gallery (horizontal line) and larval mines (vertical lines) left after an attack by the fir engraver in California. Such activity in the phloem girdles and kills the tree from within. *(Courtesy of the U.S. Forest Service.)*

Traditional control of bark beetles includes most of the direct-attack methods considered earlier, such as felling, burning, sun curing, or ground spraying by hand or power equipment.

Sanitation logging and other salvage operations have been successful in preventing the buildup of large beetle populations. Blowdowns must be salvaged quickly before epidemic beetle populations occur (Gara, Holsten, and Manewal, 1972).

A promising method of control is use of the attractant or pheromone mentioned above. The pheromones for most of the bark beetles have been identified and synthesized. It is expected that synthetic pheromones will be used to lure beetle populations away from prime timber or to trap beetles before they can do any damage.

**Wood Borers**   The damage from wood borers usually comes after the trees have been felled but before they are utilized. Some wood borers attack standing but dying trees. A tree killed by insects, fire, or other causes becomes host to ambrosia beetles which burrow into the sapwood and heartwood. Rather than eat the wood themselves, they introduce a fungus into the tunnels upon which the adults and larvae feed. Another wood boring group consists of the larvae of certain wasps, whose adult females insert an ovipositor as much as an inch into the newly felled tree and deposit their eggs (Fig. 18-8). The wasp larvae bore for one or two seasons in the solid unseasoned wood and do considerable damage. The flat-headed and round-headed wood borers are the larvae of two families of beetles which mine into the inner bark or wood of forest trees. The eggs are laid in bark crevices; the larvae burrow into the tree, making a series of rounded or flattened winding "wormholes," which make the wood worthless for lumber. The best control for such insects as these is to remove the felled tree from the forest as soon as possible. Once lumber becomes dried it is fairly safe from attack by the above group. If logs are to be used in the round form, for cabins, poles, or piling, for example, they should be peeled and treated with creosote or other chemicals.

Even seasoned sapwood in the form of finished products is not safe from damage by powder-post beetles. Treatment with paint or varnish gives the wood a protective covering. Carpenter ants (in the West) and termites

**Figure 18-8**   The wood wasp *(Urocerus, spp.)* on the bark of a white spruce in Alaska. The ovipositor (indicated by the arrow) is extended into the bark (the ovipositor sheath extends from the rear of the wasp). The wasp larvae bore into the wood. *(Photo by Ed Holsten.)*

(in the South) tunnel into stumps, logs, snags, and heartwood of living trees; but their main damage where humans are concerned is in wooden poles, fences, and the framework of buildings. Control is effected by chemical treatment of the wood with creosote or some other preservative. In the matter of protection from termites, keeping the wood dry and elevated above the ground is the best method of control.

**Terminal Feeders**   These are serious pests, especially of seedlings and saplings, in nurseries and plantations where damage has been disastrous. Damage inflicted on older trees is seldom of importance. Injury to buds and other tender growing tips is caused by a wide variety of insects such as the terminal weevils (Fig. 18-9), twig beetles, twig-boring caterpillars, aphids, midges, and scale insects. One of the most destructive members of the group is the Nantucket pine tip moth, which causes malformation of growing tips in pine nurseries and plantations in southern United States. Control is accomplished by ensuring that the best pine species for a given site is planted. For example, in east Texas, damage by the moth is reduced when shortleaf pine is planted instead of loblolly pine on sandier, drier upland sites.

**Root Feeders**   The group of insects that feed on roots is composed of white grubs, certain weevils, termites, and wireworms. Damage is most serious in forest nurseries. To control these, the soil is poisoned by one of many

**Figure 18-9**   The tip weevil *(Pissodes strobi)*, a devastating pest of white pine in the East, of Engelmann spruce in the Rocky Mountain area, and Sitka spruce in the Pacific Northwest. *(Photo by Ed Holsten.)*

available soil insecticides before planting or seeding. Test plots should be made to study the effect of the poison on the seedlings, since different soils and seedlings react differently to the various poisons. A poison incorrectly used could render the soil useless for several years.

**Gall Makers**  An insect gall is an abnormal growth formed on leaves or twigs by mechanical irritation or chemical stimulation from insects. The gall provides protection for the insect larvae while they are feeding on the tree's tissues or sucking its sap. Such galls are seen by many people without their realizing what they are. Examples are: (1) the oak-apple gall, of several oaks, caused by a wasp; (2) the aphid gall on the stem of cottonwood leaves; (3) the Cooley spruce gall, a conelike structure formed on the western spruces by an aphid; and (4) the gall midges of some pines and junipers of the West, balsam fir of the North, and a dozen or more different hardwoods of the East.

The damage to the forest from the gall makers is negligible. In spruce nurseries, plantations, or ornamentals, the presence of the Cooley spruce gall is of some concern because it does tend to stunt and disfigure the trees. Cutting off and burning the young gall before the adult aphids emerge is one means of control. Sprays may be used in early spring if the infestation becomes serious.

**Seed Insects**  Cone and seed insects destroy trees even before they can germinate from seed. These pests are most destructive to seed orchards where crops represent years of accumulated care and expense. In general, cone and seed insects lay their eggs on the outside of the cone or fruit. The developing larvae then bore through the seed coat and into the seed itself, where they subsequently feed on the endosperm. Seed-destroying insects are controlled by systemic insecticides. These highly toxic materials are sprayed on the soil at the base of the tree and migrate down into the root system. They are eventually translocated into the branches and tend to concentrate in the seeds themselves. Invading insects are then killed when they bore through the seed coating into the seed.

### In Conclusion

To keep a wildfire small, it must be detected when small. Insect infestations can also be kept small through early detection. Any forest worker or user, from the person who goes fishing to the one who just enjoys being in the woods, can act as a detector, and prompt action will keep timber mortality to a minimum. When abnormal insect activity is discovered and reported to a local forester, the report is normally transmitted to the nearest U.S. Forest Service Experiment Station. The station entomologist will review the report, and if the insect seems to be a serious threat, an on-the-spot investigation is made. Often the entomologist will call on university, privately employed, and state forest entomologists to help with the investigation. They determine the trend of the infestation, and if it is upward, they estimate the damage that will result if control measures are not taken. The threat may be of such degree that long-range silvicultural or biological controls are all that is needed, or perhaps a salvage logging operation is in order to remove the infested timber. Should these be impractical because of the extent of the buildup, the direct methods of control outlined on the previous pages will be necessary. One of the major aerial insecticide operations may even be needed—there may be no choice if the forest is to be saved.

By now, it should be apparent that forest entomology is a complicated subject requiring greater coverage than the authors have been able to offer here. For a more detailed treatment it is recommended that the interested reader consult the Bibliography of this chapter for titles of publications devoted to insects and their control.

## MAMMALS

The forest is the natural home of many game and fur-bearing animals and has served for centuries as a pasture for domestic stock. Also, it harbors numerous rodents that are interesting but likely to be considered useless, if not harmful. The food demands of these animals may become so great at times that real damage to the timber crop will occur. Particularly where islands, in a real or figurative sense, are inhabited by important game animals, the forest suffers as animal population increases. The inroads of civilization, which diminish the natural feeding and breeding grounds of certain mammals, may also drive them to feed upon bark or twigs during the winter to an injurious extent. Domestic grazing animals not only retard natural reproduction but compact the soil by trampling, injure natural cover, and expose the surface to erosion and, in the case of hogs particularly, actually consume the roots of certain young trees.

### Damage by Larger Mammals

Several members of the deer family are known to cause some damage to the forest. Moose on Isle Royale National Park in Lake Superior have formed a "browse line" about 11 ft from the ground while satisfying their food requirements. Elk have seriously injured reproduction in some Western states by overbrowsing. Most of the damage from members of this family, however, comes from the deer themselves (Fig. 18-10). Excessive browsing has actually eliminated all palatable reproduction in some forest areas, while in others which have been repeatedly overbrowsed no reproduction under 30 years of age will be found. The entire acorn crop of some oak forests has been consumed by deer where these animals are too abundant. Deer do further harm, such as deforming growth by nipping off the leaders of young trees, or damaging their trunks by debarking them when removing

**Figure 18-10**   A white tail deer contributing to the browse line in a West Virginia forest. *(Courtesy of the U.S. Forest Service.)*

the velvet from their antlers. Deer damage from browsing is greatest in the Northern states and the Rocky Mountains, where deep winter snows confine the herds to small areas. Their damage is locally severe in West Coast Douglas-fir plantations, especially on sites where it is warm and dry in the summer (causing a moisture stress) and where deer congregate in winter. Intensive wildlife management appears to be the best control against deer injury. This may involve census taking, planting and temporarily fencing food species, protecting terminal leaders with plastic tubes, logging in the winter to provide tops for food, and reducing herds by special hunts. Much will depend on the relative importance of the recreation and hunting values of the deer as compared with the value of the timber crops. Any means of speeding up the rate of regeneration until the new trees reach a height of about 5 ft (1.5 m) is useful in controlling damage by deer.

An amazing amount of second-growth timber is being damaged or killed by black bear in the Pacific Coast Region. During the spring and early summer, the bear expose the juicy cambium near the base of certain trees by scratching and biting off the tree's outer bark (Fig. 18-11). Stomach analysis of bear proved conclusively that the cambium layer is a major food item. Studies on the Olympic Peninsula of Washington State, where damage is severe, indicate that bear have killed as many as 40 trees per acre (16 trees per ha) by girdling. Douglas-fir is the bears' favorite tree, although they extend their sap-licking damage to western hemlock, Sitka spruce, and western redcedar. There has been a long history of bear damage to trees in the region extending from northern California to British Columbia, but the damage was never extensive until after World War II. The cutover lands supported a greater food supply, which resulted in a larger population of game animals, including black bear. Biologists speculate that as the second-growth forests grew older, ground plants and berries became scarce and the

**Figure 18-11** Bear damage to young Douglas-fir on a tree farm in Washington State. *(Courtesy of the Weyerhaeuser Company.)*

increased bear population had to turn to eating the inner bark of trees in order to survive. Trees in the 15- to 30-year-old range with an average diameter of 8 to 10 in. (20 to 25 cm) have been hit the hardest. There is weak evidence that shows this behavior is learned, though most biologists still feel this is an instinctive trait. Damage became so extensive on the Olympic Peninsula that for a few years bear were declared predators. To date, the only effective method of controlling bear damage is to reduce the number of bear through the use of damage-control hunters or sports harvest with extended seasons.

Rabbit damage to reproduction is a serious threat in New England, the Lake States, and the Pacific Northwest. Nipping and girdling the young shoots results in a deformed, bushy tree, if it survives at all. The control of rabbits is seldom practical because of the difficulty and expense involved. Fencing of small areas, such as forest nurseries, has been tried. Repellents have been used with good success.

The porcupine is another troublesome rodent that kills and damages trees. Damage is not confined to any one area, but in the Pacific Northwest it does extensive damage each year. In the West its favorite food is the bark of ponderosa and lodgepole pine while in the Lake States and New England it is northern hardwoods. With no need to hibernate it girdles trees 12 months of the year. If it does not kill the tree, it leaves much of the wood exposed to further attack by insects and disease. Instead of choosing to damage the poorest trees in a stand, porcupines pick the healthiest and most vigorous. As early as 1908, a bounty was offered for porcupines in New York State. The animal is becoming a greater menace each year in Oregon and southwestern Washington. Predator hunters have been trapping thousands each year in eastern Oregon trouble spots, and game hunters are asked to shoot the animal on sight. One reason for the porcupine's steady increase in numbers is that destruction from its old enemy, wildfire, has been reduced, as are the numbers of many of its natural predators. The trapping and hunting mentioned above is a major weapon against the animal. One predator, the fisher, has been reintroduced to control the porcupine. In the Northeast the recovery of the fisher has been matched by the decline of the porcupine.

By felling trees for food, lodge, and dam construction, beavers do some damage but this is limited to small areas. Trapping is the best means of control. Since in most states the animal is protected, this can be done only by state game department officials or trappers with special beaver licenses.

### Smaller Mammals

The tree squirrels, chipmunks, and white-footed mice do widespread damage to seed crops. Although seed crop loss from squirrels may be serious, control measures are seldom undertaken. During the winter when icing is severe, tree squirrels have been observed completely stripping the younger bark from sugar maples in hardwood forests in southern Michigan, apparently because their acorn caches are inaccessible. Mice present a greater problem, but they can be controlled. Tree seed is one of the preferred foods of white-footed mice, and they can destroy an entire seed crop. Until recently, artificial seeding has often been a waste of time because mice ate most of the seed before it germinated. Seed treated with poison has been used to kill mice, but this has presented only more problems. The repellents used today actually train mice to change their eating habits. Finding the treated seed distasteful, the mice look for something else to eat. This control is effective, of course, only with artificial seeding.

### Grazing Damage by Domestic Animals

Sheep grazing on the national forests of the Southwest are destructive to ponderosa pine reproduction. This is especially true in some areas during the early summer dry period, when sheep satisfy their thirst by browsing on the succulent shoots of the young pine. Aspen reproduction is a favorite food of all livestock on many Western grazing lands. By careful regulation of the number of domestic animals permitted on these lands reproduction is spared and total destruction of the cover with attendant erosion is prevented.

In the small individual forests and farm woodlands of the South, low-grade cattle and hogs at one time were turned loose to roam unfenced forest lands, destroying reproduction and trampling the soil. Riding down saplings to obtain the tender foliage was a common form of injury by cattle. The hogs, in particular, did extensive damage by grazing on tree roots. The trend in the South today is to raise either livestock or trees but not both on the same piece of land. If the woodland owner wants the forest to reproduce, cattle and hogs must be excluded by fencing.

Grazing injury is a distinct threat to forest management and must be considered along with other destructive factors in any protection plans.

### Beneficial Effect of Animals

Animal life in the forest is by no means completely villainous, as the foregoing discussion might imply. Mankind would, no doubt, be retreating before insect armies if it were not for the millions of birds that make their headquarters in the forests. Dowden (1959) indicates that woodpeckers in particular are extremely important and have been known to kill practically the entire brood of Engelmann spruce beetles in some areas. Small mammals also render a similar service. The socially shunned but helpful skunk is estimated by a field officer of the Canadian Entomological Service to have been responsible for consuming 14,520 white grubs to the acre on an 8-acre tract in Manitoba. Plant succession after fire or other catastrophe is known to be closely connected with the habits of birds and rodents, and the latter are credited by some writers with considerable service in cultivating and fertilizing poor sites. As most of the damage to the forest comes from local overpopulation, and since the interrelationships of plants and animals in the forest are complex and obscure, it is unwise to assume that widespread destruction of any animal is necessary.

## BIBLIOGRAPHY

Baker, Whiteford L. 1959. Forest Insect and Research Control, *Jour. Forestry*, **57**: 243–244.

––––––. 1972. *Eastern Forest Insects*, Forest Service, U.S. Department of Agriculture, Miscellaneous Publication no. 1175.

Balch, R. E. 1960. The Approach to Biological Control in Forest Entomology, *Can. Entomol.*, **92**:297–310

Benedict, W. V. 1959. Every Forester Has a Stake in Forest Insect Spraying, *Jour. Forestry*, **57**:245–249.

Coulson, Robert N., Thomas L. Payne, Jack E. Coster, and Mark W. Houseweart. 1972. *The Southern Pine Beetle*, Dendroctonus frontalis Zimm, *1961–1971*, Publication 108, Texas Forest Service, College Station, TX.

Crafts, E. C. 1958. A summary of the Timber Resource Review, *Timber Resources for America's Future*, Forest Service, U. S. Department of Agriculture.

Division of Forest Pest Control. 1973. *Forest Insect and Disease Conditions in the United States, 1972*, Forest Service, U.S. Department of Agriculture.

Dowden, P. B. 1959. What About Biological Control? *Jour. Forestry*, **57**:267–270.

Forest Pest Management Group. 1972. *Insects and Diseases of the Trees in the South*, U.S. Department of Agriculture, Atlanta, GA.

Gara, Robert I. 1966. What We Have Learned from New Research on the Southern Pine Beetle, *Forest Farmer*, **25**:6–7, 18–19, Atlanta, GA.

––––––, Edward Holsten, and Ernest Manewal. 1972. *Bark Beetles: Serious Pests of the Northwestern Forests*, University of Washington Arboretum Bulletin, vol. 35, no. 2, Seattle.

Graham, Kenneth. 1963. *Concepts of Forest Entomology*, Reinhold Publishing Corporation New York.

Graham, Samuel A., and Fred B. Knight. 1965. *Principles of Forest Entomology*, McGraw-Hill Book Company, New York.

Hedlin, A. F. 1974. *Cone and Seed Insects of British Columbia*, Pacific Forest Research Centre, Victoria, BC.

Keen, F. P. 1952. *Insect Enemies of Western Forests*, U.S. Department of Agriculture.

National Academy of Sciences. 1970. *Vertebrate Pests: Problems and Control*. Series on Principles of Plant and Animal Pest Control, vol. 5, Washington, DC.

Pettinger, L. F., and D. W. Johnson. 1974. *Forest Pest Conditions in the Pacific Northwest—1973*, U.S. Forest Service, Pacific Northwest Region, Branch of Insect and Disease Control, Portland, OR.

Poelker, Richard J., and Harry D. Hartwell. 1973. *Black Bear of Washington*, Biological Bulletin no. 14, Washington State Game Department, Olympia.

Rose, A. H., and O. H. Lindquist. 1973. *Insects of Eastern Pines*, Department of the Environment, Canadian Forestry Service Publication no. 1313; Great Lakes Forest Research Centre, Sault Ste. Marie, Ontario.

Salman, K. A. 1937. *The Regional Survey of Forest Insect Conditions, California Region (mimeographed), 1931–1936.* Bureau of Entomology and Plant Quaranteen, Berkeley, CA.

Smith, Ray F., Thomas E. Mittler, and Carroll N. Smith (eds.). 1973. *Annual Review of Entomology*, Annual Reviews, Inc., Palo Alto, CA.

Swingler, W. S. 1959. Keeping Forest Insects in Their Place, *Amer. Forests*, **65**: 28–45.

Van den Bosch, Robert, and P. S. Messenger. 1973. *Biological Control*, Intext Educational Publishers, New York.

Wygant, N. D., and A. L. Nelson. 1949. Four Billion Feet of Beetle-killed Spruce, *Trees*, Yearbook of Agriculture, U.S. Department of Agriculture.

# Chapter 19

# Disease and the Elements

## FUNGUS DISEASES

Trees are subject to attack by many diseases, those caused by fungi being the most important. In fact, every stand of timber is infected with some kind of fungus, although its presence may not always be detected. Frequently fungi injure or destroy trees at various stages of growth and certain ones destroy rough or manufactured forest products. Fungi reach epidemic proportions under the proper environment and become a serious threat to sound forestry (Fig. 19-1). Their attacks must be prevented and combated just as are the attacks from fire, insects, and other animals.

The causes of plant diseases were poorly understood before the Civil War. Prior to that time, any loss not attributed to fire or insects was blamed on poor soil, bad weather, or even interference from the supernatural. Today, disease in plants is generally understood to mean any disturbance or interruption in the process of nutrition, or other growth processes, resulting in partial or complete stoppage of development, or causing death. Some diseases cause hypertrophy, a condition of excess development. Of course, the function of nutrition has long ceased in logs, lumber, and manufactured

**Figure 19-1**  Examples of wood decay and the fungi that cause it. (1) Indian paint fungus (*Echinodontium tinctorium*) on western hemlock. (2) Brown cubical rot caused by *Polyporus sulphureus* on black cherry. (3) *Fomes everhartii* on red oak. (4) *Polyporus versicolor* on white oak. (5) *Fomes igniarius nigricans* on American beech. (6) The tinder fungus (*Fomes fomentarius*) on yellow birch. (7) *Daedalea quercina* on red oak. (8) Red belt fungus (*Fomes pinicola*) on Sitka spruce. (9) *Fomes rimosus* on black locust. (10) The false tinder fungus (*Fomes igniarius*) on quaking aspen. (11) The birch conk (*Polyporus betulinus*) on paper birch. *(Courtesy of The University of Michigan.)*

wooden products, but deteriorating and discoloring organisms may be active here. These organisms also cause brown, white, and soft rots, dry rots, and molds in wood, which are seldom spoken of as *diseases*. The term *disease* is applied when one speaks of any decay of heartwood in standing timber, even though it involves little interference with life processes. Therefore, it is reasonable and convenient, in discussing this entire class of injuries to forests and wood products, to think of them as diseases. The study of these diseases is called *forest pathology*. While it is the forest entomologist who is concerned with insects, it is the forest pathologist who is concerned with tree diseases. A forest protectionist is concerned with both insects and diseases, their detection and control.

### Losses from Fungus Diseases

Tree seeds suffer less from fungi than they do from insects, but starting with storage and germination of the seed there is a fungus threatening every stage of tree growth, from the damping-off diseases of tiny seedlings to destructive interior decays in the old-growth forests of the Northwest. There are specialized diseases which attack roots, stems, and foliage. There are rusts, wilts, stains, decays, and molds caused by organisms that attack the wood products as they are taken from the forest and moved through the mill. Similar diseases attack the finished products in service as containers, lumber, posts, railroad ties, or buildings.

In the previous chapter we learned that insects actually destroy more standing timber in a year in the United States than does any other factor. Disease, on the other hand, ranks number one in slowing down the growth of forests. Therefore, we see that disease is more of a factor in growth loss than in tree mortality. This, coupled with the damage to the finished product, makes it a serious problem in forests and forest products. Losses from disease when the forests stood in the way of "progress" were tolerated, or else went unnoticed. Today, something is known about most tree diseases, and although some cannot be controlled and new ones keep appearing, research continues and efforts are made to control and prevent many of them.

Diseases could be classified as (1) weakening diseases, the kinds that cause the growth loss mentioned above, or (2) killing diseases. The latter types are mostly foreign diseases that are free of natural controls and find domestic trees, which have no natural resistance to them, an easy prey. The best example of a killer disease is the chestnut blight induced by *Endothia parasitica*, brought accidentally into the United States in 1903 on nursery stock from Asia. During its first 20 years, the blight spread throughout the natural range of American chestnut (eastern United States) destroying millions of board feet of valuable timber. Though over three-quarters of a century has passed since its introduction in the U.S., no effective means of control has been discovered. Many deep taproots of chestnut still live, sending up sprouts every year, but these too become infected and die after a few years. The chestnut would come back if an effective treatment for the disease could be found. Blight-resistant Asiatic chestnut is now grown in this country, but it does not attain the commercial timber size once characteristic of American chestnut.

Another example of an imported killer is the Dutch elm disease, which may eventually bring to native elms a fate similar to that which befell the American chestnut. Introduced in 1930, Dutch elm disease has killed millions of American elms. A third foreign disease, causing widespread destruction to the five-needled pines in North America, is the white pine blister rust. These last two killer-type diseases will be discussed at greater length later in this chapter.

Today, jet airliners land in dozens of American ports of entry from many parts of the world. This accelerated means of transportation makes it possible for fungal spores (and insects for that matter) to arrive in a healthy condition. Each week prohibited plant materials are discovered in one port of entry or another, and frequently they contain a disease or insect not previously recorded for the United States. The gravity of the situation cannot be overestimated, and the enforcement and improvement of plant quarantine laws is essential. This type of legislation was first initiated in this country in 1912, with the Federal Plant Quarantine Act.

The passage of the Forest Pest Control Act by Congress in 1947 provides for better control of pests once their presence is known. In this act, the federal government has accepted the responsibility of leadership in controlling all pests on federal lands and making emergency funds available to control diseases and insects on state and private land.

### How the Fungi Gain Entrance

Most forest diseases are caused by thallophytic plants known as *fungi*. Although some fungi are useful, our chief concern lies in the destruction caused to forests, vegetable and cereal crops, and in their attacks upon humans and domestic animals.

All fungi are nongreen plants (lacking chlorophyll) and are composed of many threadlike structures called *hyphae*, which collectively are called *mycelium*. Not being able to manufacture their own food, as do plants with chlorophyll, the fungi must take it from something else. Fungi grow *parasitically* on living material or *saprophytically* on dead material. Some fungi may live for a time as a parasite and later, if the host dies, as a saprophyte.

Without getting involved in the various kinds of reproduction and stages of development characteristic of fungi, let us look at the *spore*, the minute reproductive body common to many lower plants. The spore may be wind-borne, carried by insects or other animals, or transported in water to a suitable environment, where it germinates. The hyphae invade host tissue, growing between or into the cell, secreting enzymes which help digest the wood. After feeding for a sufficient time, the mycelium near the surface develops a fruiting body characteristic of the species (Fig. 19-2). These fructifications emit millions of minute spores, which will in turn infect other suitable hosts when the required conditions of transportation, moisture, temperature, and host tissue are met. A single large shelf fungus, or *conk*, is capable of releasing more than a million spores an hour, night and day for several months. These billions of spores infect trees in the vicinity, or may be wind-borne hundreds of miles to other trees, or may be carried thousands of miles by aircraft.

The fruiting bodies and the destruction caused by the mycelia serve as a means by which the forester can recognize the disease. The symptoms may be in the form of wilting, leaf spots, leaf curl, needle cast or discoloration, blight, scabs, blisters, lesions, cankers, discolored and cracked bark, resin discharges, galls, burls, conks, and dead or broken tops. A certain conk on the outside of a tree may mean the disease extends 15 ft (4.6 m) above and below the conk; the presence of others may indicate the entire heartwood is decayed.

Fungi gain entrance to the heartwood of living trees through fire scars, broken limbs, an ax blaze, insect holes, wounds from careless logging operations, lightning strikes, storm breakage, and anything else that creates an

**Figure 19-2** Fourteen or more conks (*Fomes pini*) are visible on this western hemlock. Chugach National Forest, Alaska. *(Courtesy of The University of Michigan.)*

entrance through or damages the tree's protective tissues. Still other fungi infect the leaves, buds, roots, cambium, flowers, and fruit of trees.

### Typical Diseases of American Forests

With perhaps as many as 50,000 individual diseases capable of affecting trees in one manner or another, it seems more practical here to discuss only the most damaging ones.

**The Heart Rots**   The expression "she's punky," heard so commonly among workers in logging camps, is often followed by a laconic *"Fomes pini"* as a tree or log is discussed. At least this one fungus common to so many conifers is known to others than forest pathologists by its scientific name. Some common names by which this disease's effects are known are red heart, ring scale, and red ring rot. Its effects are not only widespread in

North America but have plagued European forests for many years and are common in other parts of the world. This rot offers an excellent example of a disease that destroys the interior of the tree almost to a pulpy mass. The tree may blow over when exposed to strong winds. Loss from heart rot is particularly high in the old-growth forests of the Northwest (Fig. 19-3). According to Childs and Shea (1967), heart rots cause more board-foot loss than any other group of diseases in the Northwest. Of the numerous heart rot fungi found here, *Fomes pini* (mostly in Douglas-fir) and *Echinodontium tinctorium* (mostly in western hemlock and true firs) are the most important. *Poria asiatica* is the cause of hollow trunks in living western redcedar.

The heart rot disease may enter the tree at any wound; frequently where a branch has been broken off. Early accounts of the disease in Germany indicate that it was most prevalent in forests near villages, where pilfering of branches was common, and in woods exposed to high winds where there were many broken branches. The cross sections of logs, if taken at frequent intervals, indicate that the irregular cylinders or cones of decayed wood may extend for short distances in either direction from a wound entrance, up into the butt log from root infection and wounds near the ground, or for the complete length of the trunk. In the latter instance,

**Figure 19-3** Heart rot on the butt end of a western hemlock. Some of this diseased tree was salvaged at the sawmill; some became pulp chips. *(Courtesy of the Weyerhaeuser Company.)*

several separate infected sections may join or overlap. The cross-sectional appearance, depending upon age and degree of the infection, is one of incomplete and irregular circles of reddish brown to very dark brown, sometimes merging into complete circular areas. The conks, also called *sporophores*, are evident on the outside of the trunk in advanced stages of the disease. Obviously, the removal of the conk is not a method of control.

Forest management, including short rotation and intermediate salvage cutting, offers practicable control for this disease. The prevention of wildfires is helpful as fire scars and other trunk wounds afford entrance for various pests. Salvaging of individual trees injured in logging is also advised.

Heart rot, caused by several species of fungi, is credited with being the greatest cause of growth loss in the forests of the United States. Were it not for this rot, a large number of conifers and hardwoods could be left to grow for many more years.

**Root Diseases**   *Poria weirii, Fomes annosus, Polyporus schweinitzii, Armillaria mellea,* and others cause or induce root rot. Such diseases attack trees of all ages, and appear on both hardwoods and conifers throughout the United States. However, the most serious infestations are in the Pacific Northwest and in the Southeast. *Poria weirii* is a real threat to the management of second-growth Douglas-fir. In a similar manner *Fomes annosus* threatens intensive management of plantations of southern pine.

*Poria weirii* enters the tree through wounded roots and roots in close association with infected roots, causing a decay in the heartwood of the butt. Conks often appear at the tree's base or in the root crotches, but more than likely there will be no sign of the disease until the tree falls. The tree's anchorage is weakened when the roots become infected, leaving the tree at the mercy of the winds. Old-growth western redcedar east of the Cascades is also seriously affected at the base, often rendering the tree commercially useless for 15 or more ft (4.6 m) up the trunk. Curtailing fire through adequate protection and reducing damage from logging have no doubt reduced the losses from this rot, however there is no known control of the disease.

An important fungus root disease on pines in the Southeast is *littleleaf*. Shortleaf pine is hit the hardest and loblolly to a lesser extent. Littleleaf disease has been the subject of considerable study since it was discovered in Alabama during the midthirties. Three researchers (Campbell, Copeland, and Hepting, 1953) found that the fungal pathogen *Phytophthora cinnamomi*, was already present in most Southeastern pine soils, but its severity differed with the drainage ability of the soil. A root system in a soil with poor aeration develops poorly and becomes a favorable host for root fungi. As the fungus attacks the newer roots, their growth is interfered with, and they lose their ability to absorb. The result is a yellowing of the foliage and, finally, death of the tree. The water content of the soil can be changed through drainage adjustments, but only over long periods of time. Planting species other than shortleaf or loblolly pine seems to be the best way to avoid the disease.

**White Pine Blister Rust** *(Cronartium ribicola)* This destructive fungus has probably been in the country since the late 1890s. The organism was first found on cultivated black currants at Geneva, New York, but it was not until 1909 that it was found on white pine seedlings imported from Germany. Unfortunately, shipments of these trees had been sent to many applicants for planting stock throughout the Northeastern and Lake States and to eastern Canada: and by 1915, in spite of control measures taken according to the best knowledge of the time, it was well established in the eastern pine belt. Today it is found throughout the range of eastern white pine, from Newfoundland to northern Georgia, and west to Manitoba and Minnesota. On the Pacific Coast the blister rust got started in 1910 on nursery stock sent to Vancouver, British Columbia, from France. All of the West Coast's five-needle pines are susceptible. Now the disease extends from British Columbia well into California and east to Montana. Death comes relatively soon to young pines, and older trees are also killed after a number of years of severe attack and may be deformed, spiked-topped, and broken off at the top in shorter time.

The life history of this fungus is complicated but interesting. The infected pines develop bark cankers which usually cause swelling and are surrounded by yellowish discoloration. From these cankers come orange-yellow spring spores to be carried by the wind to the next host. This alternate host is a currant or gooseberry bush (any member of the genus *Ribes*). The spores land on the *Ribes* leaves, and after germination, the germ tube infects the leaf tissue. After a brief period of growth the fungus mycelium produces a pustule. The pustules liberate spores, which in turn are blown to and infect other currant and gooseberry bushes, and this process is repeated all summer. The infected bushes produce hairlike columns on the underside of the leaves. Spores, produced on these columns, are carried by the wind to the pines. These spores (called basidiospores) are carried comparatively short distances and are very frail. Infection of the tree occurs through the stomata on the young pine needles, and 2 to 5 years later the bark cankers and orange-yellow blisters containing spores appear. Three established facts can be taken advantage of in controlling this fungus: (1) an alternate host is necessary if the organism is to complete its life history; (2) this particular alternate host can be eradicated; (3) the spores that infect pines are fragile and require specific weather conditions for germination and host infection. The spores from the pines can be wind-borne for as much as 100 mi (161 km) and still be viable. The return trip, however, of the spores from *Ribes* to

pine must be shorter and is surrounded with danger to the spores themselves because of their fragility. Should the alternate host be the cultivated
black currant, the fall spores can travel a full mile to infect pine; if the host
is the wild currant or gooseberry, the trip is likely to be unsuccessful if it is
longer than 900 ft (270 m). A control lies in eradicating the respective
alternate hosts within these distances.

Unfortunately, control is hard exacting work and interferes with
people's choice gardens and pastures, and even with national parks, where
Nature is supposed to have its own way.

Control presently consists of managing white pine on those sites whose
climatic conditions limit the ability of basidiospores to germinate and infect
young pine needles. In addition, several programs are underway within the
Forest Service that will result in the production of seed sources with a high
level of natural resistance. Planting stock produced from such seeds should
restore commercially important five-needle pines to their former place in
the forest.

**The Dutch Elm Disease**    This desease, induced by the fungus *Ceratocystis ulmii* causes serious concern, since elms are important shade and
ornamental trees. The disease, which spreads from one city to another
through the forest, was first observed in the United States in 1930 on elms
in Cleveland and Cincinnati, Ohio. Today the disease is found throughout
most of eastern United States and Canada, with spot infections in some
Western cities where elms have been planted.

The Dutch elm disease pathogen is dependent on one of two insects,
the native elm bark beetle and the European elm bark beetle, for its transportation from one tree to another. The latter beetle, imported into the
United States in the early 1900s was unimportant until the disease arrived.
Once inoculated by contaminated beetles, the American elm is partly or
completely killed by the disease and provides a suitable breeding ground on
which increasing populations of beetles develop.

Wilting, often accompanied by a yellowing of the leaves, is the indication of an infected area on a tree. Because the disease is spread by insects it
may be controlled, but the method is expensive. Infected parts, or even
entire trees, are burned to destroy the insects' breeding ground. Spraying
the entire bark surface is another means of control. Though many insecticides have been tested, few offer the control potential of DDT. Most Eastern cities have invested in portable power-spray equipment, capable of
reaching the tops of elms, to prevent further loss of shade trees from this
disease.

**Dwarf Mistletoes (*Arceuthobium* spp.)**    A close relative to the harmless
mistletoe used in Christmas decorations, the dwarf mistletoe is a serious

pest of Western coniferous forests. So extensive is the reduction in growth due to this disease that it is rated as one of the ponderosa pine's worst enemies. It also infects lodgepole pine, western hemlock, and Douglas-fir, mostly in the dry regions, and black spruce in the Lake States.

All dwarf mistletoes are parasitic, leafless, seed plants, whose root systems, called *sinkers*, can invade the bark and become imbedded in the sapwood of their hosts, extracting both dissolved nutrients and water (Fig. 19-4). The result is a slow-growing, weakened, poor seed-producing tree, which after years of infection may develop bark cankers or the characteristic tangled mass of twigs and needles called a *witches'-broom* that slowly starves and weakens the host.

Gill and Bedwell (1949), indicated that dwarf mistletoe, without killing a tree, may reduce its lumber production by 30 to 50 percent. These pathologists also show that the weakened tree suffers further from attacks of bark beetles and heart- and root-rotting fungi, which a healthy tree can usually resist.

This parasite has a rather unusual method of spreading. The dwarf

**Figure 19-4**  Dwarf mistletoe plant parasitizing western hemlock near Corvallis, Oregon. *(Courtesy of the U.S. Forest Service.)*

mistletoe produces small sticky seeds, which are discharged forcibly at maturity, and can travel up to 50 ft (15 m) from their source. By this method it is commonly spread to understory plants of the same host species. Therefore, it is a major problem during the regeneration phase of stand culture. On striking and sticking to a nearby young limb tip, the seed germinates and its roots penetrate the bark and the plant becomes a parasite on the tree. The seeds are carried even greater distances by birds, squirrels, and porcupines.

Control of the disease is attempted by pruning out the infected limbs, and by thinning out heavily infected understory trees and cutting all infected overstory trees. Should dwarf mistletoe become established on the main trunk, the tree must be marked for removal in the next sanitation cut.

**The Canker Diseases**   The term *canker* usually refers to a disease which causes the death of relatively localized areas of a trunk or branch. Mechanical injury, such as a heavy blow, or frost and sunscald (discussed later) can also result in a canker. Most cankers are of fungus origin. Generally, infection which results in canker formation occurred when the stem was less that 10 years old.

The most serious effect of canker diseases (which seldom kill their host) is that heart-rot fungi and wood boring insects can enter the tree through the canker. The canker itself also reduces the quality of the wood through malformation of the stem and discoloration of the wood and makes the tree more susceptible to windthrow (Boyce, 1961). Aspen is infected by both *Nectria* (Fig. 19-5) and *Hypoxylon* cankers, probably the most important cankers on hardwoods at the present time. Conifers most frequently become infected by one of several species of *Dasyscypha;* the larch canker is currently the most serious.

**The Wilts and Diebacks**   Both types of disease are usually attributed to fungi. The fungi responsible for true wilt interfere with the upward conduction of water through the tree, resulting in the tree's death. The Dutch elm disease, discussed earlier, is an example of a true wilt. Oak wilt is presently one of the nation's most serious diseases. Studies have shown that all species of oaks and closely related trees (chestnut, tanoak, and the chinkapins) are susceptible. Unfortunately, it has now spread throughout large areas of eastern United States.

Bretz (1953) points out that oak wilt can spread from an infected to a healthy tree through natural root grafts. The spores may be transmitted greater distances by birds and insects but can infect a tree only through a break in the bark. Control is possible by felling infected trees and spraying or burning the slash. Careful pruning of infected limbs may lengthen a tree's life. Bretz feels that the mechanical severing of roots connecting diseased and healthy trees may save individual trees.

**Figure 19-5** *Nectria* canker on quaking aspen in Minnesota. *(Courtesy of the U.S. Forest Service.)*

Dieback is a "condition" in which a gradual deadening, starting with the tip, advances slowly down the stem. Fungi are responsible for most dieback, although there are other causes. The most serious manifestation of this condition is birch dieback, presently killing paper and yellow birches in northeastern United States and southeastern Canada. The cause of birch dieback seems to be something other than fungi; prolonged drought and abnormally high temperatures apparently are involved.

**The Blight Diseases** Often, any sudden dying of twigs, foliage, or flowers is called a blight. Its name frequently includes the affected part (needle blight, twig blight) or the name of the tree on which it grows (cedar blight, maple blight, sweetgum blight). Even the size or shape of the tree (pole blight) may be included in the name. Blight is accompanied by symptoms of wilting, dieback, discoloration, and spotting. The cause of the disorder may be difficult to determine. Blight, it seems, is a very general term.

Pole blight, which is characterized by dieback of the entire crown, is causing considerable damage to second-growth polesize western white pine in the Inland Empire region of Washington, Idaho, and Montana. Pole blight becomes more severe in areas where soil moisture is less abundant. Sweetgum blight, another of these nebulous blight diseases, is characterized first by dieback of the crown and then the death of the entire tree. Sweetgum blight in the South also seems to refer to a condition caused by a shortage of water in certain years. The origin of maple blight in the Lake States has been even more obscure. This desease is causing concern in forest industries and public agencies, but fortunately, the rate of spread is slow.

**Needle Diseases**   There are many diseases which infect the foliage of both hardwoods and conifers. A serious needle disease of ponderosa pine in much of the Northwest is *Elytroderma* needle cast (sometimes referred to as a needle blight), which can convert the entire crown into a series of witches'-brooms and stunted, swollen branches. Growth of the tree comes to a standstill. If it does not die from the disease, insects usually finish the job.

A second needle infection worthy of comment here is the brown spot needle disease of longleaf pine, present in differing degrees over much of the Southern Forest region. Its adverse effect is that of prolonging the "grass stage" of longleaf pine, often to the point where a loss of health and vigor may cause 100 percent mortality of the seedlings. Brown spot disease can be controlled by prescribed burning. The terminal bud of longleaf pine has a remarkable resistance to fire, and by burning off the young pine's needles the disease is destroyed. The acreage burned must be large enough to prevent a serious invasion of the disease from the surrounding unburned area. Hartman (1949) indicates that it is usually necessary to burn 200 acres (80 ha) or more to prevent reinfection.

**Stains and Rots That Leave Timber Merchantable**   Blue stain and other sap stains in lumber are caused by various fungi. The organisms may start their staining in the forest or attack lumber. The colors associated with various decay fungi, for example, red heart or yellow ring rot, are caused by stains characteristic of that fungus.

Some staining fungi, although present in the wood, cause little change in the wood's original durability or strength properties. The stained wood is nonetheless discriminated against by a buyer because of its less desirable appearance. Also conditions which are favorable to blue stain growth may favor the growth of decay fungi.

The spores of stain fungi are carried by the wind, water, and bark beetles. Warm weather and ample moisture seem to promote development of most stains. Green lumber piled solidly in the hold of a ship or in a boxcar can arrive at its destination in a stained or moldy condition because of inadequate ventilation.

In warm humid areas, stain can be avoided by removing the tree from the woods soon after felling. If this is not practicable or if logs must wait for several weeks at the mill before being sawn, it may be necessary to treat with antistain solution, or store in water either by sprinkling or ponding. Reducing the moisture content of lumber, in kilns or air-drying yards, or dipping lumber in chemical baths before shipping are means employed to reduce the possibility of stain.

**Damping-off in Forest Nurseries**  This trouble, which causes small seedlings to topple over and die just after they emerge from the soil, is not due to a single organism but may be the work of any one of 30 or more species of fungi. Some of the more common genera are *Pythium, Rhizoctonia,* and *Fusarium.* These fungi invade the tender root or stem soon after the seed germinates, causing the seedling to topple over just above the ground from the destruction of tissue. This desease results in a considerable loss and affects many species of American conifers unless the nursery soil is treated. Hartig (1894), a distinguished German forester, spoke of the damping-off of beech seedlings as a disease observed but not explained by foresters in Europe as long ago as 1795. Losses are likely to be heavy in broadcast or drill seeding, where there are large numbers of seedlings per unit area of nursery bed. Chances of such loss can hardly be taken, in view of the cost of improved quality seed and the urgent need for maximum nursery output. The attack usually occurs under moist warm conditions in nursery beds and may be recognized by examination of individual stems of seedlings for lesions or moist areas exhibiting brownish discolorations. Diagnosis and treatment at this point cannot save the crop. Its value lies in prevention of recurrence the following season. This is accomplished by treating the soil with applications of fungicidal chemicals, which are usually applied as soil fumigants.

In conclusion, it should be mentioned that not all forest fungi are harmful. Some fungi are parasitic on the disease-causing fungi. In Chap. 9 the role of mycorrhiza and its soil moisture and nutrient-absorbing qualities were mentioned. The importance of fungi in keeping the earth from being choked with undecomposed piles of forest litter, or the ability of fungi to convert fallen leaves and twigs into essential humus, should not be forgotten.

## DAMAGE TO FORESTS FROM THE ELEMENTS

**Breakage and Windthrow**  The United States has had a number of classic examples of wind damage, including the historic blowdown of 1921, which traversed the western part of the Olympic Peninsula in Washington State. A swath 30 mi (48 km) wide and 70 mi (113 km) long was cut by this gale, which destroyed more than 5 billion board feet, mostly Sitka spruce and western hemlock. Because of the area's inaccessibility, the shortage of logging equipment, and lack of nearby markets, very little of this blowdown was salvaged. The Northwest suffered again in 1951 and 1958. In the latter storm, damage approached 500 million board feet on federal, state, and private forests (Fig. 19-6). The wind causing the damage blew in from the southwest with recorded velocities of 90 mi/h (145 km/h) at the mouth of the Columbia River and reached 161 mi/h (260 km/h) on Cowan Peak in Pacific County, Washington.

An earlier storm in Alachua County, Fla., destroyed millions of feet of longleaf pine, snapping off many of the trees 15 to 30 ft (4.5 to 9 m) above the ground (Pinchot, 1900). In September 1938, a hurricane hit New England and flattened more that 3¼ billion board feet of timber, about 80 percent of which was valuable softwood. In addition to timber loss, in the White Mountain National Forest alone, 150 mi (240 km) of telephone line were put out of commission, 1,000 mi (1,610 km) of foot trail blocked, roads washed out and crisscrossed with as many as 200 trees to the mile (322 trees/km) and a serious fire hazard was created over several hundred thousand acres. Building and other property losses elsewhere were enormous. Salvage operations were organized by the Forest Service on an emergency basis, and 47 percent of the wind-thrown volume was milled and used. The

**Figure 19-6**  This area, once a showpiece forest, became a tangled mass of trees in a Northwest windstorm. Note the two people. *(Photo by A. M. Prouty.)*

great tangle of overthrow and breakage create a great fire hazard, as well as an excellent breeding ground for insects.

Wind is the cause of other forms of damage to the forest. Blowing over seed trees, carrying fungus spores, fanning forest fire, and sandblasting trees are some examples. On the other hand, wind has its beneficial attributes, such as seed and pollen dissemination.

**Snow and Ice Damage**  Breakage and deformation occur occasionally in the forest from the weight of heavy snowfall. This is usually in young stands or among trees that are crowded and spindling or on slopes where the trees, in recovering an upright position, assume a bent and crooked form. Damage of the latter type usually occurs in forests maintained for protective rather than for wood-producing purposes and is not important. Breakage is combated in commercial forests by silvicultural methods to guarantee strong individuals and by favoring resistant species. Ice damage comes from the breaking of tops and branches under the weight of ice formed during glaze storms. On shade trees pruning and painting the newly exposed areas with a protective coating may prevent entrance of disease. Such practice is hardly feasible in a forest and damaged trees are generally removed during salvage operations.

**Frost Damage**  Trees planted in low spots with insufficient air drainage may be killed or damaged by frost, and these pockets should by avoided. Damage from frost is usually local and due to unseasonable low temperatures, which injure buds and tender wood when the tree is not prepared for them. Reproduction can be protected from early and late frosts by use of silvicultural systems such as the shelterwood and other selection methods.

An off-season cold snap, when the temperature stays below freezing for a sustained period, causes widespread damage, mostly to exotic species. Such a freeze serves as a rather drastic means of determining the cold resistance of an ornamental.

**Damage from Avalanches and Landslides**  To suggest a remedy for an avalanche seems arrogant and futile, but avalanches and landslides starting at high points take toll in large swaths from valuable forests lower down. Insofar as human action may be responsible or a contributing cause, it must be challenged. Steep slopes with thin soil and subject to heavy rains are likely settings for the starting of avalanches and landslides; and little can be done except to guard the grass, brush, and tree cover from fire, destruction by grazing, and improper cutting patterns. Even afforestation of high slopes or seeding with grass or herbaceous plants may be justified. Sheep particularly should be excluded from grazing on the critical slopes. The Swiss have managed their forests on a selection system to assure tree cover to hold deep snows in place.

**Damage from High Temperatures and Drought**   Droughts are natural phenomena and watering of forest plantations is usually prohibitive in cost, but drought-resistant ecotypes or genetic varieties may be used. Watering of small plantations or shelterbelt plantings may be justified because of their high value for other than timber purposes. Sunscald, injury by heat of the sun to trees with thin bark, can be guarded against by taking precautions in thinning, so that remaining trees will not be left open to full and sudden rays of the sun for long periods. Tender coniferous seedlings and certain of the hardwoods when grown in nurseries require partial shade for a time.

**Lightning**   Injury to trees by lightning is seldom important except as lightning causes forest fires, the control of which is discussed elsewhere. Individual specimens are frequently so shattered that salvage is impossible. Valuable shade trees or trees of historic importance, such as the Boundary Oak at Lincoln's birthplace in Kentucky, may justify lightning rods and cables, but such devices are not practicable in forest management.

## BIBLIOGRAPHY

Baxter, Dow V. 1952. *Pathology in Forest Practice*, John Wiley & Sons, Inc., New York.

Boyce, John S. 1961. *Forest Pathology*, 3d ed., McGraw-Hill Book Company, New York.

————. 1957. Oak Wilt Spread and Damage in the Southern Appalachians, *Jour. Forestry*, **55**:499–505.

Bretz, T. W. 1953. Oak Wilt, A New Threat, *Plant Diseases*, Yearbook of Agriculture, U.S. Department of Agriculture.

Campbell, W. A., O. L. Copeland, Jr., and G. H. Hepting. 1953. Littleleaf in Pines in the Southeast, *Plant Diseases*, Yearbook of Agriculture, U.S. Department of Agriculture.

Childs, T. W., and K. R. Shea. 1967. *Annual Losses From Disease in Pacific Northwest Forests*, U.S. Department of Agriculture, Forest Service Resource Bulletin PNW-20, Pacific Northwest Forest and Range Experiment Station, Portland, Oregon.

Division of Forest Pest Control. 1973. *Forest Insect and Disease Conditions in the United States, 1972*. Forest Service, U.S. Department of Agriculture.

Driver, Charles H., and James H. Ginns, Jr. 1968. *Practical Control of Fomes annosus in Intensive Forest Management*, Institute of Forest Products, College of Forest Resources, University of Washington, Seattle.

Eadie, W. Robert. 1954. *Animal Control in Field, Farm and Forest*, The Macmillan Company, New York.

Foster, A. A. 1959. *Nursery Diseases of Southern Pines*, Forest Pest Leaflet no. 32, U.S. Department of Agriculture.

Gill, L. S., and J. L. Bedwell. 1949. Dwarf Mistletoe, *Trees*, Yearbook of Agriculture, U.S. Department of Agriculture.

Hartig, R. 1894. *Diseases of Trees* (Sommerville and Ward Translation), George Newnes, Ltd., London.

Hartman, A. W. 1949. Fire as a Tool in Southern Pine, *Trees*, Yearbook of Agriculture, U.S. Department of Agriculture.

Hawksworth, Frank G., and Delbert Wiens. 1972. *Biology and Classification of Dwarf Mistletoe* (Arceuthobium), Forest Service, U.S. Department of Agriculture, Handbook no. 401.

Hepting, George H. 1971. *Diseases of Forest and Shade Trees of the United States*, Forest Service, U.S. Department of Agriculture, Handbook no. 386.

McNew, G. L. 1953. The Effects of Soil Fertility, *Plant Diseases*, Yearbook of Agriculture, U.S. Department of Agriculture.

Partridge, Arthur D., and Daniel L. Miller. 1974. *Major Wood Decays in the Inland Northwest*, Idaho Research Foundation, Inc., Moscow.

Pinchot, Gifford. 1900. *A Primer of Forestry*, Part I, Division of Forestry, U. S. Department of Agriculture, Bulletin no. 24.

# Part Five

# Forestry and National Planning

# How the Federal Government Practices Forestry

As discussed in Chap. 6 and elsewhere in this book recent public awareness of environmental problems has resulted in increased federal activities. This has resulted in increased grants to the states and in more intensive management of all federal activities. The public is more involved in environmental decisions, and this environmental concern is likely to increase in the future.

Sixteen federal agencies are practicing forestry or giving important aid to the practice. In the Department of Agriculture the Forest Service, with its entire resources devoted to forestry; the Soil Conservation Service, which uses forestry to further its own particular objectives; the Extension Service, which gives federal leadership to extension efforts; and the Cooperative State Research Service, which administers cooperative forestry research, are involved (Fig. 20-1).

In the Department of the Interior, the Bureau of Indian Affairs, the National Park Service, and the Bureau of Land Management manage forest lands, and the Bureau of Outdoor Recreation coordinates and promotes recreation use on forest and other lands (Fig. 20-2).

The Tennessee Valley Authority has in its unified program of resource

DEPARTMENT OF AGRICULTURE

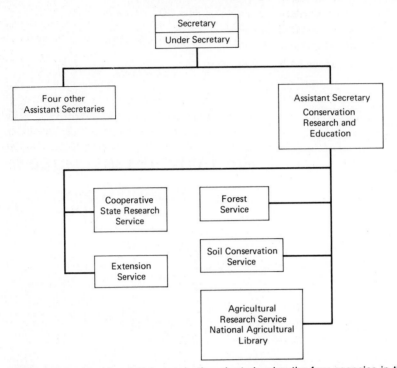

**Figure 20-1** An abbreviated organization chart showing the four agencies in the Department of Agriculture that engage in some forestry activities. *(United States Government Manual 1973-74, office of the Federal Register, National Archives and Records Service, General Services Administration, pp. 92–123.)*

conservation, development, and use a Division of Forestry, Fisheries, and Wildlife Development. In 1970 the Environmental Protection Agency was created to coordinate governmental action on behalf of the environment. The preceding does not take into account the various regulatory and credit agencies.

The Department of Commerce, which is close to the forest-products industries in its economic and statistical studies of lumber exports and imports, also furnishes information useful in forestry practice. The four agencies in the Department of Defense charged with the supervision of military reservations, maintain staffs of post foresters on certain areas. The National Oceanic and Atmospheric Administration, in the Department of Commerce, assists numerous state, federal, and private fire-control organizations by maintaining fire weather observers in certain areas. Finally, the Internal Revenue Service in the Department of the Treasury should be

DEPARTMENT OF THE INTERIOR

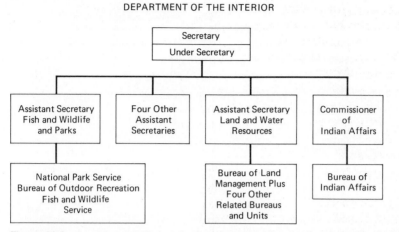

**Figure 20-2** An abbreviated organization chart showing the four agencies in the Department of the Interior that engage in some forestry activities. *(United States Government Manual 1973-74, office of the Federal Register, National Archives and Records Service, General Services Administration, pp. 259–286.)*

mentioned, since it employs people with forestry training in the valuation of timber properties.

It is hardly necessary to point out that all these activities could not be concentrated in a single bureau or department, or that the ramifications of forestry activity emphasize its importance as a federal function.

## THE DEPARTMENT OF AGRICULTURE

### The Forest Service

The organization of the Forest Service is reasonably simple and highly decentralized (Kaufman, 1960) (see Fig. 20-3). Its activities are shown as an example of one federal land-managing agency. These public lands are managed under multiple-use and sustained-yield principles.

The mission of the Forest Service is to provide national leadership in forest management, protection, and utilization, involving participation in designating national priorities for land use, formulation of programs to meet national objectives, and establishment of federal forestry policies to assure maximum contribution of environmental, social, and economic benefits to present and future generations. Accomplishment of the Forest Service mission includes three major areas of operation: (1) management, protection, and development of the 187 million acre (75.7 million ha) National Forest System; (2) cooperation with state foresters, private owners of forest lands, wood processors, and private and public agencies; and (3) conducting research activities that directly or indirectly support the Forest

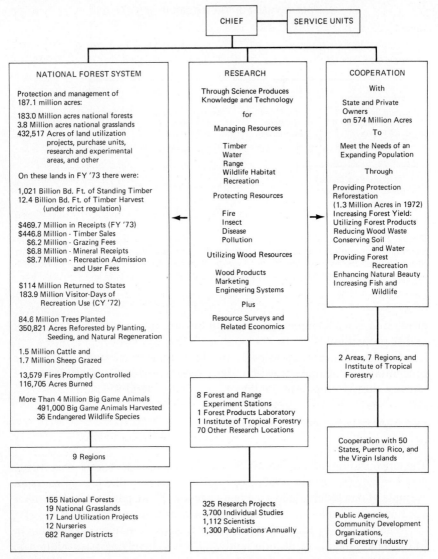

**Figure 20-3** The major activities of the Forest Service, U.S. Department of Agriculture.

Service mission, forestry and forestry-related resources (U.S. Department of Agriculture, 1974*b*).

The diagram (Fig. 20-3) shows three major divisions of activity. The greatest physical undertaking of the Forest Service is the management of the National Forest System. Location of the units in the system are shown on the map (Fig. 20-4).

**Forest-Fire Management**   The National Forest System is located in 44 states, Puerto Rico, and the Virgin Islands. These range from Maine to California and from Alaska to Texas. They have fire danger at every season and almost every cause of wildfire to cope with. There will be snow on many of the high Western forests while the severe spring fire season is on in the Carolinas. During the summer danger period in the Colorado or Wyoming lodgepole pine forests, moist green cover still exists in parts of the Appalachians. Wildfires will be fought in Michigan with plows, short-handled shovels, and water from quickly washed-in shallow wells, pumped by power or used sparingly by hand from backpack pumps. In the Pacific Northwest and Southwest, power pumps at streams and lakes, mattocklike digging tools, power saws, heavy axes, bulldozers, fire trucks, helicopters, planes, smoke jumpers and other fire fighters will be on the scene. In parts of the South, backpack pumps, tractor-drawn plows, "spankers" or beaters, and fire rakes will be in action. In the Rocky Mountain regions, airplanes carrying jumpers and supplies will be more frequently seen. There will be little confusion, for definite plans have been worked out and reviewed so that, as the first word of wildfire from a lookout tower, cabin, traveler, patrol plane, or other informant reaches a dispatcher by telephone or radio, the location is verified, and the appropriate fire-suppression force is dispatched. This will be either in the form of a single smokechaser, smoke jumper, a small crew with loaded truck ready to move on a few second's notice, a crew working on road or trail, a whole camp of emergency laborers, or a complete cooperating logging crew.

In addition to the control of wildfires there are other aspects to fire management. For example, in recent years prescribed fire has been used to improve wildlife habitat, enhance natural cover, control certain forest diseases, decrease slash and other fire hazards, and increase water yields (see Chap. 17).

**Timber Growing and Selling**   There is a large amount of mature and overmature timber on the Western national forests. The forests in all regions have crowded stands of timber in which growth is unsatisfactory. Good silviculture demands (except where needed for watershed protection and scenic areas near roads and recreational grounds) that the timber be harvested judiciously with full provision, first, for leaving a partial crop or in other ways ensuring reproduction, and second, for improving the quanti-

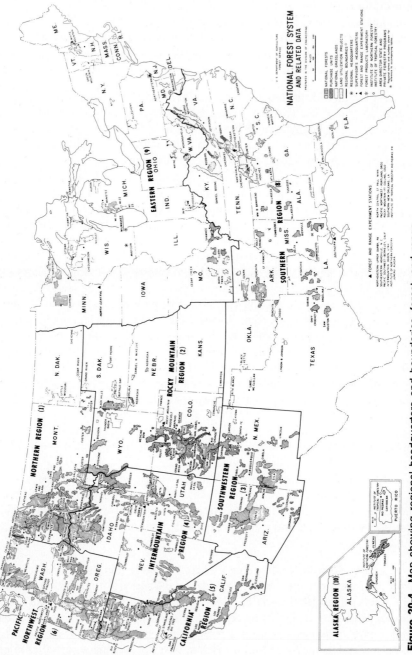

**Figure 20-4** Map showing regional headquarters and boundaries, forest, and range experiment station headquarters, and national forest system. *(Courtesy of the U.S. Forest Service.)*

ty and quality of the next crop. The Forest Service is not in the business of cutting its own timber and manufacturing it, but it does have a system by which designated stumpage (standing timber) can be sold and cut under such restriction and supervision as will accomplish these purposes.

In selling timber commercially, the Forest Service makes an estimate of an area proposed for sale in accordance with a management plan for the whole forest. It then appraises the value and sets prices on the various species within limits fixed by the Secretary of Agriculture, advertises the total amount for sale, awards the contract to the highest bidder capable of fulfilling it, and thereafter marks or designates the timber for cutting, checks up on provisions designed to prevent injury to reproduction and the residual stand, and measures the logs as a basis for periodic payments. (See Fig. 20-3 for volumes and values.) Under some contracts the purchaser deposits a fund that is used by the Forest Service for disposing of the logging slash; otherwise, the purchaser is responsible for the actual disposal. On some sales a cooperative deposit is made for planting or stand improvement.

In selecting a silvicultural method for harvest on national forest timber sales, major attention is given to the system which assures satisfactory reproduction if wildfire is controlled. Certain sale areas in Douglas-fir or lodgepole pine must depend on seeding from nearby blocks of timber or must be artificially reforested. In Fig. 20-5 the staggered settings of a timber sale are illustrated.

**Planting Trees to Reestablish Forests**   Forest planting is undertaken on the national forests to add to the nation's future supply of timber, to reestablish the forest as a self-renewing cover on denuded areas, and to

**Figure 20-5**   The staggered settings of a timber sale on the Umpqua National Forest in Oregon. *(Courtesy of the U.S. Forest Service.)*

serve as demonstrations of the practicability of reforestation projects for private owners of potential forest land (U.S. Department of Agriculture, 1974c).

In the plans (which are made far enough in advance to arrange for producing the necessary nursery stock), extent of area needing reforestation, species best adapted, planting methods, and recommendations for organizing the work are covered. The trees are very small and do not usually exceed 4 years of age. Costs of production vary from $5 to $20 or more per thousand.

Direct seeding of cutover and burned over areas by airplanes is coming into general use. Helicopters flying low and at moderate speeds are particularly useful in direct seeding. Cross-flights are employed in order to get proper seed distribution.

**Managing and Utilizing Forage Resources**    Mountain meadows, foothill grass and brush areas, sagebrush, and other scattered openings in national forests produce a vast amount of forage, which has been used for many years by local owners as pasture for their livestock (Fig. 20-6).

Fair market value fees per head of cattle, horses, sheep, goats, or hogs are charged for pasturing the animals on the national forest ranges. These aid in securing legitimate use of a natural resource, the building up of the highly important livestock industry, and continuity in the use of the range. A system of permits, preferences in allotting permission to use the range, and limits on numbers of stock allowed any one owner have been worked out on an equitable basis, and these have resulted in orderly and efficient use and building up and perpetuating the forage resources. Care is taken not to overstock the ranges, poisonous plants are eradicated, water supplies are developed, and stock is excluded from certain recreation areas.

**Figure 20-6**  Sheep grazing under paid permit in the Challis National Forest, Idaho. *(Courtesy of the U.S. Forest Service.)*

Stockmen's organizations are recognized by the Forest Service, and cooperation is frequently secured from them in forest protection and range improvement work. (See Fig. 20-3 for numbers of cattle and sheep grazed.)

**Water Conservation** Much of the nation's water supply flows from National Forest System lands. Use of these lands and their associated water resources is constantly expanding and intensifying, which has led to increasing emphasis on broad interdisciplinary planning for protection and enhancement of the water resource as a vital element of the environment. Included in this process are methods for increasing streamflow and improving water quality. In addition, watersheds are revegetated after wildfires and when needed to correct or avoid erosion (U.S. Department of Agriculture, 1974a).

**Recreational Developments** The concept of multiple use which guides the Forest Service in its administration of federal lands also provides for recreational use of those lands, where possible and desirable. As the pressure of population and demand for outdoor recreation areas has increased, so has the emphasis on this aspect of Forest Service land use. In calendar year 1972 there were 183.9 million visits to the National Forest System. The major role which the Forest Service now plays in the recreational field was considered in greater detail in Chap. 5.

**Engineering and Improvement Work** Protecting and making available the natural resources require buildings for headquarters, communication systems, fire-detection stations, firebreaks, fire roads, bridges, major and minor administrative roads, water systems, fences, recreation improvements, foot and horse trails, portage routes, and sources of gravel and other building materials. Careful design and location are required in order that installations will harmonize with the environment and will be safe for public use.

Development of these facilities involves a tremendous and continuing program of construction. At Washington, D.C., and at regional and national forest headquarters, engineering forces are maintained for this work, but most of it is supervised and actually accomplished by the field personnel. Major road and bridge construction is usually handled cooperatively by the Federal Highway Administration in the Department of Transportation.

**Use of the National Forests** It should be remembered that use of the national forests has always been a characteristic of their management. It is interesting to recall that the first set of regulations issued under the Department of Agriculture for the management of the national forests—then called forest reserves—was known as the *use book*. A letter from Secretary of Agriculture James Wilson to Chief Forester Gifford Pinchot, in 1905, repeatedly emphasized two words: *use* and *permanent*. These two words are still guiding principles.

**Research in the Forest Service**   Plans for research by the Forest Service are coordinated through the Department of Agriculture with other U.S. Department of Agriculture programs, with research at land-grant institutions and with that conducted under the McIntire-Stennis Act at forest schools. Some 3,700 individual studies require more than 1,100 highly trained and educated foresters, botanists, physicists, economists, chemists, and engineers supported by more than 2,200 technicians, clerks, and administrative personnel (U.S. Department of Agriculture, 1972). Environmental problems are of major importance. Problems attacked vary from determining the best means of abating the sprouting habits of some undesirable forest species to finding how small a log can be sawed profitably; from remote-sensing techniques which permit identification of root rot centers in Douglas-fir–western hemlock forests to securing a dependable estimate of the standing timber in the whole United States; from learning how to force a preservative into a plentiful timber, little used because of tendency to decay, to selecting the correct form, size, and age of tree to leave for seed on a timber-sale area. These men and women must be open-minded and exhibit the impartiality credited to scientists. They must be patient, accurate, and persistent, and because nobody else is assigned to that particular task, they must interpret and promote the practices that their findings establish as advisable. The Forest Service itself does not escape the lag between research and application of research findings. The more progressive timber companies are using these findings and are supporting their own research programs.

Two examples of the type of research work that has revolutionized accepted practices may be cited:

Fire management techniques have been used to improve environmental quality. These include control of smoke emissions from prescribed fires; proper location and design of fuel breaks in brushy areas, and more effective application of prescribed fires to gain certain management objectives.

The Forest Products Laboratory research is the second general example (Fig. 20-7). These forest products research studies have added millions to the earnings of the wood-using industries since the organization of the Forest Products Laboratory in 1910.

Recent findings of forest products research include a new composite wood product called COM-PLY. A house using this material is being built to field-test its value. COM-PLY lumber has particle board centers and solid wood facings. Preliminary research, done at Athens, Georgia, indicates COM-PLY can use more than 90 percent of a tree for high value lumber products. These products have less warpage and less variability in

**Figure 20-7** Forest products laboratory, Madison, Wisconsin. This institution works to increase uses of wood, decrease wood waste, and conducts other fundamental studies of forest products. *(Courtesy of the U.S. Forest Service.)*

strength and stiffness than sawn lumber (U.S. Department of Agriculture, 1974*a*).

Silvicultural experimentation is less spectacular, and yet experimental spacings in residual stands after cutting, selection of characteristically formed seed trees, and thinning and pruning experiments at many stations and on many forests have definitely shown greatly stimulated rates of growth and increment. Tree breeding is now undertaken in several of the forest and range experiment stations. Some 47 modern laboratories are maintained for long-time experiment and observation.

Grazing research has established more exact knowledge of the carrying capacities of forest ranges and has made possible the revegetation and reclaiming of worn-out ranges. Improvement of big-game habitat is being sought with studies of plant palatabilities. The socioeconomic values of outdoor recreation, including wilderness, are being evaluated.

**Cooperation with States and the Industries** Cooperation in fire control and farm and woodland forestry and advice on the practice of forestry on privately owned lands are an important segment of the Forest Service mission. Consequently, the Forest Service has an organization devoted to such services (see Fig. 20-3). State and private forest land needing protection is now organized with, and receiving help from, federal funds. Such contributions in any state may not exceed annually the total amounts spent by the state itself and the private owners. All 50 states now have this cooperative protection, 14 percent of which is financed by federal funds. Forest Service personnel in this work are students of equipment, organization, tactics, planning, and finance. Their duties take them into forest-fire fighting, equipment warehouses, state fire-research stations, fire-control training conferences, and conferences for planning and for reviewing the failures and successes of prevention and suppression effort.

Similar relations are maintained with state authorities in growing and distributing farm and woodland reforestation stock, from nurseries partially financed by federal funds, and in supplying instruction and advice to farmers. In the latter work, the Forest Service cooperates closely with the Extension Service of the Department of Agriculture. Various cooperative projects are under way in all 50 states and in Puerto Rico; and in most instances extension foresters are in the picture to work with groups of farmers and other private owners, visiting and holding demonstrations in windbreak and forest planting, farm-woodland management, and marketing of forest products. They also assist in organizing and guiding juvenile agricultural and other groups in forestry undertakings. Under the Cooperative Forest Management Act of 1950, more intensive assistance is given timberland owners by foresters employed by the states and jointly financed by federal and state governments. These and additional programs are described in Chap. 21 in greater detail.

**Human Resource Development Programs**    The development and conservation of human resources is equally as important as natural resources. Basic forestry activities are used by the Forest Service for the employment and training of minority, economically depressed, elderly, handicapped, and youth groups. A reservoir of forestry work projects is continually used for a variety of work-training projects.

**Informing and Educating the Public**    The Washington headquarters, each regional research station, state and private area, and national forest headquarters maintain special forces to deal with public requests for information. A growing public concern about environmental matters along with increased demands on all forest resources has brought about a surge in public interest and involvement. In an effort to respond to this the Forest Service carries out a number of activities to seek better understanding of natural resource issues and environmental management.

All of the information activities seek to broaden cooperative efforts with groups, organizations, and individuals from all walks of life to assure that our forest resources and the natural environment will continue to serve the needs and desires of America both now and in the future (U.S. Department of Agriculture, 1974a).

HOW THE FEDERAL GOVERNMENT PRACTICES FORESTRY

## Cooperative State Research Service (CSRS)

This agency administers federal grant funds in agriculture, agricultural marketing, and rural life, and for cooperative forestry research and research facilities. Funds are made available to the State Agricultural Experiment Stations and other designated state institutions in the 50 states and Puerto Rico, Guam, and the Virgin Islands. CSRS also administers a specific grant program for basic scientific research. A portion of these funds are earmarked for the land-grant colleges (Fig. 20-8).

The technical staff of the Service reviews research proposals received from the institutions and conducts on-site reviews of the research in progress, gives leadership in planning and coordinating the research, and encourages the establishment and maintenance of cooperation by and between the stations. They also participate in coordinating research between the experiment stations and the Department of Agriculture (see Fig. 20-3).

## The Cooperative Extension Service

The Smith-Lever Act of 1914 established the Cooperative Extension Service. This act was based on the belief that human progress can be enhanced if the products of research can be translated to the land. Technical information and other assistance is made available to individuals for a higher quality of decision making. The success of this system in developing the world's most productive agriculture has been internationally recognized.

There is a Cooperative Extension Service in each of the 50 states, the District of Columbia, Puerto Rico, the Virgin Islands, and Guam. Extension programs are now conducted in 3,150 counties and many cities.

The Extension Service carries out programs in the broad categories of agriculture, forestry, wildlife, fisheries, and other natural resource areas, including environment, home economics, 4-H clubs, and other youth and community resource development. Extension staff members live and work among the people they serve to help stimulate and educate Americans to plan ahead and cope with their problems.

Nationwide the Extension Service has about 200 staff members in Washington, D.C., and approximately 23,000 in the field. These include professional, paraprofessional, and support staff.

**Agents** Spearheading the work of the Cooperative Extension Service are the county Extension Agents. They live among the people—working with farmers, agricultural industries, homemakers, youth, and community leaders. Most of their assistance is provided through meetings, demonstrations, workshops, short courses, publications, mass media, and followup consultation.

**Extension Forestry** The concerted effort by the Extension Forester

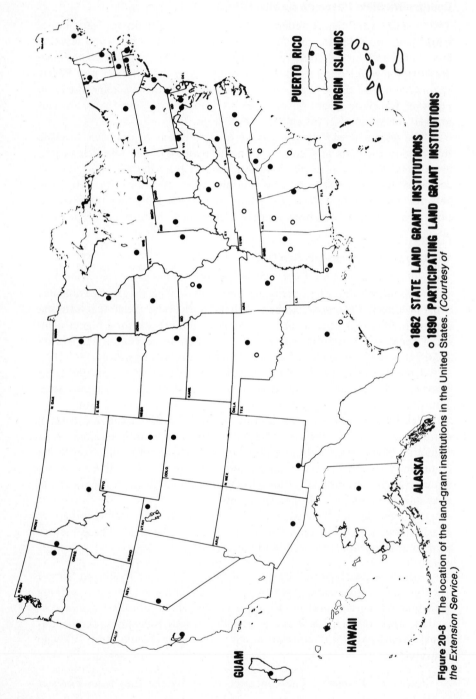

PUERTO RICO

VIRGIN ISLANDS

GUAM

HAWAII

ALASKA

● 1862 STATE LAND GRANT INSTITUTIONS
○ 1890 PARTICIPATING LAND GRANT INSTITUTIONS

**Figure 20-8** The location of the land-grant institutions in the United States. *(Courtesy of the Extension Service.)*

working within this total Extension Service delivery system is concentrated into three major areas; these are (1) forest resources management, (2) forest-products processing, marketing, and distribution, and (3) urban community in environmental forestry. The extension forestry program includes interpretive publications aimed at many levels of users; radio, television, and other media programs adapted to current needs; educationally designed short courses, workshops, conferences, meetings, field tours, and demonstrations adapted to current forestry problems on demand. The Extension Foresters also furnish educational assistance for numerous federal, state, and private agency programs. Because of the close cooperation between teaching, research, and extension, the land-grant universities are in a unique position to carry out effective forestry educational programs to train personnel to undertake research problems, to implement research, and to carry the educational messages through Extension Service (Marks, 1974).

### The Soil Conservation Service

Forestry in the Soil Conservation Service—another bureau in the Department of Agriculture—is centered in the Plant Science Division.

Soil Conservation Service forestry work differs from that of other bureaus in one very important particular—it is practically all done on private lands or public lands that are not in direct control of the Soil Conservation Service. There is a chief forester in a staff position at the Washington office, a forester at each of the four Technical Service Centers serving a group of states (West, Midwest, Northeast, and South), and some 50 foresters assigned to geographical areas usually, but not always, defined by state boundaries.

The Service works in very close cooperation with the nearly 3,000 Soil Conservation Districts, which are organized under state laws and are subdivisions of government. Conservation Districts are similar in some respects to drainage, irrigation, or sanitary districts formed under state laws. In some states Conservation District boundaries coincide with county boundaries but some Districts cover two or more counties while others contain only a part of a county.

The Service assists a Conservation District in preparing conservation agreements with landowners and in implementing the planned conservation work on individual landownerships. Where those ownerships contain land in forest or needing planting to trees, the Service assists the owners accordingly and provides technical forestry services where not available from other sources.

The Service has prime responsibility for windbreak plantings which are very important in the Great Plains states. These plantings may be for erosion control, for protection of the farmstead, or for the protection and encouragement of wildlife (Fig. 20-9).

**Figure 20-9** Pattern of windbreaks near Hecla, South Dakota. The farmstead in lower left is well protected by trees. Protection of the land is obtained by windbreaks in combination with strip cropping. *(Courtesy of the Soil Conservation Service.)*

On a broader basis the Service helps the sponsors of Resource Conservation and Development Projects and Watershed Projects (P.L. 566) and other governmental units to recognize and encourage improved forest management (Lloyd, 1974).

## THE DEPARTMENT OF THE INTERIOR

### The Bureau of Indian Affairs

The Bureau in the Department of the Interior with the longest continuous record for the practice of forestry is the Bureau of Indian Affairs. Under the present organization, it is a program of the Division of Trust Services and provides staff assistance to the Director of the Office of Trust Responsibilities. The principal activity is to manage and protect the Indian-owned forest lands under federal trust. These lands cover 12 million acres (5 million ha) of the total land area of 50 million acres (20 million ha). There are 265 established reservations or groups, plus additional scattered tracts in 26 states. Today, the commercial forest area of 5 million acres (2 million ha) supports a stand of some 36.5 billion board feet. The greater share of this footage lies in the Western states with Washington State having in excess of 15 billion board feet (Fig. 20-10). This one, plus the states of Arizona, California, Montana, New Mexico, and Oregon contain 88 percent of the timber volume in Indian ownership.

Technical forestry operations performed on Indian lands are similar to those described in foregoing pages for the national forests. However, the peculiar landownership in which tribes own land as a group, or individuals own allotted land through various patents, which may be held by an individual owner or may be in an undivided complicated heirship status, present special problems. Another challenging aspect may be found in a stated objective of Title XXV CFR, as it applies to forestry operations, and we quote:

> (3) The development of Indian forests by the Indian people for the purpose of promoting self-sustaining communities, to the end that the Indians may receive from their own property not only the stumpage value, but also the benefit of whatever profit it is capable of yielding and whatever labor the Indians are qualified to perform.

On forested reservations where the volume of timber available for cutting is in excess of that which is being developed by the Indians, open market sales of Indian timber are authorized, providing consent is given by

**Figure 20-10** Old-growth forest, mostly western redcedar, on U.S. Highway 101, in the Quinault Indian Reservation, Olympic Peninsula, Washington State. *(Photo by Grant W. Sharpe.)*

the tribal governing body for tribal timber or by the majority Indian interest of individual allotments. Mills owned by tribal entities may be found at Neopit, Wisconsin (Menominee); Red Lake, Minnesota (Chippewa); Navajo, New Mexico (Navajo); Whiteriver, Arizona (White Mountain Apache); and Warm Springs, Oregon (Warm Springs). Management is usually through a board of directors, with Indians assuming positions of importance. Many other benefits accrue to the tribes through these operations.

In 1929, Indians realized the sum of $2,818,000 from the sale of 660 million board feet. In calendar year 1973, the realization was $70,023,731 from a cut of 918 million board feet. Of these amounts in 1973, the Pacific Northwest cut 60 percent of the volume and realized 71 percent of the reported value.

Grazing is another program in the Division of Trust Services. The promulgation of the General Grazing Regulations of June 4, 1931, was the beginning of an organized program for the management of Indian range. The establishment of the range unit system eliminated "checkerboard" leasing that resulted in extensive trespass of unleased allotments.

The Indian Reorganization Act of 1934 directed the Secretary of the Interior to make rules and regulations for the operation and management of Indian ranges in accordance with the principles of conservation. New grazing regulations were promulgated on December 28, 1935, that incorporated the conservation and administrative provisions basic to the 1931 regulations.

The grazing of livestock is an active business on more than 41 million acres (16.7 million ha) of Indian land. There are 34 million acres (13.6 million ha) classified as open grazing and the remaining acreage is primarily in noncommercial timberland. Indians utilize 87 percent of the grazing capacity of their property for the grazing of horses, cattle, sheep, and goats. The gross value of livestock production from these lands exceeded $77 million of which Indian livestock raisers produced $58.5 million. Landowners received $5.5 million from grazing permits. Free grazing, authorized by tribes and individual Indians, was estimated to be worth $8.8 million. Range management has been difficult to apply because of the reluctance of the Indians to make necessary reductions in their herds (Maynard, 1974).

### The Bureau of Land Management

Some 110 million acres (44.5 million ha) of forest and woodland in the United States, including Alaska, are administered by the Bureau of Land Management. This Bureau was established in 1946 by combining the General Land Office, one of the oldest in the Department of the Interior, with the Grazing Service which had been established to handle the grazing lands in the public domain under the Taylor Grazing Act of 1934. The total

**Figure 20-11**   Ponderosa pine from BLM lands in western Montana. *(Courtesy of the Bureau of Land Management.)*

acreage of all Bureau of Land Management (BLM) lands is 470 million acres (190 million ha) (Stafford, 1974).

Much of the Bureau's forestry work consists of managing the Douglas-fir forests of the revested Oregon and California Railroad grant lands in the Pacific Northwest, but it is also concerned with the lands on the public domain of the inter-Mountain states (Fig. 20-11), and interior forests of Alaska.

The latest management practices are employed in these areas and about 500 foresters are busy marking mature timber for sale, salvaging dead timber, reforestation planning, inventorying, and reconciling various multiple uses which the Department of the Interior encourages. Such activities as fire control, road and trail maintenance, and reforestation work are usually contracted to private business. The Bureau maintains no technical forest research organization but draws frequently on the advice of the regional experiment stations of the Forest Service. As mentioned in Chap. 23 the foresters of the Bureau are paid salaries similar to other federal foresters of similar responsibility.

The question is frequently asked as to why the federal government maintains two bureaus doing similar work, such as the Forest Service and the Bureau of Land Management. The answer apparently lies in the broader land management responsibilities of the Bureau of Land Management and that the lands concerned are in the hands of the government under different laws and long-established practices of administration.

## The National Park Service

The National Park Service (NPS), a bureau in the Department of the Interior, has as its primary mission the management and conservation of the 235 areas of the National Park System for use and enjoyment by all people. Each area is primarily administered in one of three different management categories—natural, historical, or recreational, depending on the primary national significance of the area involved.

Forestry practices in the NPS areas are largely concerned with the protection against wildfire, and any fire determined to be a wildfire, that is a fire threatening valuable physical resources or endangering human life, will immediately be attacked and controlled (Fig. 20-12). However, fire has now begun to be viewed as a management tool in the NPS.

Fire management includes the *use* of fire, as opposed to the total control and suppression, as soon as possible, of each and every fire that occurs. In other words, fire may be determined necessary to perpetuate a desired vegetative or wildlife habitat. Hence, under an established fire management plan for a certain area, when purpose and research have validated the need, a natural fire (i.e., lightning caused) may be allowed to continue after detection. In some cases, in the absence of a naturally occurring fire, a fire may be initiated by an area's resource management specialist. In other cases, a fire started by other sources may also be used.

The use of conventional equipment and procedures, which may be commonly accepted and used on wildfires on lands managed by other agen-

**Figure 20-12** A fire dispatcher at her control center in Park Headquarters, Yosemite National Park, California. All fire-control measures originate from this center. *(Courtesy of the National Park Service.)*

cies, is not always employed on certain fires. This is often the case when evidence of human intrusion with twentieth century technology would long remain after the fire had been extinguished.

The commercial harvesting of trees is not permitted in areas of the NPS managed as "natural" areas. Moreover, the removal of naturally occurring hazards in certain sections of forests in areas managed as natural areas may not be employed, whereas the practice goes unquestioned in a commercial forest. The retention of naturalness in such areas is required, the perpetuation of "manicured" scenery not. It may be desirable, however, to remove certain trees which have been killed or downed by winds or attacked by insects or disease when these pose a threat to personal safety or become a reservoir for undesirable insect infestations. The removal of trees in an area managed as an "historical" or "recreational" area may also occur in conjunction with other management objectives, but is generally incidental to the area's primary purpose.

In forestry matters, technical advice and assistance are afforded the NPS by the U. S. Forest Service, a bureau of the Department of Agriculture. Such instances include the detection and control of insects and disease. In turn, the actual remedial work is accomplished by trained park service crews under the direction of the superintendent of the area involved (Guse, 1974).

### Bureau of Outdoor Recreation

This is one of the newer federal bureaus that will have a major impact on federal land management. The Bureau of Outdoor Recreation (BOR) was created April 2, 1962, and was given statutory authority under the act of May 28, 1963. It is responsible for promoting coordination and development of effective programs relating to outdoor recreation.

The Bureau carries out most of the responsibilities delegated to the Secretary of the Interior under the Land and Water Conservation Fund Act of 1965, numerous functions under the Federal Water Project Recreation Act, the Department of Transportation Act, the Wild and Scenic Rivers Act, the National Trail Systems Act and the Federal Property and Administrative Services Act. BOR has seven regional field offices in addition to its central office in Washington, D.C.

The Bureau serves as the federal focal point to assure prompt and coordinated action at all levels of government for coordinating, planning, and financing public outdoor recreation; and encouraging and assisting all governmental and private interests to conserve, develop, and utilize outdoor recreation resources for the benefit and enjoyment of present and future generations.

The BOR also has responsibility for formulating a comprehensive Nationwide Outdoor Recreation Plan that encompasses the needs and demands of the public for outdoor recreation.

## OTHER FEDERAL AGENCIES

### Tennessee Valley Authority

Operating as an independent corporate agency concerned with all natural resources, the Tennessee Valley Authority has a separate Division of Forestry, Fisheries, and Wildlife Development. Headquartered in Norris, Tennessee, the work of this division is aimed at stimulating improved management and productivity of the terrestrial and aquatic resources in the 26 million acre (10.4 million ha) Tennessee River watershed.

A variety of means for attaining these goals is employed, including stimulation of resource development and utilization action through applied research and education, direct management of land and water resources for multiple benefits on experimental and demonstration bases, basic research to improve resource potential for the future, and environmental education to develop citizen awareness of need for protection and wise use of resources.

The division is also responsible for management and operation of Land Between the Lakes, a 170,000-acre (68,000-ha) outdoor recreation and environmental education center between Kentucky Lake and Lake Barkley in western Kentucky and Tennessee. Since its inception in 1964, Land Between the Lakes has been managed under a multiple-use concept to increase its public recreation and education opportunities, to provide better conditions for wildlife, and to upgrade the quality and appearance of the forest and open lands. Opportunities are unlimited for camping, fishing, hunting, hiking, boating, and studying in the outdoors. Three large family campgrounds and 24 lake-access areas provide facilities for campers ranging from the modern to the informal. In addition, two group camps, Brandon Spring and Camp Energy, are available for those groups who would like to conduct their programs in quiet, natural surroundings. Students and their teachers may live and study at the Youth Station, an outdoor school. Here resident environmental education programs provide the opportunity for direct and firsthand learning experiences away from tightly scheduled classrooms. In 1974 visitation registration at Land Between the Lakes exceeded 2 million including representatives from every state in the Union.

Building on the 21 million acre (8.5 million ha) forest resource, specific efforts of the Division seek to improve management on privately owned lands, maintain capacity of forests to protect soil and water resources, generate greater use of available forest resources by forest products industries already producing goods valued at over $1 billion each year, help forest industries—from logger to manufacturer—in development of new products and methods of producing, regenerate the forests of the future, reclaim land and water resources damaged by mining and pollution, increase wildlife production on forest and wildlands of the Valley, and boost environmental awareness through educational programs.

The Division's programs dealing with aquatic resources are designed to establish huntable populations of resident waterfowl and improve management, productivity, and utilization of the Valley's fisheries resource supported by the more than 600,000 acres (240,000 ha) of habitat in TVA reservoirs and their tributary streams. Activities include maintaining up-to-date information on the entire reservoir system to permit assessment of changes and improving opportunities for harvest (Ripley, 1974).

### Environmental Protection Agency

In the long run this independent agency in the executive branch may have a profound effect on the practice of forestry. As will be seen, its mission gives broad authority for protection of the environment (General Services Administration, 1973–1974).

> The Environmental Protection Agency was created on December 2, 1970, to permit coordinated and effective governmental action on behalf of the environment. EPA endeavors to abate and control pollution systematically, by proper integration of a variety of research, monitoring, standard-setting, and enforcement activities. As a complement to its other activities, EPA coordinates and supports research and anti-pollution activities by states and local governments, private and public groups, individuals and educational institutions. EPA also reinforces efforts among other Federal agencies with respect to the impact of their operations on the environment, and it is specifically charged with making public its written comments on environmental impact statements and with publishing its determinations when those hold that a proposal is unsatisfactory from the standpoint of public health or welfare and to serve as the public's advocate for a livable environment.
>
> The Agency has ten regional field offices and four field environmental research centers in addition to the central Washington, D.C., office.

### The Department of Defense

The Department of Defense through the three military departments, Army, Navy, and Air Force, manages substantial areas of withdrawn and reserved federally owned lands. While these lands are primarily managed for defense purposes, activities such as grazing, timber production, and wildlife management are permitted in some areas. Separately, the Corps of Engineers has responsibility, through the Department of the Army Civil Works Program, for the administration of a number of federally owned areas. Its activities include waterway improvement, flood control, river flow regulation, and recreation development at civil works projects. It regulates the use of navigable waters of the United States (Public Land Law Review Commission, 1970). The acreages (hectares) of federally owned land by agencies are given in Table 20-1.

> The Department of Defense prescribes policies and establishes an integrated multiple-use program for the renewable natural resources in forests and wood-

**Table 20-1   Total Acreage of Federally Owned Land by Defense Agency, 1968**

| | |
|---|---|
| Department of the Army | 11.4 million (4.6 million ha) |
| Department of the Air Force | 8.5 million (3.4 million ha) |
| Corps of Engineers (Civil Works) | 7   million (2.8 million ha) |
| Department of the Navy | 3.6 million (1.4 million ha) |

lands, fish and wildlife, soil, water, grasslands, outdoor recreation and natural beauty compatible with the military mission. The conservation programs required by these DOD directives and the military mission need not, and shall not, be mutually exclusive (Department of Defense Directive, 1965).

Multiple-use management of the Department of Defense lands under the above policies has resulted in many benefits to local people and the public in general. Outdoor recreation visitors, including hunters and fishermen, have especially benefited. In addition there has been much forest planting and timber stand improvement. Timber sales, where appropriate, have resulted in improved stands. Grazing has also been carried on in some cases. Land management on these public military lands is believed to have resulted in improved public support.

## LANDOWNERSHIP PATTERNS

From the land management and landownership information previously mentioned one gets an indication of the diverse ownerships and land management objectives. Chapters 21 and 22 will also elaborate on this situation. Each federal agency has a different mission prescribed by congressional laws. Industrial owners have their objectives; small private owners may have still different aims for their lands; and state land management is generally directed by state law. While all may be managed under a multiple-use principle, there are differences.

Federal, state, and private owners work out mutual problems in fire, insect, and disease protection. They also must determine and agree on landownership boundaries, rights-of-way, and other management. All of these management activities require cooperation and coordination (Fig. 20-13).

## BIBLIOGRAPHY

Ellefson, Paul V. 1974. Focus on the Issues, *Jour. Forestry,* **72**:196.

General Services Administration. 1973–1974. Office of the Federal Register, National Archives and Records Service.

Guse, Neal G., Jr. 1974. Chief, Natural Resources, National Park Service, U.S. Department of the Interior. Personal Correspondence.

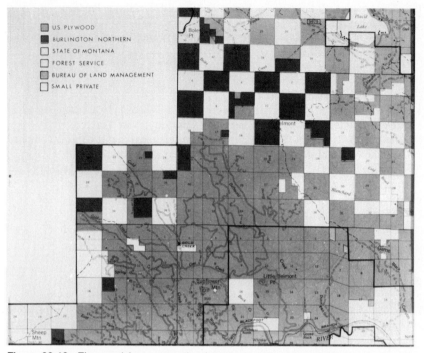

**Figure 20-13** The need for cooperation between public and private owners becomes apparent under this diverse ownership in Montana. *(Courtesy of the Extension Service, U.S. Department of Agriculture.)*

Kaufman, Herbert. 1960. *The Forest Ranger: A Study in Administrative Behavior,* published for Resources for the Future, Inc., by John Hopkins Press, Baltimore.

Lloyd, William J. 1974. Chief Forester, Soil Conservation Service, U.S. Department of Agriculture. Personal Correspondence.

Marks, Richard T. 1974. Extension Forester, U.S. Department of Agriculture. Personal Correspondence.

Maynard, Donald S. 1974. Acting Chief, Division of Tribal Services, Bureau of Indian Affairs, U.S. Department of the Interior. Personal Correspondence.

Public Land Law Review Commission. 1970. *One Third of the Nation's Land,* U.S. Government Printing Office, Washington, DC.

*Report of the President's Advisory Panel on Timber and the Environment.* 1973. U.S. Government Printing Office, Washington, DC.

Ripley, Thomas H. 1974. Director, Division of Forestry, Fisheries, and Wildlife Development, Tennessee Valley Authority, Norris. Personal Correspondence.

Stafford, Sam. 1974. Chief, Current Information, Public Affairs Division, Bureau of Land Management, U.S. Department of the Interior, Personal Correspondence.

U.S. Department of Agriculture. Forest Service. 1972. *Solving Problems on Forest and Related Lands,* Forest Service Research no. 307.

———. 1973. *The Outlook for Timber in the United States,* Forest Service Report no. 20.

———. 1974a. *What the Forest Service Does.*

———. 1974b. *Organization Chart and Mission.*

———. 1974c. *National Forest Manual.*

Van Hise, Charles R., Loomis Havemeyer, (and associates). 1930. *Conservation of Our Natural Resources,* The Macmillan Company, New York.

Widner, Ralph R. (ed.). 1968. *Forests and Forestry in the American States,* compiled by the National Association of State Foresters, Missoula, MT.

# Chapter 21

# How the States and Communities Practice Forestry

There was limited forestry activity in several states in the 1860s and 1870s. In 1885 several states moved for the first time to create a state forestry agency. From this date progress in establishing state forestry agencies came more rapidly. Until 1900 most of the forestry leadership came from the state capitals. After 1900 the national government finally assumed its responsibilities and contributed much in the ensuing decades to the development of nationwide forestry programs. It is this unique interaction between the two elements of the American federal system that makes the history of American forestry important to the evolution of the federal-state relationship in general (Widner, 1968).

The separate states of this country, in many instances, found themselves faced with problems relating to their own and privately held forest lands, more or less as an accident. They had come into possession of educational grant lands—both "school" and agricultural college tracts—tax-delinquent cutover lands, and swamp and overflow grants from the federal government, which contained considerable timber. Obviously these lands, even without the stands of timber they supported, were of some value, but they were not easy to sell, and the better of them were excellent targets for trespassers. Although the states shared the easygoing attitude of the federal government as to obligations of proprietorship involving management, they did see the need for fire control. Moreover, the forestry idea had made some headway before 1900 as outlined above. Much was heard about public forests for the nation from then until 1908; and the governors went home from the 1908 White House Conference so enthusiastic that several of the early state forestry departments were promptly modified and a number of new ones organized (Van Hise, 1930). All this is important background for considering the things that states do in their practice of forestry.

**Why the States Maintain Forestry Departments**    "The powers not delegated to the United States by the Constitution, nor prohibited by it to the states, are reserved to the states, respectively, or to the people." So reads the Tenth Amendment to the Constitution, and a state's necessary business of managing its own forest lands, real and potential, of convincing its citizens that wildfires must be controlled, of reclaiming land by tree planting, and of making it possible to reap a harvest of forest products, forest influences, and enjoyment constitutes the exercise of state powers. If federal help can be secured and is wanted, that is a different matter. State laws can be passed enabling the federal government to establish national forests within the given state, or state forestry activity can be supported sufficiently to merit federal aid in forestry action programs. On the other hand, state pride and interest helped to dictate the organization of various forestry agencies or the undertaking of state forestry work under some existing agency. Presently, all 50 states have official forestry programs (Fig. 21-1).

## TYPES OF STATE FORESTRY ORGANIZATIONS

**Type 1: Independent Forestry Boards or Executive with Headquarters Usually at State Capitals**    This particular grouping is suggested because location of the State Forester's headquarters is sometimes a measure of the character of that officer's duties. There are nine organizations of this type, and the duties of the State Forester in each instance are technical, administrative, and to some extent, policy making. The states are Arkansas, Florida, Georgia, Idaho, Louisiana, Maine, Mississippi, New Mexico, and Oregon. In all these, except Maine, the State Forester is the executive of a board or commission of five to twelve members. The Commissioner of Forestry in Maine is an independent executive, reporting directly to the governor. Some of the boards in the eight other states have administrative duties and all have a hand in policy making.

*Activities in Oregon as an Example of Type 1*    The gross land area of

**Figure 21-1**  The Washington State Department of Natural Resources practices intensive management, fertilizing 10,000 to 12,000 acres (4,000 to 4,800 ha) per year to
increase forest growth on state land. This view shows a Kaman helicopter taking off with
a fertilizer pod loaded with 1,500 pounds of urea (46 percent nitrogen). *(Courtesy of the
Department of Natural Resources, Washington State.)*

the state is 61 million acres (24.6 million ha) of which almost one-half is in
forest.

The Oregon State Department of Forestry is active in six major program areas: fire protection, insect and disease protection, management of
state forests, forest nursery, service forestry for private landowners, and
forest practices.

The department protects over 16 million acres of private and public
lands from fire, over one-half of Oregon's commercial forests. An average
of 1,057 wildfires are controlled annually, but the number can exceed 1,650.
These fires burn some 14,000 acres (5,600 ha) each year. Among the modern fire-fighting tools are aircraft for detection and fire retardant drops, a
sophisticated burning index system to measure fire danger and highly
trained fire management teams to direct control action on major fires. The
forest industry and other fire-control agencies cooperate in the protection
effort.

Insect and disease protection is provided by the department to the
same 16 million acres (6.4 million ha) that receive fire protection. Annual
aerial surveys are made of all Oregon forests to locate insect and disease

**Figure 21-2** New growth in the Tillamook State Forest crowds out an old logging trestle from its colorful past. Twelve million dollars and 24 years of the most massive reforestation effort ever undertaken by any state created this new state forest. *(Courtesy of the Oregon Department of Forestry.)*

activities. From 1972 through 1974, the Douglas-fir tussock moth was a major problem in northeastern Oregon and parts of neighboring states.

Intensive management is provided on 780,000 acres (312,000 ha) of state forests, including control of competing vegetation, precommercial thinning, commercial thinning, and timber sales. Timber sale income from these lands has averaged about $7.5 million a year. Reforestation has been a major part of this job. A principal accomplishment of the department was the reforestation and rehabilitation of the 350,000-acre (140,000-ha) Tillamook Burn into the Tillamook State Forest (Fig. 21-2).

Forestry assistance is given to private landowners by the department. Oregon has 36,000 individual owners with 5,000 acres (2,000 ha) or less. Because much of this land is very productive, landowners are encouraged to practice good forest management.

A new department program since 1972 has been administering the Oregon Forest Practices Act. This act regulates forest practices on all forest lands in the state, encouraging prompt reforestation of logged or burned lands, careful road construction and maintenance, safe use of chemicals, good logging practices, and wise slash disposal. The emphasis has been placed on industrial forest lands. Compliance has been averaging above 90 percent.

The department operates the D. L. Phipps Forest Nursery which produces over 25 million seedlings annually. These seedlings are sold to the forest industry and to the general public and are used in reforesting state lands.

Recently, the Oregon State Board of Forestry and the department have been making a broad study of the forest resources of the state to assure a future wood supply in Oregon.[1]

**Type 2: Nonforestry Administrative Boards with or without Advisory Groups and with Headquarters Elsewhere Than at State Capitals** For some peculiar reason, forestry in certain states is not considered coordinate with other state functions, even though financed and administered independently. Usually in such cases, the State Forester is located at a state educational institution. He may give a portion of his time to teaching, as in North Dakota, where the State Forester is also President of the North Dakota School of Forestry at Bottineau and responsible to the school's board of directors. Other examples include Texas, where the State Forester is located at College Station and is responsible to the board of directors of Texas Agricultural and Mechanical College. Nebraska, while it has a "Game, Forestation and Parks Commission," turns its forestry work over to an "Extension Forester" working out of the Agricultural College at Lincoln. In most of these examples, forestry functions have apparently been thought of as more closely allied to agriculture than to any other industry. Forestry work in Kansas has for many years been under the State College of Agriculture at Manhattan, while Utah's Chief Forester is located at Logan and is a member of the faculty of the College of Forestry. In 1955 Colorado shifted the responsibility of its State Forester from the Board of Land Commissioners to the State Board of Agriculture. Headquarters are at the State University of Colorado, Fort Collins. There is, of course, a wide variation in the volume of forestry activity among the states with this type of organization, and some of the most progressive forestry departments are included.

***Activities in Texas as an Example of Type 2*** Five state forests containing 6,510 acres (2,600 ha), all under management, constitute one interesting feature of the work of the Texas Forest Service. All state and federal land is under adequate fire protection, and in addition more than 11 million acres (4.4 million ha) of private forest land are organized for fire control. About 1.8 million acres (720,000 ha) of the latter class remain to be brought under

---

[1] Correspondence June 1974, Office of State Forester, Forestry Department, Salem, Oregon.

protection. One state nursery is operated with an output of 30 million seed-lings annually, available to farmers and ranchers at cost. The capacity of this nursery is being expanded. With a commercial timber stand of more than 10.4 billion board feet and an average annual fire loss amounting to $1 million, fire control draws heavily upon the time of the State Forester and his staff. Research on tree improvement and forest utilization, advice to landowners on forest management, and campaigns of education are also important activities.[2]

**Type 3: Departments of Conservation or Similar Designation Responsible to Commissions or Boards and Having Forestry as a Major Division**  A good many of the states have combined the administration of a number of natural resources, including from two to six divisions such as forests, parks, unorganized state lands, waters, minerals, and game and fish (the last two frequently combined but not always). In some states in recent years environmental protection has been added as a division, such as in the Wisconsin Department of Natural Resources. In 1970 New York estab-lished a Department of Environmental Conservation.

Michigan is an example of an almost inclusive conservation depart-ment, since it deals with everything but agricultural lands and water from the power and navigation and pollution control angles. In addition, it has a Division of Education and a Division of Field Administration, which in-cludes the functions of fire control and law enforcement. The State Forester is responsible to the director of conservation, who is in turn responsible to the conservation commission of seven members with staggered terms of office. Such terms are designed to control partisan political domination.

Pennsylvania has a Department of Forests and Waters. It administers efficiently two important natural resources, but does not include fish and game or minerals. Its commission of five members is advisory.

In all, 33 states recognize forestry on a par with other natural resources in departments similar to those of Michigan and Pennsylvania and answer-able to a policy-making board or commission.

*Activities in Ohio as an Example of Type 3*  As in the neighboring state of Michigan, Ohio's forestry work is centered in one of nineteen divisions of a conservation department known as the Department of Natural Resources. Eighteen state forests, totaling 163,757 acres (65,480 ha), were subject to harvest of around 2.5 million board feet of saw logs, round guardrails, and poles in 1973 (Fig. 21-3). Planted areas reached a total of 14,600 acres (5,840 ha). Ohio's forest nurseries have increased production of trees from 2 million in 1948 to more than 12 million in 1974. Most of these trees are distributed to landowners, including farmers, industrial concerns, schools,

---

[2] Correspondence June 1974, Texas Forest Service, College Station, Texas.

**Figure 21-3** These posts and poles were harvested from the Mohican State Forest, Ohio, in a thinning operation of pine plantings made 20 to 30 years ago. The thinning not only produced valuable products but improved the growth and vigor of the remaining stand. *(Courtesy of the Ohio Division of Forests and Preserves.)*

and organizations. A considerable amount of this nursery stock is hardwood, and demand for establishing windbreaks is brisk.

In addition to protecting state-owned lands, the Division of Forests and Preserves handles fires in 4.5 million acres (1.8 million ha) of private land in southern and southeastern Ohio. Under a special law more than 15,000 tracts of privately owned land dedicated to forest management have been certified for reduction of taxes. Assistance and advice to farm forest owners is well developed in Ohio under the Federal Cooperative Forest Management Act.

In addition to the above activities, insect and disease control and research and education projects draw heavily on the energies of the Division of Forests and Preserves.[3]

**Type 4: Departments of Conservation or Similar Designation Not Answerable to Boards or Commissions**   Minnesota and Kentucky have Divisions of Forestry within a Department of Conservation not answerable to a board or commission.

*Activities in Minnesota as an Example of Type 4*   Under a reorganization in 1973, field operations have been decentralized under Regional Ad-

---

[3] Correspondence June 1974, Division of Forests and Preserves, Columbus, Ohio.

ministrators who report to the commissioner. The divisions, including the Division of Forestry, serve as staff to the commissioner.

The land activity under the new organization has been centralized in a Bureau of Land which reports directly to the commissioner's office. The Division of Forestry in its staff function is responsible for planning, programming, procedures, evaluating, and monitoring the programs of the Department of Natural Resources and for providing leadership and assistance in forestry activities (Adams, 1974).

The forested area of Minnesota amounts to 19 million acres (7.6 million ha) or 37 percent of the total land area. 17 million acres (6.8 million ha) are commercial forest. 7.5 million acres (3 million ha) of the commercial forest land are privately owned and 9.5 million acres (3.8 million ha) are publicly owned. Of the publicly owned forest, 2.8 million acres (1.12 million ha) are federal; 3.3 million acres (1.32 million ha) are state of Minnesota; and 3.4 million acres (1.36 million ha) are in county and municipal ownership (*Forestry in Minnesota,* 1971).

Minnesota has a vigorous wildfire- and pest-control program for private, state, county, and municipal lands. Minnesota foresters actively promote private forest management. On the average 15 million trees are produced annually for planting on private and state lands.

## What Is the Best Type of State Forestry Organization?

So long as state governments with their varying traditions survive, and so long as the people of different states emphasize different objectives to be attained by the management of forest resources, there is no one best type of forestry organization. The fortunes of state forestry departments, boards, divisions, and individual state foresters, however, indicate certain principles that may be suggested for use in seeking further state forestry achievement, as follows:

1  Terms of board of commission members who make the policies for state forestry practice should be staggered; that is, there should always be carry-over members, and it is well to limit the number of those who belong to the same political party. Members should not receive salaries.

2  The general-manager or single-executive type of department should require appointment of a forester of recognized technical and administrative ability, and he or she should be removable only for cause, with a tenure of office of at least 10 years.

3  In combined natural-resource or so-called conservation departments, forestry should have financial recognition and technically capable personnel, equivalent to that of fish and game, park, and land divisions, and all employees should be selected under a civil-service system with the career-service idea well worked out.

4  Cooperative and regulatory forestry functions of the state, involving timber landowners and timber- and forest-products industries, should

be performed by the State Forester and staff. The State Forester should serve in an advisory capacity to the farm-forestry extension and reforestation work, usually centered at the state college of agriculture. The State Forester may well have direct supervision of the type of farm forestry governed by the Cooperative Forest Management Law. This person should by all means be a full-time employee, not required to teach in addition to administrative and technical work.

5   No state forestry agency should be so submerged under a broader organization that the economic aspects of forestry practice are lost in the strictly aesthetic and recreational objectives. The latter are very important but are usually more fully provided for in state and national park systems. Multiple use, with emphasis on continuous returns with due regard for all environmental values, should be the broad objective.

**Action Programs in State Forestry**   In Chap. 3 several federal laws are listed which in various ways assist state forestry programs. Congress, recognizing the national interest in the forest resources of the several states, has enacted a series of cooperative federal-state forestry programs to provide national support and coordination to the local leadership of the state forestry agencies. These programs are the Clarke-McNary Act of 1924; the Forest Pest Control Act of 1947; the Cooperative Forest Management Act of 1950; Title IV of the Agricultural Act of 1956; Title IV of the Rural Development Act of 1972, and Title X of the Agriculture and Consumer Protection Act of 1973 (forestry incentives, including urban forestry). These programs are administered by the state forestry agencies. Federal responsibilities are met by the State and Private Forestry Unit of the U. S. Forest Service, Department of Agriculture, which allocates federal funds to the several states, conducts fiscal and program audits and provides technical specialists. The programs allow for 50-50 cost sharing, but federal funds available in 1972 varied from 14 to 50 percent.

Highlights of these major programs are as follows: Under Section 2 of the Clarke-McNary Act of 1924, there were 614 million acres (248 million ha) protected in 1973 at a total cost of $137 million. Of this expenditure, $20 million was federal (or 14 percent) and $117 million was state and local (or 86 percent). During the previous 5 years (1967–1971) an annual average of 116,000 wildfires burned an annual average of 1.7 million acres (680,000 ha). Under Title IV of the Rural Development Act of 1972, a pilot program is being conducted for protection of all rural areas, including those that do not qualify under Section 2 of the Clarke-McNary Act (nonfederal timbered lands and certain nontimbered watershed lands). Since 1950 there has been a gradual reduction in area burned, total number of fires, and average size of fires.

Under the Forest Pest Control Act of 1947, there were 48 active control projects in 1972 on nonfederal lands. State forestry agencies provided $2.8 million (73 percent) to $1.1 million (27 percent) federal. Since it is estimated that there is an average annual loss of 15 billion board feet of lumber due to insects and disease, this program will probably expand in the future. More trained personnel, increased research, increased detection, and more salvage appear likely. It also appears that more attention will be given values other than timber.

Technical services and advice were provided by the states under the Cooperative Forest Management Act of 1950 in fiscal year 1973 to more than 106,000 private nonindustrial landowners on 6.47 million acres (2.58 million ha) of forest land. Advice was also given to many forest-product operators in processing primary forest products for harvesting and primary manufacture. Technical advice was also given to local governments and private agencies for development, protection, and management of forested areas and trees in urban areas. The federal funds were $4 million (25 percent) to $12 million (75 percent) for the states.

Cooperative forestation under Section 4 of the Clarke-McNary Act provides for state forestry agencies to furnish satisfactory tree planting stock. From 1968 to 1972, 3 billion seedlings were sold. In 1972, the federal government financed $214,000 (3 percent) with the states financing $6 million (97 percent). Title IV of the Agriculture Act of 1956 promotes the improvement of genetic quality of trees and the forestation of nonfederal public lands. Thirteen states now have genetically superior seed orchards (Fig. 21-4). In 1972, the federal government financed $1 million (16 percent) and the states, $5 million (84 percent). Title X of the Agriculture Act of 1973 (forest incentives) promotes forestry on nonindustrial ownerships of 500 acres (200 ha) or less. It provides for federal cost sharing for planting and timber-stand improvement under management plans approved by the state forestry agency. Urban forestry is also included. $10 million in federal funds were appropriated in 1974 under a $40 million authorization (National Association of State Foresters, 1973).

North Carolina, Texas, and Virginia have state programs that provide incentives to nonindustrial owners. Eight other states have passed some form of incentive legislation.[4]

## State Forest Practice Acts

At least 16 states have forest practice acts of some sort, and in a number of states efforts to establish such acts are actively underway. In nine of the 16 states, forest practice standards have been set forth in forest practice acts by state legislatures whereas seven states have forest practice acts which require a board or commission to establish the standards. Some states, through other state laws, have established forest practice standards though no state forest practice act exists.

---

[4] *Report of the President's Advisory Panel on Timber and the Environment,* pp. 247–248 and Appendix pp. 287–289.

**Figure 21-4** A young seed orchard of grafted slash pine. *(Courtesy of the Georgia Forestry Commission.)*

Critical to state forest practice acts is specification of forest practice standards. Just what are the "sound forest practice standards" to which landowners should adhere? The tremendous variation in local conditions affecting the establishment, growth, and survival of forest trees and other vegetation makes this an especially difficult task (Ellefson, 1974).

A summary of state laws regulating cutting practices is given in the *Report of the President's Advisory Panel on Timber and the Environment.*

## STATE, COUNTY, AND MUNICIPAL FORESTS

Of the nearly 500 million acres (200 million ha) of commercial forest land in the United States, 21.4 million acres (8.56 million ha) are owned by the states and 7.5 million acres (3 million ha) by counties and municipalities. This does not include acreages of noncommercial land used for parks, other recreation, or land otherwise not available for commercial timber production.

State forest acreages vary from only a few in some states to 3.8 million acres (1.52 million ha) for Michigan. The same is true of county and municipal forests where commercial forest acreages vary from zero or a few to a maximum of 3.3 million acres (1.32 million ha) in Minnesota (*The Outlook for Timber in the United States*, 1973).

Most of the county and municipal forest lands are managed for multiple uses. The nontimber values are increasing, but timber harvest is feasible under proper management. Numerous community or city forest watersheds are included and in some cases are being intensively managed and used by the public.

Previously in this chapter state forestry programs have been given for Oregon, Texas, Ohio, and Minnesota as examples of forestry organizations and programs. This included a discussion of the state forest programs for these four states.

### County Forestry

An excellent example of a county forest management program exists in Langlade County, Wisconsin. Langlade County is one of 28 counties in Wisconsin that has county forest land, and in each county a professional forester is responsible for the forest management program. These county forest lands comprise about half the public forest area in Wisconsin.

The total amount of land covered by forest in Wisconsin is 14.9 million acres (5.96 million ha). The vast majority, 14.5 million acres (5.8 million ha), is commercial forest land which is defined as land capable of growing industrial wood and not preserved from timber harvesting (Table 21-1). In addition, there are 374,000 acres (150,000 ha) of unproductive forest land that is incapable of growing industrial wood and about 34,000 acres (13,700 ha) of forest in the form of state and county parks (Fig. 21-5).

**Related Natural Resources Programs in Wisconsin** In addition to serving as Forest Administrator for the 121,655 acres (48,660 ha) of the Langlade County Forest, the forestry agent carries out educational respon-

**Table 21-1  Area by Ownership of Commercial Forest Land in Wisconsin**

|                                  | Acres      | Hectares  | Percentage |
|----------------------------------|------------|-----------|------------|
| State                            | 568,000    | 227,200   | 3.9        |
| County and municipal             | 2,365,700  | 946,280   | 16.3       |
| National forest                  | 1,317,000  | 526,000   | 9.0        |
| Indian and other federal         | 274,000    | 109,600   | 1.9        |
| Forest industry                  | 1,368,100  | 547,240   | 9.4        |
| Farmer owned                     | 4,809,000  | 1,923,600 | 33.1       |
| Miscellaneous private ownership  | 3,833,500  | 1,533,400 | 26.4       |
| Total                            | 14,535,300 | 5,813,200 | 100        |

*Source:* John S. Spencer and Harry W. Thorne, *Wisconsin's 1968 Timber Resource*, St. Paul, Minnesota, North Central Forest Experiment Station, Forest Service, U.S. Department of Agriculture, Resource Bulletin NC-15, p. 34.

**Figure 21-5**  Fly fishing in a Wisconsin State Forest. *Courtesy of the Wisconsin Natural Resources Department.)*

sibilities in several different areas of natural resources such as recreational development, forest-management, land-use planning and resource policy, mineral resource and mining, wildlife habitat, environmental education, program planning, and youth programs.[5]

### Urban, Community, and Environmental Forestry

In 400 urban areas and 1,900 urban counties, where approximately half our population lives, there are 124 million street and shade trees, with an estimated investment value of $31 billion and in many cases an inestimable aesthetic value. Windbreak and shelterbelt plantings are widely used in some rural settings, particularly in the Central and Western parts of the country. In these cases, sound advisory programs are utilized to protect existing investments and the proper use of trees.

[5] The above information on county forestry was furnished by Mr. Christy T. Hauge, Forestry Agent, Langlade County, Wisconsin; Dr. Gordon R. Cunningham, Extension Forester, University of Wisconsin, Madison; and Dr. Richard T. Marks, Extension Forester, Washington, D.C.

Trees and forests are becoming more important than ever in shaping the quality of the human environment. Increasingly, urbanites are influencing the future direction of all forest and land-use policy. Most of these urban dwellers have little knowledge about the establishment, protection, care, maintenance, use, enjoyment, and removal of trees within or near the city.

The growing population and expanding economy create increasing demands for land for housing, roads, parks, schools, recreational facilities, and other community services. Signs of growth are seen in sprawling suburbs, new factories, and strip developments across the countryside. Land-use planning can provide for *orderly* growth and development.

Extension educational programs in urban, community, and environmental forestry are available, not only for urban residents, some of whom are woodland owners, but also for city and village officials, developers, realtors, contractors, builders and architects, and conservation groups concerned about the future of these resources. In addition, it is important to provide information as to the values of all forest resources in our state and national economy. Included would be such basic social values as aesthetics, water quantity and quality, air purification, noise abatement, temperature amelioration, erosion control, protection and privacy, fish and wildlife habitat, recreation, and nature study.

The purely economic values of timberlands for commercial timber, fuel, and forage are included in this education program with emphasis on the utilization of salvageable material from street and shade trees.

**Problems of Urban Forestry**   The officials of most cities and smaller towns need additional knowledge of the role of trees in improving the environment, of how many trees they have, what kind they are, what condition they are in, what they are worth, and who actually owns or is responsible for the trees. Individual lot owners in our cities usually have a few trees, but most are not knowledgeable about proper care and maintenance or the selection of replacements. Most cities lack ordinances that clearly define the ownership of the trees and who is responsible for the care and maintenance of trees.

Most cities have no ordinances that define what species may be planted or where they can or cannot be planted, and the majority of cities lack adequate budgets to maintain trained personnel, adequate equipment, and a labor force to properly manage their tree resource.

People living in our cities, towns, and villages have real needs for advice, consultations, and education in the forestry field. Most of them have at least one tree, some have many trees. They all have an interest and a stake in forest policy and forests as a source of goods and services. Some actually are owners of forest lands and want information on how best to manage these lands.

## Summary

Urban forestry is the sum total of the establishment, protection, care, maintenance, use, enjoyment, and removal of trees within the city, with major emphasis on working with the private owner, the city, or the town so that maximum benefits are derived from the resource.

Urban, community and environmental forestry is being served by the Extension Service in cooperation with other federal, state, and private agencies. The Extension Service has an office serving every county in the United States. This local office has an Extension County Director, county agent, and secretarial staff. In addition, there is a staff of agents for specialized fields, depending on needs and population. In addition, each office has back-up specialist's help from the land-grant university in each state. These people can be called upon for consultation, advice, and educational meetings.

The Extension Agent in urbanized counties may well have a specialized agent in urban forestry on the county staff. This agent, in turn, can call on the university for the help of entomologists, arboriculturists, pathologists, foresters, landscape architects, horticulturists, planners, zoners, engineers, soil specialists, or whatever disciplines needed to educate, advise, or consult with the urban population (Marks, 1974).

## BIBLIOGRAPHY

Adams, Earl J. 1974. Director, Division of Forestry, Minnesota. Personal Correspondence.

Department of Defense Directive. 1965. Washington, DC.

Ellefson, Paul V. 1974. Focus on the Issues. *Jour. Forestry*, **72**:196.

*Forestry in Minnesota.* 1971. State of Minnesota, Department of Natural Resources, Division of Forestry.

General Services Administration. *U.S. Government Manual 1973–1974,* Office of the Federal Register, National Archives and Records Service.

Marks, Richard T. 1974. Extension Forester, Extension Service, U.S. Department of Agriculture. Personal Correspondence.

National Association of State Foresters. 1973. *State Forestry in the United States: Its Present Status and Needs.*

*The Outlook for Timber in the United States.* 1973. Forest Service, U.S. Department of Agriculture. Forest Resource Report no. 20.

Public Land Law Review Commission. 1968. Washington, DC.

*Report of the President's Advisory Panel on Timber and the Environment.* 1973. U.S. Government Printing Office, Washington, DC.

Ripley, Thomas H. 1974. Director, Division of Forestry, Fisheries, and Wildlife Development, Tennessee Valley Authority, Norris. Personal Correspondence.

Van Hise, Charles R., Loomis Havemeyer (and associates). 1930. *Conservation of Our Natural Resources.* The Macmillan Company, New York.

Widner, Ralph R. (ed.). 1968. *Forests and Foresters in the American States.* Compiled by the National Association of State Foresters. Missoula, MT.

# Chapter 22

# The Practice of Forestry on Private Lands

Of the commercial forest land of the United States, 73 percent is privately owned. This amounts to 363.6 million acres (145.4 million ha).

According to the Forest Service (1958) there are more than 4.5 million separate ownerships. These differ in size from 3 acres (1.2 ha) to more than 2 million acres (800,000 ha). In spite of a few large forests, the size of the average private forest is 79 acres (31.6 ha). A special study for the 1958 report determined that small ownerships predominate. The study has not been updated, but there was some evidence in 1974 that there may be 4.5 million or more since many small forests have been divided in recent years. It would appear that many changes in ownership will occur in the years ahead.

Most of the private forests are in the East, 40 percent in the North, and 48 percent in the South. The West, which supports 64 percent of the public forests, has only 12 percent of the private forests.

There is considerable variation in the size of private forests as well as a variation in the quality of forestry being practiced on them. Private forests may be conveniently divided into two categories, farm and miscellaneous private woodlands, and industrial.

**Farm and Miscellaneous Private Woodlands**   This includes small owners up to 5,000 acres (2,000 ha) and medium-sized ownerships, 5,000 to 50,000 acres (2,000 to 20,000 ha).

Commercial timberlands held by business and professional people, wage and salary workers, housewives, railroad, mining, and other corporations, and other nonfarm or miscellaneous owners represent the largest class of forest ownership. In 1970, these owners held 165 million acres (66 million ha) or 33 percent of the total area of commercial timberland.

Another 26 percent, 131 million acres (52 million ha), was classed as owned by farmers.

Many of the farm and miscellaneous private holdings include highly productive timber sites and most are close to markets for timber products. These ownerships consequently have long been of major importance as a source of timber supplies for the wood-using industries.

Until 1952 the combined area of farm and miscellaneous ownership had not shown much change. However, farm ownership dropped about 42.5 million acres (17 million ha) between 1952 and 1970, while miscellaneous private ownerships increased about the same amount. Farm abandonment and a decline in rural population has typically been associated with sales of land to nonfarm or industrial owners (U.S. Department of Agriculture, 1973).

Most small owners do not have the funds necessary for timber-stand improvement, fire protection, and taxes. Much of the land now in small ownerships was cut over in the past, cleared for farming, or used for pasture. Many of these woodlands were of great help in the building of America. The present owners will need help and incentives in building up the productivity of these forest lands.

The average owners of farm woodlands grow trees only as a side line along with their other crops and livestock farming, all too often harvesting the trees when they need ready cash, even though the trees are growing at their best.

There are many so-called small owners, such as business and professional people and wage and salary earners, making their living primarily in occupations completely unrelated to forest industries who hold their land only for the satisfaction of being a landowner or having a place to go to on time off from their primary job. Many of these owners have no intention of practicing forestry on their land.

On the other hand, there are farm woodland owners who, during their spare time, repair fences to prevent destructive grazing, mark their trees for cutting, girdle or remove weed species, prune lower limbs (Fig. 22-1), establish firebreaks, plant new trees, sell timber only when it is in the best interest of their forest, and accept advice from certain industrial, consulting, state, or federal foresters on how to manage their woodlots. Many large

**Table 22-1   Area of Commercial Timberland in the United States, by Type of Ownership and Section**

| | Total United States | | | North | |
|---|---|---|---|---|---|
| | Area | | Proportion | | |
| | Thousand | | | Thousand | |
| Type of ownership | acres | ha | percent | acres | ha |
| Federal | | | | | |
|   National forest | 91,924 | 36,769 | 18 | 10,458 | 4,182 |
|   Bureau of Land Management | 4,762 | 1,905 | 1 | 75 | 30 |
|   Bureau of Indian Affairs | 5,888 | 2,355 | 1 | 815 | 326 |
|   Other federal | 4,534 | 1,814 | 1 | 963 | 385 |
|   Total federal | 107,108 | 42,843 | 21 | 12,311 | 4,923 |
| State | 21,423 | 8,570 | 4 | 13,076 | 5,230 |
|   County and municipal | 7,589 | 3,035 | 2 | 6,525 | 2,610 |
|   Forest industry | 67,341 | 26,936 | 14 | 17,563 | 7,025 |
|   Farm | 131,135 | 52,454 | 26 | 51,017 | 20,407 |
| Miscellaneous private | 165,101 | 66,040 | 33 | 77,409 | 30,964 |
| All ownerships | 499,697 | 199,878 | 100 | 177,901 | 71,159 |

Source: The Outlook for Timber in the United States. 1973. Forest Resource Report no. 20. Forest Service, Washington, DC.

**Figure 22-1**   A farm woodland owner pruning and thinning his trees in eastern Washington State. *(Courtesy of the American Forest Institute.)*

| South | | Rocky Mountains | | Pacific Coast | |
| --- | --- | --- | --- | --- | --- |
| Thousand | | Thousand | | Thousand | |
| acres | ha | acres | ha | acres | ha |
| 10,764 | 4,306 | 39,787 | 15,914 | 30,915 | 12,366 |
| 11 | 4.4 | 2,024 | 809 | 2,652 | 1,060 |
| 220 | 88 | 2,809 | 1,124 | 2,044 | 818 |
| 3,282 | 1,313 | 78 | 31 | 211 | 84 |
| 14,277 | 5,711 | 44,698 | 17,878 | 35,822 | 14,328 |
| 2,321 | 928 | 2,198 | 879 | 3,828 | 1,531 |
| 681 | 272 | 71 | 28 | 312 | 125 |
| 35,325 | 14,130 | 2,234 | 894 | 12,219 | 4,888 |
| 65,137 | 26,055 | 8,379 | 3,351 | 6,602 | 2,640 |
| 74,801 | 29,920 | 4,051 | 1,620 | 8,840 | 3,536 |
| 192,542 | 77,016 | 61,631 | 24,650 | 67,623 | 27,048 |

pulp mills in the South, for example, are heavily dependent on farm woodlands for their very existence and maintain a staff of conservation foresters who work with the small forest owner. If the owner is practicing adequate forestry, the forest may qualify for Tree Farm certification and be included in the Tree Farm system cited later in this chapter.

In addition to the tracts of 5,000 acres (2,000 ha) or less in miscellaneous ownerships, there are an estimated 2,000 to 3,000 owners in the 5,000- to 50,000-acre (2,000- to 20,000-ha) class. The average size is estimated to be 15,000 to 20,000 acres (6,000 to 8,000 ha).

The owners of forests in medium-sized ownerships are less likely to be "absentee owners," or if they are, they likely maintain an interest in forestry. The medium-sized forest may be owned by anyone, and these holdings are fairly well distributed throughout the United States, although they are least in evidence in the Central states and somewhat more common in the South. Such a forest may be an estate, the property of a hunting club, individual owner, or of a partnership. The owners may have a small mill and supplement these holdings by buying raw material from other holders, or they may be continually on the lookout for new land to buy for incorporation into their own forest management plans.

Regardless of who owns the land, the intent to practice forestry is usually there. In fact, a forest in this category will very often support a full-time forest manager who performs the usual duties of forestry. As a result of the greater interest in forest management, this owner is usually more aware of yield taxes and other special state tax laws which are designed to encourage the practice of forestry. Because of greater property valuation, the owner of medium-sized lands is better able to obtain credit or money for improvement loans than is the small owner. Here again, the medium-sized forest owner may wish to apply for Tree Farm certification.

The estimated 4.5 million small and miscellaneous and medium-sized forest owners comprise an important segment of the total forest situation in the United States. On these lands are located over half the total commercial forest. The challenge on these lands is to meet the production of the industrial and public lands.

**Forestry Action Programs** In recent years it has become evident that more promotion and education is needed for the farm and miscellaneous private owners, especially the smaller owners. In a report of the National Association of State Foresters, 1973, the forestry action programs in wildfire, forest pest control, cooperative forest management, cooperative forestation and forestry incentives are set forth, showing present status and future objectives. These programs are now available to all 50 state forestry agencies through federal-state cooperative relationships and in turn to the private landowners. Intensified protection and technical assistance are planned.

In 1973 a forest incentives section was approved in the Agriculture and Consumer Protection Act. It directs the Secretary of Agriculture to encourage development of nonindustrial private land for timber production. This section authorizes up to $40 million annually for cost sharing, 50 to 75 percent of the cost of reforestation, timber-stand improvement and related activities. It is limited to ownerships of 500 acres (200 ha) or less. Each owner must have a plan of management approved by the State Forester. The plan becomes the basis for signed contracts of 1 to 25 years' duration (Pomeroy, 1973).

**Industrial Ownerships** A private commercial holding of more than 50,000 acres (20,000 ha) of forest land is classified as an industrial ownership. From Table 22-1, you will note there are 17.5 million acres (7 million ha) in the North, 35.3 million acres (14 million ha) in the South, 2.2 million acres (893,600 ha) in the Rocky Mountains, and 12.2 million acres (4.88 million ha) on the Pacific Coast for a total of 67.3 million acres (26.9 million ha) in industrial ownership. This represents 14 percent of the commercial forest land in the United States. It includes some of the nation's most productive timber-growing areas.

In the 1952–1970 period, areas of commercial timberland in forest-industry ownership increased by 8 million acres (3.2 million ha). Much of the increase was in the South where wood-using companies have been acquiring forest lands. A substantial part of the added acreage was purchased from farm and miscellaneous owners.

Forest industries have also turned to leasing and long-term cutting contracts to supplement fee ownership. In the South, an estimated 9 million acres (3.6 million ha) of commercial timberlands in nonindustrial ownerships were managed by the forest industries in 1970 (U.S. Department of Agriculture, 1973).

During this same 1952–1970 period there have been many improvements in the public attitudes towards industrial ownership. Prior to World War II there were few incentives for long-term forestry. Tax laws encouraged cutting. Since World War II the forest industries have been able to plan for more continuity and have given good leadership in promoting and demonstrating intensive forestry. The best forest management on private lands is being practiced on these industrial holdings.

Industrial owners, usually in the lumber, plywood, or pulp and paper business (or increasingly, all three), have a huge investment in their wood-using plants, and these must be kept supplied if they intend to stay in business. The owners of large and some medium-sized holdings see the need for, and are able to provide for, more adequate protection on their lands. Some companies are faced with a land shortage, with little chance to expand. One alternative is to increase the productivity of their present holdings.

For various reasons, then, the larger industrial forest owners are practicing intensive forestry, and it continues to improve. The expansion of industrial forestry can be partly measured by its employment of graduate foresters. Prior to World War II most forestry graduates entered government forestry service. Today, the forest industries are employing more foresters than any other employer. A discussion of how the forest industries practice forestry and employ their foresters will be considered after a brief history of industrial forestry.

## INDUSTRIAL FORESTRY IN THE UNITED STATES

The company forest is an institution which dates back before the Civil War. Familiar to most are the colorful stories of the lumberjacks, river drives, and Paul Bunyan. Colorful though they might be, they are stories of forest exploitation. These owners failed to practice forestry, but they should not be judged too harshly. For the most part, they were ignorant of even the basic ideas of good forest practice and unaware of its eventual rewards. The early land laws encouraged forest exploitation. Then too, working as they were in seemingly limitless virgin forests, there was little reason to encourage forest conservation. Also, the public at that time was not particularly willing to encourage such practice, save by criticizing neglect and failure;

and few individual Americans can honestly say that they would have done differently than the owners, if faced with the same obstacles. Let us examine a few of these obstacles.

**Handicaps in Early Private Forest Enterprises**   Inequitable taxation systems are frequently blamed for failure to practice forestry. Two features of the general property tax *are* discouraging and illustrate the point. One is the uncertainty of the amounts of probable taxes and the other is the deferred characteristic of forest crops and financial yields with which annual tax payments must be met.

High probability of loss from wildfire and other destructive agents present another handicap. Public cooperation in fire and pest control discounts this obstacle to some extent in recent years. In addition, salvage of losses is more likely in recent years.

Inequitable credit structure prevails for all natural-resource enterprises. This credit system has required high rates of interest and has been inclined to base borrowing power upon cash on hand, rather than natural resources, energy, skill, and plant, which are the elements of potential ability to pay. Even farming, which is a natural-resource industry, enjoys lower interest rates and longer term loans than lumbering and mining, and still farming has its troubles. Faulty credit structure has, no doubt, done more to bring about forest exploitation than have the desires of the lumbermen, and although recent availability of funds at lower interest rates has reflected an easing of the situation, further study and lending facilities are needed.

Uncertainty of future returns from a forest business, based upon changes in consumption habits—a phenomenon that has also affected the livestock business—and upon unpredictable future costs of operation, is another obstacle.

Another handicap that owners of timber resources place upon themselves in true American fashion is impatience with long-time enterprises as against quicker profits. More adequate supplies have done much to correct this attitude. Forest industries now are planning for permanence.

Of the obstacles mentioned, two are real. One is the probability of losses from destructive agents. The other is faulty credit structure. Some correction in taxation methods is coming. Many new tax laws have been passed, and others are now being considered, all of which are aimed at enabling the woodland owner, small and large, to practice forestry continuously.

**Early Efforts to Promote Private Forestry Practice**   Before the Forestry Division in the Department of Agriculture had any forests to manage, Gifford Pinchot, who had succeeded Dr. Bernhard Fernow as its chief in 1898, made the first real effort to promote industrial forestry on private lands. Cameron (1928) observed that Pinchot's plan of cooperation, by means of expert advice and assistance on the part of the division with owners of private timber tracts, was designed not only to promote forestry practice but also to train a force that he foresaw would someday have the national forests on its hands. The plan required large holders to pay the expenses of advisers who were to make studies and offer plans. The smaller owners were served without expense. In October 1898, Mr. Pinchot reported the total area then being managed in the Adirondacks under the plans of the Division to be slightly more than 100,000 acres (40,000 ha) (Pinchot, 1898). His own work and that of Henry S. Graves entered into these early plans. By 1905, requests for advice and assistance on no less than 2 million acres (800,000 ha) were on file with the Bureau of Forestry, and plans made for considerable areas were admitted to be sound but difficult of economic application. A few of them have persisted with varying degrees of compliance, but on the whole they were not very effective in promoting industrial forestry practice. One excellent feature of these plans was their collection of information on growth, yield, rotation, and mill-scale studies. These are areas of technical information that make dealings with timberland owners intelligible, particularly when supplemented with understanding of what makes up the costs of producing timber and lumber.

**Cooperative Approaches under the Clarke-McNary Act**    With the passage of the Clarke-McNary Act in 1924, considerable public encouragement and cooperation has been extended to private owners. It has also brought about general recognition that there is a real problem in taxing forests equitably. This cooperative law has also brought about effective systems of wildfire prevention and suppression for each forest region of the United States, with a view to perpetuating the timber crop. The cooperative approach under the Clarke-McNary Act set the stage for additional cooperative laws and assistance.

**The Minimum-Requirements Recommendations**    In 1926 and 1927, a series of bulletins (Show and Greeley, 1937) were published by the Forest Service, setting forth for each of the 12 silvicultural regions of the United States (1) a set of "minimum measures based on local physical conditions that are needed to prevent timber-bearing land from becoming barren" and (2) another set of measures listing desirable forestry practices "designed to grow reasonably complete crops of the more valuable timber trees, making full use of the real productive capacity of the land." These bulletins contain clear and concise recommendations, based on the best knowledge of their time, for guidance: first, of owners who wish only to keep their lands from becoming a liability and, second, of those who wish to make money out of forestry. Appearing during prosperous years just before the financial crash of 1929, these recommendations were impressive, and they stimulated fire-control efforts if nothing more. Indeed, the satisfactory restocking of no less than 63 million acres (25.2 million ha) of industrially owned cutover land, by the early 1930s, is credited by the Forest Service "in considerable part at least" to organized fire control and the interest and efforts of individual owners. A part of this effort, of course, dates from years before the Clarke-McNary Act of 1924 had extended federal cooperation to lands used for timber growing. Minimum measures had to do almost entirely with fire control and control of other destructive agents and with incidental provision for natural reseeding of the cutover areas. Desirable practices that were advocated include conscious planning to leave an adequate number of seed trees, well-located blocks of uncut forest where clearcutting of portions of the tracts is the only economic course, and vigorous trees of smaller diameter for both reseeding purposes and as a basis for a later logging operation when reproduction is accomplished. These trees would be well distributed over the tract and constitute more volume than that of seed trees only. Planting failed spaces, thinning, and conscious effort to control the mixture of species in the new crop were other typical recommendations for more intensive treatment.

The effect of published directions for the practice of forestry is not easy to evaluate, but it is fair to say that these suggested measures were well received by the industry, and that there was noticeable progress in the practice of industrial forestry under this constructive approach and under the steady and thoughtful leadership of Chief Forester William B. Greeley.

## Further Attempts to Improve Industrial Forestry

In the late 1920s and early 1930s, a study of the extent and character of the practice of industrial forestry (defined then as the "conscious effort to grow timber crops") was made by the Society of American Foresters. The study was confined to private ownerships in excess of 1,000 acres (400 ha) and indicated that 9 percent of the privately owned commercial timberland, aside from farms and estates, was under industrial forest management.

Other advances were made in 1934 with the adoption of the Lumber Code Authority of the National Recovery Act. A year later the NRA was declared unconstitutional and the code, as good as it was, had to go too. Many of the code's constructive woods practices were accepted by industry, however. For the short life of the code, some 250 million acres (100 million ha) of commercial timberland came under its authority and there is every reason to believe that the experiment in self-government which it afforded the industry was a convincing one. The National Lumber Manufacturers Association, concerned with the manufacturing phase of a business that employed large numbers of people and hoped to keep them employed, took over the forestry work of the code in 1935. Regional lumber associations kept the code alive, also. One of these was the American Pulpwood Association which, at a meeting in New Orleans in 1937, set up rules to cover fire control, maintenance of adequate growing stock, salvage and close utilization, cooperation with state foresters, planting, and enforcement. Although the agreement was voluntary, it carried, for one group at least, the following enforcement clause: "Each company herein represented pledges itself not to buy pulpwood from contractors who fail to comply with the above cutting regulations." An important feature of the agreement is the provision for the fullest cooperation with state foresters. The enforcement clause quoted above was not used to any great extent, the reason being given that it might have been interpreted by the Federal Trade Commission as restraint of trade.

**The American Forest Institute**   Forest industries had a reputation to build up and maintain. With their growing sense of permanence and ever-increasing use of good forest practice, they needed some way to publicize their intentions. In 1941 the American Forest Products Industries, Inc., was established to help them with this task. AFPI was renamed American Forest Institute in 1968. AFI now represents lumber, logging, pulp, paper, plywood, shingle, and other forest industries. It has now become the national public-relations organ for the forest industry, leaning heavily toward the educational program of growing trees. In its earlier years it promoted nationally, and is still coordinator of, the Tree Farm campaign started in the Pacific Northwest. Originally the National Keep Green movement was included, but this program is now dormant. Some states continue the Keep Green program as a state endeavor.

Today AFI publishes and supplies schools, Scouts, granges, other organizations, and the general public with pamphlets, posters, pictures, advertising mats, and other items on forestry, trees, fire prevention, forest products, and other similar features. AFI's materials are designed to familiarize the public with the need for and importance of managing the nation's commercial timber. These aids contain much valuable material but naturally emphasize the contribution of the industry in solving the country's forestry problem.

**The Tree Farm Movement**   This idea was conceived in the state of Washington in 1940 by a group who thought that there were more people who knew what a farm was than who knew what a forest was, and who wanted the public to think of timber-growing as farming. The first "tree farm," of 120,000 acres (48,000 ha), was dedicated in 1941 in Grays Harbor County. Soon after this, the Tree Farm idea was adopted for promotion by a joint conservation committee of two trade associations in the Northwest. Later and coincident with rapid spread of the idea, AFPI took over the national leadership and gave the program more breadth and scope.

Certificates for membership in the Tree Farm system are issued after the landowners have demonstrated their intent to manage the land accord-

**Figure 22-2**  The Tree Farm sign on the farm of Mrs. Josephine Klet, Spring Lake, Minnesota. In 1951 Mrs. Klet was certified as a tree farmer. She has planted a total of 30,000 trees on her 35 acres (14 ha) and has made three thinnings. In 1973 she was voted special recognition as an outstanding tree farmer. *(Courtesy of the American Forest Institute.)*

ing to Tree Farm standards (Fig. 22-2). A tree farm may be a single small holding or many thousands of acres, representing numerous owners who have agreed on a common program of forestry for the entire tract. AFI encourages and assists these owners in protecting their trees from fire and other destructive forces and in managing their holdings for sustained growth of forest crops. Periodic inspections by professional foresters are made to ensure compliance. There are enough teeth in the membership certificate so that violations in the form of failing to do what was agreed upon have in several instances caused revocation of the certificate.

The Tree Farm Progress Report, now kept by AFI, shows that there were ten states—Alabama, Arkansas, Georgia, Louisiana, Maine, Mississippi, North Carolina, Texas, Minnesota, and Wisconsin—on June 30, 1974, each with more than a thousand certified tree farms. Alabama, Florida, Georgia, Louisiana, Mississippi, Texas, Oregon, and Washington all had over 4 million acres (1.6 million ha) in tree-farm classification, with Arkansas not far behind. The total acreage in tree farms in 1948 was 16 million acres (6.4 million ha); in 1951, 23 million acres (9.2 million ha); in 1960, more than 50 million acres (20 million ha); and on June 30, 1974, 76.28 million acres (30.5 million ha). The total number of tree farms in 1960 was well over 15,000 and had grown to 31,446 by June 30, 1974 (American Forest Institute, 1974). This record is greatly to the credit of the forest industries, and there seems little doubt as to its future growth and spread.

**The Keep Green Movement**  Many states have organized Keep Green programs with state fire-prevention and -control committees patterned after the first one, which was launched in 1941 in the state of Washington. Faced with a loss of over 150,000 acres (60,000 ha) of timber to wildfire each year, mostly due to carelessness, the Evergreen State's forest-minded citizens came up with "Keep Washington Green," a promotional plan to drastically reduce the number of fires of human origin in the state.

Oregon began a similar plan within a few months, as did Minnesota in 1944. From these, also in 1944, came "Keep America Green," a plan to spread the program to other states. At present the national program is dormant. However, today most of the major wood-producing states have a Keep Green program directed locally. The objective is to integrate the efforts of state, federal, industrial, civic, sports, labor, and other groups toward forest protection. The effective slogan "Keep Louisiana Green" or "Keep Oregon Green" in these and numerous other states will be seen on all forms of advertising from matchfolders to huge highway signs.

**Other Industrial and Privately Sponsored Forestry Programs**  Other organizations supporting active forest conservation programs include such industrial groups as the Western Wood Products Association, American Paper Institute, American Pulpwood Association, Industrial Forestry Association, Forest Farmers Association, and several state forestry associations. Other organizations giving impetus to the promotion of forestry include the Future Farmers of America, Federation of Women's Clubs, 4-H Clubs, Boy Scouts of America, Chambers of Commerce, Isaac Walton League, American Forestry Association, Society of American Foresters, and many others.

The above groups are interested in educating their own members, timber owners, and the American public in a program of better forestry. The purpose behind such educational efforts has come with the wholesome attitude of industry—a desire to practice permanent and intensive forestry.

## How Industry Practices Forestry Today

We have seen how industry developed the tree-farm idea, and how this caught the imagination of a vast number of companies and individuals; the industry's long interest in forest protection as good business is heightened, and it has gained much new public support. Industry lands in most instances are open to the public for outdoor recreation (Fig. 22-3).

Lumber and other forest industries have employed increasing numbers of technically trained foresters, who are active in their profession as well as in the executive staffs of the industry. Traditional excellence in manufacture and new ingenuity are evident in the development of new products and the prevention of waste from the logging scene right through to fabrication and use. Most important of all, the industry is definitely growing timber for its needs, by modern cutting practices, reforestation with genetically improved stock, and other intensive management practices. It is also showing creditable interest in the lands which it does not own, but from which it draws much of its timber. Technical assistance to small private owners by industrial foresters is a major step forward in improving forest practice on small ownerships.

Industrial forestry in the United States, which is *growing* timber as a crop, must find its way in a competitive world of wood substitutes, forest

**Figure 22-3**   Quail hunting on industrial forest lands in Georgia. *(Courtesy of the International Paper Company and the American Forest Institute.)*

products imported from other countries, and even virgin timber from this country, grown without human aid.

The larger sawmills are now growing much of their needs on their own lands. The pulp and paper industry—with its huge investment in buildings, water, and specialized machinery—must stay put. The ever-increasing haul from the woodlands to the mill has long been a matter of economic concern. All this favors a company growing its own trees close to home under intensive forest management, including using forest and manufacturing residues. We have discussed the numerous ways that forestry is practiced in various parts of the country. It might be in order now to see how the company forest, which must operate under severe economic pressures, is practicing its forest management.

To get a return on a forest, forest managers must be willing to invest in their forest properties. Protection against forest destroyers and pests has already been considered in earlier chapters. In the use of silvicultural systems, a company shows its foresight and intent to stay in business. Frequently, the company will make noncommercial thinnings, prunings, apply fertilizer, or perform other acts which bring no immediate return on its investment but will show an increase in profits in future years. Figure 22-4 shows one of the long-range practices with which many forest-producing companies are concerned today.

**The Future of Forest Industries** In Chap. 24, Tables 24-1 and 24-2, data is given on site productivity. Forest industries presently have a 1970 net annual growth of 52 cu ft/acre(1.56 m³/ha) and a potential of 83 cu ft/acre (2.49 m³/ha). This compares to 38 cu ft/acre (1.14 m³/ha) net annual growth per acre in 1970 for all owners with a potential growth of 74 cu ft (U.S. Department of Agriculture, 1973).

The Report of the President's Advisory Panel on Timber and the Environment (1973) states: "Forest industry lands are of better than average quality for timber production, are generally well managed, and are being brought under intensive management more rapidly than are other classes of forest land."

The current intensive management practices of one of the largest industrial ownerships will serve to point out the trend. The example is that of Weyerhaeuser High Yield Forestry. This is a concept developed into a system. The key elements of that system, all carefully planned and controlled, are:

Clean logging to remove all usable wood and clear the land for the next crop

Preparing the ground after harvest

Growing genetically superior seedlings in tree nurseries

Planting the new crop—by hand, by machine, or by air—usually within 12 months after harvest

**Figure 22-4** *Upper,* an untouched area showing heavy growth before thinning. *Lower,* the same area after thinning, allowing rapid growth, as well as new stands of browse and grass for wildlife. Near Colville, Washington. *(Courtesy of the Boise Cascade Corporation and the American Forest Institute.)*

Controlled fertilization about every 5 years to assure rapid growth
Thinning of trees to provide space for more rapidly growing ones
Additional thinnings after 15 to 20 years
Harvest of the mature crop in order to begin the cycle all over

The end result of all these factors is better trees faster and more wood sooner (Fig. 22-5). In the South the seedling-to-harvest cycle has been reduced to 25 to 30 years. In the Douglas-fir region of the Pacific Northwest the cycle has been reduced from 80 to 100 to 45 to 60 years. Coincidental with the high-yield program are intensive protection, corollary research, and use of the lands for recreation and other purposes where appropriate (Weyerhaeuser Company, 1974).

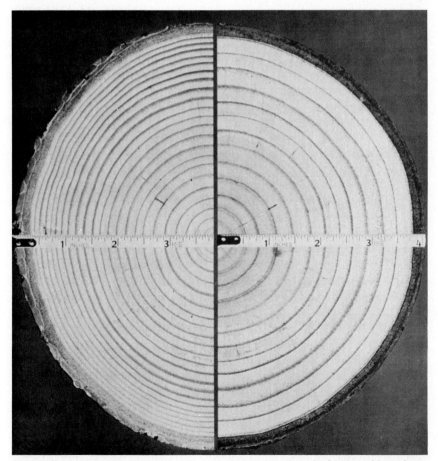

**Figure 22-5**  Managed trees grow faster. *At left,* cross section of a 24-year-old tree in an unmanaged forest. *At right,* cross section of a 14-year-old high-yield forest tree. *(Courtesy of the Weyerhaeuser Company.)*

**Research**   Industrial companies have established their own forest research organizations. Some of the following projects are examples of studies currently being undertaken:

*Control of Undesirable Vegetation*   Silvicultural systems favorable to forest reproduction are often equally favorable to the growth of undesirable brush. Chemical control of unwanted vegetation by aerial-spraying techniques will help to give seedlings a better start. In 1969 an Executive Order restricted use of certain chemicals in all phases of pesticide use, including herbicides. As acceptable herbicides are developed, they can be a low-cost method of vegetative control. When herbicides are applied, desirable species then have more room to grow.

Prescribed burning in the South, on both public and private forests, is used to prepare the seedbed for natural regeneration and to rid the young seedlings of brown spot disease.

Other site preparation techniques for planting in the South now include disking, chopping with large tractor-drawn roller choppers, with or without burning to follow. All of these methods are followed by planting which results in immediate occupation of the land by a growing crop of trees. Tractors have also been used to clear brush in the West, the Lake States, and the South with various combinations of methods for disposal of refuse.

*Forest Soils and Forest Site Identification*   A progressive timber company today knows the kind of soils found on its lands. The soil gives many clues to improved management. The best-suited species to plant may be known and thus planting failures may be eliminated. Soil-related hazards and limitations are revealed and steps can be taken to minimize them. Specialized equipment may be needed or operations may need to be timed to avoid seasonal problems (Lloyd, 1974). A soil pit of the type in Fig. 22-6 reveals the soil's physical properties, and by taking soil samples to the laboratory the chemical properties may be determined. If a company nursery is contemplated, an intensive study of the proposed location by the soil scientist is essential.

Foresters are also concerned with soil compaction from logging equipment and its effect on the soil structure.

*Forest Genetics*   Probably the greatest development in silviculture in the twentieth century has been the tremendous interest in forest genetics, or more accurately in *forest tree improvement* through tree selection and breeding techniques. Seed from trees which have the qualities of good form, rapid growth, straight limbs, desired crown to trunk ratio, windfirmness, good seed-germinating ability, wood density, and perhaps even a resistance to certain insects and diseases is collected and given special care. A Swiss invention called a "Baumvelo," a velocipede with pedals and hoops makes it possible to climb selected trees without injuring the bark (Fig. 22-7).

**Figure 22-6** A soil pit in a western hemlock forest. The approximate locations of the soil horizons are indicated by the letters. Such carefully dug pits reveal the physical properties of each horizon. *(Photo by Grant W. Sharpe.)*

**Figure 22-7** Ascending a slash pine near Savannah, Georgia. The "Baumvelo" or velocipede with pedals and hoops (instead of spurs) is one method used by forest geneticists to climb trees. *(Photo by Grant W. Sharpe.)*

**Figure 22-8** A forest geneticist using a hypodermic needle to inject selected male pollen into a plastic bag. The female flowers of this loblolly pine are bagged to protect them from unknown pollen. Seed orchard near Plymouth, North Carolina. *(Courtesy of the Weyerhaeuser Company.)*

Lightweight metal ladders, in 10-ft sections, may be strapped to a tree and allow the forest geneticist to reach the tree crown or on the larger operations the modern truck ladder. Once in the tree, he or she is able to inject pollen (from selected male cones collected in a similar manner) into sacks which protect the growing female cones. Controlled pollination is the result and, with success, the geneticist can improve on nature by developing strains and hybrids with superior characteristics (Fig. 22-8).

Tree breeding has been practiced for many years. Very successful forest-industry-financed tree improvement studies, coordinated by forestry schools, have been well established.

Seed orchards, which produce seed of highly desirable genetic characteristics in a relatively short number of years, are being developed, particularly by Southern industry. By grafting branch tips from selected trees onto young pine orchard stock, a crop of superior cones is available several years before the normal cone-producing age is reached.

**Other Research on Private Lands** This may include mechanical scarification of planting sites and its effect on growth, fertilizers and their effects on growth, seed storage, seed sowing from aircraft, game production and its effects on the forests. Other research might include integrated utilization and merchandising, watershed management, and even the use of radioactive isotopes to control parasitic diseases.

**Investment** Today a timber-producing company with plans of permanency pours a fantastic amount of money back into the business for research and development. Some of the research projects have been discussed above.

Developments include plant expansion, purchase or construction of new plants for an integrated operation, wood yards, new equipment, construction of company roads, establishment of seed orchards and nurseries, site preparation, and planting of thousands of acres of idle and cutover lands (Fig. 22-9).

**Figure 22-9** Loblolly pine growing in a company-owned forest nursery in North Carolina. The nursery holds about 28 million seedlings. *(Courtesy of the Weyerhaeuser Company.)*

No company, either pulp, plywood, lumber, or other can spend millions of dollars on its operations without knowing where it is going to get its supply of raw material. It must have confidence in its ability to continually supply its needs. Present-day industrial firms are demonstrating their willingness to invest large amounts of money and to intensify their entire operations so as to ensure their future operations.

## BIBLIOGRAPHY

American Forest Institute. 1973. *Forests U.S.A.,* Report from the American Forest Institute, Washington, DC.

———. 1974. *Tree Farm Progress Report,* Report from the American Forest Institute, Washington, DC.

Cameron, Jenks. 1928. *Development of Governmental Forest Control in the United States,* Johns Hopkins Press, Baltimore.

Clawson, Marion. 1972. *America's Land and Its Uses,* Published for Resources for the Future, Inc., The Johns Hopkins Press, Baltimore.

Greeley, W. B. 1950. Industrial Forestry, *Fifty Years of Forestry in the U.S.A.,* Society of American Foresters, Washington, DC.

Lloyd, William J. 1974. Chief Forester, Soil Conservation Service. Washington, DC. Personal Correspondence.

National Association of State Foresters. 1973. *Forestry Action Programs.*

Pinchot, Gifford. 1898. *The Adirondack Spruce,* The Critic Company, New York.

Pomeroy, Kenneth B. 1973. The Forest Incentives Program, presented at Annual Meeting, National Wildlife Federation, Washington, DC.

*Report of the President's Advisory Panel on Timber and the Environment.* 1973. U.S. Government Printing Office, Washington, DC.

Show, S. B., and W. B. Greeley. 1937. *Timber Growing and Logging Practice in the California Region,* U.S. Department of Agriculture Bulletin 1493. (Eleven others of similar title and content for different regions.)

U.S. Department of Agriculture. Forest Service. 1958. *Timber Resources for America's Future,* Forest Resource Report no. 14.

———. 1973. *The Outlook for Timber in the United States,* Forest Resource Report no. 20.

Weyerhaeuser Company. 1970. *The Keys to High-Yield Forestry: Clearcutting—Vital Tool in Forest Management. Forest Fertilization in the Pacific Northwest,* Tacoma, WA.

———. 1974. *Weyerhaeuser High-Yield Forestry: Growing Trees for Your Future.* Tacoma, WA.

Chapter 23

# Education in Forestry: Career Opportunities in Forestry

As in many other fields, the profession of forestry has undergone significant change, particularly in the last two decades. Some of the more important changes are outlined in this chapter.

Forestry was described in previous chapters as a science and an art as well as a public policy and a business. The education of foresters must, therefore, be broad. They must have, as tools with which to serve public policy or business, knowledge of the science and training in the art. Whatever culture and understanding they acquire as educated citizens will help the quality and quantity of service they render. Business administration, accounting, writing, speech, English literature, philosophy, psychology, and sociology are useful in the practice of forestry as a profession. Thorough grounding in English, mathematics, botany, zoology, geology, economics, chemistry, physics, and government is essential as a minimum, in addition to the technical forestry subjects taught in professional forestry schools. Unless the college years have been broken by opportunities for field experience as a summertime or full-time employee on some major forestry project, the graduate's equipment upon leaving the forestry school is made up principally of viewpoint and theory. These are worth money to the employer, and they are things that are not easy to buy on the open market.

However, viewpoint and theory must be supplemented as rapidly as possible by training and experience in the practice of the art of forestry. Practice is acquired outside the halls and far from the laboratories of schools. Growing demands upon foresters for service as land managers point to a longer period for general and professional education (Fig. 23-1).

**Early Problems in Educating Foresters** Brief mention was made in Chap. 3 of the beginnings of education in forestry. During the early years of this century, forestry was seen as romantic and adventuresome and promised opportunity for public service of a high order. Furthermore, there was demand for every educated forester who could be turned out, although many of these early foresters wished that their education had included business practices and studies in the art of persuasion.

**Trends in Educating Foresters** Both business and government today demand the services of graduates whose education has included special emphasis on the more scientific and social aspects of forestry and on land

**Figure 23-1** Forestry students learn about the identification, structure, and properties of wood in a wood-technology laboratory. *(Courtesy of Michigan State University.)*

use involving all natural resources. In recent years there has been increased emphasis on environmental impacts in the practice of forestry. The use of forest land for recreational purposes is increasing also, and several schools of forestry emphasize programs in this field. Wildlife management, with emphasis on ecology and on conscious manipulation of animals and their environment and differing from zoology as traditionally taught, has been developed extensively in a number of schools of forestry as a curriculum in itself or as a part of a forestry curriculum. In addition to producing wild animals for sport, the teaching of wildlife management at present includes nonconsumptive values.

Because 4 years is hardly enough time in which to get the minimum of fundamental and professional courses needed in order to command real opportunity, considerable interest has recently been shown in the 5-year course as a required plan in certain schools. Longer periods of schooling are also favored in which such combined courses as forestry and liberal arts, forestry and engineering, or forestry and business administration are offered.

### The Profession of Forestry in the United States

Forestry is a profession in the sense in which the older "learned professions," such as theology, law, and medicine, are understood. In these professions men or women have acquired some special knowledge that equips them to guide, instruct, or advise others, or to serve them in some art.

The development of specialized educational institutions is one of the signs that a profession has appeared. Other indications include the publication and accumulation of a technical literature, research activity, convening of practitioners, and improvement of technical practices by the application of the results of research. Such developments have been discussed at length in foregoing pages. It may be added here that forestry, judged by these signs, has been a profession in this country since about 1900.

**Number of Professional Foresters in the United States**   From the years 1900 through 1971, it is estimated that there have been 50,436 bachelor degrees granted in the United States. In addition, there have been 10,115 master degrees and 1,691 doctoral degrees granted (Vasey and Theoe, 1975). Of these 55,000 graduate foresters, probably 25,000 are active in the profession (Theoe, 1973b).

**Major Fields of Service**   The profession finds public opportunity for its services in federal and state, as well as county and municipal, government and in educational institutions. Several agencies of the federal government include foresters on their staffs, and they are represented in from one to three services in many of the states. County and municipal forestry is attracting more foresters in recent years.

Private demand for the services of professional foresters comes from industrial forest owners, from forest- and wood-using industries and public utilities, private estates, forestry and trade associations, and forest nurseries. There are also a number of thriving firms of consulting foresters, and a considerable number of younger foresters may be found engaged in graduate study for limited periods. Service in foreign countries, particularly in the tropics, attracts a small but persistent group.

On a functional basis, the majority of the profession is engaged in forest administration, management, and utilization, but there are growing numbers of specialists in all fields. The employment of the 25,000 active foresters in the United States as of 1971 was approximately as follows:[1]

| | |
|---|---:|
| Federal | 7,800 |
| State forestry agencies | 3,200 |
| County and city | 250 |
| Industry | 10,000 |
| Teaching | 1,400 |
| Associations | 250 |
| Consulting | 500 |
| Other | 1,600 |

**The Society of American Foresters**   Founded in 1900 the Society of American Foresters now has approximately 19,000 members, organized with objectives "to advance the science, technology, education and practice of professional forestry in America and to use the knowledge and skill of the profession to benefit society" (adopted by referendum 12-6-69). It has several grades of membership, as follows: student member, member, fellow, technician member, corresponding member, and honorary member. Graduates of forestry schools approved by the Council of the Society are admitted to membership upon proper endorsement. All, except corresponding members, must be citizens of the United States or its territories, or of Canada, or must be permanent residents of either country.

The Society publishes monthly the *Journal of Forestry,* which is the result of combining the Society's *Proceedings* with Dr. Fernow's *Forest Quarterly* in 1917. It also publishes *Forest Science,* a quarterly research magazine, the proceedings of its annual meetings, and an increasing number of technical books and bulletins.

Among other activities of the Society are the following:

Evaluation of research in forestry, through periodic surveys and standing committees, in cooperation with the National Research Council

---

[1] Series of reports on forestry employment by the 1972–1973 SAF Committee on Professional Employment, *Journal of Forestry,* November-December 1972; January, August, and October 1973; and June 1974.

**Figure 23-2** The Gifford Pinchot Building, National Headquarters of the Society of American Foresters, in Bethesda, Maryland. *(Courtesy of the National Geographic Society.)*

The formulation of a code of professional ethics for foresters

Study and development of standards in forestry education through comprehensive periodic studies, assisted by financial grants

The accrediting of forestry schools

A description of forest-cover types

The maintenance of professional standards and salaries in the employment of foresters

Promotion of international forestry relations

The classification of forestry literature

The compilation and standardization of forest terminology

Preparation and publication of the *Forestry Handbook,* a comprehensive assemblage of forestry techniques

Study and formulation of cutting practice guides for different regions of the United States

Publication of periodic summaries of development, progress, and history of forestry in the United States

The Society has 24 regional sections and 27 working groups, holds annual and sectional meetings, and for the past few years has entered actively into the influencing of legislation affecting the forestry movement through supplying technical testimony. It has its headquarters in Bethesda,

Maryland, not far from Washington D.C. (Fig. 23-2), and it employs an executive vice president and a staff of ten professional persons.

**The Canadian Institute of Forestry**   This organization was formerly known as the Canadian Society of Forest Engineers (1908 to 1950). The Canadian Institute of Forestry is a professional organization of high standards and reputation. In 1971 the CIF rolls listed 2,055 in all categories. Besides its central organization with headquarters at Macdonald College, Province of Quebec, the Canadian Institute of Forestry has 21 sections located in nine provinces.

The central purpose of the Institute as a national "technical" society is to promote the development and improvement of methods and techniques of forestry as a science and a business throughout Canada. One of the objectives of the CIF is to publish a professional and technical journal, *The Forestry Chronicle*. Since 1968, it has been published as a bimonthly journal, its stated purpose "to improve the management and use of the Canadian forest land resources and encourage a wider understanding of the problems of forestry."

In addition to the above, the CIF has been vitally interested in forestry education. This interest was manifested in the 1960s by a study (Garratt, 1971), which concerned itself with three major aspects of the subject: (1) reviewing the development of professional education in forestry and related fields since its inception in 1907; (2) assessing the current status of education and associated research in forestry and related fields; (3) setting the goals for professional and technical education in forestry and related fields during the next 10 to 20 years, based on available estimates of needs.

Forestry is taught at six universities with full 4-year undergraduate courses. In addition there are several diploma, certificate, and other programs in Canada. See Appendix D for a current listing of Canadian forestry educational offerings.

### Forestry Education in United States

In 1957 the SAF (Society of American Foresters) received a grant for a study of forestry education. This study resulted in a report by Dana and Johnson (1963). Recommendations in the report were debated within the SAF, especially by the Council of Forestry School Executives. In 1969 a symposium devoted entirely to forestry education was held at Roanoke, Virginia. In 1972 a similar session was held at Corvallis, Oregon. These and other events resulted in considerable curriculum changes in numerous forestry schools and led to a change in SAF educational requirements. The new requirements are being quoted below:

#### Educational Requirements

The SAF Council, at its November 1972 meeting, approved new educational requirements for professional forestry graduates. Effective July 1, 1973, they require that all SAF accredited and affiliated forestry schools in the United States teach the significant concepts in, and a working knowledge of, five areas of knowledge:

1  forest biology
2  forestry in the social context
3  forest resources measurements
4  forest ecosystem management
5  forest resources administration

These requirements replace 10 subject-areas formerly required by the Society since 1967: forest economics, forest protection, silviculture, forest resources management, forest resources use, dendrology, forest ecology, forest measurements, forest policy, and forest administration.

No specific courses are prescribed to cover the five new areas of knowledge, but a suggested list of preliminary basic studies is provided, and topics to be included in each area of knowledge are suggested [Fig. 23-3]. There is no attempt to dictate how this array of subject matter shall be organized into instructional units nor what relative emphasis should be given to the topics.

The proposal was developed by the Committee on Accreditation in close cooperation with the Committee on Educational Policies and the Council of Forestry School Executives. Nearly a year was spent on the proposal before presenting it to the Council, which, after considerable review and consideration, approved it.

**Rationale**  The Committee believed that the ever-increasing rate of change in the social climate and availability of technical knowledge require that professional foresters be better educated. They must be able to clearly delineate alternative strategies for attainment of a variety of management goals. Greater public interest in forest lands and the increasing complexity of knowledge undergirding professional practice call for greater diversity of expertise among professional foresters.

Professional education must adapt to the changes of the past decade and look increasingly to the future. Factors bearing upon professional education include two important elements which should affect curricular content: (1) an increasing availability of graduates of two-year technical forestry programs, and (2) a trend toward the use of engineers, landscape architects and other specialists for some work once done by foresters. The forester on the ground is increasingly a manager who must work effectively with a diverse clientele, describe technically sound alternative solutions to forestry problems and make rational decisions in view of mulitple demands upon the forest.

The specific purposes of the Committee's proposal were to (1) increase flexibility, with accompanying potential for greater diversity among schools, (2) strengthen the orientation to "people-related" problems and administrative-managerial approaches to their solution and (3) permit increased emphasis on future goals of the institution's forestry division.

**Definitions**  The following definitions of the required five areas of

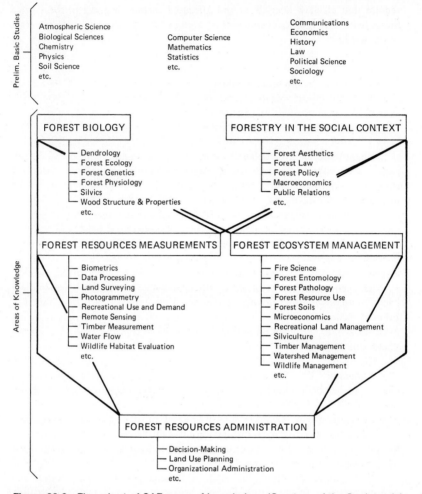

**Figure 23-3** Flow chart of SAF areas of knowledge. *(Courtesy of the Society of American Foresters.)*

knowledge have been adopted by the Council:

**1** *Forest Biology.* The biology of forest species including classification, distribution, characteristics and identification; interrelationships among environmental factors (edaphic, atmospheric and others) and the plants and animals of the forest (including forest influences). Emphasis should be on ecosystem principles, illustrated by a few selected species and types from various countries or regions, with field studies of local forests.

**2** *Forestry in the Social Context.*   Human aspects of forestry as distinguished from the biological or physical sciences: economic, legal, ethical, sociological, political, institutional and historic influences that affect the practice of forestry aimed at the full range of sustainable human benefits. Leadership in resolving forestry issues requires an understanding of each of these influences and their implications for forest policy and administration in the world as well as nationally; equally important is an understanding of resource-related organizations.

**3** *Forest Resources Measurements.*   Principles of sampling, inventory and census with illustrative applications to a variety of forest resources and environments, to various goods and services derived from the forest, and to the assessment of public opinion and preferences. Also an introduction to land surveying and to techniques of photogrammetry, remote sensing, and data processing with selected applications to forestry. Careful attention should be given to the selection of parameters for measurement.

**4** *Forest Ecosystem Management.*   The science and art of managing the forest to attain desired results. Included here are understanding of silvicultural practices as applied to representative forest types under various goals, analytical techniques for comparing management alternatives in terms of benefits and costs, principles of protecting forest resources against natural and man-caused deterioration, and harvesting methods and utilization standards for sustainable yields of forest products.

**5** *Forest Resources Administration.*   Application of administrative, organizational, economic and social principles in combination with physical and biological principles and practices to the planning, budgeting and decision-making processes.*

Figure 23-3 illustrates conceptually the flow of the five areas of knowledge in the student's formal educational experience. At the top of the diagram are suggested prerequisite courses. Below each of the required areas of knowledge are suggested course interest areas. The prerequisites and content of each, however, are to be determined by the individual institution (Duncan and Theoe, 1974).

## WHAT FEDERAL FORESTERS DO AND WHAT THEY EARN

### Positions in the U.S. Forest Service

**Forester**   Foresters are chosen from an eligible list made up of candidates who have passed an unassembled civil service examination with satisfactory grades. Admission to the civil service list is a matter of education, character, citizenship, and physical fitness. A forestry degree or immediate prospect of one is essential. War veterans are given preference in the form of additional grade points. Foresters receive further training under forest rangers or research workers. They are then in line for ranger positions and

*From Standards for Accrediting Institutions For the Teaching of Professional Forestry, Journal of Forestry, February 1976.

later for selection as staff assistants on national forests, deputy forest supervisors, or staff specialists. The work of a forester before becoming a ranger or a staff specialist frequently involves timber estimating; supervising projects to avert damage from fires, insects, and disease; measuring logs, cordwood, pulpwood, and special sale products; appraising land and timber values in trespass cases or for purchase; surveying boundaries, mapping forest types, and supervising recreation, wildlife, or watershed projects. In the research organization, detail work on numerous studies requires the forester's services under the direction of experienced scientific investigators. The beginning salary for forester (the professional assistant) depends partly on scholastic standing in college and the experience gained during the summer months. The entrance grade levels, GS-5 and GS-7, begin at approximately $9,500 and $11,500, respectively, and have automatic annual salary increases of $175.

**District Ranger** The ranger's work has become so technical and the responsibility so great that the position offers not only a stepping stone to higher administrative positions in the national forest system, but a fair life-work in itself for a person with technical training. The position entails directing the protection of an area of 50,000 to 300,000 acres (20,000 to 120,000 ha) of forest land, the development of recreational areas and uses, and the use of the forage resources in the district by domestic stock. The position requires reports on occupancy permits for everything from beehives to summer homes and the training of younger technical persons assigned as helpers. A district ranger plans and directs planting projects, keeps sales of timber and permits for the use of timber in order and within the regulations, carries on educational campaigns, enforces the laws and regulations against trespasses of several kinds, and directs the building and maintenance of physical improvements. A person can reach a salary range of approximately $15,000 to $24,000 a year as district ranger, and there are 682 ranger districts. Formerly, selections for the position of district ranger were made through special civil service examinations. At present, most of them come from the ranks and will have served as assistant rangers.

**Deputy Forest Supervisors** Persons who serve as immediate aides to supervisors in charge of national forests are commonly advanced from the ranks of district rangers, no special civil service examination being held for the position. Duties can best be described under those of the forest supervisor, whom these persons assist. The salary range for deputy supervisors is between $20,000 and $30,000.

**Forest Supervisor** Perhaps the most satisfying of all field positions in the national forest system is that of forest supervisor, who is literally the manager of a 0.5 million or more acres (200,000 ha) of timbered country, frequently mountainous in character. The objective of management is the benefiting of human welfare from the resources of the forest. Work is controlled through natural resource plans periodically revised and perfected with the assistance of a staff. There is a considerable responsibility for the continuous training of the staff. Much time is spent in the field. The job entails directing everything from hunts for lost people to the sale of 10 million board feet of standing timber, from helping fishermen in open season to addressing the state Chamber of Commerce. The salary range is from $23,000 to $38,000. The deputy acts when the supervisor is absent, or acts as a representative in the field, and is usually assumed to be in training for the position of forest supervisor.

**Regional Forester**    At the head of each administrative region in the national forest system is a regional forester who, with a staff of assistants and specialists, operates one of the decentralized groups of national forests, usually about 15 to 18 in number. This position requires an executive with the ability to assume great responsibility and who usually is a forest-school graduate. The salary ranges from $28,000 to $38,000.

**Research Foresters**    Professionally trained people who work in research are given a grade and paid a salary based on their educational level, time in service, and level of performance. As in the regions, there will be included in the forest experiment station staff, in addition to the director, an associate, several deputy directors, and specialists in numerous lines of forestry. Research is generally undertaken on a problem basis, with a project leader and staff specialists. Substations or field laboratories frequently will be directed by a project leader. They may house several projects. The work of the project leader is to prosecute and direct searches for the answers to their problems. These may be biological questions affecting frost or insect injury to forests, economic questions such as determining uses of a given species and demand for it, or perhaps silvicultural problems such as determining the proper spacing of trees in order to secure desired growth of a given group of species on a given site and for a particular age class. Solution of utilization problems and those touching timber growing for definite types of products is undertaken by the staff of the Forest Products Laboratory at Madison, Wisconsin, under its director and a staff of assistants. A few professionally trained foresters undertake utilization research, but persons trained as chemists, physicists, and engineers predominate. Salaries of experiment station directors are comparable to those of regional foresters. Other research personnel are classified according to the complexity of the job and other important factors.

**Chief Forester**    At the head of the Forest Service is the Chief or Chief Forester, formerly called the *forester*, with associate chief, five deputy chiefs, and a staff of specialists. Nine men have occupied this position since the Forest Service was created on its present basis in 1905, and one was temporarily acting in the position for several years. All of them were educated in forest schools. The work of the Chief Forester is that of an executive at the head of a major corporation, even though the Bureau is a subdivision of the greatest corporation in the country, and its stockholders are the people of the United States. This position commands a salary of $37,800.[2]

A total of about 9,500 professional people are employed by the Forest Service, and of these between 50 and 60 percent are foresters. Since land management and research problems are interdisciplinary in nature, the need is for professionals in all natural resource and related fields. This will mean a smaller percentage of foresters in the future, when compared to the total professional force.

### Professional Foresters in the Indian Service

At present, there are positions for forestry-educated personnel on the lands of the Division of Trust Services under the Bureau of Indian Affairs in the Department of the Interior. At the head of the forestry work is a staff assistant to the Director of the Office of Trust Responsibilities. The other foresters, a few of whom are Indians, hold positions similar to those in the Forest Service of the Department of Agriculture and, with the exception of research, do the same kinds of work. In the Indian Service the work of foresters must be coordinated in a general plan for the economic and social progress of the Indians who are the owners of the range and forest lands. Indians are employed for much of the nontechnical work, and as they develop they are assigned positions of considerable responsibility and work under the supervision of professional foresters or range managers. These professionals must win the respect and confidence of the Indians so as to obtain their cooperation in the management of their valuable land resources.

The training of Indians to take positions requiring skill and administrative ability is given important consideration in these enterprises. There are complicated problems in the management of more than 50 million acres (20 million ha) of forest and range lands, which includes approximately 12 million acres (5 million ha) of Indian-owned forest land under federal trust. (See Chap. 20.)

Entrance salaries for professional foresters, range managers, and range conservationists are the same as in other federal agencies, and there are good opportunities for promotion.

[2] The salary for chief and those in super grades is limited to the rate for level V of the Executive Schedule, $37,800. This rate will likely be increased in the future to comparable rates in private industry. (From General Pay Schedule, 1975.)

## National Park Foresters

The forestry profession, with its grasp of land-management problems, has contributed to the National Park Service numerous executives in positions of high responsibility. A relatively small staff of persons are employed as professional foresters and these few, assigned principally to the seven regional offices and to Washington, D. C., work through local national park staffs.

The functions of the national park foresters include the correlation of forest and fire-control activities and consist of supervising the preparation of fire-control plans and estimates, mapping of the vegetative types for protection and other purposes, reducing fire hazards, organizing insect-control and tree disease-control projects, establishing forest nurseries and supervising forest planting where necessary, protecting forest growth in campgrounds and other developed areas against preventable damage, furnishing services of special tree preservation and repair, and furnishing technical supervision for any necessary cutting of timber. The technical work of foresters in the national parks is limited to such services as may be required on areas managed for the use, enjoyment, and inspiration of the public rather than on those managed for material products.

Foresters entering the National Park Service under permanent civil service appointment frequently do so as park rangers and are eligible for advancement to assistant chief ranger, chief ranger, assistant superintendent, and on up to the higher executive positions of the service. The work of the foresters in the ranger organization is usually a combination of technical forestry and nontechnical administrative work. Where the work is entirely or principally of a technical forestry nature, the appointees may be assigned to the various professional grades of forester and to the more advanced professional grades. A general background of forestry, with special consideration of wildlife management, recreation, and an appreciation of forest-landscape principles, forms a splendid preparation for employment in the national park administration. Salaries of foresters in the National Park Service are comparable to those in other federal agencies.

## Positions in Other Federal Bureaus

**Investigative Positions**    Valuation of timber and lands for income tax purposes has required the services of a few thoroughly trained and experienced foresters in the Timber Section of the Internal Revenue Bureau in the Treasury Department, and similarly, some demand for professional services has come from the Bureau of Census in its study of forest products. The Tariff Commission has need of like talent, and the Department of Commerce, in its studies of exports and imports of forest products, offers still other professional opportunities. Salaries are similar to those of other federal agencies.

**Wildlife Management by Public Agencies**   The forestry profession has found the handling of wildlife resources to be a part of the business of forest-land management. A considerable number of forest-school graduates have qualified as biologists, with opportunities and salaries comparable to those of foresters.

**Bureau of Land Management**   With about 450 million acres (180 million ha) of natural resource lands to administer in the United States, including Alaska, the Bureau of Land Management employs nearly 500 foresters. Their work involves the managing of forests in the Northwest, Alaska, and the Inland Empire. Salaries and other benefits are comparable to those in other federal agencies.

**Promotional and Extension Work in Federal Bureaus**   The sort of guiding, explaining, and demonstrating by foresters that is designed to promote the practice of forestry on farm timber holdings and other small tracts is called extension work. It is more than teaching but is, in a sense, adult education jointly financed by the state and federal governments under the Smith-Lever Act of 1914 and the Clarke-McNary Act of 1924. Such work attracts one or more professionally trained foresters in the majority of the states. The work takes the extension forester to farmers' and woodland-owners' gatherings and onto the farms for organized demonstrations in reforestation, silvicultural management of existing forests, establishment of windbreaks, interesting 4-H Clubs of farm boys and girls in forestry work, and helping farmers to market their forest products advantageously. Extension foresters must travel a large part of the time, address many gatherings, write articles, and collect and disseminate convincing data for the promotion of forestry practices.

Public-relations work on a more general scale is highly organized in the Washington office and other headquarters of the federal agencies and attracts professional foresters to most of the positions. Their work is propaganda in the better sense and includes preparing, and in some cases delivering, radio and television talks and other public addresses and developing television shows; issuing accurate and informative news about forests and forestry; conducting fire-prevention campaigns; furnishing teaching material and exhibits to public schools and miscellaneous organizations; and making educational contacts with various individuals and groups. Compensation varies with responsibility in promotion work.

More extensive help is furnished to small-forest owners by foresters employed by states and jointly financed by the state and the federal government under the Cooperative Forest Management Act of 1950 and other cooperative programs. State foresters supervise the work of these field foresters who spend most of their time in the woods, advising forest owners on management, marketing, and other matters.

**Foresters in Soil Conservation Work**   The Soil Conservation Service in the Department of Agriculture has a staff specialist who is a forester in the Washington office and some 50 foresters assigned to specific geographical areas.

Because this bureau works exclusively on land that it controls only by cooperative agreement, a convincing type of professional forester is required for much of the work. Persons with a genius for research are also required, and the forestry profession has contributed its share of these. New foresters are selected by civil service examination. The various positions carry compensation similar to that of other federal forestry positions.

**Managing Forest Lands in the Tennessee Valley Project**   In the vast area of the Tennessee Valley, with its many ownerships and its ambitious federal project for social as well as natural resource management, the Tennessee Valley Authority (TVA) maintains a Division of Forestry, Fisheries and Wildlife Development. Salary scales for TVA professionals are comparable to those of other federal employees for similar work. There is little turnover and limited recruitment, but the work of the Authority does stimulate employment of foresters by industry and by other cooperators.

## Managing State Forests

With 50 state foresters and their assistants, state forest superintendents, fire wardens, service foresters on cooperative programs, and counterparts of many federal officers, the states employ about 3,200 professionally trained foresters in regular positions.

In state forestry agencies, the executive officer usually works under a policy-making body or commission and is faced with tasks of sorting and organizing state school lands, tax-reverted areas, and purchases of land into state forest systems; securing the cooperation of private timberland owners for fire control and reforestation; convincing the people of the state of the economic and social importance of their forests and gaining their support; and selling and exchanging state forest lands and reforesting them on a large scale. Frequently the management of recreation areas and roadside forest planting is a duty of state foresters and their force, and forest research and part-time forest-school teaching are sometimes required. There is some reason to expect that state foresters will be called upon to take a more active part in building up and administering a body of state laws regulating private forest exploitation as they have already done in such fields as compulsory fire patrol and special systems of forest taxation. In general, it should be noted that state forestry positions are not so well paid as similar federal positions, but that a high type of professional forester has been attracted to the work. The Association of State Foresters meets annually and is active, among other things, in promoting uniform cooperative practice with the federal government. Entrance salaries in state forest organizations range from $8,000 to $9,000. State foresters themselves receive from $18,000 to $24,000 on the average and more in some states.

### Teaching and Research at Forest Schools

An estimated 1,400 members of the profession are engaged in teaching at forestry and other schools (Fig. 23-4). Many of them are also engaged in research work, and a few give their entire time to the management of school forest properties. Salary scales differ widely, but these are examples of salaries based on 12-month positions: instructors, $8,000 to $14,000; assistant professors, $14,000 to $17,000; associate professors, $17,000 to $22,000; full professors, $18,000 to $26,000; heads of schools, $22,000 to $32,000. Certain universities, of course, will pay more than these figures (Walker and Theoe, 1973a).

### Positions in Private Forestry

**Managing Commercial Forests in Private Ownership**   In 1930, the figure 200 was a good estimate of the number of professional foresters in the United States who were employed by commercial firms such as lumber and paper companies, railroads, and chemical enterprises. By the early 1950s about 1,000 were actually engaged in forest-land management. Counting all of the foresters employed by industry, including safety work, sales, engineering, and straight logging, it is estimated that 10,000 would be the figure

**Figure 23-4**  A forestry professor teaching students how to use the dendrometer, an instrument which accurately measures tree diameters at any height. *(Courtesy of Michigan State University.)*

as of 1975, and of these, several hundred are in important executive positions. From this it should be apparent that demand for foresters in the service of industrial firms has greatly increased.

In Chap. 22 we learned that industrial forestry is a business in which each company must show a profit if it is to survive in this competitive field. The industrial forester is concerned with producing raw material for the employer and takes considerable pride in seeing that the lands under management are at their highest rate of productivity, generally under multiple-use management. The duties, which are varied, include taking continuous inventory measurements, aerial survey and mapping of forest properties, marking timber for cutting, organizing fire-control systems, making complete management plans, studying costs, appraising and purchasing saw logs and pulpwood, managing seed orchards and supervising logging operations. The job may also include research in soils, watershed management, forest protection, tree breeding through selection of superior trees, seeding and planting, repellents and rodent control, and the effects of applying fertilizers. The job may also entail public relations, dealing with hunters and other recreation groups, or with the neighboring small-forest owner and the forest management problems. The job may include studying the effects of wildlife, such as bear, elk, and deer, on the forest.

Entrance salaries in industry are slightly higher than those of government foresters but are parallel after a few years. Salary scales range from $10,000 to $27,000 or more. It will be noticed that industrial forestry jobs are basically similar to government positions. The greater emphasis on forest economics in industrial forestry is one of the chief differences.

**Consulting Foresters**   Individuals and partnerships of consulting foresters have been operating in the United States for more than 50 years. Services available from them include timber surveys and estimates; surface and aerial photographic mapping of timber holdings; appraisals; purchases and sales of forest properties; planning for fire and insect control; operation of portable sawmills; management of forest estates; reforestation; acting as expert witnesses in cases of trespass and in damage suits affecting forest properties; and preparing environmental impact statements. A number of larger consulting firms are controlled by engineers or professional timber cruisers who employ foresters. Earnings of foresters in these firms compare favorably with those of the employees of the younger firms of engineers and architects.

**Foresters on Private Estates**   This type of employment for professional foresters is increasing. Arboriculture and landscape work are likely to be combined with forestry duties. Compensation is comparable to state forestry work of like character.

**Managing and Serving Forestry and Trade Associations**   Several forestry and wildlife associations employ professional foresters as executives, legislative workers, and promoters of improved forestry and game-management practices. Editorial and other public-relations efforts characterize the programs of these groups. Professional foresters must be able to build up, interest, and retain adequate memberships, take decided positions on controversial legislative and other questions, and conduct campaigns of education.

Trade associations of lumbermen, paper and pulp manufacturers, and miscellaneous business firms, such as those in regional and national chambers of commerce, have used foresters in their organizations for 60 years or more. These men have promoted forestry practice among timberland-owning members, promoted legislation designed to encourage forestry practice, taken part in promoting trade in forest products, and acted as association executives. At least 500 professional foresters are so engaged at present.

Salary ranges for association managers are comparable to those of the heads of major federal bureaus, as a minimum, and exceed them in some cases. For specialists and executives, salary ranges compare with those of other foresters of like responsibilities.

### The Outlook for the Forestry Profession

Although demand has been brisk for professionally trained foresters in the years following World War II, more persons are being graduated yearly from forest schools than are being absorbed by public agencies or by private enterprise.

The following are other professional fields still in the pioneering stage, which should offer excellent opportunities to intelligent foresters with real imagination, ability, and energy: organized management and protection services to groups of comparatively small timberland owners within limited territories; sales-engineering types of service applied to marketing of forest products; specialization in real multiple-use forestry where recreation demands must predominate but not exclude other uses; interpreting and promoting the use of research data in forest utilization and forest management; acquiring and managing small forest properties for relatively short rotation products; and providing information and serving in areas of environmental concern.

**Trends in Employment**   Of the 1973 bachelor degree graduates, 1,710 found work (Theoe, 1974a) as compared to 1,371 in 1972 (Theoe, 1973c). This was nearly 55 percent of the graduates in 1973 as compared with 50 percent in 1972.

**Trends in Enrollment**   During the calendar year 1971, the 51 schools of forestry awarded an estimated 2,830 bachelor degrees, 610 master degrees, and 219 doctoral degrees. In 1971 undergraduate enrollment reached a new high of 19,313, of which 1,175 were women (Marckworth, 1975). Total number of women enrolled in the fall of 1974 was more than 2,701 (Didriksen, 1975).

A survey conducted by the Tuskegee Institute found only 18 black undergraduates in forestry schools during the 1970 spring term. For a variety of reasons blacks and others of minority groups have not been attracted to forestry, but this is slowly changing (Payne and Theoe, 1971). The total undergraduate minority enrollment by the fall of 1974 was 263 (Didriksen, 1975).

**Registration and Licensing of Foresters**   Currently 11 states have enacted forester registration acts, and 4,618 United States foresters were registered in 1973. Georgia enacted the first registration act in 1950. California enacted the most recent one in 1972. Forester registration is very popular in those states with a great deal of private land (Theoe, 1974b).

**Income and Retirement**   In 1973 all SAF members, fellows, technicians, retired members and retired fellows were mailed questionnaires. In all, 60 percent were returned. Results were compared with a 1959 and 1964 survey and information updated. Some of the highlights are found in Appendix E (pages 516–518).

**Updating the Professional**   A nationwide survey of 2,500 foresters and an equal number of other natural-resource managers was conducted by Pennsylvania State University in 1971. Results indicated that these professionals were well aware of the need to keep abreast of changes that have a bearing on their jobs.

Conclusions drawn from the survey of these professionals indicated that they were seriously concerned about the problem of keeping up with current developments and wanted better means of updating their knowledge and skills than their employers were providing. In addition they were eager for training in environmental management, pollution control, and ecosystems and wanted better and more complete knowledge on long-range planning, management techniques, and relationships with natural-resource scientists, social scientists, and planners. The study suggested that the quality and extent of current updating programs should be reassessed and work loads should be adjusted so that perhaps as much as 20 percent of the forester's time could be devoted to keeping abreast with new developments and techniques (George et al., 1974).

### Qualities Needed for Success in the Forestry Profession

To succeed in forestry there are certain indispensable qualities. Character is one, intelligence another, good health is a third. Besides these, self-confidence, courage, and qualities of leadership are frequently specified by employers. Initiative is emphasized, and so is social viewpoint, by certain public agencies and other employers. Keen interest in the outdoors and things that grow should produce both enthusiasm and contentment in this work. The following are selected from a list of 40 qualities worked out with a psychologist by a group of undergraduate students in forestry. They represent important characteristics that students believe a forester should work to develop: courage (physical and moral), ability to express oneself clearly (orally and on paper), all-round handiness, resourcefulness, good woodsmanship, mental quickness, persistence, initiative, businesslike attitude and habits, punctuality, industry, sense of humor, calmness in emergencies, optimism, self-confidence, leadership, courtesy, tact, honesty, and ability and will to cooperate and to work successfully with people.

A keen interest in the forest as a community of living organisms that will yield to human manipulation characterizes every true forester, even though he or she may spend more time with maps, adding machines, and people than with trees.

## BIBLIOGRAPHY

*Ask Any Forester.* 1968. Society of American Foresters. Washington, DC.

Bentley, William R. 1975. Educating the Professionals, *Jour. Forestry*, **73**:84–85.

Beuter, John H. 1975. Teaching, Learning, Doing: Integrated Forest Resource Management, *Jour. Forestry*, **73**:94–98.

*Careers in Forestry.* 1967. Miscellaneous Publication, rev. March 1967, U.S. Department of Agriculture.

Dana, Samuel T., and Evert W. Johnson. 1963. *Forestry Education in America Today and Tomorrow*, Society of American Foresters. Washington, DC.

Didriksen, Ralph G. 1975. Liaison Officer, Lincoln University, Data compiled on minorities enrolled in Professional Forestry Schools.

Duncan, Donald P., and Donald R. Theoe. 1974. SAF Educational Requirements, *Jour. Forestry*, **72**:306–308.

Garratt, George A. 1971. *Forestry Education in Canada*, Canadian Institute of Forestry, Macdonald College, Quebec.

George, John L., and Samuel S. Dubin. 1971. *Continuing Education Needs of Natural Resource Managers and Scientists*, Pennsylvania State University, University Park.

———, and Benjamin M. Nead. 1974. What Foresters Need to Do to Keep Up-to-Date, *Jour. Forestry*, **72**:5.

Hagenstein, Perry R. 1975. Integrated Resource Management: An Unrevolutionary Approach to Teaching, *Jour. Forestry*, **73**:87–89.

Vasey, Richard B., and D.R. Theoe. *Statistics from Schools of Forestry for 1974: Degrees granted and Enrollments,* Society of American Foresters, Washington, DC.

Payne, Brian R., and Donald R. Theoe. 1971. Black Foresters Needed: A Professional Concern, *Jour. Forestry*, **69**:295–298.

Randall, Charles E. 1969. So You Want To Be a Forester, The American Forestry Association; reprinted and slightly revised by Forest Service, U.S. Department of Agriculture.

Shirley, Hardy L. 1973. *Forestry and Its Career Opportunities*, 3d ed., McGraw-Hill Book Company. New York.

The Society of American Foresters, An Historical Summary: Part 1, The First Half Century (1900-1950), Ralph S. Hosmer; Part 2, The Past Decade (1951-1960), Henry Clepper; *Jour. Forestry*, **58**:775–779; Part 3, unpublished (1961-1973). Washington, DC.

Somberg, Seymour I., and Donald R. Theoe. 1974. State Registration of Foresters, *Jour. Forestry*, **72**:375.

Theoe, Donald R. 1972*a*. *Forestry Education in Canada* (book review), *Jour. Forestry*, **70**:175.

———. 1972*b*. Second SAF Education Symposium: Continuing Education for Foresters, *Jour. Forestry*, **70**:653–655.

———. 1973*a*. Supply and Demand in Professional Employment: Panelists Respond to the Context and the Issues (comments), *Jour. Forestry*, **71**:494–495.

———. 1973*b*. Employment of Foresters in the United States, presented to *Symposium on Manpower Concerns*, University of Massachusetts, Amherst.

———. 1973*c*. Employment Summary for Forestry Graduates, Class of 1972, *Jour. Forestry,* **71**:710–711.

———. 1974*a*. Employment of 1973 Forestry Graduates, *Jour. Forestry*, **72**:360–361.

———. 1974*b*. The Outlook for Professional Forestry, address presented at the Central Rocky Mountain Section Meeting, Denver, CO.

Thompson, Emmett F., Alfred D. Sullivan, and Donald R. Theoe. 1975. Income and Employment of SAF Members; 1974, *Jour. Forestry*, **73**:590–594.

Vaux, Henry J. 1975. The Integrated Curriculum in Contemporary Forest Education, *Jour. Forestry*, **73**:80–83.

Walker, Laurence C., and Donald R. Theoe. 1972. Forestry Employment by the States, *Jour. Forestry*, **70**:771–772.

———. 1973*a*. Forester Employment in Academia, *Jour. Forestry*, **71**:56–57.

———. 1973*b*. Forestry Employment in Industry, *Jour. Forestry,* **71**:537–538.

———. 1973*a*. Forestry Employment in Consulting Work, *Jour. Forestry*, **71**:672–673.

———. 1974. Foresters in Association Employment, *Jour. Forestry*, **72**:378.

———, and Stephen R. Hopkins. 1972. Forestry Employment in the Federal Government, *Jour. Forestry*, **70**:716–721.

Webster, Henry H. 1975. Forest Resource Management and Education: Pressure, Pain and Constructive Change, *Jour. Forestry*, **73**:75–79.

# Chapter 24

# The Trends in Forestry and National Planning

The preceding chapters have given the history, influences, and uses of the forest; the extent, character, and location of the forests; the practice of forestry; and forest protection. This concluding chapter will summarize the major trends and planning from a national standpoint.

**Is There Such a Thing as a National Plan?** A plan is an ordered decision or set of decisions on the ways in which to achieve certain objectives. Many important plans are recorded, and they may vary from a half-page memorandum to more than 100 sets of papers, including lists of objectives, maps, inventories, budgets, instructions, methods, allocations of personnel, as well as volumes, standards, and time limits for accomplishment of various tasks.

A plan is not an end in itself. It is a means to an end, and the end is more important than the means. Flexibility in a plan frequently determines whether or not it will work. Even the most skillful of planners cannot always be sure that their plans will not need to be modified as work progresses. Legislative and executive authority changes a plan into a program. The carrying out of a program, it is expected, will achieve the objectives.

We have, in the United States at present, no national plan in the sense of an exact and ordered set of decisions that this or that way is the one which will achieve the broad objectives set forth in the Declaration of Independence. We do have a positive instrument of fundamental law that we call the Constitution. At times, this has been changed in the careful and orderly manner that should characterize changes in any fundamental law. Certain programs can be set up by legislation under the Constitution, and certain policies can be followed without any special legislation. But to reduce the thousands of decisions, executive orders, policies, records, and annual changes into the common denominator of a plan is impossible and unnecessary in our form of government.

**Planning on a National Scale**    In the absence of a great single plan and of the generally feared "planned economy," we do have national planning, or planning on a national scale, for such things as health, public works, housing, highway transportation, education, national defense, and many phases of the conservation of natural resources. These efforts have grown out of the need for clearing up, and trying to pull out of, confusion wherever it exists or threatens. Cities, states, groups of states, regions, and bureaus have found it possible and to their advantage to plan their development. Without such planning, a program of public works, for example, or attempts to deal with agricultural surpluses would be much slower to start and more wasteful to maintain. Such confusion as does characterize any such projects at any time can probably be traced to hurried and insufficient planning.

During the 1960s and early 1970s, there was much activity and public concern on the subject of forest land and forests. This concern resulted among other things in four major reports published in 1973: *Report of the President's Advisory Panel on Timber and the Environment*; *Timber: The Renewable Material*; *Outdoor Recreation—A Legacy for America*: *A Nationwide Outdoor Recreation Plan;* and *The Outlook for Timber in the United States.*

In the *Report of the President's Advisory Panel on Timber and the Environment,* among the 20 major recommendations were several bearing on intensity of management of the better lands. Table 24-1 gives the area of commercial forest land in the United States by site productivity class and by ownership in 1970. Note that 296 million acres (118.4 million ha) are in the farm and miscellaneous private owner class. In acreage these lands offer the greatest opportunity for increased intensity of management. All lands could be managed more intensively.

Table 24-2 makes a comparison for all owners of the current average net annual growth with the potential growth per acre by regions. The South and Pacific Coast areas offer the greatest opportunities, but all regions have a greater potential than now realized (Ellefson, 1974). Overall, the potential is double present growth by the year 2020 (Glascock, 1973).

**Table 24-1  Area of Commercial Forest Land in the United States, by Site Productivity Class and by Ownership, 1970***

| Ownership | Total all productivity classes | | Productivity class (cubic feet per acre per year) | | | | | | | |
| --- | --- | --- | --- | --- | --- | --- | --- | --- | --- | --- |
| | | | 20 to 50 | | 50 to 85 | | 85 to 120 | | 120 or more | |
| | Million acres | Percent | Million acres | Percent | Million acres | Percent | Million acres | Percent | Million acres | Percent |
| National forest | 87 | 18 | 25 | 19 | 33 | 17 | 18 | 16 | 11 | 21 |
| Other public | 45 | 9 | 16 | 12 | 17 | 8 | 6 | 5 | 6 | 12 |
| Forest industry | 67 | 14 | 11 | 9 | 25 | 13 | 19 | 17 | 12 | 23 |
| Farm and miscellaneous private | 296 | 59 | 80 | 60 | 121 | 62 | 73 | 62 | 22 | 44 |
| Total, all ownerships | 495† | 100 | 132 | 100 | 196 | 100 | 116 | 100 | 51 | 100 |

Source: *The Outlook for Timber in the United States.* 1973. Forest Resource Report no. 20. Forest Service, Washington, DC.
*These acreage figures are for comparison only. If the reader wishes to convert each to hectares, multiply by 0.4047. Example: 87 million acres = 35.2 million ha.
†Not including 5 million acres (2 million ha) of commercial forest land classified as "unregulated" in national forests of the Rocky Mountain region.

**Table 24-2   Average Net Annual and Potential Growth per Acre, by Owner and Region, 1970***

| Region | All owners | National forest | Other public | Forest industry | Farm and miscellaneous private |
|---|---|---|---|---|---|
| | cubic feet† | | | | |
| **North:** | | | | | |
| Current | 31 | 38 | 33 | 40 | 29 |
| Potential | 68 | 66 | 59 | 72 | 69 |
| **South:** | | | | | |
| Current | 45 | 55 | 45 | 53 | 42 |
| Potential | 76 | 70 | 71 | 81 | 75 |
| **Rocky Mountain:** | | | | | |
| Current | 24 | 23 | 23 | 47 | 25 |
| Potential | 60 | 65 | 54 | 70 | 50 |
| **Pacific Coast:** | | | | | |
| Current | 45 | 27 | 60 | 65 | 58 |
| Potential | 95 | 88 | 100 | 107 | 96 |
| **Total, all regions** | | | | | |
| Current | 38 | 30 | 39 | 52 | 36 |
| Potential | 74 | 73 | 68 | 83 | 72 |

*Source: The Outlook for Timber in the United States.* 1973. Forest Resource Report no. 20. Forest Service, Washington, DC.

*Potential growth is average net growth attainable in fully stocked natural stands.

†To convert these growth figures from cubic feet per acre to cubic meters per hectare, multiply each figure by 0.06997. Example: 31 cu ft/acre = 2.17 m³/ha.

In the foreword of the report, *Timber: The Renewable Material*, a case is made for "timber as a material"; its virtues and shortcomings; its present and prospective availability measured against probable demands and constraints; the opportunities and measures needed to assure adequate supplies now and in the future; what should be done to make more efficient use of wood products, including recycling; and where the United States fits into the world wood picture. It is not, and does not purport to be, a comprehensive treatise on all products, uses, and services of forests. The great importance of the nontimber forest resources, including environmental and other nonmarket values, are recognized. The environmental impacts of timber growing, harvesting and processing, and the measures needed to overcome or minimize such impacts are discussed. The constraints on timber production and modifications required to provide for other important forest resources and the possible impact of competing uses on timber availability are dealt with in a number of places throughout the report.

*Outdoor Recreation—A Legacy for America* cites the increased needs of people for outdoor recreation. This nationwide recreation plan is concerned with major leisure-time recreation activities which normally take place out-of-doors. The plan provides guidelines for coordinating federal programs and efforts and for strengthening the cooperative relationships between various nonfederal and federal efforts. It provides the basis for establishing the roles and responsibilities of the various levels of government and the private sector in meeting outdoor-recreation needs. The plan looks at recreation as an important element in land use and land-use planning and places outdoor recreation in context with this process (Bureau of Outdoor Recreation, 1973).

*The Outlook for Timber in the United States* analyzes the timber situation as of 1970. It also recognizes that these lands must provide recreation, water, wildlife, and other similar products for the American people. Further substantial increases in future demand for timber are expected.

The following summary is quoted from the report:

In summary, if increased supplies of timber for a growing nation are desired, a number of things could be done to increase and extend timber supplies, including:

More complete utilization of logging residues, and trees lost by mortality, and greater use of recycled fibers.

Greater use of available equipment and manufacturing processes to increase output of lumber and other products from available log supplies.

Better allocation of available timber to assure use for optimum end products.

Some increase in dependence on imports of timber products.

More intensive management of all classes of forest lands suitable for timber management, by road construction, commercial thinning and salvage, reforestation with genetically improved planting stock, timber stand improvement, use of fertilizers, and better protection against fire, insects and other destructive agents—while simultaneously managing lands to assure a balance with other uses and environmental protection.

Continued development and application of new technology in timber growing, in processing of timber products, and in consumer use of wood products.

Substantial public and private investments will be necessary for such measures to increase timber supplies significantly and to improve utilization of available timber supplies. Such measures are both technically and economically feasible. They can be carried out while maintaining a balance with environmental uses of the forest (U.S. Department of Agriculture, 1973).

**Planning for Other Forestry Objectives**   There is nothing automatic in carrying out a policy of multiple use. Everything points to increasing demand for recreational and other uses, and this cannot always be reconciled with timber production. As the management of game animals for the recreation of hunting, which is in growing demand, becomes more intensive, more food, edges, and openings in forests will need to be maintained. There is also a rapidly increasing use by "hunters" with cameras, hikers, and those seeking amenity values. The management on the streams and lakes of thousands of watersheds will increase in importance. Water as a resource for human use and for the support of sport fishing will come in for attention, and the control of runoff damage in erosion and flooding may require that forest areas on steep slopes be closed to logging. Highways, airports, power-line rights-of-ways, reservoirs, schools, and even residences represent demands for space and will interfere with timber production. All of these uses will have to be planned for and reconciled with timber production. In the far-distant future, as population increases, it is not unlikely that a considerable timber-covered acreage in farms will have to be put to growing food and certain nontimber types of fiber; and because farms are near settlements, industry and subdivision developments will cut down the timber-producing area.

But success in maintaining adequate acreage and satisfactory management of forest resources does not rest exclusively upon any one set of plans, planners, or items of planning. It requires the exercise of equal zeal by public and private agencies in the use of encouragement, persuasion, and such compulsion as is proper in a democracy when necessary. It is safe to say that realistic planning will help and that the public will be more involved in land use decisions in the future.

In the field of planning ahead and periodic assessments, perhaps the most significant legislation to be enacted in recent years is the Forest and Rangeland Renewable Resources Planning Act, also known as the Humphrey-Rarick Act (P.L. 93-378) of August 1974. The act calls for long-range planning by the Forest Service to ensure that the United States has an adequate supply of forest resources in the future while maintaining the quality of the environment. It may turn out that this approach will evolve into a national plan.

The act goes into great detail, but two major requirements emerge. The Forest Service must periodically submit to Congress a Renewable Resources Assessment and a long-range Renewable Resource Program. Both of these tasks were due for the first time on December 31, 1975.

Assessments are to be updated in 1979 and every 10 years thereafter. The first program must cover the 4-year period beginning October 1, 1976, and at least each of the four fiscal decades following. The program must be updated every 5 years, always planning at least 45 years ahead. The Renewable Resources Assessment must consider *all forest, range, and related lands in the United States.* The first assessment was modeled on the timber trend reports, *but was expanded to include all forest resources.* To gather data on a more intensive basis and to cover all forest resources, the forest survey authorization has been raised from $5 million to $20 million.

In summary it can be said that forestry is a science, an art, a business, and a public policy. It has outgrown its infancy in each of these fields in the United States. Forestry is also a young and vigorous profession faced with the inspiring opportunity to forestall in America the periods of want that came to older nations before they had established forestry programs.

## Summary

Some of the important trends and forecasts in forest land uses, forest land practices, and in the profession of forestry can be summarized as follows: Population increases and other trends have led to more demand and markets for all forest resources. There is a growing competition for space and all that it entails. Prices for forest land and its commodities are at an all-time high and are forecasted to go higher. In many cases it will pay to manage forest land on a more intensive basis, especially the better timber sites.

There is a growing public interest in the forest environment, especially as it relates to air and water pollution, aesthetics, and amenity values.

Economics and public interest have increased the use of logging and mill residues. The practice of harvesting products by chipping is only one example of technology developed to meet the times.

Public interest in the environment probably will intensify, and on public lands this will mean more involvement in decisions on land use and forest land management. Environmental impact statements, now required under the National Environmental Policy Act for public lands, will be publicly reviewed prior to management decisions by the state and federal agencies. Foresters and land managers will be spending more time on public issues and in defending land-management practices.

State forest practice acts are now being revised in some states and will be used for improving private land use and forest practices, especially on the smaller ownerships.

Special emphasis is being given by forestry schools to a broader professional education. Many schools now stress increased education in socioeconomic and communication areas in addition to other technical subjects. Interdisciplinary approaches to problem solving are being emphasized.

Forest schools and employers are both providing opportunities to professionals for updating their knowledge to meet the challenges and opportunities of the 1980s and beyond.

## BIBLIOGRAPHY

Alston, Richard M. 1972. Goals and Decision Making in the Forest Service: Inter-
mountain Forest and Range Experiment Station, Forest Service, U.S. Department of Agriculture, Ogden, UT.

Barnett, Harold J., and Chandler Morse. 1963. *Scarcity and Growth: The Economics
of Natural Resource Availability*, published for Resources for the Future, Inc.,
by The Johns Hopkins Press, Baltimore.

Clawson, Marion. 1972. *America's Land and Its Uses*, published for Resources for
the Future, Inc., by The Johns Hopkins Press. Baltimore.

Cliff, Edward P. 1973. *Timber: The Renewable Material*, prepared for the National
Commission on Materials Policy, U.S. Government Printing Office. Washington, DC.

Ellefson, Paul V. 1974. Focus on the issues, *Jour. Forestry*, **72**:2–3.

Glascock, Hardy R., Jr. 1973. The View From Here, *Jour. Forestry*, **71**:682.

Phelps, Robert B., and Dwight Hair. 1974. Division of Forest Economics and Marketing Research, Miscellaneous Publication no. 1292, Forest Service, U.S. Department of Agriculture.

*Report of the President's Advisory Panel on Timber and the Environment*. 1973. U.S.
Government Printing Office. Washington, DC.

Robinette, Gary O. 1972. *Plants, People and Environmental Quality*, National Park
Service, U.S. Department of the Interior, in collaboration with the American
Society of Landscape Architects Foundation, Washington, DC.

U.S. Department of Agriculture. 1974. *Land Use Planning Assistance Available
Through the United States Department of Agriculture*.

——. Forest Service. 1958. *Timber Resources for America's Future*, Forest Resources Report no. 14.

——. 1973. *The Outlook for Timber in the United States*, Forest Resources Report
no. 20.

U. S. Department of the Interior, Bureau of Outdoor Recreation, 1973. *Outdoor
Recreation—A Legacy for America*. Washington, DC.

# Appendix A

# Legislation and Government Policy[1] Influencing the Development of Forestry in the United States, by Time Periods[2]

**Prior to 1770**  Colonial development

**1770–1890**  Period of both public land acquisition and disposal through settlement of the country, timber exploitation, development of widespread transportation facilities, and other subsidized internal improvements. Little progress toward the establishment of forest reserves or forest policy.

**1775–1783**  American Revolution.

**1820–1870**  Industrial revolution; westward expansion.

**1841**  Preemption Act: Heads of families with certain qualifications could purchase 160 acres (64.7 ha) of public land (cheaply) for their own settlement, use, and benefit. Preemptor was supposed to improve the land and erect a dwelling.

**1861–1865**  Civil War.

[1]Information on laws taken from *The Principal Laws Relating to Forest Service Activities,* Agricultural Handbook no. 453, Forest Service, U. S. Department of Agriculture, January 1974.

[2]The idea of legislation and government policy being placed in time periods came from a handout, Forestry as a Scientific Profession, by Dr. Gary Schneider, Associate Professor, Michigan State University.

**1862**  Homestead Act: Broader than the Act of 1841. Free patent after 5 years of residence and cultivation. Claimant could elect to commute or pay up and secure patent at any time 6 months after time of filing.

**1862**  Morrill Act: Several grants of public land for establishment of colleges of agriculture and mechanical arts. A second act in 1890 provided cash grants from public land sales. An amendment in 1903 provided that in case these amounts were less than amount appropriated, they could be paid from the Treasury.

**1872**  Yellowstone National Park Act: Established Yellowstone National Park as "a public pleasuring ground," and ordered preservation of resources and wonders in natural condition.

**1873**  Timber Culture Act: Offered to donate 160 acres (64.7 ha) of public land to any person who would plant 40 acres (16 ha) to trees and keep them growing for a period of 10 years. In 1878 an act reduced area and increased number of trees per acre planted. Repealed by the Forest Reserve Act in 1891.

**1887**  Hatch Act: Provided for financial assistance to states for agricultural experiment stations including forestry in research activities.

**1891–1910**  Forest Reserves established; later called National Forests; management policies of public forests created; state forestry programs initiated.

**1891**  Forest Reserve Act: Authorized President to reserve any public timber or forest growth lands and proclaim them as public reservations. Also repealed Preemption Act of 1841 and the Timber Culture Act of 1873 and halted sales of public land.

**1897**  Forest Reserve Organic Act: Provides for administration and use of existing and new forest reserves.

**1905**  Transfer Act: Jurisdiction of the forest reserves transferred from Department of the Interior to Department of Agriculture.

**1906**  Antiquities Act: Empowered the President to set aside, as national monuments, federally controlled areas containing prehistoric or historic structures, historic landmarks, or other objects of historic or scientific interest.

**1907**  Name Change Act: Forest Reserves to National Forests.

**1908**  White House Conference.

**1911–1932**  National forests consolidated; new public forests established; state forestry programs greatly improved.

**1911**  Weeks Act: Promoted cooperative fire protection with states, provided for federal land acquisition on headwaters of streams and land exchanges.

**1914–1918**  World War I.

**1914**  Smith-Lever Act: Provided for cooperative agricultural extension work between U.S. Department of Agriculture and the land-grant colleges.

**1916**  National Park Service Act: Created National Park Service in Department of the Interior, defined purposes for which national parks may be established and authorized Secretary of the Interior to make such rules and regulations as he may deem necessary for their proper use and management.

**1922**  General Exchange Act: When public interest will benefit, United States lands from the public domain in national forests may be exchanged for other lands if national forest lands are of equal or greater value—or an equal value of timber can be given in exchange.

**1924**  Clarke-McNary Act: Authorized up to $20 million annually for cooperative fire control (authorization amended in May 1972 and increased to $40 million annually); authorized a study of tax laws; distributed tree seeds or planting stock; and provided for land acquisition of watershed lands under certain conditions.

**1928**  McSweeney-McNary Research Act: Authorized and appropriated money for investigations, experiments, and tests in order to promulgate, demonstrate, and determine the best methods of reforestation and of growing, managing, and utilizing timber forage and other forest products, maintaining watersheds, forest protection and determining underlying economic considerations in forestry. Appropriated money and directed that a comprehensive forest survey be made and kept current with federal, state, and private cooperation.

**1933–1942**  Private forestry practices improved; multiple-use forestry principle established; forestry employment possibilities recognized.

**1933**  Civilian Conservation Corps (CCC) program: Attacked the problems of unemployment. CCC enrollees were used in conservation work.

**1933**  Lumber Code: Broad federal legislation to invite and assist various industries to adopt codes of fair competition as a means of improving business. Committed forest industries to leave their lands in productive condition after logging, providing certain public cooperation was extended. Declared unconstitutional in 1934.

**1934**  Taylor Grazing Act: Authorized Secretary of the Interior to establish grazing districts on certain public lands; to dispose of isolated tracts; to use 25 percent of receipts for certain range improvements and for other purposes. There were amendments to the 1934 act in 1936 to 1938 and in 1939 and later.

**1935**  Soil Conservation Service: October 1933 Soil Erosion Service established in Department of the Interior. Transferred to Department of Agriculture in March 1935 by Executive Order. Soil Conservation Act of April 27, 1935, recognized need for cooperative soil conservation and directed Secretary of Agriculture to proceed on all phases of soil conservation.

**1937** Norris-Doxey Farm Forestry Act: Authorized farm forestry in cooperation with the states.

**1941–1945** World War II.

**1942–1964** Forestry research intensified; industrial forestry practices greatly improved; multiple-use and sustained-yield concept intensified; woodland forestry practices increased.

**1946** Bureau of Land Management established: Consolidated General Land Office and Grazing Service (Taylor grazing act lands) to form the Bureau of Land Management in the Department of the Interior.

**1947** Forest Pest Control Act: Established government policy to protect all lands regardless of ownership from destructive forest insect pests and diseases. Authorized Secretary of Agriculture to cooperate with other federal, state, and local agencies and private concerns and individuals in detecting and controlling outbreaks.

**1950** Cooperative Forest Management Act: Repealed Norris-Doxey Act. Appropriated $2,500,000 to enable Secretary of Agriculture to cooperate with State Foresters in providing technical services to private landowners and processors. Raised to $5 million and then to $20 million in May 1972.

**1960** Multiple-Use, Sustained-Yield Act: Directed Secretary of Agriculture to develop and administer the renewable resources of the national forests for multiple use and sustained yield. Congress directed that the national forests should be managed for outdoor recreation, range, timber, watershed, and wildlife and fish purposes. Supplements Act of June 4, 1897, Organic Act. Defines multiple use and sustained yield.

**1962** Food and Agriculture Act: Amended previous farm bills. Among other things authorized payments for retiring cropland and continuing conservation reserve contracts under Soil Bank Act for conserving and developing soil, water, forest, wildlife, and recreation resources.

**1962** McIntire-Stennis Cooperative Research Act: Authorized Secretary of Agriculture to cooperate with the states in carrying out a coordinated forestry range and related research program. Act specifies how financial and other assistance will be given.

**1963** Bureau of Outdoor Recreation Act: Organic act for BOR establishment, Department of the Interior, April 2, 1962. Authorized Secretary of the Interior to carry out several cooperative and coordinating functions which were delegated to BOR.

**1964–present** Public participation in policy management decisions of public domain; past legislation and management programs reexamined; shift of emphasis towards environmental concerns including aesthetics.

**1964** Land and Water Conservation Act: Provided funds for expanded federal land acquisition and for grants to states for planning, acquisition, and development of recreation areas.

**1964** Wilderness Act: Established the National Wilderness Preservation System. Directed Secretaries of the Interior and of Agriculture to review additional lands within their administration within 10 years and to recommend to Congress new wilderness areas for inclusion in the system.

**1965** Clean Air Act: An act to improve, strengthen, and accelerate programs for the prevention and abatement of air pollution.

**1965** White House Conference on Natural Beauty.

**1965** Water Quality Act of 1965 with 1972 Federal Water Pollution Control Act: Set standards for water quality to be implemented largely by the states with federal guidelines and back-up enforcement authority.

**1966** Endangered Species Act: Provided for the conservation, protection, and propagation of native species of fish and wildlife, including migratory birds, that are threatened with extinction; to consolidate authorities and for other purposes.

**1968** Wild Rivers Act: Declared a national policy to preserve certain rivers in their free-flowing condition.

**1968** North Cascades Complex Act: Established the North Cascades National Park and Ross Lake and Lake Chelan National Recreation Areas.

**1968** Redwood National Park Act: Preserves significant examples of coastal redwood, *Sequoia sempervirens,* 58,000-acre (23,472-ha) National Park.

**1968** National Trails Act: Declared Appalachian Trail in the East and Pacific Crest Trail in the West as initial components of the national system. Designated 14 other trails for study for possible addition to the system as national scenic trails.

**1969** National Environmental Policy Act: The purpose of the act was to declare a national policy which will encourage productive and enjoyable harmony between people and their environment; to promote efforts to eliminate or prevent damage to the environment; to promote understanding of the ecological systems and natural resources important to the nation; and to establish a council on environmental quality.

**1973** Agricultural and Consumer Protection Act of August 10, 1973: Title X of the act allows for long-term contracts with landowners for installing conservation practices that will (1) improve fish, wildlife, and recreation resources; (2) enhance the level of management of nonindustrial private forest lands [forestry incentives contracts for owners of 500 acres (202 ha) or less by federal cost-sharing for planting and timber-stand improvement]; and (3) developing long-term cover for wildlife.

**1974** Humphrey-Rarick Act, called the Forest and Rangeland Renewable Resource Planning Act (P.L. 93-378) August 1974: The act calls for long-range planning by the Forest Service to ensure that the United States has an adequate supply of forest resources in the future, while maintaining the quality of the environment. The two major requirements are that the Forest Service periodically submit to Congress a Renewable Resources Assessment (every 10 years for all forest, range, and related lands in United States) and a long-range Renewable Resource Program (updating every 5 years and always planning at least 45 years ahead).

1974   Youth Conservation Bill: On September 2 the President signed this bill making it a permanent organization with a $60 million authorization. States can participate on a 50-50 basis. The Department of the Interior and the Department of Agriculture (Forest Service) are to jointly administer the program.

# Appendix B

**Special Forestry Metric Conversions**

| Symbol | To convert | Multiply by | To find | Symbol |
|--------|-----------|-------------|---------|--------|
| ft²/ac | Square feet per acre | 0.2296 | Square meters per hectare | m²/ha |
| ft³/ac | Cubic feet per acre | 0.06997 | Cubic meters per hectare | m³/ha |
| ft³/sec | Cubic feet per second | 101.941 | Cubic meters per hour | m³/h |
| ft/sec | Feet per second | 1.097 | Kilometers per hour | Km/h |
| gal/ac | Gallons per acre | 11.2336 | Liters per hectare | l/h |
| gal/min | Gallons per minute | 0.0757 | Liters per second | l/s |
| lb/ac | Pounds per acre | 1.1208 | Kilograms per hectare | Kg/m³ |
| lb/ft³ | Pounds per cubic feet | 16.0185 | Kilograms per cubic meter | Kg/m³ |
| No/ac | Number (i.e., trees) per acre | 2.471 | Number per hectare | No/ha |
| ton/ac | Tons per acre | 2.242 | Tonnes per hectare | t/ha |

## Metric Conversion Factors*
(Approximate Conversions to Metric Measures)

| Symbol | When you know | Multiply by | To find | Symbol |
|--------|---------------|-------------|---------|--------|
| **Length** | | | | |
| in. | inches | 2.54 | centimeters | cm |
| ft | feet | 30.48 | centimeters | cm |
| yd | yards | 0.91 | meters | m |
| ch | chains | 20.1 | meters | m |
| mi | miles | 1.61 | kilometers | km |
| **Area** | | | | |
| in.$^2$ | square inches | 6.45 | square centimeters | cm$^2$ |
| ft$^2$ | square feet | 0.09 | square meters | m$^2$ |
| yd$^2$ | square yards | 0.83 | square meters | m$^2$ |
| ch$^2$ | square chains | 404.7 | square meters | m$^2$ |
| mi$^2$ | square miles | 2.58 | square kilometers | km$^2$ |
| ac | acres | 0.405 | hectares | ha |
| **Mass (weight)** | | | | |
| oz | ounces | 28 | grams | g |
| lb | pounds | 0.45 | kilograms | kg |
| | short tons (2,000 lb) | 0.9 | tonnes | t |
| **Volume** | | | | |
| pt | pints | 0.47 | liters | l |
| qt | quarts | 0.95 | liters | l |
| gal | gallons | 3.8 | liters | l |
| ft$^3$ | cubic feet | 0.03 | cubic meters | m$^3$ |
| yd$^3$ | cubic yards | 0.76 | cubic meters | m$^3$ |
| **Temperature** | | | | |
| °F | Fahrenheit | $5/9$ (after subtracting 32) | Celsius | °C |

*Courtesy National Bureau of Standards, U.S. Department of Commerce.

# Appendix C

# Common and Scientific Names
# of Trees Mentioned in the Text

| Common name | Scientific name |
| --- | --- |
| **North America** | |
| Alaska-cedar | *Chamaecyparis nootkatensis* |
| alder, red | *Alnus rubra* |
| ash, black | *Fraxinus nigra* |
| blue | *F. quadrangulata* |
| green | *F. pennsylvanica* |
| Oregon | *F. latifolia* |
| white | *F. americana* |
| aspen, bigtooth | *Populus grandidentata* |
| quaking | *P. tremuloides* |
| baldcypress | *Taxodium distichum* |
| basswood, American | *Tilia americana* |
| beech, American | *Fagus grandifolia* |

*Source:* Adopted from E. L. Little, 1953, *Check List of Native and Naturalized Trees of the United States*, Agriculture Handbook no. 41, Forest Service, Washington, D.C.

| Common name | Scientific name |
| --- | --- |
| birch, paper (white) | *Betula papyrifera* |
| river | *B. nigra* |
| sweet | *B lenta* |
| yellow | *B. alleghaniensis (lutea)* |
| blackgum (see also tupelo) | *Nyssa sylvatica* |
| buckeye, Ohio | *Aesculus glabra* |
| yellow | *A. octandra* |
| butternut | *Juglans cinerea* |
| California-laurel | *Umbellularia californica* |
| cascara | *Rhamnus purshiana* |
| catalpa, northern | *Catalpa speciosa* |
| cherry, black | *Prunus serotina* |
| chestnut, American | *Castanea dentata* |
| chinkapin, golden | *Castanopsis chrysophylla* |
| cottonwood, black | *Populus trichocarpa* |
| eastern | *P. deltoides* |
| cucumbertree | *Magnolia acuminata* |
| Douglas-fir | *Pseudotsuga menziesii* |
| elm, American | *Ulmus americana* |
| slippery | *U. rubra* |
| fir, balsam | *Abies balsamea* |
| California red | *A. magnifica* |
| grand | *A. grandis* |
| noble | *A. procera* |
| Pacific silver | *A. amabilis* |
| Shasta red | *A. magnifica* var. *shastensis* |
| subalpine | *A. lasiocarpa* |
| white | *A. concolor* |
| hackberry | *Celtis occidentalis* |
| hemlock, eastern | *Tsuga canadensis* |
| mountain | *T. mertensiana* |
| western | *T. heterophylla* |
| hickory, bitternut | *Carya cordiformis* |
| mockernut | *C. tomentosa* |
| shagbark | *C. ovata* |
| water | *C. aquatica* |
| honeylocust | *Gleditsia triacanthos* |
| hophornbeam | *Ostrya virginiana* |
| incense-cedar | *Libocedrus decurrens* |
| juniper, Rocky Mountain | *Juniperus scopulorum* |
| larch, eastern (see also tamarack) | *Larix larcinia* |
| western | *L. occidentalis* |
| locust, black | *Robinia pseudoacacia* |
| madrone, Pacific | *Arbutus menziesii* |
| magnolia, southern | *Magnolia grandiflora* |

| Common name | Scientific name |
|---|---|
| mangrove | *Rhizophora mangle* |
| maple, bigleaf | *Acer macrophyllum* |
|   black | *A. nigrum* |
|   red | *A. rubrum* |
|   silver | *A. saccharinum* |
|   sugar | *A. saccharum* |
| mulberry, red | *Morus rubra* |
| oak, black | *Quercus velutina* |
|   bur | *Q. macrocarpa* |
|   California black | *Q. kelloggii* |
|   cherrybark | *Q. falcata* var. *pagodaefolia* |
|   chestnut | *Q. prinus* |
|   chinkapin | *Q. muehlenbergii* |
|   live | *Q. virginiana* |
|   northern red | *Q. rubra* |
|   Nuttall | *Q. nuttallii* |
|   Oregon white | *Q. garryana* |
|   overcup | *Q. lyrata* |
|   post | *Q. stellata* |
|   scarlet | *Q. coccinea* |
|   southern red | *Q. falcata* |
|   swamp chestnut | *Q. michauxii* |
|   swamp white | *Q. bicolor* |
|   water | *Q. nigra* |
|   white | *Q. alba* |
|   willow | *Q. phellos* |
| osage-orange | *Maclura pomifera* |
| pecan | *Carya illinoensis* |
| persimmon, common | *Diospyros virginiana* |
| pine, eastern white | *Pinus strobus* |
|   jack | *P. banksiana* |
|   jeffrey | *P. jeffreyi* |
|   limber | *P. flexilis* |
|   loblolly | *P. taeda* |
|   lodgepole | *P. contorta* |
|   longleaf | *P. palustris* |
|   Monterey | *P. radiata* |
|   pitch | *P. rigida* |
|   pond | *P. serotina* |
|   ponderosa | *P. ponderosa* |
|   red | *P. resinosa* |
|   shortleaf | *P. echinata* |
|   slash | *P. elliottii* |
|   sugar | *P. lambertiana* |
|   Virginia | *P. virginiana* |

| Common name | Scientific name |
|---|---|
| western white | *Pinus montieola* |
| whitebark | *P. albicaulis* |
| pinyon | *P. edulis* |
| singleleaf | *P. monophylla* |
| Mexican | *P. cembroides* |
| planertree (waterelm) | *Planera aquatica* |
| poplar, balsam | *Populus balsamifera* |
| swamp | *P. heterophylla* |
| Port-Orford-cedar | *Chamaecyparis lawsoniana* |
| redcedar, eastern | *Juniperus virginiana* |
| western | *Thuja plicata* |
| redwood | *Sequoia sempervirens* |
| sassafras | *Sassafras albidum* |
| sequoia, giant | *Sequoia gigantea* |
| spruce, black | *Picea mariana* |
| blue | *P. pungens* |
| Engelmann | *P. engelmannii* |
| red | *P. rubens* |
| Sitka | *P. sitchensis* |
| white | *P. glauca* |
| sugarberry | *Celtis laevigata* |
| sweetgum | *Liquidambar styraciflua* |
| sycamore, American | *Platanus occidentalis* |
| tamarack | *Larix laricina* |
| tanoak | *Lithocarpus densiflorus* |
| tupelo, black (blackgum) | *Nyssa sylvatica* |
| water | *N. aquatica* |
| walnut, black | *Juglans nigra* |
| white-cedar, northern | *Thuja occidentalis* |
| willow, black | *Salix nigra* |
| yellow-poplar | *Liriodendron tulipifera* |

## Hawaii

| | |
|---|---|
| ash, Mexican | *Fraxinus uhdei* |
| eucalyptus | *Eucalyptus* spp. |
| gum, flooded | *E. saligna* |
| kiawe | *Prosopis chilensis* |
| koa | *Acacia koa* |
| kukui | *Aleurites moluccana* |
| mamani | *Sophora chrysophylla* |
| ohia lehua | *Metrosideros polymorpha* |
| redcedar, Australian | *Toona ciliata* var. *australis* |
| silk-oak | *Grevillea robusta* |

# Appendix D

# Professional Forestry Instruction in the United States and Canada

The Society of American Foresters (SAF) is the official accrediting agency for professional forestry education in the United States, recognized by both the National Commission on Accrediting and the Office of Education of the U.S. Department of Health, Education, and Welfare. The Society accredits only the first professional forestry degree offered at an institution.[1]

The Society also designates Affiliated Institutions. These institutions have certified that they are building toward SAF accreditation.

The Society has evaluated only those institutions which have applied for designation as an Accredited or Affiliated Institution. Other institutions listed have not been evaluated by SAF.

The forestry degrees offered at each institution are shown by code: B (Bachelor), M (Master), and D (Doctor). The first year shown indicates the first accreditation or affiliation action by the Society, the second year shown indicates the year of last reexamination by the Society. SAF reexamines institutions approximately every 10 years (5 years after initial accreditation).

[1] *Journal of Forestry,* December 1975.

## ACCREDITED INSTITUTIONS (42)

The following institutions are accredited by the Society of American Foresters for professional forestry education:

### Alabama

Auburn University, Department of Forestry, Auburn 36830. B, M, D. 1950; 1973.

### Arizona

Northern Arizona University, School of Forestry, Flagstaff 86001. B, M. 1968; 1973.
University of Arizona, Department of Watershed Management, Tucson 85721. B, M, D. 1972; 1972.
University of Arizona, School of Renewable Natural Resources, Tucson 85721. B,M,D, 1972; 1972.

### California

University of California, Department of Forestry and Resource Management, Berkeley 94720. B, M, D. 1935; 1970.

### Colorado

Colorado State University, College of Forestry and Natural Resources, Fort Collins 80521. B, M, D. 1939; 1974.

### Connecticut

Yale University, School of Forestry and Environmental Studies, New Haven 06511. M, D. 1935; 1973.

### Florida

University of Florida, School of Forest Resources and Conservation, Gainesville 32611. B, M. 1942; 1972.

### Georgia

University of Georgia, School of Forest Resources, Athens 30601. B, M, D. 1938; 1971.

### Idaho

University of Idaho, College of Forestry, Wildlife and Range Sciences, Moscow 83843. B, M, D. 1935; 1974.

### Illinois

Southern Illinois University, Department of Forestry, Carbondale 62901. B,M, 1975; 1975.
University of Illinois, Department of Forestry, Urbana 61801. B, M. 1963; 1973.

### Indiana

Purdue University, Department of Forestry and Conservation, Lafayette 47907. B, M, D. 1942; 1970.

### Iowa

Iowa State University, Department of Forestry, Ames 50010. B, M, D. 1935; 1972.

## Kentucky

University of Kentucky, Department of Forestry, Lexington 40506. B. 1974.

## Louisiana

Louisiana State University, School of Forestry and Wildlife Management, Baton Rouge 70803. B, M, D. 1937; 1973.

## Maine

University of Maine, School of Forest Resources, Orono 04473. B, M, D. 1937; 1967.

## Massachusetts

University of Massachusetts, Department of Forestry and Wildlife Management, Amherst 01002. B, M, D. 1950; 1969.

## Michigan

Michigan State University, Department of Forestry, East Lansing 48823. B, M, D. 1935; 1973.
Michigan Technological University, School of Forestry and Wood Products, Houghton 49931. B, M. 1968; 1973.
University of Michigan, School of Natural Resources, Ann Arbor 48104. B, M, D. 1935; 1973.

## Minnesota

University of Minnesota, College of Forestry, St. Paul 55101. B, M, D. 1935; 1973.

## Mississippi

Mississippi State University, School of Forest Resources, Mississippi State 39762. B,M,D. 1966; 1972.

## Missouri

University of Missouri, School of Forestry, Fisheries and Wildlife, Columbia 65201. B, M, D. 1950; 1971.

## Montana

University of Montana, School of Forestry, Missoula 59801. B, M, D. 1935; 1968.

## New Hampshire

University of New Hampshire, Forestry Program, Durham 03824. B, M. 1959; 1970.

## New York

SUNY College of Environmental Science and Forestry, School of Environmental and Resource Management, Syracuse 13210. B, M, D. 1935; 1971.

## North Carolina

Duke University, School of Forestry and Environmental Studies, Durham 27706. M, D. 1939; 1965.

North Carolina State University, School of Forest Resources, Raleigh 27607. B, M, D. 1937; 1973.

## Oklahoma

Oklahoma State University, Department of Forestry, Stillwater 74074. B, M. 1971.

## Oregon

Oregon State University, School of Forestry, Corvallis 97331. B, M, D. 1935; 1970.

## Pennsylvania

Pennsylvania State University, School of Forest Resources, University Park 16801. B, M, D. 1935; 1972.

## South Carolina

Clemson University, College of Forest and Recreation Resources, Clemson 29631. B, M. 1962; 1972.

## Tennessee

University of Tennessee, Department of Forestry, Knoxville 37916. B, M. 1969.

## Texas

Stephen F. Austin State University, School of Forestry, Nacogdoches 75961. B, M. 1965; 1971.
Texas A & M University, Department of Forest Science, College Station 77843. B,M,D. 1975; 1975.

## Utah

Utah State University, College of Natural Resources, Logan 84321. B, M, D. 1937; 1968.

## Vermont

University of Vermont, Department of Forestry, Burlington 05401. B, M. 1971.

## Virginia

Virginia Polytechnic Institute and State University, Division of Forestry and Wildlife Resources, Blacksburg 24061. B, M, D. 1965; 1973.

## Washington

Washington State University, Department of Forestry and Range Management, Pullman 99163. B, M. 1965; 1972.
University of Washington, College of Forest Resources, Seattle 98195. B, M, D. 1935; 1975.

## West Virginia

West Virginia University, Division of Forestry, Morgantown 26506. B, M. 1947; 1969.

## Wisconsin

University of Wisconsin, Madison, Department of Forestry, Madison 53706. B, M, D. 1971.

## AFFILIATED INSTITUTIONS (8)

The following institutions offer professional forestry education and have met the standards for SAF Affiliated Institutions:

### Arkansas

University of Arkansas at Monticello, Department of Forestry, Monticello 71655. B. 1969.

### California

Humboldt State University, School of Natural Resources, Arcata 95521. B, M. 1969.

### Louisiana

Louisiana Tech University, School of Forestry, Ruston 71270. B. 1969.
McNeese State University, Department of Agriculture, Lake Charles 70601. B. 1969.

### Nevada

University of Nevada, Renewable Natural Resources Division, Reno 89507. B. 1969.

### New Jersey

Rutgers University, Forestry Section, Cook College, New Brunswick 08903. B. 1969.

### Tennessee

University of the South, Department of Forestry, Sewanee 37375. B. 1969.

### Wisconsin

University of Wisconsin, Stevens Point, College of Natural Resources, Stevens Point 54481. B. 1969.

## OTHER INSTITUTIONS (2)

The following institutions offer professional forestry education; however, they have not yet been evaluated by SAF.

### District of Columbia

Washington Technical Institute, Department of Forest Management, Washington 20008. B.

### Ohio

Ohio State University, Division-Department of Forestry, Columbus 43210. B, M, D.

## PREPROFESSIONAL FORESTRY INSTITUTIONS

Many 2-year and 4-year institutions in the United States offer preprofessional forestry study programs which may qualify students for transfer to a professional forestry school at the sophomore or junior level. Often these do not include forestry courses but lay a foundation for professional forestry education. SAF-organized Forest Technician Schools in the United States and Canada are listed.

## SAF-RECOGNIZED FOREST TECHNICIAN SCHOOLS IN THE UNITED STATES[2]

The institutions in this list have been in contact with the Society of American Foresters and have employed the SAF "Minimum Guidelines for the Training of Forest Technicians" as a self-study. The Society feels that you may wish to consider attending one of these institutions should you wish to study to become a forest technician. You should be aware, however, that other institutions beyond those listed may offer similar programs. This list does not constitute accreditation or approval by SAF.

Forest-technician graduates of these institutions are eligible for SAF-membership category of Technician Member. Full-time students in forest technology at these institutions are eligible for the Student Member category.

### California

College of the Redwoods, 1040 Del Norte Street, Eureka 95501
Lassen Community College, 1100 Main Street, Susanville 96130
Reedley College, 995 North Reed Avenue, Reedley 93654
Santa Rosa Junior College, 1501 Mendocino Avenue, Santa Rosa 95401
Sierra College, 500 Rocklin Road, Rocklin 95677

### Florida

Lake City Community College, Lake City 32055

### Georgia

Abraham Balwin Agricultural College, ABAC Station, Tifton 31794
Savannah Area Vocational-Tech. School, Savannah 31401

### Idaho

North Idaho College, Coeur d'Alene 83814

### Illinois

Southeastern Illinois College, 333 West College Street, Harrisburg 62946

[2]*Society of American Foresters, January 1976.*

### Kentucky

Forestry and Wood Technology, University of Kentucky, Quicksand 41363

### Maine

Forest Technician Program, University of Maine, Orono 04473

### Maryland

Allegany Community College, Cumberland 21502

### Michigan

Alpena Community College, Alpena 49707
Ford Forestry Center, Michigan Technological University, L'Anse 49946

### Minnesota

Brainerd Area Vocational Technical Institute, 300 Quince Street, Brainerd 56401
North Central School, University of Minnesota, Grand Rapids 55744
Vermilion State Junior College, 1900 East Camp Street, Ely 55731

### Montana

Flathead Valley Community College, P.O. Box 1174, Kalispel 59901
Missoula Technical Center, 909 South Avenue West, Missoula 59801

### New Hampshire

Forest Technician Curriculum, University of New Hampshire, Durham 03824

### New York

Paul Smith's College of Arts and Sciences, Paul Smiths 12970
Ranger School Forest Technician Program, SUNY College of Environmental Science and Forestry, Wanakena 13695

### North Carolina

Haywood Technical Institute, P.O. Box 427, Clyde 28721
Martin Technical Institute, P.O. Drawer 866, Williamston 27892
Wayne Community College, Drawer 1878, Goldsboro 27530

### Ohio

Hocking Technical College, Nelsonville 45764

### Oklahoma

Eastern Oklahoma State College, Wilburton 74578

### Oregon

Central Oregon Community College, College Way, Bend 97701
Chemeketa Community College, Salem 97303
Clatsop Community College, Astoria 97103
Lane Community College, 4000 East 30th Avenue, Eugene 97405
Mt. Hood Community College, 26000 S.E. Stark Street, Gresham 97030
Southwestern Oregon Community College, P.O. Box 518, Coos Bay 97420

Treasure Valley Community College, 650 College Boulevard, Ontario 97914
Umpqua Community College, Roseburg 97470

### Pennsylvania

Mont Alto Campus, The Pennsylvania State University, Mont Alto 17237
Williamsport Area Community College, 1005 West Third Street, Williamsport 17701

### South Carolina

Horry-Georgetown Technical Education Center, P.O. Box 317, Conway 29526

### Virginia

Dabney S. Lancaster Community College, Clifton Forge 24422

### Washington

Centralia College, Centralia 98531
Everett Community College, 801 Wetmore Avenue, Everett 98201
Green River Community College, 12401 S. E. 320th Street, Auburn 98002
Peninsula College, Port Angeles 98362
Shoreline Community College, 161st Street and Greenwood Avenue, Seattle 98133
Spokane Community College, E 3403 Mission Avenue, Spokane 99202
Wenatchee Valley College, Wenatchee 98801

### West Virginia

Glenville State College, Glenville 26351

## PROFESSIONAL FORESTRY INSTRUCTION IN CANADA

### Degree Programs

### Alberta

Faculty of Forestry, University of Alberta, Edmonton. B.

### British Columbia

Faculty of Forestry, University of British Columbia, Vancouver. B, M, D.

### New Brunswick

Faculty of Forestry, University of New Brunswick, Fredericton. B, M.

### Ontario

Faculty of Forestry, University of Toronto, Toronto. B, M, D.
School of Forestry, Lakehead University, Thunder Bay. B.

### Quebec

Faculty of Forestry, L'Université Laval, Quebec 10. B, M, D.

## Diploma, Certificate, and Other Programs (1- or 2-year)

### Alberta

Forest Technology School, Hinton (2-year)

### British Columbia

B.C. Forest Service Training School, North Surrey (1-year)[3]
B.C. Institute of Technology, Burnaby 2 (2-year)
College of New Caledonia, Prince George (2-year)
Selkirk College, Castlegar (2-year)

### New Brunswick

Maritime Forest Ranger School, Fredericton (1-year)

### Newfoundland

College of Trades and Technology, St. John's (2-year)

### Ontario

Algonquin College of Applied Arts and Technology, Pembroke (2-year)
Lakehead University, School of Forestry, Thunder Bay (2-year)
Ontario Forest Ranger School, Dorset (1-year)[4]
Sault College of Applied Arts and Technology, Sault Ste. Marie (2-year)
Sir Sandford Fleming College, Lindsay (2-year) (Information obtainable from the
Peterborough Campus)

### Quebec

College D'Enseignement general professionnel de Sainte-Foy (2-year)
Forest Ranger School, Duchesnay (1-year)
Institut de technologie de Chicoutimi, Chicoutimi (2-year)

### Saskatchewan

Kelsey Institute, Saskatoon (2-year)

[3] In-Service Training School open only to employees of the Provincial Forest Service.
[4] In-Service Training School open only to employees of the Provincial Forest Service.
Source: *The Forestry Chronicle,* vol. 51, no. 2, April 1975, p. 85., and ditto sheet "Schools
Offering Forest Technician Training".

# Appendix E

# Forest Employment and
# Income Tables

Table E-1 gives income (1974) by years of experience for all types of employment. The overall median income increased from $8,900 in 1964 to $17,000 in 1974. One-half of all incomes, within a category, are below and one-half are above the median. Within a category, 10 percent of all incomes are below the lower decile and 10 percent are above the upper decile.

**Table E-1   Income (1974) by Years of Experience for All Types of Forestry Employment Combined***

| Years of experience | Number of returns | Income (dollars) | | |
|---|---|---|---|---|
| | | Lower decile | Median | Upper decile |
| 0–1 | 48 | 4,260 | 10,010 | 14,050 |
| 2–5 | 1,521 | 8,500 | 11,300 | 15,500 |
| 6–10 | 1,248 | 11,200 | 14,830 | 20,000 |
| 11–15 | 1,291 | 13,000 | 17,500 | 24,000 |
| 16–20 | 1,117 | 14,280 | 19,980 | 27,000 |
| 21–25 | 1,197 | 14,400 | 20,500 | 31,000 |
| 26–30 | 731 | 15,000 | 22,000 | 34,000 |
| 31–36 | 256 | 15,350 | 23,500 | 36,000 |
| 36 + | 275 | 12,000 | 24,000 | 40,000 |
| Overall | 7,730[1] | 10,500 | 17,000 | 27,220 |

[1]Includes 46 returns not classified by years of experience.

*From Income and Employment of SAF Members - 1974. Thompson, Emmett F., Alfred D. Sullivan, and Donald R. Theoe. *Journal of Forestry*, September 1975.

**Education and Income**   As with the previous surveys the results emphasize that education pays. The more significant financial rewards are associated with the doctorate (Table E-2).

## Table E-2 Median Forestry Income (1974) by Educational Attainment and Years of Experience*

| Years of experience | Median income (dollars) | | | | |
|---|---|---|---|---|---|
| | Bachelor | Master | Doctorate | Technician | High school or other |
| 0–1 | 9,100 (33)* | 11,500 (12) | † (0) | † (3) | † (0) |
| 2–5 | 11,000 (1,064) | 12,630 (304) | 16,400 (89) | 9,000 (62) | † (2) |
| 6–10 | 14,440 (887) | 15,630 (212) | 19,690 (116) | 11,410 (28) | † (5) |
| 11–15 | 17,000 (900) | 18,000 (241) | 20,880 (125) | 12,800 (17) | † (7) |
| 16–20 | 19,000 (782) | 20,500 (198) | 23,750 (126) | † (7) | † (4) |
| 21–25 | 20,000 (883) | 21,400 (237) | 24,600 (106) | 16,750 (14) | † (6) |
| 26–30 | 21,300 (473) | 23,750 (154) | 26,105 (79) | † (8) | 17,850 (17) |
| 31–35 | 23,250 (156) | 23,350 (64) | 25,000 (25) | † (4) | † (6) |
| 36 + | 22,090 (158) | 24,880 (70) | 26,030 (35) | † (2) | 22,000 (10) |
| Overall lower decile | 10,200 | 11,500 | 15,810 | 7,840 | 10,960 |
| Overall median | 16,330 | 18,000 | 22,000 | 11,160 | 17,400 |
| Overall upper decile | 26,000 | 28,760 | 31,940 | 17,440 | 25,680 |
| No. of returns‡ | 5,286 | 1,492 | 701 | 145 | 57 |

*Number of returns.
†Too few returns to calculate median and deciles.
‡Forty-nine returns could not be classified for this table.
*From Income and Employment of SAF Members - 1974. Thompson, Emmett F., Alfred D. Sullivan, and Donald R. Theoe. *Journal of Forestry*, September 1975.

## Table E-3   Median Salaries by Specified Profession or Field

| Profession or field | Median yearly income | Number of persons surveyed | Year of survey |
|---|---|---|---|
| Physicians (all fields) | $39,727 | 3,928 | 1969 |
| Lawyers | 30,000 | 300,000 | 1972 |
| Dentists | 26,900 | 8,899 | 1970 |
| Bank economists | 25,000 | 164 | 1972 |
| Engineers | 17,750 | 167,225 | 1972 |
| Statistics | 16,900 | 2,953 | 1970 |
| Computer science | 16,500 | 11,324 | 1970 |
| Economics | 16,300 | 13,386 | 1970 |
| Physics | 15,900 | 36,336 | 1970 |
| Chemistry | 15,300 | 86,980 | 1970 |
| Atmospheric and space sciences | 15,200 | 6,637 | 1970 |
| Foresters | 15,090 | 7,759 | 1972 |
| Biological sciences | 15,000 | 47,493 | 1970 |
| Psychology | 15,000 | 26,271 | 1970 |
| Earth and marine sciences | 14,900 | 23,756 | 1970 |
| Anthropology | 14,700 | 1,325 | 1970 |
| Mathematics | 14,300 | 24,400 | 1970 |
| Political science | 13,100 | 6,493 | 1970 |
| Sociology | 13,000 | 7,658 | 1970 |
| Instructional staff (4-year colleges and universities) | 12,932 | · · · · · · | 1971 |
| Agricultural sciences | 12,800 | 15,730 | 1970 |
| Linguistics | 12,500 | 1,902 | 1970 |
| Librarians | 11,758 | 11,289 | 1970 |
| Engineering technicians | 10,300 | 71,000 | 1971 |
| Classroom teachers (public elementary and secondary schools) | 10,114 | · · · · · · | 1972 |

Source: Data collected by SAF National Office; information regarding sources is available from D. R. Theoe; tables and interpretation from Emmett F. Thompson, Alfred D. Sullivan, and Donald R. Theoe, 1974. Income and Employment of SAF Members, 1973, *Jour Forestry*, **72:** 82–86.

**Comparison of Forestry with Other Professions**   To answer the question how forester's incomes compare with the income of other professions, data from several other professions were assembled (Table E-3). SAF members median income is in the median range of incomes for 25 professions. Since much of the information was from 1970 surveys the comparative data with 1972 forester incomes may be low.

# INDEX

Page numbers in **boldface** type refer to pages on which there are illustrations or photographs.

A-frame log loader, 290, 291
Abney level:
  in forest mensuration, **252,** 253
  topographic mapping, 276
  for tree heights, 264, **265**
Acadia National Park, fire in, 328
Acorns, used as food, 4
Act for the Preservation of American Antiquities,
  94, 494
Adams, Earl J., 434
Adirondack Preserve, 94
Administration, forest, 190
Adventitious buds, 234
Advertising Council, The, Inc., 335, 336
Aerial photographs, **252**
  delineating insect damage, 279
  in forestry, 278, 279
  in fuel analysis, 352
  in map making, 279
AFI (American Forest Institute), 451, 453
AFPI (American Forest Products Industries,
  Inc.), 451
Africa:
  as exporter of logs, 198
  forest distribution, 195, 197
  map, 196
Age measurement, 266, **267**
Agency for International Development (AID),
  205, 206
Agriculture, Department of (*see* Department of
  Agriculture)
Agriculture and the forest, 9
Agriculture Act of 1956, 435, 436
Agriculture and Consumer Protection Act of
  1973, 43, 435, 436, 497
Air drying:
  compared to kiln drying, 313
  and moisture content, 311, 312
  stain reduction, 393
Air pollution:
  prescribed burns, 104
  from slash burning, 104
Air temperature, influences of forest on, 52
Aircraft:
  transportation of insects and disease by, 382
  use of: air drops of food and supplies, 353
    in detecting wildfires, 345, 346
    in direct seeding, 235
    in directing ground attack, 345
    in dropping retardants, **353**
    fertilizing with helicopter, **429**
    in insect control, 361, **362**
    in photography, 352
    in reconnoitering fire progress, 352
    in spraying vegetation, 243
    in transporting equipment, 353
    in transporting personnel, 341, 342
Alabama, tree farms, 453
Alaska:
  Bureau of Land Management in, 79, 419
  conks on western hemlock, **384**
  Engelmann spruce beetle, 368
  fire conditions in, 163
  forest land area, 161
  industry in, 164
  log rafts, 292
  pulpwood and paper industry in, 24, 161
  recreation, 164
  wood wasp, **370**

Alaska-cedar, 161
Alaska Native Claims Settlement Act of 1971,
  164
Alaskan forest:
  coastal forest, 161, **163**
  commercial species, 161, 163
  description, 161
  interior, 161, 163
  map, 162
  pulp industry, 161
Alberta:
  forest land area, 169
  forests of, 171
  map, 170
Albright, Horace M., 37
Alder:
  in Alaska, 163
  red, 160, 161
  furniture species, 160
Algaroba, 166
All-aged forest, definition, 186
Allen, Durwood L., 64
Allison, John W., 45
Ambrosia beetles, 370
American Antiquities Act of 1906, 94, 494
American Association for the Advancement of
  Science, 28, 29
American Fisheries Society, 95
American Forest Congresses, 41, 42
American Forest Institute (AFI), 451, 453
American Forest Products Industries, Inc.
  (AFPI), 451
American Forestry Association, 30, 41, 42, 45,
  95, 453
American forestry schools, 505–512
American Ornithologists Union, 95
American Paper and Pulp Association, 453
American Pulpwood Association, 450, 453
American Turpentine Farmers Association, 453
Ammonium phosphates in fire control, 353
Angiosperms, 116
Angle gauge, **252,** 277, 278, **278**
Animals:
  beneficial effects from, 377
  big-game, as products of forest, 64
  collecting cones in cache of, 236
  damage to forest from, 356–378
  domestic: in the forest, 9
    grazing damage from, 18, 373, 377
  effect on plant succession, 185
  effect on soil composition, 54
  essential elements, 175
  forest as home for, 4, 373
  fur-bearing, as product of forest, 64
  game, as food, 4
  small, from fields and wooded areas, 64
  transportation of mistletoe seeds by, 390
  waterfowl, 64
  wildlife management, 61–68
Annual ring:
  cell formation, 305
  cutting to bring out figure, 306
  how formed, 180
*Anthocephalus chinesis,* 167
Antiquities Act of 1906, 494
Ants, carpenter: control, 371
    damage from, 371
    prevention treatment, 313, 371
    as wood borer, 370

**519**

Aphid:
  aphid gall, 372
  Cooley spruce gall, 372
  sucking insect, 364, **364**
  terminal feeders, 371
Appalachian Trail, 497
*Arceuthobium* spp., 388
Arch, laminated, 316, **316**
Arizona, Indian lands, 416
Arkansas:
  interstate fire protection compact, 44
  state forestry, 428
  tree farms, 453
*Armillaria mellea*, 386
Army Corps of Engineers:
  functions of, 81
  outdoor recreation, 81
  road building in early national parks, 36
Ash, 149
  bending strength, 305
  black, 152
  blue, 152
  green, 152
  handles from, 152
  Mexican, 166
  Oregon, 160
  white, 131, 132, **132**, 152
    description, 131
    products from, 132, 150
Asia:
  exporter of logs, 198
  forest distribution, 197
  map, 196
Aspen:
  bigtooth, 149
  as cinderella tree, 150
  damage from livestock, 377
  heat, compared to coal, 296
  *Hypoxylon* canker disease, 390
  *Nectria* canker disease, 390
  as pulp species, 150
  quaking, 148, 156, 163, 171
    false tinder fungus, **381**
    *Nectria* canker, **391**
  and wildlife, 66
Associations supporting industrial forestry, 453
Atmosphere, influences of forest on, 50 – 53
Audubon Society, 95
Australia, nutrient deficiencies in pine, 247
Autecology, 183
Avalanche:
  damage, 395
  potential, in recreation planning, 88

Backfire, 351
Baker, Whiteford L., 357
Balch, R. E., 365
Baldcypress, 153
  products from, 155
Balloon, hauling logs by, 288 – 290, **289, 290**
Balsam wooly aphid:
  damage to true firs, 359
  example of sucking insect, 364
  as a gall maker, 361
  spread in Northwest, 357
Barge:
  log transportation, 293
  pulpwood transportation, 295
Bark, function of, **176**, 180
Bark beetles, **367, 368, 369**
  attractants, 366
  control, 365, 366, 369
  damage from, 360
  examples, 367, 368
  life history, 365 – 367

Barricades in recreation areas, 89, 90
Barrows, Jack S., 327
Basal area:
  by Bitterlich method, 277
  growth, 268
  in survey data, 276
Base lines, 270
Basidiospores, 387, 388
Basswood:
  American, 134, **134,** 135, 149, 152
    description, 134, 135
    products from, 135, 150
  flowers for honey, 150
  wood flour for plastics, 310
Baumvelo, 458, **459**
Beams, laminated, 316, **316**
Bear:
  as big-game animal, 64
  in conflict with forest management, 64
  tree injury from, 375, **375,** 376
Beaver:
  damage to forest, 376
  as fur bearer, 64
Bedwell, J. L., 389
Beech:
  American, 135, 136, **136,** 148, 152, 153
    charcoal from, 310
    description, 135, 136
    plasticity, 306
    products from, 136, 150, 152
    wildlife food from, 152
  as pulp species, 152
Beetles:
  as transporters of Dutch elm disease, 388
  as transporters of stain fungi, 392
  (*See also* specific beetles)
Belgium in FAO, 205
Bending strength of wood, 305
Benedict, W. V., 362
Benzene hexachloride (BHC), 362
Biltmore School, 33
Biltmore stick, **277**
  diameters, 263, **364**
  in forest mensuration, **252,** 253
  tree heights with hyposometer scale, 264, **266**
Binomial nomenclature, 115
Biodegradable wood, 299
Biological control of insects, 363, 365
Biological Survey, forerunner to U.S. Fish and
    Wildlife Service, 95
Biology, relation to forestry, 188
Birch:
  charcoal from, 310
  dieback disease, 391
  paper, 149, 163, 171
    birch dieback, 391
    fungus, **381**
    novelties from, 150
  river, 152
  sweet, 152
  yellow, 136 – 138, **137,** 148
    birch dieback, 391
    description, 137
    fungus, **381**
    products from, 138, 150
Birds:
  beneficial effects, 377
  as transporters of mistletoe seeds, 390
  as transporters of oak wilt spores, 390
  (*See also* specific birds)
Bitterlich method of basal area determination,
    277
Blackgum, 153
Blight, chestnut, 382
Blight diseases, 391, 392

Blowdowns and beetle populations, 369
Board-foot log rules, 253–255
  (*See also* Log rules)
Bonner, J., 174
BOR (*see* Bureau of Outdoor Recreation)
Boreal forest, 171
Borer:
  increment, **252,** 267, **267**
  marine, prevention of, 313, 314, **315**
  seed, 372
Boundary Waters Canoe Area, 219
Boy Scouts of America, 453
Boyce, John S., 390
Brandis, Dietrich, 200, 201
Breakage damage to forest, 393, 395
Bretz, T. W., 390
British Columbia:
  forest land area, 169
  forests of, 171
    map, 170
  helicopter, wildfire control, **342**
  introduction of white pine blister rust, 387
  log rafts, 292
British influence on early forestry, 198, 201
Broad arrow policy, 16, 17
Brockman, C. Frank, 75
Brown, Arthur A., 339, 354
Brown spot needle disease, 66, 392, 458
Buckeye:
  Ohio, 152
  yellow, 152
Budworm (*see* Spruce budworm)
Buffer strips:
  and logging, 103
  and wildlife habitats, 66
Building board, consumption and demand, 319, 320
Bulldozer in fire fighting, **328,** 348, **348**
Bureau of Forestry, 32, 449
Bureau of Indian Affairs, forestry and range work, 416–418
Bureau of Land Management:
  acreage of, 418
  in Alaska, 163, 164
  establishment in 1946, 79, 496
  foresters in, 476
  forestry work, 419
  grazing fees, 61
  in land surveys, 271
  Oregon and California Railroad Grant Lands, 419
  outdoor recreation, 79, 80
Bureau of Outdoor Recreation (BOR):
  functions of, 81, 421, 496
  recreation demand surveys, 74
  recreation statistics on private lands, 82, 83
  responsibilities, 421
  state-wide outdoor recreation plan, 74
Bureau of Reclamation:
  functions of, 80
  outdoor recreation, 81
Burma, early forestry in, 200, 201
Burning:
  for fuel hazard reduction, 104
  permit, sample, 334
  prescribed: in the South, 104
    in wildlife management, 66, 104
  slash, 104
  techniques, to reduce smoke, 104
Butler, O. M., 146
Butternut, 152

Cable skidding of logs, 286, **288**
Cadzow, Donald A., 4
Calhoun, John C., 23

California:
  chaparral fires, 327, **328**
  condor, 103
  early logging with oxen, 286
  fighting wildfire, **328, 347**
  fir engraver beetle, **369**
  fire lookout house, **343**
  fire scars on giant sequoia, 327
  floods, 56
  Indian lands, 416
  land ownership study, 45
  redwoods, 159
  wilderness area, **79**
  Yosemite National Park, **77, 420**
California Extension Service, 220
California-laurel, 160
Cambium, **176,** 180
Cameron, Jenks, 7, 18, 448
Cammerer, Arno B., 37
Campbell, W. A., 386
Campers, as cause of wildfires, 331
Camping, facilities for, 88
Canada:
  balsam, 297
  early timber trespass laws, 18
  exports of logs and sawn wood, 198, 199
  FAO, 205
  forest distribution, 169–171, 195
  forest land area by provinces, 169, 197
  forestry education in, 512, 513
  forests of, 169–171
    map, 170, 196
  helicopter use on wildfires, **342**
  insect control with aircraft, 362
  interstate fire protection compact, 44
  leading exporter of forest products, 169
  maple syrup production, 297
  pulpwood importation from, 24, 169
  river floating of pulpwood, 292
  timber outlook, 171
Canadian Entomological Service, report on benefits of skunk, 377
Canadian Institute of Forestry, 468
Canadian Society of Forest Engineers, 468
Candlenut, 166
Canker diseases, 390
Cants, 301
Capper bill, 37
Carabid beetles, 363
Carbohydrate in tree growth, 179
Carbon:
  in lignin, 179
  in photosynthesis, 179
Carbon dioxide:
  as raw material of wood, 177, 304
  in tree growth, 177–179
Career opportunities in forestry, 463–482
Caribbean National Forest, 168
Carpenter ants:
  control, 371
  damage from, 371
  prevention treatment, 313, 371
  as wood borers, 370
Carriage, riderless, 301, **301**
Carrying capacity of wilderness, 109, 110
Carson, Rachel, 96
Cascara, 297, 298
Catalpa:
  northern, 152
  resistance to decay, 305
Cattle:
  damage to forest, 377
  forest forage, 9
  grazing, **62**
  numbers on national forests, 404

Cattle:
  pasturing on national forests, 408
  in range management, 60, 61
CCC (*see* Civilian Conservation Corps)
Cedar:
  blight disease, 391
  resistance to decay, 305
  Spanish, 167
  (*See also* Alaska-cedar; Incense-cedar; Port-
    Orford-cedar; Redcedar; White-cedar)
Cedars of Lebanon, 11
Cells, wood, function of, 304, 305
Cellulose:
  formation in tree growth, 179
  in papermaking, 307
  percentage in wood, 307
Cemeteries in urban woodlands, 109
Central Hardwood Forest, **151**
  commercial species, 151, 152
  description, 150
  map, 148
  products from, 152
Central Park, 72
Centre International de Silviculture (CIS), 202,
  203
*Ceratocystis ulmii,* 388
Chalcids:
  control of larch sawfly, 365
  seed insect, 361
Challis National Forest, **408**
Chambers of Commerce, 453
Champlain and Hudson, observations on forests,
  146
Chaparral:
  fire, 327, **328**
  retarding run-off, 56
Charcoal:
  from chemical wood, 296
  how manufactured, 310, 311, **311**
  from lower-grade hardwoods, 150
Charlevoix, observations on Lake States forests,
  145
*Check list of Native and Naturalized Trees in the
  United States,* 147, 521
Chemical(s):
  baths, stain reduction, 393
  characteristics of wood, 306
  control of insects, 361 – 365, 370, 371
  control of vegetation, 458
  fungicidal, 393
  reaction of photosynthesis, 179
  release operations, 243
  retardants in fire control, 353
  wood, 296
Chemistry, relation to forestry, 188
Cherry:
  black, 152
    products from, 150, 152
  brown cubicle rot, **381**
  color and grain, 306
Chestnut:
  American, 149, 152
    and chestnut blight, 149, 382
  Asiatic, blight resistant, 382
  oak wilt, 390
Childs, T. W., 385
China, early forestry in, 201
Chinchona tree, 4
Chinkapin:
  golden, 160
  oak wilt, 390
Chipboard, 319
Chipmunks, damage to seed crops, 376
Chipped waste, 303

Chippewa National Forest, **240**
Chippewas, 6
Chipping machines in pulpwood harvesting, 295,
  **296**
Chips:
  in logging slash removal, 175
  use of, 303
Chlorophyll, 178, 383
Chloroplasts, 178
Christmas trees, 150, 297
Chugach National Forest, **384**
Cicadas, 364
Civilian Conservation Corps (CCC):
  establishment, 38, 95, 495
  impact of, 39
  projects, 39
  similar programs, 39
Clarke, John D., 37
Clarke-McNary Act of 1924, 37, 38, 330, 435,
  436, 449, 450, 476, 495
Classification, forest, 185, 186
Clean Air Act of 1965, 497
Cleaning to remove undesirable species, 243
Clearcutting, **184, 229, 231**
  controversy, 47, 100, 103
  method defined, 228
  misapplied, 104
  and soil movement, 102
  and wildlife, 104
  and wildlife habitat, 66
Cleveland, Grover, 31
Click beetle, 361
Cliff, Edward P., 304
Climate, as influenced by forest, 50, 51
Climax forest stands, 229
Climax stage in forest succession, 185
Clinometer:
  in forest mensuration, 253
  topographic mapping, 276
  for tree heights, 264, **265**
Clonal populations, 247
Cloquet, Minnesota, fire, 326, 327
*Closing Circle, The,* 96
Clothing from forest, 5
Coal:
  ash content comparison with wood, 296
  as fuel, 6
  heat comparison with various woods, 296
Coconino National Forest, first experiment sta-
  tion, 36
Codominant crown classification, 186, **186**
Cohesion theory, 181
Colbert, Jean Baptiste, 198
Colonial forest industries, 15
Color of wood, 306
Colorado:
  cattle grazing, photo, 62
  early forest reserves, 30
  state forestry, 431
Comité International du Bois (CIB), 202, 203
Committee on Forestry Bibliography and Termi-
  nology, 208
Common names of trees, 501 – 504
Commoner, Barry, 96
Commonwealth Forestry Bureau of Oxford, Eng-
  land, 208
Communication:
  in forestry education, 470, 471
  as a presuppression activity, 346
Community forestry, 439
Compacts, interstate for forest-fire control,
  43
Compass, **252**
  in forest mensuration, 253

Compass:
  line, 275
  in use, **265, 277**
Competition:
  of the forest, 183
  in plant populations, 242
  and reproduction, 232
COM-PLY, 410
Condor, California, 103
Cone collecting, 236, **236**
Cone insects, 372
*Congressional Globe,* 23
Conifer cones, 297
Conks, **381, 384,** 386
Connecticut, interstate fire protection compact,
  44
Connectors, timber, 320, **321**
Conner Forest Industries, 85, **85**
Conservation through utilization, 321
Consulting foresters, 479
Consumption:
  of forest products, 211
  of paper and paperboard, 24, 309
Contact poison, 364
Containerized seed, 237, **238,** 239
Continuous Forest Inventory (CFI), 279, **279**
Control time (of wildfires), 352
Controlled breeding of trees, 241
Controlled fire, 325
  (*See also* Fire, prescribed)
Conveniences from forest, 8, 9
Cooley spruce gall, 372
Cooperage stock, 296
Cooperative Extension Service, 413
Cooperative Forest Management Act of 1950, 40,
  412, 435, 436, 476, 496
Cooperative State Research Service, 413
Copeland, O. L., Jr., 386
Cordwood measurement, 261
Corners, marking, 271
Corps of Engineers:
  forestry work, 423, 424
  functions of, 81, 423
  outdoor recreation, 81
  road building in early national parks, 36
Correction lines, 271
Cost-benefit analyses, 105
Cotta, Henrich, 200
Cottonwood:
  aphid gall, 372
  black, 160, 161, 163
    products from, 160
  eastern, 152, 153
    products from, 152
  shelterbelts, 51
  wood flour for plastics, 310
Coulson, Robert N., 357
Council of Forestry School Executives, 468
  forestry education, 468 – 471
County forests, 437, 438
County government in recreation, 73
Cox, R. G., 297
Crafts, E. C., 357
Credit structure on private forests, 448
Creosote:
  control of wood borers, 370, 371
  treatment with: open tank, 313, 314
    pressure, 314
*Cronartium ribicola,* 387
Crosshauling, 290
Crown fire, 350
Crown thinning, 247
Cruiser's stick, **252,** 264
Cruising timber, 273 – 279, **277**

Cubic-foot log rules, 256 – 258
Cucumbertree, 152, 153
Cull, deducting for, in logs, 259 – 261
Cunits, 256
Cunningham, Gordon R., 439
Cunningham, Russell N., 45
Currant, blister rust, 387, 388
Cutting methods, silvicultural, 242 – 247
Cuttings:
  effect on deer population, 66
  layouts of, **282**
  to reduce transpiration, 58
Cypress (*see* Baldcypress)


D. L. Phipps Forest Nursery, 431
Dalhousie, Lord, 200
Damage to forest:
  animals, 356 – 378
  avalanche, 395
  drought, 396
  fire (*see* Wildfire)
  frost, 395
  high temperature, 396
  insect, 356 – 373
  lightning, 396
  snow and ice, 395
  wind, 393 – 395
Damping-off disease, 393
Dana, Samuel T., 26, 33, 45 – 47, 56, 468
Daniels, Jonathan, 328
Dasmann, R. F., 66
*Dasyscypha* canker, 390
Davis, Kenneth P., 339, 354
dbh (diameter at breast height):
  defined, 185
  measuring, 263, 264
DDT:
  as contributor to osprey decline, 107
  in Dutch elm disease control, 388
  persistent compound, 105
  in tussock moth control, 362, **362,** 363
Debris burning:
  as cause of wildfires, 331
  permit for, 334
  prevention of, 332, 333
Decay:
  prevention, 313 – 315
  resistance to, 305
Deciduous trees, defoliation, 365
Declaration of Principles, 1908 White House Conference, 35
Deeming, John E., 349
Deer:
  as big-game animal, 64
  in conflict with forest management, 66
  damage to forest, 373, 374, **374**
  effect of cutting practices on, 66
Defect, deducting for, 259, 260
Defense, national and forest, 10
Deficiency, density-induced, 183
Defoliation, effect on tree, 365
Defoliator insects:
  control, 364, 365
  damage from, 360
  examples, 364, 365
Demaray, Arthur E., 37
*Dendroctonus,* 368
Dendrology, application to forestry, 188
Department of Agriculture:
  forest agencies, 403 – 416
  in Puerto Rico, 168
  training wildfire control personnel, 342
  transfer of forest reserves to, 32, 33
Department of Defense, forestry work, 423

Department of the Interior:
administering early national parks, 36
administering forest reserves, 32
forestry related agencies, 416–421
national park service, 76–78
training wildfire control personnel, 342
Department of Transportation Act, 421
Desert Land Act of 1877, 27
de Soto, Don Fernando:
hardships with floods, 56
observations on Florida forests, 146
Destructive distillation, 296
Detectors for wildfires:
aerial, 345
air-ground, 345, 346
fixed-point, 343, 344
moving ground, 345
Diameter at breast height (dbh), 263, 264
Diameter growth, 268
Diameter measurement, 263, **264**
Diameter tape, **252**
in forest mensuration, 253
how used, 263
Didriksen, Ralph G., 481
Diebacks and wilts, 390, 391
Direct control of insects, 361–363, **362**
Discovery time, 346
Disease:
classification, 382
definition, 380, 381
effect on plant succession, 185
fungus, losses from, 381
growth losses from, 382
recognizing, 383
Diseased trees and wildlife, 67
Distillation, destructive, 296
Division of Forestry:
established in 1876, 29
Fernow as head, 30, 31, 201
forest reserves transferred to, 32
name change, 32
Pinchot as head, 31
Domestic grazing animals:
effect on forest, 373, 377
pasturing on national forests, 408
Dominant crown classification, 186, **186**
Donaldson, Thomas C., 21
Douglas-fir, 123, **123**, 124, 156–160, 171
bear damage, 374, 375, **375**
clearcutting, **229**
deer damage, 374
deer population, 66
description, 123, 124
dwarf mistletoe, 389
harvest cycle, 457
heart rot, 385
as leading commercial species, 158–160
products from, 124, 160
root rot, 386
seedling nutrient studies, **249**
spruce budworm, 365
volume table, 268
Douglas-fir beetle, **367**, 368, **368**
Douglas-fir Tussock moth, **362**, 365
aerial spraying, 363
control, 365
defoliation from, 365
Dowden, P. B., 377
Doyle log rule, 255
Drought damage, 396
Drury, Newton B., 37
Drying wood, 311–313
Duerr, William A., 222
Duncan, Donald P., 471

Dutch elm disease:
control, 388
insect transport of, 388
introduction of, 382, 388
as true wilt, 390
Dwarf mistletoe, **389**
how spread, 389, 390
method of control, 390
relative to Christmas mistletoe, 388
Dwellings from the forest, 5

Eagles:
nest abandonment, 103
snag protection for, 67
East Meadow Creek, 100
*Echinodontium tinctorium*, 385
Ecologists, self-proclaimed, 97
Ecology:
forest, 183, 227
relation to forestry, 188
Economic nationalism during industrial revolution, 18
Economics:
of forests, 212, 213
measuring nonmarket products, 111
and political process, 221, 222
and practice of forestry, 218
relation to forestry, 188
of wood products, 213
Economist, forest: contributions of, 213, 215–219
evaluating management actions, 219
Ecosystem:
definition, 181
knowledge of, 110
Edge to increase wildlife population, 67
Edging, 253, 254, **254**
Educating against wildfire, 335
Education in forestry:
courses in, 463
early problems, 464
requirements, 468–471
trends, 464, 465
Educational programs in recreation, 86, 87
Elements:
damage to forest from, 393–396
for tree growth, 174, 175
Elk:
as big-game animal, 64
elimination of, in eastern U.S., 63
forest injury from, 373
grazing, **65**
and human encroachment, 103
Ellefson, Paul V., 437, 485
Elm, 149
American, 138, **138**, 139, 152, 153
description, 138, 139
Dutch elm disease, 382, 388
products from, 139
products from, 152
slippery, 152
Elm bark beetle, 388
Ely, Richard T., 18
*Elytroderma* needle cast, 392
Endangered Species Act of 1966, 497
Endemic stage of insects, 358
*Endothia parasitica*, 382
Energy requirements, 12
Engelmann spruce beetle:
damage, 368
losses from, 357
Engineering:
in logging roads, 101, 102
on national forests, 409

Entomologist, forest, 372, 373, 381
Entrance charge in recreation areas, 85
Environment, forest use impacts on, 101 – 106
Environmental considerations in fire line construc-
    tion, 352
Environmental forestry, 439
Environmental impact assessments, 47
Environmental impact statements, 98, 423
    in the logging plan, 282
Environmental interactions, 183
Environmental law, 99, 100
Environmental movement, 95 – 111
Environmental problems from logging, 102
Environmental Protection Agency:
    function of, 423
    permission to use DDT, 362
Environmental resistance, 358
Environmental values:
    and forest management, 93
    managing forests for, 106
    in recreation planning, 77
    treatment of, 110, 111
Epidemic stage of insects, 358
Equipment inventory and maintenance in the log-
    ging plan, 281
Equipment use as cause of wildfires, 331
Erosion:
    accelerated, 56
    effect of slope, 55
    geologic, 56
    influence of forest on, 55
    prevention of, on farmsteads, 415
    protection from, 55
        in watershed management, 59
        in recreation planning, 88
Estate Thomas Experimental Forest, 168
Eucalyptus, 166, 207
Europe:
    forest distribution, 197
    as importer of logs and sawn wood, 198
Evaporation:
    in hydrologic cycle, 55
    influence of forest on, 53
    and photosynthesis, 181
    soil, as affected by windbreaks, 51
    of surface run-off, 55
    and transpiration, 181
    in watershed management, 57
Even-aged forest, definition, 186
Evergreen trees, defoliation, 365
Everhardt, Gary, 37
Everhart, William C., 37
Experiment station, forest: first, 34
    tree breeding at, 411
Exports and imports of forest products, 198, 199
Extension forestry, 413, 415
Extension Service, urban forestry assistance, 440

Fabrication of wood, 316 – 320
Facilities in recreation areas, 88 – 90
Fair Labor Standards Act, 283
FAO (see Food and Agriculture Organization)
Farm forestry, federal aid, 40
Farm forests, ownership, 443, 445
Farm woodlands, 443, **444**
Farms:
    converted from forests, 9
    subsidizing with forests, 19
    tree, 451 – 453
Farmstead planting, windbreaks, 51, 52, 415
Federal Highway Adminstration, cooperation
    with Forest Service, 409
Federal Land and Water Conservation Fund Act,
    74, 421

Federal Plant Quarantine Act of 1912, 382
Federal Power Commission, 100n.
Federal Property and Administrative Services
    Act, 421
Federal Tariff Act of 1789, 18
Federal Water Pollution Control Act of 1972, 497
Federal Water Project Recreation Act, 421
Federation of Women's Clubs, 453
Felling trees, 283, **284, 285**
Fence posts, 296
Fern fronds, 297
Fernow, Bernhard E., 10, 23, **30,** 31 – 33, 187,
    188, 448
    arrival in U.S., 201
    chief of Forestry Division, 30, 201
    *Forest Quarterly,* 466
Fertilizing forest soils, 247, **249,** 250
    with helicopter, **429**
Fiber cells, wood, 304
Fiber products, 303, 307
Fiber saturation point, 312
Fibers, wood, steam separation of, 303
Fighting wildfires, 350 – 352
Fir:
    balsam, 147 – 149, 177
        gall midges, 372
        hemlock looper, 365
        as lumber and pulp species, 150
        wood flour for plastics, 310
    California red, 157, 160
    Douglas (*see* Douglas-fir)
    grand, 156, 160
    heart rot, 385
    noble, 160
    Pacific silver, 160
    pulpwood from western species, 160
    shasta red, 160
    subalpine, 156, 160, 171
    white, 156, 157, 160
Fir engraver beetle, 368, **369**
Fire:
    compacts, interstate, 43, 44
    control: of brown-spot disease, 392
        plan, 338
        trends, 352 – 354
    curtailment, to prevent root rot, 386
    danger, defined, 349n.
    danger rating system, 349
    dispatcher, 346, **420**
    equipment, **328,** 347, **347,** 348, **348**
    extra-period, 352
    fighting, 350 – 352
    as a great discovery, 325
    hazard: definition of, 337
        logging debris, 232
        reduction, 337
    interstate compacts, 43, 44
    large, in North America, 326 – 329
    and lodgepole pine, 156
    management, 325, 327
        research in, 410
        in U.S. Forest Service, 347, 348
    prescribed: and air pollution, 104
        contrasted with wildfire, 325, 327
        control of brown-spot disease, 392, 458
        decrease fire hazard, 405
        eliminate disease and insects, 325, 405
        increase water yields, 405
        for livestock herbage improvement, 104
        on national forests, 405
        purpose of, 325
        removing hardwoods and brush, 325
        removing logging slash, 175, 325, 405
        research in, 410

Fire:
  prescribed: seedbed preparation, 325, 458
    site preparation, 232, 233
    wildlife cover and browse, 104, 405
    in wildlife management, 66, 67, **67**
  presuppression activities, 338 – 350
  prevention, 332, 338
    watershed management, 59
  protected areas, 330
  reporting, 346
  resistance to control, 346, 351
  resistance treatment of lumber, 314
  risk, 337
    definition of, 337
    reduction, 332 – 337
  root rot incidence, 386
  tools and equipment, **328**, 347, **347**, 348, **348**
  transportation, 346, 347
  (*See also* Wildfire)
Fire-Danger Rating System, National, 349
Fire-weather interpretation, 349
Fireman's Handbook, 349*n.*
Fireplaces in recreation areas, 88
Fish:
  in early Lake States, 62
  and forested watersheds, 64
Fish and Wildlife Service:
  from Biological Survey, 95
  fish hatcheries, 80
  and Klamath Reservation purchases, 44, 45
  outdoor recreation, 80
  refuges managed, 80
Fisher:
  as fur bearer, 64
  in porcupine control, 376
Fjelstad, Anders, 201, 203
Flakeboard, 319
Flat-headed borers, 360, 370
Flitch, 317
Floods:
  influence of forest on, 56
  potential, in recreation planning, 88
  prevention, in watershed management, 58
Florida:
  naval stores production, 297
  site preparation, **233**
  state forestry, 428
  subtropical forest, 167
  tree farms, 453
  wildfire in, 326, 328
  wind damage, 394
*Fomes annosus,* 386
*Fomes pini,* 384, **384,** 385
Food and Agriculture Act of 1962, 496
Food and Agriculture Organization (FAO),
    203 – 208
  establishment of, 202
  forestry responsibilities, 203 – 206
  specialists assigned to, 204
Food from forest, 4, 5
Food chains and persistent chemicals, 105
Foote, Cone, and Belding (advertising firm), 336
Forage resources, 9, 59 – 61
  on national forests, 408
Ford-Robertson, F. C., 187
Foreign Operations Administration (FOA), 205
Forest:
  administration, 190
  classification, 185, 186
  competition, 183
  contribution, 23, 24
  definition, 182, 187
  development, path of, 220, 221
  ecology, 183, 227

Forest:
  economist: contributions of, 213, 215 – 219
    evaluating management actions, 219
  ecosystem, 110, 181
  edge, 67
  entomologist, 372, 373, 381
  experiment station, first, 34
  fires (*see* Fire; Wildfire)
  genetics, 458
  growth determination, 268, 269
  as home for fur-bearing animals, 373
  industry (*see* Industrial forestry)
  influences: on air temperature, 52
    on atmosphere, 50 – 53
    on evaporation, 53
    on humidity, 52
    on precipitation, 53
    on soil composition, 54
    on soil temperature, 53
    on weather, 50, 51
    on wind, 51
  landscaping and silviculture, 106
  management, 189
    economic effectiveness, 219
    relationship to harvesting, 298
  measurements, 251 – 280
  mensuration, 189, 251 – 280
  openings and wildlife, 67
  ownership, U.S., 168
  pathologist, 381
  pathology, 381
  policy, 190, 191
    cooperative agreement, 46
    development of, 26
  products, 299 – 321
    in international trade, 197, 198
    (*See also* specific products)
  protection, 189, 190, 381
  regulation, 190
  reserves (*see* Reserves)
  soils: application to forestry, 188
    identification, 458
    (*See also* Soil)
  subsidies, early, 19
  succession, 185
  tree improvement, 458
  use impacts, on environment, 101
  utilization, 191
  valuation, 190
  wealth, 15
  yield, 269
Forest Farmers Association, 453
Forest Lieu Selection Act of 1897, 34
Forest Pest Control Act of 1947, 42, 383, 435
Forest Practice Acts, 436
Forest Products Laboratory, **411**
  establishment, 36, 410
  moisture content recommendations, 312
  research at, 410
Forest and Rangeland Renewable Resources
    Planning Act of 1974, 489, 497, 498
Forest Reserve Act of 1891, 494
Forest Reserve Organic Act of 1897, 31, 494
  violation of, 100
*Forest Science,* 466
Forest Science Laboratory, **238**
Forest Service, U.S.:
  acreage of, 212, 403, 404
  big-game animals, 78
  cooperation with states and industries, 411, 435
  decentralization in 1908, 34
  education programs, 412
  engineering work, 409
  established from Bureau of Forestry, 32

Forest Service, U.S.:
  forage resources, 408, **408**
  forest-fire management, 405
  foresters in, 471–474
  grazing fees, 61
  harvesting policy, 407
  in Hawaii, 166
  human resource development, 412
  information services, 412
  and Klamath Reservation purchases, 44, 45
  major activities, 403, 404
  Mineral King suit, 100
  mission, 403
  Multiple-Use Act, 46, 78
  name change, 32, 34
  outdoor recreation, **71,** 78, 79, **79, 80,** 409
  under Gifford Pinchot, 32
  planting trees, 407, 408
  positions, 471–474
  in Puerto Rico, 167, **167,** 168
  range resources, 408
  recreation, 78, 79, 409
    research in, 79
  reforestation, 407, 408
  regional structure, 406
  Renewable Resources Assessment, 489
  Renewable Resources Program, 489
  research, 36, 410, 411
  special interest areas, 78
  state cooperation, 411, 435
  stumpage sales, 407
  timber growing and selling, 405
  water conservation, 409
  Wilderness Act, 78
  wilderness movement, birth of, 95
Foresters:
  in associations, 480
  attitudes of, 97
  in Bureau of Land Management, 476
  in commercial forests, 478
  conservative background, 97
  in consulting work, 479
  and contemporary realities, 99
  duties and salaries, 471–480
  education, 463–471
    enrollment trends, 480, 481
  employment trends, 480
  in extension work, 476
  in federal positions, 471–477
  graduating in U.S., 480, 481
  income, 472–474, 516–518
    and retirement, 481
  in Indian Service, 474
  in investigative positions, 475
  licensing, 481
  and national environmental policy act, 99
  in National Park Service, 475
  number in U.S., 465
  on private estates, 479
  in private forestry, 478–480
  registration and licensing, 481
  in research, 473, 478
  Society of American, 466–468
  Soil Conservation Service, 477
  state agencies, 477, 478
  in teaching profession, 478
  in Tennessee Valley Authority, 477
  in U.S. Forest Service, 471–474
  in wildlife management, 476
  and wood processing, 320, 321
Forestry:
  beginning of, in Europe, 198–201
  Canadian Institute of, 468
  county, 437, 438

Forestry:
  definition, 187
  divisions of, 188
  early traning, 33
  education, 463–465, 468–471
    for recreation employment, 90
    requirements, 468–471
  farm, 40
  federal, 401–424
  as federal public policy, 26–47
  handbook, 467
  industrial: ownerships, 446, 447
    practice of forestry, 447–462
  and national planning, 484–490
  on private lands (*see* Private lands)
  profession of, 465–468
    qualities needed for success, 481
  schools: in Canada, 512–513
    in U.S., 505–512
  as a science, 187
  state, 40, 427–437
  urban, 437, 439–441
*Forestry Abstracts,* 208
*Forestry Chronicle,* 468
Forestry Division of FAO, 203
*Forestry Quarterly,* 33
Forests:
  of Canada, 169–171
    map, 170
  contributions, 23
  early American villages, 18
  economic importance, 212, 213
  industries in colonial times, 15–17
  and society, 219
  soil conservation, 40
  of U.S., ownerships, 168
  of world, 193
    map, 196
Forklift loader, 291, **292**
Forsling, Clarence, 203
4-H Clubs, 453, 476
Fourdrinier paper machine, **308**
Fox, as fur bearer, 64
Framing anchors, 320, **321**
France:
  in FAO, 205
  influence on early forestry, 188, 198–200
Friends of the Earth, 86
Frost:
  canker disease, 390
  damage, 395
Fruiting body of fungus, 383
Fuel:
  consumption in U.S., 7
  continuity, 351
  and fire rate of spread, 351
  and fire suppression, 350
  and fire triangle, 351
  from forest, 5–8, 296
  hazard reduction, 104
  moisture, in fire-danger rating, 349
  size, effect on fire, 351
  from waste, 303
Fuelwood, 296
Fungi:
  beneficial to forest, 393
  examples, **381**
  gaining entrance through insect holes, 360, 383
  how it infects trees, 383, 384
  and log purchases, 262
  losses from, 381
  mycorrhiza on roots, 178, 393
  prevention of attack in wood, 313–315, **315**
  (*See also* Disease)

Fur-bearing animals, 64, 373
*Fusarium* spp., 393
Future Farmers of America, 453

Galileo, 199
Gall-making insects:
  control, 372
  damage from, 361
  examples, 361, 372
Galston, A. W., 174
Gara, Robert I., 366, 369
Garbage disposal in recreation areas, 89
Garratt, George A., 468
Gene pools, 240
General Exchange Act of 1922, 495
General Land Office:
  administering forest reserves, 32*n.*
  merged with Grazing Service, 418, 496
General Sherman tree, 159
Generic name, 115
Genetics:
  considerations of trees, 240
  controls, nursery seedlings, 240, 241
  forest tree breeding, research, 411
  forest tree improvement, 458 – 461, **459, 460**
Geology, relation to forestry, 188
George, John L., 481
George Washington National Forest, **11, 80**
Georgia:
  geneticist, **459**
  hunting on forest lands, **454**
  naval stores production, 297
  pulp mill in, 309
  seed collection, **236**
  seed orchard, **437**
  state forestry, 428
  tree farms, 453
Germany:
  early fire ordinance, 327
  early management practices, 187, 188
  influence on early forestry, 33, 199 – 201
  in world forestry, 202
Getaway time, 347
Gifford Pinchot building, **467**
Gill, L. S., 389
Gin pole log loader, 290
Girdling, 243, **245**
Glascock, Hardy R., Jr., 485
Glesinger, Egon, 202, 203
Glucose in tree growth, 179, 180
Goats pasturing on national forests, 408
Gooseberry, blister rust, 387, 388
Graham, Samuel A., 357
Grain of wood, 306
Grand Canyon National Park, 94
Grant, Ulysses S., 21
Graves, Henry S., 33, 449
Grazing:
  damage from domestic animals, 373, 377
  fees, 61
  history of, in U.S., 60
  research in, 411
  in Rocky Mountain forest, 158
Grazing Service, 418, 496
Great Britain in FAO, 205
Great Idaho fire, 327
Greeley, W. B., 449, 450
*Grenzmarken*, frontier forest in Germany, 10
Grinnell, Rae H., 171
Grosenbaugh, L. R., 277
Gross national product, forests contribution, 197
Ground fire, 350
Ground water, 55

Groundwood pulp process, 307
Grouse, ruffed: and aspen management, 66
  hunting importance, 64
Growth:
  annual, of forest industry, 455
  ring, 266, 267
  (*See also* Annual ring)
  stand volume, 268
  of a tree, 175 – 180
  tree height, diameter, basal area, 268, 269
Guard cells, 181
Gum:
  flooded, 166
  from naval stores production, 297
  uses of, 297
Guse, Neal G., 421
Gymnosperms, 166
Gyppo, 283
Gypsy moth:
  biological control, 363
  defoliation from, 365
  direct control, 365

Hackberry, 152
Hair, Dwight, 213, 303, 304
Haleakala National Park, 166
Handle bolts, 296
Hardboard, consumption, 319, 320
Hardness of wood, 305
Hardwoods:
  competing with soybeans, 220
  gall midge attacks on, 372
  gypsy moth attacks on, 365
  porcupine damage, 376
Harrison, Benjamin, 29, 30
Hartig, G. L., 200
Hartig, R., 393
Hartman, A. W., 392
Hartzog, George, 37
Harvesting:
  effect on plant succession, 185
  effect on spawning streams, 282
  environmental problems, 102
  the forest crop, 281 – 298
  locations, in logging plan, 281
  methods, in logging plan, 281
  relationship to forest management, 298
  total tree, 295, **296**
Hatch Act, 494
Hatcheries, national fish, 80
Hauge, Christy T., 439
Hawaii:
  forests of, **165**
    commercial species, 165, 166
    description, 164, 165
    foreign trees in, 166
    map, 162
    products from, 165
    water production, 164
  state forestry, 166
Hawaii Volcanoes National Park, 166
Hawks, snag protection for, 67
Hazard (*see* Fire, hazard)
Heart rot:
  examples, **384, 385**
  gaining entrance to tree, 385
  growth loss from, 385, 386
Heartwood, **176,** 179
Heat:
  factor in decay, 313
  insulation of wood, 305
Heat-sensitive alarms in fire control, 352
Heel boom loader, 291, **291**

Height growth, 268
Height measurement, 264, **265, 266**
Helicopters:
    advantages over fixed-wing aircraft, 353
    in direct seedling, 408
    fertilizing with, **429**
    in hauling logs, 286, 287
    in spraying insects, 361, **362**
    in transporting fire personnel, **342,** 353
    in wildfire control, 340, 341, 353
Helitack crew, 340, 341, **342**
Helium gas in balloons, 290
Hemlock, **126**
    eastern, 125 – 127, 148, 149, 152
        description, 125, 126
        hemlock looper, 365
        as lumber species, 150
        products from, 126, 127
    mountain, 160, 161
    western, 124, 125, **125,** 156, 160, 161, 171
        bear damage, 375
        description, 125
        dwarf mistletoe, 389, **389**
        *Fomes pini,* **384**
        heart rot, 385, **385**
        hemlock looper, 365
        Indian paint fungus, **381**
        products from, 124, 125, 161
        as pulp species, 160, 161
        soil pit in, **459**
        wind damage, 394
Hemlock looper:
    aerial spraying, 363
    control, 365
    defoliation from, 365
Hennepin, Father, 15
Hepting, G. H., 386
Heriulfsson, Bjarni, observations of, 146
Hickory, 149
    bending strength, 305
    bitternut, 152
    heat of, compared to coal, 296
    mockernut, 153
    products from, 152
    shagbark, 152
    water, 153
    wildlife food from, 152
Hilman, J. B., 93*n*.
Historic areas of National Park Service, 76
Historic wildfires, 326 – 328
Hogs:
    damage to forest, 377
    pasturing on national forests, 408
Hollow box plywood beams, 318
Holly leaves and berries, 297
Holsten, Edward, 366, 369
Homestead Act of 1862, 19, 494
Homesteaders and cattlemen, 60
*Homo sapiens,* 194
Honeylocust, 152
Hooke, Robert, 199
Hoosier National Forest, **151**
Hophornbeam, 157
Horses:
    and forest forage, 9
    pasturing on national forest, 408
    in pulpwood transportation, 295
    as replacement of oxen in logging, 286
Hough, Franklin B., 28, 29, **29**
Huber's formula, 258
Huckleberry branches, 297
Hudson and Champlain, observations on forests, 146

Human encroachment on wildlife, 103
Human impact on the natural world, 210
Human resource development, 412
Human treatment of forest, 12
Humidity, influences of forest on, 52
Humphrey-Rarick Act of August 1974, 489, 497, 498
Humus, 175, 393
Hunting:
    clubs, on private forest lands, 68
    nonconsumptive, 64
Huron-Clinton Metropolitan Park Authority, **74**
Hurricane of 1938, New England, 394
Hydraulic loader, 292
Hydrogen:
    in lignin, 179
    in photosynthesis, 179, 180
Hydrologic cycle, **54,** 55
Hyphae, 383
*Hypoxylon* canker, 390
Hypsometer, Merritt, **266**
    in forest mensuration, 253
    obtaining tree heights, 264, 266

Ice and snow damage, 395
Idaho:
    aerial detection in, 345
    clearcut, **184**
    heel boom loader, **291**
    sheep grazing, **408**
    state forestry, 428
    wildfires, 327, 328, **329**
Illinois, early settlement, 19
Illinois Central Railroad, 21
Imports and exports, 198, 199
Improvement cutting, 243
    before and after, **244**
Incendiary fire:
    as cause of wildfires, 331
    prevention of, 332
Incense-cedar, 160
    pencils from, 160
Incentive programs, 436
Increment borer, **252,** 267, **267**
Increment hammer, **252,** 267
India, early forestry in, 200, 201
Indian Affairs, Bureau of, 416 – 418
Indian lands:
    cooperation in managing, 34
    termination of federal supervision, 44, 45
Indian Forest Service, 201
Indians, mills owned by, 418
Indirect control of insects, 361
Industrial forestry:
    attempts to improve, 450
    early handicaps, 448
    organizations supporting, 451, 453
    ownerships in U.S., 446, 447
    present practices, 454 – 462
    research in, 458 – 462
Industrial revolution, effect on lumber business, 18
Industries, forest, in colonial times, 15
Infrared imagery, 353
Initial point, 270
Inland Empire, 156
    pole blight disease, 391
Inland Waterways Commission, 34
Inner bark, **176,** 180
Insecticides:
    aerial application, **362**
    benzene hexachloride, 362
    carbamate, 364

Insecticides:
  DDT (see DDT)
  in direct control, 361
  phosphate, 364
  soil, 372
  systemic, 372
  zectran, 362
Insects:
  damage from, 356–373
  forest, classes, 358–361
  gall makers, 361, 372
  infestations, reporting, 372
  life cycles, 359
  and log purchases, 262
  methods of controlling, 361
    from aircraft, 362, 363
  populations, 358
  prevention of attack in wood, 313, **315**
  timber losses from, 357
  as transporters: of Dutch elm disease, 388
    of oak wilt spores, 390
    of stain fungi spores, 392
Insulation:
  board, 302
    consumption, 319, 320
  from heat and sound, 306
  products, 309
Integration of wood-using industries, 302
Interception of water, 55
Intermediate crown classification, **186,** 187
International Cooperation Administration (ICA),
  205
International Institute of Agriculture (IIA), 201,
  202
International Log Rule, 255
International Union of Forestry Research Organi-
  zations (IUFRO), 208
  organization of, 201
International Union of Societies of Foresters,
  founding of, 207
Interpretive programs:
  Fish and Wildlife Service, 80
  industrial forest lands, 85
  Jasper National Park, **87**
  miscellaneous facilities, 90
  national forests, 78
  national parks, 77
  objectives, 86, 87
  signs in, 90
  steam locomotive, **85**
Interstate compacts for fire control, 43
*Intersylva,* 202
Intolerant species, 228
  definition, 186
Inventions from forest, 8
Inventory of equipment in logging plan, 281
Investment:
  in paper mill, 309
  by private companies, 461
Iowa, early settlement, 19
*Ips,* 368
Isaac Walton League, 453
Ise, John, 18, 22
Isle Royale National Park, damage by moose, 373
IUFRO, 201

Jack pine warbler, 66, 107
Jahn, Laurence R., 64–66
James, Lee M., 220
Japan:
  chip exports to, 303
  early forestry in, 201
  as importer of logs, 198
  log exports to, 293

Jasper National Park, **87**
Jesuit explorers, 4
Job Corps Conservation Centers, 39
Johnson, Evert W., 468
Joint FAO/IUFRO Committee on Forestry Bibli-
  ography and Terminology, 208
*Journal of Forestry,* 466
Juniper, 156
  gall midges on, 372
  Rocky Mountain, **174**

Kaibab squirrel, 107
Kaiser, H. F., 213
Kansas:
  early settlement, 19
  state forestry, 431
Karlsefni, Thorfinn, observations of, 146
Kaufman, Herbert, 403
Keep Green Associations, 330
Keep Green Program, 330, 336, 337, 451, 453
Keep Washington Green, 336
Kentucky:
  lightning cable protection, 396
  state forestry, 433
  Tennessee Valley Authority in, 81
Kerf, saw, 253, 254, **254**
Kiawe, 166
Kiln:
  lumber drying, 313
  plywood manufacturing, 318
  stain reduction, 393
Kirtland's warbler, 66, **67,** 107
Klamath Reservation, 44
Knees, 194
Knesse, Allen V., 210
Knight, Fred B., 357
Knuckle-boom loader, 292, 295
Koa, 165
Kraft pulpwood process, 307*n,*
Krueger, Myron, 45
Kukui, 166

Labor needs:
  in the logging plan, 281
  in naval stores production, 297
Labrador, forest of, map, 170
Lake Chelan National Recreation Area, 497
Laminated beams, 316, **316**
Land and Water Conservation Fund Act of 1964,
  81, 421, 496, 497
Land Between the Lakes, 81, **82,** 442
Land conversion programs, reaction to, 96, 105
Land ethic, 95
Land-grant railroads, 20, 21, **21**
Land measurement units, 273
Land survey:
  marking corners, 271, 273
  metes and bounds, 270
  rectangular system, 270–273, **272**
  units of land measurement, 273
Landownership patterns, 424, **425**
Landscape architect, 106
Landslide damage, 395
Langlade County forestry work, 438
Larch:
  eastern (see Tamarack)
  western, 156, 171
Larch canker, 390
Larch sawfly:
  control of, 365
  damage from, 357
  defoliation from, 365
Lassen, L. E., 303, 304
Latin America, forest distribution, 197

Latin names, 115
League of Nations, 202
Least-cost plus-damage concept, 339
Leaves, function of, **176,** 178, 179
Leeuwenhoek, Anton van, 199
Leopold, Aldo, 63
Lewis and Clark, observations of, 146
Liberation cutting, 243
Licensing of foresters, 481
Light, effect on plant succession, 185
Lightning:
　as cause of wildfire, 331
　damage to trees, 396
　fires, detected with satellites, 354
Lignin:
　formation, in tree growth, 179
　in manufacture of plastics, 310
　in papermaking, 307
　percentage in wood, 307
Lignumvitae, 167
Liller, Neal, Battle, and Lindsey, Inc., 336
*Limnoria,* 314
Linnaeus, Carolus, 115
Lion, mountain: as big-game animal, 64
　in wilderness, 110
Litter, forest floor, 54
Little, E. L., 147, 164, 501
Littleleaf disease, 386
Livestock industry:
　history in U.S., 60
　prescribed burning to improve herbage, 104
Lloyd, William J., 416, 458
Loading logs, 290, 291, **291,** 292, **292**
Locomotive:
　first logging, 18
　in interpretive program, 85, **85**
　as wood burner, 6
Locust:
　black, 152
　fungus, **381**
　honey (*see* Honeylocust)
Log:
　crosshauling, 290
　hauling: by balloon, 288 – 290, **289, 290**
　　by cable, 286, **288**
　　by helicopter, 286
　　by oxen, 286
　　by rail, 293
　　by rubber-tired skidder, 286, **287**
　　by sleigh, 20
　　by tractor, 286, **287**
　　by truck, 293, **294, 295**
　　by water, 292, 293
　loading and unloading, 290 – 292, **291, 292**
　markets, in logging plan, 281
　scale stick, 253
　　how used, 258, 259, **259**
　scaling, 258, 259, 285
　transport, impact of, 101
　　effect of careless construction, 102
　weight, in measurements, 262
Log-rule values, variations, 255
Log rules:
　board foot, 253
　　Doyle, 255
　　how made, **254**
　　International, 255
　　Scribner, 254
　　　deduction for defect, 260, 261
　　Scribner decimal *C,* 255
　　variation in, 255
　cubic foot, 256 – 258
　　Huber, 258
　　Smalian, 256 – 258

Logging:
　camps, 283
　damage, and root rot incidence, 386
　debris: as fire hazard, 232
　　and tree reproduction, 232
　museum, 85
　and natural patterns and textures, 107, **107**
　plan, 281, 282
　residues: for destructive distillation, 296
　　for pulp chips, 295
　roads, impact of, 101, **101,** 102, **102,** 103
　waste, use of, 296
Loomis, W. E., 179
Lorentz, J. B., 200
Louisiana:
　interstate fire protection compact, 44
　keep green, 453
　state forestry, 428
　tree farms, 453
Low thinning, 247
Lumber:
　changing rates in consumption, 23
　as a colonial export, 17
　derivation of name, 300
　drying, 311 – 313
　manufacture, 300 – 302
　stains and rots, 393
Lumber Code Authority, 450, 495
Lumber lead:
　of Lake States, 150, 155
　of Northeast, 150
　of South, 155, 160
　of West Coast, 155, 160

McIntire-Stennis Act, 410, 496
McLintock, T. F., 93
McNary, Charles L., 37
Macronutrients, 250
McSweeney-McNary Research Act of 1928, 495
Madrone, Pacific, 160
Magnolia, 149
　southern, 153
Maine:
　early leader in lumber production, 150
　fires in 1794, 327
　fires in 1947, 43, 328
　interstate fire protection compact, 44
　loading pallet, **295**
　state forestry, 428
　tree farms, 453
　wildfires in, 326 – 328
Malvern Hill fire, 328
Mamani, 166
Mammals, damage to forest by, 373 – 377
Managed forest, cutting in, 284
Management:
　fire, 326, 327
　forest: definition, 189
　　relationship to harvesting, 298
　of the forest environment, 93 – 111
　resource strategies, 110
Manewal, Ernest, 366, 369
Mangroves, 167
Manitoba:
　forest land area, 169
　forests of, 171
　　map, 170
　skunk, beneficial effects, 377
Manning, Glenn H., 171
Maple:
　bigleaf, 160
　　products from, 160
　black, 152
　blight disease, 392

Maple:
  charcoal from, 310
  as pulp species, 152
  red, 152, 153
  silver, 152
  sugar, 129 – 131, **130**, 148, 152
    damage from squirrels, 376, 377
    description, 129
    hardness, 305
    products from, 131, 150
Maple syrup and sugar, 131, 297
Mapmaking:
  from aerial photographs, 279
  while cruising, 276
Maps in the logging plan, 282
Marckworth, Gordon D., 481
Marginal analysis, 217
Marine borers, **315**
  prevention of, 313, 314
Mariposa Big Tree Grove, 94
Maritime provinces:
  forest land area, 169
  forests of, 171
    map, 170
  log rafts, 292
Marking corners, 271
Marking trees for felling, 285
Marks, Richard T., 415, 439, 441
Marshall Plan (1948), 205
Martin, as fur bearer, 64
Marty, Robert, 210, 222
Maryland, national headquarters office of SAF, **467**
Massachusetts:
  early fire laws, 18
  interstate fire protection compact, 44
Massachusetts Bay, early forest regulation, 16
Mast, 9, 152
Mathematics, relation to forestry, 188
Mather, Stephen T., 36, **37**, 95
Maynard, Donald S., 418
Measurements, trends in, 279
Measuring:
  cordwood, 261, 262
  for defect, 259 – 261
  forests, 273 – 283
  land area, 270 – 273
  logs: board-foot rules, 253 – 255
    cubic-foot rules, 256 – 258
    by weight, 262
  products, 285, 286
  trees, 263 – 270
    age, 266
    diameter, 263
    height, 264, **265**, **266**
    volumes, 267 – 270
Mechanical pulp process, 307, 308
Mechanical sampling, of cruising, 274, **274**, 275
Mechanical thinning, 247
Medullary rays, 304
Menominee Reservation, 44, 45
Mensuration, forest, 189, 251 – 280
Meridians, 270
Merriam, Lawrence C., Jr., 75
Merritt hypsometer, 264, 266, **266**
Mesa Verde National Park, 76
Mesquite, 166
Metabolism, 181
Metamorphosis, 359
Metes and bounds, 270
Metric:
  conversion factors, 263
  conversion table, 499, 500
  volume measurements, 255*n.*, 257, 258, 261

Metropolitan Park Authority, 73
Mice, white-footed, damage to seed crops, 376, 377
Michigan:
  charcoal industry, 311, **311**
  early forestry training, 33
  early leader in lumber production, 150
  early logging, **19**
    with oxen, 286
  early steam sawmill, 18
  jack pine warbler management, 66, 107
  selection cutting, **230**
  state forest acreage, 437
  state forestry, 432
  thinning, before and after, **248**
  tree damage from squirrels, 376, 377
Micronutrients, 250
Midges:
  gall, 372
  terminal feeders, 371
Migratory waterfowl, 64
Mill waste, use of, 296, 302, 303
Mills:
  integration of, 302
  lumber, 300 – 302
    methods of powering, 302
  paper, investment in, 309
  pulp: in Alaska, 24
    in the South, 24
    use of wood chips, 295
Mineral Disposal Act of 1947, 42
Mineral King, 100
Mineral matter:
  as raw material of wood, 177, 304
  in tree growth, 177
Mineral substances, 174
Minimum requirements, bulletins on private forestry, 449, 450
Mining claims on national forests, 42
Mink, as fur bearer, 64
Minnesota:
  aspen management, 66
  Cloquet fire of 1918, 326, 327
  early leader in lumber production, 150
  example of state forestry, 432
  keep green program, 453
  land ownership study, 45
  machine planting, **240**
  *Nectria* canker, **391**
  red pine seedling, **238**
  state forest acreage, 438
  tree farms, **452**, 453
  windbreak, 51, **52**
Miscellaneous fires:
  as cause of wildfires, 332
  prevention of, 335
Mississippi:
  interstate fire protection compact, 44
  state forestry, 428
  tree farms, 453
Missouri, charcoal industry in, 311
Mistletoe:
  dwarf, 389, **389**, 390
  as small forest product, 297
Mixed forest, definition, 186
Moisture:
  as factor in decay, 313
  of fuel in fire danger rating, 349
  recommendations for woodwork, by regions, 312
Monongahela National Forest, clearcutting controversy, 100
Montana:
  aerial detection, 345

Montana:
  Indian lands, 416
  landownership, **425**
  logging truck, **419**
  spruce budworm damage, 357
Monuments for marking corners, 271
Moose:
  as big-game animal, 64
  Isle Royale National Park, 373
Mopping up (of wildfires), 352
Morrill Act, 494
Mt. Baker-Snoqualmie National Forest, **245**
Mount of Olives, 11
Mountain pine beetle, 368
Mountaineers, 86
Muir, John, 94
Mulberry, resistance to decay, 305
Mules in pulpwood transportation, 295
Multiple use:
  definition, 46
  and environmental policies, 98
  Sustained-Yield Act of 1960, 46, 496
  visual resources management, 106
Mumford, Lewis, 5
Municipal forestry, 437, 439
Muncipal government in recreation, 73
Museum, logging, 85
Muskeg forest type, 161, 163
Muskrat, 64
Mutualism, 242
Mycelium, 383
Mycorrhiza, 178, 393

Name Change Act of 1907, 494
Nantucket pine tip moth, 371
Nash, Roderick, 14
National Academy of Sciences, 30, 31
National Association of State Foresters, 436, 446
National Audubon Society, 86
National Bison Range, 95
National Capital Parks, 77
National Conservation Commission, 36
National Cooperative Forest Fire Prevention Program, 330
National defense and forests, 10
National Environmental Policy Act (NEPA) of 1969, 98, 99, 105, 111, 497
National Fire-Danger Rating (NFDR) System, 349, 350
National forests:
  in Alaska, 164
  engineering in, 409
  from forest reserves, 32–34
  map showing locations, 406
  mining claims, 42
  multiple use, 46
  number and acreage, 212
  as recreation lands, 78, 79, **79,** 409
  sustained yield, 46
  water conservation, 409
  (*See also* Forest Service)
National Keep Green, 451
  (*See also* Keep Green Program)
National Lumber Manufacturers Association, 450
National Park Service:
  in Alaska, 164
  areas, 77
  criticisms of, 78
  directors, 36, 37
  establishment, 36, 76, 95, 495
  fire management, 420, **420,** 421
  foresters, 475
  forestry work, 420, 421
  in Hawaii, 166

National Park Service:
  historic areas, 76
  as international consultant, 78
  interpretive program, 77
  Mineral King suit, 100
  National Capitol Parks, 77
  national monuments, 76
    act creating, 1906, 494
  national parks, 76
  natural areas, 76
  outdoor recreation agency, 75
  protection problems, 77
  recreation areas, 76
  tree removal policy, 421
  and Wilderness Act, 78
National planning, 484–490
National Recovery Act of 1933, 450
National recreation areas:
  Forest Service, 78
  National Park Service, 76
National Trail Systems Act, 421
  establishment in 1968, 497
National Wild and Scenic River System, 421
  in Alaska, 164
National Wilderness System, 220
National Wildlife Refuges (*see* Wildlife, refuges)
Nationwide Outdoor Recreation Plan, 421
Natural areas:
  of National Park Service, 76
  private lands, 83
Natural resources and recreation, 70
Nature trails in urban woodlands, 109
Naval stores production, 297
Navy:
  building of a wooden, 10, 17
  Royal, mast timbers, 16
Nebraska, state forestry, 431
*Nectria* canker, 390
Needle diseases, 392
Nelson, A. L., 357
NEPA (*see* National Environmental Policy Act)
Netherlands, the, and FAO, 205
New Brunswick:
  forest land area, 169
  forests of, 171
    map, 170
  interstate fire protection compact, 44
New England:
  and broad-arrow decree, 16
  wind damage, 394
Newfoundland, forests of, 169, 171
    map, 170
New Hampshire:
  early forest fires, 18
  interstate fire protection compact, 44
New Jersey and broad-arrow decree, 16
New Mexico:
  Indian lands, 416
  state forestry, 428
Newton, Sir Isaac, 199
New York:
  and broad-arrow decree, 16
  early leader in lumber production, 150
  early porcupine damage, 376
  interstate fire protection compact, 44
  state forestry, 432
  white pine blister rust discovery, 387
New York State College of Forestry, 33
NFDR [*see* National Fire-Danger Rating (NFDR) System)]
Noble, J. W., 29
Nonconsumptive use of wildlife, 64
Norris-Doxey Act of 1937, 40, 496

North America:
  exporter of logs and sawn wood, 198
  forest distribution, 195, 196
    map, 196
North Carolina:
  Biltmore, 31
  early fire laws, 18
  forest, **182**
  incentive programs, 436
  land ownership study, 45
  forest geneticist, **460**
  forest nursery, **461**
  tree farms, 453
North Cascades Complex Act of 1968, 497
North Cascades National Park, **159**
North Dakota, state forestry, 431
Northern Forest:
  commercial species, 147 – 149, **149**
  description, 147
  as leader: in lumber production, 150
    in pulp production, 150
  map, 148
  products from, 150
Northwest Territories and the Yukon:
  forest land area, 169
  forests of, map, 170
Nova Scotia:
  and broad-arrow decree, 16
  forest land area, 169
  forests of, 171
    map, 170
NRA (National Recovery Act), 450
Nursery, forest: damping-off disease, 393
  loblolly pine, **461**
  in Oregon, **237**
  root feeders in, 371
  seedlings, genetic controls, 241
  selecting site, 236
  shade protection, 396
Nutrient deficiencies, **249**, 250
Nutrients, effect on plant succession, 185

Oak:
  black, 151
  bur, 151, 157
  California black, 160
  cherrybark, 153
  chestnut, 151
  chinkapin, 151
  color and grain, 306
  deer damage to acorns, 373
  heat, compared to coal, 296
  live, 153
    for naval use, 17
  northern red, 149, 151
    fungus, **381**
    hardness, 305
    permeability, 305
  Nuttal, 153
  and oak wilt, 390
  Oregon white, 160
  overcup, 151
  post, 151
  products from, 152
  as pulp species, 152
  as sacred tree, 10
  scarlet, 149
  shrubby species, 156
  silver grain in, 304
  southern red, 151
    hardness, 305
    permeability, 305
  swamp chestnut, 153
  swamp white, 151

Oak:
  water, 153
  white, 132 – 134, **133,** 149
    description, 132, 133, 134
    fungus, **381**
    hardness, 305
    importance of, 151
    products from, 134, 152
    resistance to decay, 305
    wildlife food from, 152
  willow, 153
  wilt, 390
Oak-apple gall, 372
Odor of wood, 306
  from preservatives, 315
Ohia lehua, 165, **165**
Ohio:
  early settlement, 19
  example of state forestry, 432, 433, **433**
Oklahoma, interstate fire protection compact, 44
Olympic National Park, 94
  large trees, 159
Omnibus Flood Control bill, 95
Ontario:
  forest land area, 169
  forests of, 171
    map, 170
Ordinance of Waters and Forests of 1669, 199
Oregon:
  example of state forestry, 428 – 431, **431**
  Indian lands, 416
  Keep Green Program, 336, 453
  Klamath Reservation, 44
  leader in lumber production, 160
  log rafts, 292
  porcupine damage, 376
  shelterwood cutting, **230**
  staggered settings, **407**
  Tillamook fires, 326, 327
  tree farms, 453
  Tussock moth control, **362**
Oregon and California Railroad land grant, 34, 419
Organic Act of 1897, 46
Osage-orange, 152
  resistance to decay, 305
Osprey, 107
Otter, as fur bearer, 64
Outbreak of insects, 358
Outdoor recreation:
  definition, 70
  dispersed use, 79
  facilities, 88 – 90
  factors affecting the demand, 71, 72
  factors affecting the supply, 72 – 86
  on industrial forest lands, 83, 454
  interpretive programs, 86, 87
  planning small sites, 87, 88
  on private lands, 81 – 86
  on public lands, 73 – 81
  vandalism, 84, 85, 87
Outdoor Recreation, Bureau of (*see* Bureau of
    Outdoor Recreation)
*Outdoor Recreation—A Legacy for America,* 485,
  488
Outdoor Recreation Resources Review Commission, 81
Outer bark, **176,** 180
*Outlook for Timber in the United States, The,* 7, 8,
  23, 24, 155, 485, 488
Overstory release, 232
Owls, snag protection for, 67
Oxen, hauling logs by, 286
*Oxford System of Decimal Classification for For-
  estry,* 208

Oxygen:
  as factor in decay, 313
  and fire triangle, 351
  in lignin, 179
  in photosynthesis, 179
  and tree growth, 179

Pacific area, forest distribution, 197
Pacific Coast Forest:
  commercial species, **159**, 160
  description, 158, 159
  as leader in lumber production, 160
  lightning fires, 331
  map, 148
  products from, 160
Pacific Crest Trail, 497
Pallets in pulpwood transportation, 295, **295**
Palms, 167
Panshin, John A., 310
Paper and paperboard consumption:
  per person in 1970, 24
  per person in 1972, 309
  per person in 2000, 24
  in U.S., 24, 309
Paper mill, investment in, 309
Parasite (dwarf mistletoe), 388–390
Parasitic control of larch sawfly, 365
Parasitic fungi, 383, 393
Parking areas in recreation areas, 89
Parks in urban woodlands, 109
  (*See also* Outdoor recreation)
Particle board:
  consumption, 319, 320
  how made, 318, 319
  kinds, 319
  from waste, 302
Pasturing on national forests, 408
  (*See also* Grazing)
Pathology, forest, 381
Paul Bunyan, 447
Payne, Brian R., 481
Peace Corps, 206, **207**
Pearce, J. Kenneth, 293
Pecan, 153
Peeler block, **317,** 318
Pennsylvania:
  early leader in lumber production, 18, 150
  state forestry, 432
Pentachlorophenol, 314
People management, 110
Permeability of wood, 305
Permit:
  for debris burning, 333
    example, 334
  to ration wilderness, 110
Persimmon, common, 153
Personnel assignments in the logging plan, 281
Pesticides, restrictions, 45, 105
Petroleum, as fuel, 6
Pheasant, hunting importance, 64
Pheromone, 366, 369
Phillippine College of Forestry, 206
Phloem, **176**
  engraving from insects, 360
  function in tree growth, 180
Photography:
  aerial, map-making, 279
  in fire control, 353, 354
Photosynthesis, 179
Physics, relation to forestry, 188
*Phytophthora cinnamomi,* 386
Picnic tables in recreation areas, 88
Pierson, A. H., 22

Piling, 296
Pinchot, Gifford, 31, 32, **32,** 33, **35,** 394, 409, 448, 449
  pioneer in science of forestry, 201
Pine:
  butterfly, defoliation from, 365
  damage from sheep, 377
  distillation, from stumps, 310
  eastern white, 116, 117, **117,** 148, 149
    blister rust, 382, 387
    in colonial times, 16
    description, 117
    heat, compared to coal, 296
    as most desirable lumber species, 150
    products from, 117
    tip weevil, **371**
    wood workability, 305
  gall midges on, 372
  jack, 148, 171
    as lumber species, 150
    warbler, 66, 107
  jeffrey, 157, 160
  limber, 156
  loblolly, 153, **153, 236, 460**
    forest nursery, **461**
    plantings and Nantucket pine tip moth, 371
    root disease, 386, 387
    uses of, 155
  lodgepole, 156, 157, 160, 161, 171
    damage by porcupine, 376
    dwarf mistletoe, 389
    as fire type, 156
    mountain pine beetle, 368
    pine butterfly, 365
  longleaf, 153
    brown spot needle disease, 66, 392
    grass stage, 392
    naval stores from, 297
    products from, 155
  Monterey, 207
  pitch, 149, 152, 153
  pond, 153
  ponderosa, 120, **120,** 121, 156, 157, 158, 160, 171, **320**
    damage from porcupine, 376
    damage from sheep, 377
    description, 120, 121
    dwarf mistletoe, 389
    felling, **284**
    logging truck, **419**
    mountain pine beetle, 368
    needle disease, 392
    pine butterfly, 365
    products from, 121, 158
    western pine beetle, 367
  prescribed burning, 66
  red, 148
    liberation of reproduction, **245**
    as lumber species, 150
    seedling, **238**
    thinning, **248**
  root rot in southern species, 386
  seed orchard, **437**
  shortleaf, 121–123, **122,** 149, 152, 153, **153**
    description, 121, 122
    plantings and Nantucket pine tip moth, 371
    products from, 123, 155
    root disease, 386, 387
  slash, 153, **459**
    naval stores from, 297
    products from, 155
  sugar, 199, **119,** 120, 157, 160
    description, 119

Pine:
  sugar: products from, 120
  transpiration rate, 181
  turpentine beetle, 367
  Virginia, 149, 152
  western white, 117, 118, **118**, 156, 157, 160, 171
    blister rust, 382, 387
    description, 117, 118
    mountain pine beetle, 368
    pine butterfly, 365
    products from, 118
  white: in colonial times, 16
    wood flour for plastics, 310
    workability, 305
  whitebark, 160
Pine butterfly:
  control, 365
  defoliation from, 365
Pine sawfly:
  control, 365
  defoliation from, 365
Pinyon, 156
  nuts from, 297
Pioneer species, 241
Pioneers in forest succession, 185
Pisgah National Forest, **182**
Pitch, 297
Pitch out, 366
Pith, 179
Pittman-Robertson Act, 95
Plan:
  fire-control, 338
  logging, 281, 282
Planertree, 153
Planning:
  in fire control, 335
  in forestry on national scale, 484 – 490
  small outdoor recreation sites, 87
Plant quarantine laws, enforcement, 382
*Plantarum* by Linnaeus, 115
Planting nursery stock:
  by hand, **239**
  by machine, **240**
Planting seedlings:
  by hand, **239**
  by machine, **240**
  on national forests, 407, 408
  number per acre, 239
Plasticity of wood, 306
Plastics, 310
Plots:
  sample, 274
  sizes, 275
Plus trees, 241
Plywood:
  consumption in U.S., 24
  how made, 317, **317**, 318, **319**
  production, 318
  uses for, 318
Poison to kill mice, 377
  (*See also* Insecticides)
Poisonous plant eradication, 408
Pole, tree classification, 186
Pole blight disease, 391, 392
Poles:
  redwood and cedar, 305
  structures from treated, 314
Policy, forest: application to forestry, 190
  cooperative agreement, 46
  development, 26
  disposal of Public Domain, 27
  trends, 47
Pollarding, 187

Pollination, controlled, 460, **460**
Pollute, permission to, 111
*Polyporus schweinitzii,* 386
Pomeroy, Kenneth B., 45, 446
Poplar:
  balsam, 163, 171
  swamp, 153
  tulip (*see* Yellow-poplar)
  yellow (*see* Yellow-poplar)
Porcupine:
  in conflict with forest management, 64
  damage to forest, 376
  methods of control, 376
  as transporter of mistletoe seeds, 390
*Poria asiatica,* 385
*Poria weirii,* 386
Port-Orford-cedar, 160
  arrow species, 160
  strength and light weight, 305
Poster contest, fire prevention, 336
Posts:
  fence, 305
  and poles, **433**
  from redwood and cedar, 305
Powder-post beetles, 360, 370
Power equipment in fighting fire, 347 – 349
Power saws, 285
Power shears, 285, 294, **295**
Precipitation:
  in fire-danger rating, 349
  influences of forest on, 53
Precommercial thinning, 247
Predator, reintroduction, 376
Preemption Act of 1841, 19, 493
  repeal, 29
Prescribed burn (*see* Fire, prescribed)
Preservatives, wood, 313, 314
  and forestry, 315
President's Advisory Panel on Timber and the Environment, 220, 455
Presuppression activities, fire, 338 – 350
Prince Edward Island:
  forest land area, 169
  forests of, 171
  map, 170
Private forest ownerships:
  large, 446, 447
  location of, 442
  medium-sized, 443 – 446
  positions in, 478, 479
  small, 443 – 445
Private lands:
  forestry practice on, 442 – 462
    early promotion of, 448, 449
    handicaps, 448
    minimum requirements, 449, 450
    practices, 454 – 462
    research, 458 – 462
  and hunting clubs, 68
  outdoor recreation, 81 – 86, **84, 85**
Product recovery factors, 262, 263
Production of forest products, 211
Products and inventions from forest, 8
Profession of forestry:
  Canadian Institute of Forestry, 468
  fields of service, 465, 466
  number of professionals, 465
  outlook, 480
  qualities needed for success, 481
  updating professionals, 481
Professional courses of study, 468 – 471
Propaganda, 85
Properties of wood, 305, 306

Protection, forest, 189
Protectionist, forest, 381
Protoplasm, 180, 181
Pruning, 243
Public domain, disposal, 27, 28
Public hearings and the logging plan, 282
Public involvement, 47, 98
Public Land Law Review Commission, 220, 423
Public opinion, conservation clubs, 86
Puerto Rico, **167**
    Forest Service of, 168
    forests, 167, 168
    map, 162
Pulp and paper:
    from chipped waste, 303
    manufacturing process, 307 – 309, **308**
    from mill by-products, 303
Pulp and paper industry, 455
    in Alaska, 24, 161
Pulp mills:
    in Southern states, 155
    use of wood chips, 295
Pulpwood:
    consumption in U.S., 24, 309
    felling and loading, 294
    importation from Canada, 24
    industry, 455
    leading forest product, 294
    manufacturing process, 307 – 309
    in regions of U.S., 24
    transportation, 293 – 295
        by truck, 295, **295**
        by water, 292
    from wood processing residues, 307
Pure forest, definition, 186
*Pythium* spp., 393

Quail:
    hunting in Georgia, **454**
    hunting importance, 64
    prescribed burning, 67
Quasi-public lands, outdoor recreation, 83
Quebec:
    forest land area, 169
    forests of, 171
        map, 170
    interstate fire protection compact, 44

Rabbits:
    damage to tree reproduction, 376
    as fur bearer, 64
    hunting importance, 64
    reproduction browse, 235
Raccoon, as fur bearer, 64
Radar:
    in fire control, 352
    tracking stations, for lightning storms, 331
Radio equipment, use in wildfire control, 346
Railroads:
    as cause of wildfires, 331
    and cloquet fire, 327
    influence on cattle industry, 60
    land-grant, 20, 21
        violations, 34
    log transportation, 293
        distance, 282
    pulpwood transportation, 295
    ties, 296
    in Wisconsin's lumber history, 85
Random sample, 273, **274**
Range and township, 271, **272**
Range management, 59 – 61
    history in U.S., 59

Rate of spread, fire, 346, 351
Rayon, 309
Rays, wood, 304
Recovery factor of forest products, 262, 263
Recreation:
    activity-oriented, 70
    in Alaska, 164
    on county lands, 73
    dispersed use, 79
    excluding stock, 408
    facilities, 88 – 90
    factors affecting demand for, 71, 72
    factors affecting supply of, 72
    on federal lands, 75 – 81
    and local government, 73
    measuring values due to wildfire, 339
    miscellaneous facilities, 90
    on municipal lands, 73
    for nonprofit, 83
    in Pacific Coast Forest, 160, 161
    planning small sites, 87 – 90
    problems on private lands, 84, 85
    for profit, 82
    research, 79
    resource-oriented, 70
    in Rocky Mountain Forest, 158
    on state lands, 73 – 75
    (*See also* Outdoor recreation)
Recreation areas, national: of Forest Service, 78
    of National Park Service, 76
Rectangular system of surveys, 270, 273, **271**
Recycling, wood products, savings from, 303
Redcedar:
    Australian, 166
    eastern, 152
        color and grain, 306
        odor, 306
        products from, 152
    western, 156, **159**, 160, 161, 171, **417**
        damage by bear, 375
        heart rot, 385
        historic photos, **7, 22**
        leading shingle species, 160
        products from, 160
        root rot, 386
        stump house, **7**
Redwood, **129**, 159, 160, 166
    description, 128, 129
    early logging with oxen, 286
    preserved examples, 497
    products from, 129, 160
    resistance to decay, 305
Redwood National Park, 219
    Act of 1968, 497
Reforestation, Senate Select Committee on, 37
Refuges, wildlife: first established, 95
    nonconsumptive use, 64
Registration of Foresters, 481
Regulation, forest, 190
Relative humidity in fire-danger rating, 349
Release, cuttings, 242
    from overstory, 232
Religious use of forests, 10, 11
Remote-sensing, 410
Renewable Resources Assessment, 489
Replaceable wood products, 321
Report of the President's Advisory Panel on
    Timber and the Environment, 485
Report time, fire, 346
Reproduction:
    from cuttings, 177
    methods of silviculture, 227
    from root sprouting, 177

Reproduction:
  from seeds, 175, 177, 235, 236
  site preparation for, 232
  sources of, 233–239
  vegetative, 234, 235
Reproductive potential, 358
Research:
  forest: formal recognition, 36
    on private lands, 458–462
  in Forest Service, 410
    employment, 473
  by private timber companies, 410, 458–462
  recreation, 79
  wildlife, cutting practices, 66
Reserves, forest: Act of 1897, 31, 494
  additions to, 31
  under Roth, 32
  transfer to Department of Agriculture, 32, 33
Residues, trends in use, 303
Resistance:
  to control (wildfire), 346, 351
  to decay, 305
  fire, treatment of lumber, 314
Resource Conservation and Development Projects, 416
Respiration in leaves, 179
Reynolds, R. V., 22
*Rhizoctonia* spp., 393
Rhode Island:
  and early lumber business, 18
  interstate fire protection compact, 44
Ribbentrop, B., 200
*Ribes* spp., 387
Richards, E. C. M., 10
Rick, 261
Rings:
  annual, 180
  cell formation, 305
  growth, 266, 267
Ripley, Thomas H., 423
Risk:
  compared with hazard, 337
  definition, 337
  in fire-danger rating, 349, 350
  reduction, 332–337
Roads:
  logging, 101–103
  in the logging plan, 281
  in recreation areas, 89
Rocky Mountain Forest, **157**
  commercial species, 157
  description, 155, 156
  lightning fires, 331
  map, 148
  products from, 158
  pulpmills in, 24
Rolston, K. S., 297, 309
Romans, early forestry, 187, 188
Roosevelt, Franklin D., 38
  and FAO, 203
Roosevelt, Theodore, early forest reserves, 33, 34, **35**, 36
Root diseases:
  avoiding, 387
  examples, 386
  gaining entrance to tree, 386
Root feeding insects:
  control, 371, 372
  damage from, 361
  examples, 361, 371
Root hairs, 178
Root pruning of seedlings, 236

Roots, **176, 178**
  function of, 177, 178
  kinds of, 178
Rosin and rosin oils, 297
Ross Lake National Recreation Area, **57**, 497
Roth, Filibert, 32, 33
Rots and stains, 392, 393
Round-headed borers, 360, 370
Roundwood, progress in use of, 303
Royal Navy, mast timbers, 16
Rural Development Act of 1972, 435

Safety precautions in the logging plan, 281
St. Helens Tree Farm, recreation on, 84
St. Joe National Forest, **184**
Salman, K. A., 357
Salvage operation, 243, **245**
  to control heart rot, 386
Sample plot dimensions, 275
Sampling, measuring forests by, 273–275
Sandwich-board panels, 318
Sanitation:
  cutting, 243
    for bark beetle control, 369
    for dwarf mistletoe control, 390
  laws, on private lands, 85
  in recreation areas, 88
Sapling, tree classification, 185
Saprophytic fungi, 383
Sapwood, **176,** 179
Sargent, Charles S., 30, 31
Saskatchewan:
  forest land area, 169
  forests of, 171
  map, 170
Sassafras, 152
Satellites, orbiting, in fire control, 354
Saw:
  band, 301, **301**
  chain, 285
  circular, 15, 301
  gang, 301
  kerf, 253, 254, **254**
  power, 284, **284,** 285
  sash, 15
  trim, 302
Sawdust, utilization of, 303
Sawmills:
  first in America, 15
  first steam, 18
  modern, 301, **301**
  and timber needs, 455
  waste: for destructive distillation, 296
    for pulp chips, 295
Sawyer, 301, **301**
Scale insects, 364, 371
Scale sticks:
  in forest mensuration, **252,** 253
  in use, **259**
Scaler, 258, 259, **259**
Scaling:
  deduction for defect, 260, 261
  logs, 258
  in the woods, 259, 285
Scenic Hudson Preservation Conference, 100*n.*
Schenck, C. A., 33
Schlich, William, 200
School lands, 28
Schools, forestry: in Canada, 512, 513
  in U.S., 505–512
Scientific names, 115
  trees in text (Appendix C), 501–504

Scolytid beetles, 361
*Scolytus ventralis,* 368
Scott, David R. M., 227, 242
Scribner log rule, 254
    deducting for defect, 260
Seaman, Jerome F., 299
Seed, tree: collecting and storage, 235, 236, **236**
    controlling mice, 377
    damage from mammals, 377
    distribution, 194
    genetic research, 458
    how disseminated, 175
    orchards, 241, **437**, 460, **460**
    production areas, 241
    reproduction, 235–239
    sowing, 236
    stratification, 236
    superior qualities, 240, 241
Seed insects:
    control, 372
    damage, 361, 372
    examples, 361
Seedling:
    forest nursery, **237**, 461
    genetic controls, 241
    greenhouse, **238**
    growth, 177, **177**
    planting of, 239
        by hand, **239**
        by machine, **240**
    storage, 237
    transplanting, 236, 237
    tree classification, 185
    in tubes, **238**
Selection system of silviculture, 228, **230, 231**
Selection thinning, 247
Self-guided auto tours and trails, 83, 87
Semichemical pulp process, 309
Senate Select Committee on Reforestation, 37
Sequoia, giant, 159, 160
    commerical value, 159
    early fire scars on, 327
Sequoia National Park, General Sherman tree, 159
Settlers, westward advance, 19
Shade:
    cover for, in recreation planning, 88
    effect on plant succession, 185
    enduring ability, 194, 195
    protection in nurseries, 396
Shake and shingle bolts, **245,** 296
Sharpe, Grant W., 87
Shaving board, 319
Shea, K. R., 385
Shearing trees, **285,** 294
Sheep:
    big-horn, 103
        wilderness solitude, 110
    domestic: and avalanches, 395
        damage to reproduction, 377
        drive, **62**
        and forest forage, 9
        grazing, **408**
        numbers on national forests, 408
        pasturing on national forests, 408
        in range management, 60, 61
Shelter from forest, 5
Shelterbelt planting, 51, 439
    wind current, **51**
    (*See also* Windbreaks)
Shelterwood system, 228–231, **230, 231**
Shipworm damage, prevention of, 313, 314, **315**

Show, S. B., 449
Shrinkage in wood, 311, 312, **312**
Sierra Club, 86, 95
Signs in recreation areas, 90
*Silent Spring,* 96
Silk, artificial, 309
Silk-oak, 166
Silver-grain in oak, 304
Silvics, application to forestry, 189
Silviculture:
    application to forestry, 189
    cutting methods, 242–247
    definition, 227
    intermediate operations, 242–250
    methods, on national forests, 407
    reproduction methods, 227–241
    research in, 411
    use of, in forest landscaping, 106
Sinkers of dwarf mistletoe, 389
Site preparation:
    equipment used for, 233, **233**
    for tree reproduction, 232, 233
Skidding:
    cable, 286, **288**
    distances, 283
    with horses, 286
    with oxen, 286
    tractor, 286, **287**
Skok, Richard A., 222
Skunk, beneficial effects of, 377
Slab, 253, 254, **254**
    utilization of, 303
Slash:
    fire hazard, 175
    logging: definition, 175
        disposal of, 104
Slatin, Benjamin, 309
Sleigh log hauling, **20**
Smalian's formula, 256–258
Small forest products, 297
Smith, David M., 104
Smith, Hoke, 30
Smith, Captain John, observations of, 146
Smith-Lever Act of 1914, 413, 476, 494
Smoke from prescribed burning, 104
Smokechaser, 340
Smokejumper, 340, 341, **341,** 353
Smoker fires:
    as cause of wildfires, 331
    prevention of, 333
Smokey Bear Program, 330, 335–337
Snags in wildlife management, 67
Snell bill, 37
Snow:
    depth, in recreation planning, 88
    drifting, affected by windbreaks, 51
    and ice damage, 395
    preventing evaporation, 57
Society of American Foresters:
    activities, 466, 467
    definition of forestry, 187
    education requirements, 468–471
    forest types, 115
    forestry education study, 468
    founding of, 33, 466
    industrial forestry study, 450
    national headquarters, **467**
    publications, 33, 208, 209, 466
Sociology, relation to forestry, 188
Soil:
    as affected by windbreaks, 51
    application to forestry, 188

Soil:
  chemical treatment, 393
  compaction, 54
  composition, influences of forest on, 54
  effect on seedling adaption, 241
  fertility: measuring losses from wildfire, 339
    and timber harvesting, 250
  in forest ecosystems, 232
  fumigants, 393
  identification, on private lands, 458
  mineral substances, 174, 175
  moisture: effect on plant succession, 185
    effect on transpiration, 181
    influences of forest on, 54, 55
  movement, and log transport, 102
  preparation for tree reproduction, 232
  in recreation planning, 87, 88
  research, 458, **459**
  structure, 54
  systemic insecticides, to control seed insects,
    372
  temperature, influences of forest on, 53
Soil Bank Legislation, 43
Soil Conservation Service:
  establishment, 40, 95, 495
  foresters, in, 477
  forestry work, 415
Songbirds, prescribed burning for, 66, 67
Sound:
  absorption of trees, 109
  insulation of wood, 306
  response to vibrations, 306
South America:
  forest distribution, 195
  map, 196
Southern bald eagle, 103
Southern Forest, **153**
  commercial species, 153
  description, 152, 153
  as early leader in lumber production, 150,
    155
  map, 148
  products from, 155
Southern pine beetle, damage from, 357, 367
Spalding, Volney M., 33*n.*
Spanish moss, 153
Spar tree boom loader, 291
Special interest groups in environmental concerns,
  97
Species name, 115
Spiritual needs and forest, 10, 11
Splinter board, 319
Spore of fungi, 383, 387
Sporophores, 386
Spot fires, 351
Spread of fire:
  effect of fuel on, 351
  patterns from, 351
Springwood, 180
Sprouting, 243
Spruce:
  black, 148, 163, 171
    dwarf mistletoe, 389
  blue, 156
  Cooley spruce gall, 372
  Engelmann, 156, 157, **157**, 171
    tip weevil, 371
  Engelmann spruce beetle, 368
  gum, 297
  hemlock looper, 365
  light but strong wood from, 305
  red, 148, 149
    as lumber and pulp species, 150

Spruce:
  Sitka, 127, **127,** 128, 160, 161, 171
    damage by bear, 375
    damage by wind, 393, 394
    description, 127
    fungus, **381**
    products from, 128
    as pulp species, 160, 161
    tip weevil, 371
  turpentine beetle, 367
  white, 148, 157, 163, 171
    as lumber and pulp species, 150, 160
  wood flour for plastics, 310
Spruce budworm, **360**
  aerial spraying, 363
  control, 365
  damage, 357
  defoliation from, 365
Squirrels:
  cone cashes for seed, 236
  damage to seed crops, 376
  damage to trees, 376, 377
  hunting importance, 64
  Kaibab, 107
  as transporter of mistletoe seed, 390
Stafford, Sam, 419
Stagnation, 246
Stains and rots, 392, 393
Stamm, Edward P., 45
Stand density, 186
Stand improvement cutting, 243
  before and after, **244**
Stand manipulation, 228
Standards, tree classification, 186
State Forest Practice Acts, 436, 437
State forestry departments:
  action programs, 435
  status of, 40
  types, 428 – 435
State Park systems, 73 – 75
Statics, forest, 190
Stenzel, George, 293
Stereoscope, **252,** 253, 278
Stomata, 178
  function of, 181
Stone, Earl, 104
Storm King case, 100
Strategies in resource management, 110
Stratification, seed, 236
Strength of wood:
  and light weight, 305
  under weight and shock, 306
Strip cruising, 275
Succession, forest, 185
Sucking insects, **364**
  control, 364
  damage from, 359, 364
  examples, 364
Sugar and syrup industry, maple, 297
Sugarberry, 153
Sulfate pulpwood process, 307*n.*
Sulfite pulpwood process, 307*n.*
Sulla, observations on tillage and pasturage, 9
Summerwood, 180
Sundance fire, Idaho, 328
Sunlight, effect on plant succession, 185
Sunscald:
  canker disease, 390
  prevention of, 396
Superior National Forest, **149, 238**
Suppressed crown classification, **186,** 187
Surface fire, 350
Survey crew, 276, **277**

Surveyer's tape, **252**
  in forest mensuration, 253
Sustained yield, defined, 46
Sweetgum, 141, **141,** 142, 152, 153
  blight disease, 392
  description, 141, 142
  products from, 142, 152
Swine and forest forage, 9
Swingler, W. S., 357
Swiss forest management to hold snow, 395
Sycamore:
  American, 152
  products from, 152
Symptoms of disease, 383
Synecology, 183
Syracuse University New York College of Environmental Science and Forestry, 206
Systemic poison, 364

Tables, picnic, in recreation areas, 88
Tagawa, Tom K., 166
Tally methods, 276
Tally sheets, 253, 276
Tamarack, 148, 163, 171
  larch sawfly, 365
    losses from, 357
  as lumber species, 150
Tanoak, 160
  oak wilt, 390
Tar, 297
Taxation of forest lands:
  under Clark-McNary Act, 449
  handicaps of, 448
  promotional material, 84
  resulting from recreation improvement, 85
  small ownerships, 443
Taylor Grazing Act of 1934, 95, 418, 495
Telephones in wildfire control, 346
Television in fire control, 352
Temperature:
  air, influences of forest on, 52
  damage to trees, 396
  effect on plant succession, 185
  in fire-damage rating, 349
  and fire triangle, 351
  in recreation planning, 88
  soil, influences of forest on, 53–55
Tennessee Valley Authority:
  establishment of, 81
  foresters in, 477
  forestry work, 422, 423
  functions of, 81
  outdoor recreation, 81, **82**
Tent caterpillar, **366**
  control, 365
  defoliation from, 365
*Teredo,* 314
Terminal feeding insects:
  control, 371
  damage, 360, 361, 371
  examples, 360, 371
Terminal weevils, 371
*Terminology of Forest Science, Technology, Practice, and Products,* 209
Termites:
  control, 371
  damage from, 360
  prevention treatment, 313, 371
  as root feeders, 371
  as wood borer, 370
Terrain in recreation planning, 87
Texas:
  annexation, 19

Texas:
  example of state forestry, 431, 432
  incentive programs, 436
  insect damage in, 357, 371
  interstate fire protection compact, 44
  subtropical forests, 167
  tree farms, 453
Texture of wood, 306
Theoe, Donald R., 471, 480, 481
Thermal infrared imagery in fire control, 353
Thinning, 246, 247, **248, 456**
Tillage, forests cleared for, 9
Tillamook fires, 326, 327
Timber connectors, 320, **321**
Timber cruising, 273–279
Timber Culture Act of 1873, 27, 494
  repeal, 29, 494
Timber economy, impact of, in U.S., 213
Timber harvesting, 281
  impact of, 102
Timber removal costs and the logging plan, 282
*Timber Resources for America's Future,* 23
*Timber: The Renewable Material,* 485, 487
Timber Trespass Act of 1831, 28
Tip weevil, **371**
Toilets in recreation areas, 88
Tolerant species, defined, 186, 228
Tongass National Forest, 161, **163**
Tools:
  from forest, 8, 9
  used in fighting fire, 347, 348
Total tree harvesting, 295
Township and range, 271, **272**
Toxicity of preservatives, 314
Tracheids, 304
Tractors:
  as replacement of horses in skidding, 286
  in site preparation, 458
  skidding logs by, 286, **287**
  in pulpwood transportation, 295
Trails:
  in recreation areas, 89, 90
  self-guided, 83, 87, 90
Training:
  fire, interagency personnel, 342
  personnel for wildfires, 340, 341
Transfer Act of 1905, 33, 494
Transpiration:
  as affected by windbreaks, 51
  contribution to rainfall, 52
  definition, 181
  and humidity, 52
  in watershed management, 58
Transportation:
  logs, 286–293
    by air, 286–290, **289, 290**
    impact of, 101
    by rail, 293
    from stump to landing, 286–290
    by tractor, 286, **287**
    by truck, 293, **294, 419**
    by water, 292, 293
  pulpwood, 293–295, **295**
  subsidizing with forests, 19
  to wildfires, 346, 347
Travel time, 347
Tree:
  breeding, 411, 460
  caliper, **252**
    in forest mensuration, 253
    how used, 263
  definition, 175
  farm, 445, 451, **452**

Tree:
  growth, 175 – 180, 268, 269
    elements needed for, 174
  measurements (*see* Measuring)
  seed, 458
Tree Farm movement, 451 – 453, **452**
Trees:
  identification, 116
  inspiration from, 173
  intrinsic beauty of, 109
  number of species of, 115
  and their environment, 116
  in the urban forest, 109
Trefethen, James B., 64 – 66
Tropical Forests:
  description, 167, 194
  in Florida, 167
  in Puerto Rico, 167, **167,** 168
    map, 162
  in Texas, 167
Truck:
  log transport distance, 282, 283
  log transportation, 293, **291, 292, 294, 419**
  pulp transportation, 295, **295**
True bugs, 364
Truman, Harry S, 205
Trunk, Johann Jacob, 200
Trusses, laminated, 316
Tulip-poplar (*see* Yellow-poplar)
Tupelo:
  black, 149, 152, 153
  water, 153
Turkey, hunting importance, 64
Turpentine, 297
  uses, 297
Turpentine beetle, 367
Tuskegee Institute, 481
Tutankhamen, 8
TVA (*see* Tennessee Valley Authority)
Twig beetles, 371
Twig-boring caterpillars, 371

Umpqua National Forest, **407**
*Unasylva,* beginning of, 208
Undercut in tree felling, 284, **284**
U.S.S.R.:
  exporter of logs and sawn wood, 198
  forest distribution, 195, 197
    map, 196
United Nations Development Program (UNDP),
    203, 204
U.S. agencies (*see* specific agency)
Urban forestry, 108, 109, 436, 439, 440
Utah:
  ancient tree, **174**
  state forestry, 431
Utility poles, 296
Utilization:
  forest, 191
  as good conservation, 321
  of harvesting discards, 303
  of slabs, sawdust, and cores, 303

Valuation, forest, 190
Vandalism:
  and interpretation, 87
  on recreation lands, 84, 85
  sign construction, 90
Vanderbilt estate, 31
Van Hise, Charles R., 29, 428
Variable plot cruising, 277
Vaux, Henry J., 220, 222
Vegetation:
  control, 458
  in fire-danger rating, 349

Vegetation:
  in fire suppression, 350
  protection, 109
  in recreation planning, 88
Vegetative reproduction, 234, **234,** 235
Veneer:
  from Douglas-fir, 317, 318
  in plywood manufacturing, 317, **317,** 318, **319**
  from yellow birch, 150
Vermont, interstate fire protection compact, 44
Vessels, as water conductors, 304
Veteran, tree classification, 186
Viereck, Leslie A., 164
Viking observations, 146
Villages, early American, and forests, 18
Vlrginia:
  incentive programs, 436
  interpretation in, 80
Visual resources, 106
Volume growth, 268
Volume tables, **252,** 253, 267, 276
  example, 268

Wadsworth, Frank, 168
Walker, Ronald, 37
Wallboard, 302
Walnut:
  black, 142, 143, **143,** 149, 152
    description, 142, 143
    products from, 143, 152
  color and grain, 306
  nuts from, 297
  shells, wood flour from, 310
  wildlife food from, 152
War Advertising Council, 335
Warbler, jack pine (Kirtlands), 66
Washington:
  aerial detection, 345
  balloon logging, **289**
  bear damage, **375**
  farm woodland, **444**
  fertilizing with helicopter, **429**
  fire lookout, **344**
  historic logging, **22**
  Indian lands, 416, **417**
  industrial forest campground, **84**
  Keep Green Program, 336, 453
  large trees, 159
  leader in lumber production, 160
  log rafts, 292
  plywood manufacturing, **317, 319**
  porcupine damage, 376
  stump house, **7**
  tree farms, 453
  Tussock moth control, 362, 363
  wildfires, 329
  wind damage, 393, 394
Wasp:
  chalcid: control of larch sawfly, 365
    as seed insect, 361
  larvae, 370
  oak-apple gall, 372
  wood, **370**
Waste products of logging and milling, 296, 302,
    303
Water:
  absorption, by forest soils, 55
  conduction: inhibited by fungi, 390
    by tracheids and vessels, 304
  conservation, on national forests, 409
  in fire fighting, 353
    bombs, 353
  free, in wood cells, 312
  ground, 55
  hydrologic cycle, 55

Water:
  loss: through evaporation, 53, 55, 58
    through transpiration, 53, 58, 181
  production: in Hawaiian forests, 164
    in Pacific Coast forests, 161
    in Rocky Mountain Forest, 158
  as raw material of wood, 177, 304
  in recreation planning, 88
  removing from wood, 311 – 313
  storage in soil, 58
  supply: on ranges, 408
    in recreation area, 88
  surface, 55
  table, 55
  transportation of logs by, 292, 293
    distances, 282
  as transporter of stain fungi spores, 392
  In tree growth, 177, 180, 181
Water Quality Act of 1965, 497
Water resource manager, 58
Waterelm, 153
Waterfowl, 64
Watershed:
  definition, 57
  revegetated after wildfires, 409
  in urban woodlands, 109
Watershed Management, 57 – 59
Weather:
  influences of forest on, 50, 51
  interpretation in wildfire control, 349
  satellites and lightning storms, 331
Webster, Henry H., 210, 222
Wedge prism, **252**
  in forest mensuration, 253
  how used, 278, **278**
Weeks Law of 1911, 330, 494
  amendment, 38
Weevils:
  as root feeders, 361, 371
  as terminal feeders, 371
Weight:
  of logs, measurement by, 262
  and strength of wood, 305
Wenatchee National Forest, wildfire in, 329,
  **353**
West Coast Lumbermen's Association, 453
West Virginia:
  charcoal industry in, 311
  clearcutting controversy, 100
  early settlement, 19
  white tail deer in, **374**
Western Pine Association, 453
Western pine beetle, 367
Weyerhaeuser High Yield Forestry, 455, 457,
  **457**
White-cedar, northern, 147, 148
  uses, 150
White House Conference of 1908, 34 – 36, 428,
  494
White House Conference on Natural Beauty of
  1965, 497
White Mountain National Forest, 394
White pine blister rust, 382, 387, 388
Widner, Ralph, 427
Wigwam, 6
Wild Rivers Act of 1968, 497
Wild and Scenic Rivers Act, 421
Wilderness:
  carrying capacity, 109, 110
  purists, 110
Wilderness Act of 1964:
  establishment, 497
  Forest Service, 78
  injunction against Forest Service, 100
  National Park Service, 78

Wilderness areas:
  Forest Service, 78
  National Park Service, 78
Wilderness East, 219
Wilderness Society, 86
Wilderness users, threshold, 110
Wildfire:
  in Alaska, 163
  causes of, 330 – 332
    camper, 331
    children, 332
    debris burning, 331 – 333
    equipment use, 331
    incendiary, 331, 332
    lightning, 331
    miscellaneous, 332, 335
    railroad, 331
    smoker, 331, 333
  detection system, 342 – 346
  educating against, 335
  effect on plant succession, 185
  fighting, 350 – 353
  historic significance, 326 – 329
  personnel, 339 – 346
  porcupine control, 376
  presuppression activities, 338 – 350
  prevention of, 332 – 338
  prevention programs, 335 – 337
    Keep Green, 336, 337
    Smokey Bear, 335, 336
  protection from, in U.S., 330
  reporting, 346
  situation in U.S., 329, 330
  supplies and equipment, 347, 348
  suppression of, 350 – 352
Wildlife:
  and buffer strips, 66
  and clearcuts, 67
  and diseased trees, 67
  and food from trees, 152
  and forest openings, 67
  habitat on commercial forest lands, 66, 67
  habitat improvement and prescribed burning,
    104
  and human disturbance, 103
  management, 61 – 68
  nonconsumptive use, 64
  refuges: in Alaska, 164
    first, 95
    number of, 80
    visitors to, 64
  sanctuaries, in urban woodlands, 109
  and timbercutting, 108
  value to forestry, 67, 68
  windbreak planting on farmsteads, 415
Wildlife ecologist and silviculturist collaboration,
  108
Willow:
  in Alaska, 163
  black, 152
  reproduction from cuttings, 177
  in Rocky Mountains, 156
Wilson, C. L., 179
Wilson, James, 409
Wilts and diebacks, 390, 391
Wind:
  beneficial effects, 395
  breakage and overthrow from, 393 – 395, **394**
  defense from, 51, 439
  dissemination of seed, and pollination, 175,
    395
  effect on plant succession, 185
  in fire-danger rating, 349
  and fire spread, 351
  influences of forest on, 51

Wind:
  in recreation planning, 88
  as transporter of fungus spores, 387, 392
Windbreaks:
  effect on air flow, 51, **51**
  purpose, 51, 415
  in rural settings, 439
Windthrow damage to forest, 393, 394, **394**
Winema National Forest, 45
Winters, Robert K., 10, 203
Wireworms, 361, 371
Wirth, Conrad L., 37
Wisconsin:
  county forestry work, 438
  early leader in lumber production, 150
  Forest Products Laboratory, 36, **411**
  interpretive programs in, 85, **85**
  Menominee Reservation, 44, 45
  recreation on state forest, **439**
  state forestry, 432
  tree farms, 453
  wigwam in, **6**
Witches'-broom, 389, 392
Wood:
  ash content, compared with coal, 296
  bending strength, 305
  biodegradable, 299
  borers: control, 370, 371
    damage from, 360
    examples, 360, 370, **370**
  cells, 304, 305
  charcoal from, 296, 310, 311, **311**
  chemical characteristics, 306
  color, 306
  distillation, 310, 311
  fabrication, 316 – 320
  fiber products from, 23, 307
  for fireplace fuel, 296
  flour, 310
  grain, 306
  hardness, 305
  heat comparison, with coal, 296
  insulation properties, 306
  odor, 306
  permeability, 305
  plasticity, 306
  preservation, 311 – 315
  products from logs, 296
  properties, 305, 306
  raw material extraction, 211
  rays, 304
  residues, 303
  resiliency, 306
  resistance to decay, 305

Wood:
  response to sound, 306
  shrinkage, 312, **312**
  strength, 305, 306
  structure, 304
  tar, 297
  technology, 191
  texture, 306
  warmth and beauty, **300**
  workability, 305
Woodland Conservationists, 40
Woodpeckers, snag protection for, 67
Workability of wood, 305
World Forestry Congress:
  in Budapest, 1936, 202
  in Madrid, 1966, 207
  organization of, 201
  in Rome, 1926, 201, 208
*World Forestry Inventory*, 208
Wygant, N. D., 357
Wyoming:
  early forest reserves, 30
  elk grazing, **65**
  sheep drive, **62**

Xylem, **176,** 179, 180

Yale University, early graduates, 33
Yarding:
  balloon, 288 – 290, **289, 290**
  cable, 286, **288**
*Yearbook of Forest Products*, 208
Yellow-poplar, 139 – 141, **140,** 149, 152, 153
  description, 139, 140
  products from, 141, 152
  wood workability of, 305
Yellowstone National Park, establishment, 32, 72,
  94, **494**
Yield, forest, 269
Yield tables, 269, 270
Yoho, James G., 45
Yosemite Grant, 72
Yosemite National Park, 72, **77, 420**
Yosemite Valley, 94
Youth Conservation Bill of 1974, 498
Youth Conservation Corps, 39
Yukon and Northwest Territories:
  forest land area, 169
  forests of, map, 170

Zanthier, Hans Dietrich van, 200
Zectran, 362
Zeeuw, Carl de, 310